Governing States and Localities

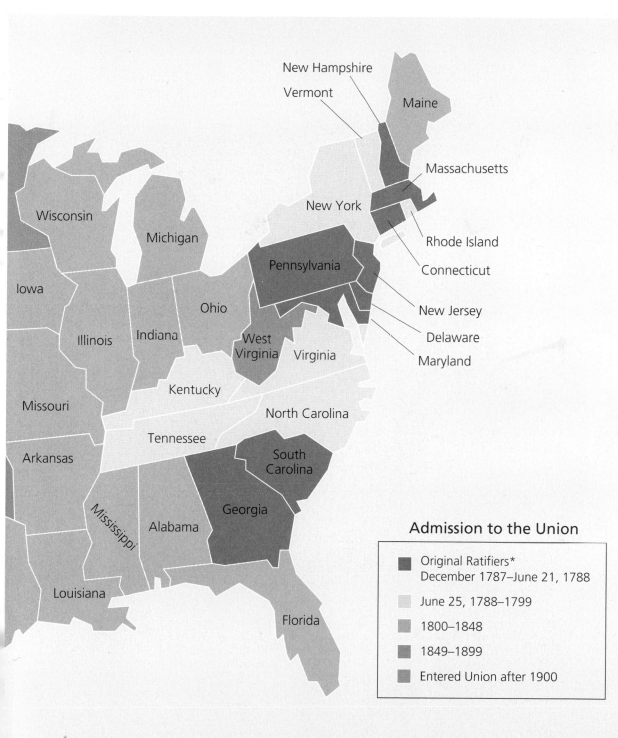

Admission to the Union

- Original Ratifiers*
  December 1787–June 21, 1788
- June 25, 1788–1799
- 1800–1848
- 1849–1899
- Entered Union after 1900

New Hampshire

Vermont

Maine

Massachusetts

New York

Rhode Island

Connecticut

New Jersey

Delaware

Maryland

Wisconsin

Michigan

Pennsylvania

Iowa

Ohio

Illinois

Indiana

West Virginia

Virginia

Missouri

Kentucky

North Carolina

Tennessee

Arkansas

South Carolina

Mississippi

Alabama

Georgia

Louisiana

Florida

Source: Bruce Wetterau, *Desk Reference on the States* (Washington, D.C.: CQ Press), 1999: 8–10.

*****Note:** Until these first nine states ratified the Constitution, it technically was not in effect.

CQ Press and **Governing** Magazine Present a New Introduction to State and Local Government

Governing States and Localities

Kevin B. Smith, *University of Nebraska–Lincoln*
Alan Greenblatt, *Governing*
John Buntin, *Governing*

with Charles S. Clark

CQ PRESS

A Division of Congressional Quarterly Inc.
Washington, D.C.

CQ Press
1255 22nd St., N.W., Suite 400
Washington, D.C. 20037

Phone, 202-729-1900
Toll-free, 1-866-4CQ-PRESS (1-866-427-7737)

www.cqpress.com

♾ The paper used in this publication exceeds the requirements of the American National Standard for Information Sciences—Permanence of Paper for Printed Library Materials, ANSI Z39.48-1992.

Cover design, interior design, and figures: Naylor Design Inc.
Composition: BMWW

Editorial/political cartoons:
Daryl Cagle at *Slate*: 57
Copyright © 1962 by Bill Mauldin. Reprinted courtesy of Mauldin Estate: 112

Historic Alabama voter registration materials: 112
Courtesy of Civil Rights Movement Veterans

Photo credits:
National Archives: 45
Massachusetts Turnpike Authority: 384
Mel Curtis/Getty Images, Inc.: xi, xx
Courtesy of the Paul P. Pressau family, photo by Stephen Aquilino: 422
Oregon Right to Life Yes on 51 Campaign: 88
Reuters: viii, x, xii, xiii, xviii, 25, 61, 64, 127, 136, 224, 250, 259, 365, 373
Courtesy of the Library of Congress: 99, 140, 195, 317, 441
AP/Wide World Photos: viii–xii, xiv–xix, 3, 12, 15, 21, 28, 34, 85, 93, 97, 105, 107, 131, 171, 176, 181, 192, 213, 220, 255, 270, 289, 295, 301, 305, 333, 336, 351, 358, 395, 409, 417, 431, 433, 453, 465, 468, 475, 492

Printed and bound in the United States of America

08 07 06 05 04   5 4 3 2 1

Library of Congress Cataloging-in-Publication Data
Smith, Kevin B.
    Governing states and localities / Kevin B. Smith, John Buntin, Alan Greenblatt.
        p. cm.
    Includes bibliographical references and index.
    ISBN 1-56802-789-3 (alk. paper)
    1. State governments—United States—Textbooks.   2. Local government—United States—Textbooks.   3. Comparative government—Textbooks.   I. Buntin, John. II. Greenblatt, Alan.   III. Title.

JK2408.S57 2005
320.473—dc22   2004020242

To my wife, Kelly
Kevin B. Smith

For Ron Elving, a great writer and student of politics, and in memory of Allan Abbott, one of my earliest teachers.
Alan Greenblatt

To Melinda
John Buntin

Brief Contents

ii Map of the United States

xii Contents

xxi Tables, Figures, and Maps

xxv Boxed Features

xxviii Preface

2 **Chapter One**

Introduction to State and Local Government: They Tax Dogs in West Virginia, Don't They?

24 **Chapter Two**

Federalism: The Power Plan

60 **Chapter Three**

Constitutions: Operating Instructions

92 Chapter Four

**Political
Culture, Political
Attitudes, and
Participation:
Venting and
Voting**

130 Chapter Five

**Parties and
Interest Groups:
Elephants,
Donkeys, and
Cash Cows**

170 Chapter Six

**Legislatures:
The Art of
Herding Cats**

212 Chapter Seven

**Governors
and Executives:
There Is No Such
Thing as Absolute
Power**

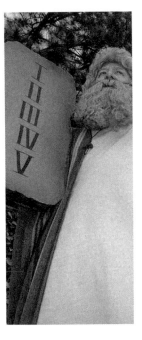

254 Chapter Eight

**Courts:
Turning Law
into Politics**

300 Chapter Nine

**Bureaucracy:
What Nobody
Wants but
Everybody
Needs**

332 Chapter Ten

**Local
Government:
Function
Follows Form**

364 Chapter Eleven

**Finance: Filling
the Till and
Paying the Bills**

394 Chapter Twelve

**Education:
Reading,
Writing, and
Regulation**

**430 Chapter
Thirteen**

**Crime and
Punishment**

**464 Chapter
Fourteen**

**Health and
Welfare: State,
Heal Thyself!**

496 Notes

519 Appendix A

520 Glossary

532 Index

Contents

Map of the United States ii

Brief Contents viii

Tables, Figures, and Maps xxi

Boxed Features xxv

Preface xxviii

Chapter 1 2

Introduction to State and Local Government: They Tax Dogs in West Virginia, Don't They?

The Impact of State and Local Politics on Daily Life 5

The Comparative Method in Practice: Yes, They Really Do Tax Dogs in West Virginia 7
  Sociodemographics 10
  Culture and History 12
  Economy 13
  Geography and Topography 15

Recognizing the Stakes 16
  Devolution 18
  Laboratories of Democracy 20

Conclusion 22

Key Concepts 23

Suggested Readings 23

Suggested Web Sites 23

Chapter 2 24

Federalism: The Power Plan

Systems of Power 28

Why Federalism?: The Origins of the Federal System in the United States 30

The Advantages and Disadvantages of Federalism   33

The Constitutional Basis of Federalism   35

The Development of Federalism   40
   Dual Federalism (1789–1933)   41
   Cooperative Federalism (1933–1980)   43
   New Federalism (1980–Present)   47

The Supreme Court: The Umpire of Federalism   52
   The Rise of Nation-Centered Federalism on the Court   53
   A Tenth Amendment Renaissance or Ad Hoc Federalism?   54

Conclusion   57

Key Concepts   59

Suggested Readings   59

Suggested Web Sites   59

Chapter 3
Constitutions: Operating Instructions

60

What State Constitutions Do: It's Probably Different than You Think   65

The Evolution of State Constitutions   69

The First Generation of State Constitutions   71

Formal Constitutional Changes   74
   Legislative Proposal   74
   Ballot Initiatives and Referendums   75
   Constitutional Conventions   78
   Constitutional Revision Commissions   79
   Ratification   79

Informal Methods for Changing Constitutions   80

Why State Constitutions Vary   81

How State Constitutions Differ   83
   Operating Rules and Selection for Office   83
   Distribution of Power   84
   Rights Granted   85
   Representative Government vs. Direct Democracy   86

Constitutions for Local Government?   90

Conclusion   90

Key Concepts   91

Suggested Readings   91

Suggested Web Sites   91

Chapter 4   **92**
Political Culture, Political Attitudes, and Participation:
Venting and Voting

State Political Cultures   96
   Elazar's Classifications   98
   Was Elazar Right?   103

Elections   104
   State Supervision of Elections   106
   Regulating the Parties   108
   Restricting Voters   110
   Voter Turnout   110

What Elections Are Used For   116
   Electing the Executive Branch   117
   Legal Offices   118
   Direct Democracy   120

Public Opinion   123
   Responding to Opinion   124

Conclusion   127

Key Concepts   129

Suggested Readings   129

Suggested Web Sites   129

Chapter 5   **130**
Parties and Interest Groups: Elephants, Donkeys,
and Cash Cows

A Primer on Political Parties   133
   What Parties Were Like   138
   Parties in the Twentieth Century   140
   How State Parties Recovered: Campaign Reform in the
      Late Twentieth Century   143

State Party Regulation and Finance   145
   State Party Regulation   145
   Campaign Finance   146

Party Competition: Why Some States Are More Competitive
than Others   149
   The Political Cultures of States   151
   Effect of Parties on Political Culture   153
   Party Factions and Activists   154
   Pragmatism vs. Idealism   156

Third Parties and Independents   157
   Difficulties of Building Support   159
   Major Party Support   160

Interest Groups and Lobbies   161

Conclusion   167

Key Concepts   168

Suggested Readings   168

Suggested Web Sites   168

Chapter 6   **170**
Legislatures: The Art of Herding Cats

The Job of Legislatures   175
    What Legislatures Do   177
    Lawmaking   178
    Representation   180
    Constituent Service   183
    Oversight   183

Organization and Operation of Legislatures   185
    Bicameralism   185
    Legislative Leadership   188
    Committees   190
    Rank-and-File Members   191
    Apportionment   193

State Legislators   195
    Professional Background   196
    Demographic Diversity   196
    Professional vs. Citizen Legislators   203

The Citizen's Whipping Boy: Legislators and Public Opinion   206

Conclusion   210

Key Concepts   211

Suggested Readings   211

Suggested Web Sites   211

Chapter 7   **212**
Governors and Executives: There Is No Such Thing as
Absolute Power

The Job of Governor   216
    Chief Legislator   218
    Head of State Agencies   219
    Chief Spokesperson for the State   220
    Party Chief   221
    Commander-in-Chief of the National Guard   222

The Powers of Governors   223
    Formal Powers   224
    Informal Powers   230

Merging Formal and Informal Powers 235

Becoming Governor and Staying Governor 236
Factors Driving Gubernatorial Elections 240
Keeping and Leaving Office 244

Other Executive Offices 248
Lieutenant Governor 248
Attorney General 249
Other Offices 251

Conclusion 252

Key Concepts 253

Suggested Readings 253

Suggested Web Sites 253

Chapter 8   **254**
Courts: Turning Law into Politics

The Role and Structure of State Courts 259
Trial Courts 260
Appeals Courts: Intermediate Appeals and Courts of Last Resort 261

Selecting Judges 264
Popular Elections 266
Appointment 271
Terms of Office 273

Judicial Compensation 277

Prosecution and Defense of Cases in State Courts 278
The Prosecutor 279
Defense Attorneys 281
Juries 286
Defendants' Rights vs. Victims' Rights 287
Sentencing 289

The Case for Court Reform 292
The Problem of Increasing Caseload 293
The Reform of Judicial Selection 295
Problems from the Lack of Sentencing Uniformity 296

Conclusion 297

Key Concepts 299

Suggested Readings 299

Suggested Web Sites 299

Chapter 9   **300**
Bureaucracy: What Nobody Wants but Everybody Needs

What Is Bureaucracy? 303

What Does Bureaucracy Do?   304
Bureaucracy as Policy Implementer   304
Bureaucracy as Policymaker   305

What Is "Enough" Bureaucracy?   307

Measuring Bureaucratic Effectiveness: It Does a Better Job
than You Think   310
*Bureaucracies Put to the Test: Who Passes and Who Fails
and Why*   311
Is There a Better Way to Run Public Programs and Services?   314

The Transformation of State Bureaucracy: From Patronage
to Professionalism   316

Politics and the Merit System   319
Public Labor Unions   319
Affirmative Action   321

If Not Merit . . . Then What?   323

The ATM Bureaucracy   327

Conclusion   329

Key Concepts   330

Suggested Readings   330

Suggested Web Sites   330

Chapter 10   **332**
Local Government: Function Follows Form

Working within Limits: The Powers and Constraints of
Local Government   337
Dillon's Rule   337
Home Rule   338

The Organization and Responsibilities of Local Governments   341
Between the County Lines   341

Municipal Governance   344
Mayor-Council Systems   345
Commission Systems   348
The Council-Manager System   348
Special Districts   350

Intragovernmental Politics   351

Participation in Local Government   357

The Road Ahead   359

Conclusion   361

Key Concepts   362

Suggested Readings   362

Suggested Web Sites   362

Chapter 11   **364**
Finance: Filling the Till and Paying the Bills

Show Me the Money: Where State Revenues Come From   368
   Sales Taxes   368
   Property Taxes   370
   Income Taxes   374
   Other Tax Revenue Sources: Cars, Oil, and Death   374
   Other Sources of Income: Fees, Charges, and Uncle Sam   377
   Insurance Trust Funds   378
   Intergovernmental Transfers   378
   Taxing Variations among State and Local Governments   379
   Explaining Tax Variations   380
   Bonds   382

The Budget Process   384
   Expenditures, or Where the Money Goes   385
   Restraints on State and Local Budgeteers   390
   Unfunded Mandates   390
   Ballot Initiatives and the Budget Process   391

Conclusion   391

Key Concepts   393

Suggested Readings   393

Suggested Web Sites   393

Chapter 12   **394**
Education: Reading, Writing, and Regulation

Organization and Leadership: Schools Have Many Bosses   398

Money Matters   402

New Pressure to Perform   407

Many Brands on the School Reform Shelf   412
   Standards and Accountability   412
   Recruiting Good Teachers   416
   Charter Schools   417
   Vouchers   419
   Privatization   420
   Home Schooling   421

Can't Tell the Players without a Program   422
   Teachers' Unions   423
   Parents' Groups   423
   National Political Parties   424
   Business Groups   424
   Professional and Advocacy Groups   425

Ever-Unsettled Issues   425

Conclusion 426

Key Concepts 428

Suggested Readings 428

Suggested Web Sites 428

Chapter 13 **430**
Crime and Punishment

Private Wrongs, Public Justice 433

Common Law, Sovereign Power 435

The Purpose of Punishment 438

New Freedoms, New Fears 440

The War on Drugs 442

Crack Cocaine 443

Harsher Punishments and Penalties: Prison Nation 445

The Return of Policing 447

Community Policing vs. the Professional Model 448

A Return to Community Policing 449

Crime, Punishment, and the Essence of Modern America 453

Trends to Watch in Criminal Justice 455
    Policing 455
    Cooperation among Law Enforcement 456
    Recidivism and the Limits of Improvement 457
    The End of Federal Support 457
    The New Criminal Frontier 457
    The Uncertain Future of the Death Penalty 459
    A New Interest in Alternative Punishment 460
    More Young People, More Crime? 461

Conclusion 462

Key Concepts 463

Suggested Readings 463

Suggested Web Sites 463

Chapter 14 **464**
Health and Welfare: State, Heal Thyself!

The Influence of Culture 469

How Government Got into the Healthcare Biz 471

The Idea of a Social Safety Net 472

The Birth of the American Safety Net 473

A Multibillion-Dollar Afterthought 474

Oops!: The Unexpected Cost of Health Insurance   475

The Devolution Revolution   477

Welfare Reform   478

The Feds Falter   480

The Rise of the Healthcare State   481

A Promising Beginning   481

Does It Work?   485

The Return of Rising Costs   485
Prescription Drugs   486
The Decline of Managed Care   486
Long-Term Care   488

The Return of Public Health   490

What Is Good Health Anyway?   492

The Future of Devolution   494

Conclusion   494

Key Concepts   495

Suggested Readings   495

Suggested Web Sites   495

Notes   **496**

Appendix A   **519**

Glossary   **520**

Index   **532**

Tables, Figures, and Maps

Tables

1-1	Politics and the Status of Women in the States: Some Variables	9
2-1	Advantages and Disadvantages of Federalism	35
2-2	U.S. Constitution's Provisions for Federalism	39
2-3	Key U.S. Supreme Court Rulings Regarding Federalism, 1992–2001	56
3-1	Procedures for Constitutional Amendment by Legislature	76
4-1	Political Cultures at a Glance	100
4-2a	Percentage of the Voting Age Population Casting Ballots in the 2000 Presidential Election	114
4-2b	Percentage of Registered Voters Casting Ballots in the 2000 Presidential Election	115
4-3	Avenues for Direct Democracy	123
5-1	Transfers from National Party Committees to State Parties, 1999–2000 Election Cycle	147
5-2	Top Ten Most Influential Interests in the States, 2002	164
5-3	Most Active Lobbying Organizations, 2000	165
6-1	Dumb Law? Or Not?	179
6-2	Ranking of States by Total Number of State Legislators, 2004	186
6-3	Ranking of States by Percentage of Legislators Who Are Women, 2004	198
6-4	Ranking of States by Percentage of Legislators Who Are African American, 2003	200
6-5	Ranking of States by Percentage of Legislators Who Are Latino, 2003	202
7-1	Formal Powers of the Governors by State	226
7-2	Ranking of the Institutional Powers of Governors, 2004	231

7-3	Ranking of the Personal Power of the Governors, 2004	237
7-4	Governors, Past and Present: Women, African Americans, and Asian American and Pacific Islanders	240
7-5	Where Do They Come From? Governors' Backgrounds	241
7-6	Recall Rules	245
7-7	The Powers of the Offices	251
8-1	Appellate Court Terms and Methods of Reappointment by State, 2004	274
8-2	Trial Court Terms and Methods of Reappointment by State, 2004	276
8-3	Judges' Salaries, 2003	278
8-4	Statistics for Prosecutorial Staff and Operations in Large Districts, 2001	280
8-5	Maximum and Minimum Annual Salary for Prosecutors in Large Districts, 2001	280
8-6	Maximum and Minimum Annual Salary of Public Defenders and Supervisory Attorneys in State-Funded Systems, 1999	282
8-7	Statistics for State-Funded Public Defender Staff and Operations, 1999	283
9-1	State and Local Government Employment by Function	308
9-2	States with the Most and the Least Bureaucracy by Number of Employees	309
9-3	States with the Most and the Least Bureaucracy by Expenditures	310
9-4	Government Performance Project, Grades at a Glance, 2001	313
9-5	States that Offer Various Online Services	328
10-1	Twenty-five Largest U.S. Counties by Population, 2000	342
10-2	Twenty-five Smallest U.S. Counties by Population, 2000	343
10-3	Most Common Forms of City Government in the United States	345
10-4	Population Change for the Ten Fastest-Growing Metropolitan Areas, 1990–2000	354
11-1	The Five States Most Reliant on Sales Tax for Revenue	370
11-2	State Individual Income Tax Rates, 2004	375
11-3	State Revenues, Expenditures, and Debt, 2000	386
11-4	Department of Health and Human Services Poverty Guidelines, 2004	389
12-1	Voter Turnout and the Timing of School Board Elections	400
12-2	Dropout Numbers and Rates in Grades 9–12 by State, 2000–2001	413
12-3	Charter School Scores	419

12-4	Types of Sanctions and Assistance for States with Policies Regarding School Sanctions, 2000	427
13-1	Percent Change in Homicides	452
14-1	Amount a Working Parent with Two Children Applying for Publicly Funded Coverage May Earn and Still Be Eligible	476

Figures

2-1	Systems of Government	29
2-2	Powers of National and State Governments	40
2-3	Key Dates in the History of American Federalism	44
6-1	The Legislative Process: How a Bill Becomes a State Law	174
8-1	State Court Structure: Illinois vs. New York	262
10-1	Strong Mayor–Council Form of Government	345
10 2	Weak Mayor–Council Form of Government	346
10-3	Council-Manager Form of Government	350
13-1	The Rise and Fall of Crime Rates: Aggravated Assault, Robbery, and Homicide Rates, 1960–2000	442
13-2	U.S. Incarceration Rate, 1920–2000	446
13-3	U.S. Incarceration Rate for Six Types of Crime	447
13-4a	Violent Crime, Arrest Rates by Age, 1976–2000	451
13-4b	Homicide, Arrest Rates by Age, 1976–1999	451
13-5	Homicides in Large U.S. Cities, 1995, 2000, 2001	452

Maps

1-1	Population by State	11
1-2	Economy by State	14
1-3	Number of Government Employees by State	17
3-1	Number of Constitutions Per State	73
3-2	Number of Amendments Adopted Per State	73
4-1	States that Currently Hold Executions	95
4-2	Dominant Political Culture by State	98
5-1	Party Affiliation Requirements for Voting in Direct Primaries	142
5-2	Interparty Competition, 1999–2003	150
5-3	Spending by Lobbyists, 2003	162

6-1	Partisan Control of State Government, 1954	189
6-2	Partisan Control of State Government, 2000	189
6-3	Full-time, Hybrid, and Part-time Legislatures	205
7-1	Women, African American, and Asian American/Pacific Islander Governors by State	239
8-1	Judicial Selection by Type of Court	266
11-1	Federal Aid to State and Local Governments, Per Capita Ranges by State, Fiscal Year 2000	379
12-1	Spending Per Student by State, 1999–2000	404
12-2	Student Enrollment in Public Schools by State, Fall 2000	405
12-3	Textbook Adoption and Open Territory States	416
13-1	Incarceration Rates (Rank) Per 100,000 Population, 2000	439
14-1	TANF Income Eligibility Thresholds	480
14-2	Highest Rates of Uninsurance	481
14-3	States as Innovators in Low-Income Health Coverage	484
14-4	Medicaid Managed Care	487
14-5	HMO Penetration Rate	487
14-6	Obesity Trends among U.S. Adults	493

Boxed Features

Local Focus

Policy in Practice

Chapter 1: Introduction to State and Local Government

A Difference that Makes a Difference   9
Is It Better to Be a Woman in Massachusetts or a Gal in Mississippi?

Local Focus   19
The Federal City

Chapter 2: Federalism

Policy in Practice   37
Preemption: The Gorilla that Swallows State Laws

A Difference that Makes a Difference   48
It Pays to Elect Republicans

Local Focus   51
The Other Federalism: State and Local Relations

Chapter 3: Constitutions

A Difference that Makes a Difference   66
State Constitutions, Educational Equity, and the New Judicial Activism

A Difference that Makes a Difference   70
The Peculiar Constitution of Early Pennsylvania

Chapter 4: Political Culture, Political Attitudes, and Participation

A Difference that Makes a Difference   107
For Whom the Ballot Polls

A Difference that Makes a Difference   112
How Some States Discourage Voters

Local Focus   125
An Online Appeal for Green Votes

Chapter 5: Parties and Interest Groups

A Difference that Makes a Difference   148
That Clean All-Over Feeling: Maine's Public Financing of Campaigns

A Difference
that Makes
a Difference

Local Focus   158
A Green Team vs. the Money Machine

Chapter 6: Legislatures

Local Focus   184
Constituent Service: Going the Extra Mile

Chapter 7: Governors and Executives

Policy in Practice   225
Governors with Gumption: Policy Innovation and Interstate Influence

A Difference that Makes a Difference   246
From State House to White House: Translating a Governorship into a Presidency

Chapter 8: Courts

A Difference that Makes a Difference   258
The New Judicial Federalism

Local Focus   270
Courting Trouble: Judicial Selection in Brooklyn

Local Focus   285
Phoenix's Flat Fees and the Death Penalty

Chapter 9: Bureaucracy

A Difference that Makes a Difference   322
Teachers' Unions and Test Scores

Policy in Practice   326
Florida Ends the Merit System

Chapter 10: Local Government

Local Focus   340
Sex and the City . . . Charter

A Difference that Makes a Difference   353
Marrying a City with a County

Local Focus   356
Loudoun County, Virginia: Caught between Sprawl and Smart Growth

Policy in Practice   360
The Feds Giveth, the Feds Taketh Away

Chapter 11: Finance

Policy in Practice   372
California's Misguided Effort to Equalize School Funding

Policy in Practice   377
Milking the Cash Cows

Policy in Practice
Are Casinos and Lotteries a Good Bet?   382

Chapter 12: Education

Policy in Practice
Do School Board Races Improve Education or Simply Create More Bumper Stickers?   400

Local Focus
Got an Alternative to Throwing Money at Schools? Tell It to Kansas City   406

Policy in Practice
How College Tuition Gets Raised   410

Chapter 13: Crime and Punishment

A Difference that Makes a Difference
Jury Power: What the Courts Don't Want You to Know   436

Policy in Practice
Is It Time to Admit Defeat in the War on Drugs?   444

Policy in Practice
Does Gun Control Work?   458

Chapter 14: Health and Welfare

A Difference that Makes a Difference
When States Go It Alone   482

Policy in Practice
Felonious Seniors   489

Local Focus
Rising from a Hospital's Ruins: Milwaukee   491

Preface

*G*overning States and Localities offers a concise and comprehensive introduction to state and local government, and does it with a difference. It is unique in that it is a collaboration between an academic and professional writers. *Governing States and Localities* rests squarely on a foundation of academic scholarship and a decade of experience teaching undergraduates about state and local government. Unlike other texts, however, this book also benefits from the input of writers and reporters from *Governing* magazine. As the preeminent publication covering state and local government, *Governing* offers unparalleled currency, data, inside knowledge, and know-how.

The involvement of *Governing* brings a fresh and contemporary perspective on state and local politics in terms of coverage and content as well as in the look and feel of the book. Taking full advantage of *Governing*'s award-winning reporting, *Governing States and Localities* deliberately follows the magazine's crisp newswriting style. The book's magazine-quality, four-color layout and design bring further life to this vital subject. The intent is to create a text that meets the highest academic and pedagogical standards while remaining engaging and easily accessible to undergraduates.

The pedagogical philosophy that provides the book's theme is the comparative method. This approach compares differences and similarities among similar units of analysis in order to explain *why* such differences exist. As scholars know well, state and local governments make excellent units of analysis for comparison because they operate within a single political system. The similarities and differences that mark their institutional structures, laws and regulations, political cultures, histories, demographics, economies, and geographies mean that they make exciting laboratories for asking and answering important questions about politics and government. Put simply, their differences make a difference.

The appeal of exploring state and local government through comparison is not just that it makes for good political science. It is also a great way to engage students, as it gives undergraduates an accessible, practical, and systematic way to understand politics and policy in the real world. Students learn why even such seemingly personal concerns as why their tuition is so darned high are not just relevant to their particular situation and educational institution, but also to the interaction of that institution with its state's political culture, economy, history, tax structure, and even the school's geographical and demographical position within the state and region. Using the comparative method, this book gives students the resources they need to ask and answer such questions themselves.

In writing this book, we made an effort to integrate local government throughout. While we have a chapter devoted solely to local government, we have placed particular emphasis on making sure that each chapter deals with local, as well as state, politics and policy. For instance, in the chapter on finance, we identify the different institutional constraints that restrict how local governments generate revenue, as well as some of the ways localities get around these obstacles. In the political participation chapter, we discuss how the different histories and cultures of cities like Camden, New Jersey, and Providence, Rhode Island, influence the political behavior of their constituents today.

Key Features

This book includes a number of elements designed to showcase and promote the main themes of the text. A set of questions at the start of each chapter engages student interest in chapter content and prompts them to begin looking systematically for answers to these questions using the comparative method. The idea is not to simply spoon-feed the answers to students, but to demonstrate how the comparative method can be used to explore and explain questions about politics and policy.

Following the comparative questions, each chapter moves on to an opening vignette modeled after a lead in a news magazine article: a compelling story, crisply written, that segues naturally into the broader themes of the chapter. Many of these opening vignettes (as well as many of the feature boxes) represent original reporting by *Governing* writers.

The feature boxes in each chapter also emphasize and reinforce the comparative theme:

- "A Difference that Makes a Difference" boxes provide clear examples of how variation between states and localities can be used to explain a wide range of political and policy phenomena. These pieces detail the ways in which a particular state's institutions, regulations, political culture, demographics, and other factors shape its constitution, the way its political parties function, how its citizens tend to vote, how it allocates its financial resources, and why its courts are structured the way they are, to name a few.

- The "Local Focus" boxes spotlight the ways localities function independently of the states and show how they are both constrained and empowered by intergovernmental ties. From battles to wrest control of their budgets from the state to constitutional restrictions on how they can tax and spend to the way that a particular municipality's political culture influences the voting behavior of its citizens, these boxes showcase the rich variety that exists in these nearly eighty-seven thousand substate entities.
- "Policy in Practice" boxes demonstrate how different states and localities have interpreted and implemented legislation handed down from higher levels of government and the consequences of these decisions. Gubernatorial policy innovators in Wisconsin and Maryland, the surprising effects of new e-government tools, and the political and policy challenges involved in tuition hikes are just some of the issues addressed.

Box themes are clearly labeled, and each has its own distinctive logo to make it easier for instructors to refer to and test on boxed material.

Another key feature that serves the comparative theme is the design and use of graphics and tables. Twenty-six full-color fifty-state maps, including three unique cartograms, provide an intuitively easy way to grasp visual representation of the differences among states and localities, whether it is a measure of the size of state economies or the different party affiliation requirements for voting in direct primaries or methods of judicial selection or state incarceration rates. Similarly, more than sixty tables and figures emphasize how states and localities differ and what these differences mean to politics and policy. State rankings of voter turnout rates, state-by-state data on per-pupil educational spending, recent regional murder rates, and many other features support comparisons made in the text.

To aid student assimilation of content, each chapter includes a set of highlighted key concepts. These concepts are defined in the margins near the text where they are introduced and are compiled into a list at the end of each chapter. To further aid the understanding and exploration of key issues and concepts, relevant Web links and lists of suggested readings, both with brief annotations, also are found at the end of each chapter. A comprehensive glossary of key concept terms follows an appendix featuring state capitals and the dates of entry into the Union and precedes the book's index.

Organization of the Book

The book is organized so that each chapter logically builds upon previous chapters. The first chapter, subtitled, "They Tax Dogs in West Virginia, Don't They?," is essentially a persuasive essay that lays the conceptual groundwork for the book. Its aim is to convince students that state and local politics are important to their day-to-day lives and to their futures as professionals and as citizens. That is, it makes the case for why students should care about state and local politics. Along the way, it introduces the advantages of the comparative method as a systematic way to explore this subject. In introducing the book's approach, the chapter provides the basic context for studying state and local government, especially the differences in economics, culture, demographics, and geography that drive policy and politics at the regional level.

The next two chapters cover federalism and state constitutions. These chapters provide a basic understanding of what state and local governments are and what powers, responsibilities, and roles they have within the political system of the United States, as well as a sense of how they legally can make different political and policy choices. The next two chapters cover political culture, political attitudes, and participation and parties and interest groups. These chapters give students a coherent sense of the important mechanisms that link citizens to state and local governments.

Chapters six, seven, eight, and nine are separate treatments of the core institutions of government: legislatures, executives, courts, and bureaucracy. There is special emphasis in each chapter on how variation in structure, powers, and responsibilities among these institutions has real-life implications for citizens of states and localities. Chapter ten focuses on local government. The final four chapters are devoted to specific policy areas: finance, education, crime and punishment, and health and welfare. These represent a selection of the most critical policy functions of state and local governments.

Ancillaries

Written by Christopher Larimer of the University of Nebraska–Lincoln, we are pleased to offer a full range of high-quality, classroom-ready instructor and student ancillaries to accompany the book. Each is specifically tailored to *Governing States and Localities*.

A CD-ROM with instructor resources is available free to adopters, including a comprehensive test bank of more than 350 true/false, multiple-choice, and short-answer questions in *CQP Test Writer* software. The test bank is easy to use as is, but instructors also may add, remove, or edit questions to their own specifications. *CQP Test Writer* software is capable of creating multiple versions of tests.

Also on the CD-ROM is a collection of more than two hundred Power-Point lecture slides tailored to the text. These slides carefully detail the core concepts of each chapter, underscoring the book's comparative principles. The slides include additional material from *Governing* magazine as well as other sources that will enhance lectures and discussion.

An Instructor's Manual with clear chapter summaries, lecture outlines, points for discussion, and sample syllabi for the course is included as well. The CD-ROM also contains .jpg and .ppt format files of all of the tables, figures, and maps in the book, as well as a handful of "bonus" visuals not found in the text. Instructors can use all of these to create additional Power-Point slides or transparency masters when covering comparative data in the classroom or in discussion groups. In addition, these visuals can be imported into exams.

A host of student resources can be found on the book's Web site at http://college.cqpress.com/govstateandlocal, including chapter summaries; self-grading quizzes for each chapter with multiple-choice, true/false, and matching questions; and a set of annotated links to important state and local Web sites.

Students and instructors alike will find *Governing* magazine's Web site especially useful for further research and in-class discussion. At www.governing.com, users of *Governing States and Localities* will find a menu of resources specially tailored to the book's content.

To help instructors bring the latest word from the states and localities to their classrooms, adopters will receive a free semester-long subscription to *Governing* magazine.

Acknowledgments

A lot of effort and dedication goes into the making of a textbook like this, only a fraction of which is contributed by those whose names end up on the cover. Appreciation must be given, first and foremost, to Peter Harkness and Alan Ehrenhalt, publisher and executive editor, respectively, of *Governing.* Getting from the glimmer of an idea to an actual game plan for the project never would have happened without their vision, enthusiasm, and generous outlay of resources—meaning, graciously letting their reporters spend company time on such an endeavor. Charles S. Clark, a former writer for the *CQ Researcher* and currently senior editor at the Association of Governing Boards of Universities and Colleges, generously agreed to share his expertise and talent by writing the chapters on local government and education. We want to express our gratitude to him for these top-rate contributions.

At the University of Nebraska–Lincoln, thanks are due to Christopher Larimer, who created the book's ancillaries, and to Daniel Braaten, who had the misfortune to be Kevin Smith's research assistant when much of this book was written. (He is recovering nicely, although any visit to a library still brings traumatic flashbacks.)

To Elise Frasier, Charisse Kiino, and Lorna Notsch, the editorial team at CQ Press responsible for much of what happened from game plan to actualization, a single word: Thanks! The word is miserly compensation for their work, effort, and dedication, and in no way makes up for all the trouble we caused. Nonetheless, the thanks are most sincerely meant. Thanks also to CQ Press's Steve Pazdan, Margot Ziperman, Paul Pressau, Joan Gossett, and Robin Surratt, who each in their various ways helped usher this book through editing and production to bring it across the finish line. To our designer, Debra Naylor, and the composition staff at BMWW, Leroy Stirewalt and Jim Taylor, we know you went above and beyond the call of duty, and we appreciate it very much.

We heartily thank our many reviewers for their careful and detailed assistance with reading and commenting on early proposals and drafts of each chapter: Sharon Alter, William Rainey Harper Community College; Jeff Ashley, Eastern Illinois University; Neil Berch, West Virginia University; Shannon Bow, University of Florida; William Cassie, Appalachian State University; Douglas Clouatre, Mid Plains Community College; Gary Crawley, Ball State University; Warren Dixon, Texas A&M University; Madhavi McCall, San Diego State University; Zachary Smith, Northern Arizona University; Kendra Stewart, Eastern Kentucky University; Charles Turner, California State–Chico, and other anonymous reviewers. We hope and expect that each of them will be able to find traces of their numerous helpful suggestions throughout this final product.

In addition, we would like to express our appreciation to a group of political scientists who pay attention not only to Washington, D.C., but also to what is happening in the rest of the country: Alan Rosenthal, Rutgers University; Larry Sabato, University of Virginia; Burdett Loomis, University of Kansas; Bruce Cain, University of California–Berkeley; Christopher Mooney, University of Illinois at Springfield; and the dean of governor-watchers, Thad Beyle of the University of North Carolina. All generously contributed their expertise when contacted by Alan Greenblatt. A special thanks also goes to Melissa Feinberg, who provided invaluable legal expertise to the chapter on state courts. Thanks to those who supported the writing of the book, both professionally and personally: Melinda Beeuwkes Buntin and Howard Husock.

Also owed thanks are the research staff at Georgetown University's Lauinger Library. Not only does the library buck current security-conscious trends by keeping its doors open to the public, but also it provides a safe haven for actual print copies of periodicals and microforms. Kudos.

Governing States and Localities

CHAPTER 1

Introduction
to State and Local Government
They Tax Dogs in West Virginia, Don't They?

Is government going to the dogs? State and local governments raise revenues in many different ways, including varying levels of income, sales, and property tax. They can tax virtually anything, including dogs. In some places a man's best friend is not only a family pet, but also a source of money for government.

Why are state and local politics important?

What is the comparative method and why is it a useful way to talk about state and local governments?

What role does state and local politics play in determining how much certain services—like a college education—cost?

Following President George W. Bush's 2003 State of the Union Address, CNN sent a reporter to gauge the reaction of undergraduates to his case for war with Iraq.

"I missed it," said an Emory University student. "There was intramural basketball in the gym."

The CNN reporter was taken aback. Bush had declared in the speech that Saddam Hussein had chemical and biological weapons and an advanced nuclear weapons program. The president had argued that Hussein's regime represented a direct threat to the national security of the United States. A few months after the speech, hundreds of thousands of Americans would be put in harm's way based on the case Bush had laid out. Under such circumstances, was intramural basketball more important than what the president had to say?

"Well," said the student, "it was the playoffs." [1]

Are college students really that disengaged from politics? If this is the reaction to a presidential case for war, how important is the topic of this book—state and local government—likely to be to them? Well, let's take a look at the "typical" college student. She is a white female between eighteen and twenty-four years old, is a full-time student at a large four-year public university, and is majoring in business or education. She is often bored with her classes, does less homework than her predecessors, and pays about $3,700 for in-state tuition and fees. She has volunteered for community service programs, prays at least once a week, and leans slightly to the left politically. She thinks that homosexual couples should have the right to marry, that marijuana should be legalized, and that affirmative action should be abolished. She has a vague idea that her state and local governments could probably do a better job addressing the issues she cares about, but she is not particularly well informed about those issues. She is not politically involved in general. She has never participated in a political campaign, thinks elected officials are not to be trusted, and does not believe that politics is really relevant to her life. [2]

"She" is a representative picture drawn from several studies that examined the characteristics and attitudes of the U. S. college population at the beginning of the twenty-first century. Yet one of the most notable things about this typical student is how *unrepresentative* she really is. College students are almost as likely to be male (44 percent) as female (56 percent), and more than 40 percent are more than twenty-five years old. One in five students is in private rather than public school, and nearly four in ten are at two-year colleges. Out-of-state students get less taxpayer support and have the tuition bills to prove it. While more college students are identifying themselves as liberals than in the past, approximately 67 percent say they are moderates or conservatives. On specific issues, 25 percent firmly oppose the legalization of homosexual marriage and large numbers oppose the legalization of marijuana.

While actual college students vary considerably from our statistical composite, our fictional student's general orientation towards politics is an accurate reflection of the undergraduate population in the United States. There certainly are exceptions, but most surveys show that college students are not particularly interested in politics. They do not see politics as really relevant to their lives. For example, in early 2001, immediately after the presidential election between George W. Bush and Al Gore, interest in politics among college students fell to all-time lows. This was one of the most hotly contested presidential elections in U.S. history, and interest actually *dropped*. A terrorist attack in September 2001, subsequent wars in Afghanistan and Iraq, and a stumbling economy in the two years that followed barely raised the importance of politics to college students.[3] Perhaps that CNN reporter should not have been surprised that intramural basketball outranked a State of the Union Address.

The variation in college students' backgrounds and beliefs, coupled with their general lack of interest in politics, presents a challenge for a textbook like this. Readers with different characteristics, expectations, and attitudes are likely to come to a course in state and local politics with different, or perhaps indifferent, expectations. The one question most readers are likely to have is: Why should I care? Fair enough. Why should you care about politics and government? More specifically, why should you care about politics and government at the state and local level? The first goal of this textbook is to make the case that *everyone*—not just college students—has a vested interest in knowing more about state and local government.

The Impact of State and Local Politics on Daily Life

Why should you be interested in state and local politics? Government at this level plays a large, if largely invisible, role in your life. Regardless of what you are interested in—money, career, religion, relationships, even sex, drugs, and rock and roll—state and local government shapes how, whether, and to what extent you will be able to pursue these interests. As an example, consider your college education. The vast majority of college students in the United States—almost 80 percent—attend public institutions of higher education.[4] Public colleges and universities are created and supported by state governments. For many readers of this textbook, the opportunity to get a college education is possible only because each state government created a system of higher education. These state governments require that taxpayers subsidize the studies of college students like you. The size of that subsidy determines the size of the tuition bill paid by most undergraduates. On average, about 36 percent of a public college's revenue comes from money the state appropriates, or sets aside. Less than 20 percent comes from tuition and fees paid by students. This means the relationship between state politics and your bank account is fairly direct: the greater the size of the state appropriation, the lower your tuition bill.[5]

If you attend a private college, you're not off the hook. State government probably still plays a significant role in covering the costs of your education. Each year, undergraduates at private colleges receive more than $2,000 in state grants or other financial aid from state or local government. Not including tuition that is several hundred dollars more than the average undergraduate at a public college receives from the state.[6]

> Regardless of what you are interested in—money, career, religion, relationships, even sex, drugs, and rock and roll—state and local government shapes how, whether, and to what extent you will be able to pursue these interests.

State governments do not just determine what opportunities are available for higher education and how much those opportunities will cost. Some states have curriculum mandates. You may be taking a course on state and local politics—and reading this book—because a state government decided that it was a worthy investment of your time and money. In Texas, for example, a state politics course is not just a good idea—it's the law. According to Section 51.301 of the Texas Education Code, in order to receive a bachelor's degree from any publicly funded college in Texas, you must successfully complete a course on state politics.

Think that's a lot of regulation? The government's role in shaping your college education is actually pretty small. Compared to the heavy involvement of state and local governments in shaping K-12 education, colleges have free rein. About 70 percent of grade school students attend public elementary and secondary schools. Local units of government operate most of these schools.[7] Private grade schools are also subject to a wide variety of state and local government regulations ranging from teacher certification and minimum curriculum requirements to basic health and safety standards. Whether you attended public or private school—or were home schooled— at the end of the day you had no choice in the decision to get a basic grade school education. Although the minimum requirements vary, every state in the union requires at least a grade school education.

State and local governments do not exist simply to regulate large areas of your life, even if it sometimes seems that way. The primary purpose of state and local governments is to provide services to their respective populations. By providing these services, state and local governments shape the social and economic lives of their citizens. Education is a good example of a public service that extends deep into the daily lives of Americans, but it is far from the only one. The roads you use to get to school are there because state and local authorities built and maintain them. The electricity that runs your computer comes from a utility grid regulated by state and/or local government. State and local governments are responsible for the sewer and water systems that make the bathroom down the hall possible. They make sure that the water you drink is safe and that the burger, sushi, or salad you bought in your student union does not make you sick.[8] State governments determine the violations and punishments that constitute the criminal law. Local governments are primarily responsible for law enforcement and fire protection. The services state and local government supply are such a part of our lives that in many cases we only notice their absence—when the water does not run, when the school is closed—rather than their presence.

The Comparative Method in Practice: Yes, They Really Do Tax Dogs in West Virginia

Recognizing the impact of state and local government may be a reasonable way to spark an interest in the topic, but interest alone does not convey knowledge. A systematic approach to learning about state and local government is necessary to gain a coherent understanding of its many activities, responsibilities, and levels. In this textbook, that systematic approach is the **comparative method**, which uses similarities and differences as the basis for systematic explanation. Any two states or localities you can think of will differ in a number of ways. For example, they really do tax dogs in West Virginia. The state authorizes each county government to assess a fee for every dog within that county's jurisdiction. This is not the case in, say, New Jersey, where dogs live tax free.[9] Texas has executed hundreds of criminals since the moratorium, or ban, on the death penalty was lifted in the 1970s. Other states have executed none. In recent elections, Georgians sent Republicans to the House of Representatives (eight of eleven seats in 2001). The people of Massachusetts sent Democrats (all nine seats in 2001). Differences between states and localities do not just involve oddities such as the tax status of the family pet or big political questions such as the balance of power in the House of Representatives. Those of you who do something as ordinary as buying a soda after class may pay more than your peers in other states or cities. Some readers of this textbook are certainly paying more in tuition and fees than those in other colleges. Why?

The comparative method answers such questions by systematically looking for **variance**, or differences, between comparable units of analysis. For our purposes, states are one comparable unit of analysis. Local governments—governments below the state level, such as county boards of com-

COMPARATIVE METHOD

A learning approach based on studying the differences and similarities among similar units of analysis (such as states).

VARIANCE

The difference between units of analysis on a particular measure.

missioners and city councils—are another. This means they have basic similarities that make meaningful comparisons possible. One way to think of this is that the comparative method is based on the idea that you can learn more about apples by comparing them to other apples rather than to oranges or bananas. Similarly, the argument is that you can learn about states by comparing them to other states. All fifty states are independent democratic governments free to make their own decisions as long as they stay within the broad confines of the single set of rules that is the U.S. Constitution. Their governmental structures are roughly the same. All have a basic division of powers between the executive, legislative, and judicial branches of government. There are different kinds and different levels of local government, but they share many of the same responsibilities. The similarities among states and among local governments make meaningful comparison possible. Their differences provide the opportunity to answer questions about politics and government.

> The comparative method is based on the assumption that you can learn more about apples by comparing them to other apples rather than to oranges or bananas. Similarly, the argument is that you can learn about states by comparing them to other states.

The states may share similar political structures and follow the same set of rules, but they make very different choices. These differences have consequences. Take, for example, college tuition and fees. As we noted earlier, there is a direct relationship between the size of a state government's contribution to higher education and a student's average tuition bill. Underlying this relationship is a set of differences that explains why your tuition bill is high (or low) compared to tuition charged by colleges in other states. Simply put, your tuition bill is comparatively higher (or lower) depending on the size of a state government's subsidy to higher education. A similar difference explains why some of you will pay more for a soda after class than others. The sales tax on a can of soda ranges from 0 to 9 percent depending on the city and state, hence different prices in different locales.[10]

Such differences can lend themselves to very sophisticated statistical analyses. A professional policy analyst can use data on state higher education funding and tuition rates at state universities and colleges to provide a precise estimate of the relationship between contributions from state government and your tuition bill: In the average state, increasing the government's contribution to higher education by one percentage point means a $65 to $75 drop in the typical student's tuition bill.[11] State appropriations make up anywhere from 14 percent to more than 50 percent of higher education revenue. These differences can literally mean thousands of dollars to you. We are not going to delve into the math underlying such analyses, but the basic logic that structures the equations is well suited for comparison. The essence of the comparative method boils down to this: Differences make a difference.

A Difference that Makes a Difference:
Is It Better to Be a Woman in Massachusetts or a Gal in Mississippi?

According to the Institute for Women's Policy Research (IWPR), it is better to be a woman in Massachusetts than a gal in Mississippi.

Why? Well, in its 2002 analysis of the status of women in the states, the IWPR had several reasons for ranking Massachusetts as the best state for women and Mississippi as the worst. For example, in Massachusetts women had greater economic autonomy and enjoyed greater reproductive rights than women in Mississippi. This is only a partial answer to the question, however. Why do women have greater economic autonomy and more reproductive rights in Massachusetts than in Mississippi?

The comparative approach to answering this question involves looking for other differences between Massachusetts and Mississippi. Differences that might explain those found between the individual indicators—such as autonomy—of the status of women. Some candidates for those explanatory differences are presented in Table 1-1. This table shows the top five and the bottom five states in the IWPR rankings, the dominant political culture in these states, and the percent of state legislators that are women. Notice any patterns?

You may have caught that each of the top five states has either a moralistic or an individualistic culture. All of the bottom five states have traditionalistic cultures. Therefore, political culture might explain some of the difference in women's status. States in which the dominant political values stress the importance of everyone getting involved might offer more opportunities for women. So might states in which such values emphasize hard work as the predominant basis for getting ahead in life. States in which the dominant political values stress leaving the important decisions to established elites might offer fewer opportunities.

Also, take a look at the proportion of females in the state legislatures. On average, almost 30 percent of state legislators in the top five states are women. In the bottom five states, that average is halved—only about 14 percent of state legislators are women. This is a difference that can have considerable impact. A number of studies show that women legislators tend to support more progressive policies, are more likely to pay attention to women's issues, and are more likely to push these issues into law.*

TABLE 1-1

Politics and the Status of Women in the States: Some Variables

Five Best States for Women	Dominant Political Culture	Percentage of State Legislators that Are Women
1. Massachusetts	Individualistic	26%
2. Minnesota	Moralistic	27.4
3. Vermont	Moralistic	30.6
4. Connecticut	Individualistic	29.4
5. Washington	Moralistic	33

Five Worst States for Women	Dominant Political Culture	Percentage of State Legislators that Are Women
46. Arkansas	Traditionalistic	16.3%
47. Oklahoma	Traditionalistic	11.4
48. Kentucky	Traditionalistic	10.9
49. Tennessee	Traditionalistic	17.4
50. Mississippi	Traditionalistic	12.6

Sources: Center for American Women and Politics, "Fact Sheet: Women in State Legislatures 2003," 2003. www.cawp.rutgers.edu/Facts/Officeholders/stwide.pdf (accessed September 18, 2003) Institute for Women's Policy Research, *The Status of Women in the States,* 2002. www.iwpr.org/states 2002/pdfs/US.pdf (accessed September 18, 2003) Daniel Elazar, *American Federalism: A View from the States* (New York: Crowell, 1966).

Thus, states that have more women in their legislatures are more likely respond to issues such as reproductive rights, violence against women, child support policies, and family leave benefits. All of these contribute to IWPR's calculations. Why is Massachusetts a better state for women than Mississippi? A comparative answer to that question is that Massachusetts has a political culture that is more likely to encourage and support political participation by women, and it also has a greater female presence in its state legislature.

*Michele Swers, "Understanding the Policy Impact of Electing Women: Evidence from Research on Congress and State Legislatures," *PS: Political Science and Politics* 34, no. 2 (2001): 217–220.

What's more, these differences can be used to answer "why" questions. For example, we know that how much a state gives to higher education helps determine how much you pay in tuition. So, you might want to know why some states provide more support to higher education than others. This is a question about one difference that can be answered by looking at other differences. What might these differences be? Well, they could range from partisan politics in a state's legislature to a state's traditions and history to its relative wealth. As a starting point for using the comparative approach to analyzing such questions, consider the following basic differences among states and among localities:

Sociodemographics

The populations of states and localities vary enormously in size, age, and ethnicity. The particular mix of these characteristics, or **sociodemographics**, in a specific state or community has a profound impact on its politics. California is the most populous state in the nation, with about thirty-four million residents. Of those thirty-four million, more than 40 percent are minorities—many of which are first-generation or second-generation immigrants—and 14 percent live in poverty. Compare this with New Hampshire, which has about 1.2 million residents, 96 percent of whom are white, and only about 7 percent of whom live below the poverty line.[12] These population characteristics present different challenges to the governments in these two states. Differences in populations are likely to promote different attitudes and policies on welfare, affirmative action, bilingual education programs, even the role and responsibilities of government in general. And it gets better. All of these population characteristics are dynamic. That is, they change. Between 1990 and 2000, the population of Philadelphia, Pennsylvania, shrank by more than 10 percent. During the same time period, the population of Phoenix, Arizona, grew by more than 20 percent. These contractions and expansions presented these two local governments with very different problems and policy priorities—the battle against urban decay and the fight for renewal versus the struggle to accommodate and serve new growth.

How are sociodemographics related to your tuition bill? Consider the age distribution from young to old of a state's population. There is less demand for college education among those over the age of sixty-five than there is among those in the traditional undergraduate demographic of eighteen to twenty-four. Given this, states with a higher percentage of their populations in the older age group face a different set of education policy pressures than those with higher concentrations in the younger group. States with large aging populations are likely to face less demand for higher education spending and more demand for public programs such as healthcare that address the needs of the elderly. Why do some states provide more sup-

MAP 1-1 **Population by State**

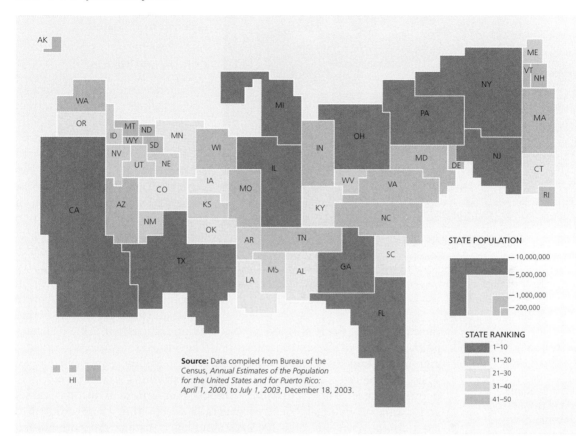

Source: Data compiled from Bureau of the Census, *Annual Estimates of the Population for the United States and for Puerto Rico: April 1, 2000, to July 1, 2003*, December 18, 2003.

port to higher education than others? At least a partial answer to this question is that different sociodemographics create different demands for higher education.

Study Map 1-1 for a moment. Believe it or not, you are actually looking at the United States. The reason the states look so strange is that this is a special kind of map called a cartogram. Instead of using actual geographical space to determine the size of a particular area represented in the map—the number of square miles in each state, for instance—cartograms use other variables to determine how size is represented. In this case, this cartogram measures the size of each state's population. This is another useful way to compare states. Notice how some states that are actually pretty big, like New Mexico at 122,000 square miles, are very small on this map because they have small populations. Other states that are actually really small, like Connecticut (only 5,000 square miles), look much bigger on this map because

Demographics and culture give each state and locality a unique "personality." In the picture above, San Francisco's Chinatown prepares for the Chinese New Year, an important event in the city's calendar. Yet while many San Francisco businesses closed in order to prepare for an official celebration, in other cities the special day passed virtually unnoticed.

they have large populations. Some states, like Virginia, don't look that different in size at all.

Culture and History

States and localities have distinct "personalities" that are apparent in everything from the "bloody bucket" shoulder patch worn by the Pennsylvania National Guard to the twang that distinguishes the speech of West Texas natives. Some states have been part of the Union for more than two hundred years and still project an Old World connection to Europe. Others, notably Hawaii and Alaska, became states within living memory and are more associated with the Old West and the exoticism of the Pacific. New York City prides itself on being a cosmopolitan center of Western civilization. The visitor's bureau of Lincoln, Nebraska, touts its small-town ambience and Middle American values. These differences are more than interesting variations in accent and local points of pride. They are visible symbols that represent distinct values and attitudes. Political scientists generally accept that these differences extend to government, and that each state has a distinct **political culture**, identifiable general attitudes and beliefs about the role and responsibility of government.

We will cover political culture, its roots, and its effects more in depth in Chapter 4. For now it is important to remember that states have different political cultures. State political cultures can be placed loosely into one of three categories: moralistic, individualistic, or traditionalistic.[13] States with **moralistic** cultures are those in which politics is the means to try to achieve a good and just society. Moralistic states such as Minnesota and Wisconsin do not have more people with morals than other states. What they do have are more citizens who are active participants in politics. These citizens see political participation as a way to contribute to the collective good. In **individualistic** cultures such as Indiana and Ohio politics is viewed as an extension of the marketplace, something in which people participate for individual reasons and to achieve individual goals. In **traditionalistic** cultures, politics is the province of elites, something that average citizens should not concern themselves with. Most states in the Deep South, including Georgia, have traditionalistic cultures.

POLITICAL CULTURE

The attitudes and beliefs broadly shared in a polity about the role and responsibility of government.

MORALISTIC

A political culture where politics and government are seen as the means to achieve the collective good.

INDIVIDUALISTIC

A political culture where politics and government are seen as just another way to achieve individual goals.

Governing States and Localities

Few states today are considered "pure" cultures. In other words, most states have elements of two of the cultures or of all three. Yet for a vast majority of states, one of these forms of political culture is likely to be dominant. Numerous studies have found that the dominant political culture shapes politics and policy in important ways. Policy change and innovation, for example, are more likely in moralistic states. Individualistic states are more likely to offer businesses tax breaks. Traditionalistic states tend to commit less public money to areas such as education.[14] Faced with similar problems, the Texas and Wisconsin state legislatures may propose radically different policy responses. These differences are at least partially a product of the political cultures that still distinguish each state. In other words, culture and history matter.

These cultural differences certainly are apparent when it comes to supporting higher education. Moralistic states commit considerably more resources to higher education than governments in individualistic and traditionalistic states. They spend about 13 percent more per capita on colleges and universities than states in the other two cultures. Since moralistic states are those in which attitudes support higher levels of commitment to the public sector, these spending differences make sense in cultural terms. Why do some states provide more support to higher education than others? Apparently, another part of our answer is that some political cultures see higher education in more communal than individual terms.

Economy

The relative size and health of a state's economy has a huge impact on its capacity to govern and provide public services. The per capita gross state product—the state equivalent to national gross product—varies from $22,516 in West Virginia to more than $46,000 in Connecticut. (See Map 1-2.) This means government in Connecticut has the ability to tap greater resources than government in West Virginia. This results in a difference to the bank accounts of citizens and to the quality and quantity of the public services they consume. State and local government revenues account for about 20 percent of personal income in Connecticut and 28 percent of personal income in West Virginia. Despite taking a smaller slice of its citizens' income, government in Connecticut can afford to spend more than West Virginia on a wide array of public services ranging from health and safety programs to environmental protection.[15] These sorts of differences are also visible at the local level. Wealthy suburbs can enjoy lower tax rates and still spend more on public services than economically struggling urban or rural communities.

Regional economic differences not only determine tax burdens and the level of public services. They also determine the relative priorities of particular policy and regulatory issues. Fishing, for example, is a sizable industry in coastal states in the Northeast and Northwest. States like Maine and

California's gross state product equals 13% of the nation's total.

MAP 1-2 Economy by State

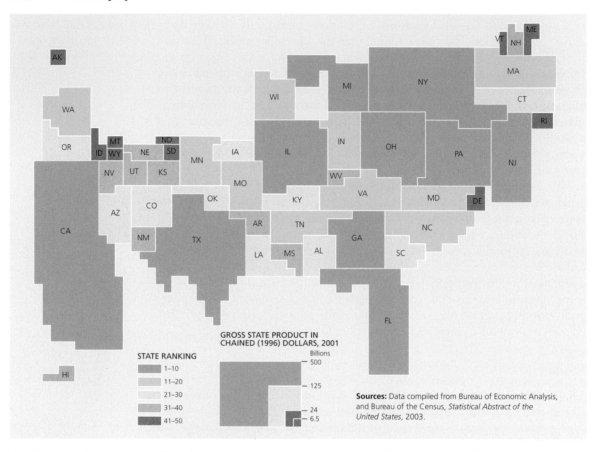

GROSS STATE PRODUCT IN
CHAINED (1996) DOLLARS, 2001

STATE RANKING

■	1–10
■	11–20
□	21–30
■	31–40
■	41–50

Billions
— 500
— 125
— 24
— 6.5

Sources: Data compiled from Bureau of Economic Analysis, and Bureau of the Census, *Statistical Abstract of the United States,* 2003.

The relative size of state economies is measured in terms of gross state product. Notice how big states with small economies (Montana and Alaska) compare to small states with big economies (New Jersey and Massachusetts).

Washington have numerous laws, regulations, and enforcement responsibilities tied to the catching, processing, and transporting of fish. Regulating the economic exploitation of marine life occupies very little government attention and resources in places such as Kansas and Nevada, although agriculture in the former and gambling in the latter create just as many policy challenges and demands for government action.

Regardless of the basis of a state's economy, greater wealth does not always translate into more support for public programs. States with above average incomes actually tend to spend *less* per capita on higher education. Why would less wealthy states concentrate more of their resources on higher education? There are a number of possible explanations. Education is a critical component of a post-industrial economy, so less well-off states may direct more of their resources into education in hopes of building a better economic future. Citizens in wealthy states may simply be better able to afford higher tuition costs. Whatever the explanation, this example shows another advantage of employing the comparative method—it shows that sometimes the obvious answers are not always the correct ones.

Geography and Topography

There is wild variation in the physical environments in which state and local governments operate. Hawaii is a lush tropical island chain in the middle of the Pacific Ocean, Nevada encompasses a large desert, much of Michigan is heavily forested, and Colorado is split by the Rocky Mountains. Such geographical and topographical variation presents different challenges to government. State and local authorities in California devote considerable time and resources to preparing for earthquakes. Their counterparts in Texas spend comparatively little time thinking about earthquakes, but they do concern themselves with tornadoes, grass fires, and hurricanes. Combine geography with population characteristics and the challenges become even more complex. Montana is a large, rural state where transportation logistics—simply getting students to school—can present something of a conundrum. Is it better to bus students long distances to large, centrally located schools? Or should there be many smaller schools within easy commuting distance? The former would be cheaper. Larger schools can offer academic and extracurricular activities that smaller schools cannot afford. But the bussing exacts a considerable cost on students and families. The latter eases the transportation burdens, but it requires building more schools and hiring more teachers, which means more taxes. Geo-

The physical environment of a state or locality helps determine the issues and problems government must attend to. In Hawaii that means being prepared to deal with road blockages and property damage caused by the occasional volcanic eruption.

graphical and population differences often not only shape the answers to such difficult policy issues, they pose the questions.

Consider the variety of seasonal weather patterns that occur within the enormous geographical confines of the United States. In Wisconsin, snow removal is a key service provided by local governments. Road clearing crews are often at work around the clock during bad weather. The plows, the crews, and the road salt, all cost money. They all require a considerable investment in administration and coordination to effectively do the job. In Florida, snow removal is low on local governments' lists of priorities for good reason—it rarely snows. On the other hand, state and local authorities in Florida do need to prepare for the occasional hurricane. Less predictable and less common than snow in Wisconsin, it only takes one hurricane to create serious demands on the resources of local authorities.

And, yes, even basic geography affects your tuition bill, especially when combined with some of the other characteristics discussed here. Many large public colleges and universities are located in urban centers because central geographical locations serve more people more efficiently. Delivering higher education in rural areas is a more expensive proposition simply because there are fewer people in the service area. States with below average population densities tend to be larger and more sparsely populated. They also tend to spend more on higher education. Larger government subsidies are necessary to make tuition affordable.

Recognizing the Stakes

The variation across states and localities offers more than a way to help make sense of your tuition bill, or to explain why some public school systems are better funded, or to understand why taxes are lower in some states. These differences also serve to underline the central role of states and localities in the American political system. Compared to the federal government, state and local governments employ more people and buy more goods and services from the private sector. They have primary responsibility for many of the issues that people care about the most, including education, crime, transportation, healthcare, and the environment. Public opinion polls often show that citizens place more trust in state and local governments than in the federal government. These polls frequently express citizens' preference for having the former relieve the latter of a greater range of policy responsibilities.[16] With these responsibilities and expectations, it should be obvious that state and local politics are played for high stakes.

> Compared to the federal government, state and local governments employ more people and buy more goods and services from the private sector. They have primary responsibility for many of the issues that people care about the most, including education, crime, transportation, healthcare, and the environment.

High stakes, yes, but it is somewhat ironic that state and local governments tend to get less attention in the media, in private conversation, and in curriculums and classrooms than their federal counterpart.[17] Ask most people to think about American government and chances are they will think first about the president, Congress, Social Security, or some other feature of the national government. Yet most American government is state and local. Five hundred and thirty-five elected legislators serve in the U.S. Congress. Thousands of legislators are elected at the state level, and tens of thousands more serve in the legislative branches of local government. The combined civilian workforce of the federal government—about three million—is almost equal in number to the single most

MAP 1-3 Number of Government Employees by State

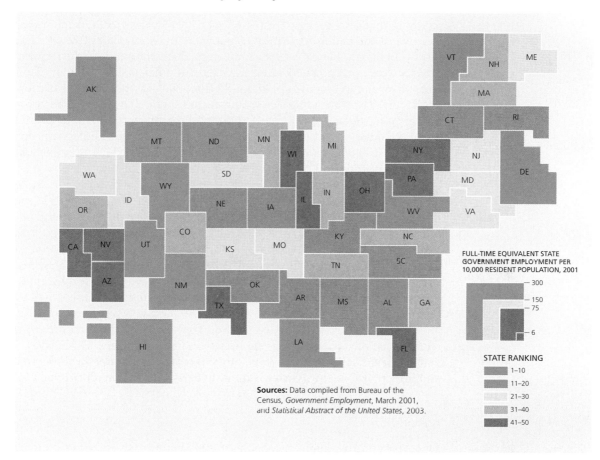

FULL-TIME EQUIVALENT STATE
GOVERNMENT EMPLOYMENT PER
10,000 RESIDENT POPULATION, 2001

— 300

— 150
— 75

— 6

STATE RANKING

1–10
11–20
21–30
31–40
41–50

Sources: Data compiled from Bureau of the
Census, *Government Employment*, March 2001,
and *Statistical Abstract of the United States*, 2003.

common category of state and local government employment—public
school teacher.[18] In terms of people, state and local governments dwarf the
federal government. Roughly five million state employees and more than
thirteen million local government employees punch the time clock every day.
(See Map 1-3). In terms of dollars, state and local governments combined
represent about the same spending force as the federal government, which
was a little more than $1.6 trillion in 1999.[19]

The size of state and local government operations is commensurate with
their twenty-first-century role in the political system. After spending much
of the twentieth century being drawn closer into the orbit and influence
of the federal government, states and localities have become much more
aggressive in asserting their independence during the past thirty years. This
maturing of nonfederal, or subnational, government has made its leaders
and its policies—not to mention its differences—one of the most important

States that are more densely
populated have fewer
employees per resident than
states that are more sparsely
populated. Why? Relatively
fewer people are required
to serve densely settled
populations than to assist
populations scattered over
large areas.

characteristics of our political system. What is at stake in state and local politics turns out to be not just what *you* are interested in, but just about anything that anyone is interested in. Consider the war on terrorism that has riveted the nation's attention in the wake of September 11, 2001. The most prominent political leaders in the immediate aftermath of the terrorist attacks were not the president or other federal officials, but Rudolph Guiliani, the mayor of New York City, and George Pataki, the governor of New York State. The reason for their prominence is simple: The responsibility for coordinating rescue efforts, evacuation, and treatment of the injured, and for maintaining social order, fell immediately to firefighters, police officers, and other arms of state and local government. The first line of homeland defense was—and will continue to be—state and local authorities.

The context of the federal system of government, and the role of state and local governments within that system, is covered more in-depth in the following chapter. Nonetheless, it is important to recognize now that governance in the United States is more network than hierarchy. The policies and politics of any single level of government are connected and intertwined with the policies and politics of the other levels of government in a complex web of interdependent relationships. The role of states and localities in these governance partnerships has changed considerably in the past few decades.

What states and localities do, and how they go about doing it, turns out to shape national life as well as the lives of individual citizens. Given what is at stake at the state and local level, no citizen can fully comprehend the role and importance of government without understanding subnational politics.

Devolution

One of the most prominent ongoing trends within the American political system is the transfer of power and policy responsibilities from national to subnational governments. A number of ideological and historical reasons lie behind this shift, but the basic impetus came from a growing belief that the national government had gone too far. It had encroached too far into jurisdictions, or areas, in which states had constitutional primacy. The increasing tide of red ink that washed over the federal budget in the 1980s and early 1990s provided another push.[20] The national government's long established *modus operandi* of tackling policy problems by providing money to the states and setting strict guidelines on its use ran into opposition in the form of popular opinion and tight budgets.

This left states in something of a quandary. During the course of a half-century or so, states had become increasingly dependent upon federal dollars to run a wide variety of popular public programs. The price for accepting the federal largesse was to agree to the strings attached to the money. While this caused some not inconsiderable grumbling about the erosion

Local Focus: **The Federal City**

Riddle me this: It is a city. It is sort of a state. It is ruled by Congress. What is it? It is the District of Columbia, otherwise known as Washington, D.C. It is also the nation's capitol, and surely the most unusual and unique local government in the country.

Technically, Washington, D.C., is a federal city. Article I, Section 8, Paragraph 17 of the U.S. Constitution gives Congress the power to rule over an area not to exceed ten square miles that constitutes the seat of national government. Yet it has never been quite clear what that means in terms of governance. Should Congress rule the city directly? Should citizens of the city be given the right to elect a representative government? If they do this, should the government be subordinate to Congress, or should it be counted as an equivalent to a state and be free to make any laws that do not violate the U.S. Constitution?

Throughout its history, these questions have been answered very differently. In the early 1800s the district was a strange collection of cities and counties, each governed by different means. Washington City and Georgetown were municipalities run by a chief executive (a mayor) and a legislature (a council). Depending on the time period, however, the mayors were sometimes appointed by the federal government and sometimes elected. In addition to the two cities, there were also two counties. Maryland laws governed Washington County. Alexandria County followed the laws of Virginia.

In the 1870s, Washington City, Georgetown, and Washington County were combined into a single governmental unit, a federal territory with a governor appointed by the president and a legislature elected by territorial residents. This eventually became the District of Columbia, or Washington, D.C. For most of its history, commissioners appointed by the federal government governed the district. It was not until 1974 that the residents of Washington, D.C., gained home rule and the right to elect their own mayor and council.

This mayor/council arrangement, however, is unlike any other municipal government in the United States. The laws passed by the council have to be reviewed and approved by Congress. The laws that govern federal-state relationships treat the district as a state, even though it is not a state and cannot operate like one. The mayor is not considered the head of a federal agency, but he or she is expected to act like one when seeking appropriations from Congress.

This odd hybrid of local, state, and federal government is reflected in the unique electoral status of Washington, D.C., voters. Voters in the district have a local vote, but only half of a federal vote. They can vote for the president, but not for a member of Congress. They can vote for a mayor and council, but they have no voting representative in Congress. Yet Congress has the power to overturn laws passed by the council. The district now has three electoral votes. Prior to 1963 it had none, and D.C. voters could not cast a ballot for president.

All this makes Washington, D.C., the nation's most unusual local government. It is the only municipality that is a creature of the United States rather than a state constitution, and as such is the only really national city in the country.

Source: Select material from Council of the District of Columbia, "History of Self-Government in the District of Columbia," 1997. www.dccouncil.washington.dc.us (accessed September 23, 2003).

of state sovereignty, generally speaking as long as the money was offered, states took it.

As the federal government sought to control its budget problems and periods of economic stress by squeezing government budgets at all levels, a consensus emerged that the national government would send less money to the states. The states, in return, would get more autonomy. This process is generically known as **devolution**. During the past twenty-five years, states began to develop their own revenue sources and became less reliant on federal grants.[21] Faced with the pressure to continue, and perhaps even expand, a broad range of public programs while getting less money from the national government, states and localities accelerated an ongoing expansion of their organizational and management capabilities and became more self-reliant. They became more financially independent and much less likely to wait for the national government to take the lead in tackling a problem. As the twenty-first century began, states had the institutional tools and the political will to aggressively assert their role as much, much more than the middle managers of the political system.

Laboratories of Democracy

Devolution gave a new relevance to a phrase coined by Supreme Court justice Louis Brandeis. He called the states **laboratories of democracy**. This metaphor refers to the ability of states—and, to a lesser extent, localities—to experiment with policy. Successful experiments can be replicated by other states or adopted by the national government. In an era in which states have greater capabilities and levels of autonomy, they are much more willing to accept the risks of innovation. It is the states, not the federal government, that are aggressively promoting new ways to solve old problems in such high profile policy areas as welfare, gun control, and education. These issues are addressed in-depth in later chapters.

How state and local governments decide to exercise their independent decision-making authority is dependent upon a number of factors. Some of these factors are external. The U.S. Constitution, federal laws and regulations, nationwide recessions, and the like constrain what states and localities can and cannot do. Increasingly, however, it is the characteristics of the state—not the firm hand of the federal government—that limits what the state decides to do.

The "big three" of these limits are wealth, the characteristics of the state's political system, and the relative presence of organized **interest groups,** or individuals who organize to support policy issues that concern them. Public programs cost money. Wealth sets the limits of possible government action. Simply speaking, wealthier states can afford to do more than poorer states. Political system characteristics are the elements of the political environment that are specific to a state. States in which public opinion is relatively conservative are likely to pursue different policy avenues than states where public opinion is more liberal. States in which Republicans dominate government are likely to opt for different policy choices than states in which Democrats dominate government. States with professional, full-time legislatures are more likely to formulate and pursue sustained policy agendas than states in which legislators are part-timers who only meet periodically. States in which the governor perceives an electoral mandate to reform government are more likely to be innovative than states in which the government perceives an electoral mandate to retain the status quo.[22] Organized interest group activity helps determine what sort of policy demands government responds to. Governments in states with powerful teachers unions, for example, will experience different education policy pressures than governments in states where teachers unions are politically weak. These factors constitute the basic ingredients for policymaking in the states. Specifics vary enormously from state to state, and the potential combinations in this democratic laboratory are virtually infinite.

Localities face more policymaking constraints than states because they typically are not sovereign governments. This means that, unlike states, local governments get their power from the level of government above them, rather than directly from citizens. The states have much greater control over local governments than the federal government has over the states. Yet while localities are much more subordinate to state government than state government is to the federal government, they do not simply take orders from the state capitol. Many local governments have independent taxing authority and broad discretion to act within their designated policy jurisdictions. These policy jurisdictions, however, are frequently subject to formal limits. The authority of school districts, for example, extends only to funding and operating public schools. State government may place lids on districts' tax rates and set everything from minimal employment qualifications to maximum teacher to pupil ratios. Yet even within this range of tighter restrictions, local governments retain considerable leeway to act independently. School districts may decide to contract out cafeteria and janitorial services, cities and counties actively seek to foster economic development with tax abatements and loan guarantees, and police commissions experiment with community-based law enforcement. During the 1990s many of the reforms enthusiastically pursued at all levels of government—reforms ranging from innovative new management practices to outright privatization of public services—had their origins in local government.[23]

What all this activity shows is that states and localities are not only the laboratories of democracy, but also the engines of the American republic.

States and localities often approach the same problem in different ways. Responding to the problem of violent crime, some governments have made it easier for citizens to carry concealed weapons. Other governments have tried to get guns off the streets by creating no-questions-asked buyback programs. In Washington, D.C., such a program was so popular that it had to be suspended because it quickly ran out of money.

> States and localities are not simply safe places to engage in limited experimentation; they are the primary mechanisms connecting citizens to the actions of government.

States and localities are not just safe places to engage in limited experimentation; they are the primary mechanisms connecting citizens to the actions of government. As the specifics of these connections vary considerably, the comparative method is an intuitive way to impose order on and make sense of politics and policy at the subnational level.

Conclusion

While pursuing the nuances and details of politics and government is not of primary interest to the typical college student, there are good reasons for developing a curiosity about state and local government. State politics determine everything from how much you pay for college to whether your course in state and local government is required or elective. Above and beyond understanding its impact on your own life and interests, state and local government is important to study because of its critical role in the governance and life of the nation. Subnational, or nonfederal, government employs more people than the federal government and spends as much money. Its responsibilities include everything from pothole repair to education to homeland security. It is difficult, if not impossible, to understand government in the United States and the rights, obligations, and benefits of citizenship without first understanding state and local government.

This textbook fosters such an understanding through the comparative method. This approach involves looking for patterns in the differences among states and localities. Rather than advocating a particular perspective on state and local politics, the comparative method is predicated, or based, on a systematic way of asking and answering questions. Why is my tuition bill so high? Why does Massachusetts send mostly Democrats to the U.S. House of Representatives? Why are those convicted of capital crimes more likely to be executed in Texas than in Connecticut? Why are sales taxes high in Alabama? Why is there no income tax in Nevada? Each of these questions can be answered by comparing states and looking for systematic patterns in their differences. The essence of the comparative method is to use one difference to explain another.

The study of state and local politics has been organized into three distinct sections. The first section consists of four chapters designed to set the basic framework, or context, for studying state and local politics. Included here are chapters on federalism, state constitutions, political participation, and political parties and interest groups. The second section covers the institutions of state and local government: legislatures, executives, courts, and bureaucracy. Although elements of local government will be discussed in all of these, there is also a separate chapter in this section devoted solely to local politics and government. The final section covers a series of distinct policy areas: budget and taxes, education, healthcare, and crime. These chapters not only cover areas of substantive policy interests, but also offer concrete examples of how a broad understanding of the context and institutions of state and local government can be combined with the comparative method to promote a deeper understanding of the politics of states and localities.

Key Concepts

comparative method (p. 7)

devolution (p. 20)

individualistic (p. 12)

interest groups (p. 20)

laboratories of democracy (p. 20)

moralistic (p. 12)

political culture (p. 12)

sociodemographics (p. 10)

traditionalistic (p. 13)

variance (p. 7)

Suggested Readings

Elazar, Daniel. *American Federalism: A View from the States.* New York. Crowell, 1966. The classic work on political culture in the states.

Gray, Virginia, and Russell Hanson, eds. *Politics in the American States: A Comparative Analysis.* 8th ed. Washington, D.C.: CQ Press, 2003. One of the better-known, comparative studies of state politics and policies. Periodically updated.

Hovey, Kendra, and Harold Hovey. *CQ's State Fact Finder 2004: Rankings across America.* Washington, D.C.: CQ Press, 2004. Comprehensive reference on all aspects of the states. Good source for comparative research.

Van Horn, Carl, ed. *The State of the States.* 3d ed. Washington, D.C.: CQ Press, 1996. Good overview of the trends in state politics and political institutions.

Suggested Web Sites

www.csg.org/csg/default. Web site of the Council of State Governments (CSG), an organization that represents elected and appointed officials in all three branches of state government. Publishes on a wide variety of topics and issues relevant to state politics and policy.

www.census.gov/statab/www/ranks.html. Bureau of the Census Web site that lists state rankings on such measures as population, per capita income, employment, poverty, and other social and economic indexes.

http://cspl.uis.edu/InstituteForLegislativeStudies/ SPPQ. Web site of *State Politics & Policy Quarterly,* an academic research journal devoted to studying state-level questions. Includes links to a publicly accessible database on state politics and policy.

CHAPTER 2

Federalism

The Power Plan

Your eyes would roll back in your head too if you were faced with the task that confronted (from left to right) Democratic Party attorney Dennis Newman; canvass board member Carol Roberts; Democratic Party attorney Ben Kuenhue; canvass board chair, Judge Charles Burton; Republican Party attorney John Bolton; canvass board member Theresa LePore; and Republican Party attorney Kevin Murphy and hundreds of election volunteers. A tragedy of errors during the 2000 presidential race between George W. Bush and Al Gore forced several Florida counties to begin recounting thousands of ballots. Ultimately, the U.S. Supreme Court ordered an end to the recounts, essentially naming George W. Bush the forty-third president of the United States. U.S. citizens got an unexpected—and headache-inducing—lesson in how federalism works.

2

What are the advantages and disadvantages of federalism?

Why do states seem to be gaining power while the federal government loses power?

Why would some businesses prefer to be regulated by the federal government rather than state governments?

On November 7, 2000, roughly 105 million Americans went to the polls intending to elect a president. Rather than a chief executive, they got a five-week lesson in **federalism.**

Federalism is a political system in which national and regional governments share powers and are considered independent equals.

FEDERALISM

Political system in which national and regional governments share powers and are considered independent equals.

In the United States, one byproduct of this decentralized approach is that the presidency goes not to the candidate who wins the most votes but rather to the one who wins the most states.

It's true. Technically, Americans do not vote directly for their president. In practice, the winner of the state's popular vote determines which set of party loyalists—Democratic or Republican—ends up in the electoral college. This is the body that actually chooses the president. Each state gets a number of electoral college delegates equal to the size of its congressional delegation. The minimum is three, since each state has two U.S. senators and at least one U.S. representative. So if the Republican candidate gets the most popular votes, the state's delegation is made up of Republican loyalists who vote for the Republican nominee. However, if the Democratic candidate wins a state's popular vote, Democratic loyalists get to be the electoral college delegates. The bottom line is that the states determine who ends up in the White House.

In 2000 the race for the presidency became a race for Florida. This single crucial state represented a cache of twenty-five electoral votes. Unlike other large electoral states such as Texas, California, and New York, the partisan loyalties of Florida's voters did not predetermine who would be going home with the state at the end of the night. Democratic candidate Al Gore could take comfort in the fact that a plurality of the state's voters were registered Democrats. Republican candidate George W. Bush had the advantage of a family connection—his brother Jeb was the state's popular governor. Florida's electoral votes were up for grabs.

Left to its own devices, who got the state's electoral votes—Gore or Bush—could have come down to the decisions made by two local officials: Palm Beach County Election Supervisor Theresa LePore and Barbara Ford-Coates, a Sarasota County tax collector. Since there is no standardized election ballot in the United States, many states, including Florida, make elections largely a local—typically county—responsibility. States and localities decide who is allowed on the ballot, what the ballot looks like, and what specific mechanism is used to cast a ballot—pulling a lever, punching a hole, making an "X" with a pencil, etc. These locally determined differences played the decisive role in 2000.

Part of LePore's job was to decide on the physical design of the ballot used in Palm Beach County. Her job was made more difficult in 2000 by the earlier activism of Ford-Coates. As part of a successful electoral reform effort a few years earlier, Ford-Coates had championed a move to make it easier for presidential candidates from minor parties—those representing the Green Party or the Libertarian Party, for instance—to get on the ballot. Rather than the four presidential candidates of 1996, LePore was faced with the difficult design task of squeezing ten candidates onto the 2000 ballot.[1]

She finally opted for the now infamous butterfly ballot design. Most observers believe that this design "confused thousands of people and apparently cost Gore thousands of votes."[2] Those few thousand popular votes were more than enough to decide the winner of Florida electoral votes. In other Florida counties, local officials found themselves dealing with similar complications and struggling to extract voter intent from half-spoiled ballots and hanging chads. A chad is the small bit of paper created when a punched-hole vote is made. A hanging chad means that the bit of paper did not separate completely from the ballot. All of this confusion triggered weeks of county-level recounts, state and federal lawsuits, and an intervention threat from the Republican-controlled state legislature. Ultimately, the issue was decided by the U.S. Supreme Court in *Bush v. Gore* (2000)—five weeks after election day. The Supreme Court disagreed with the Florida Supreme Court's interpretation of state and local electoral responsibilities, halted the county-level recount, and in effect, awarded the presidency to George W. Bush.

Few absolutes surrounded the 2000 election in Florida, but one fact it made absolutely crystal clear was the interconnected nature of federal, state, and local governments. At stake was perhaps the single most important national policy decision—who would head the executive branch of the national government. As Al Gore learned, majority rule does not count for the presidency. It is not how many popular votes you pocket, but how many states you sew up that determines whether you get to spend the next four years in the most powerful office on earth.

Even as most Americans sweated it out with Bush and Gore, much of the rest of the world looked on baffled. Yes, virtually all nations have local or regional units of government, and even the most authoritarian political system has to distribute at least some power and policy responsibilities among them. But the 2000 presidential election demonstrated that the United States is somewhat unusual. Its subnational governments—states and localities—play a central policymaking role and enjoy a high degree of independence from the central government. It is this independence that allows many of the differences across states and localities to exist and makes the comparative method a useful approach to studying them. This importance and independence are products of federalism.

Localities may not have the powers of federal or state governments, but they certainly have enough authority to make a difference in the lives of citizens. One of their powers is that of eminent domain, or the right of a government to take private property for public use. The owners of this family business, founded in 1913, were forced to sell out to the Newark, New Jersey, city government as part of a planned development project.

This system of shared powers is critical to understanding the politics of states and localities and the central role they play in the U.S. political system. The central question at the heart of it all is: Who—the federal government or the state governments—has the power to do what? The answer decides not only the presidency, but also a wide range of other far from trivial issues. In the words of noted University of Chicago law professor Cass Sunstein, the debate over the distribution of powers between the state and federal levels holds "the ultimate fate of measures safeguarding the environment, protecting consumers, upholding civil rights, protecting violence against women, protecting endangered species, and defining criminal conduct in general and banning hate crimes in particular."[3] In this chapter, we seek to provide a basic understanding of federalism, its history and evolution in the United States, and its implications for politics and governance for states and localities.

> The central question at the heart of it all is: Who—the federal government or state governments—has the power to do what?

Systems of Power

Generally speaking, a nation organized under a single sovereign government, that is, a government that depends on no other government for its political authority or power, can distribute power and responsibility throughout its political system in any of three ways. One is to concentrate power in

FIGURE 2-1 Systems of Government

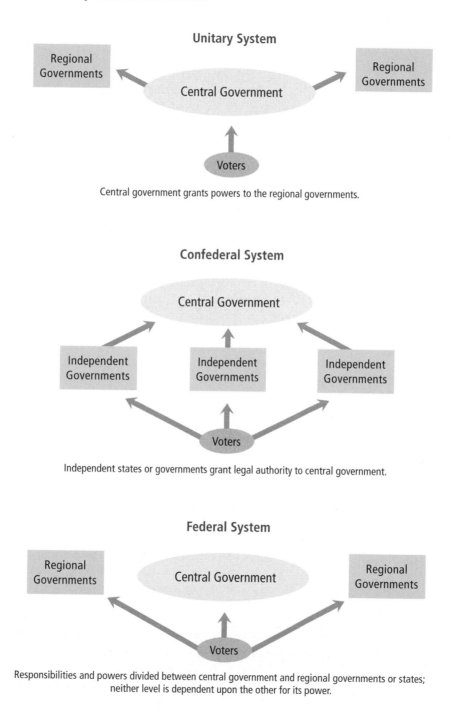

Unitary System

Regional Governments

Central Government

Regional Governments

Voters

Central government grants powers to the regional governments.

Confederal System

Central Government

Independent Governments

Independent Governments

Independent Governments

Voters

Independent states or governments grant legal authority to central government.

Federal System

Regional Governments

Central Government

Regional Governments

Voters

Responsibilities and powers divided between central government and regional governments or states; neither level is dependent upon the other for its power.

the central government. Nations in which legal authority is held almost exclusively by a central government are known as **unitary systems**. Unitary systems typically have regional or local governments, but these can only exercise the powers and responsibilities granted them by the central government. The United Kingdom is a good example of a unitary system. Although the United Kingdom has a strong tradition of local government—and has set up regional legislatures in Scotland, Wales, and (intermittently) Northern Ireland—power is concentrated in the nation's Parliament. If it so chooses, Parliament can expand or contract the powers and responsibilities of its lower governments or even shut them down entirely, which has happened periodically in Northern Ireland.

In contrast to unitary systems, confederal systems concentrate power in regional governments. A **confederacy** is a voluntary association of independent states or governments. The central government is dependent upon the regional governments for its legal authority. The United States has experimented with a confederal system twice during its history. The Articles of Confederation was the first constitution of the United States. It organized the U.S. political system as an agreement of union among sovereign states. The national government consisted of a legislature with equal representation for the states. There was no national executive branch such as the presidency and no national judiciary such as the Supreme Court. This confederal system was adopted during the Revolutionary War and remained in effect for more than a decade. The nation's founders found it wanting, however, and wrote its replacement at the Constitutional Convention of 1787 in Philadelphia. The product of that gathering—the U.S. Constitution—was ratified in 1788 and replaced the Articles of Confederation as the basis of the U.S. political system.[4] The United States' second experiment with confederacy began in 1861 at the onset of the Civil War. Those southern states that sought to secede from the Union organized their political system as a confederacy, which ended with the South's surrender in 1865.

Federal systems operate in a middle range between unitary systems and confederacies. Responsibilities in a federal system are divided between the two levels of government, and each is given the appropriate power and legal authority to fulfill those responsibilities. The system's defining feature is that neither level of government is dependent upon the other for its power. Within their defined areas of responsibility, each is considered independent and autonomous. In the United States, states are equal partners with the national government and occupy a central role in the political system.

Why Federalism?: The Origins of the Federal System in the United States

There are a number of reasons why the United States is organized as a federal, rather than as a unitary system or a confederacy. The framers of the

Constitution rejected a confederal system largely because of their experiences with the Articles of Confederation. The national government was so weak under the Articles of Confederation that prominent figures, such as James Madison and George Washington, feared it doomed the newly independent republic to failure and dissolution. These fears were not unfounded. Following the successful conclusion of the Revolutionary War in 1783, the new United States found itself in the grip of an economic recession, and the central government had little power to address the crisis. Indeed, rather than help, it actually contributed to the problem by constantly threatening to default on its debts. Independence had brought political freedom, but it also meant American-made products now were pitted in head-to-head competition with cheap, high-quality goods from Great Britain. This made consumers happy but threatened to cripple American businesses. The economic difficulties pitted state against state, farmer against manufacturer, debtor against banker, while the central government could do little but stand by and hope for the best.

As internal tensions mounted within the United States, European powers still active in the Americas threatened the nation's very sovereignty. Spain shut down shipping on the Mississippi. The British refused to withdraw from some military posts until the U.S. government paid off its debts to British creditors. George Washington believed the United States, having won the war, was in real danger of losing the peace. He said that something had to change in order "to avert the humiliating and contemptible figure we are about to make on the annals of mankind." [5]

For a loose coalition of the professional classes that called themselves Federalists, that "something" was obviously the central government. This group of lawyers, businessmen, and other individuals drawn mostly from the upper social strata began to agitate for a new constitution to replace the Articles. Their primary goal was to create a stronger and more powerful national government. Americans, however, were not particularly enthusiastic about handing more power to the central government, an attitude not so different from today. Most recognized that the Articles had numerous flaws, but few were ready to copy the example of the British and adopt a unitary system.

Two events in the fall of 1786 allowed the Federalists to overcome this resistance and achieve their goal of creating a more powerful national government. The first was the Annapolis Convention. This meeting in Maryland's capital convened to try to hammer out an interstate trade agreement. Few states sent delegates. Those who did show up had strong Federalist sympathies. They took advantage of the meeting and petitioned Congress to call for a commission to rewrite the Articles of Confederation.

The second event was Shays's Rebellion, named after its leader, Daniel Shays, a hero of the recently won Revolutionary War. The rebellion was an uprising of Massachusetts farmers who took up arms in protest of state efforts to take their property to pay off taxes and other debts. It was quickly crushed, but with further civil unrest threatening to boil over into civil war and with mounting pressure from powerful elites within the Federalist ranks, the Continental Congress was pushed to call for states to send delegates to Philadelphia in the summer of 1787. The purpose for the meeting was the rewriting of the Articles of Confederation.

The delegates formed what is now known as the Constitutional Convention. Representatives largely consisted of Federalist notables such as Washington and James Madison. Once convened, the group quickly abandoned their mandate to modify the Articles of Confederation and decided to write an entirely new constitution. In doing so, the Federalists who dominated the convention rejected confederacy as an adequate basis for the American political system. Their experience under the Articles of Confederation had taught them that a central government subordinate to the states was not much of a government at all. What they wanted was a government capable of effectively dealing with national problems, and this meant a government independent of the states. While some Federalists, most notably Alexander Hamilton, were attracted to the idea of a unitary government, such a system was never seriously considered. For one thing, there was strong popular sentiment against a unitary system. Remember that the Revolutionary War had been fought in no small part because of the perceived arrogance and abuse of a unitary system. For another, any new constitution would have to be ratified by the states, and it was highly unlikely the states were going to voluntarily agree to give up all of their powers to a national government. Federalism remained as the only practical option. Thus the establishment of a federal system of government is the central feature of the Constitution of the United States.

A federal system, however, represented more than the price that had to be paid in order to achieve a stronger national government. The Founders were attempting to construct a new form of **representative government,** a form of government in which citizens exercise power indirectly, on the basis of a paradox. Convention delegates wanted a more powerful national government, but at the same time they did not want to concentrate power for fear it would lead to tyranny. Their solution to this problem was to create a system of separated powers and checks and balances. They divided their new and stronger national government into three branches—legislative, executive, and judicial—and made each branch partially reliant on the others to carry out its own responsibilities. This made it difficult for any single group to gain the upper hand in all three divisions of government and gave each branch the power to check the excesses of the other branches. A similar set of goals was achieved by making state and national governments co-equal partners. By letting states remain independent decision makers in a wide range of policy arenas, power was divided between the national and subnational levels of government. The national government was made more powerful by the new constitution, but the independence of the states helped set clear limits on this power.

REPRESENTATIVE GOVERNMENT

A form of government in which citizens exercise power indirectly by choosing representatives to legislate on their behalf.

The Advantages and Disadvantages of Federalism

Dividing power between state and local units of government helped the Founders achieve their philosophical aims of dispersing and separating power. The newly adopted federal system overcame the immediate political challenge of getting the states to agree to a stronger national government. It also bequeathed a further set of advantages and disadvantages that have benefited and bedeviled the American political system for more than two centuries.

There are four key advantages to the federal system. First, it keeps government closer to the people. Rather than have the federal government impose a "one size fits all" policy, states have the freedom and authority to match government decisions to local preferences. This freedom also results in the local variance in laws, institutions, and traditions that characterize the U.S. political system and provide the comparative method with its explanatory strength. Second, federalism allows local differences to be reflected in state and local government policy and thereby reduces conflict. Massachusetts, for example, tends to be more liberal than, say, Alabama. California has a much more ethnically and culturally diverse population than Nebraska. Rather than have the various interests and preferences that spring from state-to-state differences engage in a winner-take-all policy struggle at the federal level, they can be accommodated at the state level. This reduces the friction among interests and lowers conflict. Third, independent subnational governments allow for flexibility and experimentation. The states, as Supreme Court justice Louis Brandeis famously put it, are "the laboratories of democracy." Successful policy innovations in one state can be adopted by other states and copied by the federal government.

Fourth, independent subnational governments make it easier to achieve at least some national goals. For example, although homeland security became a national policy priority following the terrorist attacks of September 11, 2001, the federal government was ill equipped to create emergency response plans for potential attacks in every state and every locality. It did not have the infrastructure, the resources, or the legal authority. While the national government struggled to put together an overall blueprint for homeland security, state and local governments took matters into their own hands by incorporating terrorism into their ongoing emergency response planning operations. One group, the Mid-America Regional Council (MARC), an association of 144 cities and 8 counties in the Kansas City metro area, already had a well-established arrangement that allowed local governments to cooperatively respond to emergencies. State and local organizations like MARC were well positioned to become immediate and effective terror-response agencies. The federal government simply piggybacked on these existing resources by making funds available to maximize state and local capability to combat terrorism. One set of federal grants to the MARC member Kansas City, Missouri, fire department was used to buy trailers full of special response gear and store them at strategic points throughout the metro area. The thinking was that terrorism does not respect state or municipal lines, so state and local governments in the Kansas City area must be prepared to respond accordingly.[6] So rather than create the needed emergency response infrastructure from scratch, the federal government cooperated with existing state and local organizations to achieve the broader goal of national security.

Along with its benefits, however, federalism also confers a set of disadvantages. First, while allowing local differences does keep government closer to the people, it also creates complexity and confusion. For example, if you are a nationwide business, you have to deal with state *and* federal regulations—fifty-one sets of regulations in all. That means, among other things, fifty-one tax codes and fifty-one sets of licensing requirements. Second, federalism can increase conflict as easily as reduce it. The Constitution is very vague on the exact division of powers between state and federal government. This results in a constant struggle—and a lot of litigation—in an effort to resolve what level of government has the responsibility and legal authority to take the lead role in a given policy area. Third, while federalism promotes flexibility and experimentation, it also promotes duplication and reduces accountability. Local, state, and national governments, for example, have all taken on law enforcement responsibilities. In some areas, this means there may be municipal police departments, a county sheriff's department, the state patrol, plus local offices of the Federal Bureau of Investigation and Drug Enforcement Agency. The responsibilities and jurisdictions of these organizations overlap, which means taxpayers end up paying twice for some law enforcement activities. When these agencies are unsuccessful or ineffective it also is hard to figure out who is responsible and what needs to change. Fourth, the federal system can make it hard to coordinate policy efforts nationwide. While organizations like MARC offer a well-trained, ready solution to terrorism preparedness efforts, these efforts are not uniformly duplicated in other states and other urban areas. Police and fire departments on opposite sides of a state border, or even

Local governments provide much of the nation's emergency first response capabilities. Here, Seattle police scramble over rubble and demolished buses on May 12, 2003, as part of a terrorism response exercise. The most extensive in U.S. history, the drill included hundreds of firefighters and police officers responding to the mock explosion of a radioactive "dirty bomb." Since the terrorist attacks of September 11, 2001, local authorities have been in the front lines of the war on terrorism.

Governing States and Localities

TABLE 2-1

Advantages and Disadvantages of Federalism

Advantages	Disadvantages
Allows for flexibility among state laws and institutions.	Increases complexity and confusion.
Reduces conflict because states can accommodate citizens' interests.	Sometimes increases conflict when jurisdictional lines are unclear.
Allows for experimentation at the state level.	Duplicates efforts and reduces accountability.
Enables the achievement of national goals.	Makes coordination difficult.
	Creates inequality in services and policy.

within adjacent jurisdictions in the same state, may have different communication systems. It is hard to coordinate a response to a terror attack if the relevant organizations cannot talk to each other, and the federal government cannot force state and local governments to standardize radio equipment. Finally, a federal system creates inequality in services and policies. The quality of public schools and welfare services, for example, depends heavily on the choices state and local governments make. This inevitably means that some states offer better educational opportunities and do more for the needy than others.

The Constitutional Basis of Federalism

The relationship between national and state governments is something of a sibling rivalry. It is hard to imagine either level of government getting along without the other, yet because each is independent and focused on its own interests, conflict is common. The ink was barely dry on the newly ratified Constitution before the federal government and the states were squabbling over who had the power and authority in this or that policy area. In writing the Constitution, the Founders recognized that differences between states and the federal government were likely to be a central and lasting feature of the political system. Accordingly, they attempted to head off the worst of the disputes—or at least provide a basis for resolving them—by making a basic division of powers between the national and state governments.

The Constitution grants the federal government both enumerated and implied powers. **Enumerated powers** are grants of authority explicitly given by the Constitution. Among the most important of these is the **national supremacy clause** contained in Article VI, Section 2. This states that the Constitution, "shall be the supreme law of the land; and the judges in every

ENUMERATED POWERS
Grants of authority explicitly given by the Constitution.

NATIONAL SUPREMACY CLAUSE
The constitutional clause stating that federal law takes precedence over all other laws.

state shall be bound thereby." In other words, federal law takes precedence over all other laws. This allows the federal government to preempt, or override, areas regulated by state law. In recent decades the federal government has aggressively used this power to extend its authority over states in a wide range of policy issues. So much so that **preemption** has been called "the gorilla that swallows state laws." [7]

Other enumerated powers are laid out in Article I, Section 8. This part of the Constitution details a set of **exclusive powers**—grants of authority that belong solely to the national government. These include the power to regulate commerce, to declare war, and to raise and maintain an army and navy. Article I, Section 8 also confers a set of **concurrent powers** to the national government. Concurrent powers are those granted to the national government but not denied to the states. Both levels of government are free to exercise these prerogatives. Concurrent powers include the power to tax, borrow, and spend. Finally, this same section of the Constitution also gives the national government **implied powers**. The basic idea behind implied powers is that the authors of the Constitution realized they could not possibly list every specific power the national government would require to meet the needs of a developing nation. Accordingly, they gave Congress the flexibility to meet unforeseen challenges by granting the federal government a set of broad and largely undefined powers. These include the **general welfare clause**, which gives the federal government the authority to provide for "the general welfare of the United States," and the **necessary and proper clause**, the ability for Congress "to make all laws which shall be necessary and proper" to carry out its responsibilities as defined by the Constitution.

The Constitution says a good deal about the powers of the federal government—it says very little about the powers of the states. The original, unamended Constitution spent much more time specifying the obligations of the states than it did defining their power and authority. The obligations list includes Article IV, Section 2, better known as the **full faith and credit clause**. The clause requires all states to grant "full faith and credit" to each other's public acts and records. This means that wills, contracts, and marriages valid under one state's laws are valid under all. Under the **privileges and immunities clause**, states are also prohibited from discriminating against citizens from other states. The idea here was to prevent people traveling across states or temporarily residing in a state because of business or personal reasons from becoming the target of discriminatory regulation or taxation. Other than explicitly granting the states the right to enter into compacts, or binding agreements, with each other on matters of regional concern, however, the Constitution is virtually silent on the powers of the states.

The lopsided attention to the powers of the federal government was a contentious issue in the battle to ratify the Constitution. Opponents of the Constitution, collectively known as Anti-Federalists, feared that states would become little more than puppets of the new central government. Supporters of the Constitution sought to calm these fears by arguing that states would

Policy in Practice: Preemption: The Gorilla that Swallows State Laws

It seemed a little strange that every single one of the more than three thousand taxpayers in Norwich, Vermont, would decide to become tax deadbeats at the same time. Yet that was the message the Norwich town clerk was getting throughout the summer of 1991. The town was being bombarded by phone calls and faxes from banks and mortgage companies across the country, all asking if Norwich's tax delinquents had paid off their back taxes and cleared their credit records.

In reality, there *were* no tax deadbeats in Norwich. Well, not three thousand of them at any rate. As it turned out, a credit reporting company employee hired to get copies of tax delinquency records mistakenly copied off and sent in every name on the township tax register. It was—ha, ha—just a mistake.

The Vermont legislature was not amused, especially after several similar incidents cropped up across the state. In response, it passed a law in 1992 that entitled every citizen of Vermont to one free copy of their credit record per year and forbade credit companies from passing on an individual's credit records without that individual's consent. Now it was the credit industry that was not amused. Supplying everyone with a free copy of their credit record would not be cheap and gathering individual consent created an additional administrative burden for the companies and their customers. The credit industry lobbied Congress for a federal statute, essentially asking the national government to override irritating—at least to the credit companies—state regulations such as those passed by Vermont.

As it turned out, Vermont managed to keep most of its credit privacy and protection laws on the books, although not without a fight. That fight was against the six-hundred-pound constitutional gorilla of federal preemption, which routinely swallows state laws whole. The national supremacy clause makes it clear that acts of Congress take precedence over state law, and throughout history various groups and agendas have not been shy about urging Congress to exercise this power over the states for their own benefit.

Preemption vastly simplifies interstate business transactions, so businesses are often its loudest advocates. Take your local ATM. A number of states outlaw certain ATM surcharges, viewing them as little more than attempts by large banking companies to gouge customers. Needless to say, the banking industry is not laughing and is increasingly impatient at having to deal with fifty-one sets of different—and sometimes contradictory—regulations.

The business community does often succeed in getting federal laws to preempt state laws. Recent examples include the Securities Market Enhancement Act (1999), which preempted state oversight of mutual funds, and the Telecommunications Act (1996), which gave the Federal Communications Commission the power to preempt any state or local regulation judged to discourage competition.

The three-way tussle among state preferences, national power, and the agendas of special interests such as the credit industry has produced an ironic result. In the first 200 years of its existence, Congress preempted roughly 250 state laws. In the past two decades—the era of New Federalism and devolution—it has roughly doubled that number. While devolution may have loosened federal leashes on the states, it clearly has not caged the preemption gorilla.

Source: Adapted from Ellen Perlman, "The Gorilla that Swallows State Laws," *Governing* magazine, August 1994, and Jonathan Walters, "Save Us from the States," *Governing* magazine, June 2001.

remain sovereign and independent and that the powers not specifically granted to the federal government were reserved for the states. As James Madison put it, in writing the Constitution the Federalists were seeking "a middle ground which may at once support due supremacy of the national authority," but would also preserve a strong independent role for the states.[8]

Madison and his fellow Federalists offered to put these assurances in writing. In effect, they promised that if the Constitution were ratified, the first order of business for the new Congress would be to draft a set of amendments that spelled out the limits of central government power and specified the independence of the states. Although Anti-Federalist skepticism remained, the Federalists kept their promise. The First Congress formulated a series of changes that eventually became the first ten amendments to the Constitution and are collectively known as the **Bill of Rights**.

Most of these amendments set specific limits on government power. The aim was to guarantee certain individual rights and freedoms, and at least initially, they were directed at the federal government rather than state governments. The **Tenth Amendment**, however, finally addressed the power of the states. In full, the Tenth Amendment states: "The powers not delegated to the United States by the Constitution, nor prohibited by it to the states, are reserved to the states respectively, or to the people." This provided no enumerated, or specific, powers to the states, but those implied by the language of the amendment are considerable. The so-called reserved powers encompass all of the concurrent powers that allow the states to tax, borrow, and spend; to make laws and enforce them; to regulate trade within their borders; and to practice eminent domain, which is the power to take private property for public use. The reserved powers have also been traditionally understood to mean that states have the primary power to make laws that involve the health, safety, and morals of their citizens. Yet the powers reserved for the states are more implied than explicit, and they all rest in an uneasy tension with the national supremacy clause of Article VI.

After the Tenth Amendment, the **Fourteenth Amendment** is the most important in terms of specifying state powers. Ratified in 1868, the Fourteenth Amendment is one of the so-called Civil War Amendments that came in the immediate wake of the bloody conflict between the North, or the Union, and the South, or the Confederacy. The Fourteenth Amendment prohibits any state from depriving individuals of the rights and privileges of citizenship and requires states to provide due process and equal protection guarantees to all citizens. The Supreme Court has used these guarantees to apply the Bill of Rights to state governments as well as to the federal government and to assert national power over state power in issues ranging from the desegregation of public education to the reapportioning state legislatures.

The implied powers of the federal government, the limitations set on states by the Fourteenth Amendment, and the undefined "leftovers" given to the states by the Tenth Amendment mean that the scope and the authority of both levels of government are, in many cases, dependent upon how the Constitution is interpreted. The Constitution, in other words, provides a basic framework for solving the sibling rivalry squabbles between the states and the federal government. It does not provide, however, an unambiguous guide to who has the primary power, responsibility, and authority

TABLE 2-2

U.S. Constitution's Provisions for Federalism

What It Is . . .	What It Says . . .
Article I, Section 8 (Commerce Clause)	The Congress shall have Power . . . To regulate Commerce with foreign Nations, and among the several States, and with the Indian Tribes. . . .
Article I, Section 8 (Necessary and Proper Clause)	The Congress shall have Power . . . To make all Laws which shall be necessary and proper for carrying into Execution the foregoing Powers, and all other Powers vested by this Constitution in the Government of the United States, or in any Department or Officer thereof.
Article IV, Section 3 (Admission of New States)	New States may be admitted by the Congress into this Union; but no new State shall be formed or erected within the Jurisdiction of any other State; nor any State be formed by the Junction of two or more States, or Parts of States, without the Consent of the Legislatures of the States concerned as well as of the Congress.
Article IV, Section 4 (Enforcement of Republican Form of Government)	The United States shall guarantee to every State in this Union a Republican Form of Government, and shall protect each of them against Invasion; and on Application of the Legislature, or of the Executive (when the Legislature cannot be convened) against domestic Violence.
Article VI (Supremacy Clause)	This Constitution, and the Laws of the United States which shall be made in Pursuance thereof; and all Treaties made, or which shall be made, under the Authority of the United States, shall be the supreme Law of the Land; and the Judges in every State shall be bound thereby, any Thing in the Constitution or Laws of any State to the Contrary notwithstanding.
Tenth Amendment	The powers not delegated to the United States by the Constitution, nor prohibited by it to the States, are reserved to the States respectively, or to the people.
Fourteenth Amendment	All persons born or naturalized in the United States, and subject to the jurisdiction thereof, are citizens of the United States and of the state wherein they reside. No state shall make or enforce any law which shall abridge the privileges or immunities of citizens of the United States; nor shall any state deprive any person of life, liberty, or property, without due process of law; nor deny to any person within its jurisdiction the equal protection of the laws.

TENTH AMENDMENT
Guarantees a broad, but undefined, set of powers be reserved for the states and the people, as opposed to the federal government.

FOURTEENTH AMENDMENT
Prohibits any state from depriving individuals of the rights and privileges of citizenship and requires states to provide due process and equal protection guarantees to all citizens.

FIGURE 2-2 Powers of National and State Governments

National Government Powers	Concurrent Powers	State Government Powers
Coin money		Run elections
Regulate interstate and foreign commerce		Regulate intrastate commerce
Tax imports and exports		Establish republican forms of state and local government
Make treaties	**Concurrent Powers**	Protect public health, safety, and morals
Make all laws "necessary and proper" to fulfill responsibilities	Tax	All powers not delegated to the national government or denied to the states by the Constitution
Make war	Borrow money	
Regulate postal system	Charter banks and corporations	
	Take property (eminent domain)	**Powers Denied**
Powers Denied	Make and enforce laws and administer a judiciary	Tax imports and exports
Tax state exports		Coin money
Change state boundaries		Enter into treaties
Impose religious tests		Impair obligation of contracts
Pass laws in conflict with the Bill of Rights		Enter compacts with other states without congressional consent

Source: Adapted from Lee Epstein and Thomas G. Walker, *Constitutional Law for a Changing America: Institutional Powers and Constraints,* 5th ed. (Washington, D.C.: CQ Press, 2004). 323, Table III-1.

on a broad range of policy issues. This, as we shall see, means that the U.S. Supreme Court is repeatedly thrust into the role of refereeing power disputes between national and state governments.

The Development of Federalism

Disagreements about the scope and authority of the national government broke out shortly after the First Congress convened in 1789. The issue of a national bank was one of the most controversial of these early conflicts and the one with the most lasting implications. Alexander Hamilton, secretary of the treasury under President George Washington, put together a broad program designed to get the newly empowered national government to address the nation's economic woes. Part of this program was the proposed creation of a national bank. The problem was that although Hamilton believed a central bank was critical to stabilizing the economic situation there was nothing in the Constitution that specifically granted the federal government the authority to create and regulate such an institution.

Lacking a clear enumerated power, Hamilton justified his proposal by using an implied power. He argued that the necessary and proper clause implied the power to create a national bank because the bank would help the government manage its finances as it went about its expressly conferred authority to tax and spend. Essentially, Hamilton was interpreting necessary as "convenient" or "appropriate." Secretary of State Thomas Jefferson objected, arguing that if the Constitution was going to establish a government of truly limited powers, the federal government needed to stick to its enumerated powers and interpret its implied powers very narrowly. He thus argued that the "necessary" in the necessary and proper clause should be properly interpreted as "essential" or "indispensable." Hamilton eventually won the argument, and Congress approved the national bank. Still, the issue simmered as a controversial—and potentially unconstitutional—expansion of the national government's powers.

The issue was not fully resolved until 1819 when the Supreme Court decided the case of *McCulloch v. Maryland*. This case stemmed from the state of Maryland's attempts to shut down the national bank—which was taking business from state chartered banks—by taxing its operations. The chief cashier of the national bank's Baltimore branch refused to pay the tax, and the parties went to court. The Supreme Court, in essence, backed Hamilton's interpretation of the Constitution over Jefferson's. This was important above and beyond the issue of a national bank. It suggested that the Constitution gave the national government a broad set of powers relative to the states. Key to this early affirmation of the federal government's power was Supreme Court Chief Justice John Marshall, whose backing of a broad interpretation of implied powers laid the foundation for later expansions in the scope and authority of the federal government.

The full impact of *McCulloch v. Maryland*, however, would not be felt for some time. For the most part, the federal government began to feel its way into the gray areas of its constitutional powers pretty cautiously. Federalism went on to develop in three distinct stages—dual federalism, cooperative federalism, and new federalism—and the first of these stages leaned towards the more limited role of the federal government favored by Jefferson.

Dual Federalism (1789–1933)

Dual federalism is the idea that state and federal governments have separate jurisdictions and responsibilities. Within these separate spheres of authority, each level of government is sovereign and free to operate without interference from the other. It represents something of a middle ground in the initial interpretations of how the Constitution divided power. On one side of the debate were Federalists like Hamilton, who championed a nation-centered view of federalism. They wanted to interpret the Constitution as broadly as possible to give the national government supremacy over the states.

DUAL FEDERALISM

The idea that state and federal governments have separate and distinct jurisdictions and responsibilities.

STATES' RIGHTS

The belief that states should be free to make their own decisions with little interference from the federal government.

COMPACT THEORY

The idea that the Constitution represents an agreement among sovereign states to form a common government.

NULLIFICATION

The process of a state rejecting a federal law and making it invalid within state borders.

SECESSION

The process of a government or political jurisdiction withdrawing from a political system or alliance.

NATION-CENTERED FEDERALISM

The belief that the nation is the basis of the federal system and that the federal government should take precedence over the states.

On the other side were fierce **states' rights** advocates like John Calhoun of South Carolina, who served as vice president in the administrations of John Quincy Adams and Andrew Jackson. Supporters of states' rights wanted the federal government's power limited to the greatest possible extent and saw any expansion of it as an encroachment upon the sovereignty of the states. In the 1820s and 1830s Calhoun formulated what became known as the **compact theory** of federalism. The idea was that the Constitution represented an agreement among sovereign states to form a common government. It interpreted the Constitution as essentially an extension of the Articles of Confederation, meaning that the United States was more a confederal system than a federal one. The compact theory argued that since sovereignty ultimately rested with the states, the states rather than the Supreme Court had the final say in how the Constitution should be interpreted. The states also had the right to reject federal laws and make them invalid within their own borders. This process was known as **nullification,** and the compact theory took it to an extreme. Calhoun argued that states could reject the entire Constitution and choose to withdraw, or secede, from the Union. In the 1820s national policies—especially a trade tariff—triggered an economic downturn in the southern states, creating wide support for nullification and **secession** arguments. These extreme states' rights views were not completely resolved until the Union victory in the Civil War ended them for good.

Dual federalism walked the line of moderation between the extremes of **nation-centered federalism** and **state-centered federalism**. Basically, dual federalism looks at the U.S. political system as a layered cake. The state and federal governments represent distinct and separate layers. To keep them separate, advocates of dual federalism sought to limit the federal government to exercising only a narrow interpretation of its enumerated powers. If the Constitution was to be interpreted broadly, that interpretation should favor the states rather than Congress. This became the central operating philosophy of the U.S. Supreme Court for much of the nineteenth century and is most closely associated with the tenure of Chief Justice Roger B. Taney, who served from 1836 to 1864. Unlike his predecessor John Marshall, Taney was much less sympathetic to arguments that interpreted the federal government's powers broadly.

The dual federalism doctrine gave rise to some infamous, not to mention downright notorious, landmark decisions on the powers and limitations of the federal government. Perhaps the best known expression of the philosophy came in *Scott v. Sandford* (1857). Dred Scott was a slave taken by his master from Missouri, a slave state, to Illinois, a free state, and on into what was then called the Wisconsin Territory, where slavery was outlawed by the Missouri Compromise of 1820. This federal law stipulated which new states and territories could and could not make slavery legal. After his master's death, Scott sued for his freedom, arguing that his residence in a free territory had legally ended his bondage. Scott's case was tied to the Missouri Compromise, which the Supreme Court subsequently ruled unconstitutional. Their justification was that Congress did not have the enumerated, nor the implied, power to prohibit slavery in the territories. Thus Scott remained a slave, although his owners voluntarily gave him his freedom shortly after the Supreme Court decision. He died of tuberculosis in 1858, having spent only one of his nearly sixty years as a free man.

Cooperative Federalism (1933–1980)

In theory dual federalism defines and maintains a clear division between state and national governments and sets a clear standard for doing so: If the federal government has the enumerated power to take the disputed action or make the disputed law, it has supremacy over the states in the particular case. If it does not have the enumerated power, then the Tenth Amendment reserves that power for the states and state preferences take precedence.

The problem was that its clarity in theory rarely matched the complex realities of governance in practice. State and national government have shared interests in a wide range of issues that range from education to transportation. To cleanly divide these interests into separate spheres of influence was not only hard, in many cases it was not even desired. Even at the height of the dual federalism era, state and federal governments were collaborating as much as they were fighting. The federal government, for example, owned vast tracts of land in the Midwest and West, and it made extensive grants of these lands to the states to help develop transportation and education systems. Many of the nation's best-known state universities got their start this way as land-grant colleges. In the nineteenth century the federal government also gave out cash grants to support Civil War veterans housed in state institutions, gave money to the states to support agricultural research, and loaned federal manpower—primarily Army engineers—to help state and local development projects.[9] Rather than a layered cake, some experts believe a more appropriate metaphor for federalism is that of a marble cake—the different levels of government so thoroughly mixed with each other they are impossible to separate.

Certainly as the nation became increasingly industrialized and more urban, state and federal interests became increasingly intertwined. As the nineteenth century drew to a close and the twentieth century began, the federal government undertook a significant expansion of its policy responsibilities. In 1887 it began to regulate the railroads, a policy with enormous significance for the economic development of states and localities. In economic and social terms this was roughly equivalent to the federal government of today announcing comprehensive regulation of the Internet and software manufacturers. By fits and starts, dual federalism gradually fell out of favor with the Supreme Court. The Court instead began to interpret the powers of the federal government very broadly and to allow the jurisdictions of state and national governments to gradually merge. Several events accelerated this trend. The First World War (1914–1918) resulted in a significant centralization of power in the federal government. The Second World War (1939–1945)

STATE-CENTERED FEDERALISM

The belief that states are the basis of the federal system and that state governments should take precedence over the federal government.

FIGURE 2-3 Key Dates in the History of American Federalism

Left	Year	Year	Right
Revolutionary War starts	1775	1776	Declaration of Independence adopted
Articles of Confederation ratified	1781	1783	Revolutionary War ends
Annapolis Convention	1786	1786	Shays's Rebellion
Constitutional Convention drafts new constitution	1787	1788	U.S. Constitution ratified
First Congress adopts Bill of Rights	1791		
McCulloch v. Maryland establishes that the federal government has a broad set of powers over the states	1819		
Roger Taney sworn in as chief justice; adopts dual federalism as model for federal-state relations	1836	1832	South Carolina attempts to nullify federal law
		1857	*Scott v. Sandford* demonstrates the limits of the federal government
Southern states experiment with confederacy as Civil War starts	1861	1860	South Carolina secedes from the Union in December; hostilities between North and South begin a month later
		1865	Civil War ends with Union victory; Thirteenth Amendment abolishes slavery
Fourteenth Amendment passes	1868		
		1887	Federal government regulates the railroads
Great Depression	1930	1933	Franklin Delano Roosevelt takes office; era of cooperative federalism begins
		1972	Richard Nixon begins revenue sharing
Election of Ronald Reagan and emergence of New Federalism	1980		
Supreme Court decides *Bush v. Gore;* George W. Bush receives Florida's contested electoral votes and becomes president	2000	1986	William Rehnquist becomes chief justice; Supreme Court begins to look more favorably on states' rights arguments

centralized that power even further. The need to fight global conflicts pushed the federal government to assert the lead role on a wide range of economic and social issues. Even more important to the long-term relationship between state and national governments was the Great Depression of the 1930s, a social and economic catastrophe that swept aside any remaining vestiges of dual federalism.

State and local governments were ill equipped to deal with the problems created by the Great Depression. They simply did not have the resources and, at first, the federal government was simply reluctant to act. The catalyst for a fundamental change in the nature of state-federal relations was the election of Franklin Delano Roosevelt to the presidency

The Great Depression placed enormous strain on state and local governments and spurred the development of cooperative federalism. The workers pictured above are undertaking a classic state and local responsibility—building a road—although the work itself is a part of a federally funded and administered project. This blurring of federal, state, and local responsibilities during the 1930s became the hallmark of federalism in the United States for much of the twentieth century.

in 1932. In an effort to combat economic and social malaise, Roosevelt aggressively pushed the federal government into taking a lead role in areas traditionally left to the states. The federal government in the 1930s became deeply involved in regulating the labor market, creating and managing welfare programs, and providing significant amounts of direct aid to cities. The general approach of Roosevelt's so-called New Deal agenda defined the central characteristics of **cooperative federalism**—use the federal government to identify the problem, set up the basic outline of a program to address the problem, make money available to fund that program, then turn over much of the responsibility for implementing and running it to the states and localities. This arrangement dominated state and federal relations for the next half-century.

Having all levels of government addressing problems simultaneously and cooperatively paid dividends. It combined the need to attack national problems with the flexibility of the decentralized federal system. Cooperative federalism, however, also signaled a significant shift in power away from the states and toward the federal government. The key to this power shift was money. An ever-increasing proportion of state and local budgets came from federal coffers. At the beginning of the nineteenth century, federal grants constituted less than 1 percent of state and local government revenues. By the middle of the 1930s, federal grants accounted for something like 20

COOPERATIVE FEDERALISM

The notion that it is impossible for state and national governments to have separate and distinct jurisdictions and that both levels of government must work together.

percent of state and local revenues.[10] By the 1960s the federal government aggressively began attaching strings to this money. Federal-state relations evolved into a rough embodiment of the Golden Rule of politics—he who has the gold, gets to make the rules.

Cooperative federalism is characterized by three types of federal **grants-in-aid,** which are cash appropriations given by the federal government to the states. Grants-in-aid are distinguished from each other by the constraints put on how the money can be spent. **Categorical grants** are federal funds given to states and localities for very specific programs. Recipients have little discretion on how to spend the money. Federal highway funds, for example, often come in the form of categorical grants. **Block grants** are federal funds given to states and localities for general policy areas such as education or public transportation. Recipients have more discretion on how to use the funds, although the programs the money underwrites have to stay within the policy area targeted by the grant. **General revenue sharing grants** were federal funds turned over to the states and localities with essentially no strings attached. Although popular with states and localities—from their perspective it was "free" money—this type of grant-in-aid had a short life span. Born during the Nixon administration in the late 1960s, general revenue sharing was killed by the Reagan administration in the early 1980s.

Federal grants, strings or no strings, do not sound so bad on the surface. Money is money, and a government can never have too much. The problem was that the grants were not distributed equitably to states and localities, and a central feature of cooperative federalism was the often fierce competition to control and access these revenues. The politics became complex. One form of these politics was between the states and the federal government over what type of grant should be used for a particular policy or program. States and localities favored federal grants with fewer strings. Congress and the president often favored putting tight guidelines on federal money, since this allowed them to take a greater share of the credit for the benefits of federal spending. Another form of grant politics was the competition between states and localities for access to the funds. Applying for grants became a specialized and highly prized skill. State and local governments with more professionalized and well-organized bureaucracies—or with savvy, congressional delegations with majority party influence—were better positioned to get these revenues.

Perhaps the most important dimension of the politics of grants-in-aid, however, was the federal government's increasing desire to use its purse strings to pressure states and localities into adopting particular policies and laws. Beginning in the 1960s and 1970s, cooperative federalism began a new, more coercive era with the rise of ever more stringent grant conditions. These included **crosscutting requirements,** or strings that applied to all federal grants. For example, one condition to receive virtually any federal gov-

GRANTS-IN-AID

Cash appropriations given by the federal government to the states.

CATEGORICAL GRANTS

Federal grants-in-aid given for specific programs that leave states and localities with little discretion on how to spend the money.

BLOCK GRANTS

Federal grants-in-aid given for general policy areas that leave states and localities with wide discretion on how to spend the money within the designated policy area.

GENERAL REVENUE SHARING GRANTS

Federal grants-in-aid given with few constraints, leaving states and localities almost complete discretion over how to spend the money.

ernment grant is an assessment of the environmental impact of the proposed program or policy. Accordingly, most state and local governments began writing—and defending—environmental impact statements for any construction project that involved federal funds.

The federal government also began applying **crossover sanctions**. Crossover sanctions are strings that require grant recipients to pass and enforce certain laws or policies as a condition of receiving funds. An example is the twenty-one-year-old drinking age. The federal government requires states to set this as the minimum legal drinking age as a condition of receiving federal highway funds. Increasingly, the strings came even if there were no grants. State and local governments were issued direct orders, essentially commanded, to adopt certain laws or rules such as clean water standards and minimum wage laws.[11] These **unfunded mandates**—federal laws that require state action but offer no compensation—became a particular irritant to state and local governments. Even where there was broad agreement on the substance of the mandate, subnational governments resented the federal government's taking the credit for these actions while leaving the dirty work of finding funds and actually running the programs to the states and localities. Congress eventually passed a law banning unfunded mandates in the mid-1990s, but it is full of loopholes. For example, the law does not apply to appropriations bills—the laws that actually authorize the government to spend money. In fiscal year 2004 the National Conference of State Legislatures estimated the federal government shifted $29 billion in costs onto the states. Despite the law, Congress continues to pass laws and pass the costs to the states.[12]

New Federalism (1980–Present)

Cooperative federalism's centralization of power in the national government always faced opposition from states' rights advocates, who viewed the growing influence of the national government with alarm. By the end of the 1970s cooperative federalism was also starting to face a practical crisis—the federal government's revenues could not keep up with the demand for grants. With the election of Ronald Reagan in 1980, the practical and ideological combined to create pressure for a fundamental shift in state and federal relations.

Reagan was not the first president to raise concerns about the centralization of power in the national government under cooperative federalism. A primary reason for Nixon's support of general revenue sharing, for example, was the attraction of giving states more flexibility by cutting the strings attached to federal grants. It was not until Reagan, however, that a sustained attempt was made to reverse the course of cooperative federalism. Reagan believed the federal government had overreached its boundaries and wanted to return power and flexibility to the states. At the core of his

CROSSCUTTING REQUIREMENTS
Constraints that apply to all federal grants.

CROSSOVER SANCTIONS
Federal requirements mandating that grant recipients pass and enforce certain laws or regulations as a condition of receiving funds.

UNFUNDED MANDATES
Federal laws that direct state action but provide no financial support for that action.

A Difference that Makes a Difference:
It Pays to Elect Republicans

Why do some states and localities get more federal grants-in-aid than others? At least part of the answer comes from state and local differences in partisan loyalties and demographics. Who you send to Congress—and the programs they champion—has considerable implications for where the federal government spends its grant money.

There is an old saying that "to the victor go the spoils," and in the 1990s the spoils were sweet—albeit with a definite pork-like twang—for the constituents of victorious Republican members of Congress. Following their takeover of the House of Representatives in 1994, Republicans precipitated a massive geographical shift in federal spending. In simple terms, Republican districts began to get more federal dollars than Democratic districts.

The numbers tell a fairly straightforward story. In 1995 the federal government spent an average $3.9 billion on various grants and programs in Republican and Democratic House districts. In 2001, spending in Republican House districts increased to $5.8 billion, while spending in Democratic districts increased only to about $5.2 billion. So six years after the Republican takeover of the House, GOP members of Congress were getting an average of $612 million more spent in their districts compared to their Democratic colleagues.

Thus the comparative method can help explain why federal spending varies so widely across the states—if a state's voters send members of the majority party to Congress they are rewarded with a greater share of federal grant money. It is not only the differences in partisanship that help explain the variation in federal spending, but also the geographic and demographic characteristics of the state. After 1994, federal grant dollars shifted to programs favored by Republicans, and it turns out these have distinct geographical and demographic differences from programs favored by Democrats.

For example, after 1994, spending on child care, public housing grants, and food stamps have been cut, and in some cases virtually eliminated. These are all programs traditionally favored by Democrats. Spending on direct payments to farmers, business loans, and crop insurance programs increased by as much as 700 percent. These are all programs traditionally favored by Republicans. The net result has been a shift of federal money from poor and rural—and more likely to be Democratic—areas to the more Republican suburbs and GOP-leaning farm country.

Source: Adapted from David Pace, "Majority Status Enriched GOP Areas," *Washington Post,* August 6, 2002, A13.

NEW FEDERALISM

The belief that states should receive more power and authority and less money from the federal government.

---

vision of state-centered **New Federalism** was the desire to reduce federal grants-in-aid but, in return, give states more policymaking leeway with the money they did get.

Reagan's drive to make this vision a reality had mixed success. The massive budget deficits of the 1980s made cutting grants-in-aid to states and localities a practical necessity. Reducing the federal government's influence over states and localities turned out to be another matter. Reagan, like many conservatives, was a modern heir to a states' rights perspective that dated back to the Anti-Federalist movement. This meant he believed that government should be as close to the voters as possible—in the city hall or the state capitol building—rather than far away in Washington, D.C. Yet believing that government should be closer to the people in the abstract is far different from putting that belief into practice. Taking power from the federal government did advance a core philosophical belief of the Reagan administration, but it also created problems for Reagan supporters, who were not shy about voicing their displeasure.

Core conservative constituencies such as business quickly realized that dealing with one government was much less of a headache than dealing with fifty governments. They almost immediately began to put counterpressure on the movement towards expanded state policymaking authority. The result was something of a push-and-pull, with the Reagan administration trying to shove power back to the states with one set of legislative priorities and yank it back to the federal government with another. Reagan did succeed in cutting grants-in-aid. He consolidated fifty-seven categorical grants into nine new block grants. General revenue sharing and another sixty categorical grants were eliminated entirely. This reduced the amount of money sent to the states while increasing their ability to act independently.[13] Yet Reagan also engaged in a number of fairly aggressive preemption movements and backed a number of unfunded mandates. This reduced the independence of states and forced them to fund programs they did not necessarily support.

The seeds of New Federalism had a hard time taking root at the national level, but its roots sank fast and sank deep at the state and local level. States were caught between the proverbial rock of a cash-strapped federal government and the hard place of the demand for the programs traditionally supported by federal funds. States slowly and often painfully worked themselves out of this dilemma by becoming less reliant on the federal government. They aggressively began pursuing innovative policy approaches to a wide range of social and economic problems.

Subnational governments and conservative constituencies both had their reasons for wanting New Federalism to just dry up and blow away, but their wish was not to be. "New federalists" emerged from the 1980s who included prominent Democrats and Republicans whose desire to get the states out of the federal government's shadow became an increasingly well organized and coordinated movement. Groups such as the National Governors Association and the National Conference of State Legislatures gave a powerful voice to state concerns, a voice that had an increasingly sympathetic ear in the White House. None of the first six presidents following World War II—Truman, Eisenhower, Kennedy, Johnson, Nixon, and Ford—had gubernatorial experience. Four of the next five—Jimmy Carter, Ronald Reagan, Bill Clinton, and George W. Bush—all had served as governors. Only George Bush, who took over the Oval Office from Reagan, had never held the position. This meant that the state perspective was in many ways the White House perspective. There was, as one author put it, "a developing agreement among state and national political elites that states should have greater authority and flexibility in operating public programs."[14]

Political elites were not alone in their increasing desire to push power from the federal government. Public opinion polls consistently show that Americans place more trust in state and local governments and express a

Less than 10% of Minnesota's nonelderly population is uninsured.

greater confidence in their ability to effectively manage a broad range of policies and programs compared to the federal government.[15] In the 1990s the Clinton administration picked up the pace of an orderly transition of power from the federal to the state level, an extension of New Federalism that was termed devolution. Although devolution essentially sought to reverse the trend of centralizing power in the federal government that had been created by cooperative federalism, the primary characteristic of the state-federal relations remained grants-in-aid. The Clinton administration did follow Reagan's lead and shifted authority to the states by consolidating categorical grants and federal entitlement programs into block grants. Probably the best-known example of this is the Work Opportunity Reconciliation Act of 1996, popularly known as the law that "ended welfare as we know it." The law ended Aid to Families with Dependent Children (AFDC) and replaced it with a block grant. In essence, the law reduced the federal government's financial commitment to social welfare programs and turned over primary policymaking responsibilities in this area to the states.

Like its parent, New Federalism, the devolution revolution faced strong resistance, often from an old enemy. Conservatives, at least rhetorically, still were the strongest states' rights advocates. Yet when states' rights conflicted with key portions of the conservative political agenda, conservative groups still fought tenaciously for federal supremacy over the states, just as they had during the 1980s. A good example is the 1996 Defense of Marriage Act. This federal law was proposed in the wake of movements in Hawaii and Vermont to legalize same sex unions. Now, remember, the full faith and credit clause means that a contract made under the laws of one state is legally recognized and binding in all states. If one state made same sex unions legal, it raised the possibility that the other forty-nine states would have to recognize civil unions as the legal equivalent of marriage. There was a strong push from many traditional states' rights advocates for the federal government to, in essence, grant states exceptions from their full faith and credit obligations. The Defense of Marriage Act did this. It also put the federal government into the business of defining what constitutes a marriage, an area traditionally left to the states.[16]

This was not enough to stop some states and localities from moving toward legalizing same sex unions under their own laws. In 2004 the Massachusetts Supreme Court ruled that legally prohibiting same sex marriages violated the state's constitution. This cleared the way for gay couples to marry. In the same year, the city of San Francisco began issuing marriage licenses to same sex couples before being ordered to stop by the California Supreme Court. Some viewed these developments with alarm. Although the obligation of states to recognize same sex unions was a point of legal debate in 2004, many conservatives began to call for a constitutional amendment banning gay marriage, a proposal that President George W. Bush publicly supported. Such an amendment would be in many ways the ultimate form of federal preemption. Conservatives have not limited their calls for federal

Local Focus: The Other Federalism: **State and Local Relations**

Imagine watching a riveting television ad about municipal finance. Tough to do? Well, try writing one. In 2002, that was a large part of Mike Madrid's job. A Republican political consultant, he was helping mount a campaign to urge voters to help protect the finances of local governments in California against poaching from the state.

Madrid basically had the voters on his side—polls suggest that most citizens believe local taxes should stay in the hands of local governments. Yet getting voters engaged and attentive to matters of local finance proved extremely hard. Madrid found that the complexity of the financial entanglements between state and local governments created more glazed eyes than righteous indignation in focus groups.

Local governments in California have good reason to be concerned about losing control over their own budgets. For example, in 1978 school districts controlled more than half of their revenues. Now they control only 5 or 6 percent of their budget. The state determines or funds the rest. A quarter century of initiatives has severely shrunk the discretionary budget of local governments and increasingly made them little more than dependents of the state.

The real problem is that local governments in California and throughout the nation are at a severe disadvantage in any power struggle with the state. Although collectively states are part of a federal system of government, within their own borders they essentially are considered unitary governments. In other words, local governments do not enjoy the roughly equal footing in their relations with the states that the states have in their relations with the federal government. Within any single state, power is concentrated in state government. Local governments are only allowed to exercise the powers delegated to them.

Despite this, in many ways states and localities do engage in the same sort of cooperative relationship that has evolved between state governments and the federal government. States, for example, provide a good deal of funding to local governments and place a variety of strings on how this money can be spent. Yet the power imbalance between states and localities can cause considerable friction, especially when states impose unfunded mandates on local governments, set limits on their revenue raising, direct how their budgets are to be spent, and take or withhold revenues raised from local sources. State constitutions can provide municipalities with a reasonable measure of independence, but in practical terms, if local governments are to win in a power struggle with state government they are largely dependent upon their ability to persuade the state legislature or to persuade voters to approve a ballot initiative.

Local governments are far from helpless, but the bottom line is that they have no blanket equivalent of the Tenth Amendment to protect their claims of sovereignty. Instead, state-local relations are governed by what is known as Dillon's Rule, which asserts that local governments can only exercise the powers granted to them by state governments. The rule is named after Judge John F. Dillon, who laid down the basic justification for the argument in his nineteenth century work, *Commentaries on the Law of Municipal Corporations.* At least informally, it is Dillon's Rule that ultimately solves most local-state conflicts—and the ruling is rarely on the side of localities.

Source: Adapted from Alan Greenblatt, "Enemies of the State," *Governing* magazine, June 2002, 26–31.

dominance to gay marriage, however. In the past few Congresses, conservatives have also pushed the federal government to preempt state authority in a broad array of other policy areas that range from electric utility deregulation to property rights.

The mixed commitment to New Federalism is perhaps best exemplified by the presidency of George W. Bush. Bush came to the White House directly from the Texas governor's mansion and at least on the surface was a strong supporter of the principles of New Federalism. He established the Interagency Working Group on Federalism shortly after being inaugurated and charged it with finding ways to cut through the regulatory red tape that often accompanies grants-in-aid. The group was also asked to identify additional federal programs that could be turned over to the states. Once again, the federal government was making it easier for the states on the one hand by reducing grant application hassle while making it harder for them on the other hand by giving them more programs to support with those grants. Reuben Morales, director of the federal Office of Intergovernmental Affairs, summarized the Bush administration's approach to federalism by saying, "federalism is no longer just about which level of government does what. Services and programs are more integrated than ever before . . . (and) the federal government must finds ways to be a better partner with states and localities." [17]

Three things conspired to blunt Bush's plans to accelerate the trends of New Federalism: recession, war, and his own agenda. Throughout the history of the United States, power has centralized in the national government during times of crisis—it simply is better equipped to deal with national economic challenges or international conflict. The Bush administration found itself struggling with a soft economy while also committing the nation's resources to a global war on terrorism in response to the devastating attacks of September 11, 2001. Both problems pretty much required that the federal government take a lead policy role. On top of this, key parts of Bush's agenda specifically called for a stronger federal role in areas that were the traditional responsibility of states and localities. His education proposals, such as the No Child Left Behind Act, imposed a broad set of federal standards on local schools.

All of this has conspired to make some argue that the first decades of the twenty-first century are likely to be characterized by what some have called **ad hoc federalism** rather than a continued commitment to the core principles of New Federalism.[18] Ad hoc federalism describes the process of choosing a state-centered or nation-centered view of federalism on the basis of political or partisan convenience. In other words, the issue at hand, not a core philosophical commitment to a particular vision of federalism, will determine a policymaker's commitment to state or federal supremacy.

The Supreme Court: The Umpire of Federalism

Article VI, the national supremacy clause of the Constitution, declares that the Constitution, laws passed by Congress, and national treaties are the "supreme law of the land." This does not mean that the states are always subordinate to the national government. Don't forget—the Tenth Amendment also counts as part of that supreme law. However, it does mean that

AD HOC FEDERALISM

The process of choosing a state-centered or nation-centered view of federalism on the basis of political or partisan convenience.

federal courts often have to referee national-state conflicts. Since it has the final say in interpreting the Constitution, the Supreme Court is, in effect, the umpire of federalism. Its rulings ultimately decide the powers and limitations of the different levels of government.

The Rise of Nation-Centered Federalism on the Court

Throughout U.S. history the Supreme Court has cycled through trends of state-centered and nation-centered philosophies of federalism. As we have already seen, the early Supreme Court under Chief Justice John Marshall pursued a fairly broad interpretation of the federal government's powers in cases such as *McCulloch v. Maryland*. Marshall's successor, Roger Taney, took the Court in a more state-centered direction by establishing dual federalism as the Court's central operating philosophy. The shift from dual federalism to cooperative federalism required a return to a more nation-centered judicial philosophy. Although the Court initially took a more nation-centered track in its rulings following the Civil War, it was not until the Great Depression and Roosevelt's New Deal that a decisive tilt in its rulings cleared the way for the rise of cooperative federalism and the centralization of power in the national government.

A number of New Deal programs—including the Agricultural Adjustment Act, which provided federal subsidies to struggling farmers—at first were struck down. In a series of 5–4 rulings, the Court declared these programs to be unconstitutional expansions of federal power. In 1937 a frustrated Roosevelt proposed to "pack" the Court as a way to prod it into fully accepting cooperative federalism. Under this plan, every time a justice turned seventy and did not retire, the president could appoint an additional judge to the Court. Roosevelt's scheme would have allowed him to alter the balance of power on the Supreme Court by packing it with up to six more members.

Reaction to the plan was largely negative. The proposed law reached Congress pretty much dead in the water—and is remembered today as one of the Roosevelt presidency's few public relations disasters. Law or not, however, the court-packing plan had the desired effect. As it became apparent that Roosevelt was serious about pursuing a significant shake-up, the Supreme Court switched direction and began to rule in favor of key New Deal proposals. This included upholding the constitutionality of the first Social Security Act.

The shift towards a liberal interpretation of the federal government's powers dominated the Supreme Court's operating philosophy for much of the next sixty years and is exemplified by *United States v. Darby Lumber Co.* (1941). The substantive issue at stake was whether the federal government had the power to regulate wages. The Supreme Court said yes, but the decision is of more lasting interest because of the majority opinion's dismissive comment on the Tenth Amendment. Supposedly the constitutional lockbox of state power, the Court viewed the amendment as doing little more than stating "a truism that all is retained which has not been surrendered." In other words, the Tenth Amendment was simply a basket for the "leftover" powers the federal government had not sought or did not want.

During and after the New Deal era, the Supreme Court also accelerated a trend of broadly interpreting Congress's powers to regulate interstate commerce. It did this through its interpretation of the **interstate commerce clause**. In *Wickard v. Filburn* (1942), the Court ruled that the clause gave Congress the power to regulate what a farmer can feed his chickens. In *Heart of Atlanta Motel v. United States* (1964) and *Katzenback v. McClung* (1964), the justices ruled it gave Congress the power to regulate private acts of racial discrimination. A series of such decisions over the course of more than fifty years led some judicial scholars to conclude that the Supreme Court had essentially turned the concept of enumerated and reserved powers on it head. In effect, the assumption now seemed to be that the federal government had the power to do anything the Constitution did not specifically prohibit.[19] The states and localities were drawn ever closer into subordinate satellite roles in orbit around the federal government. This situation continued until just before the turn of the twenty-first century. Once again the Court began siding with the states over the federal government.

INTERSTATE COMMERCE CLAUSE

The constitutional clause that gives Congress the right to regulate interstate commerce. This clause has been broadly interpreted to give Congress a number of implied powers.

A Tenth Amendment Renaissance or Ad Hoc Federalism?

By the mid-1990s, the Supreme Court was dominated by justices appointed by new federalists. Reagan, who had campaigned on his intention to nominate federal judges who shared his conservative philosophy, appointed four. He also elevated a fifth, William Rehnquist—originally appointed by Nixon—to the position of chief justice. Reagan's vice president and presidential successor, George Bush, appointed two more justices. The end result was a Supreme Court chosen largely by conservative Republican presidents who wanted limits set on the federal government's powers and responsibilities. The justices obliged.

A series of such decisions over the course of more than fifty years led some judicial scholars to conclude that the Supreme Court had essentially turned the concept of enumerated and reserved powers on its heads. In effect, the assumption now seemed to be that the federal government had the power to do anything the Constitution did not specifically prohibit.

In a series of narrow—mostly 5–4—decisions in the 1990s, the Court began to back away from the nation-centered interpretation of the Constitution that had dominated its rulings during the era of cooperative federalism. An early signal of this new direction was *New York v. United States* (1992). At issue in this case was the Low Level Waste Policy Amendments Act of 1985, which mandated that states establish radioactive waste facilities. The Supreme Court ruled the law unconstitutional and sided with states' rights advocates who claimed that Congress did not have the authority to force states to take responsibility for what amounted to a federal regulatory program.

United States v. Lopez (1995) was an even more significant victory for states' rights and a clear break from a half century of precedent. This case involved the Drug Free School Zone Act of 1990, which made it a federal crime to possess a firearm within one thousand feet of a school. Following a good deal of precedent, Congress justified its authority to regulate local law enforcement by using a very liberal interpretation of the interstate commerce clause. The Supreme Court disagreed and argued that the commerce clause granted no such authority. Similar reasoning was used by the justices in *United States v. Morrison* (2000) to strike down the Violence Against Women Act (VAWA). Congress had passed this law in 1994 out of concern that the states, although having primary responsibility for criminal law, were not adequately dealing with the problem of violence against women. The key provision of the VAWA gave assault victims the right to sue their assailants in federal court. Congress argued that it was authorized to pass such a law because fear of violence prevented women from using public transportation or going out unescorted at night. Such fears, the reasoning went, placed limits on economic opportunities for women. This argument made the connection to commerce and Congress's constitutional authority. The Supreme Court again rejected this broad interpretation of the commerce clause.

At the same time that it was narrowly interpreting the Constitution to limit federal power, the Supreme Court after 1990 began to interpret the Constitution broadly to expand state power. Notably, the Court made a series of rulings that broadly interpreted the Eleventh Amendment's guarantee of **sovereign immunity** to the states. Sovereign immunity is essentially "the right of a government to be free from suits brought without its consent."[20] In cases such as *Seminole Tribe of Florida v. Florida* (1996) and *Alden v. Maine* (1999), the Supreme Court adopted an interpretation of the Eleventh Amendment that limited the right of citizens to sue states for violations of federal law. These rulings not only lessened the power of the federal government over the states, they arguably gave the states more power over their own citizens.

Although these and other rulings resurrected the Tenth Amendment and underlined the independent power of the states, there was also an element of inconsistency to Supreme Court decisions after 1990. As we have already seen in *Bush v. Gore* (2000), the Supreme Court seemed to abandon its commitment to states' rights by overruling the Florida Supreme Court and ordering a halt to the contested recount of presidential ballots. In effect, the Supreme Court overturned the state court's interpretation of state law and decided the presidency in favor of George W. Bush. Another decision that favored federal power over state power came in *Lorillard Tobacco Co. v. Reilly* (2001). Here, the Court overturned a Massachusetts law that regulated the advertising of tobacco products. The Court argued that federal

TABLE 2-3

Key U.S. Supreme Court Rulings Regarding Federalism, 1992–2001

New York v. United States (1992)	Court strikes down federal law mandating that states establish radioactive waste facilities. State claim upheld.
United States v. Lopez (1995)	Court strikes down a federal law prohibiting possession of firearms near public schools. State claim upheld.
Seminole Tribe of Florida v. Florida (1996)	Court rules Congress cannot allow citizens to sue states in a federal court except for civil rights violations. State claim upheld.
Printz v. United States (1997)	Court strikes down federal law requiring mandatory background checks for firearms purchases. State claim upheld.
United States v. Morrison (2000)	Court strikes down federal Violence Against Women Act. State claim upheld.
Reno v. Condon (2000)	Court upheld a federal law preventing states from selling driver's license information. State claim overturned.
Alden v. Maine (2000)	Court rules that Congress does not have the power to authorize citizens to sue in state court on the basis of federal claims. State claim upheld.
Bush v. Gore (2000)	Court overrules Florida Supreme Court action allowing hand recounts of contested election ballots. State claim overturned.
Alabama v. Garrett (2001)	Court rules that state employees cannot sue their employees in federal court to recover monetary damages under the provisions of the Americans with Disabilities Act. State claim upheld.
Lorillard Tobacco Co. v. Reilly (2001)	Court strikes down Massachusetts laws regulating the advertising of tobacco products. State claim overturned.

law—specifically, the Federal Cigarette Labeling and Advertising Act—legitimately preempts state law on this issue.

Some scholars argue that these sorts of inconsistencies have long been characteristic of the Supreme Court's federalism rulings. It is ideology—not a firm commitment to a particular vision of state-national relations—that ultimately decides how a justice will rule in a particular case.[21] Therefore, a

CLOSED CAPTIONING PROVIDED FOR THE HEARING IMPAIRED.

Court dominated by conservative appointees will occasionally depart from the state-centered notion of federalism if a nation-centered view is more ideologically pleasing, while a Court dominated by liberal appointees will do the opposite. The Supreme Court, like the president, also finds it hard to resist the temptations of ad hoc federalism.

Conclusion

The Constitution organizes the United States into a federal political system. This means that the states are powerful, independent political actors that dominate important policy areas. Many of these policy areas are those with the most obvious and far-reaching roles in the day-to-day lives of citizens. Education, law enforcement, utility regulation, and road construction are but a handful of examples. The independence they are granted under the federal system allows states a broad leeway to go their own way in these and many other policy areas.

The resulting variation has a number of advantages, such as making it easier to match local preferences with government action and allowing states and localities to experiment with innovative programs or policies. There are also a number of disadvantages. These include complexity and difficulty in coordinating policy nationally. The interests of state and national governments overlap in many areas. Because of this and because the Constitution does not clearly resolve the question of who has the power to do what in these arenas of shared interest, conflict is inevitable.

What is the future of federalism? Whether the states' rights perspective embedded in New Federalism will evolve into the guiding principle of future state-federal relations or give way to the less predictable whims of ad hoc federalism remains to be seen. Over the past decade or so, Congress and the president have exhibited a very mixed commitment to devolution. The federal government has pushed for greater state authority in areas such as welfare and Medicaid, while simultaneously pursuing aggressive preemption of state laws in areas such as crime and the environment.[22] Broader social trends and world events are also complicating the drive to allow the states more independence. The burden of homeland security, for example, falls heavily on states and localities. Yet the federal government is directing and, with mixed success, taking the lead in coordinating these efforts. The drive for recognition of gay marriages is gaining ground in some states, and in response many who would normally consider themselves states' rights advocates are pressuring for federal dominance in this area. Finally, the states spent much of the first four years of the twenty-first century in a severe budgetary bind, even as they were asked to take on more responsibility by the federal government. The net result is not gradual flow of power from Washington, D.C., to state capitals, but an inconsistent give and take, with the supporters of national or state dominance shifting with the issue.

The federal system has evolved into a complex web of intergovernmental relationships that recognizes the practical necessity of cooperation between the various levels of government. All of this creates a situation ripe for continued conflict between state and federal governments, conflicts that in many cases will have to be resolved by the Supreme Court. The Court recently has been much more sympathetic to state claims than in the past, but it has also exhibited some inconsistency in its commitment to favoring states' rights in resolving state-federal conflicts. Yet regardless of how these conflicts are ultimately resolved, the future undoubtedly will find states and localities continuing to play a central role in the U.S. political system, both as independent policymakers and as cooperative partners with the federal government.

Key Concepts

ad hoc federalism (p. 52)
Bill of Rights (p. 38)
block grants (p. 46)
categorical grants (p. 46)
compact theory (p. 42)
concurrent powers (p. 36)
confederacy (p. 30)
cooperative federalism (p. 45)
crosscutting requirements (p. 46)
crossover sanctions (p. 47)
dual federalism (p. 41)
enumerated powers (p. 35)
exclusive powers (p. 36)
federalism (p. 26)
Fourteenth Amendment (p. 38)
full faith and credit clause (p. 36)
general revenue sharing grants (p. 36)
general welfare clause (p. 36)
grants-in-aid (p. 46)
implied powers (p. 36)
interstate commerce clause (p. 54)
national supremacy clause (p. 35)
nation-centered federalism (p. 42)
necessary and proper clause (p. 36)
New Federalism (p. 48)
nullification (p. 42)
preemption (p. 36)
privileges and immunities clause (p. 36)
representative government (p. 32)
secession (p. 42)
sovereign immunity (p. 55)
state-centered federalism (p. 42)
states' rights (p. 42)
Tenth Amendment (p. 38)
unfunded mandates (p. 47)
unitary systems (p. 30)

Suggested Readings

Ellis, Richard E. *The Union at Risk: Jacksonian Democracy, States' Rights, and the Nullification Crisis.* New York: Oxford University Press, 1990. A history of the states' rights movement and the nullification crisis of the 1820s and 1830s.

Peterson, Paul E. *The Price of Federalism.* Washington, D.C.: Brookings Institution, 1995. Overview of how federalism operates in the United States; documents how federal-state relations have evolved.

Storing, Herbert J., and Murray Dry. *What the Anti-Federalists Were For.* Chicago: University of Chicago Press, 1981. Explains why the Anti-Federalists opposed the U.S. Constitution and fought for the Bill of Rights.

Walker, David B. *The Rebirth of Federalism: Slouching toward Washington.* 2nd ed. Washington, D.C.: CQ Press, 1999. Comprehensive history of federalism in the United States and an assessment of current problems and issues.

Suggested Web Sites

www.ncsl.org/statefed/statefed.htm. Web site dedicated to state-federal issues sponsored by the National Conference of State Legislatures.

ww2.lafayette.edu/~publius. Web site of *Publius,* a scholarly journal dedicated to the study of federalism.

www.federalismproject.org. Web site of the Federalism Project, a program sponsored by the American Enterprise Institute that promotes New Federalism ideas.

CHAPTER 3

Constitutions

Operating Instructions

What's really behind this sign? The issue of judicial interpretation. In 2003, judges in Massachusetts, California, and several other states began to interpret antidiscrimination laws as being applicable to marriage. In essence, this made same-sex marriages legal. Efforts to halt such unions took the form of a proposed amendment to Massachusetts's constitution. Here, Charles Chester of Quincy, Massachusetts, speaks out. Gathering in front of the Massachusetts State House in February 2004, Chester and hundreds of other protesters urged state legislators to veto the amendment and to keep the constitution as is.

THE CONSTITUTION
DEFEND IT
don't amend it

What impact do state constitutions have on our lives?

Why do state constitutions differ?

How do they determine what state and local governments can and cannot do?

Mercedes-Benz and Alabama. The pairing of the German luxury automaker with one of the poorest states in the United States is not exactly a natural fit.

But in 1992 when then governor Jim Folsom learned that Mercedes wanted to build a new line of sports utility vehicles in the United States, he resolved to bring the plant and its 1,400 jobs to Alabama.

**CONSTITUTIONAL
CONVENTION**

An assembly convened
for the express purpose
of amending or replacing
a constitution.

To do this, he first had to overcome a variety of obstacles. Some were to be expected. These included competition from neighboring states and opposition from lawmakers who balked at offering lavish subsidies—approximately $250 million in tax breaks, rebates, and outright payments—to the automaker. One problem, however, was a bit unexpected: the state's own constitution.

Alabama's current constitution was drafted in 1901 by a small group of wealthy planters. The group had gathered in Montgomery, the state capital, for a **constitutional convention** during which they amended the document. Its primary purpose, in the words of convention chair John Knox, was to "secure white supremacy in this state." A secondary goal was to ensure the primacy of planters like Knox. Although unlikely, a coalition of sharecroppers and miners and industrial workers from Birmingham's fast-growing coal mines and steel mills would have threatened elite rule in Alabama.

To achieve these ends, Knox's constitution threw up a series of roadblocks to slow industrialization in Alabama. After the Civil War, county governments had run up big debts to build railways and modernize the state. The new constitution banned such activities. In fact, it barred counties from passing local ordinances entirely. Power was concentrated in the state government instead. The planters then proceeded to take that power and make certain it was not put to good use. To underscore their belief that the state had no role in promoting public works, they inserted a section that decreed that "the state shall not engage in works of internal improvement, nor lend its money or its credit in aid of such; nor shall the state be interested in any private or corporate enterprise." [1]

Fortunately for Governor Folsom, by the time he went after Mercedes this particular section had been amended—if not abolished. But Alabama's constitution continued to cause trouble. It provides that all money raised by the state's personal income and corporate taxes must go to education. So when Gov. Folsom offered Mercedes a cushy rebate on corporate income tax payments, Alabama's powerful teachers' union threatened to sue—an action that might have scuttled the entire deal. Ultimately, such controversies and questions helped sink Folsom's bid for reelection. A new governor mollified the teachers' union, built the plant, and created thousands of new jobs.

This routine, if large-scale, economic development initiative occurred despite Alabama's constitution, not because of it.[2] The state has one of the nation's more unusual constitutions. It has been amended 665 times and is now more than 310,000 words long. That's about the length of a one thousand-page novel. But Alabama is not the only state to have constitutional provisions that are at best quirky and at worst obsolete. Until 1999, Texas's constitution—drafted in 1876—required that the state government provide aid to indigent or disabled Confederate soldiers and mandated that it defend the population against Indians and "predatory bands."[3] Faced with such oddities, it's sometimes easy to conclude that state constitutions are quaint relics with little relevance to everyday life. Yet as Alabama discovered, nothing could be further from the truth.

State constitutions have an enormous impact on state governments and policymaking—and on us. They affect the education we receive, the employment opportunities we enjoy, the political culture of the states in which we live, and the rights we do—or don't—have, as the case may be. State constitutions and the rights and powers they provide also vary widely. Alabama's constitution makes it difficult for Alabama's chief executive to recruit businesses in ways that in other states would be routine. The constitution of Massachusetts—as recently interpreted by that state's supreme court—requires the state to provide homosexual couples with the rights and benefits of marriage. Yet until the U.S. Supreme Court struck down antisodomy laws in 2003, many other states had laws that criminalized gay sex. California's constitution embraces the idea of **direct democracy**. The **electorate**, or those individuals who can vote, can make its opinions known at the voting booth. **Ballot initiatives** and **referendums** allow voters to override the decisions of the state's elected officials—or even remove the officials entirely—with ease. New York's constitution does not. Its politicians are famously insulated from voters' demands, and decisions are made by a handful of senior elected officials.

What explains the tremendous variation among state constitutions? A state's constitution reflects its historical experiences, its political culture, its geography, and its notions of what makes good government. Alabama's constitution, for instance, reflected the fear of a planter class that believed rapid industrial development would threaten the "best" form of government—that is, planter government. Although some resisted it at the time, the state's generally traditional political culture made these ideas broadly

DIRECT DEMOCRACY
The means for citizens to make laws themselves, rather than relying on elected representatives.

ELECTORATE
Individuals who can vote.

BALLOT INITIATIVES
The process through which voters directly convey instructions to the legislature, approve a law, or amend the constitution.

REFERENDUMS
A procedure that allows the electorate to either accept or reject a law passed by the legislature.

A brand-new Mercedes-Benz, built in the company's Alabama plant, makes a dramatic entrance. The plant itself was at the center of a political drama, as the state's constitution constrained efforts by state and local officials to lure the factory and its jobs to Alabama. These problems were eventually overcome, and the result is German luxury cars being built in Tuscaloosa.

> [I]t's sometimes easy to conclude that state constitutions are quaint relics with little relevance to everyday life. Yet as Alabama discovered, nothing could be further from the truth.

JUDICIAL FEDERALISM

The idea that the courts determine the boundaries of state-federal relations.

acceptable.[4] As time passes and a constitution becomes more entrenched, it begins to shape a state's culture and determine the range of political possibilities. Alabama remained a traditional state at least in part because its constitution thwarted industrialization and modernization. And Alabama is not alone in this regard. Many of the differences in subnational politics can be traced directly to state constitutions.

In recent years, state constitutions have become more important, not less. During the 1990s, the U.S. Supreme Court handed down a number of decisions that strengthened state governments at the expense of the federal government. The Court's recent insistence on determining the boundaries of federalism and evaluating state laws and regulations—a form of activism sometimes referred to as **judicial federalism**—has even gained Chief Justice William Rehnquist the nickname "Governor Rehnquist."[5]

State supreme courts are also becoming more assertive. In 1977, Supreme Court Justice William Brennan, a former New Jersey state supreme court justice, wrote a famous article for the *Harvard Law Review* that noted that state constitutions afford their citizens another layer of rights above and beyond the rights protected in the U.S. Constitution. He urged state courts to pay more attention to these rights and assert themselves more forcefully. They have. In the past two decades, for example, seventeen state supreme courts have found school financing systems "unconstitutional." (See the feature box "State Constitutions, Educational Equity, and the New Judicial

Activism.") State governments have become even more powerful actors in the U.S. political system, and ever more assertive courts have found new rights in state constitutions. This means that the documents that both reflect and determine what state and local governments can and cannot do have become even more important to understanding politics in America.

What State Constitutions Do: It's Probably Different than You Think

Mention "the constitution," and chances are good that your listener will think instantly of the U.S. Constitution. The Founders have gotten more than 225 years of good press for their work in 1787. Schoolchildren memorize, "We the People of the United States, in order to form a more perfect Union . . ." and venerate the document's wisdom. Yet the U.S. Constitution is only half of the story. As residents of the United States we live under a system of **dual constitutionalism,** in which the federal government and state governments are co-sovereign powers. Both run in accordance with the rules laid out in their respective constitutions. Despite the important role state constitutions play in establishing our rights and organizing our local and state governments, most people know very little about them.

The U.S. Constitution and all state constitutions share some common functions: They all set forth the roles and responsibilities of governments, describe the basic institutional structure of the government, and establish procedures for these institutions to operate by. Most state constitutions reflect the influence of the U.S. Constitution. They create three primary branches of government (legislative, executive, and judicial) and provide a general governmental framework. Like the U.S. Constitution, they all contain something roughly equivalent to a bill of rights that spells out the rights of citizens and places specific limits on governmental powers. Most state constitutions place these rights firmly in the **natural law,** also known as **higher law,** a tradition that holds that these rights are not political creations but divine endowments. Such **constitutional amendments,** or changes, are meant to ensure these rights for citizens.

Yet in many ways it is misleading to compare state constitutions with their better-known federal counterpart. Consider these important differences:

Permanence. The U.S. Constitution is widely seen as the document that created the United States—the embodiment of the Founders' wisdom. As such, politicians and the public alike hold it in the highest regard. It has lasted more than two centuries and has been formally changed only twenty-seven times. In contrast, state constitutions are amended and even replaced much more frequently. Most states have replaced their original constitutions at least once. California is currently on its second constitution. New York is on its fourth. Louisiana is on its eleventh. In

DUAL CONSTITUTIONALISM

A system of government in which people live under two sovereign powers. In the United States this is government of their state of residence and the federal government.

NATURAL LAW OR HIGHER LAW

A set of moral and political rules based on divine law and binding on all people.

CONSTITUTIONAL AMENDMENTS

Proposals to change the constitution, typically enacted by a supermajority of the legislature or through a statewide referendum.

A Difference that Makes a Difference:
State Constitutions, Educational Equity, and the New Judicial Activism

Robert Frost once began a poem by proclaiming New Hampshire to be one of the two best states in the Union. He said Vermont was the other. Frost is one of the few people in history who have ever been fond of both states. For virtually everyone else, it is one or the other.

To much of New Hampshire, Vermont represents a failed experiment in socialism, a onetime dairy state where social workers now outnumber cows. To much of Vermont, New Hampshire is an enclave of wacky and irresponsible libertarians, one small step above a gun-toting militia. Just how different these two states are can be seen by their very different reactions to recent court rulings in each state.

Within a ten-month period in 1997, the supreme courts of New Hampshire and Vermont both declared that their states' finance systems violated state constitutions. The reasoning differed, but the demand was the same: Change the system.

Vermont's case, like those in most of the seventeen states that have been placed under school finance court orders in the past two decades, is an "equity" case. At the time of the decision, the poorest 5 percent of Vermont school districts were spending $3,732 per pupil per year. The richest 5 percent were spending $5,964—60 percent more. "Children who live in property-poor districts," the court said, "should be afforded a substantially equal opportunity."

New Hampshire had disparities just as bad as those across the border, but the court decision there didn't focus on equity. It focused on "adequacy." Although the decision made reference to tax burdens that were four times as high in some towns as in others, its fundamental point was that, in the poorest communities, the public schools were not meeting the test of "a constitutionally adequate education to every educable child." For instance, the mostly blue-collar residents of Franklin, a central New Hampshire mill town, were taxing themselves at a rate much higher than the residents of nearby Gilford, a property-rich town near Lake Winnipesauke. Despite its tax burden, Franklin was able to spend barely half the amount Gilford could spend, and was saddled with obsolete buildings and equipment, the highest student-teacher ratios in the state, and an inexperienced staff that turned over at a rate of 25 percent a year.

In recent years, more state school systems have been invalidated on grounds of adequacy than on

fact, one political scientist has estimated that the average state constitution lasts for only about seventy years.[6]

Length. The federal constitution is a relatively short document. At about 7,400 words, it is shorter than most chapters in this book. In contrast, state constitutions tend to be much longer—about twenty-six thousand words on average. Some are much, much longer. New York's constitution and California's ruling document are each roughly fifty thousand words long. The longest state constitution, Alabama's, is more than thirty times the length of the U.S. Constitution.[7]

Specificity. Why are state constitutions so much longer than the federal constitution and so much more likely to change? Part of the answer has to do with the different functions of the federal constitution versus those

grounds of equity. Kentucky, New Jersey, Ohio, West Virginia, and Wyoming are all struggling, as New Hampshire will need to do, to meet a court-declared adequacy standard.

Equity cases are easier to deal with than accountability cases in one key respect: just reshuffle enough tax money, and the requirement is met. In contrast, under the terms of the New Hampshire supreme court's ruling, politicians there had to come up with a spending plan that not only ensured that pupils were literate and numerate but also provided them with "knowledge of his or her mental and physical wellness" and "sufficient grounding in the arts . . . to appreciate his or her cultural and historical heritage."

The Vermont legislature moved promptly to comply with the ruling of its highest court. New Hampshire politicians did not. Many Republicans proposed responding to the ruling, which was based on the state constitution, by passing an amendment stripping the supreme court of its jurisdiction over school finance—that is, in effect changing the constitution which was, after all, the basis of the New Hampshire court's ruling. Democrats proposed complying by passing a broad-base sales or income tax or a statewide property tax, as Vermont did, and then pump much of the revenue into education. After years of acrimonious debate, the two sides agreed on a new package that raised approximately $900 million dollars through a variety of new taxes and fees. For Vermonters, New Hampshire's grudging response was a sign of its distorted priorities.

"I look across," says longtime state legislator Nancy Chard, D-Windham, "and feel sorry for them. They haven't been able to accept the court decision. There has never been in New Hampshire the kind of human concern for the citizens that Vermont has had."

For New Hampshire citizens, however, Vermont was the sad spectacle. "New Hampshire people look at Vermont," observes Keene school district assistant school superintendent Dean Haskell, "and say, 'We'd rather be here. We like local control. We can actually do things that make sense, rather than just worrying about state regulations.' "

Source: Abridged version of Alan Ehrenhalt, "SCHOOLS+TAXES+ POLITICS=CHAOS," *Governing* magazine, January 1999.

of state constitutions. The U.S. Constitution is primarily concerned with setting up the basic structures and procedures of government. State constitutions do these things too. However, state constitutions often set forth procedures and address policies in much greater detail than the federal constitution. While the federal constitution creates a framework for government, state constitutions often get into the policy details. Oklahoma's constitution, for instance, mandates that home economics be taught in school. Maryland's regulates off-street parking in Baltimore. South Dakota's requires the state prison to produce twine and cordage. Louisiana's provides instructions on how to build pipes. Political scientist Christopher Hammonds has estimated that 39 percent of the total provisions in state constitutions are devoted to specific matters of this sort. In contrast, only 6 percent of the U.S. Constitution deals with such specific issues.[8]

Embrace of Democracy. The U.S. Constitution creates a system of representative government. The Founders went to great pains to check "the whimsies of the majority" by designing a system of checks and balances. During the Progressive Era in the early 1900s, many states revamped their constitutions to do just the opposite. This was particularly true of the newer western and midwestern states where old school politics were less entrenched and where political cultures tended towards the moralistic or individualistic. Progressive reformers believed old constitutional arrangements were outmoded. Moreover, they worried that state legislatures had been captured by wealthy special interests. Their solution was to give the people the ability to amend their constitutions and pass laws directly through the use of referendums and ballot initiatives. Thus, in many cases, state constitutions championed direct democracy in a way that the U.S. Constitution purposefully did not.

> While the federal constitution creates a framework for government, state constitutions often get into the policy details. . . . [It is] estimated that 39 percent of the total provisions in state constitutions are devoted to specific matters. . . . In contrast, only 6 percent of the U.S. Constitution deals with . . . specific issues.

Finances. Congress and the executive branch can run up as much national debt as they can persuade bond buyers to swallow. In contrast, thirty-two state constitutions require the legislative and executive branches to balance their budgets. Another seventeen states have statutes requiring balanced budgets. Only Vermont can run up debt like the feds. Even state constitutions that do not require a balanced budget take a much more proscriptive, or restrictive, view of budget matters than the U.S. Constitution. California's constitution, for instance, mandates that at least 40 percent of the state budget go toward education, a requirement that has often constrained legislators' options when faced with budget shortfalls. Other state constitutions mandate a specific style and format for the laws that allow the transfer of money to the executive branch. These are known as **appropriations bills.** Sometimes the constitutions get more specific still, prohibiting legislators from attaching "riders" to appropriations bills and requiring a single subject for each bill. Riders are amendments or additions unrelated to the main bill. During the 1990s, some states, including Arizona, Colorado, Oklahoma, Nevada, and South Dakota, amended their constitutions to require supermajorities instead of simple majorities of the legislature to increase revenues or taxes.[9] Not surprisingly, state legislators sometimes try to evade these strict requirements. As a result, state judges tend to be much more involved in monitoring the budget process than their federal counterparts.

APPROPRIATIONS BILLS

Laws passed by legislatures authorizing the transfer of money to the executive branch.

There's another important and surprising difference between the U.S. Constitution and state constitutions—the scope of the documents. The U.S.

Constitution's original purpose was to organize a federal government with sharply limited powers. In contrast, state governments have a wider field of activities. As the Tenth Amendment of the U.S. Constitution makes clear, all powers not expressly delegated or forbidden to the federal government are reserved for the states. In other words, the range of responsibilities patrolled by state governments is much larger than the federal government's. Given this fact, it's not surprising that state constitutions change more quickly and tend to be longer, more detailed, and more varied.

The Evolution of State Constitutions

The first state constitutions were not technically constitutions at all. Rather, they were **colonial charters** awarded by the king of England. These charters were typically brief documents giving individuals or corporations the right to establish "plantations" over certain areas and govern the inhabitants therein. King James I of England granted the first charter in 1606. It created the Virginia Company of London, which in 1607 established the first English settlement in North America at Jamestown.

COLONIAL CHARTERS
Legal documents drawn up by the British crown that spelled out how the colonies were to be governed.

As the colonies expanded, many of these charters were amended to give the colonists "the rights of Englishmen." Just what those rights were, however, was not entirely clear. Britain's constitution was not a written document per se. It was a tradition, based on the Magna Carta of 1215 and on a shared understanding of what government should and should not do. From the start, some colonies took an expansive view of their rights and privileges. The Massachusetts Bay Colony, like other English settlements in North America, was organized as a corporation and controlled by a small group of stockholders. But while the charters of the other companies remained in England within easy reach of the British courts, Puritan leader John Winthrop took his colony's along when he sailed for the New World in 1630. This made it difficult for the English government to seize and revoke the charter if the company misbehaved or operated illegally, which it soon did. The Puritans excluded nonchurchgoers from local governments, punished people who violated their sense of morals, and generally behaved like an independent polity. This misbehavior eventually incurred the displeasure of King Charles II, who revoked the charter in 1691. Massachusetts then received a new royal charter that provided for a royal governor and a general assembly—a form of governance that lasted until the Revolutionary War nearly a century later.[10]

When the colonies won their independence, it was clear that colonial charters had to be replaced or at least modified. It was less clear what should replace them. Some colonial leaders believed that the Continental Congress should draft a model constitution that every state should adopt. Richard Henry Lee, a Virginia politician, explained the idea thusly in a letter to John Adams in May 1776: "Would not a uniform plan of government,

A Difference that Makes a Difference:
The Peculiar Constitution of Early Pennsylvania

The original American colonies were established for very different purposes. The Massachusetts Bay Colony, for example, started off as haven for a persecuted religious sect. The Puritans were determined to create, in the words of Massachusetts's first governor, John Winthrop, "a city upon a hill" to serve as an example of a holy community for all people. Other colonies, such as Virginia, began as business ventures. Still others, such as Pennsylvania, were both.

Pennsylvania's first colonial charter reflected the colony's dual purposes as a religious settlement and an investment. It illustrates how state constitutions or charters were created to serve very particular goals—and how "rights" that Americans now take for granted, such as the right to self-governance, were by no means obvious to this country's founders.

The colony started out as a business venture. In 1681, William Penn received a proprietary interest—

the controlling share—in what is now the state of Pennsylvania as repayment for a debt that England's King Charles II owed Penn's father. Penn was already deeply involved in land speculation in North America. He and eleven other investors already owned East Jersey (present-day New Jersey). Soon after buying into Pennsylvania, they acquired a lease on Delaware.

Penn, however, wasn't just a businessman. He was also a devout Quaker, a member of a peace-loving religious group that was often at odds with the official Church of England. Pennsylvania was to Penn "a holy experiment"—a unique chance to found a province dedicated to Quakerism's unique vision of equality and religious freedom.

William Markham, Penn's deputy, was sent in 1681 to establish a seat of government for Penn's new colony. Penn also instructed his representative to construct a "City of Brotherly Love"—Philadelphia. One year later,

---

UNICAMERAL LEGISLATURES

Legislatures that possess only one chamber. Nebraska is currently the only state with a unicameral legislature.

SEPARATION OF POWERS

The principle that government should be divided into separate legislative, executive, and judicial branches, each with its own powers and responsibilities.

prepared for America by the Congress, and approved by the colonies, be a surer foundation of unceasing harmony to the whole?" [11]

Adams thought not. While he liked the idea of uniform state constitutions in principle, Adams worried about what would happen in practice. He believed that effective government required a strong executive. The colonists' experience dealing with royal governors, however, had created an aversion to executive power. Adams feared that the Continental Congress would create governments dominated by powerful **unicameral legislatures** or even do away with governors altogether and create a special committee of legislators to handle the everyday business of governing. This would violate what he saw as the wise precautionary principle of the **separation of powers.**

Ultimately, despite being a unicameral body itself, the Continental Congress rejected that particular idea. What it did do was pass a resolution urging the thirteen colonies to reorganize their authority solely "on the basis of the authority of the people." [12] This set the stage for the states to create their own varied blueprints for government.

After independence was declared and secured, states convened special assemblies to draft new constitutions. Most adopted lightly modified ver-

Penn himself arrived in his fledgling colony. His first major action was to draw up a constitution, or charter, for his new colony, which he called "the Frame of Government." His second major act was to establish friendly relations with American Indians in the area—an unusual action that reflected his pacific religious beliefs.

In many ways, the Frame of Government echoed Quakerism's progressive dogmas. Penn's constitution guaranteed religious freedom to everyone who believed in God. It also set forth a humane penal code and encouraged the emancipation of slaves. In contrast, the early settlers of Massachusetts were interested not in individual religious freedom but in establishing a just Puritan society. As a result, the functions of local churches and town governments were intertwined in early Massachusetts. Indeed, the colony was governed as a virtual theocracy for its first two hundred years.

However, the Pennsylvania model was not a uniform triumph of humane liberalism. Penn did use his charter to protect his business interests. While the Frame of Government provided for an elected general assembly, it also concentrated almost all power in the executive branch of government, which was controlled by Penn and the other proprietors.

It was not long before colonists began to chafe at some of the less progressive features of William Penn's early constitution. He was forced to return to Pennsylvania in 1701 and issue a new constitution, the Charter of Privileges, which granted more power to the provincial assembly. However, the conflict between proprietary and antiproprietary forces did not diminish until 1776. That year, noted revolutionary Benjamin Franklin led a convention to assemble and approve a new constitution for the state as it struggled for independence from Great Britain.

sions of the old colonial charters. References to the king of England were deleted, and bills of rights added. Most concentrated power in the legislative branch to diminish the possibility of tyrannical governors appearing in the political arena.

The First Generation of State Constitutions

This first generation of state constitutions created powerful **bicameral legislatures**—with a few exceptions. Vermont, Georgia, and Pennsylvania opted for unicameral legislatures. Governors and state judiciaries were clearly subordinate in most cases. In fact, legislatures often appointed both the governor and judges. No one envisioned that one day a state supreme court would have the power to overrule the acts of a legislature on the grounds that its laws were unconstitutional. Indeed, the states that did provide for a constitutional review entrusted that function to a special "council of revision" or "councils of censor."

Nor did the early state constitutions embrace the now commonplace idea of "one person, one vote." Every early state constitution except Vermont's

BICAMERAL LEGISLATURES

Legislatures that possess two chambers, typically a house of representatives, or assembly, and a senate.

restricted voting access to white males who met certain minimum property requirements. Vermont gave the vote to every adult male. Supporters of a limited **franchise** defended these limitations as essential to the new republic. Without property qualifications, John Adams warned,

THE FRANCHISE
The right to vote.

> There will be no end to it. New claims will arise; women will demand a vote; lads from 12 to 21 will think their rights are not enough attended to; and every man who has not a farthing will demand an equal voice with any other, in all acts of the state. It tends to confound and destroy all distinctions, and prostrate all ranks to one common level.[13]

Indeed, Adams wanted to restrict the franchise even further by setting still higher property requirements.

In practice, the actual requirements necessary to achieve the right to vote varied widely. Some states, such as New Hampshire, let all white male taxpayers vote. This reflected the fact that New Hampshire was a state of small landowners with a fairly egalitarian political culture. However, even this fair state had a higher threshold of property ownership to meet should a man wish to hold office. In Virginia, a state with a more hierarchical political culture dominated by a small group of wealthy landowners and planters, property qualifications were stiff. Only white males who owned at least twenty-five acres and a twelve-foot by twelve-foot house, or fifty acres unsettled, or a town lot with a twelve-foot by twelve-foot house could vote. It is not entirely clear how many people met these qualifications. Most scholars, however, believe that in the more democratic northern states 60 percent to 80 percent of white males could vote. Needless to say, women and minorities could not.

Over the course of the nineteenth century, the franchise was expanded gradually, although in a very uneven and often unjust fashion. A number of southern states, for example, rewrote their constitutions to allow minorities to vote as part of the price for readmission to the Union after the Civil War. African American rights were also enshrined in the Fourteenth Amendment of the U.S. Constitution. Yet despite these protections, gains for African Americans proved short-lived. In the last decade of the 1800s, African Americans' ability to vote and to participate in all aspects of society was harshly limited by the passage of **Jim Crow laws**. These laws provided for the systematic separation of races, sharply restricted access to the franchise, and permitted the outright intimidation of African Americans. Women fared only slightly better. Wyoming began to allow women to vote in 1869. By 1912, only thirteen states had followed suit. It took the Nineteenth Amendment, ratified in 1920, to secure the right to vote, or suffrage, for all women nationwide. This was also the culmination of the Suffrage Movement of the nineteenth century.

JIM CROW LAWS
Measures passed in the last decade of the nineteenth century that sought to legally and systematically separate blacks and whites.

The limitations on the franchise imposed by many early state constitutions did little to promote good governance. State legislatures quickly

MAP 3-1 Number of Constitutions Per State

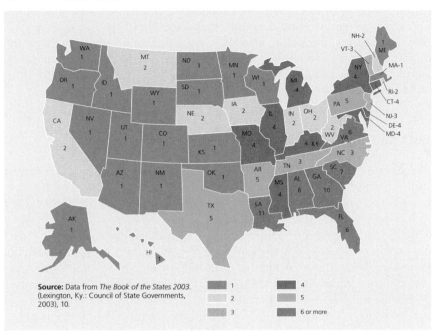

Source: Data from *The Book of the States 2003*. (Lexington, Ky.: Council of State Governments, 2003), 10.

Legend: 1, 2, 3, 4, 5, 6 or more

MAP 3-2 Number of Amendments Adopted Per State

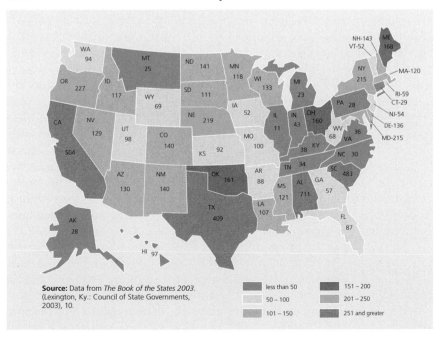

Source: Data from *The Book of the States 2003*. (Lexington, Ky.: Council of State Governments, 2003), 10.

Legend: less than 50, 50 – 100, 101 – 150, 151 – 200, 201 – 250, 251 and greater

developed an impressive record of corruption and fiscal extravagance. As a result, new territories entering the Union, such as Indiana and Mississippi, opted for elected governors, as did older states that began to revise or replace their constitutions in the 1820s. By 1860, South Carolina was the only state with a governor selected by the legislature.[14] The era of unlimited legislative power did not last very long. In hindsight, the nineteenth century would be seen as a period of tumultuous constitutional change.

Formal Constitutional Changes

Every state constitution provides a method for making changes. Fourteen states actually require citizens to periodically vote on whether or not they want to convene a constitutional convention. Voters can decide if they want to amend or replace their state's constitution.[15]

In the early nineteenth century, suggesting such change could be an exciting—and dangerous—business. In 1841 a patrician attorney and renegade lawmaker by the name of Thomas Wilson Dorr convened an illegal constitutional convention. Its task was to replace Rhode Island's colonial charter with a more modern and progressive constitution. The aged document still limited the franchise to voters owning land valued at $134 or more at a time when other states had long since abandoned such requirements. When Dorr's supporters elected him "governor" the following year on a platform that proposed allowing all white males—even Catholic immigrants, a group viewed with great suspicion—to vote, the sitting governor ordered him arrested and tried for treason. Thus began the Dorr War, or Dorr's Rebellion. His supporters then attempted to seize the arsenal in Providence but were repelled when their cannons failed to discharge. A month later, Dorr and his followers tried again. This time a force of militiamen and free blacks from Providence repelled them.[16] Still, Rhode Island's establishment got the hint. A new, more liberal constitution was quickly enacted.

The amendment process has since become a bit more routine in most states. Amending or replacing a state constitution is typically a two-step process. First, a constitutional amendment or a new constitution must be proposed—and meet a certain threshold of support. Then it must be ratified.

There are four primary ways to propose changes to state constitutions: legislative proposals, ballot initiatives or referendums, constitutional conventions, and constitutional commissions.

In 2000 Florida voters amended their constitution to allow fewer protections against cruel and unusual punishment in death penalty cases.

Legislative Proposal

Most attempts to change a state's constitution begin with a legislative proposal. Forty-nine state constitutions allow the state legislature to propose constitutional amendments to the electorate as a whole.[17] In seventeen states, a majority vote in both houses of the legislature suffices to send a constitutional amendment on for **ratification**. However, most states require a supermajority—two-thirds or three-fifths of the electorate—for a constitutional amendment to go into effect. Some states set the bar even higher. The constitutions of eleven states—Delaware, Indiana, Iowa, Massachusetts, Nevada, New York, Pennsylvania, South Carolina, Tennessee, Virginia, and Wisconsin—require their legislatures to vote for a constitutional amendment in two consecutive sessions before it can be ratified.[18] In principle, some state legislatures can also propose completely new constitutions to voters. However, no state legislature has successfully proposed a wholesale constitutional change since Georgia did so in 1982.

Ballot Initiatives and Referendums

Eighteen states give voters another way to propose constitutional amendments—ballot initiatives or popular referendums. These ballot measures offer citizens a way to amend the constitution or to enact what is new legislation without working through the legislature. Citizens have the option of circulating a petition that calls for a vote on their proposal. If they gather enough signatures, the proposal then goes onto the statewide or countywide ballot at the next opportunity for yea or nay vote. The result is legislation without the legislature. South Dakota was the first state to provide ballot initiatives, in 1898, but it was only after Oregon embraced them in 1902 that the push for direct democracy really got underway. In the sixteen years that followed, nearly two dozen states followed Oregon's lead. The last state to approve ballot initiatives was Massachusetts in 1918.

How ballot measures work in practice varies widely from state to state. In Oregon, supporters of a constitutional amendment or new law must first gather signatures for a petition requesting a statewide referendum on the measure. Oregon's constitution requires that the number of signatures be equal to or greater than 8 percent of the total voter turnout for all candidates for governor in the last election. Petitions that meet this requirement are then put to a statewide vote. California, Illinois, and Missouri have similar thresholds. Each requires that at least 8 percent of the total number of voters who voted for governor in the last election sign a petition to get a proposed constitutional amendment onto the ballot before it can go before the public. Other states, however, have lower thresholds. In Massachusetts, for instance, it takes only about 25,000 signatures to get a ballot initiative or referendum onto the ballot.[19]

Ballot measures typically combine the proposal and ratification stages of the amendment process. Once a proposed amendment is on the ballot, it usually requires a simple majority to pass and become part of the constitution. Some state constitutions do require supermajorities.

RATIFICATION

A vote of the entire electorate to approve a constitutional change, referendum, or ballot initiative.

TABLE 3-1

Procedures for Constitutional Amendment by Legislature

Legislative Vote Required for Proposal			Consideration by Two Sessions Required[a]		
Majority	**3/5 Majority**	**2/3 Majority**	**No**		**Yes**
Arizona	Alabama	Alaska	Alabama	North Carolina	Delaware
Arkansas	Florida	California	Alaska	North Dakota	Iowa
Connecticut[f]	Illinois	Colorado	Arizona	Ohio	Indiana
Hawaii[g]	Kentucky	Delaware	Arkansas	Oklahoma	Massachusetts
Indiana	Maryland	Georgia	California	Oregon	Nevada
Iowa	Nebraska	Idaho	Colorado	Rhode Island	New York
Massachusetts[h]	New Hampshire	Kansas	Florida	South Dakota	Pennsylvania[i]
Minnesota	North Carolina	Louisiana	Georgia	Texas	South Carolina[j]
Missouri	Ohio	Maine[l]	Idaho	Utah	Tennessee[m]
Nevada		Michigan	Illinois	Washington	Vermont
New Jersey[o]		Mississippi[p]	Louisiana	West Virginia	Virginia
New Mexico[q]		Montana[r]	Kansas	Wyoming	Wisconsin
New York		South Carolina[s]	Kentucky		
North Dakota		Texas	Maine		
Oklahoma		Utah	Maryland		
Oregon[t]		Washington	Michigan		
Pennsylvania[v]		West Virginia	Minnesota		
Rhode Island		Wyoming	Mississippi		
South Dakota			Missouri		
Tennessee[w]			Montana		
Vermont[x]			Nebraska		
Virginia			New Hampshire		
Wisconsin			New Mexico		

Source: Data compiled from *The Book of the States, 2003* (Lexington, Ky.: Council of State Governments, 2003), 12–13.

Notes:
[a] Connecticut, Hawaii, and New Jersey each require that if a supermajority is not achieved in one session (3/4, 2/3, or 3/5, respectively), a simple majority must be achieved in a second session. In Connecticut, an election must have intervened between the first and second sessions. If a supermajority is not achieved in the first session, Hawaii requires a majority vote in each house in two sessions. New Jersey requires a majority of all members of each house for two successive sessions.
[b] Connecticut has no referendum.
[c] Not required.
[d] Majority of all citizens voting for governor.
[e] Majority voting in election or three-fifths voting on amendment.
[f] Three-fourths vote in each house at one session or majority vote in each house in two sessions between which an election has intervened.
[g] Two-thirds vote in each house at one session or majority vote in each house in two sessions.
[h] Majority of members elected sitting in joint session.
[i] Emergency amendments may be passed by two-thirds vote of each house, followed by ratification by majority vote of electors in election held at least one month after legislative approval. There is an exception for an amendment containing a supermajority voting requirement, which must be ratified by an equal supermajority.
[j] Two-thirds of members of each house, first passage; majority of members of each house after popular ratification.
[k] Majority vote on amendment, except an amendment for "new state tax or fee" not already in effect on November 7, 1994. This requires two-thirds of voters in the election.
[l] Two-thirds of both houses.
[m] Majority of members elected to both houses, first passage; two-thirds of members elected to both houses, second passage.
[n] Majority vote on amendment must be at least 50 percent of the total votes cast at the election (at least 35 percent in Nebraska); or, at a special election, a majority of the votes tallied which must be at least 30 percent of the total number of registered voters.

Governing States and Localities

TABLE 3-1 *(continued)*

Vote Required for Ratification				Limitation on Number of Amendments Submitted at One Election[b]		
Majority Vote in Election	**Majority or Supermajority Vote on Amendments**		**Other**	**No**		**Yes**
Minnesota	Alabama	Nebraska[y]	Delaware[c]	Alabama	New Hampshire	Arkansas
Tennessee[d]	Alaska	Nevada	Illinois[e]	Alaska	New Jersey[z]	Idaho
Wyoming	Arizona	New Hampshire		Arizona	New Mexico	Iowa
	Arkansas	New Jersey		California	New York	Kansas
	California	New Mexico[aa]		Colorado	North Carolina	
	Colorado	New York		Delaware	North Dakota	
	Connecticut	North Carolina		Florida	Ohio	
	Florida[k]	North Dakota		Georgia	Oklahoma	
	Georgia	Ohio		Hawaii	Oregon	
	Hawaii[n]	Oklahoma		Illinois	Pennsylvania	
	Idaho	Oregon[bb]		Indiana	Rhode Island	
	Indiana	Pennsylvania		Kentucky	South Carolina	
	Iowa	Rhode Island		Louisiana	South Dakota	
	Kansas	South Carolina		Maine	Tennessee	
	Kentucky	South Dakota		Maryland	Texas	
	Louisiana[u]	Texas		Massachusetts	Utah	
	Maine	Utah		Michigan	Vermont	
	Maryland	Vermont		Minnesota	Virginia	
	Massachusetts	Virginia		Mississippi	Washington	
	Michigan	Washington		Missouri	West Virginia	
	Mississippi	West Virginia		Montana	Wisconsin	
	Missouri	Wisconsin		Nebraska	Wyoming	
	Montana			Nevada		

[o] Three-fifths of all members of each house at one session or majority of all members of each house for two successive sessions.

[p] The two-thirds must include not less than a majority elected to each house.

[q] Amendments concerning certain elective franchise and education matters require three-fourths vote of members elected and approval by three fourths of electors voting in state and two-thirds of those voting in each county.

[r] Two-thirds of both houses.

[s] Majority of all citizens voting for governor.

[t] Majority vote to amend constitution, two-thirds to revise ("revise" includes all or part of the constitution).

[u] If five or fewer political subdivisions of the state are affected, majority in state as a whole and also in affected subdivisions is required.

[v] Emergency amendments may be passed by two-thirds vote of each house, followed by ratification by majority vote of electors in election held at least one month after legislative approval. There is an exception for an amendment containing a supermajority voting requirement, which must be ratified by an equal supermajority.

[w] Majority of members elected to both houses, first passage; two-thirds of members elected to both houses, second passage.

[x] Two-thirds vote in senate, majority vote in house, first passage; majority both houses, second passage. As of 1974, amendments may be submitted only every four years.

[y] Majority vote on amendment must be at least 50 percent of the total votes cast at the election (at least 35 percent in Nebraska); or, at a special election, a majority of the votes tallied which must be at least 30 percent of the total number of registered voters.

[z] If a proposed amendment is not approved at the election when submitted, neither the same amendment nor one which would make substantially the same change to the constitution may be again submitted to the people before the third general election thereafter.

[aa] Amendments concerning certain elective franchise and education matters require three-fourths vote of members elected and approval by three fourths of electors voting in state and two-thirds of those voting in each county.

[bb] Majority of all citizens voting for governor.

Constitutional Conventions

The most freewheeling approach to changing or replacing a state constitution is to convene a constitutional convention. Massachusetts, whose constitution was drafted in 1780 and is the nation's oldest, was the first state to adopt a constitution via a convention. Most other states quickly followed. Currently, the only states that make no provisions for changing their constitutions through the use of constitutional conventions are Arkansas, Indiana, Mississippi, New Jersey, North Dakota, Pennsylvania, Texas, and, ironically, Massachusetts. Evidently, once was enough.

A constitutional convention typically begins when a state legislature passes a resolution that calls for a statewide referendum on whether a convention should be held. If a majority of the electorate votes in favor of the proposal, then the next step is to hold elections for convention delegates. In most states, a law is passed that provides for electing convention members from local election districts in much the same way that legislators are elected. (See Chapter 4.) Of course, there are exceptions. The legislatures of Georgia, Louisiana, Maine, South Carolina, South Dakota, and Virginia can call a constitutional convention without the approval of the electorate. Alaska and Iowa hold automatic constitutional assemblies every ten years.

Once delegates are selected, a constitutional convention can convene. Members are free to amend, revise, or even replace their state's constitution. A constitutional convention has virtually unlimited discretion in making such changes. It can amend the existing document in any way it sees fit or even write an entirely new constitution. Ultimately, its handiwork goes before the electorate as a whole to be voted in or cast out.

> [A constitutional convention] can amend the existing document in any way it sees fit or even write an entirely new constitution. Ultimately, its handiwork goes before the electorate as a whole to be voted in or cast out.

Or it can do nothing at all. In 1974, Texas convened a convention to rewrite its creaky 1876 constitution. Members spent several months drafting a new constitution, but when it came time to vote on their handiwork, a majority of the delegates unexpectedly came out against it. The next year the state legislature voted to put the constitution the convention had drafted to the public anyway as a referendum. The voters turned it down.[20]

State legislators tend to be wary of constitutional conventions and rarely convene them. The reason for this caution is that once convened, a constitutional convention can theoretically reexamine any and all aspects of state and local government. Lawmakers who approve a convention might end up initiating a process that leads to more far-reaching changes than they had expected. Increasingly, the average voter seems to share this skepticism. In 2002, Alabama governor Don Siegelman's plan to call a convention to draft a new constitution was derailed when Siegelman lost his reelection bid. Voters in Alaska, New Hampshire, and

Montana also rejected referendums that would have provided for constitutional conventions. In fact, the last constitutional convention was held in 1986 in, you guessed it, Rhode Island.[21]

Constitutional Revision Commissions

If constitutional conventions are for the bold and trusting, then **constitutional revision commissions** are often the cautious technocrat's preferred route to constitutional change. Constitutional revision commissions typically consist of a panel of citizens appointed by the governor and/or by the state legislature. Between 1990 and 2000, seven states—Alaska, Arkansas, California, Florida, Oklahoma, New York, and Utah—have convened constitutional commissions to consider changes to the state constitutions.

Two states go even further in their enthusiasm for constitutional commissions. Florida's constitution includes a requirement that a constitutional revision commission convene every twenty years, regardless of whether people are dissatisfied with the constitution or not. It also gives the commission a power unique among constitutional revision commissions—the right to present proposed changes directly to voters for their approval or rejection. Florida's last constitutional revision commission met in 1998. It recommended thirteen changes to the state constitution, including a proposal to allow local governments to expand the background checks and waiting period requirements on gun sales. That led the head of Florida's chapter of the National Rifle Association (NRA) to decry the proposal as a power grab and to issue a warning that gun owners might vote down all constitutional changes, even changes with universal support, should the proposal pass.[22] The commission refused to back down. Six months later, more than 70 percent of voters supported the measure.

The other state with an unusual constitutional revision commission is Utah, the only state whose commission is permanent. Utah Constitutional Revision Commission members are appointed by the governor, the leaders of both houses of the legislature, and by sitting commission members. Unlike Florida's commission, Utah's constitutional revision commission can only issue its recommendations in the form of a public report to the governor.

Ratification

Once an amendment has been proposed and found acceptable, it must be ratified before it can go into effect. In most states, this is a straightforward process. First, the proposed constitutional amendment or new constitution is put before the voting public in the next statewide election. Then the electorate either approves or rejects it. Two states add a twist to this process. In South Carolina, a majority of both houses of the state congress must vote to approve a constitutional amendment—after the successful popular referendum—before the amendment goes into effect. In Delaware, approval by

CONSTITUTIONAL REVISION COMMISSIONS
Expert committees formed to assess a constitution and suggest changes.

a two-thirds vote in two successive general assemblies gets a constitutional amendment into effect. As already discussed, the ballot initiative essentially combines the proposal and ratification stages. Once a proposed amendment is qualified for the ballot, it usually requires only a simple majority to become part of the constitution.

Informal Methods for Changing Constitutions

In recent years, voters and legislators nationwide have generally resisted making major changes to their states' constitutions. However, many state constitutions have changed dramatically in informal ways. The most common route of informal constitutional change is via state supreme courts. For instance, when a court interprets an existing constitution in a way that creates a new right, such as the right to an adequate or equitable education discussed earlier in the earlier feature box, "State Constitutions, Educational Equity, and the New Judicial Activism." Sometimes constitutional changes also come about from **judicial review**. In December 1999, the Vermont Supreme Court ordered the state legislature to pass a law providing for gay marriage. Their rationale? The court found that because the state constitution was "instituted for the common benefit, protection and security of the people," the state government could not refuse to provide the benefit of marriage to gay people. To those who objected that the state constitution, which was enacted in 1793 and is a model of brevity at 8,200 words, said nothing about gay marriage, the court explained that its job was "to distill the essence, the motivating idea of the framers," not to be bound by eighteenth-century notions of jurisprudence.[23] In November 2003, the Massachusetts Supreme Court followed suit, prompting efforts nationwide to amend the U.S. Constitution to explicitly define marriage as the union between of a man and woman.

State constitutions can also change when other branches of government successfully lay claim to broader powers. For example, Rhode Island's legislature has used its strong constitutional position—a clause in the state constitution says the General Assembly "can exercise any power" unless the constitution explicitly forbids it—to take control of functions that most states delegate to governors. In Rhode Island, legislators not only sit on the boards and commissions that oversee a range of state agencies, they also dominate the board that sets the salaries for high-ranking executive branch officials. Not surprisingly, this has given the legislature a great deal of power over executive branch decisions. In short, Rhode Island has just the type of government that John Adams feared.

Southern states such as Florida, Mississippi, and Texas also tend to have constitutions that provide for weak governors. In these cases, this arrangement is a legacy of the post–Civil War **Reconstruction** period. During Reconstruction the victorious Union Army forced most of the former Confederate

JUDICIAL REVIEW
The power of courts to assess whether a law is in compliance with the constitution.

RECONSTRUCTION
The period following the Civil War when the southern states were governed under the direction of the Union Army.

Governing States and Localities

states to replace their constitutions. Reconstruction ended in 1876, and the Union troops withdrew. With the exception of Arkansas, North Carolina, and Tennessee, most southern states abandoned their revised constitutions in favor of new constitutions that greatly weakened gubernatorial powers.[24] For example, in 1885 Florida passed a constitution that took away the governor's right to appoint his own cabinet. Members were elected instead. Although it has been amended many times since, that constitution is still in effect today. As a result, Florida has one of the weakest governorships in the country.[25]

Of course, state legislatures do not always gain the upper hand. In states whose constitutions give governors the edge, some chief executives have been very aggressive in expanding their powers. While their techniques do not involve written amendments to the state constitutions themselves, they do affect the distribution of powers within state government—a function that is a primary concern of state constitutions.

There's another way to change state constitutions—simple neglect. Sometimes state governments just stop enforcing obscure or repugnant sections of their state constitutions, effectively changing the constitution in the process. No politician today would dare to argue for denying the vote to individuals simply because they are poor or don't own land or belong to a minority group, yet until 1999 Texas's constitution contained a provision that limited the right to vote to citizens who owned land and paid a poll tax. The state government had stopped enforcing these objectionable requirements long before but had neglected to actually repeal them. Likewise, Alabama's constitution outlawed interracial marriages until an amendment overturned the ban in 2000, a provision that had been informally dropped years earlier.

Why State Constitutions Vary

We have seen that state constitutions vary widely from state to state. What explains these differences? Four factors seem particularly important—historical circumstances, political culture, geography, and changing notions of good government.

To better understand how historical circumstances and culture can create a constitution—and then be shaped by that constitution—consider the case of Texas. The Lone Star State's current constitution was written in 1876, soon after federal troops had withdrawn and Reconstruction had ended. During Reconstruction, a strong unionist governor backed by Federal troops had governed the state, centralized police and education functions in state hands in Austin, and generally defied the white Democrats who had been in power before the Civil War. So Texas followed in the footsteps of other southern states and drew up a constitution whose purpose was to ensure that the state would never again have an activist state government. Toward that end, the new constitution allowed the legislature to meet only infrequently, limited the governor's power over the executive branch, and provided for an elected judiciary. The document's sole progressive feature was a provision that for the first time allowed women to continue to own their own property after they were married.[26]

White Democrats' antipathy to Reconstruction explains much of the content of Texas's 1876 constitution. Texas's political culture explains why its constitution has endured to the present. Political scientist Daniel Elazar has classified Texas as a "traditionalistic/individualistic" state—a state that, in Elazar's words, "places a premium on limiting community intervention" and "accepts a natural hierarchical society as part of the ordered nature of things."[27] While Elazar's categories have blurred in recent years, state constitutions continue to bear out his categories. In short, Texas's constitution is well suited to its political culture—a culture that views strong, activist government with suspicion.

In contrast, a constitution that allowed the legislature to meet only every other year would suit a moralistic state poorly. Not surprisingly, moralistic states like Minnesota, Wisconsin, and Michigan allow their legislatures to meet far more frequently than does Texas. Because they envision fairly robust styles of governance, constitutions in these states allow their legislature to meet throughout the year, creating what are, for all intents and purposes, full-time professional legislatures.

New England's propensity for short, framework-oriented constitutions is a variation based noticeably on geography. One political scientist has hypothesized that such a variation may reflect the fact that New England states are small and relatively homogenous and that their citizens are thus less inclined to fight to include policies they support in their states' constitutions.[28]

Of course, history, political culture, and geography aren't the only factors that determine the kind of constitution a state will have. Another important factor is the changing sense of what works best. In the early nineteenth century, many states concluded that a system in which the legislature operates with unbridled power simply did not work well. So they changed their constitutions in ways that strengthened the chief executive. Eighty years ago, groups like the National Municipal League argued that state constitutions should be more like the federal constitution—that is, that they should be much shorter documents that provided a framework for governance rather than long documents that get into the details of the policies. That argument gave rise to the **model constitution**, a kind of ideal that states interested in "improving" could adopt. During the 1960s and 1970s, many states did revise their constitutions in ways designed to make their governments more effective.

> Of course, history, political culture, and geography aren't the only factors that determine the kind of constitution a state will have. Another important factor is the changing sense of what works best.

MODEL CONSTITUTION

An expert-approved generic or "ideal" constitution that is sometimes used by states as a yardstick against which they can measure their existing constitutions.

Since the mid-twentieth century, however, some political scientists have questioned the assumptions behind the model constitution movement. To these revisionists, the fact that most state constitutions outside of New England are long and policy rich is actually a good thing—a healthy sign of an engaged electorate. Revisionists argue that while Americans have essentially left it to the U.S. Supreme Court to interpret and on occasion to change the federal constitution, citizens have defended their right to participate by shaping their state constitutions.[29]

How State Constitutions Differ

The most obvious ways in which state constitutions differ involve their length and ease of amendment. These are not simply cosmetic differences. Rather, they almost always reflect the different functions state constitutions serve. Vermont has the shortest state constitution. Like the U.S. Constitution, its goal is primarily to establish a framework for effective government. This is true to a lesser extent of other states in New England as well.

In contrast, constitutions in other regions of the country tend to be longer and more specific in their policy prescriptions. In most states, voters and interest groups who want to accomplish a goal like increasing state spending on education will lobby the governor or the legislature. In California, a state with a long, policy-specific constitution that provides for a high degree of direct democracy, they often attempt to amend the constitution instead. While the majority of political scientists wring their hands about this tendency, it undeniably gives Californians a role in shaping their constitution that voters in regions of the country like New England lack.

Operating Rules and Selection for Office

State constitutions create varying organizational structures and operating rules for the constituent elements of state government. They establish different methods and requirements for serving in state politics. Some of these differences reflect the historical differences among states, as well as different political cultures and geography. Other differences reflect different notions of what makes good government. Sometimes these notions can be quite quirky. Consider the following, for example. To serve as the governor of Oklahoma, a state of 3.4 million people, you must be at least thirty-one years old. In contrast, to lead California's population of thirty-four million, the chief executive need only be eighteen. You can lead one of the nation's largest states, but don't try to get a beer or a glass of wine at your fundraisers!

In addition, state constitutions differ widely in how many statewide elected positions they create and how those positions are filled. One of the most important such differences has to do with the judiciary. At the federal level, judges are selected by the president and approved by the U.S. Senate. Things work very differently in the states. Most give their governors the right to nominate state supreme court justices, often from a list of names chosen by a judicial screening commission. Eighteen states—Arkansas, Georgia, Idaho, Illinois, Kentucky, Louisiana, Michigan, Mississippi, Missouri, Nevada, North Carolina, North Dakota, Ohio, Oregon, Pennsylvania, Texas, Washington, and West Virginia—select their supreme court justices and lower level judges in elections. Many states use a hybrid of appointment and elections called the Missouri Plan to select and retain judges. Named after the state in which it was first adopted, the plan calls for a governor to appoint a judicial nominating commission. This commission then recommends candidates to fill vacancies on the bench. It presents a list of three carefully vetted, or selected, candidates to the governor, who selects one to fill the vacancy. The nominee assumes the office, but first must be approved by the voters, usually during the next general election. Once approved, the judge faces periodic retention elections. As long as the voters approve, the judge retains office.[30]

Seemingly small institutional differences can have a big impact on how state governments work. A governor with strong veto powers, for example, may have an easier time getting a recalcitrant legislature to consider the executive's point of view on a particular piece of legislation than one who does not. Elected judges are more likely to uphold the death penalty in capital crimes than those more insulated from the ballot box.[31] In short, the different operating rules embedded in state constitutions lead to very different types of governance.

Distribution of Power

State constitutions make very different decisions about where power should reside. While all state constitutions make at least a bow toward the principle of the separation of powers, in actuality, many have given one branch of government a preponderance of power. Under some state constitutions, the reins of government are clearly in the hands of the legislature or general assembly. Other states have amended their constitutions in ways that give their governors the upper hand.

As previously discussed, some state constitutions clearly give the state legislature an advantage over the governor in the struggle for preeminence. Rhode Island is the classic example. Yet while strong state legislatures may still be the norm, in recent decades, constitutional changes in many states have bolstered their governors' powers. More than forty state constitutions now give governors the important power of the **line-item veto**, the ability to veto certain portions of appropriations bills while approving the rest. Exactly what counts as an item, and thus what is fair game for a governor's veto pen, is often unclear. As a result, line-item veto court cases have become a common part of the legal landscape.

LINE-ITEM VETO

The power to reject a portion of a bill while the rest remains intact.

Some states go even further. Twelve states allow governors to reduce spending by striking a digit from the amount appropriated. Wisconsin's state constitution even allows a governor the power to strike out an appropriation entirely and write in a lower figure. Former Wisconsin governor Tommy Thompson pushed the power of the partial veto to strike passages and even individual words from bills that came to his desk. In some cases, Thompson would strike individual letters from bills, creating entirely new words and meanings, and changing the entire meaning of the legislation. Critics came to call Thompson's creative writing "the Vanna White veto." In one case, Thompson used the Vanna White veto and his Scrabble skills to transform a piece of legislation from a bill that set the maximum detention period for juvenile offenders at forty-eight hours to one that allowed for a ten-day detention period, a move that enraged the Democratic legislature.[32] Voters later amended the constitution to prohibit that particular veto maneuver. Yet despite the controversies that surrounded such actions, during his record fourteen-year reign, none of Thompson's more than 1,900 budget vetoes were ever overturned by the legislature.[33]

Wisconsin governor Tommy Thompson looks more like Evel Knievel than Vanna White on his Harley Davidson Road King. A Harley is fitting, though, and not just because the motorcycles are made in Wisconsin. His use of Vanna White veto powers—the ability to strike single words from bills—gave him a reputation for riding over the wishes of the state legislature.

The power structures set up by the constitutional schemes of some states resist easy classification. Take Texas. The fact that the legislature meets for only five or six months every other year might lead one to think that power in Texas would reside primarily with the governor. Not so. In fact, the Texas constitution arguably makes the office of lieutenant governor the most powerful in the state. In Texas, the lieutenant governor presides over the senate, appoints senate committees and assigns bills, and chairs the powerful Texas Legislative Council, which is responsible for researching and drafting bills. Indeed, many observers attribute George W. Bush's two successful terms as governor to his close relationship with his lieutenant governor, Bob Bullock, a Democrat.

Rights Granted

State constitutions not only create different mechanisms of governance and give governments different sets of constraints and powers, they also confer different rights to citizens. For example, the U.S. Constitution does not explicitly create a right to privacy, although the U.S. Supreme Court did define a limited right to privacy in *Griswold v. the State of Connecticut*

(1965). In contrast, Montana's constitution states that "the right to individual privacy is essential to the well-being of a free society and shall not be infringed without the showing of a compelling state interest." [34] As a result, courts in Montana—and Kentucky and Tennessee—have interpreted their state constitutions to protect adults' freedom to engage in consensual oral or anal sex—sex acts that until quite recently were illegal in many other states. [35]

Representative Government vs. Direct Democracy

One of the most striking differences among state constitutions is the degree to which they have or have not embraced direct democracy. While most Americans celebrate the United States as a democracy, the Founders believed that they were establishing something different—a representative democracy. This is a form of government in which qualified representatives of the public make the decisions. Direct or pure democracy was viewed with suspicion by most of the Founders. "[A] pure democracy, by which I mean a society consisting of a small number of citizens, who assemble and administer the government in person, can admit of no cure for the mischiefs of faction," warned James Madison, one of the primary authors of the U.S. Constitution, in his famous argument for the document in *The Federalist,* No. 10:

> A common passion or interest will, in almost every case, be felt by a majority of the whole . . . and there is nothing to check the inducements to sacrifice the weaker party or an obnoxious individual. Hence it is that such democracies have ever been spectacles of turbulence and contention; have ever been found incompatible with personal security or the rights of property; and have in general been as short in their lives as they have been violent in their deaths. [36]

In other words, Madison believed that entrusting a simple majority with the power to carry out its will would lead to fickle and tyrannical behavior and a government that teetered between anarchy and autocracy.

The U.S. Constitution's solution to the problem of pure democracy was to create a representative government or, as Madison saw it, government by a small group of elected officials "whose wisdom may best discern the true interest of their country." [37] In accordance with this belief, the U.S. Constitution created an upper chamber—the Senate—whose members would be selected by state legislatures from among their eminent men. The document also created an electoral college to elect the president. Both of these decisions were made to insulate the federal government from the whims of the majority. The Constitution makes no provision for direct democratic processes. There is not a single federal office *directly* elected by the entire nation. Indeed, as we saw in 2000 with the election of George W. Bush, the electoral college system can result in a candidate winning the presidency after losing the popular vote.

The creators of the federal government took great care to ensure it was insulated from direct democratic processes. Many states decided to do just the opposite during the Progressive Era. By giving their citizens the chance to make laws and change their constitutions directly, the Progressives sought to circumvent legislatures and executives they viewed as beholden to wealthy special interests. As Robert M. La Follette, a leader of the Progressive Party in Wisconsin and later a governor and senator from the state put it:

> The forces of the special privileges are deeply entrenched. Their resources are inexhaustible. Their efforts are never lax. Their political methods are insidious. It is impossible for the people to maintain perfect organization in mass. They are often taken unaware and are liable to lose at one stroke the achievements of years of effort. In such a crisis, nothing but the united power of the people expressed directly through the ballot can overthrow the enemy.[38]

For politicians like La Follette, direct democratic mechanisms, such as the ballot initiative and the referendum, represented the general populace's best hope for breaking the power of political bosses and the moneyed interests. Between 1902 and 1918, direct democracy enjoyed a great vogue in the states. Sixteen states adopted the ballot initiative in that fourteen-year period. After the First World War, ballot initiatives lost some of their luster as popular enthusiasm for Progressive ideas waned. Only five states—Alaska (1959), Florida (1968), Wyoming (1968), Illinois (1970), and Mississippi (1992) have amended their constitutions to allow for ballot initiatives since the end of the Progressive Era.[39]

For much of their existence, initiatives and referendums were used sparingly. Then came Proposition 13 in California. In the 1970s, taxpayer activist Howard Jarvis and retired real estate salesman Paul Gann launched what at first seemed a foolishly impractical campaign to roll back California property taxes and cap the rate at which they could grow. Their campaign struck a cord with many Californians. The state's booming economy had sent property values skyrocketing. Higher property assessments led to higher real estate taxes, which created a huge revenue boom for state and local governments. Indeed, at the time the state government had a $5 billion annual surplus. Yet despite the public outcry for relief from rising property costs, Gov. Jerry Brown and the politicians in Sacramento could not agree on a tax reduction plan.

In 1978, California voters passed Proposition 13 and took the decision out of their hands. It directed the state to roll back real estate taxes to 1975 levels and decreed that property assessments could not increase by more than 2 percent a year, regardless of inflation. Most localities previously had reassessed real estate taxes every two years. Proposition 13 decreed that property could only be reassessed when it was sold. The legislation also cut property tax receipts in half and marked the beginning of

In 2002, Oregon citizens voted on seven ballot initiatives, the most by any state.

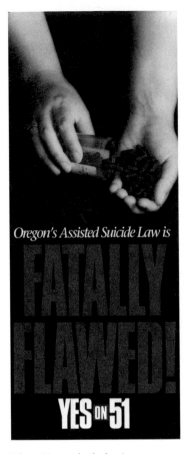

Oregon's Assisted Suicide Law is

FATALLY FLAWED!

YES on 51

When citizens take the law into their own hands, they literally may be making life and death decisions. Ballot initiatives allow citizens to bypass the legislature and make law themselves. The poster above urges voters to support Oregon's Measure 51, a proposal seeking to overturn a previous ballot initiative legalizing physician-assisted suicide.

a nationwide "taxpayer revolt." The revolt culminated in the election of former California governor Ronald Reagan to the presidency two years later.

For California's political establishment, the passage of Proposition 13 was viewed with great trepidation. Politicians worried that it would cripple their ability to pay for the schools and infrastructure that had contributed so much to California's post–Second World War successes. These fears proved well founded. In the wake of Proposition 13, California went from having one of the best funded public school systems (in the top third in terms of per pupil spending) to having one of the worst (in the bottom third). The proposition put such draconian limits on the ability of local government to raise revenues that municipalities and counties became increasingly dependent on the state for their funding—so much so that ten years later, in 1988, California teachers' unions would push through Proposition 98, which mandated that 40 percent of California's general revenue go to education.[40]

Besides complicating government finances and drastically reducing the flexibility of lawmakers in California, the success of Proposition 13 revived interest in ballots in the twenty-four other states in which they were permitted. In the three decades from 1940 through 1970, there was an average of nineteen ballot initiatives per two-year election cycle in the United States. In the 1980s, that number shot up to fifty initiatives in the average election cycle. In the 1990s, it hit seventy-six ballot initiatives per election cycle.[41] Many of these initiatives were proposed constitutional amendments. Their sheer numbers indicate that states with the initiative are now engaged in an almost continuous cycle of changing their constitutions. These changes are increasingly less about broad questions of good governance and more about pushing narrow agendas.

In the past two decades, ballot initiatives have been used to push through some of the most controversial political issues in the entire country. Oregon voters used a ballot initiative to narrowly—51 percent to 49 percent—approve physician-assisted suicide in 1994. In California, voters have used initiatives to impose some of the nation's strictest term limits on elected officials, to end affirmative action (Propositions 209 and 96), to deny education and health benefits to families of illegal immigrants (Proposition 87), and to recall a sitting governor and replace him with an action movie star.

The initiative process has become big business. Several companies are devoted to gathering signatures and getting issues placed on the ballot for anyone who can afford their services. Billionaire financier George Soros; Peter Lewis, the head of the Cleveland-based Progressive Corporation; and Phoenix entrepreneur Jon Sperling, founder of the for-profit University of Phoenix, have each funded medical marijuana referendums in Alaska, Arizona, Nevada, and Oregon.

Governing States and Localities

To those who have used them successfully, ballot initiatives are a nifty way to circumvent a hostile legislature and act on the will of the majority. This is particularly true of the various medical marijuana initiatives mentioned above. To date, six states—Alaska, Arizona, California, Maine, Oregon, and Washington—have approved the use of medical marijuana through ballot initiatives. In contrast, only one state legislature, Hawaii's, has approved a medical marijuana initiative. To supporters of medical marijuana, the existence of ballot initiatives has allowed the silent majority to express their opinions on an issue that most politicians are reluctant to address.

But most political scientists and close observers of state politics have a different viewpoint. To them, ballot initiatives only reinforce the wisdom of the Founders in their decision to keep direct democratic processes out of the U.S. Constitution. A number of those who have examined initiatives conclude that they have been hijacked by those with deep pockets. Individuals who use them to further their own self-interests.

Veteran *Washington Post* political reporter David Broder describes the ballot initiatives in scathing terms:

> At the start of a new century—and millennium—a new form of government is spreading in the United States. It is alien to the spirit of the Constitution and its careful system of checks and balances. Though derived from a reform favored by Populists and Progressives as a cure for special-interest influence, this method of lawmaking has become the favored tool of millionaires and interest groups that use their wealth to achieve their own policy goals—a lucrative business for a new set of political entrepreneurs.[42]

Exploiting the public's disdain for politics and distrust of politicians, interest groups with deep pockets now have a mechanism to literally rewrite state constitutions to advance their own agendas. For example, in 1997 Microsoft cofounder and Seattle Seahawks owner Paul Allen made an end-run around a balky state legislature and spent $6 million on a ballot initiative that required the state to foot much of the cost for a new stadium for his team. It proved to be a good investment; the initiative passed by 51 percent. While this was welcome news for many football fans, most political scientists probably see it as an illustration of the VERY problem Madison identified in *The Federalist* No. 10. In some ways the initiative has created a very odd form of governance, where citizens live under laws that are often resisted by their elected governments. With its ability to make sweeping changes in state constitutions, the initiative process threatens to radically change the American system of government in the next few decades.

Exploiting the public's disdain for politics and distrust of politicians, interest groups with deep pockets now have a mechanism to literally rewrite state constitutions to advance their own agendas . . . the very problem Madison identified in *The Federalist* No. 10.

Constitutions for Local Government?

For the most part, substate governments, or **special districts,** such as school districts, counties, and many municipalities, are considered subordinate arms of the state. While they may seem like autonomous political units, they in fact operate under state constitutions and at the discretion of state governments. The courts have generally viewed only the federal government and the states as sovereign entities with the right to determine how their authority should be exercised. The authority and power of local governments is largely confined, if not outright dictated, by the states.

There are some exceptions to this rule. The **municipal charter** is a key example. In a rough sense, these charters are similar to the charters that served as the governing documents for the original colonies. Legally, most municipalities are corporations, and their charters describe the purposes of the municipality and the processes for achieving these objectives. A charter is not a constitution, but rather a grant of authority derived from a constitution or from state law. Some states have **home rule,** which allows municipalities the right to draft and amend their own charters and to regulate local matters within their jurisdictions without interference from the state. Some states have municipal home rule provisions in their constitutions. Others grant municipal home rule through legislation. Municipal home rule means that some local governments are operated by charters that "can take on many characteristics of a constitution." [43] Even in the most liberal home rule states, however, state constitutions and state law generally take precedence over municipal charters.

Conclusion

Though you rarely read about them in the newspaper—much less hear about them on the evening news—state constitutions play *the* critical role in defining the possibilities of politics in most states. All state constitutions set the basic structure of government, apportion power and responsibilities to particular institutions and political actors, and determine the rights and privileges of citizenship. State constitutions reflect states' distinctive political cultures and, in time, reinforce or alter those traditions.

Yet beyond this common core of shared functions, state constitutions vary greatly. Some protect and extend the rights of the individual beyond the guarantees of the U.S. Constitution, while others do not. Perhaps the single biggest difference among state constitutions is the degree to which they serve as a venue for policymaking. In western states, whose constitutions provide for a high degree of direct democracy, advocates and interest groups often attempt to enshrine their policy positions in the state constitution. As a result, these states have long, detailed constitutions. In contrast, the constitutions of the eastern states, particularly in New England, more closely resemble the U.S. Constitution.

State constitutions tend to have a bad reputation with political scientists, for understandable reasons. While many function well, in more than a few instances, they play an outright disruptive role. In states like Alabama and Texas, antiquated state constitutions have made it difficult for state governments to promote economic development—a function that most people believe the state government should play. In California and other states, interest groups have used the constitution to ensure that the state's general revenues flow towards the programs they support. In the process, they have greatly reduced elected officials' ability to make spending decisions on their own.

But as political scientist Christopher Hammonds has argued from another perspective, the fact that constitutions continue to be a contentious venue for politics in many states is not necessarily all bad. While it is still theoretically possible to change the U.S. Constitution, for all practical purposes, we as a society have given that right over to the U.S. Supreme Court. It takes an extraordinarily contentious issue, such as gay marriage, to provoke talk about changing the federal constitution. In contrast, citizens have refused to give up their right to tamper with and tweak their state constitutions. Is that all bad?

Key Concepts

appropriations bills (p. 68)

ballot initiatives (p. 63)

bicameral legislatures (p. 71)

colonial charters (p. 69)

constitutional
  amendments (p. 65)

constitutional
  convention (p. 62)

constitutional revision
  commissions (p. 79)

direct democracy (p. 63)

dual constitutionalism (p. 65)

electorate (p. 63)

the franchise (p. 72)

home rule (p. 90)

Jim Crow laws (p. 72)

judicial federalism (p. 64)

judicial review (p. 80)

line-item veto (p. 84)

model constitution (p. 82)

municipal charter (p. 90)

natural law or
  higher law (p. 65)

ratification (p. 75)

Reconstruction (p. 80)

referendums (p. 63)

separation of powers (p. 70)

special districts (p. 90)

unicameral
  legislatures (p. 70)

Suggested Readings

Book of the States. Lexington, Ky.: Council of State Governments. The single best source of information on state constitutions. Updated yearly, it includes a chapter written by a leading researcher with the latest state constitution news.

Tarr, G. Alan. *Understanding State Constitutions.* Princeton, N.J.: Princeton University Press, 1998. Offers the most detailed look at state constitutions and avoids the tendency to view them as inferior versions of the federal constitution.

Suggested Web Sites

www-camlaw.rutgers.edu/statecon. Web site for Rutgers University Center for State Constitution Studies.

CHAPTER 4

Political Culture, Political Attitudes, and Participation

Venting and Voting

Nine-tenths of democracy is just showing up. Whether it is voting, speaking before a city commission or town council, or contacting a legislator, participation is the key to getting government to pay attention to citizen interests. In a democracy, government can only hear those who exercise their right to get involved. Here Ronald Hoormann flexes his political muscle at a meeting of the Pinckneyville, Illinois, city council which after citizens input unanimously voted to ban lewd entertainment at the local bar.

4

Why do some states remain more conservative—or more liberal—than others over long periods of time?

How do politicians tune in to what citizens are thinking?

Thirty-eight states have a death penalty statute on the books, and support for the death penalty runs fairly high across the country. Yet nearly all executions take place in a handful of states in the South and Southwest.

According to Franklin Zimring, a University of California, Berkeley, law professor, this is not mere coincidence.

He notes that most legal executions take place in those states that had a history of lynching—mob killing of African Americans—and other vigilante violence during the late nineteenth and early twentieth centuries. These states include Alabama, Florida, Georgia, Louisiana, Mississippi, and Texas.[1]

The notion that mob behavior a hundred years ago determines state policy today may sound far-fetched. But states do have **political cultures** that are surprisingly durable. Despite the homogenizing influence of uniform federal requirements, national television networks, and chain department stores, states have retained to a surprising degree their own distinct identities. Vermont, for instance, and Texas are very different places. The state of Vermont offers nearly universal health insurance to children living there. In 2000, it became the first state to offer same-sex couples the chance to enter into civil unions. This gave gay and lesbian couples some of the legal rights enjoyed by married couples. It is hard to imagine such a law passing in Texas. In fact, Texas governor Rick Perry signed a bill in 2003 that banned same-sex marriages or civil unions. A much more conservative state that was briefly an independent republic between periods of control by Mexico and the United States, it has long cherished that heritage. In keeping with its independent, individualistic spirit, Texas does not collect a state income tax and imposes low taxes in general. In exchange, Texans expect a low level of services from their government.

The different histories of Vermont and Texas—or of California and Kansas, for that matter—go some way toward explaining why these states are so different. Such differences also reflect the different values of their residents and impose different levels of restrictions on citizens and businesses. But history alone is not enough of a guide. Variations in how a state runs and maintains its political institutions are part of a state's self-perpetuating political culture. For instance, some states have legislative processes that are more open to the public than others. All of the states have differing political systems that allow parties greater or lesser control of the nominating process. Some states allow for direct election of high-ranking positions,

POLITICAL CULTURE

A set of beliefs that prevails within a state over an extended period of time.

such as state supreme court justices, while those jobs are filled through executive appointments in other states.

Just as each state's political culture is a result of its unique set of political practices and traditions, there are certain factors that cause a particular state's culture to remain largely the same over time. State political cultures historically have been maintained through elections—not the outcome of a particular race, but the actual mechanics of how the elections are run. Federal laws and court decisions have reduced differences between state election laws, but there still are variations in how states allow parties to nominate their candidates and in how difficult they make it for citizens to register to vote. Those differences have profoundly affected how many people—and what sorts of people—actively participate in the political process. That sorting process shapes political culture as well.

That is only one part of the answer, however. In the modern age of polling and instant news, citizens express political opinions constantly, not just at election time. Their attitudes are the bedrock of a state's political culture. Legislators, governors, and other officials try, with varying degrees of success, to take into account public opinion and sentiment on a broad range of issues, such as tax policy, reproductive rights, environmental regulations, and, yes, the death penalty. People's positions on these issues will often vary by state. Residents of the coastal Mid-Atlantic states, for example, are more likely to favor strong environmental protections than ranchers in the Plains states. Aside from housing different opinions, however, states may differ widely in terms of how loudly and effectively citizens can make those opinions known to their elected officials. At one extreme, nearly half of the states allow citizens to write their own laws via the ballot initiative process. Other states may lack enough infrastructure—news media, public interest lobbyists, local think tanks, and community and philanthropic groups—for legislators to have any firm idea of what their constituents believe, save through word of mouth.

All state governments may at first glance look the same: each has a governor, a legislature, and similar bureaucracies and court systems. States,

MAP 4-1 States that Currently Hold Executions

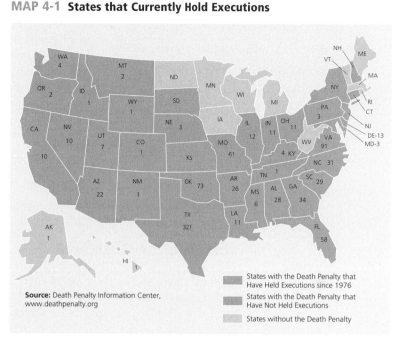

Source: Death Penalty Information Center, www.deathpenalty.org

States with the Death Penalty that Have Held Executions since 1976

States with the Death Penalty that Have Not Held Executions

States without the Death Penalty

> A state's political culture is derived from its history—the circumstances of its founding and its founders—and is perpetuated over time by the way in which it runs and maintains its political institutions.

however, with their different economies, histories, and rules for government interaction with the public, still remain distinct from one another. Why do some states stay more conservative—or more liberal—than others over long periods of time? How do politicians know what citizens are thinking, and how do they translate that knowledge into policy? A state's political culture is derived from its history—the circumstances of its founding and its founders—and is perpetuated over time by the way in which it runs and maintains its political institutions. These are the dynamics we will explore in this chapter.

State Political Cultures

Robert E. Lee was in some ways an unlikely choice to serve as the South's leading general during the Civil War. He was Lincoln's first choice to lead the Union Army and considered slavery a "moral and political evil." Yet Lee's allegiance to his native Virginia made him feel obligated to fight for the Confederacy. "With all my devotion to the Union," he wrote to his sister, "I have been not been able to make up my mind to raise my hand against my relatives, my children, my home." [2] After the war, he testified to Congress that Virginia's act of withdrawal from the United States "carried me along as a citizen of Virginia."

It is hard to imagine a citizen today feeling that kind of loyalty to Virginia or, for that matter, Louisiana, Michigan, or Wisconsin. Indeed, the South's loss in the Civil War greatly diminished the argument that states were autonomous actors within the federal system, since the war proved that the United States itself was more than the sum of its parts. Americans now identify more strongly, in other words, with their country than with their state.

As we explored in Chapter 2, the triumph of the central government in recent years has further blurred some differences between the states. Federal requirements now set baselines for all states to meet in a wide variety of policy areas, including health and welfare spending, educational testing, and environmental standards. To cite just one example of federal supremacy among hundreds, in 2002 a federal judge ordered the governor of South Carolina to end his blockade against federal shipments of plutonium into the state. "It is a sad day for South Carolina when the governor, who has taken an oath to uphold the Constitution, must be ordered by a court to obey it," the judge said. [3] Loyalty to the nation and its laws trumps any state's self-interest.

The sense of a state's unique identity is a diminished thing compared to what it was in the founding days of the republic. Profound differences between the states do still exist, however. Even today, where a person lives says a lot about that person's values and what he or she cares about. We have a sense of this on a local level. We feel like we can guess some things about college students, for instance, based on whether they choose to live in a sorority on campus or in an apartment off campus. We can infer that a person who lives in a high-rise apartment complex downtown has different likes and dislikes than a person who lives in a four-bedroom house near a suburban office complex.

It's the same, to some degree, with states. Most people—just under 60 percent—live in the state where they were born.[4] This is a major reason

why state political cultures tend to be fairly stable, as values are passed down both by political institutions and within families. But the United States is a mobile place. More than twenty million people packed up and moved between states during the latter half of the 1990s.[5] Most of them were following the economy as a higher number of jobs opened up in the South and West. Many people, however, do choose where to live based on whether they think they would feel comfortable with their neighbors, whether they want to enjoy a year-round outdoor lifestyle, or whether they are willing to pay higher taxes to support strong public schools.

So, with all these people pulling up stakes and the federal government, the media, and mass marketing driving nails into the coffin of state individuality, why is it that states still have pronounced differences in political culture? There are many reasons. Some we have already mentioned, including history, residents' values, and political processes and traditions. States also have different economies—wealthier states are typically better able to afford innovative or experimental programs and professionalized legislatures with large staffs that seek out and implement ideas. States with heavy urban populations may devote more attention to social services and infrastructure concerns, such as mass transit. Rural states may be less attentive to these issues, and states with an urban-rural mix may be prone to political infighting between regions. Some states are dominated by one party or the other for a long period of time, which tends to stifle change, since policy innovation often occurs when a new party first takes power.

Political scientists have long wrestled with questions of political culture. No one has come up with an explanation that seems to explain every difference on every issue. In Chapter 1, we briefly discussed the most influential of these explanations, put forth by Daniel J. Elazar. Elazar's classification of state political cultures has proved to be a useful way for explaining

Political culture is stable, even though many Americans are mobile. An influx of new people into a booming state, such as Nevada, can bring different opinions and orientations towards politics as well as new suburbs and strip malls. The newcomers, however, also may find themselves adopting the values of their new community.

why states have different attitudes about abortion, the environment, welfare spending, and many other matters. His explanation is worth outlining in some greater detail here.

Elazar's Classifications

In his 1966 book *American Federalism: A View from the States*,[6] Elazar argued that politics in each state were shaped by three important factors: **sectionalism,** which means that states in geographic clusters, as in the South or New England, tend to influence one another and share certain expectations; **migration patterns,** the patterns of settlers moving west and, later, people leaving farms in favor of cities; and—you guessed it—the state's political culture, its history, habits and customs regarding government, people's expectations from government, and the types of people who actively participate in politics and government.

For Elazar, people's religious and ethnic backgrounds and their migration patterns were the dominant influences in establishing cultures. He proposed that three types of settlers and their descendants tended to move across the country in almost a straight, westward line. Per the three types of settlers, Elazar divided the states into three different types of political cultures—moralistic, individualistic, and traditionalistic. Let's define what Elazar meant by each of these categories and look at some specific examples of each type.

MAP 4-2 Dominant Political Culture by State

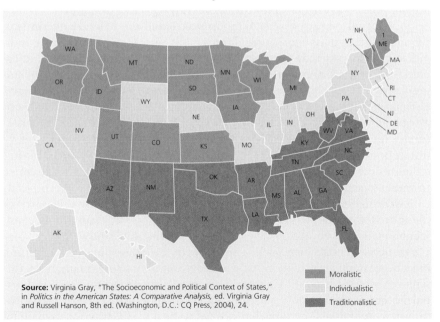

Source: Virginia Gray, "The Socioeconomic and Political Context of States," in *Politics in the American States: A Comparative Analysis*, ed. Virginia Gray and Russell Hanson, 8th ed. (Washington, D.C.: CQ Press, 2004), 24.

Governing States and Localities

Politics is basically viewed as a good thing in moralistic states. Civic involvement and public service are pleasurable duties. The government is a vital force in trying to promote the public interest and "is considered a positive instrument with a responsibility to promote the general welfare."[7] Politics and government serve the advancement of society as a whole, so it is expected that all citizens have a duty to take an active interest in them. People who do not vote should be ashamed. Although government service is considered something worthwhile and beneficial to engage in, the work of politics should not be handed over to political professionals. Moralistic states have high levels of competition between the parties because each person's and each politician's motivations are supposed to spring from serving the community, rather than a particular party or agenda.

They no longer try people for witchcraft in New England, although some of the values of the Puritan settlers remain embedded in the region's political culture. Moralistic states, which share a Puritan heritage, are associated with progressive politics and policy. As noted in Chapter 3, however, the same moral fervor that fed a desire to build the best possible society at times inspired extreme actions and reactions.

The moralistic states tend to be clustered in the country's northern tier—in New England, the upper Midwest, and the Pacific Northwest. Elazar pointed out that the Puritans who settled the Northeast had come to the New World seeking religious freedom. The political culture where they settled reflects their desire to use politics to construct the best possible society. This moralistic political culture spread with their Yankee descendants and with other northern European settlers into the Great Lakes region and westward into Oregon, Washington, and parts of California.

Wisconsin is a classic moralistic state. First settled by Yankees and later by Scandinavians, Germans, and Eastern Europeans, the state has long had a reputation for policy innovation, based on its early adoption of the direct primary, through which voters, rather than party officials, pick candidates for public office, and on its creation of a workers' compensation system. It was in the forefront of consumer protection and environmental protection during the 1970s and welfare reform during the 1990s. The state also has a highly developed political culture, with high **voter turnout** rates and a professional legislature that works nearly year-round.

Residents of individualistic states view the political system as simply another way to advance one's own social and economic interests. Government is meant to be utilitarian. It should provide the services that the people demand but lack the ambition to create a "good society" or intervene in private activities. Politics is a career like any other—a business, if you will—in which officeholders expect to be paid like professionals. Political parties are, in essence, corporations that help to maintain and support the industry. Politicians look at government as a way to promote their own

VOTER TURNOUT

The percentage of eligible citizens who register to vote and do vote.

TABLE 4-1

Political Cultures at a Glance

	Elazar Classification		
	Moralistic	**Individualistic**	**Traditionalistic**
Role of Government	Government should act to promote the public interest and policy innovation.	Government should be utilitarian, a service provider.	Government should help preserve the status quo.
Attitude of Public Representatives	Politicians can effect change; public service is worthwhile and an honor.	Businesslike. Politics is a career like any other, and individual politicians are oriented towards personal power. High levels of corruption are more common.	Politicians can effect change, but politics is the province of the elites.
Role of Citizens	Citizens actively participate in voting and other political activities; individuals seek public office.	The state exists to advance the economic and personal self-interest of citizens; citizens leave politics to the professionals.	Ordinary citizens are not expected to be politically involved.
Degree of Party Competition	Highly competitive	Moderate	Weak
Government Spending on Services	High	Moderate; money goes to basic services but not perceived "extras."	Low
Political Culture	Strong	Fragmented	Strong
Most Common in . . .	Northeast, northern Midwest, Northwest	Middle parts of the country, like the Mid-Atlantic; parts of the Midwest, like Missouri and Illinois; parts of the West, like Nevada and California	Southern states, rural areas

power and dole out favors. Individualistic states breed and accept a relatively high level of corruption. As long as the expected services are provided—the roads are paved and the trains run on time—citizens put up with a lot. Why? They believe that politics is a dirty business best left to the professionals. "Both politicians and citizens look upon political activity as a specialized one," Elazar writes, "and no place for amateurs to play an active role."[8] Political programs exist to deliver benefits such as contracts and jobs to a chosen few—friends or political associates of current officeholders—not to build parks and police forces that benefit everyone equally.[9]

The English, Scottish, Irish, and Germans who initially settled the middle parts of the country, including Maryland, New Jersey, and Pennsylvania, brought this "every man for himself" attitude with them. They had come to the United States in search of a better life and individual opportunity. The state political systems they created reflected that desire. Their individualistic political culture then was carried by their descendants into places like Illinois and Missouri and as far west as Nevada and parts of California.

Case in point: New Jersey was settled by waves of poor and uneducated European immigrants seeking the American Dream, especially after the Civil War. More recently, the state has attracted many African Americans and Latinos and is currently home to one million foreign-born residents. For all its mix of ethnicities, New Jersey "has always been more of a polyglot than a melting pot," says political scientist Maureen Moakley, with each ethnic group keeping to its own kind.[10] The result is a fragmented political culture. Residents lack a strong allegiance to the state, with many of them working in and identifying with cities outside of the state—Philadelphia to the south and New York to the north and countless put-down jokes about New Jersey in between.

In part because people feel more connected with their local communities than with the state, New Jersey has strong home rule laws, in which the state's five hundred-plus localities have much more power in relation to the state than is generally the case. That sense of parochialism historically has been enhanced by the power of local parties and politicians and generally has operated at the county level and provided plenty of fodder for scandal. A series of recent bribery and corruption scandals has left citizens there turned off to politics. The federal investigation into Democratic Party fundraising there has extended into the office of Governor James McGreevey and has resulted in numerous indictments surrounding alleged bribes involving the former Hudson County executive and Democratic Party leader. A poll conducted in 2003 found that only one resident in twenty-five could correctly identify which party controlled that state's governorship and two legislative chambers.[11] "Politics," says Moakley, "is generally viewed as a necessary evil and most New Jerseyans take care to place some distance between themselves and the public order."[12]

Certain localities in and out of New Jersey have become well known for their individualistic political cultures, such as Camden, New Jersey; Nassau County, New York; Providence, Rhode Island; and Chicago, Illinois. In these places—especially during the first decades following World War II—politics came to be viewed as a dirty business, with elected officials prone to corruption and known to give favors to their friends. Nevertheless, people respected politicians who could deliver the goods, the ones who ran effective building programs and kept the city running well. The respect may be gone these days, but the residents still need what the politicians can deliver.

The third type of state encompasses the southern parts of the United States. Traditionalistic states are, as their name would suggest, fundamentally conservative, in the sense of preserving a well-established society. Like moralistic states, traditionalistic states believe that government serves a positive role. The difference is that traditionalists believe the larger purpose of government and society is to maintain existing social orders. Traditionalistic states are very hierarchical, with most of the power held by a small number of elites. Everyone knows his or her role and sticks to it. Elites at the top of the social structure are expected to play a dominant role in government. "Those who do not have a definite role to play in politics are not expected to be even minimally active as citizens," according to Elazar. "In many cases, they are not even expected to vote." [13] Traditionalistic states tend to be rural, where large agricultural and other land-based or resource-based concerns are major economic drivers, rather than a broader mix of competing commercial activities. Government spending is often relatively low and party competition usually is weak.

Like the settlers of the individualistic states, the first southerners also sought personal opportunity. The pre-industrial, agrarian economy of the South, however, led to a culture that for quite some time was little more than a variation on the feudal order of the European Middle Ages. In this hierarchical system, laws and the political culture reinforced the strong positions held by wealthy landowners and farmers at the expense of sharecroppers and African Americans. As far back as the 1830s, Alexis de Tocqueville noted that "as one goes farther south . . . the population does not exercise such a direct influence on affairs. . . . The power of the elected official is comparatively greater and that of the voter less." [14]

The South's changing economy—along with the huge influx of former northerners into states such as Florida and Georgia—has altered the region's political culture. But the more things change, the more they remain the same. Georgia, Mississippi, and South Carolina are several southern states still arguing about state policies in regard to Confederate flags, symbols of southern secession in the Civil War.

The rebel flag may not fly over its capitol, but perhaps no state is as traditionalistic as Robert E. Lee's home of Virginia. As University of Virginia government professor Larry J. Sabato notes, "It's no accident that many candidates in this state have been elected using the slogan, 'For a Virginia Worthy of Her Past.'" [15] The Old Dominion dominated politics in the republic's early days and produced a wildly disproportionate share of the nation's founders and other leaders. Five of the country's first ten presidents hailed from Virginia. As in many southern states, Virginia's political institutions helped to preserve white dominance by such measures as keeping African Americans segregated in "blacks only" schools and medical facilities. Dominated for decades before the civil rights era by U.S. senator Harry F. Byrd Sr., D-Va., and his cronies and for a couple of centuries before that by a rural aristocracy, Virginia, however, did have traditions of civility that blunted its racist policies to some extent. Residents of the commonwealth never gave much support to the Ku Klux Klan, and, in the 1920s, the state

Queen Elizabeth I—the "Virgin Queen" and Virginia's namesake—graces this traditionalistic state's senate seal, adopted in 1981.

passed one of the nation's earliest and strongest anti-lynching laws. It is worth noting that Virginia is the only state that has ever elected an African American to its highest office, when conservative Democrat L. Douglas Wilder was elected governor in 1989.

Despite all of this, blue-blooded aristocrats have long run the state and political participation among average citizens is quite low. For much of the twentieth century, turnout rates for statewide elections were well under 20 percent. In 2002, U.S. senator John Warner, R-Va., won reelection without facing major party opposition for the second time. A year later, close to 66 percent of the seats in the state House of Delegates were not contested by one of the major parties. That was partly the effect of **redistricting**—the way that each district's boundaries were redrawn following the census—which made the seats less competitive, but also had a lot to do with tradition.

Like states, some cities have traditionalistic political cultures. A case in point is Memphis. Edward Hull "Boss" Crump ruled the city from his first election as mayor in 1909 until his death in 1954. Even though his later years were spent in Congress, he still ran the city. He took a paternalistic attitude toward African Americans, believing them inferior, and kept them from voting. Instead, he doublecounted the votes of loyal supporters, let them vote even if they were not registered, and trucked people in from nearby Arkansas and Mississippi to vote.

REDISTRICTING
The drawing of new boundaries for congressional and state legislative districts, usually following a decennial census.

Was Elazar Right?

Political scientists have built on Elazar's formulation as a model to seek answers as to why states enact different laws in such issue areas as the death penalty, environmental law, and affirmative action. Many experts express skepticism about his model because it is impressionistic. This means that Elazar's work is based more on anecdote and on sometimes slippery demographic categories than on hard data. His categories cannot be proved through empirical data. "I have never been especially impressed with his typology," says Greg Shaw, a political scientist at Illinois Wesleyan University. "I just don't think it's all that useful." [16] Shaw thinks that if you want to understand how state policymakers arrive at a decision, it is more useful to think about the effect of prevailing ideologies within the state combined with its ability to pay for programs. Historical culture is not a pivotal factor in any decision making.

Many political scientists share Shaw's doubts. There are certainly other factors beyond religious and ethnic makeup that help explain a state's political culture, including its economic strength. Nevertheless, Elazar remains tremendously influential among political scientists mainly because nobody has come up with a better explanation as to why some states stay conservative over long periods of time while others remain more liberal. Elazar's reasoning is largely based on sectionalism—the sense that this is a big enough country to allow for important regional differences. And there is

> . . . . there is quite a bit of evidence . . . that states tend to resemble their neighbors to a fair extent. Policymakers are more likely to worry about how their rates of taxation or teachers' salaries stack up against neighboring states than against national averages, for instance, because residents and businesses are more likely to move to an attractive state next door than anywhere else.

quite a bit of evidence that, despite the blending effects of federal requirements and the swapping of information by officeholders through national organizations, states tend to resemble their neighbors. For instance, policymakers are more likely to worry about how their state's rates of taxation or teachers' salaries stack up against neighboring states than against national averages because residents and businesses are more likely to move to an attractive state next door than anywhere else.

Impressions may be misleading, but they can also shape reality. If liberals perceive Texas as conservative, they will be less inclined to move there. The opposite is true of conservatives who would not want to live in a more liberal state such as Vermont. Political scientists who have constructed their own models since Elazar's work was first published have found that the political cultures of states do not shift very easily or very often.[17] Admittedly, Elazar's roadmap may not always be accurate. What he says about a state's political culture may not be a perfect predictor of how that state will respond to any given policy challenge. But he does offer a pretty good sense of the territory.

Elections

State political cultures are preserved primarily through elections, when a majority, or **plurality**, of voters elect officials who more or less reflect their political beliefs. Elections for public office are the fundamental process of representative democracies. More bluntly, they are the main way that the will of the people connects to and influences the actions of government. Each state must determine what constitutes a valid vote. Election laws are set and controlled by them. There is much variation between states as to how easy or how hard they make it for citizens to vote. Some of those differences have been smoothed away in recent years by federal laws and court decisions. Differences do remain, however, and they are largely reflective of the types of political cultures Elazar described and that we have outlined.

These differences, in turn, affect national politics. The way that people vote in their own state—the type of access that they have to the ballot—helps determine the success or failure of presidential candidates and the makeup of Congress. For about one hundred years after the Civil War, for example, Republicans were not a true national party. They had next to no presence in the South, which resented Republican intrusions during the Civil War and Reconstruction in support of abolition, suffrage, and equal opportunity for African Americans. Times and political parties change, however. The Republican Party of the nineteenth century bares a closer resemblance in some ways to the Democratic Party of today than to its twenty-first century Grand Old Party descendant. That is one reason Democrats held the region for decades. These days, the South is one of the pillars of Republican strength. The region's continuing conservatism now fits well within the GOP.

Southern states and the less populous, rural states in the Mountain West tilt toward Republican interests and form a bloc that helps elect presidents through its disproportionate share of the electoral college. The electoral college gives a minimum of three votes to each state, regardless of population. The influence of less populous states is increased at the expense of larger ones. Political analyst Steven Hill calls this "affirmative action for low-population states."[18] This is one reason why George W. Bush won the presidency in 2000 despite losing the popular vote. The U.S. Senate—which gives two seats to every state regardless of size—further expands the influence of smaller, less populous states.

Elections may be how citizens can speak out for their beliefs and they may give states a voice in national politics, but you wouldn't know it from the interest they generate in the general public. Sadly, the franchise appears to be a diminished thing, with the act of voting on the decline. People do not feel well connected to government. Fewer than half of the voting age population cast ballots in presidential elections. In elections in which congressional or statewide offices are at the top of the ticket, the percentage drops below 40 percent.

Voter turnout is a puzzle political scientists have been trying to explain for a long time. In moralistic states, turnout tends to be high. In other places, such as here in Grandview Heights, Ohio, on March 2, 2004, there are not enough voters to keep poll workers busy.

For municipal elections, turnout rates are generally below 20 percent.

Voting tends to pick up for competitive races—when voters feel like they have a genuine choice. The major political parties, however, have reconciled themselves to the reality that millions of people feel their vote does not count. Turnout rates are particularly abysmal for traditional college students and other young people. In an online chat in 2003, political analyst Stuart Rothenberg wrote, "All non-voters are irrelevant and unimportant, and I am skeptical about efforts by the right, left or radical center to motivate large numbers of non-voters. It seems that every election we talk about bringing new people into the system, but the 2004 contest is likely to be about which party motivates its base and sways swing voters."[19] Unquestionably, we have created an odd paradox as a nation. We like elections—we hold more of them than any other country on earth—yet we consistently score one of the lowest voter turnout rates of any democracy in the world.

State Supervision of Elections

It seems obvious to say, but elections are fundamental to democracy. They are the source of authority for governmental decisions and power. They are when a majority of eligible citizens presumably give their blessing to office-holders who will determine the course of policy. Elections are the main conduit for citizens to express their pleasure or displeasure with governmental decisions. If voters are unhappy with the decisions their elected officials have made, they can turn them out of office during the next election. For all the system's faults, politicians and parties have to win approval from voters at regularly scheduled intervals if they are to remain in power.

The U.S. Constitution gives states the authority to determine "the times, places and manner of holding elections." In nearly every state, the secretary of state has the practical duty of running elections—setting dates, qualifying candidates, and printing and counting ballots. In a few states, the lieutenant governor or a state election board may oversee these chores. The states, in turn, rely on counties or, in some cases, cities to run the polls themselves. The localities draw precinct boundaries and set up and supervise polling places. In many cases they have the main responsibility for registering voters. Following the election, county officials count up the ballots and report the results to the appropriate individual, such as the secretary of state, who then tabulates and certifies the totals.

Each state's election code determines the specific details about ballots, perhaps most importantly, the order in which offices and candidates will appear. This varies considerably among states. By 1992, about 80 percent of the states had replaced paper ballots with punch cards, machines in which voters pulled a lever next to the names of the candidates of their choice, or optical scan voting machines.[20] Voters in some states use electronic systems resembling ATMs. All but a handful of states tabulate votes for write-in candidates, although victories or even significant showings by such candidates are few and far between.

The style of ballots varies. California currently uses a random alphabet system to decide the order in which candidate names will appear and rotates the starting letter of that alphabet in each state assembly district. The **office group ballot**, also known as the **Massachusetts ballot**, lists candidates' names, followed by their party designation, under the title of the office they are seeking (governor, state representative, etc.). The other major type of ballot is called the **party column ballot**, or the **Indiana ballot**, which "arranges the candidates for each office in columns according to their party designation." [21] About twenty states make it even easier for citizens to vote

OFFICE GROUP (MASSACHUSETTS) BALLOT

Ballots in which candidates are listed by name under the title of the office they are seeking.

PARTY COLUMN (INDIANA) BALLOT

Ballots in which the names of candidates are divided into columns arranged according to political party.

A Difference that Makes a Difference: For Whom the Ballot Polls

The legitimacy of all democratic governments rests on the faith that election outcomes represent the true preferences of voters. In the United States, that faith was sorely tested by the 2000 presidential election.

Watching election officials try to divine the presidency by reading hanging chads made at least this much clear: voting machinery matters. How ballots are designed, how they are marked by voters, and how they are examined and tallied by election officials plays an important role in determining electoral fortunes.

Practically all the mechanics of voting are left to state and local authorities. What ballots look like, what voters must do to indicate their preferences, and how election officials tally those preferences differs enormously from state to state. Talk about a difference that can make a difference. Eliminate the butterfly ballot and the hanging chads in a handful of Florida counties and President Al Gore would have had to deal with the recession and 9/11.

This is not just a matter of determining who ends up in office. The core issue is the franchise, the matter of whether some citizens' votes are more likely to be counted than others. Certainly in Florida, it was the poorest localities—which typically mean heavily minority areas—that had the least modern voting machinery. The possibility that really haunts the democratic process here is the possibility that voters' preferences are being mis-

The Help America Vote Act (HAVA) brought point and click democracy to many voting booths. HAVA pushed localities to replace paper punch ballots with hi-tech electronic voting machines that leave no hanging chads.

counted because their state and local governments—for whatever reason—could not or did not invest in the basic infrastructure of voting.

In the wake of the 2000 election, the federal government passed the Help America Vote Act (HAVA), which was designed to head off a repeat of the Florida fiasco by helping state and local governments replace rickety, outdated voting machines. While well-intentioned, HAVA has only gone so far in addressing the problem. The basic difficulty is that HAVA demands state and local governments upgrade the voting infrastructure without covering the costs.

HAVA made about $1.5 billion available to the states to help buy new voting machines, but that doesn't come near to covering the cost. County commissioners in Utah County, Utah, for example, found in June that purchasing new touch-screen voting technology would represent an extra $140,000 burden to local taxpayers. At the time, the county was so strapped for money it was putting government employees on one-day, unpaid furloughs to try and balance the books. That makes buying equipment that will be used a couple of times a year a very painful purchase.

The commissioners, nonetheless, anted up. The varying probabilities of a vote being accurately counted (or not counted at all) turns out to be a difference most of us would like to see go away.

Source: Donald F. Kettl, "Congress Promised to Stop Imposing Mandates on States and Localities without Paying Them. But the Temptation Is Irresistible," *Governing* magazine, August 2003. www.governing.com/archive/2003/aug/potomac.txt (accessed April 26, 2004).

for party nominees—voters can cast a **straight ticket** vote for all of the party's nominees with one punch or pull of the lever.

Regulating the Parties

A state's authority to print ballots gives it enormous control over what parties and candidates get presented to voters. Until the late nineteenth century, parties themselves printed ballots, which obviously encouraged voters to select a straight ticket of their chosen party's nominees. The advent of the **secret ballot**—also known as the **Australian ballot**—led the states to print their own ballots and, therefore, to determine which parties should appear on ballots. "From there," writes Kay Lawson, a retired San Francisco State University political scientist, "it seemed but a short step to requiring that parties show a minimum level of support to qualify." [22]

The Republican and Democratic parties are themselves regulated at the state level by a bewildering array of varying state laws. Some states provide detailed regulations for party organization, activities, and nominating procedures. Others are silent on many specific matters. According to political scientist V. O. Key, the traditional Democratic one-party control of the South, although now a thing of the past, led to the introduction of the political primary. Primaries give voters a real say in who ultimately will hold an office, since they have no real choice in the general election. [23] These days, nearly every state holds primary elections for picking party nominees for state offices, although some states, such as Virginia, still nominate candidates at party conventions. We will have a fuller discussion of political parties in Chapter 5.

While the major parties feel their share of state ballot regulation heat, some states seem out to fry new or minor parties and independent candidates. Prior to a 1968 Supreme Court decision, *Williams v. Rhodes,* it was possible for states to have no mechanism in place to qualify new parties for their ballots. Even today, according to Richard Winger, editor of the newsletter *Ballot Access News,* new parties in eleven states cannot qualify for the ballot before they have picked their candidates, who must be listed on their ballot access petition—the collection of voters' signatures. [24]

The Court's decision meant that a state no longer could require a certain percentage of signatures be collected in each county. That did not mean that states could no longer burn aspiring parties or candidates, it just made lighting the matches a bit more of a challenge. Nine states changed their laws to require signatures be collected in each congressional district. This kept ballot access elusive for candidates or parties with most of their support in a particular city or region. Fifteen states also placed time constraints on when signatures can be collected—California and Ohio require new parties to qualify even before the election year begins. Virginia blocks petitioners from gathering signatures outside of their home congressional district. In Texas, voters who participated in major party primaries are not allowed to sign a petition to get a new party on the ballot. The state also requires citizens to know and affix their voter registration numbers next to their signatures on petitions. Similarly, Alabama, Arkansas, New York, and Virginia require signers to supply their precinct numbers. Quick—what's your precinct number?

As if it wasn't hot enough already, in a 1971 decision, *Jenness v. Fortson,* the Supreme Court upheld a Georgia law that requires minor parties or independent candidates to collect signatures that represent five percent of the total number of votes cast in the last election for the office. Independent or minor party candidates for governor in 2006 will have to accrue 101,295 signatures to qualify for the gubernatorial ballot. That is a lot of signatures for a new political player, and it is more than double the amount of votes the one minor party candidate for the office received in 2002. Not surprisingly, no new minor or independent candidate has qualified for the ballot in Georgia since 1964.[25] The Supreme Court ruling emboldened several other states to erect strict barriers against access to the ballot. States such as Alabama, North Carolina, Oklahoma, and West Virginia have the most difficult requirements for parties and candidates to get around. In West Virginia, for instance, the law requires circulators who are trying to collect signatures to tell everyone they approach, "If you sign my petition, you can't vote in the primary." That happens not to be true—but it is the law. Why make a law requiring circulators to fib to voters? Well, the fib benefits the major parties by keeping out the competition, and the major parties write the laws.

For third parties and independent candidates, it can be a real challenge to gain access to the ballots on any of the states discussed here. Given what we know about Elazar's theory about southern, or traditionalistic, states, and their hierarchical attitude toward politics, it should not surprise us that these states have the most restrictive ballot access laws. That does not mean that hundreds of minor party and independent candidates have not overcome all these hurdles and more to win spots on statewide ballots. A couple of them have even won election as governor—in Minnesota in 1998 and Maine in 1994 and 1998. Their place on a ballot one year, however, is no guarantee that members of their parties will qualify the next time around. Alabama requires that a minor party poll at least 20 percent of the vote for governor in order to win automatic qualification for the next ballot. Half a dozen other states require at least 10 percent. Given all the restrictions, Lawson concludes, "The laws have been effective in keeping minor parties off the ballot in election after election."[26]

Why all the restrictions? Keeping minor parties off the ballot naturally helps the two major parties. Those who are in power control the rules that keep them in power. In Georgia, bills to loosen the state's restrictions have been introduced at least seven times over the last twenty years. They have always failed.

Restricting Voters

States do not just regulate the access of parties to the ballot. They also regulate the interaction of citizens with that ballot. They determine who can register to vote and how they can register. Changes in federal law over the years have removed many of the initial barriers states had imposed that restricted voting rights based on property ownership, literacy, race, sex, and age. But there are still differences among states in terms of how easy they make it for citizens to register—a necessary step toward having the chance to vote in every state except North Dakota, which does not require voter registration.

In the early years of the nation, most eastern states required citizens to own property in order to vote. Those requirements diminished over time, in large part because the western frontier states lacked the type of class structure that reinforced them. The eastern states, however, soon came up with the idea of imposing literacy tests. New immigrants had to demonstrate knowledge of the state constitution or other complex issues to the satisfaction of the local election official.[27] Native whites who were illiterate were often exempted from this requirement. Southern states took up literacy testing as a means of keeping African Americans from voting, since they generally received inadequate educations in schools segregated by race. Literacy tests remained a part of the southern legal landscape until the federal Voting Rights Act of 1965 barred them.

Several amendments to the U.S. Constitution expanded voting rights to cover women and minorities. The Fifteenth Amendment was passed following the Civil War and was meant to end discrimination against black men seeking to vote. Until the civil rights movement of the 1960s, however, it was effectively bypassed through literacy tests, intimidation, and other means for a century. The Voting Rights Act of 1965 gave the federal government authority to review state requirements for registration and voting. In 1964, the Twenty-Fourth Amendment banned the use of poll taxes meant to keep blacks and other poor people from voting. Women received the right to vote with the ratification of the Nineteenth Amendment in 1920. The voting age was lowered to eighteen by the Twenty-Sixth Amendment in 1971. In 1993, Congress passed a law known as "motor voter" registration, which requires states to allow citizens to register to vote when they take tests to receive their driver's licenses.

Why all of the effort to get people registered to vote? The purpose of registering voters is to prevent fraud. It prevents people from voting more than once or outside of their home jurisdictions. This reason makes sense, but throughout the nation's history, many states have used registration laws as a means of making voting inaccessible to some. (See Box 4-2.)

Voter Turnout

It's never been easier to register and to vote, yet fewer and fewer people are actually doing either. Motor voter produced an initial spike in registration, but had little or no effect on the numbers of people voting. According to Curtis Gans of the Committee for the Study of the American Electorate, voter turnout rates have declined by about 25 percent over the last forty years.[28] There are countless reasons why voter turnout has declined, including a general disaffection with politics and government, a measurable decline in civic education and newspaper reading, a weakening of civic-minded institutions such as student government and unions, and the changing role of political parties away from engaging and educating voters and toward raising money and providing services to candidates.

Turnout rates are in decline, but they are not declining uniformly across the states. The reasons some states have turnout rates 20 percentage points higher than others have to do with many factors, but the main reasons are political culture, demographics, and party competition. The variations in voter registration laws at this point have relatively little effect.

In general, the closer you live to Canada, the more likely you are to vote. The states with the turnout rates above 60 percent for the 2000 presidential election—Maine, Minnesota, Wisconsin, etc.—are all in the northern tier of the country. The states with lower turnout rates, including Arizona, Hawaii, Nevada, and Texas, are all in the South or far West. What explains the difference? Culture, for one thing. Elazar's theory about moralistic states appears to hold up, at least as far as voter turnout goes. "You're talking about states with fairly vigorous political parties, communications media that do cover politics and an educational system more geared toward citizen engagement than other parts of the country," says Gans. A big state like California has a mix of cultures—individualistic and moralistic—according to Elazar.

The moralistic states also tend to be homogenous in terms of population. People are more likely to vote if they are better educated, if they are elderly, and if they are white. "In states with high percentage of minorities, you're going to have low turnout," says Steven Hill, a senior analyst for the Center for Voting and Democracy. "States with higher voter turnout, such as Minnesota and Maine, tend to be fairly white states."[29] The moralistic states historically have bred strong two-party competition. This tends to increase turnout. Citizens in states or districts dominated by one party or the other tend not to vote as eagerly. Their candidate of choice is certain to win—or to lose, if they are an "orphaned" voter whose party is weak in their home state.

Voter turnout rates actually have increased in the South, where many of the historical impediments against registration and voting have declined. There also is more competition between the major parties than has been the case for more than one hundred years. But the region has merely stabilized at a slightly lower turnout rate than the rest of the country. Its high proportion of African Americans and its historical legacy of suppressing their votes and the votes of some whites has kept its turnout rates sluggish even though African Americans do tend to vote more than other minorities, such as Latinos.

New Hampshire had the best turnout among young voters in the 2000 primaries.

A Difference that Makes a Difference:
How Some States Discourage Voters

Thirty years ago, a political scientist named Robert H. Blank came up with a formula for ranking states according to how easy they made it for their citizens to vote. He came up with fifteen different criteria, including whether they allowed people to vote by absentee ballot for any reason (which was true of thirty-six states); whether they kept polls open for a uniform twelve hours across the state (twenty-nine states); whether they allowed people to register to vote within one month of an election (thirty-five states); and whether they required people to establish residency in the state for more than a year before they could register to vote (twelve states).[a]

According to Blank's scale, traditionalistic states, such as Alabama, Arkansas, and Mississippi, made it hardest for people to vote. These states typically tried to maintain a hierarchical political structure in which white, non-elite citizens—and all African Americans—were discouraged from playing an active role. Obviously, attempting to disenfranchise—keep from voting—people was the most blatant way possible to limit access to political decision making. Conversely, the states that did the most to make it easier to register and to vote, such as Idaho, Michigan, and Minnesota, were moralistic states that encouraged political participation among the widest number of people possible. Raymond E. Wolfinger and Steven J. Rosenstone found that voting participation was highest in individualistic states in which government is seen as a marketplace for advancing self-interest among people who had a direct interest access to government jobs and contracts.[b]

Since Blank's survey, many of the differences in voting and registration laws among the states have been done away with because of federal intervention. A federal court in 1972 ruled that states could not cut off registration any sooner than thirty days before an election. This effectively eliminated longer state residency requirements. The federal government in 1995 adopted a "motor voter" law, based on a law pioneered in Michigan, to allow citizens to fill out a registration form whenever they applied for a driver's license. Previously, some states had restricted registration so that prospective voters had to show up

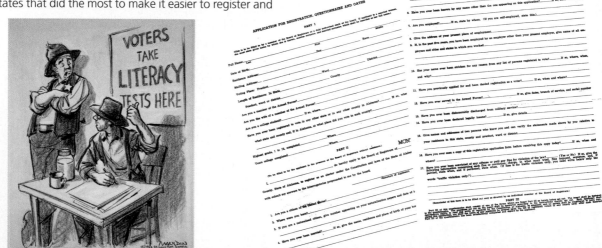

Although once a common voting requirement, literacy tests always flunked Democracy 101. States that required literacy standards used them mainly as a way to disenfranchise minorities. Whites, literate or not, were often exempt, and the standards were unevenly applied. The white male test taker in this cartoon has a much higher chance of passing the test than a minority even though he obviously is not qualified. In addition to literacy tests, voters were required to complete lengthy registration forms, like the four-page example seen here from 1950s

at a county registrar's office during limited business hours.

There are still differences among the states, though. North Dakota does not require voters to register at all, while some states, including Minnesota, allow voters to register to vote on election day itself. Since 1998, Oregon has conducted all of its elections exclusively by mail, which means that citizens do not need to leave their homes to vote and do not have to vote on one specific day. No question, the states that make it easier for their citizens to vote tend to have the highest voter turnout.

Given the many changes in election laws in recent decades, however, the difference in turnout rates has become less pronounced. Voting in southern states still lags behind the rest of the country, but by a much smaller amount than in the days of poll taxes and literacy tests. And some of the reforms have not made that much difference. Motor voting produced a surge in registration of about five percentage points during the first two years of its operation,

but did not lead to higher voter turnout rates in subsequent elections.

States that make registration harder do discourage voters—but then, their entire political cultures are based on limiting participation. The reverse is true of states with high voter turnouts. Differences in registration laws do not explain their higher levels of political participation as well as their generally inclusive cultures. People tend to vote when they are given a choice—when they think their vote matters. This is why more people vote in states that have healthy competition between the major parties, rather than being dominated by just one of them. Other factors explain voting turnout rates as well. People who are better educated, have higher incomes, are white, or are older vote more than people who are young, poor, poorly educated, or members or minority groups.

[a] Robert H. Blank, "State Electoral Structure," *Journal of Politics* 35, no. 4 (November 1993): 988–994.

[b] Raymond E. Wolfinger and Steven J. Rosenstone, *Who Votes?* (New Haven, Conn.: Yale University Press, 1980).

Alabama. These forms asked such questions as, "Give names and addresses of two persons who know you and can verify the statements made above by you relative to your residence in this state, county, and precinct, ward or district." and "Are you a college student? If so, where?" Compare that to the simple one-page Alabama voter registration form of today. The form can be printed out, completed, folded, and mailed like a postcard.

TABLE 4-2a

Percentage of the Voting Age Population Casting Ballots in the 2000 Presidential Election

Rank	State	Percent to Total Voting Age Population	Elazar Classification	Rank	State	Percent to Total Voting Age Population	Elazar Classification
1	Minnesota	68.8	Moralistic	26	Pennsylvania	53.7	Individualistic
2	Maine	67.3	Moralistic	27	Virginia	53	Traditionalistic
3	Alaska	66.4	Individualistic	28	Illinois	52.8	Individualistic
4	Wisconsin	66.1	Moralistic	29	Utah	52.6	Moralistic
5	Vermont	64	Moralistic	30	Kentucky	51.6	Traditionalistic
6	New Hampshire	62.5	Moralistic	31	Maryland	51.6	Individualistic
7	Montana	61.5	Moralistic	32	New Jersey	51	Individualistic
8	Iowa	60.7	Moralistic	33	Florida	50.6	Traditionalistic
9	Oregon	60.6	Moralistic	34	New York	50.4	Individualistic
10	North Dakota	60.4	Moralistic	35	North Carolina	50.3	Traditionalistic
11	Wyoming	59.7	Individualistic	36	Alabama	50	Traditionalistic
12	Connecticut	58.4	Individualistic	37	Tennessee	49.2	Traditionalistic
13	South Dakota	58.2	Moralistic	38	Indiana	49	Individualistic
14	Massachusetts	57.6	Individualistic	39	Oklahoma	48.8	Traditionalistic
15	Missouri	57.5	Individualistic	40	Mississippi	48.6	Traditionalistic
16	Michigan	57.5	Moralistic	41	Arkansas	47.8	Traditionalistic
17	Washington	56.9	Moralistic	42	New Mexico	47.4	Traditionalistic
18	Colorado	56.8	Moralistic	43	South Carolina	46.6	Traditionalistic
19	Nebraska	56.5	Individualistic	44	West Virginia	45.8	Traditionalistic
20	Delaware	56.3	Individualistic	45	California	44.1	Individualistic
21	Ohio	55.8	Individualistic	46	Georgia	43.8	Traditionalistic
22	Idaho	54.5	Moralistic	47	Nevada	43.8	Individualistic
23	Rhode Island	54.3	Individualistic	48	Texas	43.1	Traditionalistic
24	Louisiana	54.2	Traditionalistic	49	Arizona	42.3	Traditionalistic
25	Kansas	54.1	Moralistic	50	Hawaii	40.5	Individualistic

As previously mentioned, there are many other factors that determine rates of voter turnout. Elderly people tend to vote a lot—which is one reason why Social Security and Medicare are always important political issues. Young people, by contrast, rarely vote. People who are wealthy also tend to vote more than the poor, while people with higher levels of education vote much more regularly than people with limited educations. These are some of the reasons why a high-income state with an educated population, such

TABLE 4-2b

Percentage of Registered Voters Casting Ballots in the 2000 Presidential Election

Rank	State	Percent to Registered Voters	Elazar Classification	Rank	State	Percent to Registered Voters	Elazar Classification
1	Wyoming	97.1	Individualistic	26	Tennessee	65.3	Traditionalistic
2	Oregon	78.9	Moralistic	27	Delaware	64.8	Individualistic
3	Connecticut	77.9	Individualistic	28	Louisiana	64.7	Traditionalistic
4	Colorado	76.6	Moralistic	29	South Carolina	64.3	Traditionalistic
5	Minnesota	74.7	Moralistic	30	Nebraska	64.2	Individualistic
6	Washington	74.6	Moralistic	31	Pennsylvania	63.1	Individualistic
7	Maryland	74.5	Individualistic	32	Ohio	62.4	Individualistic
8	Virginia	74	Traditionalistic	33	Rhode Island	62.4	Individualistic
9	Maine	73.9	Moralistic	34	Texas	62.4	Traditionalistic
10	Iowa	71.4	Moralistic	35	New York	61.8	Individualistic
11	Arizona	70.5	Traditionalistic	36	Michigan	61.7	Moralistic
12	California	69.8	Individualistic	37	New Mexico	61.5	Traditionalistic
13	Vermont	68.9	Moralistic	38	Missouri	61.1	Individualistic
14	Idaho	68.9	Moralistic	39	West Virginia	60.7	Traditionalistic
15	Utah	68.6	Moralistic	40	Kentucky	60.4	Traditionalistic
16	Massachusetts	68.2	Individualistic	41	Alaska	60.3	Individualistic
17	Florida	68.1	Traditionalistic	42	Arkansas	59.2	Traditionalistic
18	Nevada	67.8	Individualistic	43	Montana	58.9	Moralistic
19	New Jersey	67.7	Individualistic	44	Hawaii	57.7	Individualistic
20	South Dakota	67.1	Moralistic	45	Mississippi	57.1	Traditionalistic
21	Georgia	66.9	Traditionalistic	46	North Carolina	56.9	Traditionalistic
22	Illinois	66.5	Individualistic	47	Oklahoma	55.3	Traditionalistic
23	New Hampshire	66.4	Moralistic	48	Indiana	54.5	Individualistic
24	Kansas	66	Moralistic	49	Wisconsin*	—	Moralistic
25	Alabama	65.9	Traditionalistic	50	North Dakota**	—	Moralistic

*Data not available.
**Has no voter registration.

Source: Federal Elections Commission. www.fec.gov/pages/ 2000turnout/2000turnout.xls (accessed April 9, 2004).

Notes: The voting age population includes all persons over the age of 18, including a significant number of people not able to vote in U.S. elections.

as Connecticut, has much higher turnout rates than a low-income state where the population is poorly educated on the whole, such as Hawaii.

A competitive election will draw a crowd even in a state that normally has low voter turnout. When people feel like they have a real choice, they are more likely to make the effort to vote. A close, three-way race for governor, as took place in Minnesota in 1998, will produce record turnout, while a yawner between a popular incumbent and a no-name opponent will make people sit on their hands. Some states tend to have competitive politics, with the two major parties enjoying roughly the same level of support. Some states are "one-party states," with Republicans or Democrats dominant. One-party states will rarely have competitive elections—but when they do, voter turnout is certain to go up.

In his bestselling 2000 book, *Bowling Alone,* Robert Putnam notes that moralistic states such as Minnesota and the Dakotas have much higher rates of volunteering, attendance at public meetings, and "social trust," as measured by polls, than traditionalistic states. In other words, voter turnout is just one indication of the overall sense of civic engagement in a place. States with strong "socializing institutions"—anything from membership organizations to news media that still cover politics—are more likely to be places where people are engaged enough to vote.

What Elections Are Used For

Forty-nine states elect a governor and two sets of state legislators—senators and members of a state House of Representatives. Nebraska's one-chamber legislature is the only exception. Beyond that, there is quite a bit of variation among the states in what they allow people to vote for. Some states allow voters to pick a number of statewide office holders, such as attorney general and secretary of state, while in a few places these are appointed positions. Judges are the product of the voting booth in most places but not in about a dozen states. Roughly half the states allow voters to make policy decisions directly through ballot initiatives and referendums.

A look at state elections shows that states have quite different rules about who gets to vote for whom. That in turn can affect how a state makes policy. A governor who can appoint his entire cabinet is likely to have better success at pushing through his own policies than one who has to contend with a group of elected officials each with his own agenda.

All this is putting aside local elections, which also vary considerably. Some cities, such as San Francisco, allow voters to elect a mayor directly. Others, such as Richmond, Virginia, have what is called a council-mayor format. The city council picks one of its own members to serve as mayor. The same holds true for counties. In some places a county commission will pick its own leader, while in others voters may pick a county executive on their own. Local elections are, for the most part, **nonpartisan.** Candidates

NONPARTISAN ELECTIONS

Elections in which candidates do not have to declare party affiliation or receive a party's nomination; local offices and elections are often nonpartisan.

do not run under a party label—but, again, there are exceptions, such as the highly partisan elections for mayor of New York City.

Electing the Executive Branch

In New Jersey, voters elect only their governor among all of their statewide officeholders. This has helped create one of the most powerful governorships in the country. It wasn't always so. For centuries, New Jersey governors were much weaker players than the legislature. They were limited to a single term with weak veto and appointment powers. County officials in the state were also quite powerful, at the expense of state officials. That all changed, however, beginning with the new state constitution of 1947. The constitution was pushed through by reformers of the moralistic strain that was always present, although usually not dominant, in New Jersey politics. The reformers got new powers for the state's governors, including the ability to succeed themselves, authority to appoint not just cabinet officials but about five hundred board and commission members, and broad authority to reject legislation. New Jersey's governors now can veto all or part of many bills and can issue a conditional veto, meaning he or she can reject portions of a bill while suggesting new language for it.[30]

Compare all of that influence with the limited powers of the governor of Texas. In Texas, the governor is only one of twenty-five elected statewide officials—and is not even the most powerful one among them. That distinction belongs to the lieutenant governor. In most states, the lieutenant governor holds a purely symbolic office, with little to do but wait around for something crippling to befall the governor. New Jersey does not even bother with the office of lieutenant governor. In Texas, the lieutenant governor is the president of the state Senate and therefore wields tremendous influence over the course of legislation.

In Texas, the governor can recommend a budget, but he has no authority to make the legislature grapple with it seriously. Compare that to Maryland, in which legislators can only accept or defeat the governor's spending proposals but make no fresh additions of their own. The Texas governor gets to appoint the secretary of state and members of many boards or commissions, but many of the latter serve staggered terms. This means that the governor has to work with people who were appointed by his predecessor in office. As recently as a government reorganization bill debated in 2003, efforts have been put forth to provide the governor with more power. Generally, they have gone nowhere. The state's so-called **plural executive system** illustrates the desires of the framers of the 1876 state constitution to keep too much power out of the hands of any one person or institution. They believed in a separation of powers not just between branches of government but within the executive branch.[31] The weakened powers of the governor are a reflection of the distrust Texans had for strong government, in keeping with their constitution's many restrictions on raising taxes.

PLURAL EXECUTIVE SYSTEM

A state government system in which the governor is not the dominant figure in the executive branch, but instead is more of a first among equals, serving alongside numerous other officials who were elected to their offices rather than appointed by the governor.

A couple of other southern and traditionalistic states, such as Georgia and Alabama, divide power within the executive branch. In 1999, Alabama Democrats in the state Senate sought to strip control of their chamber along with other powers from Republican lieutenant governor Steve Windom. They could have done it if only he had left the Senate floor. Windom refused. To stay present and to keep control of the chamber for that day, and thus for the rest of his term, he urinated into a plastic jug in the chamber.[32]

Other states chart more of a middle-of-the-road course, electing a handful of statewide officials. In most states, voters elect a lieutenant governor, treasurer, secretary of state, and attorney general. A few states elect other officers as well, such as an insurance commissioner. Some observers believe that appointed officials are removed from political concerns and can make decisions without regard to partisan interests. Others believe that having individual officers answer directly to the public makes them more responsive. Regardless, the fact that many statewide officeholders run for office independently of the governor gives them a power base of their own.

Attorneys general, treasurers, or other statewide officials often have aspirations toward becoming governor themselves one day. This leads inevitably to conflict with the sitting governor. During the 1980s in Texas, for example, Democratic attorney general Mark White frequently sparred with Republican governor Bill Clements and eventually unseated him. Today, in Texas, every statewide officeholder is Republican, but that has not put an end to squabbling within the executive branch. Caroline Keeton Strayhorn, the state comptroller, has frequently provoked the governor and lieutenant governor, accusing them of using dishonest budget numbers and raising fees excessively. "Sounds like the primary started early this year," Lieutenant Governor David Dewhurst said in 2003.[33]

Legal Offices

In most cases, voters pay comparatively little attention to candidates running for some executive branch offices. Races for state treasurer or secretary of state just are not seen as all that exciting. Most often, the party that wins the governorship will take the lion's share of the secondary executive branch offices anyway, so there is not much mystery. These are offices often pursued by legislators or other politicians looking to move up the political ladder. They hope these second-tier positions will firm up their resumes during future bids for prominent offices such as governor.

One office for which the majority-party-takes-all dynamic no longer holds is that of attorney general, the chief law enforcement officer in the state. For many years, Democrats completely dominated these positions. That began to change in the late 1990s. For one thing, the job came to be seen as a more important stepping stone to the governorship than in the past, so Republicans became increasingly unwilling to concede this training post. For another, state attorneys general, who traditionally had concentrated on law enforcement or consumer protection disputes within their states, had joined in a series of "multistate" settlements that represented an important challenge to corporate interests. They forced a series of settlements in 1998, for instance, that pushed the major tobacco companies to change their marketing strategies and pay states an estimated $246 billion over twenty-five years.

Some Republicans believed that these activist attorneys general were engaging in "government lawsuit abuse"—not targeting criminal behavior but instead going after companies to achieve changes in policy and regulation that could not be accomplished in the legislative arena. They founded the Republican Attorneys General Association (RAGA) as a campaign wing to elect members of their party to the office and funneled contributions from businesses and conservative interest groups that were threatened by the new activism. "Historically . . . attorney general races were off most business people's radar screens," according to Bob LaBrant of the Michigan Chamber of Commerce. In the new environment, he says, "there's greater incentive to get involved in an attorney general race because of the increased involvement of attorneys general across the country in litigation against the business community." [34]

Such interest group money and influence does make a difference. In 2002, the Law Enforcement Alliance of America, an arm of the gun lobby, ran an estimated $1.5 million late-season ad campaign that helped keep the Texas attorney general's office in Republican hands. This was an expanded version of the U.S. Chamber of Commerce's effort in Indiana in 2000, when a $200,000 ad campaign was widely viewed as a leading factor in driving an incumbent Democrat out of office.[35] All told, Republicans have improved their numbers since RAGA's founding from just twelve attorneys general in 1999 to twenty in 2003. Both parties now believe that campaigns for attorney general will remain more expensive and competitive than they had been historically.

A related phenomenon is affecting judicial elections, which traditionally were sleepy affairs. All but eleven states hold some type of election for judicial posts. This may mean direct election by voters or retention elections used by voters to grant another term to justices appointed by the governor or the state legislature. Until the mid-1990s, judicial campaigns were cheap and fairly ho-hum. What campaign contributions candidates did receive mainly came from trial lawyers, along with unions and other constituencies allied with the Democratic Party. As with the attorney general office, all of that began to change during the 1990s. Republicans and their business allies grew weary of seeing their legislative victories in areas such as tort law and workers' compensation overturned by high courts. In 2000, candidates in supreme court races in twenty states raised a total of $45.5 million dollars— a 61 percent increase over the previous record. On top of that, interest groups spent about $16 million in five states with important races—Alabama, Illinois, Michigan, Mississippi, and Ohio—far outpacing any spending by similar groups in the past.[36]

Direct Democracy

In addition to electing officials to state and local offices, voters can participate in some form of **direct democracy**. In about half the states, voters can pass legislation on their own through ballot initiatives or referendums, which are also available in hundreds of municipalities across the country. In twenty-four states, citizens can petition to place a piece of legislation or constitutional amendment on the ballot for approval or rejection by voters. Also in twenty-four states—mostly the same states—citizens can petition to review a law passed by the legislature and the governor, which they then can accept or reject.

When citizens or groups other than elected officials put a measure on the ballot to become a law, that is called a popular initiative. When citizens put a measure on the ballot to affirm or reject an action of the legislature or other political actor, this is called a popular referendum. When the legislature places a measure on the ballot to win voter approval, it is called a legislative referendum. Some referendums are nonbinding—expressing the will of the people but not becoming law—but most are binding and do have the force of law once passed.

In all fifty states, the legislature or other government agencies can refer a proposition to the ballot for voter approval. This may consist of a constitutional amendment, bond issue, or other matter. This is the legislative referendum just mentioned.

In the decades following independence, citizens in several northeastern states ratified new constitutions. Congress subsequently made legislative referendums for constitutional amendments mandatory for all new states entering the union after 1857.[37] The notion of popular referendums and initiatives, however, took root after the efforts of reformers from the Populist and Progressive movements. These individuals sought to give citizens more influence over state political systems that they saw as dominated by moneyed interest groups such as banks, railroads, and mining companies. A majority of the states that have adopted the popular initiative process, under which citizens can collect a certain number of signatures to place issues directly on the ballot, did so in the late 1800s and early 1900s. Most of these states are in the West or Upper Midwest, which had political cultures that welcomed the idea of populist control. Much of the opposition in the eastern and southern states grew out of racist concerns that to give people direct authority for making laws would give too much power to African Americans or new immigrants such as the Irish.

Recent ballot initiatives and referendums have covered a wide range of topics, from legalizing marijuana and allowing physician-assisted suicide to making sure that pregnant pigs are housed in large enough pens—an amendment to the Florida constitution approved by voters in 2002. Many initiatives have to do with tax and spending issues. Sometimes voters send contradictory signals. For instance, in Washington State, voters in recent years have approved limitations on property and other taxes, while at the same time approving expensive programs such as teacher pay increases and class size limitations.

Far and away the most famous and influential ballot initiative was Proposition 13, approved by California voters in 1978, which limited property tax rates and made other changes to the state's tax and spending laws. The initiative was copied successfully in Michigan and Massachusetts, and most states soon placed limitations on their own property tax rates. The success of the proposition fueled the modern initiative movement. There were only eighty-seven statewide initiatives proposed during the entire decade of the 1960s. Since 1978, however, there have been about three hundred initiatives proposed per decade. Ninety-three statewide initiatives were placed on ballots in 1996 alone. That appears to have been the peak year, with supporters of the initiative process complaining that state legislatures have placed new restrictions on ballot access and signature collection.

> Recent ballot initiatives and referendums have covered a wide range of topics, from legalizing marijuana and allowing physician-assisted suicide to making sure that pregnant pigs are housed in large enough pens—an amendment to the Florida constitution approved by voters in 2002.

Another piece of evidence of the power of initiatives is the idea of legislative term limits, which exist in nearly every state that allows ballot initiatives but in only a couple of states that do not. Congressional term limits were a popular idea during the 1990s and were approved in a number of states, but the U.S. Supreme Court ruled in 1995 that states cannot unilaterally alter constitutional requirements for holding federal office.

Those who favor the initiative process say that it gives voters a chance to control government directly. Voters know that they are voting for an environmental safety program, or a campaign finance law, as opposed to voting for candidates who say that they favor these things but who act differently once in office. Initiative states tend to have lower state spending per capita, but that gap generally is bridged by local spending, which tends to run higher in initiative states.[38]

Critics of the initiative process say that it creates more problems than it solves. Since voters are presented with a straight "yes" or "no" choice about spending more on, say, elementary and secondary education, they are not taking into account other competing state priorities, such as transportation or colleges, the way legislators must. Voters can say, as in Washington, that they want both lower taxes and more services and leave legislators and governors few tools for balancing the budget or responding to economic recessions.

Those opposed to initiatives also say that the idea that they express the popular will better than elected representatives can sounds good in theory but is flawed in practice. In many states—particularly California—initiatives have become big business. They are not necessarily expressions of grassroots ideals any more. Instead, they are proposed and paid for by wealthy individuals or interest groups, such as teachers' unions or gambling casinos.

Beyond initiatives and referendums is perhaps the ultimate expression of popular dissatisfaction—the **recall**. Recalls of local officials are allowed in thirty-six states and 61 percent of U.S. municipalities—more local governments than allow initiatives or referendums. Like ballot initiatives, recall laws are mainly byproducts of the intention of early twentieth-century reformers to make state governments more responsive to average citizens. Recalls of state officials are allowed in eighteen states. The most famous example of a recall took place in 2003, when California governor Gray Davis was recalled and replaced by Arnold Schwarzenegger.

Before that election, recalls were fairly common at the local level but rare among states. Over the past one hundred years, there have been fewer than two dozen recall elections involving state officials, including legislators.[39] The last governor to be recalled before Davis was Lynn Frazier of North Dakota back in 1921. Frazier, the state attorney general, and the agricultural commissioner each lost his office after a grassroots movement swelled against scandals in Frazier's ranks. The only other governor who has ever faced a scheduled recall election was Evan Mecham of Arizona, until the legislature saved voters the trouble by removing him from office in 1987.

California makes the recall process pretty easy, requiring fewer signatures as a percentage of the number of people who voted in the last election for the office than in other states. California only requires 12 percent, while most states require 25 percent and Kansas requires 40 percent. Gray Davis was unpopular, having won reelection the year before by a small plurality. He also had come to be blamed for the state's $38 billion deficit and electricity crisis.

The purported sins of Davis were not unique to him, however, and many political observers expect that the California recall, like Proposition 13, will demonstrate the power of direct democracy and soon be copied in other states. Talk of recalling the governor quickly spread to other states, including Minnesota, Nevada, and Wisconsin. The mere threat of such an action may cow some officials into avoiding unpopular decisions, such as raising taxes. "In the past, you could do something unpopular at the beginning of your term in hopes that memories would decay and there would be perspective by the end of your term," said Bruce Cain, director of the Institute of Governmental Studies at the University of California, Berkeley. "Now what we have because of the recall is more of a permanent campaign. The threat of a recall is very powerful, and in policy debates you can keep the heat on a governor."[40]

RECALL

An occasion for citizens to collect signatures and then vote on the ouster of an incumbent politician prior to the next regularly scheduled election.

TABLE 4-3

Avenues for Direct Democracy

State	Popular Referendum	Ballot Initiative	Constitutional Amendment by Initiative	Recalls of State Officials	State	Popular Referendum	Ballot Initiative	Constitutional Amendment by Initiative	Recalls of State Officials
Alabama	No	No	No	No	Nebraska	Yes	Yes	Yes	No
Alaska	Yes	Yes	No	Yes	Nevada	Yes	Yes	Yes	Yes
Arizona	Yes	Yes	Yes	Yes	New Hampshire	No	No	No	No
Arkansas	Yes	Yes	Yes	No	New Jersey	No	No	No	Yes
California	Yes	Yes	Yes	Yes	New Mexico	Yes	No	No	No
Colorado	Yes	Yes	Yes	Yes	New York	No	No	No	No
Connecticut	No	No	No	No	North Carolina	No	No	No	No
Delaware	No	No	No	No	North Dakota	Yes	Yes	Yes	Yes
Florida	No	Yes	Yes	No	Ohio	Yes	Yes	Yes	No
Georgia	No	No	No	Yes	Oklahoma	Yes	Yes	Yes	No
Hawaii	No	No	No	No	Oregon	Yes	Yes	Yes	Yes
Idaho	Yes	Yes	No	Yes	Pennsylvania	No	No	No	No
Illinois	Yes	Yes	Yes	No	Rhode Island	No	No	No	Yes
Indiana	No	No	No	No	South Carolina	No	No	No	No
Iowa	No	No	No	No	South Dakota	Yes	Yes	Yes	No
Kansas	No	No	No	Yes	Tennessee	No	No	No	No
Kentucky	Yes	No	No	No	Texas	No	No	No	No
Louisiana	No	No	No	Yes	Utah	Yes	Yes	No	No
Maine	Yes	Yes	No	No	Vermont	No	No	No	No
Maryland	Yes	No	No	No	Virginia	No	No	No	No
Massachusetts	Yes	Yes	Yes	No	Washington	Yes	Yes	No	Yes
Michigan	Yes	Yes	Yes	Yes	West Virginia	No	No	No	No
Minnesota	No	No	No	Yes	Wisconsin	No	No	No	Yes
Mississippi	No	Yes	Yes	No	Wyoming	Yes	Yes	No	No
Missouri	Yes	Yes	Yes	No	Total # of States	24	24	18	18
Montana	Yes	Yes	Yes	Yes					

Sources: Data compiled from the Initiative and Referendum Institute at the University of Southern California, http://iri.usc.edu/statewide-ir.html (accessed April 13, 2004); *The Book of the States 2003* (Lexington, Ky.: Council of State Governments, 2003), and the National Conference of State Legislatures, www.ncsl.org/programs/legman/elect/recallprovision.htm (accessed April 13, 2004).

Public Opinion

Randall Gnant, the former president of the Arizona Senate, says that there is quite a contrast between the politics of today and those of the 1800s. Back then, he says, "It seemed that everybody took part in the political process—there were torchlight parades, party-run newspapers for and against candidates." Today, "We're into sort of a reverse kind of period. Now, almost nobody participates in the electoral process—voter turnout rates are abysmally low." But that does not mean that citizens are not paying any attention to the political process. Given the importance of talk radio, the Internet, and other media that quickly spread public opinion—at least a share of it—the old idea that voters agree to a sort of contract with politicians whom they elect to a two-year or four-year term is rapidly becoming dated. Voters are more than willing to express their displeasure about a given policy well before the next scheduled election day. "Try to get somebody interested in electing a candidate and they just don't want to get involved," Gnant points out. "But they are perfectly willing to get involved if somebody does something they don't want them to do."[41]

Unfortunately, citizen opinion usually does not register loudly enough to result in a recall or other formal protest. On most issues that come up before policymakers at the state level, citizen opinion hardly seems to exist or be formulated at all. Although, can you really blame voters? How many citizens are going to take the time to follow—let alone express an opinion about—an obscure regulatory issue concerning overnight transactions between banks and insurance companies?

This lack of interest, or at the very least, this lack of time, begs an important question. If citizens do not or cannot make their feelings known on every issue addressed in the hundreds of bills that wend through the average state legislature each year, how can legislators know that their votes will reflect the will of their constituents? After all, as political scientist V. O. Key once wrote, "Unless mass views have some place in the shaping of policy, all the talk about democracy is nonsense."[42]

Responding to Opinion

Let's be realistic—state legislators cannot know what majority opinion is in their district about every issue they confront. On most issues, they do not hear from any constituents at all. A few high-profile concerns, such as tax increases or legalizing casino gambling, may lead a newspaper or an interested party to conduct a statewide poll—but even on the rare occasions in which there are polls on a state issue, these polls will not break down opinion in each legislative district. Given the absence of specific information each legislator, or gubernatorial aide, has about how constituents view a particular area, public officials have to rely on a series of clues.

Some political scientists have taken data from various nationwide polls, broken it down by state, and seen how well elected officials have reflected the general ideology and desires of the public in their states.[43] What they found is that average state opinion does seem to get reflected in the policy decisions made in individual states. What does average state opinion mean? It is the type of things we were discussing earlier when talking about Daniel Elazar's classifications of the states. Some states tend to be more liberal

Local Focus: **An Online Appeal for Green Votes**

Baltimore mayor Martin O'Malley was somewhat taken aback by an illustration of a restoration project for a seventy-year-old steel-arch bridge. He was surprised for a couple of reasons.

First, O'Malley had had little input in the project, which had been designed long before he took office. In other words, the design was pretty much a surprise to him, and he wasn't too wild about the overall vision. Second, the color was . . . well, red. Very red.

The problem was that O'Malley discovered the eye-catching color scheme when he unveiled the artist's illustration at a groundbreaking project in August 2003. That's usually a little too late to start making big changes to large public works projects, and O'Malley knew better than to get into a fight over such a "minor" thing as color at such a late stage.

Still, that meant the bridge was going to end up rusty red. What to do? O'Malley decided to turn to cyberdemocracy for help. Rather than spend his political capital fighting the color scheme, he put the matter up for a vote on the city's Web site. For a week in October, citizens could view two different versions of the proposed bridge project. One with the bridge in the originally proposed red and one with the bridge painted in a bright Kelly green, which was O'Malley's preferred alternative.

The idea was that by pulling in green votes and getting clear public backing for his preferred color choice, it would force the decision against red. At least that was the plan. More than five thousand votes came in. Green lost.

Not exactly a transformational moment for democracy, but it does represent what can rightly be called a new form of interactive government. O'Malley used the Internet as a way to allow citizens to participate directly in a government decision. Picking bridge colors may not be seen as high stakes stuff, but it shows that technology can be used to provide citizens with a new outlet for influencing what government does. Web polls are a new form of political participation that can be done relatively quickly and at relatively low cost. They allow government to get a quick read on public opinion.

As O'Malley discovered, though, giving citizens new ways to participate does not mean they will tell government officials what they want to hear. The bridge is red.

Source: Christopher Swope, "Governors and Mayors Learn to Love the Give and Take of Governing Interactively," *Governing* magazine, March 2004. www.governing.com/archive/2004/mar/interact.txt (accessed April 26, 2004).

overall, while others are more conservative. The average citizen's desire—whether in a conservative state like Texas or a more liberal one like Vermont—tends to be pretty well reflected by state laws on issues that range from abortion restrictions to welfare spending, the death penalty, environmental protections, and gay rights.[44]

How does this happen? For one thing, elected officials devote an enormous amount of time trying to gauge how opinion is running in their districts. They may not hear from constituents on every issue, but they pay close attention to those concerns that are registered through letters and phone calls. They go out and seek opinion by attending religious services and civic events where they can hear the concerns of constituents directly. They use surrogates—such as newspaper articles and interest groups—as ways of determining what is on their constituents' minds. Susan Herbst, a political scientist now at Temple University, spent some time a few years back hanging out with legislators in Springfield, Illinois. She found that the media were important in shaping public opinion by giving a voice to average people in their stories. The media also shaped the terms of debate. Herbst noted that people in the capital thought that lobbyists were often good indicators of how people felt about an issue: "Staffers seem to think that the nuances and intensity of public opinion are best captured in the communications of interest groups."[45]

That is not to say that using interest groups as surrogates can't be misleading sometimes. The National Rifle Association, for example, may call upon its state members to send letters to legislators in numbers that dwarf those mustered by gun control advocates—even in places where a majority favors gun control. "Intense minorities can come off potentially sounding like majorities when in fact they're not," says Illinois Wesleyan University political scientist Greg Shaw.[46] Legislators like to think that they have a pretty good sense of whether a mail-writing campaign has sprung up spontaneously or shows signs of having been organized—everyone signing their name to the same form letter, for example—but sometimes this is easier said than done.

Formal interest groups do not represent every constituent. Some people may favor environmental protection, but not give money to the Sierra Club or the World Wildlife Fund. Some older people actually resist the invitations to join AARP at cheap rates. Still, legislators do gain some sense of how active such groups are in their states and whether they seem to have favorable support at home. A lot of this is inexact, but legislators learn from talking to people about whether their constituents are most upset about crime or transportation problems. They are convinced that if they vote for things that voters broadly support, such as mandatory sentencing guidelines for drug offenders or limits on welfare benefits, they will be rewarded politically.

A legislator's major fear is of being punished politically. Not getting reelected can be the death knell of a political career. It is important to note, however, that if legislators or governors did not broadly reflect the wishes of the populace that elected them, they would never have won their positions in the first place. In this age of computer-assisted redistricting, legislative districts in particular are shaped according to a local political culture that tends to lean in one ideological direction or another. A liberal is not going to get elected to a conservative district, ninety-nine times out of a hundred.

Once elected, legislators who want to get reelected are careful not to stray too far from public opinion in their districts, as best as they can perceive it. They cannot know what public opinion is about the specifics of every bill—but the fact that not every individual is paying close attention to state politics does not mean that legislators can do whatever they want. Political officials recognize that lobbyists and other interested parties are watching their voting records carefully and can use such information against them, if necessary. "Legislators aren't worried about what their constituents know—they are worried about what an opponent might do with their record in the next election," says Paul Brace, a Rice University political scientist. They act, therefore, as if there is someone or some group out there who has a chance of using a potentially unpopular record against them. "Legislation is written in minutiae, but you know if you vote for it, you'll get an opponent who can dumb it down and use it against you in the next election, and you won't do it." [47]

Some states offer less opportunity for using a politician's record against him. In a moralistic state such as Minnesota, there are more daily newspapers paying close attention to state policy matters than in, say, individualistic Wyoming. There are more public interest groups and state-level think tanks closely monitoring St. Paul than there are monitoring Cheyenne. Citizens in states with higher levels of civic engagement are more likely to be able to keep their politicians "honest"—reflecting voters' overall policy desires—than citizens in less-engaged states.

In a state like Idaho or Maryland, one party so completely dominates state politics that only rarely are politicians voted out of office because their records do not reflect public opinion. But even Idaho Republicans or Maryland Democrats can lose—if only in the party primary—if voters sour on their records. All of the state capitals have engendered enough of

Kathleen Kennedy Townsend served two terms as Maryland's lieutenant governor and comes from one of the nation's most well known and respected political families. That background, however, was not enough to win the governor's office, nor was the fact that Maryland traditionally votes Democratic. Here she gives a concession speech after losing to Republican Robert Ehrlich for the state's top office in 2003.

an echo chamber that examines and discusses the work of legislators and other elected officials for an overall sense of their records—conservative or liberal, sellout or crusading—to be known to people who care enough about politics to vote. If those records do not reflect local opinion, the job will go to someone else in the next election.

Conclusion

The political cultures of the states are not as distinct as they were 150 years ago. Revolutions in communication, transportation, and national policies have made the states more like one another than they were during the nineteenth century. Still, states do have political cultures that differ from one another. Vermont is different from Texas is different from Oregon is different from Alabama.

It's difficult to explain why for every difference. Sometimes factors seem to feed on each other. States in which citizens are highly educated tend to be more supportive of government. This means that government spends more on programs such as education, which makes citizens more highly educated. It's hard to know whether a state is liberal on some issues or conservative on others because of its region or its history. These factors and others do combine, in sometimes unpredictable patterns, to form a fairly consistent political culture within a state.

State political cultures are preserved mainly through elections, which express the popular will through the selection of elected officials who make and implement policies. State and local officials have less ability to control who participates in the political process because of the many changes in voting laws passed at the federal level. Nevertheless, voter turnout remains low nationwide. State officials still maintain a lot of control over whom citizens can vote for through their regulation of political parties and their ability to decide who deserves to get their names onto ballots.

Which officials citizens get to vote for differs depending on where they live. In most states, citizens vote for several statewide officials such as governor, attorney general, and secretary of state. In others, they might vote only for the governor. Similarly, in some localities, citizens elect the mayor directly while in others the mayor is chosen by the city council from among its own membership. Some states allow people to vote directly for judges, while judges are appointed to office in other states. Some localities allow people to vote for school boards. In others, these positions are appointed.

In general, citizens vote for enough officeholders with the authority to control policies that the majority's will generally becomes law. However, since polling is done far more often at the national level than it is at the local or even state level, officeholders sometimes have only an anecdotal sense of what their constituents are thinking. They do pay close attention to what clues they are given and monitor opinion as closely as they can. If they do not create the types of policies that most people want, they are well aware that they are not going to stay in office for long. All these factors—election laws that give voters a greater or lesser chance of expressing their political wishes, combined with the resulting efforts of legislators and other elected officials to fulfill those wishes as best they can—help to preserve the distinct political culture of a state, county, or city.

Key Concepts

direct democracy (p. 120)

migration patterns (p. 98)

nonpartisan elections (p. 116)

office group (Massachusetts) ballot (p. 106)

party column (Indiana) ballot (p. 106)

plural executive system (p. 117)

plurality (p. 104)

political culture (p. 94)

recall (p. 122)

redistricting (p. 103)

secret (Australian) ballot (p. 108)

sectionalism (p. 98)

straight ticket (p. 108)

voter turnout (p. 99)

Suggested Readings

Elazar, Daniel. *American Federalism: A View from the States,* 3d ed. New York: Harper Collins, 1984. The classic work on political culture in the states.

Patterson, Thomas. *The Vanishing Voter.* New York: Knopf, 2002. A political scientist seeks to explain why voter turnout is falling.

Wolfinger, Raymond, and Steven Rosenstone. *Who Votes?* New Haven, Conn.: Yale University Press, 1980. A classic study of voter participation in the United States.

Suggested Web Sites

www.lwv.org. Official Web site of the League of Women Voters. Provides a wealth of voter education information.

www.nass.org/sos/sosflags.html. Official Web site of the National Association of Secretaries of State. Secretaries of state typically serve as chief election officials, and their offices have primary responsibility for recording official election outcomes.

www.rockthevote.com. Rock the Vote is a non-profit voter education organization geared towards younger citizens.

CHAPTER 5

Parties and Interest Groups

Elephants, Donkeys, and Cash Cows

Politics on the hoof? Special interest groups are often seen as the cash cows of the political system, helping to stock campaign war chests for candidates and political parties. No matter how partisan or narrow the interest, however, both political parties and special interest groups prefer to present their ideas and actions as serving the public good.

5

Why are political parties weaker than they used to be?

Why are political parties stronger in some states than in others?

Colonel Aureliano Buendia was a young man when he learned the difference between his country's Liberals and Conservatives in the Gabriel Garcia Marquez novel *One Hundred Years of Solitude.*

Liberals, his father explained, fight the authority of the church and the central government and recognize the rights of illegitimate children. Conservatives are defenders of public order and morality.

Buendia grew up to lead the Liberal revolutionary forces, without success, in nearly twenty years of civil war. Eventually, his political advisers suggest that he renounce the party's longstanding fight against clerical influence and the rest of the Liberal platform he had been introduced to years before. One adviser, however, speaks against the idea. He points out that they are merely adopting the Conservative platform because it is more popular, even though it represents everything they have fought for so long. Buendia sees things differently. What it means, he says, is "that all we're fighting for is power." [1]

This is the classic cynical view of **political parties**, those organized groups that hope to win political power by controlling a variety of elective offices, such as mayor or governor. They shift with the winds and pursue whatever policy stances bring them power—even if these stances directly contradict what the parties stood for during the last election. Ever since George Washington warned against "the baneful effects of the spirit of party" in his farewell address, many Americans have taken his words to heart. Political disaffection—that feeling that voting really does not make a difference—is why more than half the adult populace of voting age does not do so, whether they are registered or not, and why no presidential candidate has received a majority of the vote since 1988. "People feel disconnected from parties and think there's no difference between the parties, despite our rhetoric being different," said Royal Masset, the political director of the Texas Republican Party. [2]

Real, non-rhetorical differences do exist between the Democratic Party and the Republican Party. Without dwelling too much on specific points, this chapter explains the role of parties in American politics. We will look at how parties—including minor, or third, parties—have evolved; how parties function at the state and local levels; and how their influence differs from

POLITICAL PARTIES

Organizations that choose, support, and nominate candidates for elected offices.

Governing States and Localities

state to state. In addition, we will take a look at interest groups—individuals, corporations, or associations who seek to influence the actions of elected and appointed public officials in behalf of specific companies and causes.

Political parties are not as dominant in American life as they once were. From roughly the 1820s until the 1940s, parties were a prime organizing force in this country. They provided citizens not only with a political identity, but also were a major source of social activity and entertainment—and, in many cases, jobs. Today, parties are not as effective at getting people out to vote or even at organizing them around an issue. However, they do remain important to candidates as a kind of "brand name" identification and as fund-raisers.

Although there are two major national parties, they play larger roles at the state level than they do as national forces. Their respective strength varies widely from state to state and is affected by such factors as the different ways states regulate parties, the differences in the historical roles that parties played within each state, and the amount of competition between the major parties within a given state. In general, the more closely balanced the two main parties are in a state, the more likely that they will have well-funded and well-organized party organizations.

A Primer on Political Parties

Political parties recruit candidates for offices and provide them with support for their campaigns. They give candidates money or help them to raise it and offer logistical and strategic assistance. Just as importantly, they help coordinate a candidate's message with those of other candidates running for other offices under the party's banner.

Since the 1850s, the vast majority of candidates have run as members of either the Democratic or the Republican Party. Democrats as we know them today evolved from **factional splits** in the earliest days of the American republic. The country started without a two-party system, but factions soon developed. The Federalists, led by Alexander Hamilton, favored a strong central government with power rooted in the industrial north. The Democratic Republicans, led by Thomas Jefferson, emerged as the party opposing the Federalists. They argued for states' rights against a "monarchical" rule by the aristocracy and declared that farmers, craftspeople, and shopkeepers should control their own interests without interference from the capitol.

Jefferson's party, which eventually morphed into the Democratic Party, dominated politics throughout the first half of the nineteenth century. That same time period saw the creation of numerous parties—Whigs, Know-Nothings, Barnburners, Softshells, Hunkers, and Free Soilers. They all had some success, but the Democratic Party of Jefferson and Andrew Jackson dominated so completely that, as the main source of political power, the

FACTIONAL SPLITS OR FACTIONS

Groups that struggle to control the message within a party; for example, a party may be split into competing regional factions.

party split into factions, with Northern and Southern Democrats arguing over the expansion of slavery. That argument created an opening for a new major party.

The Republican Party was formed in 1854 in opposition of slavery. It soon replaced the Whig Party, which had been formed in 1834 to protest the spoils system politics of Andrew Jackson. The Republicans, also known as the "Grand Old Party" (GOP), quickly enjoyed congressional success. Following the election of Abraham Lincoln in 1860, they dominated the presidency for decades to come. Their antislavery stance, however, guaranteed that they were practically nonexistent in the South until the civil rights era of the 1950s and 1960s. Democrats reemerged as the nation's dominant party in the 1930s, when Republicans were forced to take the blame for the Great Depression. The Democrats' New Deal coalition of Southerners, union workers, African Americans, the poor, and the elderly drove American politics well into the 1960s but fragmented after that, resulting in a loss of political control.

Since then, Democratic majorities at the congressional and state levels have eroded, while Republicans have held the presidency for most of the past thirty years. In the early part of the twenty-first century, Republicans controlled the White House and Congress. They also gained a majority of seats in state legislatures for the first time in fifty years—but their majorities were not overwhelming. Democrat Al Gore won a plurality of the presidential vote in 2000, even as he lost the electoral college vote to Republican George W. Bush. Basically, the two parties have spent the past decade at roughly equal strength.

It is no secret that contemporary politics are highly competitive. Neither side enjoys a consistent advantage nationally. Candidates from either party are capable of winning statewide offices in nearly every state. Overall support for the parties is, however, split along regional lines, with Democrats enjoying more support along the West Coast, the Upper Midwest, and the Northeast, while Republicans are dominant in the South, the Plains states, and the Mountain West. (Ironically, for a party created to oppose slavery, today its greatest support is from those areas where slavery once was legal.)

While people are familiar with the Republican and Democratic parties, political parties actually take many different shapes. When people refer to Democrats or Republicans, they are really referring to officials belonging to two umbrella groups that cover a wide variety of parties. Each of the national parties is in reality a consortium of state parties. Party chairs and other representatives from the state parties dominate national party committees. State parties, in turn, are consortiums of local parties. In some states, local parties are defined by counties. In others, they are defined by congressional districts. Although both the Democratic and Republican parties are active in every state, some state and local parties are more active than others. Parties in densely populated states such as Florida and California are well-funded, professionally run organizations. In less-populated states like Montana or Idaho, the parties have a very small full-time staff and take on more help for just the few months leading up to an election.

Particular states may have particular dominant political parties, but overall, most other western-style democracies have much stronger political parties than those in the United States. For example, in the United States, party leaders are not able to nominate candidates of their own choosing. Most candidates are now chosen directly by the voting public through primaries. In fact, even a party's top nominee—its presidential candidate—may not have been the first choice of party leaders. This is much different than is the case in, say, Great Britain. There, political parties are much more centralized. Leadership within the party translates more cleanly into leadership in government. The party, not voters, selects the party's nominee for prime minister.

Here, the national Republican and Democratic parties are essentially made up of state parties. The Republican National Committee, for instance, is made up almost exclusively of state party chairs and one male and one female representative from each state. Representatives from the territories—Puerto Rico, Guam, and the U.S. Virgin Islands, among others—form the rest of the body. U.S. political parties tend to be regulated at the state level. The ways in which they raise and spend money, their organizational structures, and the rules they follow to nominate candidates and place them on ballots all are subject to differing state regulations. How much power the national parties have in relation to the state party shifts over time, as we shall see.

That is not to say that parties are not collections of interests. They are conglomerations of people who share some overlapping ideology, or set of political, economic, and social beliefs. These days, Democrats are supported largely by prochoice groups and gun control advocates. Democrats also tend to be environmentalists, trial lawyers, labor union members, and African Americans. Republicans gain support from corporate and small businesses and antiabortion groups. Party members tend to advocate respect for private property and rights for gun owners. These differences, though, are far from absolute. For many people partisanship represents a psychological attachment to a political party—a sort of "brand loyalty"—rather than a rational assessment of personal beliefs and party stance. Other groups are made up of so-called **swing voters** who might support candidates of either major party. This group includes farmers, suburban voters, and the elderly. Their votes cannot be taken for granted, so they are highly sought after. Young people tend not to vote at all, which is why their issues are generally ignored. Pulling together as wide an assortment of interests as they can, political parties help voters and groups connect with the government while furthering their own ideals.

Political parties, however, remain different from other groups that participate in the political process, including interest groups. As already noted, political candidates run under a single party label, such as Republican,

> [P]arties are collections of interests. They are conglomerations of people who share some overlapping ideology, or set of political, economic, and social beliefs.

Democratic, or Green. They campaign for office and are nominated as members of that party. In the meantime, an interest group may support them, but their candidacies are not based on their affiliation with the group. It did not recruit and support them to run in its name. The interest group, in fact, might be supporting candidates from a variety of parties.

These same candidates may still rely on parties to serve as conduits to interest groups and voters, but the importance of parties to individual candidates has not been as great recently as in the past. Academics have noted a shift to **candidate-centered politics** over the past thirty years or so. What they mean is that parties play less of a role in determining who is going to run for what office. Instead, candidates, in effect, select themselves. Ambitious people interested in politics and government run for the offices of their choice, rather than working their way up the ranks in roles the parties might have chosen for them. Arnold Schwarzenegger decided in 2003 to give up his acting career to run for governor of California and won the support of the state's Republican Party. In the old days,

CANDIDATE-CENTERED POLITICS

Politics in which candidates promote themselves and their own campaigns rather than relying on party organizations.

a party's gubernatorial candidate first would have had to put in years in lower offices. He or she would have had to earn the support of party leaders throughout the state before running for the state's highest office. And there's more. Today's candidates are not only self-selecting, they also are less likely to rely exclusively on the party for fund-raising help. In an age of heavy television advertising, they rely on their ads to get their messages out, as opposed to party workers and volunteers.

Parties still are a primary mechanism for the organization of government. Except for Nebraska, which is nonpartisan, all other state legislatures are organized by party. If the Democrats have a majority of the seats in the Maine House of Representatives, for example, the Speaker and other top leaders will be Democrats, and the party will control each committee as well. Not everyone agrees with this sys-tem. George Norris, a U.S. senator from Nebraska who promoted many changes to his home state's political system during the 1930s, argued that state politicians should be nonpartisan. That way,

The political action here is not on the racetrack, it's in the stands. "NASCAR dads" emerged in 2004 as swing voters who were courted heavily by both major political parties. This was because stock car fans were seen as representing a block of voters with weak partisan preferences. In other words, these were citizens who could make the difference in a close election.

he claimed, they would be judged on their record dealing with issues at home, rather than on the question of whether they adhered to positions taken by national parties.

Some things have changed, however. Once the dominant force in U.S. politics—deciding who would get to run for what office and with how much support—today's political parties are such loose conglomerations of differing interests that they might be better described as marketing organizations. They are brand names that individual candidates choose to apply as a shortcut to identification in the marketplace. For example, to say that you are a Democratic candidate provides voters with a fairly reliable indication that you are for handgun legislation. Republicans—those who run for office, if not all rank-and-file party members—nearly always feel the opposite. In other areas, however, such as crime, welfare, and some trade issues, the distinction between party officials is less clear.

Given the overall decline of strong **voter identification** with either major party, today's politics centers much more around individual candidates than around party politics. Parties have found a new role as support organs. They offer consulting and fund-raising services to self-selected aspirants. They have become "basically what you might call holding companies," says Walter Dean Burnham, a political science professor at the University of Texas. "They organize cash and spread it around." [3] But now parties are being forced to adapt to legal restrictions on those functions as well. A federal campaign finance law passed by Congress in 2002 and upheld by the Supreme Court in 2003 makes it more complicated for parties to spend money on activities designed to register voters or encourage them to vote. As a result, candidates are relying less and less on parties and more and more on their own resources. Although parties still play important roles, often candidates are raising their own money, producing their own TV ads, and creating their own campaign organizations.

This does not mean political parties have become any less important to state and local politics. What they do and how they do it has changed considerably, but democratic politics—and this certainly includes politics in states and localities—is virtually unthinkable without political parties. As a theoretical ideal, or baseline, political scientists use the **responsible party model** as a way to measure and assess political parties. The responsible party model holds that political parties should present clear policy options to voters, that voters will cast ballots based on the options they favor the most, that in office parties try to create and implement the programs they promise, and in the next election the parties are judged by their performance in delivering these programs. In short, this model views political parties as connecting the wishes of citizens to government programs and policies, organizing the government to deliver on those wishes, and acting as the agents used to hold government accountable for delivering on what it promises. These are all highly valuable services to democratic politics, and despite all their changes, political parties have always served these roles, and still do.

VOTER IDENTIFICATION

When a voter consistently identifies strongly with one of the parties and can be considered, for example, a Democrat or Republican.

RESPONSIBLE PARTY MODEL

The theory that political parties offer clear policy choices to voters, try to deliver on those policies when they take office, and are held accountable by voters for the success or failure of those policies.

Of course, how well parties serve these functions varies from state to state. To have some semblance of a responsible party model you need at least two competitive political parties offering voters clear choices on policies and programs. You also need parties that actually try to deliver on these policies on programs once they secure a controlling influence in government. Finally, you need voters that pay attention to what the party in power is doing and vote accordingly. States in which only one party is competitive at the polls or where there is consistently low voter turnout are less likely to fulfill the promises of the responsible party model.

What Parties Were Like

In their early years, political parties in the United States were a lot more than just brand identifiers and fund-raisers. Many of the social services now provided by local governments, such as food assistance and job placement services, were the province of political parties throughout much of the nineteenth century. For all of the contemporary complaints about the "liberal media" or the domination of talk radio by conservative hosts, today's nonpartisan media is a far cry from the newspapers of the late nineteenth century, which were often openly affiliated with a particular party. The pro-Republican *Chicago Tribune,* upon learning that a Democrat had won the 1876 presidential election, ran a headline that read: "Lost. The Country Given Over to Democratic Greed and Plunder."[4] Such an openly partisan statement is unimaginable in the mainstream media today.

People's party loyalties were so strong because so many of their livelihoods revolved around party interests. Party machines doled out jobs, government contracts, and other benefits to their workers and supporters. The idea was that "offices exist not as a necessary means of administering government but for the support of party leaders at public expense," as one political scientist wrote of nineteenth-century party cliques in New York State.[5]

Politics in many cities and some states was totally dominated by these usually indigenous party machines. In Rhode Island, the Democratic Party was dominant through much of the twentieth century, and party leaders accepted little dissent. Only a handful of free-agent candidates were able to pry nominations away from those who had been endorsed by the party. In Providence, the state capital and largest city, only three individuals held the office of mayor from 1941 until 1974. Two of those men were state Democratic Party leaders. Over the same thirty-year period, only two chairs headed the Providence Democratic Party. Both of them doubled as head of the city's Department of Public Works. Party leaders controlled 2,800 jobs, doling them out roughly equally among the various wards, or political districts, within the city. [6]

The close links connecting control of jobs, government spending, and party activity were hardly unique to Rhode Island. Chicago; Long Island,

New York's Nassau County; and Pennsylvania were all home to legendary **political machines**, which were also called party machines or machine politics. A longstanding joke about Chicago politics held that, because they were kept on election rolls, as many dead people voted as living ones. In Oklahoma, the state gave control of most government jobs—the decision-making power over hiring and firing workers—to individual officeholders. These individuals were not afraid to exploit such control for their own benefit. "I have 85 employees—garage men, road workers, janitors, elevator operators—and they work for me when I need them," said a county commissioner. "These people care if I stay in office."[7]

The machine system was self-perpetuating, with control of jobs and power and offices feeding off of one another. "Each succeeding election was viewed not as a separate contest involving new issues or new personalities," writes political scientist Joel Sibley, "but as yet another opportunity to vote for, and reaffirm, an individual's support for his or her party and what it represented."[8] Party machines and rival factions ran "slates," or specific lists, of endorsed candidates for different offices and lent their backing to favored candidates. Sometimes this support came at a price. For instance, contenders for the West Virginia General Assembly once had to pay between $250 and $400 for the honor of being listed on one of the various slates in Kanawha County, in which the state capital of Charleston is located.

Given party contacts and contracts with private sector entities, party control of jobs often extended well beyond the borders of government. Sometimes—as was the case in Jersey City, New Jersey—the machines would charge an automatic kickback of, say, three percent of public employee salaries. Such lean trimmings were not always enough to slake their greed. Clear cases of corruption, such as extorting union funds, running gambling operations, and taking kickbacks on government contracts, often led to the election of reform candidates for mayor and other city and state offices.

There were backlashes against such obvious corruption. In New Orleans, a Democratic Party political machine called the Old Regulars ruled the city from the 1890s until the mid-1930s. By then, they were the only political force left in Louisiana outside of the populist governor, Huey Long. In 1934 and 1935, Long concentrated all of his powers on changing the machine's management. He limited local control over jobs and triggered a police investigation. He even sent the National Guard into New Orleans. In the end, the machine had no choice but to accept a new city leader and get on board the Long bandwagon.[9]

Breaking up the machines usually took a less drastic effort. For one thing, in many states, such as Alabama, Florida, and Michigan, there was little

POLITICAL MACHINES
Political organizations controlled by a small number of people and run for selfish or partisan ends; controlled party nominations for public office and rewarded supporters with government jobs and contracts.

> "I have 85 employees—garage men, road workers, janitors, elevator operators—and they work for me when I need them," said a county commissioner. "These people care if I stay in office."

Huey Long was nicknamed "Kingfish," and the implication of royalty was fitting. He served as governor of Louisiana from 1928 to 1934, went on to the U.S. Senate, and was considering a presidential run before his assassination in 1935. The head of one of the most powerful political machines of the twentieth century, as a political boss he controlled Louisiana politics with an iron fist and a mix of populist appeal and demagoguery.

patronage—the ability of elected officials or party leaders to hand out jobs to their friends and supporters, rather than hiring based on qualifications. Therefore, there was little motivation to build up a machine. In some places, like Texas, nineteenth-century political parties were weak. They helped administer election code and tried to remain acceptable to all candidates. In other places, disgust over corruption in politics led to antimachine statutes, such as the imposition of civil service requirements on many government jobs and tougher anticorruption laws. The widespread use of **nonpartisan ballots** for municipal offices is the direct result of reforms imposed in reaction to political machines. These ballots, which do not list candidates by political party, are designed to separate city government from party voting.

California may be the best example of a state that had such a progressive reaction against machines. The state was hostile toward parties, lacked any type of patronage system, and held nonpartisan elections. Precinct and ward organizations were weak, while individual candidates were assertive.[10] Party organizations were once banned from endorsing candidates

in primary contests. The law also limited state party chairs to two-year terms and required the rotation of chairs on a geographical basis every two years. In 1989 the U.S. Supreme Court threw out the statute and declared it unconstitutional.[11] California was the exception to the rule. Throughout the 1800s, most states essentially treated parties as private associations and chose not to regulate them. This remains the position of many other countries today. But during the twentieth century that all changed in the United States. States began to regulate parties as though they were public utilities. We will examine such state regulation of political parties later in this chapter.

Parties in the Twentieth Century

At the dawn of the twentieth century, political machines were generally locally based, and local parties were much more important political actors than state parties in states with powerful, big-city machines. Elsewhere, state parties were often funded and controlled by corporate interests—in many cases by just one interest, such as the DuPont Corporation in Delaware or the Anaconda Copper Company in Montana. Following the Progressive Era reforms in states such as California, state parties became little more than empty shells. As late as the 1970s, many state parties lacked permanent headquarters and were run out of their chairs' homes.[12]

State parties lost much of their ability to influence **primary elections**. Such elections had been used to determine a party's nominees for offices in **general elections** against other parties' nominees. It used to be that parties picked their nominees through **party conventions**—meetings of a few hundred party officials or supporters. Party leaders closely controlled most votes. In primaries, by contrast, the general public has a chance to cast a secret ballot. This gives party officials less direct control of the nominating process. Some states, such as Virginia, still allow for the option of nominating candidates by party conventions, but every state now has a system in place to nominate candidates by primaries. Every party holds a statewide convention, and many hold conventions at the local or district level as well. Nowadays, practically anyone who cares to attend a state or local convention can do so. But it still takes some effort or connections to attend a national party convention, especially as a voting delegate.

Direct primaries allow rank-and-file voters to choose nominees for public office through means of a direct ballot. This contrasts with the convention system in which the role of voters is indirect—voters choose delegates to a convention, and the delegates choose the nominee. At the state level, there are three basic types of direct primaries. **Closed primaries** allow only registered party members to vote in the party's primary, meaning that you must be a registered Democrat to vote for the Democratic nominee for office or a registered Republican to vote for the Republican nominee. This type of primary helps prevent **crossover voting**, which is when the member of one party votes in another party's primary—a Democrat voting in a Republican primary, for instance. This practice is not allowed in all states. **Open primaries** allow independents—and in some cases members of both parties—to vote in any primary they choose. **Blanket primaries** list all candidates from all parties on a single ballot and allow voters to effectively mix and match which primary they participate in. Voters can vote in one party's primary for a particular office, then switch to another party's primary for another office. In 2000 the Supreme Court invalidated blanket primaries in *California Democratic Party v. Jones*. The only blanket primary now remaining is Louisiana's, which is a nonpartisan blanket primary. If no candidate wins an outright majority in the primary, the two top vote getters—regardless of party—go on to a general election face-off. A **runoff primary** sometimes occurs if no candidate receives a majority of the vote. In that case, the top two candidates face off. Map 5-1 shows the state-by-state breakdown of the three main types of primaries.

In contrast to the relative openness of primaries is the "smoke-filled room"—an area at a convention that is closed off to the public in which

PRIMARY ELECTIONS

Elections that determine a party's nominees for offices in general elections against other parties' nominees. Participation in primary elections is sometimes limited to voters registered as members of that particular party.

GENERAL ELECTIONS

The decisive elections in which all registered voters cast ballots for their preferred nominees for a political office.

PARTY CONVENTIONS

Meetings of party delegates called to nominate candidates for office and establish party agendas.

CLOSED PRIMARIES

Nominating elections in which only voters belonging to that party may participate. Only Democrats can vote in a closed Democratic primary, for example.

CROSSOVER VOTING

When members of one party vote in another party's primary. This practice is not allowed in all states.

party barons, each possibly puffing on a big cigar, choose a candidate of their liking. It is one of the classic images in American politics. Examples of such cronyism abound. At the 1912 Republican national convention, President William Howard Taft had to stave off a challenge from his predecessor, Theodore Roosevelt. Roosevelt had been able to demonstrate his popularity among the party's rank and file by winning every primary that year, save the Massachusetts primary. At the time, however, only a dozen states even held primaries. Taft retained the support of the national party machinery and dominated delegate selection in nonprimary states. Ultimately, he controlled the convention. Taft was renominated, but not reelected. Roosevelt bolted the party, angrily maintaining that Taft's nomination thwarted the will of the "honestly elected majority" of GOP delegates. The split within Republican ranks was enough to elect Woodrow Wilson, only the second Democrat at that point to win the White House since the Civil War.[13]

As late as 1968, party officials had selected about 600 delegates out of 2,600 to the Democratic Party—almost 25 percent—two to four years ahead of the party's national convention. Senator Eugene McCarthy had made such a surprisingly strong showing in the New Hampshire primary that he drove President Lyndon Johnson from the race. But Johnson's backing was still enough to help his vice president, Hubert H. Humphrey, win the support of delegates controlled by party officials. McCarthy believed party rules had cheated him, so he proposed that all delegates be chosen—through "proce-

MAP 5-1 Party Affiliation Requirements for Voting in Direct Primaries

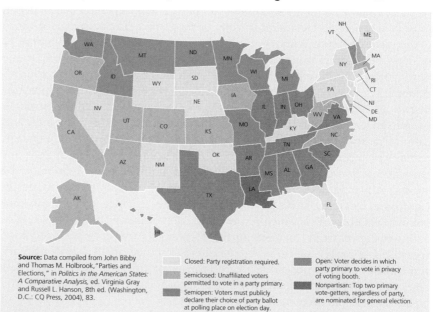

Source: Data compiled from John Bibby and Thomas M. Holbrook, "Parties and Elections," in *Politics in the American States: A Comparative Analysis,* ed. Virginia Gray and Russell L. Hanson, 8th ed. (Washington, D.C.: CQ Press, 2004), 83.

Closed: Party registration required.

Semiclosed: Unaffiliated voters permitted to vote in a party primary.

Semiopen: Voters must publicly declare their choice of party ballot at polling place on election day.

Open: Voter decides in which party primary to vote in privacy of voting booth.

Nonpartisan: Top two primary vote-getters, regardless of party, are nominated for general election.

dures open to public participation"—in the same year in which the nominating convention took place.

Humphrey recognized that McCarthy and Senator Robert F. Kennedy, both of whom had campaigned on anti-Vietnam platforms, had taken 69 percent of the primary vote. Respectful of what that number meant, he wanted to reward their followers with a consolation prize. So Humphrey coupled McCarthy's changes with one proposed by Senator George McGovern. McGovern wanted to see delegations demographically match—or at least reflect—the composition of the states they represented. More and more states threw up their figurative hands as they tried to meet each of these new requirements. Taking the path of least resistance, they decided that the easiest thing to do was to hold a popular vote primary. There had been only fifteen Democratic primaries in 1968, but by 1980 there were thirty-five. Conventions were reduced to little more than coronation ceremonies.[14]

How State Parties Recovered: Campaign Reform in the Late Twentieth Century

There aren't many smoke-filled rooms at conventions anymore. Candidates already have been selected by primary voters at that point. Yet conventions are still important networking occasions for officeholders and activists. They provide occasions for parties to change their internal rules. The action for candidates now, however, is in the primary and general election seasons. This is when they have the chance to woo voters directly, if not personally. Candidates no longer need hierarchical machines to reach voters. The decline of party machines was followed in time by the advent of televised campaign commercials as the dominant mode for trying to persuade citizens to vote.

The increasing reliance on campaign ads, ironically, has led to restored strength for state and national political parties and has spelled the decline of local party strength in federal elections. The move from greeting potential voters in person at party dinners and county fairs to airing TV ads has meant that politicians have had to run more professional campaigns. They hire pollsters to figure out what issues will resonate best in their ads. Consultants help shape their message on these issues, and media gurus produce the ads and place them during favorable time slots. Once more changing with the times, state parties became important clearinghouses in connecting candidates with consultants. Eventually, they evolved into important consulting organizations themselves.

Every Democratic and Republican state party now has a full-time chair or executive director. Most have other professional staff as well who handle fund-raising, communications, field operations, and campaigns.[15] In general, Republican state parties tend to be better funded and, therefore, are better run. Democratic state parties, however, often gain equivalent support from their allied groups, such as public sector unions.

With their massive computer databases, maintained and updated from year to year, political parties help candidates target and reach voters who are sympathetic to their messages. Parties also play an important role in helping interested groups and potential contributors determine which of the party's candidates have a realistic shot at winning. The major parties are not the voter organizers they were in the machine days, when individuals were encouraged to vote "early and often." Parties, however, do still contact up to 25 percent of the electorate in any election cycle. Individuals contacted by parties have a much higher tendency to vote than people who are not contacted, possibly because they feel like the party thinks their votes matter and that's why they were called. While the national parties typically play a greater role in polling and developing issues, "local and state parties [are] particularly important for registering voters and conducting get out the vote campaigns." [16]

One state chair of the 1950s exemplified the move parties made toward professionalized consulting services. Ray Bliss took over the Ohio Republican Party after it suffered an electoral drubbing in 1948. He immediately began to identify and recruit better candidates. He also looked at ways to encourage citizens to vote, noting that in 1948, 140,000 rural Republicans did not vote and 150,000 potential Republican voters in urban areas were not even registered. Following Bliss's registration and get out the vote drives, Ohio Republicans in 1950 reelected a U.S. senator, won three statewide offices, and regained control of the state legislature. [17]

Today, Republicans in Ohio are so dominant that they control every statewide office and both chambers of the state legislature. The Democratic candidate for state attorney general in 2002 tried to turn this hegemony into a campaign issue, complaining, "What has happened in Ohio is that in many ways we have turned government over to the business community with this one-party rule." [18] Voters did not agree with his assessment, and Republicans continued their dominance.

This is not to say that minority parties do not play an important part in politics. Minority party members enviously keep close tabs on the governing party, and they alert the public and the press to every perceived misstep and abuse. It also is important for minority parties not to get demoralized and to continue to offer voters alternative choices, so that candidates from their parties will be in place once the public is ready for a change. For instance, conservative Republicans dominated the Arizona Senate during the late 1990s. It seemed certain that Arizona Speaker of the House Jeff Groscost would join their ranks in 2000, since he was running in a Senate district that heavily favored the GOP. Late in the campaign season, however, Groscost was implicated in a scandal that led to a massive tax break that aided SUV owners—including a Groscost friend who sold the vehicles—and cost the state hundreds of millions of dollars. Groscost was beat by his previously unknown Democratic challenger, and the Senate ended up under divided control between the parties.

The two parties remain so closely competitive nationally today that political scientists refer to a period of **dealignment**, meaning that neither party is dominant. In earlier periods of American history, one party or another generally dominated politics, meaning it held most of the important offices. The two major examples are Republican dominance from the time of the Civil War into the 1920s and the Democratic New Deal coalition, which held power from the presidential election of 1932 into the 1960s. The 1932 election of Franklin D. Roosevelt was the best example of a **realignment**. This means that popular support switched from one party to another. Neither party has pulled off a similarly lasting realignment since then—and voters seem about equally supportive of both major parties—so political scientists are calling the early twenty-first century a period of dealignment.

DEALIGNMENT

When no one party can be said to dominate politics in this country.

REALIGNMENT

When popular support switches from one party to another.

State Party Regulation and Finance

It is important to note that the parties, although they are most active during the campaign season, do not dry up and blow away once an election is over. Not only is there planning for the next election . . . and the one after that . . . and the one after that, in perpetuity, but parties also play an important role in actual government operations. Granted, parties no longer are able to run government strictly to perpetuate their own power, as was true to a certain extent in the machine era. But they still help their most important supporters maintain access to officeholders and other officials.

Most municipal governments are organized on a nonpartisan basis like the Nebraska state legislature. Every other state legislature is organized by party. In other words, if the Democrats hold a majority of the seats in a state's House of Representatives, they not only control the leadership, schedule, and agenda of the House, but other Democrats chair House committees as well. There are exceptions and examples of shared power, particularly when partisan control of a legislature is tied, but these are rare. The more normal state of affairs is for the majority party to rule.

State Party Regulation

With all of that in mind, remember that states did not regulate political parties until the beginning of the twentieth century, when the progressive backlash against machine abuse led states to intervene. Political scientists now refer to parties as equivalent to public utilities, such as water and electricity, which the public has a sufficient interest in to justify state regulation.[19] Political parties, after all, are the main conduit for contesting elections and organizing government. The legal justifications states have used to regulate parties revolve around registration requirements—twenty-seven states register voters by party—since party names are printed alongside those of their candidates on ballots.

Thirty-eight states regulate aspects of the structure of their state and local parties, often in explicit detail, in order to avoid antidemocratic, machine boss control.[20] A state sometimes determines, for instance, how the members of a state party's central committee should be selected and how often that committee will meet. It can specify what party organization can name a substitute candidate if a nominee dies or withdraws prior to an election. Such regulation is practiced whether it is in regard to a state party in Minnesota or a local party in Pennsylvania.

Interestingly, a relatively limited number of state parties have challenged the laws in their states in the wake of the 1989 Supreme Court decision, mentioned previously. The Court ruled that the state of California did not have the authority to dictate how political parties are organized. The major parties in New Jersey did adopt a number of changes in party structure, but for the most part the parties seem satisfied with the way things are being run under the systems imposed on them by the states.

Nineteen eighty-nine was not the first time nor the last time the U.S. Supreme Court weighed in on the political party issue. The nation's highest court has issued a number of other decisions in recent years to clarify the legal rights of parties. In a series of cases emanating from Illinois during the 1970s and 1980s, the Court made it clear that "party affiliations and support" are unconstitutional bases for the granting of a majority of government or public jobs, except at the highest levels.[21] In 1986, it ruled that the state of Connecticut could not prevent independents from voting in Republican Party primaries, if the GOP welcomed them.[22] This precedent, which allowed the parties rather than the state to determine who could participate in a party's primary, was later followed in several other states. The parties have not always gotten their way, however. In 1999 the Court determined that states have the constitutional right to regulate elections and prevent manipulation. The ruling blocked a new party in Minnesota from "fusing" with the state's Democratic Party by nominating candidates for election that the Democrats had already nominated.[23]

Campaign Finance

INDEPENDENT
EXPENDITURES

Ad campaigns or other political activities that are run by a party or an outside group without the direct knowledge or approval of a particular candidate for office.

In 1996, the U.S. Supreme Court lifted federal limits on how much parties could spend. Under the new rules, a party could spend as much as it liked to support a candidate, as long as the candidate did not approve the party's strategy or ads or have any say over what the party was doing. The Court decided that no one had the right to restrict **independent expenditures**, or those activities that are run without the candidate's knowledge or approval. "We do not see how a Constitution that grants to individuals, candidates, and ordinary political committees the right to make unlimited independent expenditures could deny the same right to political parties," wrote Justice Stephen G. Breyer.[24]

In addition to this legal windfall, state parties already were exempted from a number of federal campaign finance limits. In 1974 and 1976, Congress enacted laws that limited the amount of money candidates could collect from individuals and **political action committees,** or PACs. Congress revised the law in 1979 after complaints from party leaders that the new laws almost completely eliminated state and local party organizations from participating in presidential campaigns. The old law, party leaders contended, put too many restrictions on how parties could spend money during a presidential election year. The revised law lifted all limits on what state and local parties could raise or spend for "party building" activities. These included purchasing campaign materials, such as buttons, bumper stickers, and yard signs, and conducting voter registration and get out the vote drives.[25]

It quickly became clear that the laxer restrictions were broad enough to allow for the purchase of TV ads and other campaign-related activities with so-called **soft money** donations, which were nominally meant to support party building. Restrictions on how parties spent soft money, which was raised in increments of $100,000 and more from corporations, unions, and wealthy individuals, were nearly meaningless—as long as the parties did not coordinate directly with candidates. Parties violated the spirit, if not the letter of the law, with state parties acting as virtual soft money laundering machines for the national parties and for each other. In 2002, Congress revisited the issue and enacted the McCain-Feingold campaign finance law, which blocked the national parties from collecting soft money donations.[26]

POLITICAL ACTION COMMITTEES

Groups formed for the purpose of raising money to elect or defeat political candidates. They usually represent business, union, or ideological interests.

SOFT MONEY

Money that is not subject to federal regulation that can be raised and spent by state parties. A 2002 law banned the use of soft money in federal elections.

TABLE 5-1

Transfers from National Party Committees to State Parties, 1999–2000 Election Cycle

National Party Transfers	Hard	Soft	Total
Republican			
National committee	$33,853,563	$93,017,578	$126,871,141
National congressional committee	10,957,743	15,852,920	26,810,663
National senatorial committee	10,689,700	20,485,179	31,174,879
Total			184,486,683
Democratic			
National committee	41,892,535	73,087,085	114,979,620
Congressional campaign committee	15,383,695	34,707,004	50,090,699
Senatorial campaign committee	24,388,338	37,444,869	61,833,207
Total			226,903,526

Source: Federal Election Commission, "Party Fund-Raising Escalates," press release, January 12, 2001, 8–9, as cited in John Bibby and Thomas M. Holbrook, "Parties and Elections," in *Politics in the American States: A Comparative Analysis,* ed. Virginia Gray and Russell L. Hanson, 8th ed. (Washington, D.C.: CQ Press, 2004), 79.

A Difference that Makes a Difference:
That Clean All-Over Feeling: Maine's Public Financing of Campaigns

Many people believe politics is inherently corrupt. This belief is compounded by the fact that campaign funding comes from individuals, corporations, and unions with a direct interest in the policies and decisions elected officials make once in office. For this reason, the public financing of campaigns has long held appeal for reformers. "I think it's a very freeing feeling," says [Maine state Representative] Marilyn Canavan, who helped draft a public finance law as head of the state ethics commission. "It means I can make decisions that are right for the people of Maine, and not be concerned in the least whether any campaign contributions are forthcoming."[a]

Through a ballot initiative, Maine has set up a voluntary system of public campaign finance for state legislative offices.[b] Anyone who wishes to pursue any state office is granted enough free money to run a credible campaign, as long as a sufficient number of $5 contributions are received upfront to show the candidate's serious intent. In 2002 more than half of Maine's candidates for the legislature renounced private funding in favor of taking the public money.

But whether Maine has really succeeded in lessening the role of special interests in state politics is a more complicated question. Since there are no restrictions on what the parties can spend—even on behalf of publicly financed candidates—there are those who see the new law as likely to attract more special interest money, not less. Among those skeptics is a former Maine governor, Angus King. The so-called clean elections law, he says, "has a gigantic loophole that really bothers me. You're running as a clean candidate, but the party can spend a million dollars on your behalf. To me, that undermines the whole premise. What you've really done is add a layer of public money to the old system." As if to prove his point, legislative leaders in Maine—even some who initially opposed the clean elections law—have been building up political action committees that raise hundreds of thousands of dollars they can spend supporting candidates of their choice.

A number of other states have enacted partial public finance laws of one sort or another during the past three decades. Some have achieved modest success. Candidates in Minnesota, for instance, tend to abide by spending limits and receive some public financing in return. More commonly, however, public financing has been a failure and largely for one reason. The money available—usually from voluntary tax checkoffs, in which taxpayers designate a few dollars from their tax returns to be spent on campaign finance—is insufficient to pay for the campaigns it is supposed to cover. Wisconsin, for example, became a pioneer when it enacted a public financing law in the late 1970s. But spending limits in Wisconsin have not been raised since 1986, and participation in the voluntary tax checkoff has fallen below 10 percent. That means that the amount of public financing grants has dropped to the point where no serious legislative or gubernatorial candidates are willing to choose them instead of taking private contributions.

Maine's law allows for inflationary adjustment, and the state has a small population and a low-key political system with a tradition of informal personal campaigning. A clean elections budget of $18,000 comes closer to full funding of a state senate election in Maine than it does almost anywhere else in the country.

Still, the state's lobbyists and pressure groups are adapting to the law, changing the way they interact with candidates seeking office. Rather than treating candidates like charities, writing out checks and declaring themselves done, interest groups are recruiting candidates themselves, and then running issue ads to support them. Such ads do not fall under the clean elections law limits. "People are changing strategies to do the same things they've always done," says Ed McLaughlin, president of the Maine Chamber of Commerce's political wing. "I expect as time goes by and people get savvy about what they can and cannot do, you're going to see more money come into campaigns. I think part of the intent of the public in passing this law was to take money out of politics. It ain't gonna happen."

[a] Adapted from Alan Greenblatt, "That Clean All-Over Feeling," *Governing* magazine, July 2002, 40.
[b] Arizona has a similar system.

The state parties themselves, meanwhile, are no slouches at raising money. According to one study, state parties raised $307 million on their own and received approximately $227 million more in transfers from national parties during the 2000 election cycle. (See Table 5-1.) It probably will not seem surprising that much of the transferred money was spent on issue ads that attacked federal candidates.[27] No matter what limitations are placed on campaign finance, money finds its way into the system, because the U.S. Supreme Court has held that political expenditures are equivalent to free speech. "There is no way to stop the flow of interested money and there will always be constitutional ways around the restrictions enacted into law," says University of Virginia government professor Larry J. Sabato. "What is so fundamental is that politics and government determine the allocation of goods and values in society. Those goods and values are critical to the success or failure of hundreds of interest groups and millions of individuals. Those groups and individuals are going to spend the money to defend their interests, period."[28]

Party Competition: Why Some States Are More Competitive than Others

The Republican Party came out of the 2002 elections with control over many of the nation's political institutions. Republicans held the White House, the U.S. House of Representatives, and they regained control of the Senate. They defied predictions and held onto a majority of governorships. For the first time since 1952, the party came out ahead in the total number of state legislative seats. Yet their victories did not represent political breakthroughs that they could necessarily bank on. All of the Republican majorities were quite narrow, reflecting the level of parity between the two major parties that has kept both of them from firm political dominance for a decade.

Just how narrow were some of the margins? Republicans had only two more governorships than Democrats. Both congressional chambers were nearly tied. Following the 2002 elections, Republicans held 49.6 percent of the nation's 7,400 legislative seats, while Democrats trailed just slightly with 49.4 percent of the seats. Republicans held a slight edge in the number of state chambers and legislatures they controlled, but the margins were often slim. In fact, a vacancy in any of a dozen legislative chambers could result in a change of party control.[29]

Perhaps just as striking as the overall level of parity between the Democratic and Republican parties at the national level is the fact that competition between them is just as healthy at the state level. (See Map 5-2.) Historically, most state political cultures have heavily favored one party or the other. A well-known example of this is the old Democratic "Solid South." For more than a century, most Southern voters were "yellow dog" Democrats, meaning they would sooner vote for a yellow dog than for a Republican. From

MAP 5-2 Interparty Competition, 1999–2003

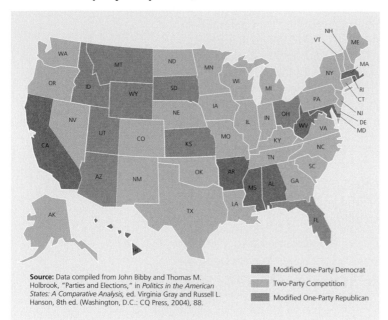

Source: Data compiled from John Bibby and Thomas M. Holbrook, "Parties and Elections," in *Politics in the American States: A Comparative Analysis,* ed. Virginia Gray and Russell L. Hanson, 8th ed. (Washington, D.C.: CQ Press, 2004), 88.

Modified One-Party Democrat

Two-Party Competition

Modified One-Party Republican

How can something like competition be measured? In the 1970s, Austin Ranney developed a scale, the Ranney index, a method of measuring interparty competition that calculates a number of factors that measure the degree of competition in each state. These include the percentage of seats won by each party in the house and senate at each election, how long either party controlled the governorship and legislature, and the proportion of time those offices have been divided between the two parties.

1880 to 1944, all eleven states of the old Confederacy voted for Democrats in every presidential election—with a couple of exceptions in 1920 and 1928—elected only Democrats and a few independents governor, and elected only Democrats to the U.S. Senate after popular voting for senators began in 1916.[30] The Democratic hegemony in the South began to break up with the civil rights era that began, roughly, with the elections of 1948.

In actuality, either party starts out with a fair chance of winning statewide elections in just about every state. That is actually a big change. Republicans are now about even—or dominant—politically in the South, but they have lost their edge in the Northeast, which is now one of the more Democratic sections of the country. Republicans hold the advantage in most states of the Mountain West, but Democrats are stronger along the Pacific Coast. All of this was perhaps most noticeable in the 2002 gubernatorial elections, when old party strangleholds finally broke. Georgia elected a Republican governor for the first time since 1868, ending the longest drought for either party in any state before or since. The GOP also took the governor's mansion in other states that had traditionally gone Democratic. These states included Maryland, which elected a Republican for the first time since 1966, and Hawaii, which chose the Grand Old Party for the first time since 1959. Democrats, meanwhile, won in Illinois, Michigan, Maine, and Wisconsin for the first time in well over a decade. They seated governors in Arizona, Kansas, Oklahoma, and Wyoming—states that had been supporting mostly Republicans in recent years.[31] Of the twenty-four new governors elected in 2002, twenty wrested control from a governor of another party.

Why the decline of one-party dominance in nearly every state? One factor is the increased mobility of the American population. People once put down roots and perpetuated the political culture of their families—now they are constantly shifting. The many Northeasterners who have moved into the South, for example, do not hold the same cultural memory of the Civil War that kept many conservatives from supporting Republicans. Immigrants to California have made the state more Democratic—Republicans politically misplayed their hand with California Hispanics by pushing

Governing States and Localities

an anti-immigrant ballot initiative during the 1990s—but the departure of many conservative voters who moved to other Western states such as Colorado and Utah has made the Golden State more Democratic as well.

All of that said, there are still plenty of places that are dominated by a single party. Republicans currently control every statewide office in Texas and seized control of the legislature with the 2002 elections. That means that Democrats have less power in Texas now than they have had for more than a century. That in turn means that interest groups are more likely to support Republican candidates, because they believe that members of that party will have more say in the function of state government. Once a party loses power, it is at a disadvantage in recovering power. Its traditional allies also will have a harder time pushing their agenda.

Interest groups recognize the fluid nature of political power. Trial lawyers are one of the most important Democratic constituencies, for example, because of their ability to contribute large amounts of campaign cash. In Florida, a state that has become more Republican in recent years, trial lawyers are splitting their donations and support. They are lining up more and more often behind Republicans, because they want to get a hearing from the currently dominant party. Some groups, however, are forever on the outs in certain states and communities. Environmentalists have a harder time pushing their legislation in Michigan, because of its dependence on the automotive industry, than they do in California. Labor unions have a harder time organizing in traditional right-to-work states in the South than in the Midwest or Northeast.

Also important to remember is that even though the majority of state legislative chambers are politically competitive, most of the seats within them are not. Legislative districts are redrawn following each decennial census. Given computerization and other tools, political leaders are able to predict the likely voting patterns of people on a block-by-block basis. Following the 2000 census, nearly every district in the country was redrawn in such a way that it became reasonably safe for a candidate of one party or another. In other words, there are now many safe Democratic districts and safe Republican districts, but not a lot of districts that are competitive. That means that most of the competition for a seat will take place in the primary race of the dominant party. If a seat looks likely to support a Republican, several qualified candidates might run for the GOP nod. The Democratic nomination probably will not stimulate as much competition.

The Political Cultures of States

As we have discussed before, in the mid-1960s, political scientist Daniel Elazar divided states into three political cultures: moral, traditional, and individual.[32] "Moral political culture focuses on the common good, traditional political culture on limited government, and individual political culture is non-ideological and self-interested," summarizes a more recent political scientist.[33] The moralist culture centers its politics on a notion of a public good or public interest. The individual takes a backseat to the good of the society. New England, the Upper Midwest, and the West Coast were home to moral political culture. The traditionalist culture also accepts the use of government as an active player, but its conception is more elitist, with the upper classes and other powerful interests seeing themselves at the top of a pyramid that provides social services to the lower classes but does not afford them a share of political power. The South was the home of traditionalist culture. The individualist culture views society essentially as a marketplace, with government held to a minimal role. According to Elazar, the states in the middle of the country, from the Mid-Atlantic through the Plains into the Mountain West, had individualist cultures.

Many of these generalizations are less true now than they were when Elazar came up with his model. The federal government has taken a greater role since then in a number of programs that were once the province of state and local governments, such as transportation and health care. In a sense, it has leveled the playing field and forced the states to make their government activity more uniform. Still, while much has changed, a state's initial conception of itself as either a progressive place providing generous services or a state that keeps both taxes and government services down still informs the way policymakers act in the state today.

Wisconsin, for example, has a shared-revenue system that distributes about a billion dollars a year to local governments. A remnant of the Progressive Era, this system is designed to equalize payments across the state on a per capita basis, so that even residents of poor areas can count on a minimum level of services. Faced with a budget deficit topping $1 billion in 2002, Governor Scott McCallum sought to eliminate the payments, both to save money and to force layers of local government to consolidate. When he unveiled his plan, he noted that there were fifty-four units of government within a ten-mile radius of where he stood in downtown Madison. Residents fought back with a public relations campaign that challenged the honesty of McCallum's numbers. Their campaign also described the services they would be forced to cut if his plan went through. His proposal went nowhere in the legislature, and he was defeated for reelection.[34] In Wisconsin, it seemed, the old political culture trumped McCallum's modern conservative ideas about making localities fend more for themselves.

Texas, by contrast, has historically been less enamored with government. A reflection of this is the fact that it is one of only seven states without a personal income tax. The state is pretty stingy when it comes to funding local government. The national average of state aid to cities is more than $200 per person—in Texas it is about $3 per person.[35] Like most other states early in the twenty-first century, Texas faced a major budget shortfall, but the GOP, the state's majority party, had no interest in raising taxes. "The idea that they'll pass a tax bill doesn't compute," said state senator Bill Ratliff.[36] In Texas and elsewhere, longstanding resistance to the idea of extensive gov-

In 1999, Wisconsin redistributed $1.1 billion for county health and human services.

Governing States and Localities

ernment services has led states to balance budgets by cutting spending from levels reached during the prosperous 1990s rather than by raising taxes.

Effect of Parties on Political Culture

Democrats are generally more liberal, favoring governmental solutions to social problems. Republicans are generally more conservative, preferring a limited role for government. These are not hard and fast rules, but they are true most of the time and have been true for many decades. As a result, the dominance of one party over the other has had an effect on the political culture of many states. Where there have been successful efforts to mobilize low-income voters through class-based appeals, in places such as Louisiana, Mississippi, and Minnesota, government has gotten bigger. If these individuals put someone into office, they expect the support and social programs they were promised. It is equally unsurprising that politicians who have come to power promising not to raise taxes have kept government growth in check. In New Hampshire, William Loeb, the editor of the Manchester *Union Leader,* came up with the idea of challenging political candidates to sign a no tax pledge. The pledge became embedded in the state's political culture. Within thirty years New Hampshire was transformed from a relatively high revenue state, one that could depend upon gaining adequate monies from taxes to fund public programs, to a low revenue state.[37] The result? Among other things, New Hampshire was the only state in the country not to offer universal kindergarten classes as recently as 1997.

What may be surprising is the fact that when the parties *really* held real sway—when the machines were more important than any individual office-holder—they were not much interested in expanding government either. Machine politicians wanted to maintain their grip on the government jobs and contracts they already had. This would seem to make sense for a conservative machine, like that run by Senator Harry Byrd in Virginia from the 1920s to the 1960s. After all, Byrd and his acolytes shared a respect for balanced budgets and a small public sector. But party machines in general, even progressive ones, were usually not expansionistic. In the machine era, party officials squabbled more over who got control of what government jobs than about changing the number or nature of those jobs. They certainly did not present new government-based solutions to problems. Keeping jobs tied to political loyalties discouraged the creation of a professionalized bureaucracy that could hold onto its job.

In the meantime, the public did not want corrupt machine politicians to control any more of their money than necessary. Interest groups, such as unions, that might have wanted an expansion of government programs, did not hold enough influence to promote them.[38] As the parties and political machines weakened, however, candidates, party activists, and interest groups became free agents, free to promote all manner of new programs and government expansion.

Party Factions and Activists

Parties are no longer able to reward their followers directly with jobs or other payoffs. Decisions handed down by the U.S. Supreme Court have made it clear that party affiliation is not a constitutional basis to decide government hires. Therefore, activism and working for a party have become largely volunteer activities. And since people seldom work for free unless they believe in something very strongly, political volunteers have become more ideological. People work for candidates and parties because they believe in specific causes, such as handgun legislation or rights for small business owners.

Just because jobs are no longer the parties' golden eggs does not mean that politicians and parties do not seek to pluck favors from their constituents through policies or promises. Both major parties court the elderly with assurances of healthcare benefits, such as providing prescription drugs through Medicare. The reason is that senior citizens vote and thus are worth courting. Young people, by contrast, do not vote. Only 13 percent of all people aged eighteen to thirty voted in the November 2002 elections.[39] That self-disenfranchisement, or separation, is one big reason why state politicians never hesitate to cut state aid to universities and pass along college costs to students through tuition increases.

Each party has its main constituent groups, but that does not mean that both parties do not try to poach supporters from the other side. Democrats have been at pains in recent years to present a friendly face to business interests, while Republican president George W. Bush has courted Teamsters and building trade unions. Remember, however, that each party is a kaleidoscope of interest groups and can only appeal so much to any one group before it risks alienating support among other groups.

It is obvious that you cannot simultaneously support higher pay for teachers and cutting educational budgets. That is why politicians must perform the neat trick of motivating the true believers within party ranks to support their candidacy during a primary election without pinning themselves down so much that they do not appeal to members of the other party and independents during the general election. Overall, the more contentious the issue, the more a party generally must try to blur its differences with the other party. Yet candidates do not want to promise so much to their core supporters—known as the "base"—that they cannot reach other voters. If you promise a lot of money for public transportation, that might help you in the city but hurt you in the suburbs.

Both major parties try to appeal to as much of the populace as possible. But their supporters sometimes care more about promoting an issue than they do about winning elections. Interest groups now raise their own funds and use them freely to promote their issues in campaigns. We'll talk about how interest groups lobby governments a little later in this chapter, but it is worth examining quickly the type of role they can play in contemporary politics.

A 1998 special election for a vacant congressional seat based in Santa Barbara, California, demonstrated the difficulty that the parties have in maintaining discipline in message and candidate selection. Congressional Republican leaders, both in Washington and in Southern California, favored a state representative who was a liberal on social issues. They thought he had the right profile to win in the progressive-leaning district. Local and national conservative activists, however, were unwilling to accept this candidate. Two conservative Christian groups, the Catholic Alliance and the Christian Coalition, each distributed one hundred thousand voter guides at churches and other venues in the days leading up to the special primary in support of a more conservative candidate. That candidate won the GOP nomination but lost the general election.[40]

Numerous interests took an active role in that particular general election campaign that fall, including groups that favored term limits, antiabortion and prochoice advocates, labor unions, environmental organizations, and antitax groups. In fact, the amount of money the candidates spent on their own campaigns was most likely dwarfed by the amount spent by these and other outside groups. This has become more the rule and less the exception in recent years. In Wisconsin, political races often are dominated by issue ads run by the Wisconsin Manufacturers and Commerce and the Wisconsin Education Associations Council. Because these groups care so much about, respectively, taxes and education, these issues dominate many races. Politicians and parties have no control over such ads, so they cannot control the agenda. Anything else the candidates might want to emphasize is likely to be drowned out. Nobody disputes that taxes and schools are important, but making them the only subjects detracts from other equally important issues.[41]

By the 1980s, it appeared that candidates were fairly free agents. They were rid of the old party machine apparatus and able to set their own agendas and spread their own messages, largely through broadcast ads. Twenty years later, times have changed again. Yes, candidates are more independent, almost choosing themselves for party nomination and spending sums they have raised to get into the public eye. Campaigns, however, have become such big business that these funds and this self-motivation often are not enough. Plus, candidates need votes, and to get these votes they must join ranks with party officials and interest groups, who tend to take the candidate's ball and run away with it. Candidates become mere pawns in campaigns that have been overtaken by deep-pocketed interest groups. They stand on the sidelines and watch as parties or other groups run the greater volume of ads, redefining their campaigns for them.

It is easy to become confused about who is the most powerful—candidates, interest groups, or political parties and in which situations they hold that power. What is important to remember is that all three are vital parts of the political process and that their relative importance varies depending

In 1997 and 1998 in New Jersey, the Democratic and Republican parties received $212,500 from four groups with unidentifiable "special interests."

on the time and place. It is impossible to illustrate every variation, but none of them are ever either nothing or everything. Their roles are entwined.

Pragmatism vs. Idealism

Interest groups, just like parties, are most likely to play a prominent role in races that are closely contested or that can tip the partisan balance in a legislature. Redistricting at both the federal and state legislative levels, however, has grown so sophisticated—with so much emphasis placed on making districts safe for incumbents—that relatively few of these races are closely contested. Much of the action takes place in primary contests. If a district is drawn so that it will be likely to elect a Republican, then when the seat has no incumbent, you will find a large number of candidates contending in the GOP primary. Fewer Democrats will bother trying. But in true "swing" districts, where either party has a shot at winning, both major parties and all of their allies will spend as much money as they can muster to win.

In these cases, party leaders grow frustrated when interest groups trumpet issues that do not appeal to a wider public, as was the case in the California congressional race we just discussed. The main goal of parties is to win elections, so they are much more interested in fielding candidates who fit the profile of the office in contention than they are in promoting a specific ideology. The Republican National Committee, for example, defeated an attempt in 1998 to pass a party resolution that would have blocked the party from giving any money to candidates opposed to a ban on late-term abortions. Social conservatives were angry that the national committee had spent $760,000 supporting the reelection effort of New Jersey governor Christine Todd Whitman, who had vetoed a state ban on the procedure. "I'm about as pro-life as anybody," said Bob Hiler of Indiana's national committee, "but I just cannot accept a situation in the Republican Party where there is a litmus test if you want to join or be a candidate. I respect the decisions of our national party leaders to place money where it needs to go to ensure that we win that seat."[42]

With just two broad-based national parties, neither can afford to preach an unyielding gospel on any single issue. The people most interested in politics may be motivated by their investment in a particular issue, but if they hang around long enough, they come to realize that no one can win all the time. Perversely, the parties that are best able to keep their troops in line and satisfied with less than perfect ideological purity are the parties currently out of power. In other words, the desire to get back into the White House or to hold majority control of a legislature is often strong enough to convince all the quarreling factions to back someone who looks like a winner— even if that candidate is not "perfect" on all of the issues.

But the fact that both parties spend a good deal of time blurring their positions on the most important issues of the day to try to appeal to the most people while alienating the fewest number has made a lot of voters sour on them. As Colonel Aureliano Buendia discovered in *One Hundred Years of Solitude,* many Americans believe that politicians do not stand for anything and are more interested in preserving power than doing the right thing. That is a major reason why voters have become more independent in recent decades and have refused to give lifelong allegiance to one party or the other in the same way that their grandparents did. "It probably would have been better for the parties if the public had become more negative rather than more neutral toward them," writes political scientist Martin Wattenberg. "Negative attitudes can easily be turned into positive attitudes by better performance or a change in policies. To induce people to care about political parties once again may well be more difficult."[43]

Third Parties and Independents

Since millions of people are disenchanted with the Republican and Democratic parties, for a variety of reasons, why isn't there more of a movement toward establishing a viable third, or minor, party as an alternative? After all, in most other democracies, there are numerous parties with strong support. In countries such as Israel and Italy, the leading party typically does not have enough seats in parliament to construct a government on its own and has to enter into a coalition with other parties.

In the 2000 presidential election, Green Party candidate Ralph Nader won 10% of the vote in Alaska, his highest nationwide.

That has never been the case in the United States for a number of reasons. Democrats and Republicans, as we have been exploring, have established wide networks of contacts and supporters—individuals and groups who have long loyalties to one party or the other. They have officeholders at all levels who can help with strategy and fund-raising.

The major parties also have many institutional advantages. For one thing, the United States favors a winner-takes-all system in which the highest vote getter in a district wins. In some countries, seats are distributed on a percentage basis, so that if a party gets 5 percent of the vote it receives about 5 percent of the total seats available. But if a party only took 5 percent of the vote across the United States, it probably would not win a seat anywhere. In 1992, Texas computer billionaire Ross Perot, the most successful third party presidential candidate in decades, took 19 percent of the vote but did not carry a single state.

For the 1996 presidential race, Perot established the Reform Party, which he called his gift to the American people. Perot used that gift himself, running for a second time but not doing nearly so well. He had a hard time getting on the ballot in some states—the rules differ in many places and are often complicated. In the state of New York, for instance, a candidate must collect a certain number of signatures from each of the congressional districts that serve as petitions to allow him on the ballot. Many candidates with less financial means than Perot have had difficulty gaining access to ballots. Perot himself was excluded from the presidential debates. The com-

Local Focus: A Green Team vs. the Money Machine

It may be hard to believe, but when Gavin Newsom, the San Francisco mayor who in 2004 became the first public official to issue licenses for same-sex marriages, ran for that office he was considered a conservative. Newsom, a Democrat, was nearly beaten in 2003 by a fellow county supervisor running as a Green Party candidate. Mayoral elections in San Francisco, like many other elections for local offices nationwide, are nominally nonpartisan—meaning candidates do not run under a party banner—but Newsom's win demonstrated the continuing power of party support and the difficulties minor party candidates have in breaking into the system.

Even though San Francisco is one of the most liberal cities in the country, Green Party members accounted for only 3 percent of San Francisco's registered voters in 2003. The party has attempted to build national support by running candidates for local offices. When San Francisco moved to a system of electing supervisors by district, rather than citywide, neighborhood activists were given a chance to win local seats, and thus gain access to higher and more influential positions.

One of those activists, Matt Gonzalez, would go on to challenge Newsom in 2003. Gonzalez was a dyed-in-the-wool liberal. He represented the famed Haight-Ashbury neighborhood, the center of 1960s hippie culture. A son of an immigrant and a former punk musician, he had sponsored the city's initiative to raise the minimum wage to the highest level in the state. Gonzalez ran well behind Newsom in the mayoral election, but because Newsom did not win a majority the two faced off the following month in a runoff election.

Newsom, on the other hand, was the son of a politically connected state judge. Outgoing mayor Willie Brown had appointed him supervisor and had supported his run for mayor. He was the beneficiary of aggressive campaigning from many other local and national Democratic figures, perhaps most notably former president Bill Clinton. For San Francisco, Newsom actually was considered relatively conservative. His pro-business views and his attempt to reform the city's system of giving financial support to the homeless were not the sort of stands usually taken by the city's Democratic officials.

Gonzalez came on strong by appealing to younger residents put off by the old Democratic machine and Newsom's personal wealth and establishment lineage. But at the end of the day, it was that establishment that carried Newsom, barely, across the finish line. Other Democrats helped him raise money—Newsom outspent Gonzalez by a 5-to-1 margin—and the party's organizational strength proved decisive. More people actually voted for Gonzalez on election day, but the Democratic Party's ability to facilitate absentee voting helped account for Newsom's slim margin of victory.

In a post-mortem on the election, another local supervisor noted, "The problem is that progressives are not comfortable raising money. It's anathema to them. It's remarkable what [the Gonzalez campaign] did, but you need some more money to be able to compete. You need to be a little grownup about it."*

*Joe Garofoli, "Gonzalez Supporters' Next Big Challenge," *San Francisco Chronicle,* December 14, 2003, A1.

mission running the debates—composed of officials from the Democratic and Republican parties—decided he was not showing enough strength in the polls to warrant being included.

Excluded though he was, Perot nevertheless took 8 percent of the vote in 1996. This was enough to guarantee the Reform nominee in 2000 a spot on all fifty state ballots, as well as $12 million in federal campaign funds. With Perot out of the running, however, the Reform nomination dissolved into chaos. Two separate conventions nominated two separate candidates. The states were left having to decide which candidate deserved the spot on the ballot. "There are no statutes to guide us," said Mike Cooney, Montana secretary of state. "The Reform Party needed to resolve this issue before it got to this point. It's an internal party problem that has been foisted upon the states and put us all in a bad situation." The eventual Reform nominee proved not to be as much of a factor in the race as Green Party nominee Ralph Nader. The Reform Party seemed to have self-destructed. Several of the old minor parties that had taken up its banner soon returned to their original names, such as Minnesota's Independence Party.

Difficulties of Building Support

Many Democrats blamed Nader for the defeat of their candidate, Al Gore. Gore won more popular votes than Republican George W. Bush but was defeated in the electoral college. Some people believe that a third party candidate will never be anything more than a "spoiler" who deprives major party candidates of needed votes. Others believe that third parties help present a real and needed alternative to the Democrats and Republicans. Unless the major parties are challenged, the thinking goes, they will never change.

The major parties, however, have proven quite adept at co-opting the most popular ideas presented by third party candidates. Both Democratic and Republican candidates of the 1990s took the idea of a balanced federal budget more seriously because Perot had raised the issue. During the 1930s, Franklin D. Roosevelt lifted many of the ideas of Socialist candidate Norman Thomas. When faced with the rare strong minor party challenge, a major party candidate can argue that he offers the best vehicle for presenting any shared ideals—and stands a better chance of beating the other major party candidate. As noted earlier, Perot's 1992 showing was the best by a third party candidate since Theodore Roosevelt's in 1912—and neither one of them came close to winning.

Minor party candidates have enjoyed more success running for lower offices, but not much. Within a state or a legislative district, there is a better chance that an individual will enjoy enough personal popularity to equalize the playing field against Democrats and Republicans who typically are better funded and connected. Still, there have been only five governors elected during the last fifty years who were not either Democrats or Republicans. Two of those five—Walter Hickel of Alaska and Lowell Weicker of Connecticut—had earlier won statewide office as Republicans. Another two were elected in Maine, a state noted for the independent-mindedness of its electorate. The fifth, Jesse Ventura of Minnesota, served only one term, and the would-be successor from his Independence Party finished a distant third in 2002.

At the legislative level, things are just as grim for third party candidates. Following the 2002 elections, there were only 23 third party state legislators in the United States, out of a total 7,382. Each of these candidates had dedicated followers. But from a pragmatic perspective—say, as a voter or an interest group interested in seeing your agenda into law—it probably makes better sense not to support a person who will hold just one vote and instead support a Democrat or Republican who has a chance of serving in the majority party.

A few minor parties have enjoyed a period of success in certain states, such as the Progressive Party during the 1920s in Wisconsin and the Farmer-Labor Party during the 1930s in Minnesota. Over time, though, these parties have been unable to survive the loss of early, popular leaders or have been absorbed by one of the major parties. For example, the official name of Minnesota's Democratic Party is still the Democratic Farmer-Labor Party. The Liberal Party of New York boasted a New York City mayor in the 1960s named John Lindsay. New York is one of the few states that allow candidates to be listed multiple times on a ballot, as the nominee of, for instance, both the Liberal and the Republican parties. In 1980, U.S. Senator Jacob Javits was denied the nomination of the state's Republican Party and ran on the Liberal line. He succeeded only in splitting the votes of liberals, moderates, and Democrats and helping to elect a more conservative Republican. The Liberal Party disbanded in 2003 after failing to garner enough votes in the previous year's gubernatorial contest to maintain its guaranteed spot on state ballots. "Parties, I suppose, have a life span," said Dan Cantor, executive director of the Working Families Party. "They had their heyday in the [19]50s and [19]60s. It looks like they have come to a full stop." [44]

Ultimately, it is the states that print the ballots and have the authority to decide which parties' nominees are going to be listed on them. It is the states that grant ballot access to parties based on their having won a minimum percentage of the vote in a previous statewide general election. The threshold varies from 1 percent in Wisconsin to as much as 20 percent in Georgia. Such high institutional barriers make minor parties' complaints about two-party dominance of American politics about as fruitless as trying to hold back the tide.

Major Party Support

One other reason minor parties have trouble gaining traction is that people are not, in the main, terribly unhappy with the major parties. The major parties, after all, do devote themselves to appealing to as broad a range of citizens as possible. That said, voter identification with the parties has declined. Some states once allowed voters to vote a straight ticket, meaning they could pull one lever to vote for all the Democratic or Republican candidates on the ballot. Such procedures are now considered quaint. Voters are more and more willing to divide their ballots, a practice called **ticket splitting**. One voter joked, "I vote for the man for president, and give him a Congress he can't work with."

In 1960, the Gallup Organization found that 47 percent of respondents identified themselves as Democrats, 30 percent as Republicans, and just 23 percent as independents or members of other parties. By the 1990s, those numbers had converged. Polling by the Pew Research Center for the People and the Press over a fifty-four-month period in the mid-1990s found an average of 33 percent of the respondents called themselves Democrats, 29 percent Republicans, and 33 percent independents, with a handful naming other specific parties.[45] Other contemporary polls found that same division.

Most of those independents are not true independents, however. What this means is that their preferences generally do lean toward one major party or the other. "Partisan loyalties in the American populace have rebounded significantly since the mid-1970s, especially among those who actually turn out to vote," concluded political scientist Larry M. Bartels in 2000.[46] Pure independents, those who do not lean toward either party, peaked at 16 percent in 1976. Twenty years later, true independents were just 9 percent of the populace.[47]

The Republicans and Democrats have dominated American politics for 150 years. They have met every challenge—both ideological and structural—and found a way to preserve their near-total control. "If there's any lesson of history about the two major parties in American politics," says political scientist Jeff Fishel, "it is that they're incredible adaptive survivors. They lost the monopoly they had, particularly on candidate recruitment and finance. That certainly does not mean that they're going out of business, just that they have to compete with other groups."[48]

Interest Groups and Lobbies

As should be apparent by now, interest groups have always been important sources for candidates—both of money and of volunteers and other services. They are those organizations that take a direct interest in political activity—both in terms of supporting candidates during an election season and lobbying elected and appointed government officials over policy and spending matters. They differ from parties in that politics and elections are not their whole reason for being. As political scientist Frank J. Sorauf notes, "The American Medical Association devotes only part of its energies to protecting its interests through political action. Not so the political party. It arises and exists solely as a response to the problems of organizing the political process."[49] In other words, the American Medical Association (AMA) may spend millions of dollars annually trying to affect elections and legislation, but it devotes more of its energy to educating its members, promoting good health techniques, and other private activities.

Interest groups basically come in three flavors. One is a membership group, like the AMA or Sierra Club, made up of individual members. A second type is the trade association, which represents individuals or organizations

MAP 5-3 Spending by Lobbyists, 2003

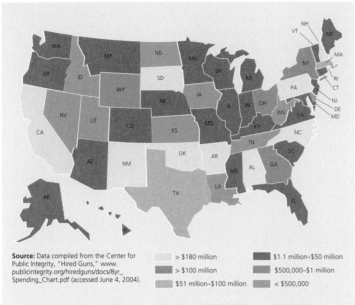

Source: Data compiled from the Center for Public Integrity, "Hired Guns," www.publicintegrity.org/hiredguns/docs/8yr_Spending_Chart.pdf (accessed June 4, 2004).

- > $180 million
- > $100 million
- $51 million–$100 million
- $1.1 million–$50 million
- $500,000–$1 million
- < $500,000

Note: Nine states did not track overall lobby spending totals in 2003: AL, AR, NH, NM, NC, OK, PA, RI, SD. For the first time, MO and ND reported spending totals in 2003. See the Center for Public Integrity's Web site for full information on each state's reporting rules.

Total for all states reporting: $715,930,207

CONTRACT LOBBYIST

A person who works for different causes for different clients in the same way that a lawyer will represent more than one client.

---

in a particular industry or field, such as the National Restaurant Association or the Association of Trial Lawyers of America. The third group is the individual institutions themselves, such as Microsoft and General Motors. The larger groups are bound to have lobbyists on staff or devote a significant portion of their executives' time to lobbying.

People and organizations have a constitutional right to petition the government for redress of grievances. That means that they have the right to complain to lawmakers and regulators about their disagreements with laws and how they are enforced. That's what lobbying is. It is worth noting that government runs some of the most active lobbies. The White House maintains a lobbying shop to try to persuade Congress of the wisdom of its policies. Municipal governments hire lobbyists and associations to protect their interests in their state capitals. There are about 45,000 lobbyists working in state capitals, and the number of associations and related groups has quintupled over the last fifty years.[50]

Any interest group, however, might also hire a **contract lobbyist**. This is usually a lawyer or former government staffer or elected official who is valued for possessing valuable insider knowledge and contacts within a particular state capital. Contract lobbyists generally have a number of clients, as a lawyer would. About 20 percent of lobbyists registered to ply their trade in a given capital are contract.[51] They play an insider's game, using their relationships and contacts to convince legislators that they should or should not pass a bill. Lobbyists ignore the executive branch at their peril, since spending decisions and regulatory action are carried out there, but more lobbying activity happens in the legislative arena. "You don't change their minds," said a California lobbyist, "You find ways of making them think they agreed with you all along."[52]

Legislators often rely on lobbyists to provide them with information, whether it is simply data about an industry's economic outlook or their opinions about whether a bill would cost jobs in legislators' districts. Legislators are always grappling with many issues at once—the state budget, education, the environment, and so on. It is up to lobbyists to keep legislators and their staffs apprised of who favors a particular bill, and who would benefit or be hurt by it. Lobbyists build up relationships with legislators over time, and legislators come to trust some of them for reliable information, even if they hold a differing position on an issue.

In contrast to a contract lobbyist is a **cause lobbyist**—who promotes a single-issue agenda, such as medical marijuana and campaign finance reform. A cause lobbyist often plays an outsider's game, using the media to sway public opinion and pressure public officials. Groups who do not have an economic interest in legislative outcomes are able to get away with that tactic because their ideological position is clear for all to see.

Using the media effectively can be trickier for private corporations and other entities directly affected by legislation. The media nearly always portray this third type of lobbyist in a negative light. If a politician sponsors a bill favoring a particular industry and individuals in that industry have made substantial donations to his campaign treasury, there are bound to be stories written about that money trail. Numerous states, including Kentucky, Minnesota, and Massachusetts, have passed ethics laws in recent years that preclude lobbyists who used to wine and dine legislators from giving them anything of value, even a cup of coffee.[53]

As mentioned earlier, some interest groups tend to be loyal to one party or the other, particularly groups with ideological agendas. But interest groups as a whole do not give most of their support to candidates of a particular party. They give most their support to *incumbents* of either party. There are a number of reasons for this. One is that incumbents are reelected the vast majority of the time, so betting on their victory is pretty safe. It makes more sense, pragmatically speaking, to curry favor with someone who possesses power than with someone who does not. Even if the incumbent does not subscribe to an interest group's entire program, the group may find it is able to work with the individual on an issue or two.

Another reason that interest groups favor incumbents is because their campaign contributions are based more on rewarding public officials for positions they have already taken than they are based on trying to persuade them to take new positions altogether. In other words, if a legislator has already demonstrated support for gun owners' rights, the NRA will be inclined to support him. The group does not give donations to gun control advocates in hopes of changing their minds. The money follows the vote, in most cases, rather than the other way around.

The adoption of gift bans and other ethical restraints has done nothing to retard the lobbying industry or deter interest groups. Too much is at stake in too many state capitals for corporations, unions, or cause activists not to play an active role. At the beginning of the twentieth century, as noted earlier, one or two powerful home-state companies dominated many state political cultures. State capitals remained old boys' clubs, where just a few powerful interests typically held sway, until about World War II. Since then, states have come to rival Washington in terms of the buzz of activity among competing interests.

CAUSE LOBBYIST

A person who works for an organization that tracks and promotes an issue, for example, environmental issues for the Sierra Club or gun regulation for the National Rifle Association.

TABLE 5-2

Top Ten Most Influential Interests in the States, 2002

Ranking	Organization
1	General business organizations
2	Schoolteacher organizations (National Education Association and American Federation of Teachers)
3	Utility companies and associations (electric, gas, water, telephone/telecommunications)
4	Insurance: general and medical (companies and associations)
5	Hospital/nursing home associations
6	Lawyers (predominantly trial lawyers, state bar associations)
7	Manufacturers (companies and associations)
8	General local government organizations (municipal leagues, county associations, elected officials)
9	Physicians/state medical associations
10	General farm organizations (state farm bureaus, etc.)

Source: Data compiled from Clive S. Thomas and Ronald J. Hrebnar, "Interest Groups in the States," in *Politics in the American States: A Comparative Analysis,* ed. Virginia Gray and Russell L. Hanson, 8th ed. (Washington D.C.: CQ Press, 2004), 119.

About 1,100 different occupations are regulated by states today, and fighting among those industries is neverending. Art therapists, for instance, want their profession recognized by more state legislatures so that they will be guaranteed reimbursement from insurance companies. Mental health counselors, on the other hand, do not want the added competition and oppose such recognition. Orthopedic surgeons and podiatrists face off over who gets to treat ankle injuries and force legislators to debate whether the ankle is part of the foot. (The Colorado legislature decided it was, opening up the field to podiatrists.) Dog groomers fight veterinarians for the right to brush canine teeth.[54]

Beer is regulated at the state level, which is why Anheuser-Busch hires lobbyists in all fifty states. Insurance is also regulated at the state level. Many more industries, in fact, are turning their attention to the states because that is where the federal government and the courts have sent the power. The states have assumed authority over issues such as securities regulation and have taken the lead on issues that have not progressed in Congress. The federal government has failed in recent years to regulate health maintenance organizations, but more than forty states have passed bills addressing the topic over the last decade.

The active role of the state in regulating economic and social activity has induced some industries, such as pharmaceutical companies, to maintain lobbies that are just as powerful in the states as they are in Washington. Others, such as the oil industry, have a major presence at the federal level but are weaker players in most states, because they have no local presence. National companies that are not based in a particular state are likely to hire local contract lobbyists to lend clout to their causes. The consumer products company Johnson & Johnson has its own lobbyists but also maintains memberships in its home state in the New Jersey Chamber of Commerce, the state's Business and Industry Association, and the New Jersey Health Products Company Group. It also belongs to industry associations in California, Illinois, Massachusetts, and elsewhere. At the national level, Johnson & Johnson belongs to the Pharmaceutical Research and Manufacturers

TABLE 5-3

Most Active Lobbying Organizations, 2000

Ranking	Organization	Number of States Registered in
1	Anheuser-Busch Companies Inc.	50
2	American Insurance Association	48
3	Brown & Williamson Tobacco Corporation	47
4	Lorillard Tobacco Company	46
5	AT&T Corporation	45
6	UST Public Affairs, Inc.	43
7	MCI WorldCom Inc.	43
8	Pfizer Inc.	43
9	National Federation of Independent Businesses	42
10	RJ Reynolds Tobacco Company	41
11	Motion Picture Association of America	41
12	Health Insurance Association of America	40
13	Variable Annuity Life Insurance Company	40
14	Pharmacia & Upjohn Company	40
15	American Cancer Society	40
16	State Farm Insurance Companies	38
17	Glaxo Wellcome Inc.	38
18	Alliance of American Insurers	37
19	Merck & Co. Inc.	37
20	Wyeth-Ayherst Laboratories	37
21	National Rifle Association Institute for Legislative Action	37
22	AFLAC Inc.	36
23	Eli Lilly and Company	36
24	Smokeless Tobacco Council Inc.	35
25	National Association of Independent Insurers	35
26	Wine Institute	35
27	Teachers Insurance & Annuity Association/ College Retirement Equities Fund (TIAA-CREF)	34
28	Dehart & Darr Associates Inc.	34
29	AARP	34
30	Household Financial Group Ltd	32

(Table continues on next page)

TABLE 5-3 *(continued)*

Ranking	Organization	Number of States Registered in
31	3M Company	32
32	American Council of Life Insurance	31
33	General Motors Corporation	31
34	Philip Morris Management Corp	30
35	Allstate Insurance Company	30
36	American Heart Association	30
37	Distilled Spirits Council of the US (DISCUS)	30
38	Golden Rule Insurance Company	29
39	Enron Corp	28
40	Pharmaceutical Research & Manufacturers of America	28
41	Alliance of Automobile Manufacturers	28
42	GTECH Corporation	27
43	Johnson & Johnson	26
44	Novartis Pharmaceutical Corporation	26
45	United Transportation Union	26
46	West Group	25
47	American Petroleum Institute	25
48	Waste Management Inc.	25
49	American Express Company	25
50	Prudential Insurance Company of America	25

Source: Center for Public Integrity, "Fourth Branch State Project," 2000. www.publicintegrity.org (accessed June 4, 2004).

of America, the Health Care Industry Manufacturers' Association, and still more groups.[55]

When an industry has relatively little credibility, it will often turn to allies to represent the public face of its cause. Tobacco companies favor hiring lobbyists who have earned the respect of state legislators as former colleagues or by working for other, less controversial clients. They also seek other groups to take the lead on a lot of their fights. When a state considers legislation that will regulate smoking in public places, for example, the most public opponents are more likely to be restaurant groups rather than the tobacco industry. "We're going to participate in a very upfront way," said a Philip Morris spokesman. "But like any other industry, we're going to look to people who share that point of view on any given issue" to take a role as well.[56]

As in the case of tobacco companies fighting smoking bans, lobbyists spend the majority of their time playing defense, trying to kill bills they believe would harm their companies or clients. Still, interest groups and their desires stir up much of the activity in state capitals. "Frankly, the legislature in New Jersey exists for the lobbyist," said one lobbyist there.[57] What he was suggesting was that the governor may want five or six bills passed during a session, while individual legislators may want one or two of their own passed as well. The remaining 99 percent of the thousands of bills introduced in a given year are a wish list of wants and needs by the lobbyists and the interests they represent.

Conclusion

The essential job of political parties is to nominate candidates for public office. They no longer control many government jobs, but despite changes in campaign finance laws, they have maintained their positions as leading fund-raising organizations. They also perform many other functions in American democracy. They aggregate and articulate political interests and create and maintain majorities within the electorate and within government. They are not the dominant organizing forces they once were, in part because voters and candidates have become more independent than they were a century ago. Parties, however, do still play important roles in recruiting political candidates, supporting them financially and logistically, and helping them market themselves to like-minded voters.

For the past 150 years, two major parties—the Democrats and the Republicans—have dominated American politics. Few candidates not belonging to either of these parties have won office at any level of government. In most cases, their victories were based on personal appeal rather than support for the third party they represented. The Republican and Democratic parties have been able to adapt to changing times and tastes in ways that have kept them in power, if not always in perfect favor.

Interest groups in recent decades have become less centralized in a small number of industries within each state. Fewer state political cultures are dominated by one group or even a few. With states regulating more industries, interest groups have proliferated, so that there are now more lobbyists than elected officials. Interest groups help push agendas subscribed to by individuals or corporations. Other interest groups push back.

Their primary mission is winning as many political offices as possible, so the parties, with varying success, collate and mute the ideological agendas of their interest group allies. Parties cannot afford to have any one group's ideas play such a prominent role that it alienates other groups or voters. It is a difficult balancing act between trying to appeal to the majority of voters at any given time, while also standing for clear enough principles that most people are willing to support them.

Key Concepts

blanket primaries (p. 141)

candidate-centered politics (p. 136)

cause lobbyist (p. 163)

closed primaries (p. 141)

contract lobbyist (p. 162)

crossover voting (p. 141)

dealignment (p. 145)

factional splits or factions (p. 133)

general elections (p. 141)

independent expenditures (p. 146)

nonpartisan ballots (p. 140)

open primaries (p. 141)

party conventions (p. 141)

patronage (p. 140)

political action committees (p. 147)

political machines (p. 139)

political parties (p. 132)

primary elections (p. 141)

realignment (p. 145)

responsible party model (p. 137)

runoff primary (p. 141)

soft money (p. 147)

straight ticket (p. 161)

swing voters (p. 135)

ticket splitting (p. 160)

voter identification (p. 137)

Suggested Readings

Gould, Lewis. *Grand Old Party: A History of the Republicans.* New York: Random House, 2003. An excellent recent history of the Republicans from Abraham Lincoln to the present day.

Greenberg, Stanley. *The Two Americas: Our Current Political Deadlock and How to Break It.* New York: Thomas Dunne Books, 2004. A Democratic pollster traces the history of the parties since World War II and explains why neither has maintained dominant political support.

Jewell, Malcolm E., and Sarah M. Morehouse. *Political Parties and Elections in the American States.* 4th ed. Washington, D.C.: CQ Press, 2000. Shows how and why political parties vary at the state level.

Rosenthal, Alan. *The Third House: Lobbyists and Lobbying in the States,* 2d. ed. Washington, D.C.: CQ Press, 2001. A primer on how interest groups operate in and influence state legislatures.

Witcover, Jules. *Party of the People: A History of the Democrats.* New York: Random House, 2003. Companion to Lewis Gould's *Grand Old Party,* traces the Democratic Party from its Anti-Federalist antecedents to Bill Clinton.

Suggested Web Sites

http://politicsorg.com/Lobbying. Provides links to dozens of lobbyists and associations in Washington and in the states.

www.dnc.org. Web site of the Democratic National Committee.

www.rnc.org. Web site of the Republican National Committee.

www.politics1.com. Provides links to candidates for most major offices in all the states.

www.followthemoney.org. Web site of the National Institute on Money in State Politics, which tracks political donations and lobbying in all fifty states.

CHAPTER 6

Legislatures
The Art of Herding Cats

While running a legislature has been compared to herding cats, legislators themselves are sometimes compared to other animals. Here a Texan expresses her opinion of "Chicken Ds," the more than four dozen Texas House Democrats who in 2003 left the state. These legislators objected to a redistricting plan being pushed through the legislature by the Republican majority. Unable to get their concerns addressed by House leaders, they bolted the state in order to deny the House a quorum and thus shut down the legislature.

6

Why do so many citizens think that legislatures accomplish so little—or accomplish the wrong thing altogether?

What constraints do legislatures face in making effective legislation?

Why are some legislators more powerful than others?

State legislatures operate in complex ways, especially when it comes to how members negotiate with their colleagues as they attempt to make laws.

Their basic dynamics, however, are fairly similar to how you and your friends decide what movies to rent.

Let's say—for the sake of argument—that a group of your women friends wants to rent a chick flick, while the guys insist on watching $100 million worth of things blowing up. If there are six women and five men and all votes are counted as equal, then you'll be watching a DVD featuring Julia Roberts and a wedding. Similarly, if Democrats hold fifty-three seats in the Indiana House of Representatives and Republicans have only forty-seven, most of the time the Democrats are going to get their way. This is called **majority rule**.

But bills do not always pass according to predictable partisan majorities. Let's change our movie-rental scenario. Now it is just you (a young woman), your roommate (also a woman), and your boyfriend. You would like to watch that Julia Roberts movie, but your roommate wants to watch a thriller. Betraying you, you feel, your boyfriend agrees with her! Something similar happens regularly in legislatures, when some members abandon their fellow Democrats or Republicans to vote with the opposing party. For instance, most Democrats might want to pass stricter gun control laws, but some of their rural, more conservative Democratic colleagues might block them by joining with the GOP. This is called **coalition building**.

By the next night, though, your boyfriend might have come to the realization that it is not smart policy for him to favor your roommate's taste over yours. In his heart, he would rather watch what the roommate wants to watch, but he knows he is better off in the long run if he agrees to watch your favorites. In much the same way, legislators often vote for bills that they do not particularly like in order to win support for other priorities. They might want to curry favor with their party leaders, or they might simply want to earn a colleague's help in the future by voting for the colleague's pet bill now. This is called trading votes, or **logrolling**.

Or maybe you have learned that you cannot count on your boyfriend to stick up for you when it's time to head out for the video store. You know you are going to end up renting a movie—it's a Sunday, and your whole suite is bored from reading about state and local government. So you go around to all your pals in the dorm and plant the idea that what would

MAJORITY RULE

The process in which the decision of a numerical majority is made binding on a group.

COALITION BUILDING

The assembling of an alliance of groups to pursue a common goal or interest.

LOGROLLING

The practice in which a legislator will give a colleague a vote on a particular bill in return for that colleague's vote on another bill to be considered later.

Governing States and Localities

really be fun tonight would be watching one of the old *Star Wars* movies. Legislators—and other people concerned with what legislators are up to—do this all time. They try to solicit support from people who are going to vote long before a vote actually takes place so that the result will come out the way they want. This is called lobbying and is similar to the kind of lobbying interest groups do, as we saw in Chapters 4 and 5.

But let's say while you are busy polling your friends that one of them unexpectedly says that she hates *Star Wars* worse than poison, that she refuses to watch *Star Wars*, and, what's more, since her DVD player is the only one on the floor that's working, there is no way you are going to watch *Star Wars* at any point this semester. This sort of thing often happens in legislatures. If there is a bill to increase state spending for abortion clinics, for instance, you can bet that one or more legislators will do everything in their power to block that spending.

> John Dingell, the longest-serving member of the U.S. House of Representatives, perhaps best described the strange relationship between the actual substance of a bill and how it moves through the House when he said in 1984, "If you let me write procedure and I let you write substance, I'll screw you every time."

There are many ways that an adamant opponent can stop a hated piece of legislation, including **filibusters**—endless debates in the Senate. Another way is to attach unwanted amendments, or **riders**, to a bill. The road to a bill's passage into law is twisty and sometimes full of unexpected hurdles. John Dingell, the longest-serving member of the U.S. House of Representatives, perhaps best described the strange relationship between the actual substance of a bill and how it moves through the House when he said in 1984, "If you let me write procedure and I let you write substance, I'll screw you every time."

In all fairness, legislatures were not designed to be simple. The congressional system was designed to be difficult enough to prevent new laws that have not been properly thought through and debated from bothering everybody. "The injury which may possibly be done by defeating a few good laws will be amply compensated by the advantage of preventing a number of bad ones," wrote Alexander Hamilton in *Federalist Paper*, No. 73. Therefore, most state legislatures share the basic structure of the U.S. Congress, with a House chamber and a Senate chamber that both must approve a bill before it can go to the governor to be signed into law. That means that even if a bill makes its way through all the circuitous steps of getting passed by the House, including **committee** fights and winning a majority in the chamber, it can easily die if the Senate refuses to sign off on an identical version. To use our video renting comparison one more time, this is like getting every member of your family to finally agree to rent some animal movie, but then having your neighbors refuse to watch it because they all want to see something starring Matt Damon. Getting the 150 or so legislators who serve in every state to agree on anything is one of the toughest tricks in politics.

FILIBUSTERS

Debates that under Senate rules drag on, blocking final action on the bill under consideration and preventing other bills from being debated.

RIDERS

Amendments to a bill that are not central to its intent.

COMMITTEE

A group of legislators formally tasked with considering and writing bills in a particular issue area.

FIGURE 6-1 The Legislative Process: How a Bill Becomes a State Law

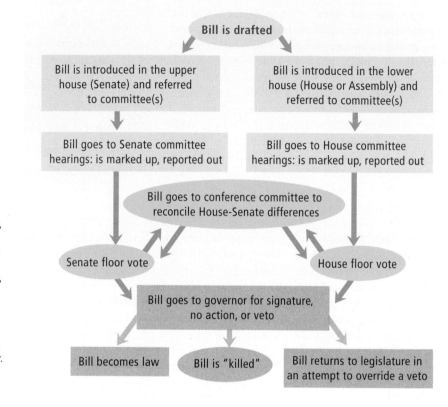

This model provides a general sense of how a bill moves through state legislatures. Note, however, that there is a good deal of variation in this process from state to state. Nebraska's unicameral system, for instance, means that bills do not pass through simultaneous House and Senate processes. In many states, bills also have to go through more than one reading before getting out of a chamber.

The consequence of this complexity is a grave misperception by the general public about how well legislatures work and how competent individual legislators are. Legislatures work hard. Thousands of bills and constituent complaints are addressed every year, but their institutional structures make it difficult for them to respond quickly to the issues of the day. The early part of the twenty-first century also finds the electorate split politically in most states, as well as nationwide, so it is especially difficult to reach an agreement that pleases everyone. The fact is, legislators are more honest than ever and are working to address more complicated problems than in the past. But the public's perception is that they are not getting the job done. Recent studies show that the average person is not in touch with what his or her legislature is up to, considers the legislature to be unnecessarily contentious, and thinks legislators are guilty of talking when they should be acting. Many people believe that legislators are too cozy with the special interest groups that provide them with campaign contributions and perhaps other favors. Voters wonder why their representatives do not simply vote the "right" way and go home.

The problem is that there is no "right" way. Many cross currents blow through every legislature. Some legislators represent liberal **districts**—others represent conservative areas. Some represent cities, while others represent farmlands grappling with entirely different, nonurban issues. Legislators acting in good faith will come to different conclusions about what is the right approach to take on any number of issues, from education and transportation to job creation and taxes. All sides get to present their most convincing arguments, but only rarely can a majority of members of a legislature come to an agreement that pleases them all. In their disagreement, they reflect the different opinions of their **constituents**, the citizens back home—which is precisely the way the system is supposed to work.

Let's say that you and your friends are still arguing about the chick flick versus the action picture. Only this time, each movie has an even number of fans. In the end, you decide that you will watch something entirely different, an old comedy you have all seen but are willing to watch again. None of you is thrilled—none of you gets to watch exactly the kind of movie you were hoping for—but all of you can live with the choice. This is called **compromise**, and it is the kind of agreement legislators make more than any other. This chapter will give you a sense of how legislators come to their decisions, who they are, what they do, and how they organize themselves in their institutions. Localities—city and county governments—typically have some form of legislature as well. These will be covered in Chapter 10.

The Job of Legislatures

You may have heard of the Segway. It is a device introduced with much hype and fanfare on national television at the end of 2001 that moves individuals around at speeds of up to twelve miles per hour. The device is undoubtedly cool, with its five gyroscopes and ten onboard computers to keep its rider balanced and to change directions with the simplest weight shift. But it cannot do anybody much good unless it can be ridden on sidewalks. At the time the product was unveiled, motorized vehicles were banned from sidewalks in all but three states. Segway LLC, the maker of the device, decided to change all that.

The company had a hot product, which it incorporated into a lobbying strategy—legislators were allowed to take rides on the machine at capitol receptions. Seeing how easy the Segways were to ride and to stop, legislators could not think of any reason they should not allow the devices on their state's sidewalks. In fact, they thought the devices might alleviate all sorts of transportation problems. Segways would cut down on air pollution, revitalize downtowns where parking cars is a problem, and provide easily accessible mobility to the elderly and handicapped. Safety advocates, who worried about the possibility of sixty-nine-pound machines barreling into pedestrians, were hardly heard. Segway bills passed through several legislatures

DISTRICTS

Geographical areas represented by members of a legislature.

CONSTITUENTS

Residents of a district.

COMPROMISE

The result when there is no consensus on a policy change or spending amount but legislators find a central point on which a majority can agree.

Lobbyists are sometimes seen as taking legislators for a ride, but perhaps not quite so literally as this. As part of its lobbying effort to make sure its premier product was not regulated off of city sidewalks, the maker of the Segway gave state legislators across the country a chance to try out the unique personal transportation system. This was an effective tactic and headed off the regulatory threat. Here Connecticut state senator George Gunthor puts the Segway through its paces.

without hearings or substantive debate. By the summer of 2004, forty states had passed bills to allow Segways on sidewalks. It looked like the remaining states would soon fall into line.[1]

It was a remarkable achievement, especially for a new company. It was also a classic example of how legislatures are *not* supposed to work. A special interest group—a single company, in fact—was able to use a $1 million public relations and lobbying campaign to work its will with legislators all across the country. Usually attempts to get states to pass uniform laws sputter along, with perhaps only a handful of states taking up an issue during any given session. The federal Centers for Disease Control and Prevention (CDC), for instance, crafted model legislation in 2002 for states to strengthen their public health response to terrorist attacks and many other emergencies. By the middle of the year, the bill had been introduced in only nineteen states and enacted into law in just six.[2]

Fairly or not, rightly or wrongly, the differing fates of the Segway and the public health laws are examples of how the public gets its negative opinion of legislatures. Segway was able to curry favor through private receptions and joyrides. Meanwhile, in the face of a dreaded public health threat, legislatures could not even agree on the powers they wanted to give their governors in case of a biological emergency. They were not able put aside their difference to serve the public good.

This caricature represents a commonly held sense of how "politics as usual" works but it also baldly overstates the problems with legislatures and unfairly maligns them. A lot more goes on than the public realizes or sees, and this creates a very skewed view. Case in point, the Segway bills were actually an example of legislators happy to help out a new technology they believed was safe, would create jobs, and would help correct other problems. And the success of the Segway blitzkrieg really was quite unusual. The fate of the CDC bill, by contrast, was quite typical. However, while the exact legislation initially proposed was not widely embraced by many states, legislatures across the country did pass other, specially tailored laws to deal with public health risks unique to their situations. Hawaii's legislature, for example, passed a plan to create a nursing branch in its public health department that could respond to hurricanes and tsunamis (tidal waves). Unfortunately, the governor did not agree with the legislators and vetoed the program. Connecticut's General Assembly—as the state's entire legislature is called—passed separate laws that ensured that the state could respond to a catastrophic event at its nuclear power facility and that make special plans for children and youth in a homeland security emergency.

What Legislatures Do

All state legislatures share three basic purposes:

- They pass laws and create policy for their states.
- They provide representation for the citizens in their districts in state government—including offering personalized constituent service to help residents sort out their problems with the state government.
- They oversee the governor and the executive branch and some private businesses through public hearings, budget reviews, and formal investigations.

State legislatures might all address similar issues, including taxes, budgets, and a broad range of other matters such as regulating office safety and requiring parental notification when minors seek abortions. Differences in timing, state history, and political culture, however, may cause one state's laws on a topic to differ widely from those of other states. Occasionally, legislatures are pressured to pass uniform laws—as when the federal government insisted that the states raise their legal drinking ages to twenty-one or risk losing highway funding. Louisiana, with its proud tradition of public drinking, resisted the longest.

More often than not, laws are adapted to the local scene and are not easily molded to match other states' versions. Large insurance companies are regulated at the state level. They would love to have their agents qualified to sell in every state rather than having to take fifty different qualifying exams. But only a few states have acted on the proposal. "I'm still not sure what happens if Michigan says you can be an insurance agent if you can sign your name with your eyes shut, and New York says you've got to take a three-year course," said Alexander Grannis, chair of the insurance committee in the New York Assembly. "What happens if someone screws up—if we cancel a Michigan guy's license to practice here for malpractice, does that mean Michigan can retaliate and cancel a New Yorker's right to practice there?"[3]

Within a given state, the media and the public manage to register every failure of a legislature while failing to give the institution enough credit for its successes in balancing all the competing interests within the state. Ethics

> "I'm still not sure what happens if Michigan says you can be an insurance agent if you can sign your name with your eyes shut, and New York says you've got to take a three-year course. . . . What happens if someone screws up—if we cancel a Michigan guy's license to practice here for malpractice, does that mean Michigan can retaliate and cancel a New Yorker's right to practice there?"

scandals generally receive greater coverage than substantial debates, yet legislators debate and pass laws that cover everything from levels of Medicaid health insurance funding to clean water protections to aid for local governments to workers' compensation payments to the price of milk. In most legislatures, 90 percent of the bills receive almost no media attention and are of interest only to those they directly affect. The media—and with it, the voting public—pay attention only when issues that affect the broadest range of people are considered, such as increases in property tax rates. Legislators do not have the luxury of tuning out when complex and boring but important issues crop up.

State senators and representatives fight their biggest fights over budgets. Most of their power is derived from the fact that with the approval of the governor they can set fiscal policy, including tax rates. How much the state devotes to each of its programs is a way of revisiting all the problems that never go away. How much is enough to spend on education? How much of that education tab should the state pick up? While public schools traditionally were funded by local property taxes, most states now pick up one-third of the bill or more. How much money for health care? How big an investment should the state make in roads? How much can be spent overall before the state is taxing individuals and businesses too highly? Practically every state has a constitutional requirement to balance its budget every year, so legislators cannot spend what they do not take in from tax receipts. State legislatures annually address hundreds of such issues, large and small.

Lawmaking

Legislatures tend to be reactive institutions. After the 1999 school shootings at Columbine High School in Littleton, Colorado, a flurry of gun control legislation was introduced in legislatures across the nation although not all of it was ultimately passed into law. But these bills truly were indeed only a flurry compared to the blizzard of bills introduced annually. The New York state legislature grappled with more than 21,000 bills in 2002,[4] while even much mellower Montana takes up about 1,500 a year.[5] Despite this amount of activity—or perhaps because of it—legislators do not go looking for issues to address. The typical bill is introduced for one of several reasons. It is a bill that has to be considered, such as the annual state budget. It is a bill dealing with a common problem modeled after another state's legislation. Or, it is something that an individual or a group outside of the legislature wants considered. These outside influences include constituents, the governor, and lobbyists.

It may not always seem like it, but constituents can have a lot of influence in government. In Massachusetts, for instance, legislators are obliged to consider petitions to introduce bills on any topic a state resident wants. During the debate over same-sex marriages in 2004, for instance, various groups petitioned the legislature with the approaches they favored. They ef-

TABLE 6-1

Dumb Law? Or Not?

Where	Law	Why
State of Arizona	Camel hunting is illegal.	The U.S. Army once experimented with using camels in the Arizona desert but eventually gave up. The remaining camels were set free and are now protected.
Detroit, Michigan	Any person seen throwing an octopus onto the ice at a Red Wings hockey game at the Joe Louis Arena will be jailed.	The first octopus was tossed on the ice on April 15, 1952, during the Red Wings' Stanley Cup playoff run. Devoted fans Pete and Jerry Cusimano, fishmonger brothers, tossed a mollusk onto the ice during the game on that fateful night. Back then the National Hockey League (NHL) consisted of six teams. A team only needed eight victories (two best-of-seven playoff series) to win the Stanley Cup. Each tentacle of the octopus symbolized one playoff victory. The Red Wings won the cup that year, and since then octopi have made periodic appearances. The law exists to protect the participants of playoff games.
State of North Carolina	Organizations may not hold their meetings while the members present are in costume.	To discourage the Ku Klux Klan (KKK), certain measures such as this one were taken. The KKK was known for their use of white hooded costumes during meetings and demonstrations for purposes of remaining anonymous, as well as to inflict fear on others. By making these actions illegal, the organization's power was weakened somewhat.
Memphis, Tennessee	Panhandlers must first obtain a $10 permit before begging on downtown streets.	Panhandlers were becoming so numerous and aggressive in downtown Memphis, a main tourist area, that it was decided that something needed to be done. The law gave local police much more leverage. The ordinance is mainly targeted at "aggressive panhandlers," who are more likely than "passive panhandlers" to scare off tourists and therefore reduce tourism income.
Austin, Texas	Wire cutters cannot be carried in your pocket.	In the days of the old Wild West, cowboys would cut barbed wire fences of property owners in order to allow their cattle herds to pass through. To prevent such acts, this ordinance was passed.

Source: www.dumblaws.com (accessed June 4, 2004).

fectively filed their own amendments. Governors and the executive branch are also powerful players in the legislative process. They promote ideas they want legislators to work on. These can be bills designed to quickly address relatively small-scale problems, such as the $4 million program to combat wasting disease in deer that the Wisconsin legislature approved in 2002, or larger issues that might be debated for years.[6]

For example, the legislature in Washington State has battled for several years over funding for transportation projects in the Puget Sound area. In

2001, legislators failed to agree to Governor Gary Locke's proposal to spend $9 billion more on roads, despite Locke calling them into three special sessions. That was in part because Republicans and Democrats had a hard time coming to agreement on changes in contracting laws that require workers to be paid a union wage in rural areas.[7] Finally, lobbyists representing a client such as Segway LLC often will promote draft legislation in hopes that a member of the legislature or General Assembly—as legislatures are known in Colorado, Georgia, Pennsylvania, and several other states—will sponsor it as a bill.

Remember, however, that a success as great as Segway's is unusual. Lobbyists may promote bills, but they also devote an enormous amount of energy trying to kill other bills. The state acts as referee between a lot of competing interests. Any change in state law that someone views as a positive step is likely to adversely affect—or at least frighten—someone else. What gun control advocates want, the gun owners' rights groups will try to stop. Legislators react most strongly to bills in which they have a personal stake or that they know will affect their constituents directly. Let's say that environmentalists are concerned about water quality on a river and want to require new water filters at a paper mill. The mill's owners, concerned that the cost of the filters will be exorbitant, warn that they will have to lay off three hundred employees if the bill goes through. A legislator from that area will have to worry about whether creating a healthier environment is worth being accused of costing people their jobs. Other legislators who live clear across the state from the river and its mill, though, will hold the deciding votes. The people directly affected—the company, the workers, downstream residents worried about pollution—will all try to portray themselves as standing for the greater good. If no side is clearly right, and favoring one side or the other can do political damage, the bill easily could die. Legislators could then be accused of doing nothing, but they will merely be reflecting the lack of statewide consensus about how to solve the problem.[8]

Representation

The primary jobs of legislators are to formulate the law and to keep an eye on the executive branch, but their primary responsibility is to provide **representation** to their constituents. Basically, they ensure the interests of those they speak for are properly considered as part of decision making at the state level. Sometimes legislators address issues because their constituents are having problems that only a change in the law can address. Medicaid is a shared federal-state program that provides health insurance to the poor. It is an entitlement program, which means that anyone who meets its eligibility requirements is supposed to receive help. But not everyone who is eligible receives that help. In 2001, Garnet Coleman, a Democrat who represented parts of Houston in the Texas House of Representatives, decided to try to change that. The state at that time required as many as fourteen different forms from parents before their children could enroll in Medicaid, and they had to be recertified every few months. Coleman sponsored legislation to reduce all that paperwork to a single four-page form. That change alone was expected to put one-third of the state's 1.4 million uninsured children on the Medicaid rolls.[9]

Coleman simply wanted to change current rules to make it easier for people who were eligible to be able to apply. Except that Texas, with its tradition of fiscal conservatism, was not about to vote to expand its Medicaid program. Other states with histories of greater governmental generosity had expanded their Medicaid programs throughout the 1990s in order to widen the pool of people eligible for coverage. Vermont, for example, vastly enlarged its Medicaid program so that all children in families with incomes under 300 percent of the poverty line—about $50,000 for a family of four—would be eligible. Today, with Medicaid costs rising faster than the level of inflation, states are wondering whether they can continue to be generous without asking the federal government to take on a bigger share of the program's costs.

Huge jury awards could go up in smoke depending on how legislatures deal with tort reform. Tobacco companies, hospitals, and others who are frequently targeted by lawsuits are pressuring state governments to place caps on the punitive damages juries can award. Trial lawyers, on the other hand, are pressuring legislatures to leave things as they are. The stakes are high. For example, in 2000 attorney Madelyn Chaber convinced a San Francisco jury to award Leslie Whiteley, a smoker, $20 million in a lawsuit against tobacco companies.

If a problem is real and persistent enough, a state's legislature will address it eventually. Sometimes there is a general recognition that just such a long-festering problem needs to be fixed. That does not mean the fix is going to be easy. Pennsylvania's supreme court is elected—and therefore its justices have their own reelection prospects to worry about—and so its members have been loath to address the issue of school funding equity, or making sure kids get an adequately funded education even if they live in poor districts. The Pennsylvania legislature met in special session in 2002 to try to solve the problem, without success, but at least it is still trying. Several states, including Mississippi, Pennsylvania, and West Virginia, have changed their tort laws, laws that cover damages to individuals, in the last couple of years. They have done this in order to help their doctors and trauma centers afford medical malpractice insurance. Addressing medical malpractice issues is difficult in part because trial lawyers object to any limitations on punitive damages that people can receive from lawsuits after suffering injury or death as a result of medical negligence.

The reason that this objection by trial lawyers is important is that trial lawyers are influential in Democratic politics. This is perhaps especially true in the Deep South, which has a reputation for hefty jury verdicts. States like Alabama and Mississippi traditionally have been hostile to trade unions, with "right to work" laws that have made it difficult for the unions to organize. Elsewhere, in the Midwest and Northeast, where unions are active, they are important donors to Democratic candidates. But where unions are weak, trial lawyers have become the major source of funding for Democrats. The role of such interest groups was discussed in Chapter 5.

Legislatures often finish their work on an issue not because of outside pressure but because of internal changes. A leadership change in the Arizona Senate in 2001 brought with it solutions to longstanding issues that included understaffing in the state's highway patrol, underfunding in the state's mental health system, and provisioning for water through new contracts. Legislators even managed to repeal antiquated sex laws that made it a crime for unmarried couples to live together.[10] States with stagnant leadership or long-term control by one party or the other have a harder time making breakthroughs. New York is a prime example. Republicans have long controlled the Senate, Democrats have long controlled the Assembly, and the two refuse to agree on certain issues. The Senate majority leader for years has refused to allow a vote on a gay rights bill, while the Assembly Speaker will not permit a vote on banning late-term abortions. Legislators in one chamber regularly refuse to allow votes on the other chamber's versions of those bills that the Senate and Assembly do agree on, including a stricter drunk driving law.[11]

Before a bill can even get far enough to be debated, the idea for it must be developed. To get ideas for bills, legislators turn to each other, to staff, to colleagues in other states, and to outside sources, whether it is a company with a cause of its own, like Segway, or a think tank interested in pushing change. Minnesota has an unusually fertile landscape when it comes to ideas for the legislature. More than 750 foundations are active in the state's public life. During the mid-1990s, thirty of them matched funds with the legislature to help nonprofit groups plan for federal budget cuts and changes in welfare law.[12]

In addition, the state capitol of St. Paul has the now-unusual benefit of being able to mine two major metropolitan daily newspapers—the *Pioneer Press* and the *Star Tribune*, which serves the capitol's "twin city" of Minneapolis. Once upon a time, numerous communities were served by two or more competing newspapers. Today, consolidations and foldings have forced most areas to make due with one, if that. Fortunately for Minnesota's legislators, both Twin City papers actively cover public policy. Perhaps as a result, the state was the first to ban smoking in restaurants, the first to allow schoolchildren choice among public schools, the first to allow charter schools, and the first to enact requirements that people holding comparable jobs receive comparable pay. Such engagement from the media—and, by extension, interest from the public—has become fairly rare. We will talk about how the media cover state legislatures a little later on in this chapter.

Constituent Service

Aside from debating and passing laws, legislators devote a good deal of time and energy to **constituent service**. They help clear up those problems citizens are having with public agencies or even private companies. They also act as liaisons between their constituents and unelected parts of the government in the executive branch, the bureaucracy that everyone knows and loves to hate.

Legislators and their staffs spend incredible amounts of their time dealing with constituent service requests, also known as **casework**.[13] Residents of a state may experience all manner of frustration coping with state laws or may merely want assistance in sorting through regulatory requirements. One of the advantages of an **incumbent** is being able to dole out this kind of personalized help. Some legislators have staff members devoted solely to helping constituents. This is particularly true in their district offices—their offices located in the area they represent, as opposed to their capitol offices. Typical issues include tracking down deadbeat dads for child support, figuring out how to receive proper health coverage under Medicaid programs, or knowing what federal agency to contact with questions about military matters. "I spend a tremendous amount of time on constituent service," says Tennessee senator Rosalind Kurita, D-Clarksville. "When we are in session, I probably make five or six calls a day and easily that many emails and letters. To me, that is one of the most important things we do."[14]

No one objects to a senator like Kurita helping a seven-year-old boy who has outgrown his wheelchair figure out how to receive a new one through the state's health insurance program. The problem is that attempts to help individuals sometimes morph into policy decisions. That is, a legislator might not only write a letter to help a particular person, but write a bill that changes the way the state approaches a program, such as health insurance. Helping an individual may be all well and good, but changing the system based on the personal story of one person is not necessarily the best way to change policies that will affect thousands.

Oversight

Under the U.S. system of checks and balances, legislatures are charged with **oversight,** the task of making sure that the governor and the executive branch agencies are functioning properly. The executive branch is called the executive branch because it executes the laws written by the legislature. Legislators are only doing their job when they call governors and executive branch agencies to account through hearings, investigations, and audits for how they are carrying out those laws. Unfortunately, the most ubiquitous form of oversight is a legislator intervening with administrative agencies on behalf of constituents or constituent groups in ways that are "episodic and punitive."[15]

CONSTITUENT SERVICE
The work done by legislators to help those in their voting districts.

CASEWORK
The work undertaken by legislators and their staffs in response to requests for help from constituents.

INCUMBENT
A person holding office.

OVERSIGHT
The role the legislature takes in making sure that the implementation of its laws by the executive branch is being done properly.

Local Focus: Constituent Service: Going the Extra Mile

When John Medinger was a member of the Wisconsin State Assembly, he worked back-breaking hours to do his job—and to make sure that his constituents knew he was doing his job. He needed to let people know how seriously committed he was to representing them and their interests, because Medinger is a Democrat who represented a Republican district.

He drove the 137 miles to the capitol in Madison and the 137 miles back home to La Crosse three times a week, even when the legislature was not meeting. When he was in La Crosse, he was in perpetual motion. "If I don't have anything to do at home," he said, "I go sit in a coffee shop and shoot the breeze. I might be home two nights a week to tuck my kids in. I go to every pancake breakfast and every rummage sale. I am always looking for something to do. If there's nothing else, I go to a basketball game and mingle with the crowd."

All that work paid off politically. One year, Medinger got a perfect 100 rating from the AFL-CIO but was rated at 29 by the Wisconsin Association of Manufacturers. The La Crosse chamber of commerce endorsed him for reelection anyway. As Medinger once said, "There are some Republicans in my district who could run against me and make my life miserable. . . . But the Republicans can't come up with candidates who will put in 100-hour weeks. So they don't make it."[a] The

fact is, no one who interacts with legislators doubts that they work hard. They keep long hours meeting with colleagues, constituents, lobbyists seeking a favor for their clients, and business leaders from their districts and across the state.

For all of the clear evidence that politicians work hard, some people still question whether all of the meeting and studying and debating those legislators do actually accomplish anything. "A politician's day is long," says satirist P. J. O'Rourke. "He gets into the office early, reads newspaper clippings with his name highlighted, submits to a radio interview with Howard Stern, goes to a prayer breakfast and an ACLU lunch, checks opinion polls, meets with an NRA delegation, makes a friendly call to Al Sharpton, sits in the Inland Waterways Committee hearing room drawing pictures of sailboats and seagulls on a notepad, proposes National Dried Plum Week, votes "yea" (or is it "nay"?) on something or other (consult staff), exercises with the president, recovers from a faked charley horse after being lapped on the White House jogging track, watches the signature machine sign letters to constituents, returns a corporate campaign contribution to WorldCom, speaks at a dinner supporting campaign-finance reform, goes home, gets on the phone, and fundraises until all hours."[b]

[a] Quoted in Alan Ehrenhalt, *The United States of Ambition* (New York: Times Books/Random House, 1991) 133.
[b] P. J. O'Rourke, "No Apparent Motive," *Atlantic Monthly,* November 2002, 34.

For example, several years ago, the Arkansas Livestock and Poultry Commission filed suit against a livestock sales barn for failure to meet state regulations of an infectious livestock disease called brucellosis. The senator from that district placed language to weaken those regulations on the bill to fund that commission, which prompted the commissioner to resign.[16] The commissioner had taken the funding cut as a signal that his authority was being undermined, so he quit. That kind of scattershot approach—helping a particular constituent at the expense of the public good—is by its nature inequitable. The point of bureaucratic norms is to make sure that regulations and laws are applied fairly across the board.

The real problem comes when legislators make decisions based on anecdotes and the personal accounts of people they meet instead of on objective data and evidence. Undoubtedly, it is important for legislators to hear about the real-world experiences of their constituents. Since they cannot meet with everybody, however, they need to rely on reports and studies to get a complete picture. They otherwise might be swayed too greatly by personal interactions. The danger of the increased need for politicians to raise significant finance treasuries is not so much that their votes can be bought, but that they are much more likely to meet with people or interest groups who give them campaign contributions. Campaign donors often give money simply so that they can have access to a legislator when they hand over the check. That means that people who do not or cannot give money may not get heard.

Unfortunately, oversight is pretty far from the minds of most legislators. Staff aides regularly perform audits and evaluations, but legislatures only make sporadic use of them. Most oversight comes in a less systematic way, through budget reviews and committee hearings. In states that impose limits on the number of terms that legislators can serve, there is even less opportunity to perform oversight. Members have less time to become expert in a particular area and so they often rely more heavily on expert testimony from the very executive branch that they are meant to oversee.

Organization and Operation of Legislatures

The U.S. system of representative democracy was designed to be messy. One recent book argued that the institutions of democracy should be more popular because they work pretty well, but conceded, "The American political system was not designed for people to understand." [17] Legislatures were created because, even in colonial days, this country was too large and its problems too complex to be addressed by its vast numbers of individual citizens. We elect legislatures in our republican form of government to argue out our problems in a single time and space in sessions at the capitol. The ranks of the legislature have become far more diverse over the last thirty years. Although the average state legislator is still a white male, there are twice as many African Americans and nearly six times as many women serving in legislatures today than there were in 1970. Also over the past thirty years or so, legislatures have become better equipped to do their job by hiring better staff and receiving more professional training. None of these changes, however, have made state legislatures any more popular with the public.

Bicameralism

Legislatures are not, of course, a random group of people hanging around a house and picking a movie to watch. Every state has a constitution that describes a body that can pass state laws. In every case but Nebraska, which has a unicameral, or one-house legislature, legislatures are bicameral, or divided into two houses, pretty much like the U.S. Congress. As mentioned

TABLE 6-2

Ranking of States by Total Number of State Legislators, 2004

Ranking	State	Total Members	Senate Members	House Members
1	New Hampshire	424	24	400
2	Pennsylvania	253	50	203
3	Georgia	236	56	180
4	New York	212	62	150
5	Minnesota	201	67	134
6	Massachusetts	200	40	160
7	Missouri	197	34	163
8	Maryland	188	47	141
9	Connecticut	187	36	151
10	Maine	186	35	151
11	Texas	181	31	150
12	Vermont	180	30	150
13	Illinois	177	59	118
14	Mississippi	174	52	122
15	North Carolina	170	50	120
15	South Carolina	170	46	124
17	Kansas	165	40	125
18	Florida	160	40	120
19	Indiana	150	50	100
19	Iowa	150	50	100
19	Montana	150	50	100
22	Oklahoma	149	48	101
23	Michigan	148	38	110
24	Washington	147	49	98
25	Louisiana	144	39	105
26	North Dakota	141	47	94
27	Alabama	140	35	105
27	Virginia	140	40	100
29	Kentucky	138	38	100
30	Arkansas	135	35	100
31	West Virginia	134	34	100

TABLE 6-2 *(continued)*

Ranking	State	Total Members	Senate Members	House Members
32	Ohio	132	33	99
32	Tennessee	132	33	99
32	Wisconsin	132	33	99
35	California	120	40	80
35	New Jersey	120	40	80
37	Rhode Island	113	38	75
38	New Mexico	112	42	70
39	Idaho	105	23	70
39	South Dakota	105	35	70
41	Utah	104	29	75
42	Colorado	100	35	65
43	Arizona	90	30	60
43	Oregon	90	30	60
43	Wyoming	90	30	60
46	Hawaii	76	25	51
47	Nevada	63	21	42
48	Delaware	62	21	41
49	Alaska	60	20	40
50	Nebraska	49	49	n/a

Source: Adapted from National Conference of State Legislatures. www.ncsl.org/programs/legman/about/numoflegis.htm (accessed April 15, 2004).

earlier in this chapter, one chamber is normally called either the House of Representatives or General Assembly and the other is called the Senate. The Tenth Amendment of the U.S. Constitution reserves all powers not given to the federal government for the states, and state legislatures can write any state law that does not interfere with federal laws.

The House, or Assembly, is considered more of a "people's house," with its members representing fewer people for shorter terms than their colleagues in the Senate. The House always has more members, known as state representatives, than the Senate. There are 163 representatives in the Missouri General Assembly, for example, but only 34 senators. There are some exceptions, but often it is the case that senators serve four-year terms, while House members have to be reelected every two years. The two chambers operate independently, with separate leaders, committees, and agendas, although both chambers have to pass the same version of a bill before it can be sent to the governor to be signed into law or vetoed. Nebraska, with its unicameral legislature, is the one exception.

Legislative Leadership

Most legislatures have essentially the same leadership structure, at least for their top positions. Before the beginning of a session, each House votes in its Speaker. This is generally someone picked beforehand by a **caucus**, or meeting, of members of the majority party. The majority leader and the minority leader rank just below the Speaker of the House. "Majority" and "minority" refer to the respective strength of the major parties. Either the Democratic or Republican party may hold the majority of seats in a chamber. Less than 1 percent of all state legislators are independent or members of so-called third parties. In the Senate, the top leader is known as the president, president pro tem, or the majority leader.

Certain aspects of the leadership positions remain constant across all the states. For example, a Speaker will typically preside over daily sessions of the House or Assembly, refer bills to the appropriate committees, and sign legislation as it makes its way over to the Senate or governor's desk. Leaders appoint committee chairs—in some states, all the members of committees—change committee jurisdictions, and offer staff or legislative help to rank-and-file members. They also often help with campaigns, including financial help.

The amount of power invested in the office of Speaker or Senate president does vary by state, however. In the Texas Senate, leadership powers are invested only in the office of lieutenant governor. Lieutenant governors do not normally possess much formal power, but in Texas, they appoint committees and committee chairs in the thirty-one-member body and decide which bills are considered and when. In some older legislatures, such as New Jersey and Massachusetts, the Senate president performs all of those functions, presides over debates, counts votes, and ensures member attendance. In California, those powers rest with the Senate president pro tem. But regardless of how the formal duties are divided up, usually there is one individual who emerges as holding the most power and speaking for the chamber in negotiating with the other chamber and the governor.

Tim Ford has been the Speaker of the Mississippi House since 1988. Mike Miller started his run as president of the Maryland Senate back in 1987. Often when one party has been in command of a legislature for a long time, but the voters are ready for a change, voters will signal their desires by unseating a top leader. This happened in the 2002 elections, when the Speakers in the Georgia and Maryland Houses lost their seats.

With the exception of Nebraska, where parties are actually banned in the nonpartisan unicameral legislature, legislatures are divided along party lines. Not only does the majority party get to pick the top leader, it gets to fill nearly all of the important committee chairs as well. A party majority is worth much more than the comfort of knowing that your fellow Democrats or Republicans will help you outvote the opposition on most bills. To hold

CAUCUS

A closed meeting of members of a political party.

MAP 6-1 Partisan Control of State Government, 1954

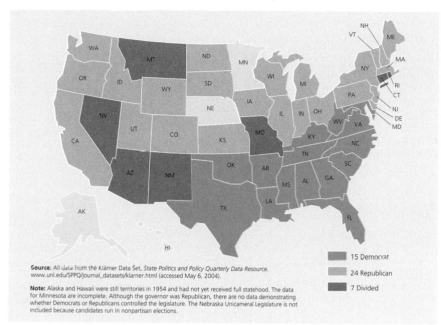

Source: All data from the Klarner Data Set, *State Politics and Policy Quarterly Data Resource*. www.unl.edu/SPPQ/journal_datasets/klarner.html (accessed May 6, 2004).

Note: Alaska and Hawaii were still territories in 1954 and had not yet received full statehood. The data for Minnesota are incomplete. Although the governor was Republican, there are no data demonstrating whether Democrats or Republicans controlled the legislature. The Nebraska Unicameral Legislature is not included because candidates run in nonpartisan elections.

Legend:
- 15 Democrat
- 24 Republican
- 7 Divided

MAP 6-2 Partisan Control of State Government, 2000

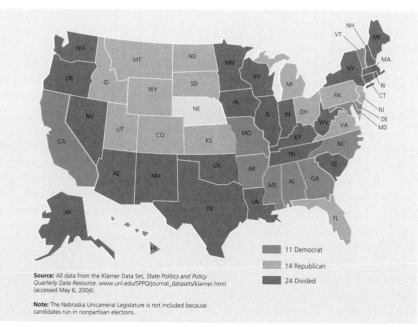

Source: All data from the Klarner Data Set, *State Politics and Policy Quarterly Data Resource*. www.unl.edu/SPPQ/journal_datasets/klarner.html (accessed May 6, 2004).

Note: The Nebraska Unicameral Legislature is not included because candidates run in nonpartisan elections.

Legend:
- 11 Democrat
- 14 Republican
- 24 Divided

the leadership and chair positions means that the majority party gets to set the agenda—deciding which bills will be heard for a vote. Democrats from the 1950s into the early 1990s held a two-to-one edge in number of legislative seats and controlled many more chambers than the GOP. In recent years, however, Republicans have pulled into near-ties both in terms of raw numbers of legislators and in how many chambers they control. At the end of World War II, all but seven of the forty-eight states had united governments, meaning one party controlled the governorship and both legislative chambers. By 1986, only twenty-one of fifty states had united governments.[18] The increasingly competitive nature of legislative politics has meant that every election cycle since 1984 has resulted in at least one tied chamber somewhere.[19]

Committees

Regardless of party control, committees are where most legislative work gets done. Legislators are divided into committees—usually about fifteen or twenty per chamber—that grapple with particular issues, such as education, transportation, or taxes. Thousands of bills are introduced annually in each legislature. Most of these bills never reach the "floor" where the full House or Senate meets. Basically, they never make it past the committee stage in order to be debated or voted upon by the House or Senate as a whole. Instead, they are sent to the appropriate committee, where they may be debated and amended, but usually they die without a hearing. Just as the Senate president, House Speaker or other leader sets the agenda for floor action on bills, so the committee chair decides which bills are going to be heard and receive priority treatment at the committee level.

Members try to serve on the committees where they will have the most influence. The most prestigious committees are the budget committees that set tax and spending levels. Other committees debate policy, but unless funding is provided to pay for those policies, they do not matter very much. Seats on a finance or appropriations committee are highly sought after, but members will also "request appointment to committees, which will give them the most visibility and interest in their districts."[20] Thus, senators from rural districts may want to serve on an agriculture committee. Representatives who previously served on city councils may want seats on the local government committee. Any member can introduce legislation on any topic, but members of the education committee, for example, are more likely to introduce and influence bills that affect schools. When an education bill is being debated in the full House or Senate, other members, who have other specialties, will turn to members of the education committee for guidance about what a bill would do and how they should vote. The same holds true for other issues such as transportation and health care.

Rank-and-File Members

Not every legislator, of course, can be a leader. The majority of legislators—those who provided leaders with their votes—are known as **rank-and-file members** of the legislature. No legislator can be fully versed on the details of each of the dozens of bills that confront them every day during a session. They turn to many sources for information on how to vote. There is a classic notion, posited by political philosopher and statesman Edmund Burke, that divides legislators into **delegates**, who vote according to the wishes of their districts, and **trustees**, who vote according to their own consciences.[21] Given the proliferation of legislation, however, members never hear from a single constituent on probably 90 percent of the bills they must consider. Instead, they rely for guidance on staff, other legislators, interest groups and lobbyists, executive branch officials, foundations, think tanks, and other sources.

The fact that legislators cannot rely solely on their own judgment to vote is the source of many people's sense that legislators' votes can be bought—or at least rented. This is ironic, considering that political scientists note that most of the time most legislators are extremely attentive to their districts and vote according to their sense of their desires. Their primary goal, after all, is to win reelection. In addition, most states have made it tougher for lobbyists to get lawmakers' attention. It is difficult under the new ethics rules for a lobbyist to spring for a legislator's cup of coffee, much less treat for lunch. In Kentucky, for example, there are fewer of the nightly receptions that once kept Frankfort well fed, and lobbyists are prohibited from making any personal contributions to candidates for the legislature. "A lot of the principal lobbyists are still here, so folks have had to learn to adapt," says Bobby Sherman, head of the Kentucky legislature's nonpartisan research staff. "It's more work for them. They have to build relationships in a different way, and information delivery is much more important."[22]

All of this is necessary because, as with most things, times have changed. It used to be that rank-and-file members voted pretty much the way they were instructed by their party leaders. In Connecticut, the legislature of the early 1960s was an assemblage of party hacks—members beholden to the party chair for patronage. This meant that most of the legislature's important decisions were made in small meetings to which the public—and even most rank-and-file members—were not invited.

Examples still exist of members caving in to party or leadership pressure. In his book *Experiencing Politics*, former state representative John McDonough, a Democrat, recounts one afternoon in the fall of 1995 when he was sitting on the floor of the Massachusetts House of Representatives. The chamber was preparing to vote on a huge tax break for Raytheon, a locally based defense contractor. McDonough thought the tax break was a terrible idea. He considered it a form of corporate blackmail. So he pushed the little

RANK-AND-FILE MEMBERS
Legislators who do not hold leadership positions or senior committee posts.

DELEGATES
Legislators who primarily see their role as voting according to their constituents' beliefs as they understand them.

TRUSTEES
Legislators who believe they were elected to exercise their own judgment and to approach issues accordingly.

red button on his desk and voted against it. Then the majority whip—the party's head vote-counter—came over to see him. "The Speaker wants a green [light] from you on this," the whip said. That did not make any sense to McDonough. The tax break was passing easily. His vote was not needed. The whip did not answer his question. "He just does," she said. So, McDonough tells us, he caved. A few months down the road, he had his own favorite bill coming up, and he wanted the Speaker's help. He did not want to take any chances. He walked right back to his desk and switched his vote. It was a classic example of trading votes. "Was my switch," he asks, "an example of naked, opportunistic self-interest or of a hard trade-off necessary to achieve a higher good? Anyone can characterize my action either way. The most honest answer is that both perspectives contain some degree of truth." [23]

Former Oregon House Speaker and current mayor of Portland, Oregon, Vera Katz has a reputation as a legislator who relies on her people skills even more than the authority of her office to get things done. While some legislative leaders get things done by playing political hardball, Katz gets things done by getting others to play nice.

Such practical decisions are made all the time. Nevertheless, leaders today carry much less weight with members than they did even a generation ago. Leaders these days are no stronger than members want them to be; they often lead by listening. Consider two examples from about a decade ago. Connecticut House Speaker Irving Stolberg was considered a brilliant legislator, but he was heavy handed as a leader. When he met with his lieutenants, it was not to consult them on strategy but rather to tell them what the strategy would be. Many of the Democrats under him thought he abused his power, so they coupled their votes in 1989 with House Republicans and drove him out.[24]

Compare this to a story from across the country the next year. In May 1990, months of work on a workers' compensation reform package threatened to go to waste during a meeting in the office of Oregon House Speaker Vera Katz. Bob Shiprack, chair of the labor committee, grew impatient as the conversation got stuck on the topic of how chiropractors would be treated under the law, so he stormed out. Katz, rather than ordering him to get back to work, ran after him and mothered him, soothed him, and sympathized with his exhaustion. "It disarmed me," Shiprack said. "Vera loves to disarm." Katz's tactic worked and the workers' compensation package went though.[25]

Leaders cannot bully their way through the way they did a generation ago for two reasons. One is that members do not rely as extensively on

Governing States and Localities

party leaders any longer to manage or fund their campaigns. Legislative leaders still control massive amounts of money. The Senate president in Maine, for example, has raised $250,000 in each of the last two election cycles, in a state where legislative races can still be won with a few thousand dollars. But today's rank-and-file member has greater access to expert advice for hire and separate sources of money, whether from political action committees (PACs) run by industries or labor unions or elsewhere.

The other factor we have already touched upon—members do not have to rely on leaders as much as they once did for information about bills or for help writing legislation. The proliferation of lobbyists and the **professionalization** of legislatures have meant that members have their own resources to draw upon.[26] We will talk more about what it means for a legislature to become more professional in the next section of this chapter.

PROFESSIONALIZATION

The process of making legislators' positions full-time jobs.

Apportionment

One more issue that profoundly affects all legislators is **apportionment**. Following the U.S. census, which occurs every ten years, each state draws new lines for its legislative districts. In states with more than one member of congress, congressional districts are redrawn as well. The **redistricting** process is the most naked exercise of political power in the states. The incumbent party will do everything it can to preserve its hold or, preferably, increase its numbers. Each party will seek to draw the maximum number of districts possible that are likely to elect members of its own party. With the increase in the number of divided governments, though, that has become a trickier task to pull off. The two major parties will fight each other as best they can to make certain that the other side does not gain the upper hand. "Just like there are no atheists in foxholes, there are no nonpartisans in redistricting," says Paul Green, director of the School of Policy Studies at Rockefeller University in Chicago. "You use whatever leverage you can."[27]

We've already discussed how Democrats control New York State's General Assembly and Republicans hold the reins in the Senate. Both sides must like things that way, because they continually draw district maps to preserve that status quo. But New York has been losing population—relative to other states—for decades. This translates into a lost congressional seat or two every ten years. In 2001 the legislature came up with a map that sliced and diced counties and towns in an effort to create new districts that balanced competing political interests in the state. Monroe County, which includes Rochester, was home to 735,000 residents following the 2000 census, more than enough to earn its own congressional seat. Instead, the county was cut into four different congressional districts, including one that stretches one hundred miles in a thin strip along the Niagara River and the Lake Ontario shore to link parts of Buffalo and Rochester and their Democratic precincts.

APPORTIONMENT

The allotting of districts according to population shifts. The number of congressional districts a state has may be reapportioned every ten years.

REDISTRICTING

The drawing of new boundaries for congressional and state legislative districts, usually following a decennial census.

GERRYMANDERS

Districts clearly drawn with the intent of pressing partisan advantage at the expense of other considerations.

MALAPPORTIONMENT

A situation in which the principle of equal representation is violated.

Political maps that link disparate communities or have odd shapes that resemble earmuffs or moose antlers are known as **gerrymanders,** after Elbridge Gerry, an early nineteenth-century governor of Massachusetts. **Malapportionment** occurs when districts violate the principle of equal representation. In the past, some state legislative districts could have many times the number of constituents as other districts. Votes in the smaller districts, in effect, counted for more. Relatively few people in, say, a sparsely populated rural district would have the same amount of representative clout in the legislature as an urban district with many times the rural area's population.

Legislatures draw the maps in most states, but there are exceptions. Since the 1980s, Iowa's political maps have been created by the nonpartisan Legislative Services Agency. The agency instructs its computers to draw one hundred House districts and fifty Senate districts according to rules that keep population as equal as possible, avoid splitting counties, and keep the districts compact. In contrast to legislature-drawn maps, the agency does not consider party registration, voting patterns, or the political territory of incumbents. Largely as a result, partisan control of the Iowa legislature flips every ten years. Other states use other commission models. In New Jersey, a bipartisan commission composed of six Democrats and six Republicans is charged with the task of coming up with a plan that can command a majority. If it cannot—which is typical—the chief justice of the state supreme court appoints a thirteenth member to the committee as a tiebreaker. In 2001, the new maps landed the Democrats a majority, and they were able to retake control of the General Assembly for the first time in a decade and also pulled into a tie in the Senate.

Partisanship is the dominating concern of redistricting, but it is not the only one. Issues of representation also play a big part. African Americans are overwhelmingly Democratic, but some blacks joined with Republicans following the 1980 and 1990 censuses to create black majority districts, especially in the South. For African Americans, their deal with the GOP offered the advantage of creating districts in which blacks were likely to be elected. It wasn't that they *joined* the Republican Party, they simply allied themselves with the GOP to draw **majority-minority districts,** which guaranteed the election of more African Americans but also made neighboring districts more likely to elect Republicans. An additional benefit for Republicans was that concentrating African American voters into a relatively few districts weakened Democratic chances in neighboring districts. Following the Voting Rights Act of 1982, the federal Justice Department encouraged state legislators to create majority-minority districts whenever possible, until a series of U.S. Supreme Court decisions during the 1990s put an end to the practice. In a confusing and often contradictory series of rulings, the Court ruled that race could not be the "predominant" factor in redistricting.[28]

In most state legislatures, the major goal of redistricting following the 2000 census seemed to be protecting incumbents. Members of the two major parties colluded to draw few competitive districts, preferring to know

MAJORITY-MINORITY DISTRICTS

Districts in which a minority group, such as African Americans or Latinos, make up a majority of the population or electorate.

they would run in "safe" Republican-leaning or Democratic-leaning districts. Drawing districts that were politically safe for current officeholders necessarily meant creating fewer new districts that were likely to elect minorities. That was true even for Hispanics, who were the fastest-growing minority group in the United States during the 1990s. Latinos accounted for 60 percent of the population growth in Texas and 80 percent of the growth in California.[29] Nevertheless, the California legislature and the Texas judicial panel that drew that state's maps did not go out of their way to draw new Hispanic-majority districts. Hispanics held only about two hundred state legislative seats in 2001, and their number did not rise appreciably in the 2002 elections.

As you have seen, incumbents usually get their job security, but the results for everyone else are pretty mixed. In part because of the uncertainty caused by the Supreme Court's decisions, black legislators followed the 2000 census by devoting more energy to preserving the districts they had won than to creating new African American–dominated districts. Hispanics, for their part, did not follow the "strange bedfellow" coalition strategy blacks had pursued with Republicans and chose instead to push for more Hispanic-majority districts through a series of mostly unsuccessful lawsuits that challenged the new political maps.

THE GERRY-MANDER. (Boston, 1811.)

One of the most powerful beasts in politics is the gerrymander. Gerrymanders result when political districts are drawn to achieve partisan ends rather than to create meaningful units of representation. Most often gerrymanders are carried out by the party in power as a way to improve their chances of continued electoral success.

State Legislators

If you were to make a composite drawing of the average state legislator, he—and it would be a he—would be white and in his forties or fifties. He would have had at least some college education, an income topping $50,000, describe himself as moderate or conservative, and would have lived in the community he is representing for at least ten years.[30] There are many, many exceptions to all of the aspects of this composite. The type of person who runs for state legislative office has changed a good deal over the past thirty years—there are far more women and African Americans in office and fewer lawyers—but nonetheless, the type of middle-to-upper-middle-class American male described above still predominates.

The nation's 7,400 state legislators come from all manner of backgrounds, particularly in the states where the House and Senate meet only for part of the year. In the full-time legislatures, such as California and New Jersey, the legislators tend, not surprisingly, to be career politicians who have served in local or other elected office or perhaps as members of a legislative staff. In part-time legislatures, like Arkansas and Indiana, members come from many different walks of life, devoting perhaps one third of their working hours to politics while earning their living through some other means.

Professional Background

Some employers encourage the political hopes of their employees because they know legislative service can be good for business. This holds true most obviously for professions most directly affected by state lawmaking, such as big business. Buddy Dyer kept up his law practice while serving in the Florida Senate and in 2002 had to respond to complaints that his bills would have protected industrial company clients from fines and lawsuits. His defense? "Probably not a bill that goes through the Legislature" that does not affect one of his firm's clients.[31]

Consider public education. Teachers' unions are usually among the most effective lobbying groups in any state, but schools do not necessarily have to rely on outsiders to influence the legislature. Teachers themselves are often members of legislatures, and employees of other institutions of higher learning also may serve. Harold Moberly is chair of the Kentucky House Appropriations Committee, which helps determine spending levels for all state agencies, but he also wears another hat as director of student judicial affairs for Eastern Kentucky University. His dual role gives his home campus a big say in legislative arguments about higher education funding. Moberly is just one of a half-dozen legislators in the state who work for public colleges and universities.[32] In Maine, state law requires that teachers be granted leave if they want to run for office. Maine's legislature meets for only one-half of the year, every other year. But even that chunk of time is enough to play havoc with a person's work schedule, and there's a good deal of concern in the state that retirees are coming to dominate the legislative chamber.

The reality is that retired persons account for only about 15 percent of state legislators nationwide. About the same number of legislators are lawyers—a big decline from past decades. In New York, 60 percent of the Assembly and 70 percent of the Senate used to be made up of lawyers.[33] Nowadays, the dominant group in legislatures nationwide are people with business backgrounds. They make up about 30 percent of today's legislators. The remaining half or so come from education, health care, real estate, insurance, or agriculture.

Demographic Diversity

The number of women legislators has risen dramatically since the "second wave" feminist era of the late 1960s and early 1970s, but their numbers are still far from reflecting the female share of the overall population. In 1970, women held just 4 percent of all state legislative seats.[34] Their numbers doubled quickly, to 8 percent of all legislators by 1975, and they climbed to 18 percent by 1991. But after reaching 21 percent by 1997, the total number of women legislators has remained pretty steady.[35] Only five states—Arizona, Kansas, New Mexico, Oregon, and Washington—could brag in 2001 that a third or more of their legislators were women.[36]

The number of women entering the legislatures may not be growing exponentially, but the type of women holding House and Senate offices has changed. In the old days of the 1970s—about a decade before most readers of this book were born—most women running for office came to politics later in life than men. They had not been tapped to run by party professionals or other "queenmakers." Instead, they jump-started their own careers, drawn into the policy realm out of concerns about their children's schools or their local communities. Men may know from the time they are in school that they want to run for office, says Barbara Lee, who runs a foundation dedicated to helping women run for office, but women often find out later in life that it is important to enter the game because of their specific concerns and experiences.[37] That dynamic has changed to some extent. Women now enter politics at ages comparable to men. But they still tend to care about a set of issues—education, health care, and the environment—that are noticeably different from the top priorities of men—taxes and budgets.

Back in the 1970s, when the first relatively large numbers of women legislators entered the capitols, they tended to be less politically ambitious and less likely to enter the ranks of legislative leaders than men. They devoted more attention to constituent service matters and tended to serve on education, health, and welfare committees. They also tended to have less education and come from jobs that were not as good as those held by their male counterparts. During the 1980s, the average socioeconomic status of women legislators had improved, and they were serving on a broader range of committees, but they were mostly still focused on issues of women, family, and children. By the 1990s, women legislators held about 15 percent of all legislative leadership positions but were still unlikely to serve on tax committees.[38] Their party backgrounds had become more varied, but they were still more conservative—although they still were more liberal than men—and they were also significantly more likely to initiate legislation than their male colleagues.[39] Women are also more likely than men to have success in getting their priority bills through the legislative process.[40]

Women, however, do not alter the fundamental political dynamics in legislatures, perhaps because they remain a fairly tiny minority in most states. For example, women legislators, by and large, favor reproductive rights, but they do not have an especially powerful impact on a given state's policy regarding this issue. Whether a state devotes much funding toward abortion programs or places a number of restrictions on such programs, including requiring parental notification, depends more on whether the state's overall political culture is liberal or conservative than on whether women make up a large minority of legislative caucuses.[41]

Still, women legislators do tend to bring up issues and concerns that are not going to be raised by an all-male legislature. This fact is even more true

TABLE 6-3

Ranking of States by Percentage of Legislators Who Are Women, 2004

Ranking	State	Total Number of Legislative Seats	Total Number of Women State Legislators	Percentage of Total Seats
1	Washington	147	54	36.7%
2	Colorado	100	34	34.0%
3	Maryland	188	63	33.5%
4	Vermont	180	56	31.1%
5	California	120	36	30.0%
5	Oregon	90	27	30.0%
7	New Mexico	112	33	29.5%
8	Connecticut	187	55	29.4%
9	Delaware	62	18	29.0%
10	Nevada	63	18	28.6%
11	Kansas	165	46	27.9%
12	Illinois	177	49	27.7%
13	Hawaii	76	21	27.6%
14	Minnesota	201	55	27.4%
14	New Hampshire	424	116	27.4%
16	Wisconsin	132	36	27.3%
17	Maine	186	50	26.9%
18	Arizona	90	25	26.7%
18	Idaho	105	28	26.7%
20	Massachusetts	200	51	25.5%
21	Florida	160	40	25.0%
22	Montana	150	37	24.7%
23	Michigan	148	35	23.6%
24	New York	212	47	22.2%
25	Utah	104	23	22.1%
26	Georgia	236	51	21.6%
27	Missouri	197	42	21.3%
28	Iowa	150	31	20.7%
29	North Carolina	170	35	20.6%
30	Ohio	132	27	20.5%

TABLE 6-3 *(continued)*

Ranking	State	Total Number of Legislative Seats	Total Number of Women State Legislators	Percentage of Total Seats
31	Rhode Island	113	23	20.4%
32	Alaska	60	12	20.0%
33	Texas	181	35	19.3%
34	West Virginia	134	25	18.7%
35	Nebraska	49	9	18.4%
36	Indiana	150	27	18.0%
37	Wyoming	90	16	17.8%
38	Tennessee	132	23	17.4%
39	Louisiana	144	24	16.7%
40	Arkansas	135	22	16.3%
40	North Dakota	141	23	16.3%
42	South Dakota	105	17	16.2%
43	New Jersey	120	19	15.8%
44	Virginia	140	20	14.3%
45	Pennsylvania	253	35	13.8%
46	Oklahoma	149	19	12.8%
47	Mississippi	174	22	12.6%
48	Kentucky	138	15	10.9%
49	Alabama	140	14	10.0%
50	South Carolina	170	16	9.4%
	Total	7,382	1,655	22.4%

Source: Adapted from Center for American Women and Politics (CAWP). www.cawp.rutgers.edu/Facts/Officeholders/stleg.pdf (accessed April 15, 2004).

of issues of concern to minorities. African Americans have made gains similar to women in legislatures over the past thirty-five years, growing from a microscopic minority to a larger minority still not reflective of their overall share of the population. Their numbers have doubled to about 595—less than 10 percent of all the legislators nationwide.

Although it is both dangerous and wrong to generalize about any group, the interests of African Americans as a whole have long been fairly stable and predictable. "On questions of public policy, ideology, and candidate choice," writes Kerry L. Haynie in his recent book on black state legislators, "African Americans have been the most cohesive and consistent policy subgroup in United States politics."[42] The timing of the increase in numbers of

TABLE 6-4

Ranking of States by Percentage of Legislators Who Are African American, 2003

Ranking	State	Total Number of Legislative Seats	Total Number of African American State Legislators	Percentage of Total Seats
1	Mississippi	174	45	26%
2	Alabama	140	35	25%
3	Louisiana	144	31	22%
3	Maryland	188	42	22%
5	Georgia	236	49	21%
6	South Carolina	170	32	19%
7	Illinois	177	28	16%
8	Florida	160	23	14%
8	Michigan	148	20	14%
8	New York	212	30	14%
8	North Carolina	170	24	14%
8	Ohio	132	18	14%
8	Tennessee	132	18	14%
14	New Jersey	120	16	13%
15	Arkansas	135	15	11%
15	Nevada	63	7	11%
15	Virginia	140	15	11%
18	Missouri	197	17	9%
19	Texas	181	15	8%
20	Connecticut	187	13	7%
20	Indiana	150	11	7%
20	Pennsylvania	253	18	7%
23	Wisconsin	132	8	6%
24	California	120	6	5%
24	Delaware	62	3	5%
26	Colorado	100	4	4%
26	Kansas	165	7	4%
26	Kentucky	138	6	4%
26	Rhode Island	113	4	4%
30	Massachusetts	200	6	3%

TABLE 6-4 *(continued)*

Ranking	State	Total Number of Legislative Seats	Total Number of African American State Legislators	Percentage of Total Seats
30	Oklahoma	149	5	3%
30	Oregon	90	3	3%
33	Alaska	60	1	2%
33	Iowa	150	3	2%
33	Nebraska	49	1	2%
33	New Mexico	112	2	2%
33	Utah	104	2	2%
33	Washington	147	3	2%
39	Arizona	90	1	1%
39	Hawaii	76	1	1%
39	Minnesota	201	2	1%
39	New Hampshire	424	4	1%
39	Vermont	180	1	1%
44	Idaho	105	0	0%
44	Maine	186	0	0%
44	Montana	150	0	0%
44	North Dakota	141	0	0%
44	South Dakota	105	0	0%
44	West Virginia	134	0	0%
44	Wyoming	90	0	0%
	Total	7,382	595	8.1%

Source: National Conference of State Legislatures. www.ncsl.org/programs/legman/about/afrAmer.htm (accessed April 15, 2004).

black state legislators was fortunate. Since the 1970s, decisions about several issues of importance to African Americans, including Medicaid, student aid, school lunch, community development, welfare, and environmental protection, have devolved from the federal level to the states.[43] In his study of how representatives in Arkansas, Illinois, Mississippi, New Jersey, and North Carolina acted in three different sessions, Haynie found that 55 percent to 82 percent of African American legislators introduced bills that addressed issues of particular interest to blacks. White legislators, by contrast, almost never introduced such legislation. In only one of the three years that Haynie studied (1969, 1979, and 1989) did more than a quarter of nonblack legislators introduce even one bill of interest to blacks.[44] It may

TABLE 6-5

Ranking of States by Percentage of Legislators Who Are Latino, 2003

Ranking	State	Total Number of Legislative Seats	Total Latino State Legislators	Percentage of Total Seats
1	New Mexico	112	44	39%
2	California	120	27	23%
3	Texas	181	37	20%
4	Arizona	90	14	16%
5	Colorado	100	10	10%
6	Florida	160	14	9%
7	New York	212	15	7%
8	Illinois	177	10	6%
8	New Jersey	120	7	6%
10	Connecticut	187	5	3%
11	Delaware	62	1	2%
11	Kansas	165	3	2%
11	Maryland	188	4	2%
11	Massachusetts	200	4	2%
11	Nebraska	49	1	2%
11	Nevada	63	1	2%
11	Rhode Island	113	2	2%
18	Georgia	236	3	1%
18	Idaho	105	1	1%
18	Indiana	150	1	1%
18	Michigan	148	1	1%
18	North Carolina	170	2	1%
18	Oregon	90	1	1%
18	Utah	104	1	1%
18	Washington	147	1	1%
18	Wisconsin	132	1	1%
18	Wyoming	90	1	1%
28	Alabama	140	0	0%
28	Alaska	60	0	0%
28	Arkansas	135	0	0%

TABLE 6-5 *(continued)*

Ranking	State	Total Number of Legislative Seats	Total Latino State Legislators	Percentage of Total Seats
28	Hawaii	76	0	0%
28	Iowa	150	0	0%
28	Kentucky	138	0	0%
28	Louisiana	144	0	0%
28	Maine	186	0	0%
28	Minnesota	201	1	0%
28	Mississippi	174	0	0%
28	Missouri	197	0	0%
28	Montana	150	0	0%
28	New Hampshire	424	1	0%
28	North Dakota	141	0	0%
28	Ohio	132	0	0%
28	Oklahoma	149	0	0%
28	Pennsylvania	253	1	0%
28	South Carolina	170	0	0%
28	South Dakota	105	0	0%
28	Tennessee	132	0	0%
28	Vermont	180	0	0%
28	Virginia	140	0	0%
28	West Virginia	134	0	0%
	Totals	7,382	215	3.20%

Source: National Conference of State Legislatures. www.ncsl.org/programs/legman/about/Latino.htm (accessed April 15, 2004).

sound obvious, but black issues are much more likely to be addressed when African Americans are serving in state legislatures.

More African American legislators does not mean changes in voting trends, however. Voting remains polarized along racial lines. Whites will support African American incumbents but are often reluctant to vote for black newcomers. The main reason for the growth in the number of black legislators, therefore, has been the creation of majority-black districts.[45]

Professional vs. Citizen Legislators

Legislatures, which were strictly white male playgrounds in the past, have become more inclusive of women and minorities and more attentive to their concerns. But the biggest changes in legislatures over the past thirty-five years have come in the very ways that they do business. Where once legislatures were sleepy backwaters in which not much got done—and even less got done ethically—now many chambers are highly professional operations with resources that rival the U.S. Congress. Most legislatures used to meet for a short time every other year. These days all but a handful meet every year and, in a few cases, nearly year-round. "No single factor has a greater effect on the legislative environment than the constitutional restriction on length of session," two leading legislative scholars wrote long ago.[46]

The most pronounced differences among states are between "professional" legislatures that meet full-time, pay members a high salary, and employ large numbers of staff, and "amateur," or "citizen," legislatures that meet part-time, have members who usually hold other jobs, and have smaller staffs. To some extent, all legislatures have become more professional. Even "amateur" legislators devote a third of their time to legislative work. In the early 1940s, only four states—New Jersey, New York, Rhode Island, and South Carolina—met in annual sessions, but that number has climbed continuously.[47] Today, only five states do not meet in regular annual sessions. Expenditures per legislator have increased in nearly every state above the rate of inflation, and today, the most professional legislatures have resources that rival Congress.[48]

There are many variations among states as to how professional their legislatures are, which profoundly affects their effectiveness, how much institutional strength they have compared to governors, and how popular they are with the public. Some disagreement still exists about whether professional legislators really do a better job than their citizen-legislator cousins. Typically, however, the more professional a legislature is, the more effective it is at the essential jobs of drafting and passing laws and overseeing the governor and the executive branch. Each of the more populous states, except Texas, has a highly professional legislature. These professional legislatures are able to provide more resources to their chambers. This allows these chambers to keep up with the wider variety of interests that larger states much deal with compared to most of their smaller neighbors. Legislatures in some states, such as Massachusetts and California, meet essentially year-round, while a part-time legislature like the one in Arkansas meets for only ninety days only in odd-numbered years.

Larger states have the money to invest in the full-time legislatures that are necessary to keep on top of issues facing their more complicated and developed economies and diverse populations. The reason that Texas, the second-largest state, has a part-time legislature is that state's general dislike or distrust for government in general. Texas is one of only four states that does not impose an income tax, so a legislature that meets only part-time every other year is in keeping with its general low-tax, low-service point of view. Other states have a tradition of embracing more expansive government. States with strong progressive traditions, such as Minnesota and Wisconsin, have long utilized full-time, professional legislators with substantial staffs at their command. The Northeastern states have maintained their traditional interest in hands-on government, which grew out of their old practices of self-government, including town hall meetings and the like. These states boast some of the largest legislatures. The New Hampshire House is the most extreme example, with 400 members, each representing about 3,400 people. California's legislature is one of the best equipped and most professional in the country. It has to be, considering that each member of the Assembly has more than 423,000 constituents.

Some states impose severe restrictions on the meeting times of their legislatures. In Colorado, the entire legislature is known as the General Assembly, not just one chamber. The state constitution limits the House and the Senate to no more than 120 days per year. Sometimes such limits are honored mostly in the breach. The governor may insist that the legislature meets in special session to address a budget crisis or other issue that cannot wait until the next regular session. Or the legislature may simply carve out a little more time for itself, as happened in 2002 in North Carolina. House rules require that the chamber be shut down by 9 P.M., so members stopped the clock one night at 8:50, essentially "freezing time," so they could continue debate until 3:35 A.M. and finish a session that had run for months longer than expected.[49]

Just like most of us, legislators feel intensely the pressure to get their work done on time. The fact that they have deadlines—for passing budgets or for adjournment—usually keeps them focused—in much the same way that a final exam will make college students finally hit the books at term's end. Newspapers, however, routinely write stories that criticize legislatures for missing their budget deadlines. The reality is that a legislature is pretty cheap to operate—in no state does its cost top much more than one-half of 1 percent of the state budget—but elected officials know that their overtime does not play well with voters.[50] The *Orlando Sentinel*, for instance, ran a pretty typical piece in 2002 criticizing the Florida legislature for meeting in special session at a

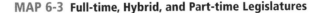

MAP 6-3 **Full-time, Hybrid, and Part-time Legislatures**

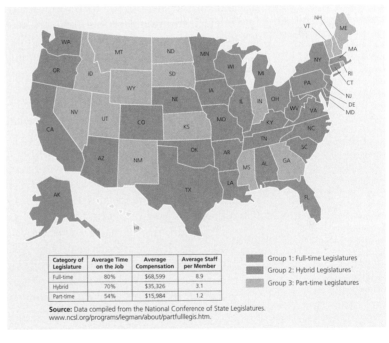

Category of Legislature	Average Time on the Job	Average Compensation	Average Staff per Member
Full-time	80%	$68,599	8.9
Hybrid	70%	$35,326	3.1
Part-time	54%	$15,984	1.2

Group 1: Full-time Legislatures
Group 2: Hybrid Legislatures
Group 3: Part-time Legislatures

Source: Data compiled from the National Conference of State Legislatures. www.ncsl.org/programs/legman/about/partfulllegis.htm.

cost of about $25,000 a day to the state. That amount, the paper said, was almost enough to pay a teacher's salary for a year.[51] Such stories are one reason why legislatures, as they get more professional and better at their jobs, remain unpopular with the public. Map 6-3 shows the breakdown of full-time, hybrid, and part-time legislatures among the states.

The Citizen's Whipping Boy: Legislators and Public Opinion

Thirty or forty years ago, legislatures were, to put it bluntly, sexist, racist, secretive, boss-ruled, malapportioned, and uninformed. Alabama's legislature was an extreme but representative case. In 1971 it ranked fiftieth out of the fifty state legislatures in independence, fiftieth in accountability, and forty-eighth in overall performance in a Ford Foundation study. Yet, just three years earlier, 65 percent of the respondents in a statewide poll had judged the institution favorably. By 1990, the legislature had freed itself of its institutional racism, secrecy, and malapportionment and was fully equipped to gather information and operate in a new, state-of-the-art legislative facility. That year it got an approval rating of 24 percent.[52]

Performance and approval ratings and other information about legislators and what they are up to is out there in the open for all to see. Legislatures are much more transparent institutions than the other branches of government and certainly are more open about what they are up to than private sector groups such as businesses or unions. This is not to say that many legislative decisions are not still made behind closed doors, but they are acted upon out in the open. Interested citizens can find out how their legislators have represented them by paging through their voting records on the Web, by reading the newsletters their representatives and senators mail to them, and, in about a third of the states, by watching the legislature in action on TV.

All of this transparency and openness, and legislatures still manage to get a bad rap. It is a curious reality of U.S. political life that state legislatures have, by and large, gotten much better at their jobs. Their membership better reflects the population as a whole now more than ever. They have reformed themselves and have become more honest, ethical, and competent in the process. Yet, to the average person, they are still out-of-control institutions that would do less harm by not meeting at all.

By now, however, it should be evident that legislatures, just like books, cannot be judged by the average person's perception of their covers. State legislatures have become more efficient and effective units of government over the past thirty years. At the federal level, Congress has punted on many of the major domestic issues of the last several years, but state legislatures have picked up those balls and run with them. Consider healthcare. Congress has not been able to come up with a prescription drug plan for seniors, but the Maine legislature did. Congress could not pass a bill to regulate health maintenance organizations (HMOs), but more than forty state legislatures did. Congress rejected President Bill Clinton's health insurance program in 1994 and barely has talked about covering the forty million-plus uninsured individuals since then. But numerous states, including Georgia, Texas, and Vermont, have tinkered with their Medicaid plans to provide health insurance to people by the tens of thousands.

Yet, for all that, legislatures are as unpopular as they have ever been. Following the terrorist attacks of September 11, 2001, polls indicated that the public's faith in government had been restored. Firefighters and cops became popular figures, but elected representatives did not bask in the same sort of glow for very long. If anything, legislators have become more unpopular than they were a generation ago. The increases in staff, in salaries, and in other professional tools that legislators have acquired in recent decades probably have made them better at their jobs. But as they have become more professional, legislatures also have become greater targets of disdain for a public that believes it has little or no use for professional or career politicians. Amateur legislatures hold a stronger appeal to deeply rooted American desires for limited government and limited governmental power.

To a large extent, the general public looks at large staffs and good salaries not as ways of ensuring that the legislature does its job in a professional manner. Instead, these increases in legislative resources are seen as yet more proof that politicians want to exploit their offices for personal gain. "The public does not want the same thing out of a legislature that you think they might want," says John Hibbing, a University of Nebraska political scientist who has written about the unpopularity of legislatures. "The public wants a legislature whose members are not in a position to feather their own nests."[53]

Legislators have done a poor job of selling the idea that what they do is important and necessary in a democracy. And the media are more concerned with dramatizing conflicts than explaining what are sometimes awfully dry policy matters; therefore, it has not helped legislators to make their case. A primary job of the media in a democracy is to report on what the government is up to, but less and less media attention is devoted to legislatures. Books about such media failings are even more tiresome, if you can believe it, than books about state and local government. But a few points are worth making here.

One such point is that ever since Watergate, the scandal that forced President Richard Nixon to resign in 1974, the press has taken an adversarial position toward government. People in government, including legislators, are not very good in the first place at getting out the good news about what they are doing or publicizing their successes. Reporters are by their nature skeptics and are good at covering scandals and mistakes. "Skepticism is not just a personality quirk of journalists," says one reporter. "It's a core value, the wellspring of all our best work."[54] The media have made boo-boo coverage practically the mainstay of government reporting. This is not true in

100 percent of the cases, of course, but the press's general attitude toward government was summed up well a few years ago by a reporter in Pennsylvania who told a public official, "Your job is to manage the public business and mine is to report when you do it wrong."[55]

Reporters may be too cynical about what legislators are up to, but a bigger problem might be that there are so few reporters watching them. An American Journalism Review survey in 2002 found that there were only 510 daily newspaper reporters covering state capitols—about one-sixth the number of journalists who cover the Super Bowl. That is an average of about ten reporters per state, but Nevada, for instance, had only five full-time statehouse reporters. The number of capitol reporters in some other states, such as Michigan, had dropped by nearly half in the previous decade or so. The numbers are even weaker for television coverage.[56]

Earlier we touched briefly upon how unusual it was that each of Minnesota's Twin Cities had a daily newspaper. Well, one effect of fewer newspapers can be fewer reporters to cover more areas. Another is intense competition for readership, and quite honestly, "sex sells." At least that is what the media argue. You may have heard this "chicken or the egg" argument. On the one hand, the media claim that people want to read about scandals and wrongdoing and not about state legislatures and policy issues. So, the media give the public what it wants. The people, on the other hand, claim that they are sick of reading about dirty politicians. They say they do not read about state legislatures and policy issues because the media seldom cover these topics. Which claim actually came first? Which is actually right? The world may never know.

Fewer reporters translate into fewer stories about what legislators are doing to earn their taxpayer-financed livings. The more populous states, such as New York and Florida, still boast a relatively sizable capitol press corps, but even in these states the legislatures lose out because their stories get lost in the clutter of other news. The South Dakota legislature, when it is in session, is a major source of news in that underpopulated state, but the Illinois General Assembly loses out to coverage of other activities in Chicago and and the surrounding area.[57] As a result of diminished coverage, says Gary Moncrief, a political scientist at Boise State University, "I'm not sure the American public is very attuned to the inner workings of legislatures and the fact that they probably do work better today than thirty or forty years ago."[58]

All of this means that the amateur legislatures are much more popular with their constituents than the more professional chambers. The urge to return legislatures to their more humble but lovable position as citizen institutions has been the main driver behind the term limits movement. Limits on the number of terms an individual may serve in the House or Senate have been approved in most of the states that allow ballot initiatives. As of mid-2004, there were seventeen states with term limits, and this number may go up if voters in other states approve limits in the future. The limits range from a low of six years of service per legislative chamber in states such as Arkansas and Maine to twelve years service in Nevada, Oklahoma, and Utah. Term limits are especially strict where the public thinks there was not enough turnover in the legislature. "The lower the existing turnover rate in the legislature," a pair of political scientists concluded in 1996, "the harsher the term limits they tend to adopt."[59] In California, for example, Assemblyman Willie Brown became the poster child for a term limits initiative because of his fourteen years as the Assembly Speaker. That state now has term limits that match the strictest limits in the nation. In 1990 California voters sent an even stronger message. Even as they limited terms, they also cut the legislature's budget and staffing levels by 40 percent—the third cut in six years. The same year, Colorado voters imposed eight-year term limits on legislators and limited sessions to no more than 120 days a year.

There is little doubt among legislators and the people who deal with legislators that term limits make them less effective in patrolling the behavior of the executive branch and in understanding, debating, and addressing complex issues. The public loves term limits, however. Polls suggest that about 75 percent of the public favors them. "With new people in office, you have people with real world experience," says Stacie Rumenap, president of U.S. Term Limits, a group that advocates limits. "Under term limits, you might have a schoolteacher sitting on the education committee."[60] That sort of suggestion is often made about term limits—you get rid of the professional politicians and get people who know what the real problems are because they themselves are real.

Professional or part-time politician, voters like people who cut through the clutter surrounding issues and offer solutions. The public's attitude is often one of "just the facts, ma'am, and spare me the details." Think about how much ridicule Al Gore received during his presidential campaign in 2000 for being a wonk who knew too much about congressional bill numbers and specific policy decisions. Policy competence in legislators is often similarly viewed as a negative. The idea is that if they are too distracted by details and special interest wishes, they will never shut up and actually do something to serve the common good.[61] Political nominees are eager to appeal to this public sentiment. "I just want to get things done," one candidate said in 2002 in a typical statement. "Hewing to the party line—any party's line—does not interest me."[62]

The problem with this worldview is that there is no such thing as an easily defined common good. No one likes Osama bin Laden, but agreement stops soon after that. Like terrorism, gun control is another such hot-button topic. After each mass murder in a schoolyard, there are calls for stricter gun control laws. Yet a large proportion of the public does not want gun owners' rights trampled on. There is no consensus on this issue, just as there is no consensus on whether SUVs should be banned to save the environment or whether the best way to address a state budget deficit is to cut funding for health coverage or to raise taxes.

In Wyoming, 77% of voters cast their ballots to institute legislative term limits.

The American electorate is clearly divided, as reflected by the tied presidential election of 2000, an evenly divided U.S. Congress, and the near-parity in total numbers of Republican and Democratic legislators. In 2002, Democrats controlled eighteen legislatures, Republicans controlled seventeen legislatures, and fourteen legislatures were split. Even in states in which one party clearly dominated, there was still plenty of disagreement. The GOP controlled both of Florida's legislative chambers in 2002, but House and Senate Republicans were barely speaking to each other after fights about redistricting, regulation of banking and insurance, and a $10 billion battle over sales tax exemptions.[63]

If there is no agreement in your dorm room about whether to rent "Titanic" or "The Sixth Sense," why should anyone in a society as diverse as ours expect easy agreement about taxation, budgets, health, guns, and the environment? Legislators simply reflect the messiness of public opinion. No matter which way they decide an issue—even if it is only to decide to maintain the law as it stands—they are bound to make some people angry. People would prefer decisions to be neat and simple and harmonious. Maybe that is why no one likes legislatures.

Conclusion

Legislatures have one of the toughest jobs in the political system. It's hard enough trying to get a group of friends to agree on what movie to rent. Imagine trying to get a hundred or more people—many of whom flat out oppose your preferred choice—to sign off on something as controversial as, say, a welfare bill. Now imagine trying to do that over and over again: putting in the research; negotiating; meeting; balancing partisan interests, special interests, and constituent interests; and finally, hammering out an agreement that no one is fully satisfied with and everyone is willing to criticize. That gives some idea of the reality of a legislator's job.

Historically speaking, legislators today do their jobs more effectively and more fairly than at any other time. For this achievement, they are mistrusted and disliked. Why? Ultimately it is perhaps because a legislature can never give the people everything they want. Democracy is simply not set up to do this because people want very different things. Legislatures do not really create conflict, they simply reflect the disagreements that exist in the electorate. Or at least they do if legislators are reasonably effective at representing the preferences of their constituencies. What democracy promises, and what state legislatures largely deliver, is not what everyone wants—on most issue no such option exists—but reasonable compromises that most people can live with. Like a group with differing tastes in movies, legislatures are successful when they can agree on second best.

Key Concepts

apportionment (p. 193)

casework (p. 183)

caucus (p. 188)

coalition building (p. 172)

committee (p. 173)

compromise (p. 175)

constituents (p. 175)

constituent service (p. 183)

delegates (p. 191)

districts (p. 175)

filibusters (p. 173)

gerrymanders (p. 194)

incumbent (p. 183)

logrolling (p. 172)

majority-minority districts (p. 194)

majority rule (p. 172)

malapportionment (p. 194)

oversight (p. 183)

professionalization (p. 193)

rank-and-file members (p. 191)

redistricting (p. 193)

representation (p. 180)

riders (p. 173)

trustees (p. 191)

Suggested Readings

Loomis, Burdett A. *Time, Politics, and Policies: A Legislative Year.* Lawrence: University Press of Kansas, 1994. A year in the life of the Kansas state legislature.

Neal, Tommy. *Lawmaking and the Legislative Process.* Phoenix, Ariz.: Oryx Press, 1996. A nuts and bolts guide to how legislatures work, published by the National Conference of State Legislatures.

Rosenthal, Alan. *The Decline of Representative Democracy: Process, Participation, and Power in State Legislatures.* Washington, D.C.: CQ Press, 1998. A political scientist's comprehensive look at the work of state legislatures and how that work is changing.

Rosenthal, Alan. *Heavy Lifting: the Job of the American Legislature.* Washington, D.C.: CQ Press, 2004. This book argues that the success of state legislatures is best measured by the effectiveness of their processes, not by the specific product of their legislation.

Rosenthal, Alan, et al. *Republic on Trial: The Case for Representative Democracy.* Washington, D.C.: CQ Press, 2002. After examining the many flaws of legislators, as well as other political leaders, the authors conclude that these leaders still do a pretty good job representing the public's interest.

Suggested Web Sites

http://stateline.org. A foundation-sponsored news service that provides daily news about state government.

www.alec.org. Web site for the American Legislative Exchange, an influential conservative organization that drafts model legislation. Both legislators and private sector interests are members.

www.csg.org. Web site for the Council of State Governments, which provides training and information to state government officials.

www.ncsl.org. Web site of the National Conference of State Legislatures that includes a wealth of information about legislative structures and procedures as well as the major issues faced by legislators.

CHAPTER 7

Governors and Executives

There Is No Such Thing as Absolute Power

The evolution of man? Not exactly, but these wax figures certainly represent the evolution of one man's career. Arnold Schwarzenegger is not the first actor to turn politician, but he may be one of the first to make such effective use of a changing political environment. In 2003, California's voting public turned against recently reelected governor Gray Davis and demanded that he leave office. Schwarzenegger used his powerful personal connections to fellow Republicans, including President George W. Bush, and his links to America's royal family, the Kennedys, through his wife, Maria Shriver (a Kennedy relative), to beat out more than 130 other candidates running for the newly opened governor's seat.

How did governors get to be such powerful players, when for much of American history their offices were weak?

Why do some states still give their governors more pomp than power?

Marissa Mathy-Zvailer, a sixteen-year-old Albuquerque, New Mexico, theater employee was killed there one July night in 2003 when she refused the sexual advances of twenty-two-year-old Dominic Akers. Akers had previously been convicted of child molestation, but his sentence had been suspended.

Outrage that such a person was free to roam the streets led to intense media coverage of the murder and, perhaps most importantly, commanded the attention of the state's freshman governor, Bill Richardson.

Richardson, a former congressman and United Nations (UN) ambassador, already had proven himself to be an **activist governor**, but few projects matched the speed with which he drafted and passed a law that required tougher penalties for sex offenders. Richardson called the legislature into special session and within four months of her death "Marissa's Law" was on the books.

Although getting Marissa's Law passed wasn't Richardson's initial reason for calling the special session, it nonetheless was an impressive display of the governor's power to control the political agenda of a state. Richardson spotted a problem and he did something about it. Like many governors, Richardson held the power to order the legislature to work. Only he—not the legislators—determined what they would work on during that special session. During the same session, Richardson also persuaded legislators to pass a $1.6 billion roads and transportation package. A governor, however, needs help to get things done. Richardson could not convince the legislature to pass, or even seriously consider, an ambitious tax package that had been his original motivation for calling the special session.

Such a mixed record of success is not unusual for governors. They often can call the shots in terms of what bills legislators will consider, but they are not very effective unless they can persuade legislators to pass those bills. Richardson quickly bragged of his victories in a series of radio ads paid for by his campaign committee. New Mexico legislators, who felt that Richardson was trying to bully them into accepting his agenda without their input, warned that they had the power to stop him whenever they felt like it. "We in the legislature have the power to say 'no' to anything," noted Max Coll, the chair of the House Appropriations and Finance Committee. "Pretty soon, we'll have the wagons circled."[1]

ACTIVIST GOVERNOR

A governor who takes a leading role in setting the political agenda of the state, as opposed to a governor who views himself or herself more as a manager, or caretaker.

Governors walk this political tightrope every day of every term. Historically, governors in U.S. politics have held more token prestige than real governmental strength. They appear to have enormous power, but they can get hardly anything done without the cooperation of others. They can't pass laws without legislators, they can't implement policy without assistance from state agencies, and they can't create jobs without the private sector.

Still, governors are the prime political actors in virtually every state. Some are notably more successful than others, but all are seen leaders. In most states, the governor sets the agenda, largely determining what policy issues will be pursued and how the state budget will look. They are unique among state-level politicians in terms of the media attention they can attract. This helps them promote their causes, but they must rely on other institutional players if they are going to accomplish more than making speeches. Legislators have to be persuaded to pass the laws. Governors also need to convince state agencies and departments to pursue and implement programs that they like or need. Such programs may include setting up tax breaks for companies moving to the state or coming up with policies that will preserve open spaces.

Recently, governors have become a lot better equipped to control the rest of the executive branch. For more than one hundred years after the founding of the American republic, governors were strong in title only, with little real power. In fact, they were hardly more than figureheads. Throughout the last decades of the twentieth century, however, governors were given more and more formal control over the machinery of government as the federal government shifted greater control of many programs, including welfare, to the states. They have more time to serve than they once did and enjoy greater authority to appoint the top officials in virtually every government agency. These changes were the result of changes in laws in many states that were specifically designed to strengthen the office of governor in hopes of creating greater accountability and coherence in government. They are now, with few exceptions, not just the most famous politicians in their states but also the most powerful.

Governors are expected to be the leading cheerleaders for their states. They are expected to attract business and jobs, to set the political tone, to manage state affairs. They serve as the primary face and voice of government during natural disasters or other crises. With this much power, of course, comes a great deal of expectation. If a state is not doing well—if it is losing more jobs than its neighbors during a recession, for example, or is running a budget deficit—voters and the media will hold the governor responsible. They are like

> Throughout the last decades of the twentieth century, however, governors were given more and more formal control over the machinery of government as the federal government shifted greater control of many programs, including welfare, to the states.

mini-presidents in each state. Like the president, the governor commands the lion's share of political attention in a state, is generally seen as setting the agenda for the legislative branch and is basically the lead political actor—the figure most likely to appear on television on a regular basis. As with the president, governors tend to receive the blame or enjoy the credit for the performance of the economy.

And, like the president, a governor shares responsibility for running the government—implementing laws; issuing regulations; and doing the work of building the roads, maintaining the parks and other public functions—with the help of a cabinet. Presidents appoint their cabinet officials to run the Departments of Defense and Agriculture and the like. Governors have no foreign policy responsibilities, of course, but they will have help in running state-level departments of agriculture, finance, environmental protection, and such. In most cases, in most states, the governor appoints officials to head those departments. But some other statewide officials, such as attorneys general, are often elected on their own and may even represent another party. We will explore the roles of these other executive branch officials.

How did governors get to be such powerful players, when for much of U.S. history their offices were weak? Why is this so? How is it even possible? Why do some states still give their governors more pomp than power? This chapter will look at how the office of governor has changed over the years. We will examine the types of power governors can command by virtue of the office and which powers they must create out of the force of personality. We'll look at what sorts of people get elected governor and how they get elected. Finally, we will survey some of the other important statewide offices, such as lieutenant governor and attorney general.

The Job of Governor

Following the American Revolution, governors had very little power for one simple reason—distrust. Colonial governors, appointed by the British, had imposed unpopular taxes and exploited their positions to make themselves rich. Americans did not want to invest too much power into individuals who might turn not into mini-presidents but instead into mini-dictators. There was no national president, after all, under the original Articles of Confederation. In the states, most of the power was disbursed by giving it to many individuals in the form of legislatures. Governors in all but three of the original states were limited to one-year terms. While in office, they were not given control over state departments and agencies. Separately elected individuals, boards, or commissions ran these instead. One North Carolina delegate said after his state's constitutional convention that the governor had been given—"Just enough [power] to sign the receipt for his salary."[2]

The number of agencies grew as government became more complex towards the end of the nineteenth century. Lack of central control over these agencies, however, meant that states had difficulty functioning coherently. The U.S. Constitution had done much to improve the political structure in the United States—but not for governors. Governors still lacked the authority to perform in a way that the public expected given their position at the top of the political pyramid. This problem persisted well into the twentieth century. Lynn Muchmore, a political scientist, summed up the sort of frustrations governors had as late as the 1980s in terms of getting various parts of government to act as they wished. Muchmore laid out a theoretical case of a governor elected on a platform of promoting growth in the state's rural areas and documented the difficulties he had in making good on those promises.

In this scenario, the new governor finds that the highway department, which is run by a separate commission, had decided a decade ago to complete urban segments of the state's road system. This decision siphoned money away from plans to develop better roads in rural areas. The board that oversees public colleges and universities has a policy of phasing out satellite campuses in favor of investing in three urban campuses. The state's department of commerce will not work in any county that does not have a local economic development corporation. Many rural counties lack such corporations because they do not have the population or tax base to support them. The state legislature has passed restrictions that deny new businesses breaks on rural utility rates.[3] Despite his promises, the governor's battle to help rural areas was an uphill one.

Not every scenario is so extreme, but it is often the case that state organizations not headed by people appointed by the governor—and therefore not answerable to him or her—will have their own constituencies and concerns. They will not have in mind the big picture of how the different parts of state government can best work together to promote the general good. Only the governor sees the whole field in that way.

Governors, in recent decades, have been granted greater powers in hopes that states will function more efficiently. Only New Hampshire and Vermont still have two-year gubernatorial terms. The rest of the states have four-year terms. Only Virginia limits its chief executive to one term—although two-term limits are common among the states. Governors now have much more power over appointments than they once did. This means that they are able to put their own teams in place to carry out their policies. They have become important symbols of the state not only at home but also as ambassadors who promote their states to businesses that they hope to attract in other states and abroad.

Terry Sanford, a former governor of North Carolina, summed up the contemporary job of governor well:

> The governor by his very office embodies his state. He must . . . energize his administration, search out the experts, formulate the programs, mobilize the support, and carry new ideas into action. . . . Few major undertakings ever get

off the ground without his support and leadership. The governor sets the agenda for public debate; frames the issues; decides on the timing, and can blanket the state with good ideas by using his access to the mass media. . . . The governor is the most potent political power in the state.[4]

Governors must be multitaskers. They propose legislation, which has to win approval from the legislature. They can implement regulations that help clear up how those laws actually are applied to individuals, businesses, and other groups. Increasingly, in recent years, governors have become their states's strongest advocate and public relations person, traveling to promote tourism and help close deals with out-of-state trading partners who might locate offices or operations in their states. We will explore all these roles in some detail below.

Chief Legislator

Just as the president does not serve in Congress, governors do not sit as parts of state legislatures. Like the president, however, they have enormous influence over the work legislatures do. Governors outline their broad proposals in inaugural and annual state of the state addresses. They and their staffs then work with individual legislators and committees to translate these proposals into bills.

Some governors are better at getting what they want from legislatures than others. Why? Part of it is personal charm, but a lot of it has to do with the powers granted to a governor in a given state. In Texas, for instance, most of the influence that the executive branch holds over legislation is given to the lieutenant governor, not the governor. Governors all vary in terms of how much authority they have in blocking bills they do not like through use of the **veto,** or rejection of the bill. Those variations in authority help to determine how much clout a governor has in the legislature.

Governors never get everything they want from state legislatures, but governors do have a great deal of impact on what bills become laws. There are a number of reasons for this. In every state except North Carolina, bills almost never become law without the governor's signature. Governors can veto them. Legislators can get around a veto, but that often means that they have to pass the bill again by a **supermajority vote.** Supermajority votes are usually votes of two-thirds or more. Since it is hard enough to get both legislative houses to agree on a bill in the first place, such a large agreement rarely happens. If you can't pass a law without the governor's approval, it stands to reason that you will want to work with him in order to create a version of the bill that will win such approval.

Another factor that makes governors enormously influential in the legislative process is their command of state budgets. In nearly every state, the main responsibility for creating a state budget rests in the office of the gov-

VETO

The power to reject a proposed law.

SUPERMAJORITY VOTE

A legislative vote of much more than a simple majority, for instance, two-thirds of a legislative chamber voting to override a governor's veto.

ernor. The governor proposes budgets that detail the amount of money that will go to every state agency, welfare program, highway department, and school district. There are often restrictions on how a state must spend much of its money from year to year, whether because of old laws or federal requirements. But a governor gets the first crack at deciding how most of the state's money is going to be spent.

Maryland's governor is the nation's most powerful in terms of setting a state budget, the result of changes prompted by a serious deficit in 1916 for which the legislature took the blame.[5] There, once the chief executive lays out the budget, the legislature cannot add any more money to fund individual departments or programs or shift money among those programs. They *can* reduce the size of appropriations, but can't create programs of their own. In the other states, legislators have more power to tinker. In New York State in 2003, the legislature passed its own budget by overriding the governor's veto. Usually, however, the governor's blueprint gets passed, with legislators only making changes here or there. "As far as legislators are concerned," one political scientist wrote, "the ability to create the budget is so powerful that it becomes *the* major tool for a governor in achieving his legislative programs."[6]

Governors get to decide, for instance, whether bridges are going to be built in particular districts. In order to get those bridges—or any other goodies they might want—legislators often have to give governors what they want in terms of passing their major initiatives. "Any legislator who says he needs nothing from the governor's office is either lying or stupid," according to one observer of the Alabama political scene.[7] Legislators who belong to the governor's party are inclined to help out anyway, because they will be perceived as part of the same team when facing voters in the next election.

> "Any legislator who says he needs nothing from the governor's office is either lying or stupid," according to one observer of the Alabama political scene.

Some governors choose only to focus on a few big issues and leave many small matters to the prerogative of the legislature. Others tackle a wide range of problems. How much success a governor enjoys varies greatly according to his or her individual abilities and skills. Yet there is no question that a governor is the most likely person to set the main agenda for the legislature and the state.

Head of State Agencies

As mentioned above, governors at one time had very little control over who ran their states' departments. This meant that people with other agendas could set policy over taxes or health or other issues. Even today, for instance, Texas voters elect twenty-five different statewide officials. Texas

New Mexico governor Bill Richardson is able to turn small talk into big business deals because of his previously established connections to national, international, and business leaders. He has met with such dignitaries as Mexican president Vicente Fox to negotiate deals meant to improve the economy of his financially flagging state. Given the increasing responsibility of states to generate revenue to fund public programs, governors like Richardson are finding it ever more important to use their presence in the public eye to sell their states' attributes.

governors cannot hire their own choices for positions such as comptroller (the state's chief financial officer), agriculture commissioner, or state supreme court justices.

In most states, that has changed in recent times. Only about half of the governors chose their own cabinet officials in 1969, but nearly all of them do today.[8] In fact, the current trend is to try to merge even large departments so that they do not work at cross purposes or duplicate work. In Massachusetts, for example, Governor Mitt Romney created a "supercabinet" position in 2003 that oversaw the state's economic, consumer affairs, and labor departments in hopes of coordinating their budgets and activities. His other attempts to consolidate more power in the governor's office through a major reorganization of the government structure, however, were rejected by the legislature.

The power to appoint people to run state departments offers obvious benefits for governors. They can pick their own people who they know will pursue their policy preferences. If they fail, they can be fired. How much influence a governor has over state education policy, say, or environmental protection still depends on the amount of energy and time the governor can afford to devote to these issues, as opposed to everything else that must be done. One Arkansas governor said that a governor "will spend almost as much time keeping his staff and his cabinet and the people around him happy as he does keeping his constituency happy."[9]

In other words, governors who can appoint their own people to run the government cannot count on their accomplishing everything they want. Just like any other boss, governors may be disappointed in the performance of the people working for them. The ability to hire and fire people, however, as well as the ability to determine how much money their departments are going to get, means that governors are truly the leaders of the executive branch of government.

Chief Spokesperson for the State

New Mexico is a case in point in terms of how a governor can change not just a few policies, such as sex offender laws, but also a state's overall public climate. There, Governor Bill Richardson has worked hard to send signals that the state government wants to be as friendly as possible to business growth. New Mexico has the forty-seventh lowest per capita income in the country, so Richardson didn't even wait until his inauguration in January 2003 to begin his sales pitch for his programs and for the state. The day after his election, he got on a plane to talk to executives in California's Silicon Valley in hopes of persuading them to set up operations in New Mexico.

Since then, he has lured movie shoots to the state with an $85 million investment fund. Richardson has helped double the state's trade with Mexico during his first year in office, using his international connections from his days as UN ambassador to begin a relationship with Mexican president Vicente Fox. Richardson proudly boasts he calls CEOs on a daily basis and "sucks up to them big time."

Other governors perform similar chores. Former Wisconsin governor Tommy Thompson used to host business executives from Minnesota at the opening of fishing season to show off the state's outdoor activities and to try to convince them to locate new facilities there. In order to combat a significant decrease in travel and tourism in the months following the terrorist attacks of September 11, 2001, Florida governor Jeb Bush wrote letters of thanks to every group that agreed to hold its convention in the state. Governors regularly send out press releases about their role in helping to land new jobs and companies through tax incentives, the creation of cooperative biotechnology ventures, or other economic development activities.

They speak out in other roles as well. Their images appear in tourism brochures. Governors are sure to let the media know that they have bet some celebrated state product against other governors when their teams are in major bowl games or World Series. More substantively, governors have become important lobbyists in Washington, seeking more federal money for their states. They are the only people that lobby in Washington who can be sure that members of Congress and cabinet officials will meet with them directly, rather than having them meet with staff.

Basically, their main role as chief face of the state is now in sales. They promote their states' benefits to economic interests. They pitch the virtues of low tax rates, good roads and transportation systems, livable communities, well-educated workforces, and anything else that they can think of that might seem attractive to a business locator. Their desire to have good packages to sell has had an effect on their policies, with most governors afraid to make any moves that might be perceived as unfriendly to business.

Party Chief

Governors are also the leading figures for their party in their states. U.S. senators arguably might be more influential figures, but governors are more important politically at home. Governors command more foot soldiers. They may be able to call on thousands of state workers, whereas a senator's staff numbers in the dozens at best. Not all of a governor's workers will be loyal members of the same party—in fact, changes in patronage laws and the creation of civil service workers mean that governors appoint far fewer state employees than they did some decades ago. Governors, however, will have more people whose jobs depend on them than will any other elected official.

Governors often pick state party chairs of their liking. They help to recruit and raise money for candidates for other statewide offices and the legislature. They use the media attention they attract to campaign for those they support. State parties are not as important as they were forty years ago, so governors now devote less energy to political activities than to the nuts and bolts of their own jobs. This does not mean they do not have to pound the political pavement. They are still the titular heads of the party in their states, and no modern politician can avoid the duties of raising campaign contributions.

Governors often are seen as the building blocks toward putting together a winning electoral map in presidential races. It is taken as an article of faith among pundits and other political experts that governors can help swing their states toward the presidential nominee of their choice through their media presence and ability to sway some percentage of their states' votes. This may not be true, at least in most cases. George W. Bush, then the governor of Texas, did receive a major boost toward capturing the Republican presidential nomination in 2000 when every other Republican governor endorsed him. To the surprise of some, however, they did not help him much in the general election. Republicans then held eight out of the ten largest states, but Bush only carried three of them.[10] Unquestionably, however, having a popular governor on your side certainly won't hurt you politically.

Commander-in-Chief of the National Guard

Even in this country's earliest days, when governors had few powers, each governor's military position was strong, "with all states designating him as commander-in-chief."[11] Southern governors perhaps most famously used their power to control the National Guard in resisting desegregation during the 1950s and 1960s. The National Guard in each state is a state agency, but the president has the power to federalize the Guard, calling up units to perform federal service. That happened in the civil rights era, when the Guard suddenly worked for the feds against governors resisting integration. Today's National Guard is more likely to fight alongside federal soldiers, in such places as Iraq, than to resist them. Regardless of where the soldiers are deployed, governors maintain their positions as heads of the Guard nonetheless.

Governors do not use the Guard as their private armies. Instead, they can call out the Guard to respond to natural disasters or riots. Milton Sharp, governor of Pennsylvania during the 1970s, remembered his years in office in terms of emergency response to floods, a pair of hurricanes, droughts, ice storms, fires, and a gypsy moth infestation rather than in terms of law-making and policy agenda setting.[12]

Most governors naturally hope to avoid having their **tenure** defined by natural disasters or other factors outside of their control. As we have seen, governors have to attend to many political tasks during their time in office—dealing with the legislature and as head of government. How much success they have in setting their own courses during their times in office depends on the amount of power they control. That power, in turn, varies a good deal by state and depends not just on the **formal powers** of the office but also on the amount of power individuals in that office can create for themselves.

The Powers of Governors

Anyone who follows sports understands that natural ability does not necessarily translate into success. Some players look great on paper—they're strong, they can run fast, they have whatever skills would help them dominate their sport. But for whatever reason, players like that sometimes squander their talent and are shown up by weaker athletes who nevertheless have a greater understanding of the game, who work harder, or who simply find a way to win.

It's the same with governors. Some of them look incredibly strong on paper, and their states' constitutions give them powers that their neighbors can only envy. Nevertheless, states that have set up the governor's office to be strong end up, sometimes, with weak governors. Conversely, states in which the governor's official powers are weak sometimes can have individuals in that office who completely dominate their states' politics. They are able to exploit the **informal powers** of their office—they have managed to create personal powers, as opposed to relying on relatively weak institutional powers.

When we talk about the powers of governors, we obviously do not refer to an ability to cast spells or turn back armies with their wands. However, if you want to understand why some governors are considered successful or powerful and why others are quickly forgotten even by their supporters, there is an obvious place to start. You need to look at what sorts of power governors are given by right of taking that office. If they do not have the tools to influence policy, they will have a much harder time winning political victories. Yet every governor, even those whom state law does not grant much authority, has enough stature to possess the possibility of success.

Let us outline the different types of powers that governors actually do have, both formal—the roles that come as part of the necessary equipment of the office—and informal powers that these individuals create for themselves by using their office as a platform.

TENURE

The time a governor spends in office.

FORMAL POWERS

The powers explicitly granted to a governor according to state law, such as vetoing legislation or appointing heads of state agencies.

INFORMAL POWERS

The things a governor is able to do, such as command media attention or persuade party members, based on position, not on formal authority.

Rick Perry had big shoes to fill when he took over as governor of Texas for then president-elect George W. Bush. Formerly the lieutenant governor under Bush, Perry was accustomed to wielding power. In fact, by becoming governor, he may actually have lost some clout, since in Texas the lieutenant governor holds more institutional power than the governor. Bush also had been a very popular governor, however, and had put his personality and personal connections to good use. Still, when Perry put on the ten-gallon hat of the Texas governorship, he picked up where Bush left off—he ranks third in the nation on scales that measure the personal gubernatorial powers.

Formal Powers

Most governors have a wide variety of formal powers granted to them by state constitutions or other laws. Among the most important of these are appointing officials to run state agencies, the power to veto legislation, the power to craft budgets, the power to grant pardons, and the power to call legislatures into session. We'll examine each of these aspects of a governor's job description in this section.

The Power to Appoint. As mentioned earlier, the first governors in this country lacked **appointment powers**. They could not pick their own people to run state agencies, which made those agencies more independent. Nowadays, governors can pick their own teams, which gives them greater authority to set policy. When John Engler served as governor of Michigan during the 1990s, for example, he put in place a series of appointees with a strong ideological commitment to limited government. These appointees helped him carry out his desire to shrink the state's government. His contemporary, Ann Richards of Texas, set out to change the face of state government by changing the faces of the people within it—appointing women, blacks, and Hispanics to replace the white men who had always run things in Austin.

APPOINTMENT POWERS

A governor's ability to pick individuals to run state government, such as appointing cabinet secretaries.

Since governors cannot run their states alone, they must rely on the work of people they appoint to help carry out broad policy desires. Governors who want to offer people living in public housing more opportunities to buy their homes will have a better chance of succeeding if they can appoint a housing director who shares those views than governors who have to work with housing directors who answer to independent commissions that oppose privatizing public housing.

Having loyal foot soldiers on your team rather than free agents is important for governors who want things done their way. This is not the only benefit the power of appointment carries with it. Governors get to appoint dozens and sometimes thousands of people to full-time government jobs and to commissions and boards. For instance, if you are attending a public college, chances are that the governor appointed the board of governors of your school or university system. These are considered plum jobs and giving them out is a way for a governor not only to influence policy but also to reward campaign contributors or other political allies.

Governing States and Localities

Policy in Practice: Governors with Gumption: Policy Innovation and Interstate Influence

Governors are the masters of their political domains—their own states. Sometimes, however, they have an effect that reaches far beyond their own state boundaries. Their ideas can spread to be emulated by their colleagues and can even affect federal policy.

In a political arena that considers governors in general to be great lobbyists in Washington, there are some who stand out as the greatest of the great. Few have had an impact equal to that of Tommy Thompson. Thompson served as Wisconsin's governor from 1987 until President George W. Bush put him in charge of the Department of Health and Human Services (HHS) in 2001. While governor, Thompson petitioned the HHS for waivers from federal welfare law requirements. One of his first acts upon taking office had been to bring together a group of welfare mothers to tell him their stories. He wanted to learn about the obstacles that made it difficult for them to get and keep jobs.

Using these personal stories as motivation, he created a program called Wisconsin Works. The program requires virtually all welfare recipients to work, either at regular jobs that the government has subsidized or in community service. The state increased its spending on child care, health, transportation, and other support services. The combination of Wisconsin's welfare reforms and a healthy economy helped the state cut its welfare caseload by about 65 percent during Thompson's first decade in office, saving more than $1 billion.*

One of Thompson's main pulpits for spreading his gospel of reform and renewal was the National Governors Association (NGA). The association is designed as a clearinghouse for governors from around the country to exchange information, as well as to lobby on behalf of the states in Washington. Thompson's experiments

were imitated elsewhere. The innovations that he and other governors came up with formed the backbone of the 1996 federal welfare law. The restructured law put time limits on how long a person could stay on welfare and imposed new work requirements.

In 2001, Maryland governor Parris Glendening—one of Thompson's successors as NGA chair—used the position to push a very different agenda. Glendening was tired of seeing farmland and open fields in his state torn up in favor of development. He thought that new houses and businesses should be built near existing houses and businesses, rather than sprawling through the countryside. The excessive development only led to long commutes and environmental degradation.

His Smart Growth Act, which became Maryland law in 1998, is designed to steer the state's money toward the expansion of roads and other infrastructure in such a way as to discourage sprawl and encourage development and redevelopment in settled communities. It does not prevent builders or local governments from creating new projects on virgin land. It merely says that the state no longer subsidizes such projects.

The idea took root, at least for a while. Other governors initially followed Glendening's example. Within a few years, however, sprawl had become a high-profile issue in at least thirty states. Nearly a dozen of these previously had passed sprawl control measures more or less similar to Maryland's.

Thompson's changes in welfare law were an example of moving the national debate by influencing Congress. Glendening's story is about having an impact by providing a model for—and offering guidance to—other states. In both cases, governors of relatively uninfluential states were able to promote big ideas that changed people's lives across the country.

* Ellen Perlman, "The Welfare Risk-Taker," *Governing* magazine, December 1997, 32.

TABLE 7-1

Formal Powers of the Governors by State

State	Budget Power		Line-Item Veto Power	Authorization to Reorganize through Executive Order	Power to Appoint Leaders of the Bureaucracy
	Full Responsibility	Shared Responsibility			
Alabama	Yes		Yes	Yes	Yes
Alaska	Yes		Yes		Yes
Arizona	Yes		Yes	Yes	Yes
Arkansas		Yes	Yes	Yes	Yes
California	Yes		Yes		Yes
Colorado	Yes		Yes		Yes
Connecticut	Yes		Yes		Yes
Delaware	Yes		Yes	Yes	Yes
Florida	Yes		Yes		Yes
Georgia	Yes		Yes	Yes	Yes
Hawaii	Yes		Yes		Yes
Idaho	Yes		Yes		Yes
Illinois		Yes	Yes	Yes	Yes
Indiana		Yes		Yes	Yes
Iowa	Yes		Yes		Yes
Kansas	Yes		Yes		Yes
Kentucky	Yes		Yes		Yes
Louisiana		Yes	Yes		Yes
Maine	Yes				Yes
Maryland	Yes		Yes		Yes
Massachusetts	Yes		Yes	Yes	Yes
Michigan		Yes	Yes	Yes	Yes
Minnesota	Yes		Yes	Yes	Yes
Mississippi		Yes	Yes	Yes	Yes
Missouri	Yes		Yes	Yes	Yes
Montana		Yes	Yes	Yes	Yes
Nebraska		Yes	Yes		Yes
Nevada	Yes				Yes
New Hampshire	Yes				Yes
New Jersey	Yes		Yes		Yes

TABLE 7-1 *(continued)*

State	Budget Power		Line-Item Veto Power	Authorization to Reorganize through Executive Order	Power to Appoint Leaders of the Bureaucracy
	Full Responsibility	Shared Responsibility			
New Mexico	Yes		Yes		Yes
New York		Yes	Yes		Yes
North Carolina	Yes			Yes	Yes
North Dakota	Yes		Yes	Yes	Yes
Ohio	Yes		Yes		Yes
Oklahoma		Yes	Yes		Yes
Oregon	Yes		Yes		Yes
Pennsylvania	Yes		Yes		Yes
Rhode Island	Yes				Yes
South Carolina		Yes	Yes		Yes
South Dakota	Yes		Yes	Yes	Yes
Tennessee	Yes		Yes	Yes	Yes
Texas		Yes	Yes		Yes
Utah	Yes		Yes		Yes
Vermont	Yes			Yes	Yes
Virginia	Yes		Yes	Yes	Yes
Washington	Yes		Yes		Yes
West Virginia	Yes		Yes		Yes
Wisconsin	Yes		Yes		Yes
Wyoming	Yes		Yes		Yes

Source: Adapted from *The Book of the States 2003* (Lexington, Ky.: Council of State Governments, 2003), 188–189.

Of course, there is a downside to the power of appointment, which is the risk of picking the wrong people. Earlier, we talked about former Pennsylvania governor Milton Sharp, who remembered his administration mainly as a time of dealing with natural disasters. It is little wonder he prefers to remember his time in office that way, because many of his appointments turned into natural disasters of his own making. His secretary of property and supplies was sent to prison for contracting irregularities. The same fate befell a member of his turnpike authority. Other members of his administration came under ethical shadows as well. Even though Sharp himself was never touched by scandal, subsequent candidates—including the man who would succeed him as governor—ran campaigns against corruption. They won office by pledging to clean up Harrisburg.[13]

Still, the ability to appoint the heads of departments that run areas such as prisons, public schools, highways, and utilities helps define a governor's overall power and influence. In some states, governors can pick their own top people without needing the approval of the legislature. In other states, they do need such approval. Rhode Island voters will have the chance in 2004 to strengthen the governor's appointment powers and weaken the legislature's reach into the executive branch through a ballot referendum that would ban legislators from serving on boards and commissions. In Texas, a legislative attempt to strengthen the governor's weak appointment powers was defeated in 2003. The primary reason for this was that legislatures and governors often have adversarial relationships—each can be the enemy of the other. If one is able to keep the other from gaining more power, it is unlikely that it will pass up the opportunity.

Power to Prepare State Budgets. We mentioned earlier that their ability to shape a state's budget may be the most powerful weapon governors have. It gives them enormous influence in their dealings with the legislature. The same is true in terms of their ability to maintain control over state agencies. In most states, agencies and departments submit their budget proposals to a central budget office that works as part of the governor's team. The governor's ability to deny them funds or shift money to departments helps make sure that agencies remain focused, at least to some extent, on the governor's priorities.

A governor can use the budget process to override old agency decisions, to make sure that the transportation department, for example, fully funds bike trails that had previously been ignored. Even when an agency has some independence about how it spends its money, a governor can persuade its officials to fund other priorities—a new law school at a state university, for example—by threatening to withhold some percentage of its overall budget.

Power to Veto. In talking about the governor as chief legislator, we mentioned the governor's ability to veto legislation in every state except North Carolina. Legislators can override vetoes, but that rarely happens because of supermajority vote requirements. Members of the governor's own party are usually reluctant to vote to override a veto. That means that if the governor's party holds just one-third of the seats in a legislative chamber, plus one, a veto is likely to be sustained—meaning the governor wins.

Legislators, therefore, try to work with governors or their staffs in order to craft a version of a bill that the governors will sign. There is little point in passing a bill if you know it is going to be rejected. Of course, sometimes legislatures pass a bill just to get it vetoed, making the governor's opposition known publicly. That happened sometimes when Gary Johnson was governor of New Mexico during the 1990s. Johnson would not support any bill that increased the size of government, and so he ended up vetoing more than seven hundred bills. Legislators sent him bills that would increase funding for popular programs, such as education, in hopes that his vetoes would make him look bad. Whether that happened or not, Johnson almost always won the political battle. Not only was the legislature unable to override his vetoes except in one instance, but he also was reelected for a second term.

All but seven governors—those in Indiana, Maine, New Hampshire, Nevada, North Carolina, Rhode Island, and Vermont—have a power known as the line-item veto, meaning they can reject just a portion of a bill. If there is a bill funding education, for example, the governor can accept all of it except for an increase in funding for a school in the district of a legislator who is a political enemy. Governors can use the line-item veto to try to cut spending, as when New York governor George Pataki eliminated spending for more than one thousand items from the state budget in 1998. The governor's ability to cut legislators' pet projects out of the budget forces most to support that governor's major initiatives. Congress tried to give the president line-item veto authority, but the U.S. Supreme Court ruled the practice unconstitutional in 1998.

When Tommy Thompson was governor of Wisconsin during the 1990s, he used the line-item veto to an unusual degree. Some governors can strike not only projects from bills, but individual words and letters as well. Thompson became notorious for vetoing just enough letters to completely alter the meaning of a bill. The courts upheld his right to do so, but that power was soon curbed.

Power to Grant Pardons. One clichéd motif of movies and television is to depict a prisoner about to be put to death, only to be spared by a last-minute pardon from the governor. Governors, like the president, can forgive crimes or commute (change) sentences if they feel a person has been unfairly convicted. They sometimes act on the recommendations of pardon boards, but the decision to pardon is theirs alone and not reversible.

A famous, recent example of the use of pardon power was in Illinois in 2003. During his last week in office, Governor George Ryan pardoned 4 prisoners condemned to death and commuted the sentences of all 167 other death-row prisoners to life in prison. Ryan had grown concerned that the number of death row cases that were being overturned because of new evidence, such as DNA lab work, indicated that the death penalty was being unfairly and inequitably assigned. He appointed a commission to study the application of the death sentence and became convinced that the state could not impose the death penalty with absolute certainty that innocent people would not be put to death. The move gained Ryan international celebrity among death penalty opponents but was criticized by prosecutors and others at home.

Not all governors use their pardon powers in such a high-minded way. In Tennessee in 1979, Lamar Alexander was sworn in as governor three days early to prevent outgoing governor Ray Blanton from commuting the sentences of any more prisoners. Blanton already had granted fifty-two last-minute pardons, and the FBI already had arrested members of his staff for extorting money to sell pardons, paroles, and commutations.

The Power to Call Special Sessions. Most legislatures meet only part-time and generally have fixed session schedules. When necessary or desired, however, every governor has the power to call legislatures into special session. Nearly half the nation's governors have the ability to set the agenda of a special session. This means that legislators can only deal with those issues that the governor wants addressed.

Special sessions can be useful for governors who want to deal with an issue right away. In recent years, many governors have called special sessions when the state's revenues have fallen short so that the legislatures can help them cut spending. Sometimes, special sessions allow legislators to focus on a complex issue, such as changing medical malpractice liability laws. Such issues might get lost in the shuffle of a regular session, when most attention is devoted to passing a budget.

Although governors can call special sessions, they typically will not enjoy success unless they can work out deals on their pet bills in advance. "If a governor calls a special session without knowing what the outcome's going to be," said Mississippi House Speaker Tim Ford, "it's chaos for everybody." Working without a deal already in place, legislators will sit around reading newspapers and eating snacks while their leaders try to hammer out an agreement with the governor. They resent having to give up time from their regular jobs to sit idly in the capitol.

Governors may be able to call legislators into special session, but they cannot necessarily make them do anything. In Iowa in 2002, Governor Tom Vilsack called the legislature back in hopes they would increase funding for education and health, but the legislature adjourned after a single day without debating any bill. "We just came in and went home," said House Majority Leader Christopher Rants. Vilsack then signed a package of budget cuts he had accepted in meetings with legislators and went on to call a second special session later in the month.[14]

Sometimes, the fact that governors have to resort to the use of such powers as calling special sessions or issuing vetoes is a sign of weakness. What it may show is that they could not get what they wanted from their legislatures during the regular course of business.

Informal Powers

The powers outlined previously are spelled out in state constitutions and statutes. Governors either have line-item veto authority or they do not. Much of the outcome of a governor's program, however, depends on individual ability to wield informal powers—the ability to leverage the power and prestige of the office into real influence in a way that may not be replicated by successors. Governors may be personally popular, have a special

TABLE 7-2

Ranking of the Institutional Powers of Governors, 2004

State	Separately Elected Executive Branch Officials	Tenure Potential	Appointment Powers	Budgetary Powers	Veto Powers	Party Control	Total Score	Rank
Utah	4	5	3	3	5	5	4.2	1
Alaska	5	4	3.5	3	5	4	4.1	2
New York	4	5	3.5	4	5	3	4.1	2
West Virginia	2.5	4	4	5	5	4	4.1	2
Colorado	4	4	3.5	3	5	4	3.9	5
New Jersey	5	4	3.5	3	5	3	3.9	5
North Dakota	3	5	3.5	3	5	4	3.9	5
Ohio	4	4	3.5	3	5	4	3.9	5
Tennessee	4.5	4	4	3	4	4	3.9	5
Illinois	3	5	3	3	5	4	3.8	10
Nebraska	4	4	3	4	5	3	3.8	10
Maryland	4	4	2.5	5	5	2	3.7	12
Minnesota	4	5	2.5	3	5	3	3.7	12
Montana	3	4	3	3	5	4	3.7	12
New Mexico	3	4	3	3	5	4	3.7	12
Pennsylvania	4	4	4	3	5	2	3.7	12
South Dakota	3	4	3.5	3	5	4	3.7	12
Connecticut	4	5	2.5	3	5	2	3.6	18
Florida	3	4	2.5	3	5	4	3.6	18
Hawaii	5	4	2.5	3	5	2	3.6	18
Maine	5	4	3.5	3	2	4	3.6	18
Massachusetts	4	5	3.5	3	5	1	3.6	18
Michigan	4	4	3.5	3	5	2	3.6	18
Delaware	2.5	4	3.5	3	5	3	3.5	24
Idaho	2	4	2	3	5	5	3.5	24
Iowa	3	5	3	3	5	2	3.5	24
Kentucky	3	4	4	3	4	3	3.5	24
Louisiana	1	4	3.5	3	5	4	3.4	28
Washington	1	5	3.5	3	5	3	3.4	28
Kansas	3	4	3	3	5	2	3.3	30
Oregon	2	4	3	3	5	3	3.3	30
Wisconsin	3	5	2	3	5	2	3.3	30
Arizona	2.5	4	4	3	5	1	3.2	33

(Table continues on next page)

TABLE 7-2 *(continued)*

State	Separately Elected Executive Branch Officials	Tenure Potential	Appointment Powers	Budgetary Powers	Veto Powers	Party Control	Total Score	Rank
California	1	4	4	3	5	2	3.2	33
Missouri	2.5	4	3	3	5	2	3.2	33
New Hampshire	5	2	3	3	2	4	3.2	33
Texas	2	5	1	2	5	4	3.2	33
Virginia	2.5	3	3.5	3	5	2	3.2	33
Wyoming	2	4	3.5	3	5	2	3.2	33
Arkansas	2.5	4	3	3	4	2	3.1	40
Georgia	1	4	2	3	5	3	3.0	41
Nevada	2.5	4	3.5	3	2	3	3.0	41
Oklahoma	1	4	1	3	5	4	3.0	41
South Carolina	1	4	2	2	5	4	3.0	41
Indiana	3	4	2.5	3	2	3	2.9	45
Mississippi	1.5	4	2	3	5	2	2.9	45
Alabama	1	4	3	3	4	2	2.8	47
North Carolina	1	4	3.5	3	2	3	2.7	48
Rhode Island	2.5	4	3	3	2	1	2.6	49
Vermont	2.5	2	3.5	3	2	2	2.5	50

Source: Thad Beyle, personal data for 2004. For previous years, see www.unc.edu/~beyle.

Notes:

Separately elected executive branch officials: 5 = only governor or governor/lieutenant governor team elected; 4.5 = governor or governor/lieutenant governor team, with one other elected official; 4 = governor/lieutenant governor team with some process officials (attorney general, secretary of state, treasurer, auditor) elected; 3 = governor/lieutenant governor team with process officials and some major and minor policy officials elected; 2.5 = governor (no team) with six or fewer officials elected, but none are major policy officials; 2 = governor (no team) with six or fewer officials elected, including one major policy official; 1.5 = governor (no team) with six or fewer officials elected, but two are major policy officials; 1 = governor (no team) with seven or more process and several major policy officials elected.

Tenure potential: 5 = 4-year term, no restraint on reelection; 4.5 = 4-year term, only three terms permitted; 4 = 4-year term, only two terms permitted; 3 = 4-year term, no consecutive elections permitted; 2 = 2-year term, no restraint on reelection; 1 = 2-year term, only two terms permitted.

Appointment powers: cover six major functional areas: corrections, K-12 education, health, highways/transportation, public utilities regulation, and welfare. The six individual office scores are totaled and then averaged and rounded to the nearest .5 for the state score. 5 = governor appoints, no other approval needed; 4 = governor appoints, a board, council, or legislature approves; 3 = someone else appoints, governor approves or shares appointment; 2 = someone else appoints, governor and others approve; 1 = someone else appoints, no approval or confirmation needed.

Budgetary powers: 5 = governor has full responsibility, legislature may not increase executive budget; 4 = governor has full responsibility, legislature can increase by special majority vote or subject to item veto; 3 = governor has full responsibility, legislature has unlimited power to change executive budget; 2 = governor shares responsibility, legislature has unlimited power to change executive budget; 1 = governor shares responsibility with other elected official, legislature has unlimited power to change executive budget.

Veto powers: 5 = governor has item veto, and a special majority vote of the legislature is needed to override a veto (3/5's of legislators elected or 2/3's of legislators present); 4 = has item veto with a majority of the legislators elected needed to override; 3 = has item veto with only a majority of the legislators present needed to override; 2 = no item veto, with a special legislative majority needed to override a regular veto; 1 = no item veto, only a simple legislative majority needed to override a regular veto.

Party control: The governor's party - 5 = has a substantial majority (75% or more) in both houses of the legislature; 4 = has a simple majority in both houses (under 75%), or a substantial majority in one house and s simple majority in the other; 3 = split control in the legislature or a non-partisan legislature; 2 = has a simple minority (25% or more) in both houses, or a simple minority in one and a substantial minority (under 25%) in the other; 1 = has a substantial minority in both houses.

Total power score: sum of the scores on the six individual indices divided by six to keep 5-point scale.

Ties in rankings reflect actual value.

gift for working with legislators, or have some other skills that help them do their jobs well but that are not based on any authority that the state granted.

Popular Support. One thing that will help a governor wield power is popular support. A governor who wins with 51 percent of the vote has all of the same formal powers as a governor who wins with 73 percent, but the more popular governor is clearly going to have an edge. Legislators and other officials will accept more readily the need to go along with a popular governor's program because they believe that program it what most voters in the state want. This is especially true if the governor ran strong in their districts. In a case like this, "Legislators cannot fail to be impressed," according to political scientist Alan Rosenthal, "for if there is one thing they are sensitive to it is the number of votes candidates receive." [15]

It is a long time between gubernatorial elections—four years in most cases—so in order to maintain and build on their popularity, governors do all sorts of public relations work. They never fail to alert the press to all their good deeds, they appear in other forums—groundbreakings, dedications, state fairs, church socials—where they can impress the public, and they propose legislation that they believe will be popular. The fortunes of governors rise and fall with the health of the economy of their states, but individual governors can make themselves more or less popular depending on how well they appear to address the problems of the day.

Party Support in Legislature. Having members of their own party dominate the legislature certainly helps governors get their agendas passed. Governors can be successful if the other party controls the legislature, but it is a lot tougher. The reasons are fairly obvious. Republican legislators want to see a Republican governor succeed, and the same holds true for Democrats. Voters perceive politicians belonging to the same party as being part of the same team. Therefore, the political fortunes of these politicians will be tied to one another's during the next election. Members of the same party are likely to hold similar positions on such issues as taxes, levels of social service spending, and the environment. "Governors are far more likely to influence legislators from their own party," a pair of political scientists concluded in 2002.[16] Each party naturally is going to try to strengthen the power of the institution it controls and weaken the one it does not, but a party that controls both the executive and legislative branches is going to be able to push through legislation in a cooperative fashion.

Governors are more likely to grant favors to legislators of their own party or raise money for them. This, in turn, makes those legislators more likely to support their programs. Some governors curry favor with legislators because they used to be legislators themselves and still have friends in the House or Senate. One-time Tennessee governor Ned McWhorter, for example, was a longtime legislator before taking the top office. He concentrated his attention on a few pet initiatives, such as a major overhaul of the state Medicaid system, and went along with whatever his pals in the legislature were thinking on most other matters.

Unified control of government is no guarantee of success for the governor, however. There certainly have been plenty of governors who were able to work well with legislatures controlled by the other party. But having to do so only made their jobs tougher. Governors need at least a large enough minority of their own party to sustain their vetoes. This is the only definite way to ensure real influence over the legislative process.

Unfortunately for governors, divided control of state governments has become common in recent decades. Voters are more likely to split their tickets and vote for nominees of different parties for different offices. Divided government is likely to make the governorship more difficult, since governors must try to convince political competitors to get with their programs. Cooperation becomes consorting with the enemy.

Political scientists have built on the work David R. Mayhew has done in studying divided power between Congress and the White House to examine divided power in the states. It was once commonly thought that divided power necessarily meant that less work got done. That does not appear to be the case. What it may mean is that different types of bills become law. In other words, a Democratic governor might work with a Republican-controlled legislature to create lots of laws, but the nature of these laws might be very different from what it would have been if the governor had worked with a Democratic legislative majority. A Democratic governor working with a Democratic-controlled legislature should be able to pursue legislation more in keeping with his party's principles and desires than a Democratic governor who has to compromise with a GOP-controlled legislature.

"[E]ach party attempts to strengthen the institution it commands and to weaken the institution controlled by the opposition," noted one political scientist.[17] In other words, if Republicans hold the governorship, they will try to make that office more powerful at the expense of a Democratic legislature and vice versa. But because power is shared under divided government, the two parties cannot just attack each other's program. If they share power, they also share responsibility in the eyes of the voters, and so they have to work together to forge compromises on central issues such as the budget.

Conflict is more likely if the party in opposition to the governor's holds both legislative chambers. If each party controls one chamber, the governor is much more likely to claim victory.[18] It is all a matter of leverage and pressing the advantages your party has.

Ability to Communicate. We've already touched upon the advantage governors have over legislators in regard to media exposure. There is no law that says newspapers and TV stations have to pay more attention to pronouncements from the governor—but that is what happens anyway. Anything legislators say and do takes a back seat. The governor is a single, well-known individual who is important to every voter in the state. A legislator, by contrast, even a powerful one, is just one legislator among 120 or 150 legislators and represents a district that is only a fraction of the state.

Smart governors are aware of the power of the mass media in helping to spread their messages. Contemporary governors have large public relations staffs that deal exclusively with the media and make sure that their governors' faces appear on television regularly. A governor's fame adds to the grandeur of the office, making the officeholder appear more potent to legislators, to aides, and to other people who deal with the governor. Power builds on power, in the sense that a governor who becomes famous for pushing through a landmark change in law becomes a more formidable presence in the state as the governor turns to the next policy battle.

Based on campaign spending per vote, New Hampshire's governor's race was the nation's most expensive in 2002 at $42.77 per voter.

Governors have to play both an "inside" game and an "outside" game. They have to appeal both to capital insiders and to the public at large. A governor who makes every move based on the ability to turn it into a press release or who appeals to the public by bashing the "corruption" in the capital may score points with the media and the public but soon will have few friends in the legislature. In Illinois, Rod Blagojevich was elected governor by railing against the corruption of state government and did not change his theme song once he took office. He refused even to establish a permanent residence in the state capital of Springfield, spending most of his time at home in Chicago. "We're going to keep fighting to reform and change the system and give the people a government that stops spending their money like a bunch of drunken sailors," he said toward the end of his first year in office. Needless to say, the legislators who Blagojevich had likened to drunken sailors were not eager to cooperate with him any more than they had to—even though his own party had a majority in both chambers.

Blagojevich is not alone in his criticisms. Many governors have bashed the legislature. What they have found is that although it made them popular with the public it did not help them get their agendas passed. When he was elected governor of California in 2003, Arnold Schwarzenegger continually threatened to take his agenda directly to the people through ballot initiatives and referenda if the legislature refused to go along for his ride. Yet even Schwarzenegger will not be able to take more than a handful of issues to voters if he cannot get his agenda passed in the legislature.

Merging Formal and Informal Powers

Roy Barnes, who served one term as governor of Georgia from 1999 until 2003, said back during his days in the state legislature, "When you are called down to the governor's office, it is a very impressive office, you're talking to the governor, and you know that he controls things that could be good or ill for your district. He controls grants, he controls roads, and other things."[19] In other words, the formal powers of the governor—the ability to control projects—merge with the informal powers—the mystique of the office—to influence legislators and other supplicants.

When Carroll Campbell became governor of South Carolina in 1987, that state's governor's office was among the weakest in the nation. The state's government consisted of seventy-nine separate administrative agencies, and the governor had sole appointment power in only ten of them. Campbell spent three years arguing that the modern executive needs more power to run a state well. He devoted nearly all of his attention to the office, using all of his informal powers—the ability to persuade, the ability to keep an issue in front of voters and legislators through use of the media—in order to increase his formal powers. In the end, he won. In 1993, the legislature restructured the government. They consolidated the administration into seventeen departments and gave the governor the power to appoint the directors of twelve of them.

The importance of being dealt such a fine political hand of cards can't be stressed enough. Governors with constitutional authority to set the budget, appoint their own people to spend that budget and implement their plans, and a line-item veto to keep legislators intimidated are going to have a lot easier time than their neighbors who lack some or all of those tools. One of those neighbors may be a more skilled politician and ultimately may have more success. People today expect the governor to be a powerful figure in the state and, in most cases, the governors have the tools to be just that. If only because of the power and prestige of the office and the ability to command media attention, a governor holds enormous influence in determining what issues are brought to the forefront and how they are handled.

Becoming Governor and Staying Governor

This chapter has described governors as the most powerful and important political actors in their states. It should come as little surprise then, given the history of politics in this country, that middle-aged white males have dominated the job. Women are being elected governor with greater frequency, but there are still plenty of states that have yet to elect a woman for the top job. In 2004, eight women served as governor, the highest number that had ever served at one time. There have been a handful of Latino and Asian governors. In 1873, P. B. S. Pinchbeck, the black lieutenant governor of Louisiana, was elevated to the post of acting governor for forty-three days, but only one African American has ever been elected as governor of any state.[20] Douglas Wilder of Virginia held the job during the first half of the 1990s.

Many nonpoliticians have been elected governor, including movie star Arnold Schwarzenegger of California, former wrestler Jesse Ventura of Minnesota, and business executives Mark Warner of Virginia and Craig Benson

TABLE 7-3

Ranking of the Personal Power of the Governors, 2004

State	Governor or Governor-elect as of 2004	Electoral Mandate	Position on Ambition Ladder	Personal Future	Job Performance Rating in Public Opinion Polls	Personal Powers Index Score	Rank
Delaware	Ruth Ann Minner, D	5	5	4	na	4.1	1
Kansas	Kathleen Sebelius, D	4	5	5	na	4.7	2
Colorado	Bill Owens, R	5	5	3	5	4.5	3
Iowa	Tom Vilsack, D	4	5	5	4	4.5	3
Louisiana	Kathleen Blanco, D	3	5	5	5	4.5	3
Michigan	Jennifer Granholm, D	3	5	5	5	4.5	3
South Dakota	Mike Rounds, R	5	3	5	5	4.5	3
Texas	Rick Perry, R	5	5	5	3	4.5	3
Wisconsin	Jim Doyle, D	3	5	5	5	4.5	3
New Mexico	Bill Richardson, D	5	3	5	na	4.3	10
Arkansas	Mike Huckabee, R	4	5	3	4	4.0	11
California	Arnold Schwarzenegger, R	5	1	5	5	4.0	11
Illinois	Rod R. Blagojevich, D	4	3	5	4	4.0	11
Kentucky	Ernest Fletcher, R	4	3	5	4	4.0	11
Maine	John Baldacci, D	3	3	5	5	4.0	11
Maryland	Robert L. Ehrlich, Jr., R	3	3	5	5	4.0	11
Minnesota	Tim Pawlenty, R	4	3	5	4	4.0	11
New York	George E. Pataki, R	5	3	5	3	4.0	11
North Carolina	Michael F. Easley, D	3	5	4	4	4.0	11
Ohio	Bob Taft, R	5	5	3	3	4.0	11
Oregon	Ted Kulongoski, D	3	5	5	3	4.0	11
South Carolina	Mark Sanford, R	4	3	5	na	4.0	11
Alaska	Frank H. Murkowski, R	5	3	5	2	3.8	23
Arizona	Janet Napolitano, D	2	5	5	3	3.8	23
Hawaii	Linda Lingle, R	3	2	5	5	3.8	23
Nebraska	Mike Johanns, R	5	2	3	5	3.8	23
New Hampshire	Craig Benson, R	5	1	5	4	3.8	23
Rhode Island	Don Carcieri, R	4	1	5	5	3.8	23
Tennessee	Phil Bredesen, D	3	2	5	5	3.8	23

(Table continues on next page)

TABLE 7-3 *(continued)*

State	Governor or Governor-elect as of 2004	Electoral Mandate	Position on Ambition Ladder	Personal Future	Job Performance Rating in Public Opinion Polls	Personal Powers Index Score	Rank
Connecticut	John G. Rowland, R	5	3	5	1	3.5	30
Georgia	Sonny Perdue, R	3	3	5	3	3.5	30
Idaho	Dirk Kempthorne, R	5	3	3	3	3.5	30
Indiana	Joseph Kernan, D	1	5	4	4	3.5	30
New Jersey	James E. McGreevey, D*	5	2	5	2	3.5	30
North Dakota	John Hoeven, R	4	1	4	5	3.5	30
Pennsylvania	Edward G. Rendell, D	4	2	5	3	3.5	30
Vermont	Jim Douglas, R	2	5	4	3	3.5	30
Florida	Jeb Bush, R	5	1	3	4	3.3	38
Massachusetts	Mitt Romney, R	3	1	5	4	3.3	38
Mississippi	Haley Barbour, R	4	1	5	na	3.3	38
Missouri	Bob Holden, D	2	5	4	2	3.3	38
Montana	Judy Martz, R	3	5	4	1	3.3	38
Nevada	Kenny Guinn, R	5	1	3	4	3.3	38
Oklahoma	Brad Henry, D	2	3	5	na	3.3	38
Utah	Olene Walker, R	1	5	1	5	3.0	45
Alabama	Bob Riley, R	2	3	5	1	2.8	46
Virginia	Mark R. Warner, D	3	1	3	4	2.8	46
Wyoming	Dave Freudenthal, D	2	1	5	na	2.7	48
Washington	Gary Locke, D	5	2	1	2	2.5	49
West Virginia	Bob Wise, D	3	3	1	2	2.3	50
Average score	—	3.7	3.2	4.3	3.7	3.7	—

Source: Thad Beyle, personal data for 2004. For previous years, see www.unc.edu/~beyle.

Notes:

Electoral mandate: 5 = landslide win of 11 or more points; 4 = comfortable majority of 6 to 10 points; 3 = narrow majority of 3 to 5 points; 2 = tight win of 0 to 2 points or a plurality win of under 50%; 1 = succeeded to office.

Position on ambition ladder: 5 = steady progression; 4 =former governors; 3 = legislative leaders or members of Congress; 2 = substate position to governor; 1 = governorship is first elective office.

Personal future: 5 = early in term, can run again; 4 = late in term, can run again; 3 = early in term, term limited; 2 = succeeded to office, can run for election; 1 = late in final term.

Job performance rating in public opinion polls: 5 = over 60% positive job approval rating; 4 = 50 to 59% positive job approval rating; 3 = 40 to 49% positive job approval rating; 2 = 30 to 39% positive job approval rating; 1 = less than 30% positive job approval rating; na = no polling data available. [Source: Author's data]

Personal powers index score: the sum of the scores for EM, AL, PF, JP divided by 4 and rounded to the nearest number, except for those states without a governor's job performance rating where the sum is divided by 3 and rounded to the nearest number.

*In August 2004, McGreevey announced his intention to resign from office in November 2004, to be replaced by state senate president Richard Cody.

MAP 7-1 Women, African American, and Asian American/Pacific Islander Governors by State

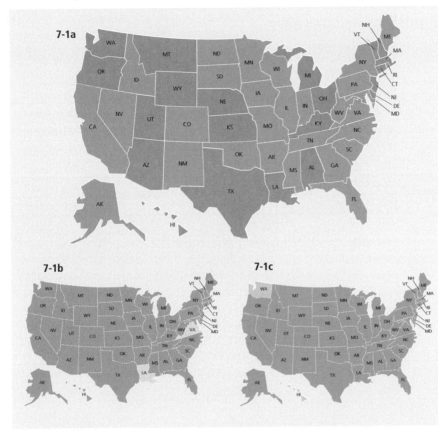

7-1a Women Governors

Alabama
Arizona
Connecticut
Delaware
Hawaii
Kansas
Kentucky
Louisiana
Massachusetts
Michigan
Montana
Nebraska
New Hampshire
New Jersey
Ohio
Oregon
Texas
Utah
Vermont
Washington
Wyoming

7-1b African American Governors

Louisiana
Virginia

7-1c Asian American/ Pacific Islander

Hawaii
Washington

Sources: Data compiled from GenderGap.com, www.gendergap.com/government/governor.htm (accessed April 14, 2004); National Governors Association, www.nga.org/governors/1,1169,C_TRIVIA^D_2118,00. html, and www.nga.org/governors/1,1169,C_TRIVIA^D_2119,00.html (accessed May 13, 2004).

of New Hampshire. Most governors, however, have had a good deal of previous government experience. They have served in the U.S. Congress, the state legislature, or other statewide positions such as lieutenant governor and attorney general or even state supreme court justice. Only a handful of independent or third party candidates have been elected governor in recent years, including Ventura in 1998 and Angus King of Maine in 1994 and 1998.

One qualification for modern governors is quite clear—they must have the ability to raise money. Gubernatorial campaigns have become multimillion dollar affairs, particularly in heavily populated states in which television ads are expensive to run because the media markets are competitive and costly. The total campaign costs for the thirty-six governors' races in

TABLE 7-4

Governors, Past and Present: Women, African Americans, and Asian American and Pacific Islanders

Women			
Miriam "Ma" Ferguson, D-TX	1925–1927; 1933–1935	Ruth Ann Minner, D-DE	2001–present
Nellie Tayloe Ross, D-WY	1925–1927	Judy Martz, R-MT	2001–present
Lurleen Wallace, D-AL	1967–1968	Janet Napolitano, D-AZ	2003–present
Ella Grasso, D-CT	1975–1980	Linda Lingle, R-HI	2003–present
Dixy Lee Ray, D-WA	1977–1981	Kathleen Sebelius, D-KS	2003–present
Vesta Roy, R-NH	1982–1983	Jennifer Granholm, D-MI	2003–present
Martha Layne Collins, D-KY	1984–1987	Olene S. Walker, R-UT	2003–present
Madeleine Kunin, D-VT	1985–1991	Kathleen Blanco, D-LA	2004–present
Kay Orr, R-NE	1987–1991		
Rose Mofford, D-AZ	1988–1991	**African American**	
Joan Finney, D-KS	1991–1995	Pinckney Benton Stewart Pinchback, R-LA	1872–1873
Barbara Roberts, D-OR	1991–1995	L. Douglas Wilder, D-VA	1990–1994
Ann Richards, D-TX	1991–1995		
Christine Todd Whitman, R-NJ	1994–2001	**Asian American/Pacific Islander**	
Jane Dee Hull, R-AZ	1997–2003	George Ariyoshi, D-HI	1974–1986
Jeanne Shaheen, D-NH	1997–2003	John Waihee, D-HI	1986–1995
Nancy Hollister, R-OH	1998–1999	Benjamin Cayetano, D-HI	1995–2002
Jane Swift, R-MA	2001–2003	Gary Locke, D-WA	1997–present

2002 was $840 million—a jump of 63 percent over the campaigns conducted only four years earlier.

Factors Driving Gubernatorial Elections

Like the Winter Olympics, gubernatorial elections in most states have been moved to the second year of the presidential term in what are called "off-year" elections. Thirty-four states now hold their gubernatorial elections in the off-year. Another five states—Virginia, New Jersey, Kentucky, Mississippi, and Louisiana—hold their elections in odd-numbered years. Nine states—Delaware, Indiana, Missouri, Montana, New Hampshire, North Carolina, North Dakota, Utah, and Vermont—hold their elections at the same time as the presidential contest. In addition, New Hampshire and Vermont, the only states that have clung to the old tradition of two-year terms, hold elections for governor every even-numbered year.

The majority of governors are elected in the even-numbered off-year because states want to insulate the contests from getting mixed up in national

TABLE 7-5

Where Do They Come From? Governors' Backgrounds

Governors with Military Service	Governors with Previous Government Experience	Governors' Educational Background
Sonny Perdue (GA)–Air Force	Bob Riley (AL)–U.S. House	Bob Riley (AL)–University of Alabama
Frank Murkowski (AK)–Coast Guard	Frank Murkowski (AK)–state legislature, U.S. Senate, State Commissioner of Economic Development	Frank Murkowski (AK)–Seattle University
Joseph Kernan (IN)–Navy	Janet Napolitano (AZ)–state attorney general	Mike Huckabee (AR)–Ouachita Baptist University
Ernest Fletcher (KY)–Air Force	Mike Huckabee (AR)–lieutenant governor	Janet Napolitano (AZ)–Santa Clara University
Ted Kulongoski (OR)–Marines	Bill F. Owens (CO)–state legislature	Arnold Schwarzenegger (CA)–University of Wisconsin, Superior
Edward Rendell (PA)–Army	John G. Rowland (CT)–state legislature, U.S. House	Bill F. Owens (CO)–University of Texas, MA
Rick Perry (TX)–Air Force	Ruth Ann Minner (DE)–state legislature, lieutenant governor	John G. Rowland (CT)–Villanova University
	Jeb Bush (FL)–state secretary of commerce	Ruth Ann Minner (DE)–GED, some college
	Sonny Perdue (GA)–state legislature	Jeb Bush (FL)–University of Texas, Austin
	Linda Lingle (HI)–mayor	Sonny Perdue (GA)–University of Georgia, PhD
	Dirk Kempthorne (ID)–U.S. Senate, mayor	Linda Lingle (HI)–California State University, Northridge
	Rod Blagojevich (IL)–state legislature	Dirk Kempthorne (ID)–University of Idaho
	Joseph Kernan (IN)–lieutenant governor, mayor, city controller	Rod Blagojevich (IL)–Pepperdine University, JD
	Tom Vilsack (IA)–state legislature, mayor	Joseph Kernan (IN)–University of Notre Dame
	Kathleen Sebelius (KS)–state insurance commissioner	Tom Vilsack (IA)–Albany Law School, Union University, JD
	Ernest Fletcher (KY)–U.S. House, state legislature	Kathleen Sebelius (KS)–not available
	Kathleen Blanco (LA)–lieutenant governor, state legislature	Ernest Fletcher (KY)–University of Kentucky, MD
	John Baldacci (ME)–state legislature, U.S. House	Kathleen Blanco (LA)–University of Louisville, Lafayette
	Robert Ehrlich (MD)–state legislature, U.S. House	John Baldacci (ME)–University of Maine, Orono
	Jennifer Granholm (MI)–state attorney general	Robert Ehrlich (MD)–Wake Forest University Law School (JD)
	Tim Pawlenty (MN)–state legislature	Mitt Romney (MA)–Harvard University Business School and Law School, MBA, JD
	Haley Barbour (MS)–U.S. Senate, Director of White House Office of Public Affairs	Jennifer Granholm (MI)–Harvard Law School, JD
		Tim Pawlenty (MN)–University of Minnesota, JD
		Haley Barbour (MS)–University of Mississippi Law School, JD
		Bob Holden (MO)–Harvard University, Kennedy School of Government

(Table continues on next page)

TABLE 7-5 *(continued)*

Governors with Military Service	Governors with Previous Government Experience	Governors' Educational Background
	Bob Holden (MO)–state legislature, state treasurer	Judy Martz (MT)–attended Eastern Montana College
	Judy Martz (MT)–lieutenant governor	Mike Johanns (NE)–Creighton University, JD
	Mike Johanns (NE)–mayor	Kenny Guinn (NV)–Utah State University, PhD
	*James McGreevey (NJ)–state legislature, mayor	Craig Benson (NH)–Syracuse University, MBA
	Bill Richardson (NM)–U.S. House	*James McGreevey (NJ)–Georgetown University, JD, Harvard University, MA
	George E. Pataki (NY)–state legislature, mayor	Bill Richardson (NM)–Fletcher School of Law and Diplomacy, Tufts University, MA
	Michael Easley (NC)–state attorney general	George E. Pataki (NY)–Columbia University, JD
	Bob Taft (OH)–state legislature, secretary of state	Michael Easley (NC)–North Carolina Central University School of Law, JD
	Brad Henry (OK)–state legislature	John Hoeven (ND)–Northwestern University, MBA
	Ted Kulongoski (OR)–state legislature, state attorney general, state insurance commissioner, state supreme court	Bob Taft (OH)–University of Cincinnati Law School, JD, Princeton University, MA
	Edward Rendell (PA)–mayor	Brad Henry (OK)–University of Oklahoma College of Law, JD
	Don Carcieri (RI)–U.S. House	Ted Kulongoski (OR)–University of Missouri, JD
	Mark Sanford (SC)–U.S. House	Edward Rendell (PA)–Villanova Law School, JD
	Mike Rounds (SD)–state legislature	Don Carcieri (RI)–Brown University
	Phil Bredesen (TN)–mayor	Mark Sanford (SC)–University of Virginia, MBA
	Rick Perry (TX)–state legislature, lieutenant governor, commissioner of agriculture	Mike Rounds (SD)–South Dakota State University
	Olene Walker (UT)–lieutenant governor, state legislature	Phil Bredesen (TN)–Harvard University
	Jim Douglas (VT)–state legislature, secretary of state, state treasurer	Rick Perry (TX)–Texas A&M University
	Gary Locke (WA)–state legislature	Olene Walker (UT)–Stanford University, MA; University of Utah, PhD
	Bob Wise (WV)–state legislature, U.S. House	Jim Douglas (VT)–Middlebury College
	Jim Doyle (WI)–state attorney general	Mark Warner (VA)–Harvard University Law School, JD
	Dave Freudenthal (WY)–U.S. Attorney for Wyoming	Gary Locke (WA)–Boston University, JD
		Bob Wise (WV)–Tulane University College of Law, JD
		Jim Doyle (WI)–Harvard University Law School, JD
		Dave Freudenthal (WY)–University of Wyoming College of Law, JD

Sources: Compiled from National Governors Association Online, www.nga.org/governors/1,1169,,00.html, and governors' Web sites.

*In August 2004, McGreevey announced his intention to resign from office in November 2004, to be replaced by state senate president Richard Cody.

issues. They want voters to concentrate on matters of importance just to the state instead of diverting their attention to federal issues brought up in presidential campaigns. This was the desire and the intent. But the plan has not been a 100 percent success. Elections for governors are often the biggest thing on the ballot, so voters use the races as a way of expressing their opinions about who is *not* on the ballot. In 1994, when antipathy was running high against Democratic president Bill Clinton, Republicans not only took control of both houses of Congress but also won a majority of the governorships for the first time in more than a decade. In 2002 and 2003, when Republican president George W. Bush was generally popular, Republicans did better than had been expected in gubernatorial contests.

Overall, however, governors' races are still less prone to follow national trends than, say, elections for the U.S. Senate. The reason? Voters understand that the governor's position is important in and of itself. They consider state-level issues carefully when choosing a governor. The dominant concern in most gubernatorial contests is the state economy. Even the most powerful politicians have only limited control over the economy at best, but voters tend to reward or punish the incumbent party based on the performance of the economy. If a state is faring poorly or doing considerably worse than its neighbors, the incumbent party is likely to struggle.

Economic matters certainly play a role in elections if the state budget is in trouble. Voters consider budget crises a sign of bad management and will take their anger out on the governor in many instances. In 2002, most state budgets were suffering shortfalls as revenues dipped due to a recession. Only a dozen governors were reelected that year, whereas a record two dozen freshman governors took office. Of those new governors, fully nineteen succeeded a governor of another party or an independent. In other words, voters in many states were ready for a change and blamed the incumbent party for the state's money problems.

For most of the twentieth century, Democrats dominated gubernatorial contests, but they lost their edge to Republicans starting in 1993. Since then, Republicans have won 62 percent of the time—98 gubernatorial elections out of 158. The GOP held twenty-eight out of fifty states in 2004. Yet, in general, momentum over the last several years has swung back and forth between the parties. In 2002, the two parties showed that they are each competitive in nearly every state. Republicans were elected governor for the first time in decades in states such as Hawaii, Maryland, and Georgia. Democrats, on the other hand, were elected in places where their party had struggled for years to win a statewide office, including Kansas, Wyoming, and Oklahoma.

Since gubernatorial elections attract a great deal of media attention, voters are more likely to vote for the person rather than the party. Indeed, voters more often use party as a guide in lower-profile contests such as state legislative races. Voters are better informed about individual gubernatorial candidates. One reason is greater news coverage of the races. Another important factor is the amount of money that candidates for governor spend to publicize themselves. Candidates create extensive organizations that promote their campaigns and use all the modern techniques of political consultants, polling, and media buys. Voters are far more likely, even in less-populous states, to get to know the candidates through TV ads and brochures than through speeches or other personal appearances. In 2002, New York governor George Pataki spent $44 million to win a second term. Even so, he still was outspent by a third party candidate who spent more than $75 million of his own money. The Democratic candidate in Texas, Tony Sanchez, spent $76.3 million in his losing effort. California governor Gray Davis spent $64 million winning reelection that year, but he was recalled in 2003. Arnold Schwarzenegger won the special replacement election that was held on the same day as the recall.[21]

Keeping and Leaving Office

For all of the potential upsets, the office of governor is a pretty stable one these days. States used to change governors just about every chance they got, but that is no longer the case. According to political scientist Thad Beyle, states changed governors by an average of more than two times apiece during the 1950s. By the 1980s, though, turnover occurred on average just over once a decade. During the 1990s, the rate climbed back up a bit, so that the average state changed governors 1.4 times.

It is not unusual to see governors get reelected by vote margins that top 70 percent. Not only are they in charge of setting policy, but they also actually get things done. They educate children, build roads, respond with help when miners get trapped. Translation? They are generally viewed more favorably than legislators. From a constituent's standpoint, what do legislators do, after all, except vote, and their votes tend to be highly partisan. Governors, on the other hand, have to compromise because of the number of people they must deal with. Of course, there are governors who are polarizing figures, but in the main they are less contentious figures than legislators or members of Congress.

Governors are rarely booted out of office prematurely. In June 2004, Connecticut governor John Rowland resigned after being investigated by the legislature for accepting gifts from a contractor with business before the state. Faced with possible **impeachment** and a federal criminal investigation, Rowland, one of the nation's longest serving governors at the time, chose to step down. In 2003, Gray Davis was the first governor recalled, or asked to leave office, since Lynn Frazier of North Dakota was booted from office more than eighty years earlier on charges of corruption. Voters felt that Davis had dug California into such a deep hole financially that the state would take years to recover. His liberal views on such issues as gay marriage had also stirred up controversy. Arnold Schwarzenegger succeeded Davis in the most publicized state election of modern time.

IMPEACHMENT

A process by which the legislature can remove executive branch officials, such as the governor, or judges from offices for corruption or other reasons.

Arizona governor Evan Mecham was impeached and convicted in 1987 for impeding an investigation and lending state money to a car dealership that he owned. The previous conviction dated back to 1929, when Henry Johnston of Oklahoma was removed for general incompetency by a legislature with possible political motives. In 1998, the U.S. House of Representatives impeached President Bill Clinton for lying about his sex life, but the

TABLE 7-6

Recall Rules

State	Specific Grounds for Recall	Signature Requirement	Petition Circulation Time	Election for Successor
Alaska	Yes	25%	Not specified	Successor appointed
Arizona	No	25%	120 days	Simultaneous (5)
California	No	12%	160 days	Simultaneous (6)
Colorado	No	25%	60 days	Simultaneous (6)
Georgia	Yes	15% (1)	90 days	Separate special
Idaho	No	20% (1)	60 days	Successor appointed
Kansas	Yes	40%	90 days	Successor appointed
Louisiana	No	33.3% (1)	180 days	Separate special
Michigan	No	25%	90 days	Separate special
Minnesota	Yes	25%	90 days	Separate special
Montana	Yes	10% (1)	3 months	Separate special
Nevada	No	25%	60 days	Simultaneous (5)
New Jersey	No	25% (2)	320 days (4)	Separate special
North Dakota	No	25%	Not specified	Simultaneous (5)
Oregon	No	15% (3)	90 days	Separate special
Rhode Island	Yes	15%	90 days	Separate special
Washington	Yes	25%	270 days	Successor appointed
Wisconsin	No	25%	60 days	Simultaneous (5)

Eighteen states permit the recall of elected officials. This table lists the requirements to recall those officials. Rules for recalling legislators and judges may differ.

Source: Adapted from the National Conference of State Legislatures by Alan Greenblatt, "Recall Rules," in "Total Recall," *Governing* magazine, September 2003, 26.

Notes: Signature requirement is % of votes cast in last election for official being recalled. Exceptions: (1) % of eligible voters at time of last election; (2) % of registered voters in electoral district of official sought to be recalled; (3) % of total votes cast in officer's district for all candidates for governor in last election. (4) Applies to governor or U.S. senator; all others 160 days. (5) Recall ballot consists of a list of candidates for the office held by the person against whom the recall petition was filed. The name of the officer against whom the recall was filed may appear on the list. (6) Recall ballot consists of two parts: The first asks whether the officer against whom the recall petition was filed should be recalled. The second part lists candidates who have qualified for the election. The name of the officer against whom the recall was filed may not appear on this list.

A Difference that Makes a Difference:
From State House to White House: Translating a Governorship into a Presidency

How big of an advantage is it to run for the presidency as a sitting governor as opposed to some other position? About as big as they come. For more than a quarter of a century, every occupant of the White House except one has come to the presidency fresh from the governor's seat.

Four out of the last five presidents were previously governors—Jimmy Carter, Ronald Reagan, Bill Clinton, and George W. Bush. The one exception was Bush's father, George H.W. Bush, who came to the Oval Office after serving as Reagan's vice president. Very early in the 2004 presidential campaign season, it looked as though two former governors—Bush of Texas and Howard Dean of Vermont—were destined to go head to head.

In late July 2004, however, it was John Kerry, long-time senator from Massachusetts, who emerged as the Democratic nominee. Prognostication is always risky, but given Kerry's long and public record as a legislator the odds are not on his side. Compare the record of governors to holders of other offices: no sitting U.S. senator has been elected president since 1960. No

member of the U.S. House has been elected since James Garfield, all the way back in 1880.

What makes governors such attractive candidates for the nation's most powerful office? And what makes other legislators so *un*attractive?

For one thing, governors are the only other politicians who have run governments that are anywhere near as complicated as the federal government. Given the complex nature of some state governments, it may even be a toss-up sometimes as to which is the more difficult—ruling one state or ruling all fifty. True, governors do not formulate foreign policy, but they do have to become experts in running departments that cover everything from taxes and education to public health and public safety. Governors have to run things. Members of Congress just vote. "Because the presidency is no place to begin to develop executive talents, the executive career-ist clearly is preferable to the legislator," writes political scientist Larry J. Sabato.[a]

Furthermore, legislators have to vote "yes" or "no" on thousands of issues, so they leave a long paper trail. A trail that is a clear record bound to contain more con-

Senate failed to convict him. A few governors, including Fife Symington of Arizona (1997), Jim Guy Tucker of Arkansas (1996), and Guy Hunt of Alabama (1993), have resigned following criminal convictions.

A more common threat to gubernatorial staying power is term limits. Governors in thirty-six states are limited to two terms or two consecutive terms in office. The governor of Utah can spend no more than three terms in office. The only two states that have two-year terms instead of four-year terms—Vermont and New Hampshire—place no limits on the number of terms a governor may serve. Howard Dean served five full terms as governor of Vermont before running for president in 2004.

So what do governors do once they leave office? Several of them, like Dean, run for higher offices like the presidency. Four out of the last five presidents, in fact, were governors in their last jobs before winning the White House. (See Box 7-2.) Not surprisingly, once in office, these former

troversial elements than any governor's list of bridges built and budgets balanced. Legislators' records are often distorted in smear campaigns that make use of attack ads and mudslinging. Their vote for a $300 billion bill becomes defined by one tiny provision it contained.

Congress is a major part of official Washington, and legislators hardly can say they have no connection with what occurs there. Conversely, governors running for the White House can always claim they are Washington "outsiders" who are going to sweep in and clean up the town. Former governor-turned-president Clinton reportedly advised Senator Joe Biden, D-Del., that senators had to overcome big handicaps to run for president. Not only did they have their records to explain, but they also had forgotten how to speak the language of the average person. "When you get to Washington, the only people you talk to are the elites: elites in the press, elites among the lobbyists, elites that you hire on your own staff," Clinton told Biden. "You're not regularly talking to ordinary, everyday people."[b]

Governors have to talk to "real people" every day. By contrast, the out-of-touch image of Congress and Washington in the public mind hampers members of Congress seeking national office. "It could probably be shown by facts and figures that there is no distinctly native American criminal class except Congress," Mark Twain wrote. Governors running for national office invariably present themselves as fresh alternatives to the tired habits of Washington, promising to change the culture and tone of the nation's capital.

That they fail to do so is almost a given. That opens up the field for the next fresh face from the state of California or Arkansas or Texas. Do not forget that all of the recent governors turned presidents came from the South or West—reflecting the growing populations and political power of these regions.

[a] Larry J. Sabato, *Goodbye to Good-Time Charlie,* 2nd ed. (Washington, D.C.: CQ Press, 1983), 33.
[b] E. J. Dionne Jr., "Govs 4, Senators 0. Tough Odds," *Washington Post,* January 4, 2004, E4.

governors appoint other governors to positions in their administrations. They understand that these individuals know and understand what it means to lead and how to delegate and get things done. Former Texas governor George W. Bush appointed five former governors to cabinet positions and an ambassadorship after moving into the Oval Office in 2000. Governors also regularly run for the U.S. Senate. An even dozen senators serving in 2004 had previously been governors.

But many politicians find that being governor—able to make and implement decisions, with a large staff and all the machinery of state government at their disposal—is the best job they'll ever have. Entering the Senate or serving as a cabinet official is generally considered a step up the professional ladder from being a governor. Still, Dirk Kempthorne, who gave up a Senate seat to run for governor of Idaho in 1998, said that many of his colleagues regretted having to give up the governorship to come to Washington and be just one more legislative voice among a hundred. "They all said that being governor is the best job in the world," Kempthorne said upon taking office. "I'm ready to find out." [22]

Other Executive Offices

Only the president is elected to the executive branch of the federal government. The vice president is the president's running mate and is elected as part of a package deal. The heads of all the cabinet departments—Defense, Transportation, Energy, Agriculture, and so on—are appointed by the president, subject to Senate approval. For the most part, the voters do not get to say who gets in and who stays out.

Things work differently at the state level. The governor is the only statewide official elected in every state. Most states, however, also have several other statewide officials elected in their own right. This is a holdover from earlier times when the governor was not invested with much power and authority was distributed among a number of officeholders. Texas still has two dozen officials elected statewide, while New Jersey only elects the governor. Most states have a handful of officials elected statewide, and we'll outline the responsibilities of a few of them here.

Lieutenant Governor

The office of lieutenant governor traditionally has been seen as something of a joke. Lieutenant governors have nothing to do but wait for their governors to resign or die so that they can accrue some real power. That situation has changed just over the last few years. The early years of the twenty-first century saw nearly every state struggling to balance its budget. Some states, such as Virginia and Georgia, initially responded by slashing the budgets and the powers of their lieutenant governors' offices. In other places and in other times, the shortfalls, combined with the new security demands created by the terrorist attacks of 2001, convinced governors that there was plenty of work to go around and that they should utilize the skills of their running mates and partners.

In Nebraska, for example, Governor Mike Johanns appointed Lieutenant Governor Dave Heineman to head all of the state's homeland security efforts immediately after the September 11 attacks. Minnesota's lieutenant governor Carol Molnau was given charge of the state's Department of Transportation after her election in 2002 and saved the state the $108,000-a-year expense of hiring a separate transportation secretary. Similarly, right after the 2003 election, Kentucky's new lieutenant governor, Stephen Pence, was named secretary of the Department of Justice, which put him in charge of public safety, corrections and law enforcement, the state police, and vehicle enforcement. "It's rare that the lieutenant governor doesn't have some specific duties," says Julia Hurst, director of the National Lieutenant Governors Association.[23]

In the cases cited here, power was granted to the lieutenant governor because of the desire of the governor. The next person to hold the office may have very different responsibilities or nothing to do at all. In many states, though, the lieutenant governor's responsibilities are laid out by law. In Indiana, for example, the lieutenant governor's portfolio includes the Departments of Commerce and Agriculture. In half the states, the lieutenant governor presides over the state Senate and has varying degrees of authority in each of these states. In Texas and Mississippi, lieutenant governors play much more than a ceremonial role. Not only do they preside over the Senate, but they also set the agenda and appoint senators to committees. In both states, the lieutenant governor often is referred to as the most powerful figure in the state, with authority in both the executive and legislative branches.

Twenty-four states elect their governors and lieutenant governors as part of the same ticket. In eighteen other states, the two are elected separately. The other eight states—Arizona, Maine, New Hampshire, New Jersey, Oregon, Tennessee, and Wyoming—don't elect lieutenant governors, although in Tennessee the Speaker of the Senate is given the title. Electing the governor and lieutenant governor separately can be a cause of mischief, especially if the people elected are not from the same party. Lieutenant governors often assume the powers of the governors when their bosses are out of the state. During the 1970s, Republican Mike Curb of California had a lot of fun appointing judges and issuing **executive orders** while Democratic governor Jerry Brown was busy out of the state doing, among other things, his own presidential campaigning.

Attorney General

Perhaps the statewide office that has undergone the greatest transformation in recent years is that of attorney general. Always referred to as the top law enforcement officer in the state, the duties of the attorney general have sometimes been quite minimal, with most criminal prosecutions being taken care of at the county level. But attorneys general have become major political players, finding new power by banding together in multistate consumer protection cases against Microsoft, financial firms, toymakers, drug companies, and shoemakers Reebok and Keds, among many other examples.

The granddaddy of all such cases were the lawsuits filed against the tobacco companies during the mid-1990s. The attorneys general argued that the cigarette makers had engaged in fraud and caused a great deal of

EXECUTIVE ORDERS

Rules or regulations with the force of law that governors can create directly under the statutory authority given them.

sickness and health conditions that the states ended up paying to treat through Medicaid and other programs. An initial agreement with the industry failed to be ratified by Congress. Instead, in 1998 the attorneys general settled their lawsuits with the companies on their own. The tobacco companies had to pay the states an estimated $246 billion over twenty-five years. More recently, New York attorney general Eliot Spitzer has gotten as much attention as any other state official and has been featured prominently in *Time* and *Newsweek,* among other national media outlets, for pursuing cases against brokerage firms and mutual funds.

New York attorney general Eliot Spitzer has made enough noise about big business corruption to catch the ear of not only fellow political officials, but also the general public. Spitzer, shown here in December 2003 crusading to curb Internet spam, has been aggressive in prosecuting corporate accounting crimes, among other causes. Some critics claim that attorneys general pursue such cases as much to help raise their own level of recognition and influence as to help their constituencies.

Not surprisingly, there has been a backlash against these newly powerful officials. One of the great philosophical divides in U.S. politics lies between those with opposing views of how business should be regulated. There are those who believe that businesses have a right to conduct their affairs with a minimum of interference from state governments, which can only hinder their productivity and profits. Others believe just as strongly that conducting business in a state is a privilege that confers with it a number of responsibilities that the state has the duty to enforce. The majority of state attorneys general over the past few years have acted as if they were members of the "privilege" camp, and that has fueled the rise of groups designed to combat what the business sector sees as excessive regulatory activism.

Attorneys general have traditionally been Democrats, their campaigns funded by trial lawyers. In recent years, the U.S. Chamber of Commerce and many business groups have spent millions trying to defeat "activist" attorney general candidates. "Historically . . . attorney general races were off most business people's radar screens," says Bob LaBrant of the Michigan Chamber of Commerce. Today, "there's greater incentive to get involved in an attorney general race because of the increased involvement of attorneys general across the country in litigation against the business community."[24] The Republican Attorneys General Association was founded in 1999 to elect candidates who believed that their colleagues had gone too far in pursuit of business regulations and the revenues such cases can generate. The number of GOP attorneys general climbed from twelve in 1999 to twenty by 2003.

When any aspect of government extends its power, there is the likelihood of a counter-reaction by some other part of government or by the media or other private sector forces against it. And the main battleground is always the ballot box. Voters elect those candidates they feel will get the most done for themselves and for their states.

TABLE 7-7

The Powers of the Offices

| | In many states, | |
Lieutenant Governors . . .	Secretaries of State . . .	Attorneys General . . .
Preside over the senate	File and/or archive state records and regulations; other corporate documents	Institute civil suits
Appoint committees	Administer uniform commercial code provisions	Represent state agencies and defend and/or challenge the constitutionality of legislative or administrative actions
Break roll-call ties	Publish state manual or directory, session laws, state constitution, statues, and/or administrative rules and regulations	Enforce open meetings and records laws
Assign bills	Open legislative sessions	Revoke corporate charters
May be assigned special duties by governor	Enroll and/or retain copies of bills	Enforce antitrust prohibitions against monopolistic enterprises
Serve as cabinet member or a member of an advisory body	Register lobbyists	Enforce air, water pollution, and hazardous waste laws in a majority of states
Serve as acting governor when the governor is out of state		Handle criminal appeals and serious statewide criminal prosecutions
		Intervene in public utility rate cases
		Enforce the provisions of charitable trusts
		Enforce open meetings and records laws

Sources: Compiled from the National Lieutenant Governors Association, www.nlga.us/Members.htm (accessed May 13, 2004); *The Book of the States 2003* (Lexington, Ky.: Council of State Governments, 2003), 215, 221, and 224; and the National Association of Attorneys General, www.naag.org/ag/duties.php (accessed May 13, 2004).

Other Offices

In 2003, New Mexico governor Bill Richardson convinced voters to approve a referendum that gave him the power to name the state's top education official directly. Richardson knew he would receive the credit or blame for running the schools anyway, so he wanted to have the power to shape policy in that office by being the boss of the person who ran it.

Every state elects its governor and most states elect a lieutenant governor and attorney general. In terms of what other offices are held by elected officials—as opposed to officials appointed by the governor or boards and commissions—the states vary widely. The theory behind electing many officials directly is that it gives the public a greater voice in shaping a variety of state programs, instead of just selecting a governor and leaving it all up to him or her.

Only a few states, including Georgia, Montana, and Oregon, elect a state superintendent of education. In Nebraska, a state board of education is elected and the board in turn selects a superintendent. Several states, mostly in the South, directly elect their secretary of agriculture. An increasing number of states allow citizens to vote for an insurance commissioner. Most states elect a secretary of state who, in turn, regulates elections in those states. Many states run their executive branches similarly—if there isn't an elected agriculture secretary there is certain to be an appointed one.

Some believe, however, that electing separate department heads makes too much of government political. A state treasurer who has to worry about getting reelected might not make politically unpopular but fiscally necessary decisions to make sure that the state's books are balanced. The other trouble with electing officials is that the departments they head will squabble over money and power instead of being part of a team that is working together to promote the greater good.

Conclusion

How did governors become the most important political figures in their states? Over the years, their offices have become the center of state power, with more and more authority given to them. The power of governors now matches, in most cases, the prestige they have always enjoyed. It is always a balancing act when trying to weigh the interests of direct citizen selection of their leaders versus the need to have professional people appointed to pursue a coherent policy promulgated by a single, accountable leader. Currently, the pendulum is swinging in favor of investing more power within the office of the governor.

Once weak, unable to set policy or budgets, governors have become unquestioned leaders. They are able to select cabinets that run most of the state agencies according to the governors' priorities. Sometimes their staff picks prove to be embarrassments, but they are able to fire bad people in hopes of seeing their agendas pushed forward. Many positions are designed with staggered terms so that governors cannot appoint their own people to every position. Strong governors, though, are able to combine their power of appointment with their ability to command attention from the mass media in order to set the terms of political issues and their direction in their states. That clout extends to the judicial branch, with most governors able to appoint most state judges.

Their control of budgets and veto authority provides governors with enormous sway over the legislative branch as well. While they never get everything they want from their legislatures, they almost always get more of what they want than other individual legislators.

The unrivalled power of governors and their ability to command attention from the media and political donors makes them the leading political actors at the state level. Their ability to put people to work in shaping policy and campaigns, as well as their ability to raise money, makes them players in political races ranging from local and legislative contests all the way, in many instances, to the presidency.

Governors, in short, are the top dogs in the states.

Key Concepts

activist governor (p. 214)

appointment powers (p. 224)

executive orders (p. 249)

formal powers (p. 223)

impeachment (p. 244)

informal powers (p. 223)

supermajority vote (p. 218)

tenure (p. 223)

veto (p. 218)

Suggested Readings

Behn, Robert D., ed. *Governors on Governing.* New York: Greenwood Press, 1991. Sixteen sitting governors talk about what they do.

Herzik, Eric B., and Brent W. Brown, eds. *Gubernatorial Leadership and State Policy.* New York: Greenwood Press, 1991. A collection of essays by political scientists on the roles and powers of governors.

Congressional Quarterly's Guide to U.S. Elections, 4th ed. Washington, D.C.: CQ Press, 2001. Part Four contains records of all gubernatorial primary and general elections since 1776 as well as a host of other data pertaining to governors.

Rosenthal, Alan. *Governors and Legislatures: Contending Powers.* Washington, D.C.: CQ Press, 1990. An examination of the role of governors and their relations with the other policymaking branch of government.

Sabato, Larry J. *Goodbye to Good-Time Charlie,* 2nd ed. Washington, D.C.: CQ Press, 1983. An overview of the role of governors and how it has changed since World War II.

Suggested Web Sites

http://library.cqpress.com. CQ Press's Electronic Library has an online voting and elections collection with a component for gubernatorial elections.

www.csg.org. Web site of the Council of State Governments, a forum for state officials to swap information on issues of common concern, such as drugs, water, and any number of other policy matters.

www.naag.org. Web site of the National Association of Attorneys General, which has become increasingly prominent as state attorneys general have banded together on a number of high-profile cases.

www.nga.org. Web site of the National Governors Association, which shares information among governors and also lobbies the federal government on their behalf.

www.stateside.com. Web site of Multistate Associates, a lobbying firm that keeps close tabs on policies and actions in the states.

CHAPTER 8

Courts
Turning Law into Politics

It was not Moses, but state judge Roy Moore who put the Ten Commandments in an Etowah County, Alabama, courtroom in 1997. Civil libertarians saw politics, not divine guidance, in this act and accused Moore of using his position of public authority to promote religion. Moore's supporters, rallying at the Alabama state capitol, made their views clear in dress as well as words. In 2003, divine intervention failed to save him from being removed from office after a similar attempt to display the holy laws.

8

Why are some states' judges elected and some appointed?

Why are some states' courts more likely to impose the death penalty than others?

When President George W. Bush suggested in 2004 that the U.S. Constitution be amended to ban gay marriages, a major reason he cited was **activist judges.**

Bush thought that judges in Massachusetts and other states had overstepped their bounds by interpreting antidiscrimination laws as applying to marriage.

ACTIVIST JUDGES

Judges who act as independent policymakers by creatively interpreting constitutions and statutes.

The idea that judges are creating new laws by misinterpreting or misapplying old ones is a common complaint, particularly among conservatives in recent years.

Such complaints are one big reason the job of judge has become a lot more political. When judges' rulings don't rubberstamp the political goals of the legislative and executive branches, the first words heard are "activist judges." Explicitly political arguments once were limited to the executive and legislative branches. Judges, often appointed to life terms, were meant to keep above the passions of the day and stick to strict legal interpretations based on precedent instead of their own opinions.

That all has changed. The decisions judges make have become highly political. In many states, judges are elected to their positions and, as such, must answer to the will of the voters. That means, for instance, that because there is broad public support for capital punishment, elected judges are more likely to uphold such decisions than judges appointed to the position. Also, elections for state judges have become much more expensive affairs, with interest groups funding high-cost campaigns. After all, what is the point of getting new legislation passed if a judge throws it out as unconstitutional?

The pressure on judges to be friendly to political whims has made for a major shift in how both the public and the judges themselves view the role of the judiciary. Fewer people seem to buy the old idea that judges are impartial observers of the law. Court decisions sometimes appear explicitly political, as when the New Jersey Supreme Court, dominated by Democratic appointees, allowed the Democratic Party in 2002 to substitute its nominee for the U.S. Senate long after the apparent deadline had passed. Or as in 2000, when the U.S. Supreme Court overruled a Florida Supreme Court decision on recounting ballots, which pretty much handed the presidential election to Bush over Vice President Al Gore.

More and more judicial action takes place in state courts. When people complained on old TV shows about how they felt abused or ripped off by their friends, those friends would often say, "Don't make a federal case about it." In the real world of crime and legal conflict, there are actually relatively few federal cases, since those involve violations of federal law, constitutional rights, or lawsuits that cross state borders. In 2002, only 341,393 cases went to trial in U.S. district courts. By comparison, approximately ninety-two million cases were filed in the lowest state courts that same year.[1]

With the exception of celebrity trials like the O. J. Simpson murder case, state courts operate largely below the public's radar. Yet they are enormously important institutions. They have the awesome responsibility to resolve the vast majority of the nation's disputes. If you crash your car or your landlord evicts you, if you get divorced and fight for child custody, if your neighbor's tree lands in your yard, or if your employer won't pay you, then you'll find yourself in a state court. State courts are also where virtually all criminal cases are tried, from drunk driving to murder, misdemeanors to capital offenses. If you get a serious enough traffic ticket, you will find yourself in a state court.

State courts even decide whom you legally can have sex with or marry. Indeed, it was the courts that stopped states from arresting people for interracial marriages. Almost twenty years before the U.S. Supreme Court gave the constitutional okay in 1967, the California Supreme Court struck down a statute forbidding interracial marriages in the 1940s. The California court held that Andrea Perez, a Latina then considered white, could marry Sylvester Davis, an African American, and ruled that marriage is "a fundamental right of free men." It did so over strenuous dissents that accused the court's majority of imposing its will on the legislature.[2]

Today, state courts are at the forefront of another marriage issue. In Massachusetts, the state supreme court held in a controversial 4-3 decision that "the right to marry means little if it does not include the right to marry the person of one's choice." They found no constitutional basis to deny the protection, benefits, and obligations of civil marriage to two people of the same sex who want to marry, especially when it put children of such unions at a disadvantage. When the legislature started constructing a civil union law to satisfy this decision, based on one demanded by a Vermont state court, the Massachusetts court said just forget it.

The court clarified its initial opinion—only marriage would satisfy the Massachusetts constitution—and explained that "the history of our nation has demonstrated that separate is seldom, if ever, equal." Each state has the right, just as Massachusetts did regarding gay marriage, to be the final interpreter of its own, unique constitution. The increasing reliance on state constitutions as a source of rights in recent years has been termed the New Judicial Federalism. By May 2004, more than six hundred gay and lesbian couples had registered to be married in the state.

In Massachusetts at least, the extremely polarizing political issue of gay marriage was resolved by supreme court justices who were appointed to the bench and are entitled to serve until their seventieth birthday without ever

A Difference that Makes a Difference: The New Judicial Federalism

A century ago, state supreme courts were described as so quiet, "you could hear the justices' arteries clog." [a] No one says this today, and the New Judicial Federalism is one big reason why.

This doctrine describes a newfound reliance on state constitutions to protect those rights not covered by the U.S. Constitution. Under the principles of federalism, each state has its own justice system—distinct from those of its neighbors and from the federal system—and its own constitution. The U.S. Constitution is the supreme law of the land, and no state court can interpret its own state's constitution in a way that limits rights secured by the federal charter. States are free, however, to interpret their own constitutions any way they like, except for that single proviso.

For most of the country's history, state constitutions were overlooked. Rarely were they relied on to overturn state laws, especially on the basis of civil rights. But starting in the early 1970s, state supreme courts increasingly began to use state constitutions as independent sources of rights. By 1986, Justice William J. Brennan characterized the "[r]ediscovery by state supreme courts of the broader protections afforded their own citizens by their state constitutions [as] . . . probably the most important development in constitutional jurisprudence in our time." [b]

In many legal areas, the actual impact of judicial federalism on civil liberties has not been all that sweeping. It is still true that most state court judges continue to interpret state constitutions in lockstep with interpretations of the U.S. Constitution. One commentator found, however, that in approximately one out of every three constitutional decisions, state courts extended rights beyond federal levels. [c] In some areas, such as the inter-pretation of rights to exercise religion freely and in search and seizure rulings, state courts, relying on their own constitutions, have continued to grant rights after the U.S. Supreme Court's interpretation of the Constitution took a more conservative and restrictive turn.

In other cases, state courts rely on unique constitutional provisions. For instance, state constitutions, unlike the federal document, often commit state governments to the achievement of particular policy ends. New Jersey's constitution requires a "thorough and efficient system of free public schools," Illinois requires the state to "provide and maintain a healthful environment for the benefit of this and future generations," and the New Mexico constitution requires bilingual education. Relying on explicit provisions like these, state supreme courts have ordered legislatures to restructure the way they finance public education when inequalities are so extreme they rise to the level of constitutional violation.

Today, the new judicial federalism is well established, with more and more cases raising state constitutional issues, sparking a renewed interest in these once over-looked documents. State supreme court justices are more likely now to take a fresh look at their own constitutions than to slavishly follow the interpretations of the U.S. Supreme Court. Activists also have focused more attention on state constitutions, mounting campaigns to amend them to either extend or curtail rights.

---

[a] G. Alan Tarr, "The New Judicial Federalism in Perspective," *Notre Dame Law Review* 72 (1997): 1097.
[b] William J. Brennan, *National Law Journal,* September 29, 1986, at S–1.
[c] James N.G. Cauthen, "Expanding Rights under State Constitutions: A Quantitative Appraisal," *Albany Law Review* 63 (2000): 1183, 1202.

---

facing an election. Therefore, they really are not swayed by public opinion. Because the Massachusetts decision was rooted in the state constitution, it is final and cannot be appealed to the U.S. Supreme Court. This leaves those who oppose gay marriage with only two legal options. They can try to amend the state's constitution to define marriage as only available to het-erosexual couples, or, as Bush wants, amend the U.S. Constitution.

Unhappiness with judicial thinking is not limited to social issues. In 2004, Kentucky state legislators considered blocking courts from ordering them to pass laws and increase taxes. This happens from time to time—for example, in states with constitutions mandating equal education, courts order legislators to find new ways to provide more money for schools to meet constitutional requirements. Legislators never like it when courts tell them what to do, but it has been understood since the U.S. Supreme Court's 1803 decision in *Marbury v. Madison* that the judiciary can override the actions of the other branches of government. That power is why everyone from Kentucky legislators to the governor of Massachusetts to the president of the United States complains about activist or overreaching judges when the courts make decisions that they don't like.

This chapter provides an introduction to state court systems. We look first at the different types of courts and the different ways these courts are structured. We then focus on the different ways state court judges are chosen and retained and the controversy these processes create. Many issues surround each of the players in the state justice system, from prosecutors and defenders to victims and jurors, and we will explore these before looking at some possible areas of reform.

When it comes to the courts, it quickly becomes obvious that there is no "right way" in which they operate. Each of the fifty states, the District of Columbia, and Puerto Rico has its own unique court system. Sometimes, it seems as if every county in every state has its own way of doing things. From judicial selection to sentencing reform, states have organized their justice systems to meet the needs of their unique political pressures and social dynamics.

In 2004, Massachusetts became the first state to provide homosexual couples the same marriage rights as heterosexual couples. Conservative critics said that the controversial state supreme court decision that allows same-sex marriage just about takes the cake as an example of liberal judicial activism.

The Role and Structure of State Courts

There are two basic kinds of court cases—**criminal cases** and **civil cases**. Criminal cases involve violations of the law, with the government prosecuting the alleged perpetrator, or criminal. Prosecuting perpetrators in criminal court is similar to suing people in civil court. Civil cases involve disputes between two private parties, such as a dry cleaner and a customer with badly stained pants. In civil cases, individuals sue each other, usually for financial judgments. Both types of cases start out in **trial court**. If the parties in a case cannot reach agreement through a **settlement** or a **plea bargain**, they go to trial.

Inevitably every trial has a winner and a loser. Those unhappy with the trial's outcome can file an **appeal**. Most states have two levels of courts that hear appeals from trial court judgments. The appeal first goes to an **intermediate appellate court**, which reviews the original trial's record to see if any errors were made. After the appellate court has ruled, parties who still are not satisfied can attempt to appeal to the highest state court of appeals, usually called the **state supreme court**. In most states, this court does not automatically have to take an appeal, but can pick and choose among cases, typically choosing those whose resolutions will require a clarification of the law. Such resolutions could set a **precedent** that has consequences well beyond the specifics of the case being appealed.

A state supreme court is the highest legal body in the state court system. This gives it the ultimate power to interpret the state constitution. Its decisions are almost always final. Only the U.S. Supreme Court outranks the highest state courts. Even the nine justices in Washington, D.C., however, cannot review—that is, come up with a new decision for—a state supreme court judgment unless it violates the federal constitution or federal law.

When such federal issues are involved, there is no question but that state courts must follow the rulings of the federal courts. The chief justice of the Alabama Supreme Court, Roy S. Moore, learned this lesson in 2003 after placing a two-and-a-half ton monument to the Ten Commandments in the rotunda of the state supreme court building. Federal judges ordered him to move it, ruling that such a display violated the First Amendment's separation of church and state. He refused and ultimately was removed from office for having tried to place himself above the law.

Trial Courts

Almost ninety-six million cases were filed in state courts in 2003. Nearly two-thirds of them involved traffic offenses. The number of civil and criminal cases was roughly equal—16.3 and 15.4 million cases, respectively—and there were 6.6 million domestic and juvenile cases.[3] The vast majority of these millions of cases were resolved through plea bargains or settlements. Only a small minority ever went to trial.

When parties do go to trial, they appear before a state court judge in what is often referred to as a **court of first instance**. In this court, nothing has been determined, nothing is a "given." The trial is a blank canvas on which the parties can introduce documentary and physical evidence, such as fingerprints or DNA. Witnesses can testify as to what they saw or heard, and experts can try to help explain complex evidence.

The judge presides over the introduction of evidence; rules on objections, which occur when either of the parties thinks that the other party has said or done something wrong, and issues of admissibility, or whether or not it is all right for specific evidence or facts to be included in the trial; and instructs the jury as to the relevant laws. The judge further instructs the jury that they must apply the laws as stated to the facts as they find them. It is the jury, however, that must decide what the facts are. In **bench trials**, this is done by the judge. The jury or the judge must decide who and what to believe and what happened. Unless this decision is based on a legal mistake, such as improper evidence, hearsay testimony (testimony based on rumor), or a misleading statement of the relevant law, the result typically will be upheld on appeal. The business of the trial court is to examine the facts to resolve the dispute. Subsequent appellate courts review the trial court's application of the law to those facts.

The key distinction among state courts is between **general jurisdiction trial courts** and **limited**, or **special jurisdiction, trial courts**. A general jurisdiction trial court hears any case not sent to a special court whether it is civil or criminal. The kinds of cases that can be tried in special jurisdiction courts are statutorily limited. Some are limited to cases of less seriousness, such as misdemeanors or civil cases that involve small amounts of money. Others are limited to the types of parties involved, such as juvenile offenders or drug abusers.

Not all states make this distinction between trial courts. Illinois has no limited jurisdiction courts. On the other hand, New York, the state with the largest number of judges, is also the state that relies most heavily on limited jurisdiction courts. Over 3,000 of the state's 3,645 judges sit on limited jurisdiction courts.[4] (See Figure 8-1.) In states that do not rely on limited jurisdiction courts, appeals go directly to appellate courts. In states that make the distinction, some issues can be appealed from limited jurisdiction courts to general jurisdiction courts.

Appeals Courts: Intermediate Appeals and Courts of Last Resort

When one of the parties in a trial is dissatisfied with the outcome, that party can challenge the result by filing an appeal. As a general rule, an appeal cannot be based on mere dissatisfaction with the trial's result. Appellants do not get a free second chance to try their whole case. Appellate courts do not decide issues of guilt or innocence or ensure that trials were conducted perfectly. Instead, an appeal must state that there were legal errors in the original trial. But it is not enough to say that an error occurred. Courts also require the error to be **prejudicial**. That is, the error affected the outcome of the case. Appellants have to argue that there was a good chance the result would have been different if the error had not been made. This often is a very challenging argument to make.

There is no one way that all of the states decide how to hear appeals from the trial courts. States have made different decisions about how many levels of review to grant an appeal, how to choose which cases can be appealed, and how many judges will hear an appeal. These decisions combine to form different appellate court structures.

COURT OF FIRST INSTANCE
The court in which a case is introduced and nothing has been determined yet.

BENCH TRIALS
Trials in which no jury is present and a judge decides the facts.

GENERAL JURISDICTION TRIAL COURTS
Hears any civil or criminal cases that have not been assigned to a special court.

LIMITED, OR SPECIAL JURISDICTION, TRIAL COURTS
Hears cases that are statutorily limited by either the degree of seriousness or the types of parties involved.

PREJUDICIAL ERROR
An error that affects the outcome of a case.

FIGURE 8-1 State Court Structure: Illinois vs. New York

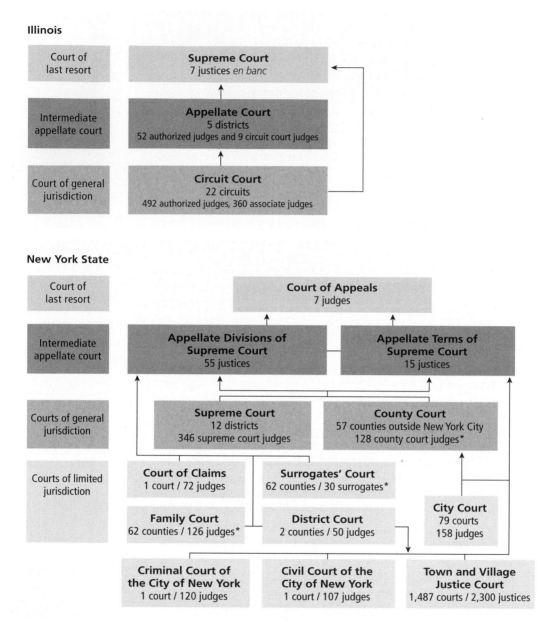

Source: Adapted from *State Court Caseload Statistics, 2003: Supplement to Examining the Work of State Courts, 2003,* a joint project of the Conference of State Court Administrators, the Bureau of Justice Statistics, and the National Center for State Courts' Court Statistics Project. www.ncsconline.org/D_Research/csp/2003_Files/2003_SCCS_Front.pdf (accessed July 18, 2004).

*Unless otherwise noted, numbers reflect statutory authorization. Many judges sit on more than one court, so the number of judges in this chart does not reflect the actual number of judges in the system. Fifty county court judges also serve surrogates' court and six county court judges also serve family court.

Not all states, for example, have both an intermediate appellate court and a supreme court. Back in 1957, only thirteen states had intermediate appellate courts. Today, eleven states and the District of Columbia still resolve all of their appeals with only one level of review. These states, including Delaware, Montana, North Dakota, Rhode Island, South Dakota, Vermont, and Wyoming, are less populous—eight have populations under one million—and thus tend to have fewer cases to resolve. Smaller populations give rise to relatively more manageable caseloads.

The sheer volume of appeals makes it impossible in the majority of states for one appellate court to hear and resolve every appeal. To deal with burgeoning caseloads, most states have created another tier of review. In these states, appeals go first to an intermediate appellate court. Only after they have been reviewed at this level can they move on to the court of last resort, usually the state supreme court. The intermediate court makes it possible for the state judicial system to hear many more appeals and creates the possibility of a second level of appeal.

Intermediate appellate courts range in size from three judges in Alaska, Alabama, Hawaii, and Idaho, to ninety-three judges in California. States with the most judges at the intermediate appellate level usually divide their jurisdictions into specific regions. California, for example, divides these judges into nine appellate divisions. By contrast, New Jersey, with thirty-two appellate judges, has the largest appellate court not divided into judicial regions.[5] Regional divisions make the courts more convenient, but also create a danger. All these different courts may come up with different rulings on the same or similar issues. This has the potential to set different, possibly conflicting, precedents for future litigation.

State appellate courts also vary in terms of whether they have **discretionary** or **mandatory jurisdiction**. In other words, in some states the courts have a right to pick and choose which cases they hear. Other states force judges to consider each case, believing that everyone has the right to an appeal. It is widely accepted that losers in a single-judge court ought to have a right to at least one appeal to a court with multiple judges.[6] This one appeal, however, is generally considered sufficient to correct any prejudicial errors made in the trial courts. Even in states in which the court of last resort has discretionary jurisdiction, capital punishment appeals may be mandatory.

Two tiers of appellate courts allow petitioners to have the right to one appeal to the intermediate appellate court, followed by the possibility of a further appeal to the court of last resort. Such a structure allows the supreme court or other courts of last resort to choose whether or not to hear cases that might have relevance beyond the parties in the case, allowing them to make the law clear to others.

One more variable in the state court system structure involves the number of judges at each level who hear a particular appeal. At either the appellate court level or at the court of last resort level, judges may hear an appeal

DISCRETIONARY JURISDICTION

Occurs when a court decides whether or not to grant review of a case.

MANDATORY JURISDICTION

Occurs when a court is required to hear every case presented before it.

en banc, or all together, or they may sit in smaller **panels**, typically of three judges. Sitting in panels may be more convenient, since courts sit simultaneously in different locations. This allows more appeals to be heard and makes the courts more convenient to the parties. However, like regional divisions, this may lead to similar problems of unifying doctrine created by various courts at the same level.

States that use panels have a variety of techniques to limit divergence among panels. These include conferencing drafts of opinions *en banc*. This means that the panel's draft opinions are circulated among all the judges, even those not on the panel. Two states have created two supreme courts with different subject matter jurisdiction, rather than have one supreme court sit in panels. Texas and Oklahoma have one supreme court with largely civil jurisdiction and one court of last resort that hears only criminal appeals. Each of these courts sits *en banc*. In Texas, the intermediate appellate court has both civil and criminal jurisdiction. In Oklahoma, the intermediate appellate court has only civil jurisdiction—all criminal appeals go directly to the court of last resort for criminal cases. A few states have created intermediate appellate courts with differing subject matter jurisdictions and then a single court of last resort.

States have mixed and matched all these variables to come up with different ways to organize the appellate court review process. The most common pattern, adhered to by half the states, involves making an intermediate appellate court, sitting in panels, consider all appeals. The decisions of these panels are then subject to review by a court of last resort, such as a supreme court, sitting *en banc*. Usually, this court can hear just the cases it sees fit to hear. States without an intermediate court of appeals often make their courts of last resort hear all the cases that are sent to them. However, two such states, New Hampshire and West Virginia, hear all appeals through a supreme court with discretionary review. The supreme courts in these two states get to pick and choose their cases. In the District of Columbia, all appeals are heard by a court of appeals with nine justices who often sit in panels of three.

In other words, if you lose your case, you will have at least one chance—and usually more than one chance—to get your appeal heard. But you will face a legal labyrinth that involves variations of courts and judges and panels and rules. All of these variations add up to one more reason to hire a good lawyer.

Selecting Judges

How the judges bestowed with such extraordinary discretion to make decisions that impact countless lives are selected is a significant political decision. Historically, such decisions have generated tremendous controversy, and the controversy continues today. Why is there no clear consensus on such an important issue? Controversy is perhaps inevitable. The judiciary is one of the pillars of the U.S. political system, but at the same time, we want to believe that judges are above politics. We like to think that they are independent and will rule only as justice requires, based on the specific facts presented and the applicable law. Of course, judges are only human, subject to all that entails. That's why we want them held accountable for their decisions. These competing values—independence and accountability—tug judges in different directions. Focusing on independence leads to the appointment of judges for lifetime tenures, similar to those of judges in the federal system. Focusing on accountability supports the public elections of judges. This is not just an academic issue. How a state structures its courts and chooses its judges may impact the types of decisions made by individual judges.

Almost no two states select judges the same way. The states, however, can be roughly divided into two camps of almost equal size. The first group includes states that choose judges through popular elections, either partisan or nonpartisan. In partisan elections, judicial candidates first run in party primaries and then are listed on the ballot with a designation of their political party. Candidates in nonpartisan elections run on the ballot without any party label. States in the second group have either the governor or the legislature appoint judges, whether or not the governor or legislature is limited to choosing from names advanced by a nominating committee.

To make matters even more confusing, many states use different methods to choose judges at different levels of their judiciaries. States might, for example, choose trial judges by popular election and appoint supreme court justices. What's more, many states employ different methods by region. In Arizona, for example, trial courts in counties with a population greater than 250,000 choose judges through merit selection. Less populous districts rely on nonpartisan elections. Indiana holds partisan elections in a portion of its judicial districts and nonpartisan elections in others. Finally, some states that generally elect their judges fill mid-term judicial vacancies by appointment.

How states choose their judges has been historically volatile. Movements to change the methods for judicial selection rise up, gain popularity, and then, eventually, are supplanted by the next big reform. How a state originally chose its judges had much to do with which reform was in vogue at the time the state entered the Union and ratified its constitution. No single judicial reform ever succeeded in completely replacing earlier methods, however, and so, there is tremendous variation among the states in the way they select judges.

Under the U.S. Constitution, the president, with the advice and consent of the Senate, appoints all federal judges. Similarly, the original thirteen states chose to appoint judges, giving the appointment power to one or both houses of the legislature, and less commonly to the governor, either alone or with the consent of the legislature.[7]

MAP 8-1 Judicial Selection by Type of Court

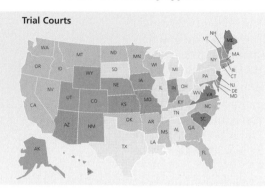

Trial Courts

Intermediate Appellate Courts

State High Courts

Partisan elections	Gubernatorial or Legislative Appointment
Nonpartisan elections	Different types of elections in different countries or judicial districts
Merit selection	No intermediate appellate court

Source: Data compiled from the American Judicature Society. www.ajs.org/selection/sel_state-select-map.asp (accessed May 21, 2004).

Note: In instances where candidates are in any way affiliated with a particular party (through nominations at party conventions, or through party slates, for instance), those types of elections are considered partisan.

Then, in the mid-1800s, during the presidency of Andrew Jackson—a period marked by distrust of government and movement toward increased popular sovereignty—the appointive system came under attack. Every state that entered the Union between 1846 and 1912 provided for some form of judicial elections.[8] At the dawn of the twentieth century, concern that judges were selected and controlled by political machines led to a movement for nonpartisan elections. By 1927, twelve states employed this practice.[9]

During the second half of the twentieth century, judicial reformers focused on persuading states to adopt a new method of choosing judges, referred to as merit selection. Nominating committees under this system submit a list of names from which the governor selects a judge. Missouri became the first state to adopt such a judicial selection method in 1940, which is why judicial merit selection is sometimes referred to as "the Missouri Plan." The movement enjoyed considerable success from the 1960s to the 1980s. The number of states that embraced merit selection for choosing supreme court justices grew from three in 1960 (Alaska, Kansas, and Missouri) to eighteen by 1980.[10]

Recently, however, this reform movement appears to have lost momentum. Approximately half of the states still rely on merit selection for some or all of their judges, and no merit selection state has returned to selection through elections. However, since 1990, most states that have considered adopting merit selection, whether for trial courts or appellate level courts, have rejected it. In Florida, for example, a 2000 initiative for the merit selection of trial court judges appeared on the ballot and was soundly defeated in every county.[11] Each method for selecting judges and the issues they raise will be addressed at length in the sections that follow.

Popular Elections

Why do some states elect judges? Elections allow greater popular control over the judiciary and more public accountability for judges. Proponents

266

Governing States and Localities

argue that such elections are compatible with this country's democratic traditions and that voters can be entrusted to make as good of choices for judges as for legislators or mayors. To some, the appointment of judges smacks of elitism and there is a worry about old-boy networks—judges getting appointed because they are the cronies or political allies of elected officials.

Some argue that electing judges can increase the representation of women and minorities on the bench. Several studies have found no correlation between selection method and diversity, although one recent researcher did find a slightly lower proportion of minorities selected through merit selection than the proportion of minorities on state courts across the country.[12] Nationwide, as of 2002, 22 of the 365 state supreme court justices were African American and 97 were women.[13]

Not everyone is so convinced. Those on the other side of the argument are critical of judicial elections in general, whether partisan or nonpartisan. They focus on what they see as a threat to the independence of the judiciary posed by the introduction of politics into the selection process. The tone of judicial elections has deteriorated substantially and in a manner that some fear could damage the image of the judiciary. Qualified candidates for office could choose to opt-out.

It's about more than a debate about ideas, however. How a state chooses judges has a very real political impact, with consequences for judicial impartiality, campaign fundraising, the role of interest groups, and the character of judicial campaigning. Some point to these problems as reasons to move away from selecting judges through judicial elections and toward a merit selection system. Others argue that the problems can be addressed without abandoning elections altogether, but rather, by tinkering with them. Die-hard supporters of elections see the increased politicization of judicial elections as positive because greater competitiveness translates into more meaningful choices for voters.

Before jumping into the consequences of elections, it is important to remember that elections for state court judges, when they are held, can be either partisan or nonpartisan. Most or all of the judges in eight states—Alabama, Illinois, Louisiana, Michigan, Ohio, Pennsylvania, Texas, and West Virginia—are selected through partisan elections. Another five states (Indiana, Kansas, Missouri, New York, and Tennessee) select some of their judges this way.[14] Nonpartisan elections are held to select most or all judges in thirteen states—Arkansas, Georgia, Idaho, Kentucky, Minnesota, Mississippi, Montana, Nevada, North Carolina, North Dakota, Oregon, Washington, and Wisconsin—and some judges in another seven states—Arizona, California, Florida, Indiana, Michigan, Oklahoma, and South Dakota.[15] In some cases labeling a popular election partisan or nonpartisan may be a distinction without a difference. All Ohio judges and Michigan Supreme Court justices run without party labels on ballots, but the candidates are chosen through party primaries or conventions, and the parties are heavily involved in judicial campaigns.[16]

The legislative and executive branches are clearly political. Representatives of the people are chosen and held accountable through elections. Why shouldn't judges be elected like other powerful players in the political system? Because the judge's role is supposed to be different. Judges decide specific cases and controversies based on hearing the evidence. They are supposed to rely only on statutes, case precedent, and constitutional law. They are not supposed to rule based on the wishes of those who elect them or with the next election in mind.

A lot rides on the public's belief that a judge will be neutral and impartial. That belief underpins the willingness to bring disputes to the courts and to abide by the results. Judges cannot, as political candidates do, make campaign promises about future decisions without undermining respect for the impartiality and independence of the judiciary. For the same reasons, judges cannot represent specific interest groups or constituents or even the will of the majority. There are times when all judges, doing their jobs properly, are compelled by the law to make unpopular judgments or to protect the rights of those without political power.

In 1999, U.S. Supreme Court justice Anthony Kennedy pointed out in an interview that there are times for every judge when the law requires the release of a criminal whether the judge likes it or not. To characterize a judge in that case as "soft on crime" betrays a misunderstanding of the judicial process and the constitution.[17] In the same television interview, Justice Stephen Breyer also expressed concerns about the way judicial elections require judges to court public opinion. He asked, "Suppose I were on trial. Suppose somebody accused me. Would I want to be judged by whether I was popular? Wouldn't I want to be judged on what was true as opposed to what was popular? . . . We have a different system. And our system is based upon . . . neutrality and independence."[18]

Is this how it really works? Or only how it is *supposed* to work? The highly charged issue of capital punishment makes a useful test case. Why are some courts more likely to impose the death penalty than others? Some research indicates that state supreme court justices facing reelection in states in which capital punishment is particularly popular, are reluctant to cast dissenting votes. Researchers Paul Brace and Melinda Gann Hall found that—among politically comparable states—rulings to uphold death sentences are more likely in states with elected judges.[19] Not only that, but the closer supreme court justices are to reelection, the more likely they are to support capital punishment.[20]

Texas and Florida share at least one thing in common—hundreds of inmates on death row and a high volume of death penalty appeals. But the similarity stops there. Texas justices are elected in partisan elections, and they almost never reverse a death sentence. In Florida, however, supreme court justices are merit selected, and the court has one of the nation's highest reversal rates.[21] It is not misguided for a judge facing reelection to fear reversing a death sentence. There are numerous examples of state supreme court justices who were labeled as soft after opposing the imposition of capital punishment in a particular case and were voted off the bench. This occurs even when the opinions are later held to be correct by the U.S. Supreme Court.[22]

The effects of judicial selection ripple out beyond those cases that tackle politically volatile issues like capital punishment. Professor Steven Ware reviewed all arbitration decisions made by the Alabama Supreme Court from 1995 to 1999. Justices there are selected through partisan elections, and this period encompassed a shift in the court majority from Democrats to Republicans. In virtually every case—even those that involved bland issues of law that appeared ideologically neutral—Ware found a direct correlation between voting and campaign contributions.[23] The Democrats, funded mostly by lawyers that worked for the plaintiffs, opposed arbitration. The Republicans, financed primarily by business interests, favored it.

Campaign financing also raises issues of improper influence on the judiciary. Candidates running for judicial office must raise money. Frequently, this money comes from the very people who have a vested interest in the outcome of cases that are or will be before the judge. The funds required to run a campaign have been rising steadily, particularly in state supreme court races. In 2000, the average campaign expenditure was $400,000 and, in sixteen races, the average expenditure topped $1 million.[24] Recently, in Michigan, at least $16 million was spent in a contentious race for three supreme court seats.[25] Much of this money comes from lawyers, litigants, and other groups with an interest in the outcome of litigation.[26]

Why do these groups contribute so much money to judicial elections? As with any other political donation, there is at least some truth to the cynic's sense that campaign contributions are a good investment. The president of the Ohio State Bar concluded, "The people with money to spend who are affected by court decisions have reached the conclusion that it's a lot cheaper to buy a judge than a governor or an entire legislature, and he can probably do a lot more for you."[27] Even if justices do not allow campaign contributions to affect their decisions, the appearance of a conflict already has been created. A 2001 survey found that eight out of ten people believe campaign contributions to judges influence decisions.[28]

> The president of the Ohio State Bar concluded, "The people with money to spend who are affected by court decisions have reached the conclusion that it's a lot cheaper to buy a judge than a governor or an entire legislature, and he can probably do a lot more for you."

Single-issue interest groups may target a judge for a specific ruling on a topic such as capital punishment, abortion, or same-sex marriage. Groups may criticize or praise the judge, taking the case completely out of its legal context. Such groups have joined together in the type of coalitions formed in other partisan political contests. Given the power of interest groups, law professor Gerald Uelmen has observed that judicial independence is most endangered in states with growing death row populations without any exe-

Local Focus: Courting Trouble: Judicial Selection in Brooklyn

Charles Hynes, district attorney for Brooklyn, New York, does not go looking for cases of judicial corruption. But neither has he shied away from prosecuting them. His indictments of judges and political leaders have earned him the enmity of his own party. More importantly, they have cast a very public light upon a broken judicial selection process. The cases involve charges of bribery and corruption, and Hynes is investigating numerous judges. What has really hit home with the public, however, is Hynes's allegation that one judge, Gerald Garson, accepted bribes to fix, or influence the outcome of, divorce and child custody cases. Garson maintains his innocence, but in February 2004, a rabbi and his daughter pleaded guilty to paying $5,000 to an intermediary they understood would bribe Garson in a custody case. "These are family cases, where people are so much more vulnerable," says Fern Schair, chair of the Committee for Modern Courts, an advocacy group. "These aren't commercial cases."

Beyond the prosecution of judges, what has gotten Hynes, 68, in a world of political trouble is twice indicting New York State representative Clarence Norman, longtime head of the Brooklyn Democratic Party. Party officials are being targeted in cases surrounding judicial corruption because they are the ones who pick the judges. The way most judges are selected in New York is a vestige of the machine politics of an earlier day. The process is complex, but basically, the leader of the dominant party within a district—whether Democratic in New York City or Republican upstate—gets to pick who is nominated at a closed convention. Convention attendees then rubberstamp that choice.

Judges are elected, but voters are not given any real choice. The minority party usually does not bother running its own candidate and may even give its nod to the other party's nominee. "Any suggestion that the

Bribery and corruption charges left New York judge Gerald Garson standing before the bench rather than presiding from it. Garson, the target of an investigation by Brooklyn District Attorney Charles Hynes, was charged with accepting bribes to fix the outcomes of divorce and child custody cases.

office of the state Supreme Court is an elective office where the citizen has an unfettered right to vote is an illusion," Hynes says. Party leaders not only choose whom they want, many have done so with more regard to party loyalty and fundraising than to legal capability or scholarship. Garson, for example, had been a party treasurer in Brooklyn.

Although judicial candidates are barred from making direct contributions to the party, they can buy tickets to expensive party functions. They also can be pressured in other ways. One of the indictments of Norman, the party chief, charged him with coercing judicial hopefuls into buying services from a favored campaign consultant.

In 2002, the *Buffalo News* ran a lengthy series about problems with the state's judicial-selection system, but Hynes's indictments have brought the arcane process its greatest attention yet. Changing the process for picking judges would take the votes of two consecutive legislatures, which is unlikely to happen anytime soon. That's why reformers now are pushing for short-term fixes that would inject merit or increased voter say into the process.

Source: Alan Greenblatt, *Governing* magazine, May 2004. From www. governing.com/archive/2004/may/players.txt (accessed May 28, 2004).

cutions, states with laws requiring parental consent for abortions by minors, and states that allow statutory enactments or constitutional amendments by initiative.[29] In two states, Ohio and Kentucky, these three judicial landmines have come together. Both states elect supreme court justices in highly partisan and expensive races on a recurring basis.

Judges' campaigns are generally subject to codes of judicial conduct, but interest group money is free from such rules. As a result, ads sponsored by these groups tend to be more harsh and negative than ads sponsored by candidates. One study found that 80 percent of the ads sponsored by interest groups were negative attack ads, compared to 27 percent of ads sponsored by candidates and political parties.[30] Campaigns rely heavily on thirty-second TV spots, which can do little more than offer simplistic sound bites about complicated issues. In the 2000 elections for the Michigan Court of Appeals, the word "pedophile" ran in huge type near the name of the judge the GOP was accusing of upholding a light sentence for a pedophile. In that same race, the Democratic Party ran ads that declared that the incumbents had ruled "against families and for corporations 82 percent of the time"— a claim the *Detroit Free Press* found "border[ed] on the bogus."[31]

Added to this mix of expensive campaigns and thirty-second TV spots is the fact that ordinary citizens have very little information with which to make informed choices about judicial races. Voters commonly vote only for candidates at the top of the ticket, like governors or senators, and leave the ballots for judicial candidates incomplete.[32] Lack of voter participation undermines the public's ability to keep the judiciary accountable. It makes judges more vulnerable to single-issue groups.

In partisan elections, the additional danger is that the political parties may expect favors from the candidates they put forward. In 1976, the Michigan Supreme Court decided a redistricting case in a way that favored Republicans. In the next election, the Democratic Party refused to renominate the court's Democratic chief justice.[33] Chief Justice Thomas Phillips of the Texas Supreme Court has asked, "When judges are labeled as Democrats or Republicans, how can you convince the public that the law is a judge's only constituency? And when a winning litigant has contributed thousands of dollars to the judge's campaign, how do you ever persuade the losing party that only the facts of the case were considered?"[34]

Appointment

States in which judges are appointed rather than elected can be put into two general categories: **pure appointive systems** and merit selection systems that rely on a nominating committee.

Federal judges have always been selected through a pure appointive system. The president appoints judges who, if they are confirmed by the Senate, "shall hold their Offices during good Behavior." No state, however, employs precisely this method of judicial selection.

In four states—California, Maine, New Hampshire, and New Jersey—the governor appoints state court judges without a nominating commission. That is, these governors are not limited in their selections to a list of names provided by someone else.[35] Judges' nominations still require some kind of second opinion, however. In Maine, the governor appoints judges subject to

PURE APPOINTIVE SYSTEMS

Judicial selection systems in which the governor appoints judges alone without a nominating commission.

confirmation by a legislative committee whose decision may be reviewed by the Senate. In New Jersey, the state senate must confirm the governor's appointees, who then serve an initial seven-year term, after which the governor may reappoint them. A special five-member elected council confirms a judicial appointee in New Hampshire. California's governor appoints judges after submitting names to the state bar for evaluation. Unlike other judges in pure appointive systems, however, judges appointed in California serve short initial terms and are then subject to retention elections at the first general election and every twelve years after that.[36] In **retention elections**, judges run unopposed. The voter may only indicate either a simple "yes" or a "no" on the question of whether the judge should be retained.

Virginia is the only state in which the legislature appoints all state judges without a nominating committee. A majority vote of both houses of the Virginia General Assembly is required to appoint any judge.

Merit selection, initially endorsed by the American Bar Association in 1937, was conceived as a way to limit the intrusion of politics into judge selection.[37] Currently, most states that appoint judges rely on a method of merit selection through nominating committees. Twenty-four states and the District of Columbia rely on a merit selection plan for the initial selection of some or all judges. Another ten states use such plans to fill midterm vacancies at some or all levels of court.[38]

What puts the merit into merit selection? It is misleading to describe it as if it were a single method for selecting judges because the details vary considerably from state to state. At its core, it requires that the state assemble a nonpartisan nominating committee. This committee forwards a list of names from which either the governor or the legislature chooses a judge. How a partisan, distrustful legislature solves the problem of creating a nonpartisan committee differs in almost every state. Some require parity of political party affiliation for the commission members. Others have adopted extremely complex methods to assure the impartiality of its nominating commissions.

A case in point is Tennessee. The fifteen commission members are chosen as follows: First, the Speaker of the Senate appoints three members from a list submitted by the Tennessee Trial Lawyers Association, three members from a list submitted by the District Attorney General Conference, and one nonattorney. Next, the Speaker of the House appoints two members from a list submitted by the Tennessee Bar Association—whose list may not contain personal injury or criminal defense attorneys—one member from a list submitted by the Tennessee Defense Lawyers Association, three members from a list submitted by the Tennessee Association of Criminal Defense Lawyers, and one nonlawyer. Finally, the speakers jointly appoint one nonattorney.[39]

Got all that? Even after the composition of the nominating commission is determined, states have different ways to choose its chair, the most influential position. In some states, including Maryland, New Hampshire, and Utah, the governor can exert considerable control over the commission through the ability to appoint its chair.[40] Other states, such as Alaska, Arizona, Colorado, and Utah, designate the chief justice of the state supreme court as chair. Some states allow the commission to choose its own chair, and, finally, New Mexico's constitution designates the dean of the University of New Mexico Law School as the chair of the state's judicial nominating commission.[41]

Usually, the governor chooses the judge from the list forwarded by the commission. In South Carolina and Connecticut, the nominating committee forwards a list of names to the legislature, which then meets in joint session, appointing judges by a majority vote.[42]

The ways in which judges are retained after being appointed initially also vary. In most states, judges appointed through merit selection serve shorter initial terms, usually one or two years. After that, they participate in retention elections. These special elections were conceived as a means to provide some public participation in the selection of judges while avoiding the intrusion of politics. In some states, notably California and Tennessee, this has backfired. Retention elections have become as fiercely partisan as popular elections.

Some merit selection states have dispensed with elections altogether. For instance, in Connecticut, Delaware, Hawaii, and New York, judges are reevaluated and reappointed by the judicial selection commission. In Vermont, after an initial appointment through merit selection, a judge receives an additional term as long as the General Assembly does not vote against it.[43]

Terms of Office

The length of a judge's tenure is another element in the balance between judicial independence and judicial accountability. In the federal court system, judges serve life terms, limited only by "good behavior." Judges can only be removed through an impeachment process for cause. This life tenure is considered an important element, perhaps the most important element, in assuring the independence of the federal judiciary.[44] There has never been a conviction of an impeached federal judge solely on the basis of an unpopular judicial decision in the federal system.[45]

With only a few exceptions, state court judges serve fixed terms of office and must therefore seek reappointment or reelection. The rare exceptions include judges in Rhode Island, who serve life terms, and judges in Massachusetts and New Hampshire, who hold their positions until the age of seventy. Judges in states with fixed terms typically serve for less than ten years. New York judges serve the longest terms in the states—fourteen years—before mandatory retirement kicks in at age seventy. (See Tables 8-1 and 8-2.)

Shorter tenures bring with them the increased danger that political interests and pressures will intrude into judicial decision making. Giving judges

TABLE 8-1

Appellate Court Terms and Methods of Reappointment by State, 2004

State	Initial Term	Subsequent Terms	Method of Reappointment
Alabama	6	6	Reelection
Alaska	3	10	Retention election
Arizona	2	6	Retention election
Arkansas	8	8	Reelection
California	12	12	Retention election
Colorado	2	10	Retention election
Connecticut	8	8	Governor renominates; legislature reappoints
Delaware	12	12	Governor reappoints from judicial nominating commission; senate consents
Florida	1	6	Retention election
Georgia	6	6	Reelection
Hawaii	10	10	Nominating commission
Idaho	6	6	Reelection
Illinois	10	10	Retention election
Indiana	2	10	Retention election
Iowa	1	8	Retention election
Kansas	1	6	Retention election
Kentucky	8	8	Reelection
Louisiana	10	10	Reelection
Maine	7	7	Governor reappoints; senate confirms
Maryland	1	10	Retention election
Massachusetts	To age 70	—	—
Michigan	8	8	Reelection
Minnesota	6	6	Reelection
Mississippi	8	8	Reelection
Missouri	1	12	Retention election
Montana	8	8	Nonpartisan election
Nebraska	3	6	Retention election
Nevada	6	6	Reelection
New Hampshire	To age 70	—	—

TABLE 8-1 *(continued)*

State	Initial Term	Subsequent Terms	Method of Reappointment
New Jersey	7	To age 70	Governor reappoints; senate confirms
New Mexico	>1	8	Retention election
New York	14	14	Governor reappoints from nominating commission; for supreme court senate must consent
North Carolina	8	8	Reelection
North Dakota	10	10	Reelection
Ohio	6	6	Reelection
Oklahoma	1	6	Retention election
Oregon	6	6	Reelection
Pennsylvania	10	10	Retention election
Rhode Island	Life	—	—
South Carolina	10	10	Legislative reelection
South Dakota	3	8	Retention election
Tennessee	<2	8	Retention election
Texas	6	6	Reelection
Utah	3	10	Retention election
Vermont	6	6	Vote of general assembly
Virginia	12	12	Legislative reelection
Washington	6	6	Reelection
West Virginia	12	12	Reelection
Wisconsin	10	10	Reelection
Wyoming	1	8	Retention election

Source: Data compiled from the American Judicature Society. www.ajs.org/js/select.htm (accessed May 24, 2004).

longer terms allows them to be judged on a more complete record. A judge can more easily put some distance between a particular controversial decision and the election. To look at this another way, research indicates that judges with longer terms of office are more willing to manifest partisanship than judges with shorter terms. For example, researchers Paul Brace and Melinda Gann Hall found that Democrats with long terms are least likely to support capital punishment, whereas Republicans with long terms are the most likely to support it. This led them to conclude "term length influences the willingness of individual justices to express their partisanship."[46]

TABLE 8-2

Trial Court Terms and Methods of Reappointment by State, 2004

State	Initial Term	Subsequent Terms	Method of Reappointment
Alabama	6	6	Reelection
Alaska	3	6	Retention election
Arizona	2 or 4, depending on population of county	4	Retention election
Arkansas	4 or 6	4	Reelection
California	6	6	Reelection
Colorado	2	6	Retention election
Connecticut	8	8	Governor renominates; legislature reappoints
Delaware	12	12	Governor reappoints from judicial nominating commission; senate consents
Florida	6	6	Retention election
Georgia	4	4	Reelection
Hawaii	10	10	Nominating commission
Idaho	4	4	Reelection
Illinois	6	6	Retention election
Indiana	2 or 6	6	Retention election
Iowa	1	6	Retention election
Kansas	>1 or 4	4	Retention election
Kentucky	8	8	Reelection
Louisiana	6	6	Reelection
Maine	7	7	Governor reappoints; senate confirms
Maryland	1	15	Nonpartisan election
Massachusetts	To age 70	—	—
Michigan	6	6	Reelection
Minnesota	6	6	Reelection
Mississippi	4	4	Reelection
Missouri	1 or 6	6	Retention election
Montana	6	6	Nonpartisan election

TABLE 8-2 *(continued)*

State	Initial Term	Subsequent Terms	Method of Reappointment
Nebraska	3	6	Retention election
Nevada	6	6	Reelection
New Hampshire	To age 70	—	—
New Jersey	7	To age 70	Governor reappoints; senate confirms
New Mexico	>1	6	Retention election
New York	14	14	Reelection
North Carolina	8	8	Reelection
North Dakota	6	6	Reelection
Ohio	6	6	Reelection
Oklahoma	4	4	Reelection
Oregon	6	6	Reelection
Pennsylvania	10	10	Retention election
Rhode Island	Life	—	—
South Carolina	6	6	Legislative reelection
South Dakota	8	8	Reelection
Tennessee	<2	8	Retention election
Texas	4	4	Reelection
Utah	3	6	Retention election
Vermont	6	6	Vote of general assembly
Virginia	8	8	Legislative reelection
Washington	4	4	Reelection
West Virginia	8	8	Reelection
Wisconsin	6	6	Reelection
Wyoming	1	6	Retention election

Source: Data compiled from the American Judicature Society. www.ajs.org/js/select.htm (accessed May 24, 2004).

Judicial Compensation

In addition to selection and tenure, compensation is one of the bellwethers for assessing independence of the judiciary. How a state determines the salaries of its judges and whether that salary can be reduced makes a difference. The U.S. Constitution forbids reducing federal judicial salaries as a protection for judges who make unpopular decisions. Not all state constitutions include this proscription. In Florida, for instance, the constitution

TABLE 8-3

Judges' Salaries, 2003

Court of Last Resort Judges		Intermediate Appellate Court Judges[a]		Trial Court Judges	
Top Five		**Top Five**		**Top Five**	
California	$162,409	California	$152,206	Delaware	$137,400
Michigan	159,960	Georgia	152,139	New Jersey	137,165
Illinois	158,103	Illinois	148,803	New York	136,700
Georgia	153,086	Alabama	147,302	Michigan	135,966
New Jersey	152,191	Michigan	147,163	California	133,052
Bottom Five		**Bottom Five**		**Bottom Five**	
Montana	$89,381	Oregon	$88,000	Montana	$82,600
North Dakota	92,289	Indiana	90,000	Wyoming	83,700
Wyoming	93,000	New Mexico	91,469	North Dakota	84,765
West Virginia	95,000	Mississippi	94,700[b]	New Mexico	86,896
New Mexico	96,283	Mississippi	95,500[c]	West Virginia	90,000

Source: Data from *Book of the States 2003* (Lexington, Ky.: Council of State Governments, 2003), 251.

Note:
[a] Data not available for some states' appellate court justices' salaries.
[b] Circuit court judges
[c] Court of appeals judges

does not prevent the legislature from amending state laws to reduce salaries to discipline judges for unpopular decisions.[47]

According to the National Center for State Courts, twenty states have created independent judicial compensation commissions to advise their legislatures on judicial salary levels. The goal of these commissions is to determine the amount necessary to retain and recruit qualified judges and to eliminate the need for judges to lobby for their own salaries. States without such commissions rely on a variety of methods to eliminate partisan bickering over judicial salaries. The District of Columbia links salary increases to those of federal judges. Judges' salaries in South Dakota are linked to annual increases of other state employees. In Pennsylvania, salary increases are tied to increases in the Consumer Price Index. (See Table 8-3.)

PROSECUTOR

A government official who conducts criminal cases on behalf of the people.

Prosecution and Defense of Cases in State Courts

Criminal cases at the state court level most often involve a face-off between two state or county employees. The **prosecutor** pursues the case on behalf of the people and usually seeks incarceration of the accused. Little difference exists among the states in the selection of the chief prosecutor—an elected county official almost always fills the position. The individual often is politically ambitious and views the tenure as chief prosecutor as a stepping-stone to higher elected office. For this reason, the policies of prosecutors tend to reflect the specific wishes of the county voters.

Private attorneys defend those individuals who can afford their services. In many cases, however, a **public defender**, an attorney also on the public payroll, represents the accused. Public defenders fulfill the state's constitutional requirement to provide indigent defense services. There is much more variety in how states organize their systems of indigent defense than in their systems of prosecution. Some are organized into statewide public defenders systems. Others have statewide commissions that set guidelines for local jurisdictions—sometimes distributing limited state funds to local programs that follow specific standards. Still others delegate the responsibility of how to provide and fund indigent defense entirely to the counties.

The competing values of state oversight and local control play out differently depending on the cultural and political realities of each state as well as any practical concerns involved. Even some states with statewide public defenders offices exclude rural areas where the case volume would make supporting such offices impracticable. In the current climate of runaway costs, increased caseloads, and widespread litigation-challenging programs, the trend has been towards more state oversight.

The Prosecutor

Commentators have gone so far as to say that the prosecutor has become the "most powerful office in the criminal justice system."[48] The prosecutor's office is run by an attorney referred to, depending on the state, as the chief prosecutor, district attorney, county attorney, commonwealth attorney, or state's attorney. Whatever the title, this lawyer represents the public in criminal and other cases.

Prosecutorial authority comes from the state, but these are essentially local offices. Authority is over a specific jurisdiction—usually a county. County governments fund chief prosecutors' offices, although close to half of these offices also receive some portion of their budgets from state funds.[49] Nationwide, there are more than two thousand state court prosecutors' offices, employing more than seventy thousand attorneys, investigators, and support staff.[50]

Most chief prosecutors serve jurisdictions with less than one hundred thousand people. About one-third of the chief prosecutors' offices had a total staff of four or fewer.[51] The top 5 percent of prosecutors' offices, however, serve districts with populations of five hundred thousand or more. That is almost half the entire U.S. population.[52] In 2001, these large offices handled approximately 66 percent of the nation's serious crimes and had a median budget of more than $14 million.[53] The Los Angeles County district

TABLE 8-4

Statistics for Prosecutorial Staff and Operations in Large Districts, 2001

	Offices serving a population of . . .	
	1,000,000 or more	500,000 to 999,999
Number of prosecutor's offices	34	80
Population served, 1999	1,478,630	680,854
Total staff size	456	195
Salary for chief prosecutor	$136,700	$118,656
Budget for prosecution	$32,114,944	$10,946,771
Felony cases closed in twelve months	12,079	4,921

Source: Adapted from Bureau of Justice Statistics. www.ojp.usdoj.gov/bjs/pub/pdf/scpld01.pdf (accessed May 25, 2004).

TABLE 8-5

Maximum and Minimum Annual Salary for Prosecutors in Large Districts, 2001

	Offices serving a population of . . .	
	1,000,000 or more	500,000 to 999,999
Assistant Prosecutor, entry level	$44,260 to 56,568	$38,250 to 50,500
Assistant Prosecutor, 5+ years experience	$55,503 to 76,800	$51,500 to 65,00
Supervisory Attorney	$74,387 to 121,720	$66,834 to 99,670

Source: Adapted from Bureau of Justice Statistics. www.ojp.usdoj.gov/bjs/pub/pdf/scpld01.pdf (accessed May 25, 2004).

LEGISLATIVE OVER-CRIMINALIZATION

The tendency of government to make a crime out of anything the public does not like.

attorney's office has the largest staff, consisting of more than 2,700 people.[54] (See Tables 8-4 and 8-5.)

A state's chief prosecutors have enormous discretion in the conduct of most of their responsibilities. The prosecutor makes all decisions as to whether or not to prosecute, whom to prosecute, and with what cause of action to prosecute. Discretion in charging is, in the words of one scholar, "virtually unchecked by formal constraints or regulatory mechanisms, making it one of the broadest discretionary powers in criminal administration."[55] Charging decisions are enormously important, particularly in states in which statutory guidelines set minimum sentences or in which the same act can be subject to a number of different charges.

Several reasons exist for giving prosecutors such broad powers. One is the trend toward **legislative over-criminalization**. This is the legislative tendency to make crimes out of everything that people find objectionable[56] By creating a large number of broadly defined crimes, legislatures have made it impossible to enforce all the criminal statutes even as they have made it possible to charge a single act under multiple, overlapping provisions.[57]

A second reason for a prosecutor's broad discretion is the need to individualize justice. Each case involves a unique set of facts and issues and requires careful weighing of the evidence. The severity of the crime must be balanced against the probability of sustaining a conviction to determine how best to spend limited resources. Prosecutors have been reluctant to publish general guidelines regarding their charging decisions. A Florida prosecutor stated that his office declines to prosecute drug cases when the amount of cocaine is deemed too small. But he refused to say just how much is too small. Understandably, he worried that drug smugglers would package their shipments in such a way to get under this arbitrary limit and escape prosecution.[58]

There are some limits to prosecutorial authority. For instance, the trial process itself. In many jurisdictions, the government first must obtain an **indictment**—or a formal criminal charge—from a **grand jury**. The U.S. Supreme Court has noted that the grand jury historically has been regarded as the primary protection for the innocent. However, only prosecutors and their witnesses appear before grand juries; no members of the defense are present. Prosecutors are able to offer their interpretation of the evidence and state the law and have no obligation to inform the grand jury of evidence of a defendant's innocence. Grand juries hear only one side of the case and almost always indict.

At trial, juries must determine guilt beyond a reasonable doubt. The possibility of **jury nullification** exists if the jury doesn't believe a case should have been brought to court. Trials rarely come into play as a check on the discretion of prosecutors—few cases charged ever end up going to trial. Most are resolved through plea bargaining. Plea bargaining is another area in which prosecutors have broad discretion. Judges rarely question or second-guess plea bargains reached between the prosecutor and defendant. Prosecutors ultimately have to answer to voters, since more than 95 percent of all chief prosecutors are chosen through election.[59]

There are positive and negative aspects to subjecting the prosecution of local crimes to the political process. On the positive side, the person deciding which laws to enforce and how to enforce them is answerable to the people of that district. More worrying is that political pressures—rather than the facts of a case—may guide the exercise of prosecutorial discretion. Prosecutors, for example, may choose not to charge politically connected friends. Some attributed the multibillion dollar savings and loan scandal of the 1980s and 1990s to the reluctance of prosecutors to subject friends and political allies to criminal indictment.[60] Discretion can also be misused when race enters the equation. Studies have shown that when the victim is white and the defendant is black, prosecutors are much more likely to seek the greatest possible punishment.[61]

Defense Attorneys

Anyone with even a casual acquaintance with TV crime dramas knows that after the police make an arrest they must inform the suspect of certain rights. One is that "you have the right to an attorney. If you cannot afford one, one will be appointed to you." This right derives from the Sixth Amendment: "In all criminal prosecutions, the accused shall enjoy the right . . . to have the assistance of counsel for his defense." In 1963, the U.S. Supreme Court found in *Gideon v. Wainwright* that this right to counsel is so fundamental and essential to a fair trial that the Constitution requires a lawyer be provided to the poor at state expense. Nine years after *Gideon*, the Court extended this right to counsel to all criminal prosecutions, state or federal, **felony** or **misdemeanor**, which carry a possible sentence of imprisonment.

INDICTMENT

A formal criminal charge.

GRAND JURY

A group of between sixteen and twenty-three citizens that decides if a case should go to trial; if yes, an indictment is issued.

JURY NULLIFICATION

Occurs when a jury returns a verdict of "Not Guilty" even though jurists believe the defendant is guilty. The jury cancels out a law that it believes is immoral or was wrongly applied to the defendant.

FELONY

A serious crime, such as murder or arson.

MISDEMEANOR

A less serious crime, such as shoplifting.

TABLE 8-6

Maximum and Minimum Annual Salary of Public Defenders and Supervisory Attorneys in State-Funded Systems, 1999

State	Assistant Prosecutor, entry level	Assistant Prosecutor, 5+ years experience	Supervisory Attorney
Alaska	$45,000 to 61,000	$55,000 to 75,000	$63,000 to 86,000
Colorado	$35,124 to 45,816	$54,480 to 73,008	$60,528 to 86,376
Connecticut	$41,612 to 46,808	$54,759 to 66,622	$57,217 to 100,406
Delaware	$36,000 to 43,000	$45,401 to 106,565	$— to 88,000
Iowa	$35,152 to 44,033	$44,033 to 68,286	$58,718 to 85,466
Massachusetts	$28,600 to 28,600	$42,000 to 42,000	$76,500 to 76,500
Missouri	$30,500 to —	$50,232 to —	$— to —
New Hampshire	$31,018 to 42,770	$48,204 to 52,754	$41,020 to 59,254
New Jersey	$40,965 to 47,873	$47,873 to 83,955	$63,198 to 91,000
New Mexico	$28,941 to 43,410	$44,834 to 67,253	$47,669 to 71,502
Rhode Island	$38,000 to 42,000	$42,000 to 46,000	$50,000 to 58,000
Vermont	$29,500 to 32,500	$39,000 to 42,000	$57,000 to —
West Virginia	$32,000 to —	$35,000 to 40,000	$55,000 to 78,000
Wisconsin	$37,087 to 93,108	$38,200 to 93,108	$42,829 to 98,850

Source: Adapted from Bureau of Justice Statistics. www.ojp.usdoj.gov/bjs/pub/pdf/sfids99.pdf (accessed May 25, 2004).

Note: Hawaii, Maine, Maryland, Minnesota, North Carolina, Oregon, and Virginia information not available.

— : Information not provided or not known

The Court has also made it clear that the Sixth Amendment guarantees "the right to the *effective* assistance of counsel." If an attorney was unprepared, drunk, or sleeping during a trial, that can be grounds for appeal.

No money came along with the constitutional mandate for counsel. And its scope is tremendous, since most criminal defendants in the United States cannot afford to pay for legal services. In 1991, about three-quarters of state prison inmates reported that they were represented by a court-appointed lawyer.[62] In 1999, in the nation's one hundred largest counties, criminal defense programs for the indigent (poor) received an estimated 4.2 million cases and spent an estimated $1.2 billion.[63] Sixty percent of this funding came from county governments. State governments pay 25 percent of the total funding.[64] Twenty-one states are funded almost exclusively by state sources, twenty use a combination of state and county funds, and nine use only county funds.[65]

TABLE 8-7

Statistics for State-Funded Public Defender Staff and Operations, 1999

State	Total Staff	Total State Indigent Defense Expenditures	Total Number of Cases Received	Chief Public Defender Appointed by	Salary of Chief Public Defender
Alaska	147	$11,460,400	29,983	Governor	$80,000
Colorado	380	31,394,830	64,179	Independent board or commission	90,590
Connecticut	348	25,095,150	56,327	Independent board or commission	110,524
Delaware	119	7,306,700	36,290	Governor	88,000
Hawaii	132	7,539,608	39,870	Governor	77,964
Iowa	199	30,720,729	61,232	Governor	75,000
Maine	—	6,999,820	—	—	—
Maryland	784	39,286,313	—	Board of Trustees	—
Massachusetts	190	62,200,000	7,143	Independent board or commission	95,760
Minnesota	636	46,400,000	178,175	Independent board or commission	89,627
Missouri	558	28,202,699	73,738	Independent board or commission	100,932
New Hampshire	127	10,667,700	15,522	Corporate board of directors	80,000
New Jersey	870	72,975,000	96,752	Governor	98,225
New Mexico	258	22,895,400	53,911	Governor	83,700
North Carolina	200	62,680,384	48,375	Judges	90,224
Oregon	—	32,564,390	—	—	—
Rhode Island	81	6,105,017	12,750	Governor	80,000
Vermont	68	5,829,246	12,703	Governor	62,000
Virginia	334	67,480,333	51,375	Independent board or commission	—
West Virginia	203	22,454,009	33,556	Independent board or commission	66,500
Wisconsin	—	61,590,139	124,171	Program advisory board	101,859

Source: Adapted from Bureau of Justice Statistics. www.ojp.usdoj.gov/bjs/pub/pdf/sfids99.pdf (accessed May 25, 2004).

Note: — : Information not reported or not known

Not only did the mandate come with no funding, but it also lacked any specifications as to how indigent services must be provided. States and localities, as a consequence, have devised differing systems, with the quality of service provided varying tremendously. Three primary models have emerged throughout the nation, with most states employing one or a combination of public defender programs, **assigned counsel**, and **contract attorneys**. The method chosen may vary from county to county in a state, or a state may rely primarily on one type and use either of the other types for casework overload or the inevitable cases involving a conflict of interest.

ASSIGNED COUNSEL

Private lawyers selected by the courts to handle particular cases and paid from public funds.

Among the nation's one hundred most populous counties in 1999, public defender programs were operating in ninety counties, assigned counsel programs in eighty-nine counties, and contract programs in forty-two counties.[66] Public defenders usually serve metropolitan areas and assigned counsel programs, or contract programs, serve less populous regions.

Public defenders are a salaried staff of attorneys. They provide criminal legal defense services either as employees paid directly by the government or through a public or private nonprofit organization. Large public defenders offices generally employ attorneys who are trained and supervised and are supported by a staff of investigators, paralegals, and clerical staff.[67] The American Bar Association has observed, "When adequately funded and staffed, defender organizations employing full-time personnel are capable of providing excellent defense services."[68] In thirty states, a public defender system is the primary method used to provide indigent criminal defendants with lawyers.[69]

Another system is called assigned counsel—private attorneys are chosen and appointed either on a systematic or an *ad hoc* basis and are paid from public funds. Depending on the state, individual judges, assigned counsel program offices, or the court clerk's office may make the appointments. In the oldest type of assigned counsel program, judges make *ad hoc* assignments of counsel. Sometimes the only basis for these decisions is whoever is in the courtroom at the time. These arrangements frequently are criticized for fostering patronage, particularly in less populated counties.

Most states appoint lawyers from a roster of attorneys available for assigned cases. These rosters are compiled in various ways. Generally, assigned counsel need do no more than put their names on a list to be appointed to cases. There is no review of their experience, qualifications, or competence. Some states, particularly those with organized plans administered by an independent manager, may require specific training before attorneys can be included on the roster. In Maine, all attorneys in the local bar are included on the roster unless they choose to be removed.[70] Assigned counsel are generally paid either a flat fee or an hourly rate, in some cases subject to an overall fee cap. Many are paid at very low rates, such that only recent law school graduates or those who were previously unsuccessful in the business of law will agree to take assignments.[71]

Contract attorney programs are another way to provide defense services. A state, a county, or a judicial district will enter into a contract for the provision of indigent representation. These contracts can be awarded to a solo attorney, a law firm that handles both indigent and private cases, a nonprofit organization, or a group of lawyers who joined together to provide services under the contract. The parties may agree to accept cases on a fixed-fee per case basis or to provide representation for a particular period of time for a fixed fee.

Fixed-fee contracts are viewed by some as quick fixes that allow the funding body to limit costs and accurately project expenses for the coming year. However, such contracts have been criticized severely by the courts and

Local Focus: Phoenix's Flat Fees and the Death Penalty

You know you're in trouble when you're facing the death penalty and your lawyer would rather go to jail himself than work on your case. In the late 1990s, Phoenix attorney Mike Terribile represented convicted murderer Richard Rivas, but as the case entered the sentencing phase, he refused to do any more work. The reason? Terribile said the flat fee he had received from Maricopa County to handle the case as a contract attorney was not enough to cover his costs. He appealed the payment contract to a judge, saying he would refuse to prepare Rivas's defense if he was turned down, even if that meant being held in contempt and jailed.

As in many jurisdictions, the Maricopa County Public Defender's Office simply can't handle all the indigent cases they receive. To alleviate the problem, the county contracts with private attorneys to handle the overflow. The county generally pays about $64,000 for a set of eight cases. Maricopa County administrator David Smith says that's plenty. "If a case settles with just a few hours'

work, they [still] get the $8,000," Smith says. He says that there is a provision in the contract that allows for extra compensation if a case gets complicated, but notes that 97 percent of the cases in the county are plea-bargained out. "We expect that it will all even out."

Terribile, who once chaired a statewide indigent-defense committee, said he hadn't taken on any more county cases, and he's not alone in refusing the work. Inadequate defense is a major reason why the American Bar Association has called for a death penalty moratorium. "You go to any death penalty state and start asking questions about counsel in those cases and, with very few exceptions, there are substantial problems," says Tye Hunter, of North Carolina's Indigent Defense Services Commission.

Source: Adapted from Alan Greenblatt, *Governing* magazine, March 2001. www.governing.com/archive/2001/mar/glimpses.txt (accessed May 28, 2004).

national organizations like the American Bar Association. Few states rely on them to provide representation for all or even a majority of their indigent defense cases. Instead, they are more commonly used to handle public defender overload or conflicts. Sometimes, a public defenders office also will contract out a specific category of cases, such as juvenile or traffic offenses. Of the total amount spent on indigent criminal defense in the nation's one hundred largest counties, only 6 percent was spent on contract programs.[72]

Regardless of the model used by a county or state, all depend on adequate funding to successfully provide "effective assistance of counsel." Inadequate funding leads to lawyers carrying impossible caseloads. Overburdened lawyers make crucial decisions based on too little fact investigation and inevitably pressure clients to plead guilty.[73] Many indigent defense systems are plagued by lack of funding and resources, high attorney workloads, and little or no oversight over quality of services—problems that could result in the conviction of innocent people.[74] "Providing genuinely adequate counsel for poor defendants would require a substantial infusion of money and indigent defense is the last thing the populace will voluntarily direct its tax dollars to fund," writes attorney David Cole. "Achieving solutions to this problem through the political process is a pipe dream."[75]

Yet, how secure would you feel if you were wrongly accused of a felony in Virginia, where your appointed lawyer could be paid only $395 to defend

> "Providing genuinely adequate counsel for poor defendants would require a substantial infusion of money and indigent defense is the last thing the populace will voluntarily direct its tax dollars to fund," writes attorney David Cole. "Achieving solutions to this problem through the political process is a pipe dream."

you? If you don't plead guilty quickly, your lawyer will lose money on your case. In a number of jurisdictions, systemic challenges have been mounted against underfunded and overburdened public defenders, assigned counsel programs, and contract attorneys. Some of these have led to successful injunctions or settlements, increased funding for indigent defense, and improved the administration of such programs.[76] Furthermore, the defense community and organizations like the American Bar Association have been focusing on the need for standards for indigent criminal representation. The goal is to educate those policymakers who design systems by which these legal services are delivered.

Juries

If you vote, pay a utility bill, or drive you may be called to jury duty at some point in your life. You may be asked to decide whether a defendant in a capital case lives or dies; whether someone spends the rest of his or her life in prison; whether a civil plaintiff, injured and unable to work, should be able to collect damages; or whether a civil defendant must be bankrupted by the large amount of damages ordered to be paid. Service on a jury may require spending days or weeks listening to intricate scientific evidence and expert testimony, listening to conflicting testimony, and deciding who is credible and who is not to be believed. Or, you may spend one day in a large room with other potential jurors, break for lunch, and go home at the end of that day without ever hearing a single case.

The right to a jury trial in state criminal proceedings is granted by the Sixth Amendment. Not all criminal prosecutions trigger the right to a jury trial—minor offenses involving a potential sentence of less than six months do not require juries. Neither do juvenile proceedings, probation revocation proceedings, or military trials.

The jury's role in a trial is that of fact-finder. The judge has to ensure a fair and orderly trial, but it is the jurors who must determine the facts of the case. In some instances, parties may agree to forego a jury trial and instead choose a bench trial in which the judge serves as both judge and jury. In a criminal bench trial, the judge alone decides guilt or innocence.

Differences and similarities in how judges and juries rule have been the subject of much research and review. Standard stereotypes might lead one to think that juries would be less able to separate emotion from reason than judges. That they would decide cases more generously for injured plaintiffs and that grisly evidence in criminal cases may motivate them to decide based on passion or prejudice. Not so. For instance, research shows that civil plaintiffs in products **liability** and medical malpractice cases have more success before judges in bench trials.[77]

Historically, juries have been composed of twelve people who must come to a unanimous verdict. Since 1970, however, a series of U.S. Supreme Court decisions has allowed states to move away from this standard.[78] In state jury trials, whether unanimity is required depends on the size of the jury. A conviction by a twelve-member jury may be less than unanimous, whereas a six-member jury must have unanimity. A majority of states continue to require twelve-member juries to make unanimous rulings in felony criminal cases, but seven states use six-member or eight-member juries for noncapital felonies. Two states, Louisiana and Oregon, do not require a unanimous verdict in such cases.[79] Most states provide for civil juries of six members or eight members. Those that still require twelve members typically allow parties to agree to smaller juries. Unanimity is not required in most civil trials—instead, most states provide for verdicts based on a supermajority of either five-sixths or two-thirds.

States develop and maintain master lists from which they identify potential jurors. Their sources include driver's licenses, motor vehicle registration, telephone directories, tax rolls, utility customer lists, voter registrations, and lists of actual voters. It is very hard to avoid ever being called in for jury duty. Jurors must be residents of the county in which the court sits and must generally be eighteen years old, although in Alabama and Nebraska the minimum age is nineteen and in Mississippi and Missouri it is twenty-one. States also usually have some sort of requirement regarding literacy and the ability to understand, communicate in English, or both. South Carolina requires at least a sixth-grade education, and Tennessee explicitly excludes those of "unsound mind" and "habitual drunkards." Most states also require that jurors not be convicted felons.

Typically, the provisions for selecting a juror are the same for all the trial courts within a state, although some make distinctions between limited and general jurisdiction courts. The formal process of jury selection begins with a *voir dire* examination. This is the process by which prospective jurors are interviewed and examined. Some may be excused following a challenge by one of the attorneys in the case. The primary purpose of this is to impanel, or select, an impartial jury. If it appears during the questioning that a particular juror is biased or has a particular view of the case, that juror may be stricken **for cause**. There is no limit on the number of challenges a party can make for cause. In addition, each party receives a certain number of **peremptory challenges**, meaning the lawyers can kick off jurors for any reason other than race or gender.

Defendants' Rights vs. Victims' Rights

Crime typically involves at least two actors: a perpetrator and a victim. Traditionally, the criminal justice system in the United States interposes the ideal

---

LIABILITY

A legal obligation or responsibility.

VOIR DIRE

The interviewing and examination of potential jurors.

FOR CAUSE CHALLENGE

Occurs when a lawyer asks the judge to excuse a potential juror because the individual appears to be biased or unable to be fair.

PEREMPTORY CHALLENGES

Used by lawyers to dismiss potential jurors for any reason except race or gender.

of public prosecution between the two. That is, all crimes are crimes against the state. The prosecutor, representing the public and not any particular individual, sees that justice is done objectively and fairly. The public's interest, under this system, is distinct from the victim's interest in retribution.

Numerous provisions in the Bill of Rights balance the rights of criminal defendants against the powers of the state. These "defendants' rights" include:

- the right to be presumed innocent until proven guilty,

- the right to be safe from arrest or searches and seizures unless the government has made a showing of probable cause,

- the right to a lawyer,

- the right to a jury trial,

- the right to confront witnesses,

- the rights to due process and the equal protection of laws, and

- if proven guilty, the right to punishment that is not cruel and unusual.

The Framers' concerns in creating these rights were of overreaching government power. They worried that innocent people otherwise might be railroaded into jail on charges they never had a chance to adequately defend themselves against. There is no mention of the rights of crime victims.

In the last two decades, this balance has undergone a radical transformation. Defendants still have all of the rights listed, but now state courts are increasingly balancing them against a new class of victims' rights. The movement advocating an increasing role for the victims of crime has become a formidable force and has achieved tremendous success in enacting legislation in all the states. The momentum started in 1982, when a president's task force on victims of crime described the United States justice system as "appallingly out of balance." That's not to say that victims were helpless—the number of state laws addressing victims' rights was already in the hundreds. By 1998, however, the number of crime victim–related statutes had soared to more than twenty-seven thousand. Twenty-nine states had passed victims' rights constitutional amendments.[80]

Today, every state has either a constitutional amendment or a statutory scheme that protects victims' rights. Some predict that the next amendment to the federal constitution will be a victims' rights amendment. Supporters frequently argue that the justice system favors defendants over victims and that, without modification, the system itself constitutes a second victimization. On the other hand, civil rights organizations fear that some victims' rights laws upset the system of checks and balances in the nation's criminal justice system and undercut the basic due process protections designed to keep innocent people out of prison.

The specifics of victims' rights laws vary among the states. A variety of statutes or amendments guarantee that crime victims receive monetary compensation, notice of procedural developments in the case, protection from offender harm, and more attentive treatment from the justice system. The more controversial of such laws are directed toward providing victims with a significantly greater involvement in the actual prosecutions. This includes providing victims the right to confer with the prosecutor at all stages, including plea bargains; the right to attend all stages of the case, even if the victim will be called as a witness; and the right to introduce victim impact statements at the sentencing phase of the trial.

Perhaps the most controversial and interesting of the victims' rights laws concern victim impact evidence. This may be particularly true in capital cases in which impact statements have been described as "highly emotional, frequently tearful testimony coming directly from the hearts and mouths of the survivors left behind by killings. And it arrives at the precise time when the balance is at its most delicate and the stakes are highest—when jurors are poised to make the visceral decision of whether the offender lives or dies." [81] In 1991, the U.S. Supreme Court reversed itself and ruled that impact statements that detailed the particular qualities of the victim and the harm caused to the victim's family could be admissible in capital sentencing hearings.[82] Today, all states allow victims' impact evidence at the sentencing phase of the trial. Most of the states with the death penalty allow it in capital trials.

States have made a number of attempts to balance the rights of victims with the rights of the accused. They have made provisions for compensation of victims, the right to confer with the prosecutor, and the right to introduce victim impact statements to the court. Here, victims' rights advocates escort relatives of some of those shot by convicted D.C. sniper Lee Boyd Malvo into Virginia's Chesapeake Circuit Court in November 2003.

Sentencing

The state prison population has ballooned in the last twenty years, from less than 320,000 in 1980 to a total of almost two million today.[83] Corrections has been one of the fastest growing items in state budgets and averaged 7 percent of state budgets by 2000.[84] In most states, the judge holds a separate sentencing hearing after the jury finds the defendant guilty. In capital cases, the Supreme Court has held that only a unanimous jury, and not the judge, can sentence a defendant to death.[85] Thirteen states have provisions for a sentence of life without parole if the jury is unable to reach agreement.[86] In noncapital cases, by contrast, it is almost always the judge who sets sentence. Only in Arkansas, Missouri, Texas, and Virginia does the jury choose the sentence. In all states but Texas, the judge is free to disregard the jury's decision.

Sentencing policy involves the balancing of value judgments, such as the perceived severity of the crimes and the perceived severity of different punishments, with the relevance of mitigating circumstances. It must include considerations of the costs to taxpayers and to society of incarceration. Surveys indicate that attitudes on sentencing follow regional patterns, "with residents of New England demonstrating the greatest tendency to be lenient and residents of central southern states displaying the least leniency." [87] It is not surprising then that state sentencing laws vary and that the punishment a convict faces depends not just on what that person did but also on where the crime was committed. Voters in California and Oklahoma, for instance, view drug offenses differently. In California state courts, a cocaine dealer is subject to a two-year to four-year prison term. The same offense in Oklahoma brings a minimum of five years and a maximum of life imprisonment.[88]

The amount of discretion given to judges also varies from state to state. Depending on the type of crime or where the defendant is charged, the sentence can be a matter of "do the crime, do the time" or whatever the judge or parole board thinks is best.

A few decades ago, it was possible to talk of a predominant American approach to criminal sentencing. At all levels of the nation's criminal justice system, a concern for rehabilitation and deterrence led states to embrace **indeterminate sentencing**. Legislatures set very wide statutory sentencing margins within which judges had the discretion to impose sentence for imprisonment with little fear of appellate review. The sentence was indeterminate because the parole board, not the judge, had ultimate control over the actual release date. Under this system, the discretion of judges and parole boards was necessary to tailor punishment to the specific rehabilitative needs of the individual defendant. This practice led to wide discrepancies in the sentences imposed for those convicted of the same crime.

Indeterminate sentencing came under attack from several angles during the 1970s. The lack of guidance for judges led to the potential for discrimination in sentencing based on such factors as race, ethnic group, social status, or gender. There was also criticism of the ability of parole boards to successfully identify whether inmates had or had not been rehabilitated. Finally, rehabilitation lost favor as the country entered an era of tough-on-crime rhetoric and a "just desserts" theory of criminal sentencing.[89] Sentencing reform sought to replace indeterminate sentencing with **determinate sentencing**. This led to the adoption of federal sentencing guidelines—a structured system of binding sentencing rules that greatly limited judicial discretion in sentencing in the federal courts.

In contrast to the federal court system, there has been no single sweeping sentencing reform across all fifty states. Some states have made wholesale changes to determinate sentencing laws, but most continue to use indeterminate sentencing.[90]

Yet indeterminate sentencing does not necessarily mean more lenient sentencing. It just means that the actual amount of time served may vary depending on the judge or the findings of a parole board. For instance, Los Angeles Lakers star Kobe Bryant was charged with felony sexual assault in

INDETERMINATE SENTENCING

The judge sentences an offender to a minimum and a maximum time in prison. A parole board decides how long the offender actually will remain in prison.

DETERMINATE SENTENCING

The judge sentences an offender to serve a specific amount of time in prison depending on the crime.

Colorado. The sex offense statutes there are considered among the harshest in the country. Any sentence on a sex assault charge can mean the possibility of life imprisonment. In part, the severity of the sentence depends on the results of a battery of tests. These results are used by judges in sentencing and by parole boards to determine if the prisoner is a continued threat. They include plethismograph tests, which involve placing an electric band around the penis in an attempt to measure deviant thoughts as the person is shown images of abusive behaviors. Described as "very Clockwork Orangish" by Don Recht, former head of the Colorado Defense Bar, the results are studied carefully nonetheless. Under Colorado's indeterminate sentencing, a convicted sex offender is released only when deemed safe to reenter society.

Most states still rely on indeterminate sentencing, but all states have adopted at least some features of determinate sentencing, although in greatly differing degrees. When it comes to sentencing reform, "the states have served as hothouses of experimentation during the last thirty years, with so much activity that the diversity of provisions among the states has become exceedingly complex."[91] Some of the major reforms adopted include sentencing guidelines, **mandatory minimum sentences** that are imposed for conviction of specified crimes, **habitual offender laws**, and **truth-in-sentencing laws**. With the implementation of these reforms, the time served in prison has been increasing as a percentage of the sentence imposed. In 1993, the percentage of a sentence an offender spent in prison was 31.8 percent; that percentage had increased to 43.8 percent by 1999.[92]

All fifty states and the District of Columbia have enacted some form of mandatory minimum prison sentencing.[93] These laws limit judicial discretion by requiring that individuals guilty of specific crimes must go to jail no less than a specified length of time. Such crimes include drug possession or trafficking, drunk driving, or sexual offenses. The mandatory sentencing laws also may take effect if certain acts enhanced the severity of the underlying crime. For instance, if deadly weapons were involved. If a crime involved the use of a deadly weapon, New Mexico requires an additional year for the first offence or three additional years for a second offense. Use of a firearm to commit a crime in Nevada requires a doubling of the sentence for the underlying crime. In Ohio, use of a deadly weapon requires an additional term of three to six years.[94]

Habitual offender laws also are common among the states. These statutes impose more severe sentences for offenders who previously have been sentenced for crimes. California's "three-strikes and you're out" law was a prototype of this kind of legislation. The laws state that if a defendant convicted of a felony has one prior conviction for a "serious" or "violent" felony, the sentence is doubled. Defendants convicted for a felony with two prior convictions for "serious" or "violent" felonies receive a life sentence without possibility of parole. The law has been severely criticized for its "unbending harshness," but has withstood constitutional challenges.[95] Twenty-four states have enacted some form of "two or three strikes" legislation. One such

MANDATORY MINIMUM SENTENCES

The shortest sentences that offenders may receive upon conviction for certain offenses. The court has no authority to impose a shorter sentence.

HABITUAL OFFENDER LAWS

These statutes impose harsher sentences for offenders who previously have been sentenced for crimes.

TRUTH-IN-SENTENCING LAWS

These laws give parole boards less authority to shorten sentences for good behavior by specifying the proportion of a sentence an offender must serve before becoming eligible for parole.

state is Michigan, in which the sentence is one and a half times the maximum sentence on the second conviction and twice the maximum sentence for a third conviction.[96]

Another sentencing reform movement began in the 1990s. Known as truth-in-sentencing, these laws reduce the amount of discretion parole boards have to shorten sentences for good behavior. They do this by specifying the proportion of a sentence that offenders must serve before they may be considered for parole. Thirty-nine states have adopted some form of truth-in-sentencing laws.[97] Most, however, still have a parole board with some discretionary release authority and a system in which the incarcerated felons can accumulate "good time" under a specified formula. Arkansas, Louisiana, Vermont, and Wyoming are among the many states that provide for a day of "good time" for each day—or less—served. North Dakota grants five days of "good time" for every month served.

These formulas also can be complicated by the accumulation of work or education credits. Some states, like Illinois, have cut through the confusion by eliminating the good time credit for certain serious offenses. Others have eliminated it altogether. Michigan eliminated the concept of good time for all felony offenses committed after December 2000, and the District of Columbia has not offered it since 1994.[98]

As states reduce judges' discretion and increase time spent in prison, a considerable burden has been placed on the facilities and personnel of the prison system. In response to this, most states are exploring sentencing options for their less serious offenders that are less severe than imprisonment but more serious than ordinary probation.[99] One such option is house arrest. This requires the offenders to remain in their residences for the duration of their sentences. They often are required to wear electronic bracelets around the wrist or ankle that sends a continuous radio signal to verify their location.

Many states rely on "intensive probation." This form of probation involves much closer supervision by parole officers with smaller caseloads than the norm. Parolees under these programs typically are required to hold a job, submit to urinalysis, pay restitution to victims, and perform community service. To alleviate prison overcrowding, some states release prisoners to "halfway" houses that assist with reintegration into the community. Young first-time offenders may be sentenced to "boot camps" for shorter periods and submitted to strict military discipline. Nonviolent offenders may be offered work release; weekend sentencing; alcohol, drug, or mental health treatment; or release subject to appearance at daily reporting centers.

The Case for Court Reform

How state courts are organized is not static and carved in stone. States constantly evaluate practices and modify procedures to adapt to demographic, economic, and political conditions. This section discusses some reforms being adopted or at least being discussed in most states. Specialized courts to handle drug offenses or family matters are currently in vogue to accommodate increasing caseloads, as are attempts to streamline and speed up court dockets. Given the controversy surrounding judicial elections, discussed in detail in earlier, many states aren't waiting for major reforms to merit selection but instead are focusing on modifying elections to minimize the problems posed by the need for campaign contributions. Finally, this section addresses some of the pressures to reform that stem from the lack of uniformity within a given state and across the country.

The Problem of Increasing Caseload

Nationwide, violent crime rates are down. State courts have nonetheless found themselves on the frontlines dealing with the results of societal problems such as substance abuse and family violence since the 1980s. From 1984 to 1999, the U.S. population grew by only 12 percent. The number of juvenile cases grew by 68 percent during the same period, and the number of domestic relations cases grew by 74 percent. Criminal cases, mostly misdemeanors, grew by 47 percent.[100]

In reaction to such growth, many states have created "problem-solving courts." These include community courts, domestic violence courts, mental health courts, and drug treatment courts. Their purpose is to deal decisively with low-level nonviolent crimes. The solutions often involve closely monitored treatment plans meant to stop the revolving door of **recidivism,** or relapses into criminal behavior. Drug courts, with their focus on treatment for nonviolent drug-addicted offenders, contribute to the decline in violent crimes and save local and state governments millions of dollars annually from reduced incarceration rates.

States also have been experimenting with integrated family courts. These courts adopt a holistic approach to all the issues that affect a single family in a single court system. Such integrated courts can address issues more efficiently, especially in cases in which delays can leave children in foster care limbo. Many individuals who appear in such family courts traditionally have been forced instead to face multiple proceedings in multiple courts: assault in county courts, custody disputes in family courts, divorce issues in yet another court. The current trend is to put all of a family's problems before a single, informed judge to eliminate conflicting orders and multiple appearances. New York, with a pilot Integrated Domestic Violence Court, estimates that the court has slashed the number of cases from more than three thousand to less than nine hundred, reducing delay and duplication and increasing cost-effective case management.[101]

This increased focus on court administration and case management has not been confined to the criminal side of the court calendar. Until just a few years ago, crowded civil dockets and multiyear waiting periods were

RECIDIVISM

A return to, or relapse into, criminal behavior.

relatively common in many states. "Back in the 1980s, there was no incentive for an insurance company to settle a case for the first year," says Bill Sieben, who was then president of the Minnesota Trial Lawyers Association. "They knew the case wasn't even going to be nearing a trial for several years." [102] This is becoming less and less true as states focus on clearing their overcrowded and overly cumbersome civil dockets. Tom Phillips, chief justice of the Texas Supreme Court, attributes faster-clearing caseloads primarily to the rise of the managerial judge.[103] Most trial judges may insist on a strong case-management system, but a generation ago, when caseloads were smaller and more manageable, not many of them did.

In recent years, not content with merely handing down verdicts, forceful judges have seized control of their courts and made it clear that things will run according to their schedules, not at the convenience of lawyers who never seem quite ready to go to trial. "A very strong component of civil cases is, just set a trial date and the case will go away," says Kevin Burke, chief judge of the Hennepin County Court in Minnesota. "Left to their own devices, lawyers aren't necessarily going to manage it to a speedy resolution." [104]

State initiatives to speed up dockets, or court case schedules, have included an increased reliance on **alternative dispute resolution**. In certain types of cases such resolutions now are mandated, and lawyers are required to inform their clients about alternatives to standard court fights. These alternatives usually involve hashing things out in front of an expert mediator. Some courts have been creative in finding appropriately authoritative experts. Hennepin County courts, for instance, refer dry cleaning disputes—stained pants, torn dresses, and busted buttons—to a retired owner of a dry cleaning business for speedy resolution. An accountant may resolve a financial dispute. These innovations increase the efficiency of the court system and free up trial judges for more complex cases.

Several states are experimenting with a **rocket docket** patterned after an innovation in a Virginia federal court. In essence, these fast-track dockets impose tight, unbending deadlines on lawyers in the handling of pre-trial motions and briefs. At the Vermont Supreme Court, the rocket docket applies to cases that present no novel issue likely to add to the body of case law. Rather than all five justices sitting *en banc* to hear these cases, each month they split and rotate through a smaller and less cumbersome panel of three that is able to reach consensus more quickly. The panel releases its decisions within twenty-four hours in 99 percent of the cases.

In Colorado, rapid population growth has led to mounting lawsuits, and courts increasingly have turned to **magistrates** to resolve less important cases. Often a local official or attorney hired on contract, these magistrates have helped the state to stay on top of an 85 percent increase in case filings despite only a 12 percent increase in the number of judges. The magistrates issue preliminary decisions that must then be upheld by a judge, but this is a formality in most cases. This modification is credited with enabling more routine cases to be handled efficiently and allowing more time for more

---

ALTERNATIVE DISPUTE RESOLUTION

A way to end a disagreement by means other than litigation. It usually involves the appointment of a mediator to preside over a meeting between the parties.

ROCKET DOCKET

Fast-track cases that often have limited, specific deadlines for specific court procedures.

MAGISTRATES

Local officials or attorneys granted limited judicial powers.

complex cases, but some have complained to the Colorado Bar that this reliance on contract attorneys to serve as magistrates decreases the accountability of the judges and does not yield sufficiently clear precedent to provide guidance to the attorneys who must practice before them.[105]

The Reform of Judicial Selection

Nationally, 87 percent of all state judges face partisan, nonpartisan, or retention elections or some mix of the above.[106] As discussed earlier, the trend in recent years has been for these elections to become more and more like elections for legislative and gubernatorial offices—loud, nasty, and expensive. Some fear that this will lead to a blurring of the distinction between the judicial and political branches of government and throw into question the independent decision making of the judiciary.

Indeed, the U.S. Supreme Court's decision in *Republican Party of Minnesota v. White* (2002) may have brought politics closer than ever to the judicial elections process. A five to four majority ruled that the First Amendment did not allow the government "to prohibit candidates from communicating relevant information to voters during an election." This includes judicial candidates who wish to speak publicly about disputed legal matters. At the same time, the Court acknowledged the core responsibility of judges to "be willing to consider views that oppose [their] preconceptions, and remain

In contrast to states that use the merit system to select judges, Pennsylvanians choose theirs through partisan elections. On May 7, 2003, the five candidates for the Democratic nomination for state supreme court, (from left to right) Judge James Lynn, Judge John Herron, Judge James DeLeon, Judge Max Baer, and Judge Cheryl Allen, faced off at a debate in Harrisburg, the state capitol. This was the first year that judicial candidates were permitted to discuss political issues.

open to persuasion when the issues arise in a pending case." Today, states that hold elections for judicial offices, such as Ohio, Pennsylvania, and Wisconsin, feature public debates among judicial candidates similar to those held for candidates for legislative office.

The major reform movement of the latter half of the twentieth century was the merit selection of judges described previously. This movement was initially very successful but, after being adopted by roughly half the states, has stalled in recent years. Since 1990, all of the legislatures that have considered merit selection have rejected it. States seeking to adopt merit selection face both cultural and political obstacles. They face an ingrained cultural belief that elections are a critical part of our democracy not to be sacrificed without a fight. Combined with this is the political reality that in most states change to merit selection would require the legislative supermajority and public approval necessary for constitutional change.

Recognizing these barriers to adopting merit selection, reformers are focusing on improving popular elections to minimize the threat they pose to judicial independence and impartiality. For example, the unprecedented level of interest group activity in judicial elections has led to recommendations to require the disclosure of campaign contributions. This is an area with First Amendment implications that requires states to tread very carefully. Some states focus their reforms on the dangers inherent in campaign financing and are experimenting with public financing of judicial campaigns. They hope that this will reduce the potential of campaign contributions to influence or to create the appearance of influencing outcomes. In Wisconsin, revenue to publicly fund the campaigns of state supreme court candidates comes from a $1 state tax return check-off. Beginning in 2004, North Carolina provides full public financing of elections for appeals court and supreme court candidates who accept spending limits. Revenues to pay for the financing are raised by both a state tax return check-off and a voluntary $50 increase in attorney bar dues.[107]

Problems from the Lack of Sentencing Uniformity

Since the 1970s, sentencing reform movements have concerned themselves more and more with the sentencing disparities that occur when judges and parole boards have broad discretion in the sentencing of criminal offenders. Many states felt pressure to reform sentencing, but how they responded varies substantially. State sentencing guidelines, adopted by a minority of states, are not as rigid as new federal guidelines. State judges also tend to have more discretion than federal judges.

A parallel trend in criminal law has involved the increased federalization of crimes that were once the sole domain of the states. Many street crimes, such as low-level gun and drug offenses, are now federal offenses. Law enforcement officials have the choice of sending such cases to federal or state prosecutors and courts, and the cases are subject to the differing sets of sentencing guidelines. The trend away from discretion in sentencing has led to some uniformity nationwide in sentencing in federal courts. Ironically, however, the federal sentencing guidelines and the increased federalization of local crimes have increased the sense of randomness in sentencing within communities. Depending on whether an offender is charged in state court or federal court for the same offense can lead to huge disparities in the sentence.

Nationwide, drug and weapons violations result in sentences that are an average of three times longer in federal courts than in state courts.[108] In some cases, the essentially random chance of being charged in federal court can lead to a death penalty, even where local voters have twice rejected capital punishment, as in the District of Columbia. In some areas, prosecutors have been suspected of "shopping" for either a state or federal trial depending on the race of the offender. In a region of Massachusetts in the late 1990s, white crack dealers were tried exclusively in state courts, while many black dealers were tried in federal courts.[109] When two members of the same community, who do the exact same thing, are subjected to drastically different treatment, it undermines confidence that justice is being done. This was one of the concerns that led to the passage of sentencing reforms in the first place.

Conclusion

State and local courts play a profound role in their state governments. They resolve civil disputes and hand out justice in criminal cases. They also protect the citizens of their states from unconstitutional behavior by the political branches of government. Despite the importance of this role, or perhaps because of it, judicial systems differ tremendously from state to state. There are organizational differences from initial trial to final appeal. Judges in some states are elected by voters and in others are appointed by the governor. Such differences reflect a state's unique orientation towards the values of politics, law, judicial independence, and accountability.

The focus in this chapter has been on the players involved as a case works its way through the judicial system. In a criminal case, the elected prosecutor has tremendous freedom to decide what charges to bring against an accused criminal. Anyone charged with crimes has the right to an attorney, and the state must provide attorneys to those unable to afford their own. Usually a public defender takes the case. If a plea bargain is not reached, the case goes to trial, and the fate of the accused rests in the hands of a panel of ordinary citizens who were called to jury duty. Potential jurors are selected from a pool of individuals who may have done something as simple as paying a utility bill. This does not mean, however, that there is anything simple about a jury's task. Often, this group holds the future of another individual in its hands.

If found guilty and sentenced to incarceration, the length of time an offender actually spends in jail depends a lot on how the values of rehabilitation, deterrence, and retribution have played out in a particular state's political system. Differences here can have enormous impact. One state may try a nonviolent drug offender in a special drug court that focuses on treatment. Another may try the same offense in a general trial court in which the judge has no choice except lengthy incarceration under rigid minimum sentencing guidelines.

None of the choices states make in structuring their courts are fixed and unchanging. States are always responding to altered societal or political realities, experimenting with what works, and adapting to political movements. Some of the areas of reform and change looked at in this chapter were triggered by the political rise of victims' rights movements, by the realities of changing caseloads, or by a perception that the selection of judges has become increasingly political.

Key Concepts

activist judges (p. 256)

alternative dispute
  resolution (p. 294)

appeal (p. 260)

assigned counsel (p. 283)

bench trials (p. 261)

civil cases (p. 259)

contract attorneys (p. 283)

court of first instance
  (p. 260)

criminal cases (p. 259)

determinate sentencing
  (p. 290)

discretionary jurisdiction
  (p. 263)

en banc (p. 264)

felony (p. 281)

for cause challenges (p. 287)

general jurisdiction trial
  courts (p. 261)

grand jury (p. 281)

habitual offender laws
  (p. 291)

indeterminate sentencing
  (p. 290)

indictment (p. 281)

intermediate appellate
  court (p. 260)

jury nullification (p. 281)

legislative over-
  criminalization (p. 280)

liability (p. 287)

limited, or special
  jurisdiction, trial
  courts (p. 261)

magistrates (p. 294)

mandatory jurisdiction
  (p. 263)

mandatory minimum
  sentences (p. 291)

misdemeanor (p. 281)

panels (p. 264)

peremptory challenges
  (p. 287)

plea bargain (p. 259)

precedent (p. 260)

prejudicial error (p. 261)

prosecutor (p. 278)

public defender (p. 279)

pure appointive
  systems (p. 271)

recidivism (p. 293)

retention elections
  (p. 272)

rocket docket (p. 294)

settlement (p. 259)

state supreme court
  (p. 260)

trial court (p. 259)

truth-in-sentencing
  laws (p. 291)

voir dire (p. 287)

Suggested Readings

Brace, Paul and Melinda Gann Hall. "Studying Courts Comparatively: The View from the American States." *Political Research Quarterly* 48 (March 1995): 5–29. This study examines how politics and methods of judicial selection effect capital punishment decisions in state supreme courts. The authors conclude that

party affiliation and whether judges are elected has an impact on how death penalty cases are decided.

Carp, Robert A., Ronald Stidham, and Kenneth Manning. *Judicial Process in America,* 6th ed. Washington D.C.: CQ Press, 2004. A comprehensive look at the state and federal court systems in the United States. Covers the foundations, history, organization, and processes of U.S. courts as well as other issues like policy implementation and judicial decision making.

Rottman, David, et al. *State Court Organization 1998* Washington, D.C.: Bureau of Justice Statistics, 2000. A basic overview of how the fifty states organize their state court systems. Includes everything from qualification requirements to selection methods to the number of courts and full-time judges serving in a state.

Ware, Steven. "Money, Politics and Judicial Decisions: A Case Study of Arbitration Law in Alabama." *Journal of Law and Politics* 15 (1999): 645. This article presents the results of a study of 106 decisions by the Alabama Supreme Court from January 18, 1995, through July 9, 1999. The study shows the correlation between campaign funding and judicial rulings.

Suggested Web Sites

http://w3.abanet.org/home.cfm. Web site of the American Bar Association, the largest voluntary professional association in the world, with a membership of more than 400,000.

www.ajs.org. Web site of the American Judicature Society, a nonpartisan organization with a national membership that works to maintain the independence and integrity of the courts and increase public understanding of the justice system.

www.ojp.usdoj.gov/bjs. Web site for the Bureau of Justice Statistics that includes information and statistics on a variety of areas, including courts and sentencing and crimes and victims.

www.ncsconline.org. Web site of the National Center for State Courts, an independent non-profit organization that assists court officials to better serve the public.

www.JusticeatStake.org. Web site of the Justice at Stake Campaign, a nonpartisan effort working to keep courts fair and impartial.

CHAPTER 9

Bureaucracy

What Nobody Wants but Everybody Needs

Waiting in line and filling out forms are what most people associate with public agencies. Here, customers go through these age-old bureaucratic rituals at the Department of Motor Vehicles in Newark, New Jersey.

9

Why do we have so much bureaucracy?

How good—or bad—of a job does it really do?

For Avigayil Wardein, setting up a lemonade stand was a way to earn a little pocket money and maybe learn a few business basics.

She earned a little pocket money all right, but ended up learning more about bureaucracy than business.

In summer 2003, the six-year-old set up shop at the end of her mom's driveway in Naples, Florida. She quickly began attracting business from thirsty passersby. Within days, however, the police arrived to shut Avigayil down. In Naples, city regulations require a permit for all temporary businesses. Avigayil had not gone to the appropriate agency, filled out the necessary forms, and paid the required $35 permit fee. Since this temporary business permit expires as soon as a vendor shuts down for the day, complying with the rules meant Avigayil was faced with paying $35 a day to satisfy city hall bureaucracy. That was five dollars more than her record daily take.

A public agency ensnaring a six-year-old's lemonade stand in red tape and demanding a daily thirty-five bucks as the price of staying open? One more example, as if we needed it, of everything that is wrong with government bureaucracy, right? Bureaucracy is overbearing, interfering, and a needless complication in citizens' lives, right?

Wrong. In this story, bureaucracy turns out to be more the understanding hero than the heartless villain. Avigayil's lemonade stand was temporarily shut down as the result of a citizen complaint. A neighbor had called city hall and protested the illegal operation of a business. Technically, the complaint was accurate and the city was legally obligated to respond. An officer was duly dispatched to shut down Avigayil, although he bought a glass of lemonade and was mostly apologetic about the whole process. The city then gave Avigayil a fistful of daily permits—more than enough to keep her business legal for the summer—and waived the fees. She was back in business.[1]

The permits are actually a reasonable rule. They are not designed to shut down lemonade stands run by entrepreneurial elementary school students, but rather to control temporary vendors like hotdog stands. Left unregulated, the latter could operate anywhere at any time, creating the potential for traffic problems, neighborhood nuisances, and unscrupulous business practices. Avigayil's story highlights bureaucracy's paradoxical nature. On the one hand, it does mean rules and red tape that are inconvenient at best and defy common sense at worst. Yet bureaucracy does not produce or enforce these rules just for kicks. Like as not there are good reasons for the rules, and someone wants the bureaucracy to enforce them.

Bureaucracy represents what is perhaps the political system's greatest contradiction. We do not particularly like it, yet we seem unable to live without it. Like a trip to the dentist, bureaucracy often is inconvenient, involves too much paperwork, and can result in a certain amount of pain. Ultimately, however, it turns out to be good for us.

In this chapter we are going to explore this workhorse of the American political system—the state and local bureaucracies that implement and manage most public programs and services. We will try to understand what bureaucracy is and why it plays such an important role. Most importantly, we will try to use the comparative method to arrive at some explanation of why the American political system has so much bureaucracy when many citizens seem to value it so little.

What Is Bureaucracy?

For our purposes, **bureaucracy** is the public agencies and the public programs and services these agencies implement and manage. Thus, **bureaucrats** are simply the employees of the public agencies. These agencies—generically known as government bureaucracies—are usually located in the executive branches of state and local governments. Although these agencies are very different in terms of the programs and services they manage and deliver, the vast majority of them are organizationally very similar. There is a specific set of organizational characteristics associated with bureaucracy:

Division of labor. Labor is divided according to task and function. Most large bureaucracies, for example, have separate technical, personnel, and financial specialists.

Hierarchy. There is a clear vertical chain of command. Authority is concentrated at the top and flows down from superiors to subordinates.

Formal rules. Bureaucracies are impartial rather than impulsive. They operate on the basis of rationally formulated guidelines and standardized operating procedures.

Maintenance of files and records. Bureaucracies record their actions.

Professionalization. Employees of bureaucratic organizations get their jobs on the basis of qualification and merit.[2]

Virtually all large, complex organizations have these characteristics, not just government agencies. General Motors (GM) and IBM have these characteristics and can thus be considered bureaucratic organizations, even though they are private companies. What separates a public bureaucracy like the Department of Motor Vehicles or the local school district from a private bureaucracy like IBM is a difference in goals. In the end, what

BUREAUCRACY

Public agencies and the programs and services they implement and manage.

BUREAUCRATS

Employees of public agencies.

PROFESSIONALIZATION

Bureaucratic employees earn their jobs based on qualifications and merit.

separates public bureaucracies from private bureaucracies is not what they are, but what they do.

What Does Bureaucracy Do?

Public bureaucracies play two fundamental roles in state and local political systems. First, they are the key administrators in the democratic process. They are charged with carrying out the decisions and instructions of elected public officials. This is the central focus of the academic discipline of public administration. Their second role is more controversial. Bureaucracies not only carry out the decisions of the democratic process, as it turns out, they have a fairly important say in what those decisions are.

Bureaucracy as Policy Implementer

The first job of bureaucracy is to be the active manifestation of the will of the state. This is just a fancy way of saying that bureaucracy does what the government wants or needs done.[3] The whole process is known as **policy implementation**. Agencies implement policy by issuing grants and contracts, enforcing laws and regulations, or undertaking and managing programs directly. For example, when elected officials decide to build a new road, they do not adjourn the legislature to go survey land, drive bulldozers, and lay asphalt. It is a public agency that negotiates to buy and survey the land. It is the agency that either issues the contracts to build the road or takes on the job of construction using its own employees and equipment. This is what makes private and public bureaucracy different: IBM and GM exist to make money, while public agencies exist to serve the public interest by turning the decisions of elected officials into concrete reality.

It is a job staggering in its scope and complexity. Citizens ask government for a lot: roads, education, health benefits, safe drinking water, parks, reliable power grids . . . the list is virtually endless. Governments respond by passing laws that create programs or policies, which then must be put into action and then managed or enforced. Governments respond, in other words, with bureaucracy. State and local bureaucracies manage not only state and local programs, but federal programs as well. The federal government relies on state and local agencies to implement the vast majority of its welfare, education, and highway programs.[4]

POLICY IMPLEMENTATION

The process of taking the expressed wishes of government and translating them into action.

> Citizens ask government for a lot: roads, education, health benefits, safe drinking water, parks, reliable power grids . . . the list is virtually endless. Governments respond by passing laws that create programs or policies, which then have to be put into action and then managed or enforced. Governments respond, in other words, with bureaucracy.

In their roles as implementers, managers, and enforcers, state and local government bureaucracies shape the day-to-day lives of citizens more than any other part of government.[5] The single largest form of bureaucracy in the United States is a fundamental part of virtually every community: public schools. Employing nearly three million teachers, public schools serve almost fifty million students and have a combined budget of $384 billion.[6] Other public agencies regulate and set licensing requirements for professions ranging from lawyers to bartenders. Think of the need to ensure that professionals are qualified to deliver the services they sell. Look around at all the public libraries, swimming pools, and parks that offer recreational and educational opportunities at little to no cost. Think of programs for garbage removal, law enforcement, and fire protection. From the barber who is licensed to cut our hair to the street sweeper who is hired to clean the paths we walk, bureaucracy literally covers us from our heads to our toes.

Cutting Red Tape? Most people do not associate barbers or beauticians with bureaucracy. Yet most barbers must be licensed and regulated by state and/or local government.

Bureaucracy as Policymaker

The second fundamental role of the bureaucracy is more controversial than its job as the government's agent of implementation. Public bureaucracies not only help translate the will of a government into action, in many instances they actually determine the will of the government. Put bluntly, bureaucracies don't just do policy they also make it.[7] They do this in at least three different ways.

The first way is through what has been called the power of the street-level bureaucrat. **Street-level bureaucrats** are the lower-level public employees who actually take the actions that represent government law or policy. In many cases, street-level bureaucrats have the discretion, or ability, to make choices about what actions they do or do not take. In making these choices, they are essentially making policy. For example, the street-level bureaucrat associated with speed limits is the traffic cop. This public employee is actually on the highway with a radar gun making certain that motorists abide by the speed limits specified by state or local law. The legislature may have passed a law setting a maximum highway speed of sixty-five miles per hour, but if the traffic cop decides to go after only those motorists doing seventy-five miles per hour or faster, what really is the speed limit that motorists must obey? And who has set that limit? Arguably, it is not the legislature, but rather the street-level bureaucrat.[8]

This is not to suggest that street-level bureaucrats are power hungry tyrants. In many cases they have no choice but to make choices. On a road

STREET-LEVEL
BUREAUCRATS

Lower-level public agency employees who actually take the actions that represent law or policy.

where speeding is common, it may be impossible to stop every leadfoot. Does it not make more sense to concentrate on the most flagrant offenders, who pose the most risks? Street-level bureaucrats have to balance the goals, laws, and regulations relevant to their agencies with the practical demands of the day-to-day situations they deal with. That often means making, not just implementing, policy.

The second way in which bureaucracies make policy is through rulemaking. **Rulemaking** is the process by which laws or mandates approved by legislatures are turned into detailed written instructions on what public agencies will or will not do.[9] Rules are necessary because most laws passed by legislatures express intention. They do not specify the details of how to make that intention a reality. For example, the Nebraska state legislature created the Nebraska Games and Parks Commission to enforce a number of laws relating to hunting, fishing, wildlife preservation, and boating. The details of enforcing those laws—such as setting permit fees, determining bag limits for particular types of fish, and designating no-wake zones on lakes—are rules established by the commission rather than laws passed by the legislature. This makes sense. The legislature would quickly become bogged down if it had to delve into the myriad details that must be addressed to put a public program into action. These details are left to individual agencies.

Once a rule is approved, it typically becomes part of a state's administrative code, which is the bureaucratic equivalent of state statutes. These rules have the force of law—violate them and you could face fines. Just ask anyone who has ever been caught fishing without a license. Given this, rules are not left to the discretion of the street-level bureaucrat. Most state agencies have to follow a well-defined process for making rules. This process includes seeking input from agency experts, holding public hearings, perhaps listening to special interests. The Nebraska Games and Parks Commission is required to give public notice of any intention to create a rule and must hold a public hearing to allow interested parties to have their say. If this sounds a lot like the process of making laws in a legislature, it is. Rulemaking is probably the most important political activity of bureaucracy. In effect, it is a large lawmaking operation that most citizens do not even know exists.

Finally, bureaucracies also contribute to policymaking directly by pursuing political agendas. Street-level discretion and rulemaking are passive policymaking—in the sense that they involve bureaucrats responding or not responding to something such as a speeding car or a newly signed bill. Yet bureaucracies and bureaucrats also take *active* roles in politics. This is done in a number of ways. At the state and local level, the heads of many public agencies are elected. Such positions include everything from county sheriff to state attorney general. As elected officials, these agency heads often make campaign promises, and once in office they try to get their agencies to deliver on them. The visibility and importance of these elected state and local agency heads have increased with the rise of New Federalism. They

---

RULEMAKING

The process of translating laws into written instructions on what public agencies will or will not do.

---

now are widely recognized as critical players in the process of policy formulation, not just policy implementation.[10] Therefore, some agencies will be the tools used to deliver on a political agenda. It is also true that other bureaucrats, not just elected agency heads, try to influence policy. As we shall see a little later, unions are powerful political actors in many states, lobbying for better pay and benefits and getting actively involved in election campaigns.

The implementation and political roles of bureaucracy make it a particular target for citizen concern and, at times, scorn. Government bureaucracy has a terrible reputation for inefficiency, incompetence, and mismanagement.[11] It is easy to see that we need some bureaucracy. Somebody has to manage all those programs and services we want from government. Yet many question whether we have too much bureaucracy, and still others are concerned about the powerful political role of what are mostly unelected officials. Why do we have so much bureaucracy? How good of a job does it really do? Could we not get by with less of it? Is there no better way to run public programs and services? Is there too much bureaucracy and too little democracy in state and local government? These are reasonable questions that the comparative method can help answer.

What Is "Enough" Bureaucracy?

Most people believe that whatever its merits, there is too much bureaucracy in government and in our lives. Undeniably, state and local government has a lot of bureaucracy. How much? Some insight into the size and scope of state and local agencies can be gleaned from Table 9-1, which lists the number of employees on state and local government payrolls by function. Combined, state and local governments have almost eighteen million full-time and part-time employees. Most of these—approximately thirteen million versus five million—are employees of local rather than state government. Local or state, the vast majority of these individuals work in what we would recognize as a bureaucracy.

The numbers contained in Table 9-1 confirm that there are a lot of state and local bureaucrats, but numbers alone give little insight into whether there is too much or too little bureaucracy. In reality, the size of the bureaucracy and the extent of its role in the day-to-day life of any given individual vary from state to state and locality to locality for two main reasons. First, in each locality, citizens make different kinds of demands on each state and local government agency. Some localities will need more of one particular resource, while others will need less. In Eden Prairie, Minnesota, the public will demand more cross-country ski trails, and in Yuma, Arizona, they will need more public swimming pools. As a result, the size and role of the public sector can vary significantly from place to place—more demand equals more bureaucracy.

TABLE 9-1

State and Local Government Employment by Function

Function	Total Individuals (in thousands)	State Government (in thousands)	Local Government (in thousands)
Elementary and secondary education	7,116	58	7,058
Higher education	2,679	2,156	523
Hospitals	999	433	565
Police protection	954	105	849
Corrections	714	473	241
Streets and highways	575	254	321
Public welfare	546	242	304
Other government administration	492	62	430
Utilities	491	34	456
Judicial and legal	430	163	262
Financial administration	427	172	255
Fire protection	411	0	411
Natural resources	215	169	46
Social insurance	89	89	0
State liquor stores	9	9	0
Other	1,829	448	1,381
All functions	17,976	4,877	13,099

Source: Adapted from *The Book of the States 2003* (Lexington, Ky.: Council of State Governments, 2003), 459.

> The size and role of the public sector can vary significantly from place to place—more demand equals more bureaucracy.

Second, there is no universally agreed upon yardstick to measure what constitutes a "reasonably" sized bureaucracy. Where one person sees a bloated public sector over-regulating citizens' lives, a second sees the same set of agencies providing important public goods and services. At the very least, to compare the size of bureaucracy across states and localities we need to explore not just the total number of public employees, but also the size of a specific public sector relative to the size of the public it serves. Table 9-2 shows one way to do this. It lists the states with the five largest and the five smallest bureaucracies as measured by the number of government employees per every 10,000 citizens.

By this measure, the mostly large, urban, and populous states have the *smallest* bureaucracies. More rural, less populous states, conversely, have the *largest* bureaucracies. How can this be? Why would North Dakota have more bureaucracy than California? The answer is actually pretty simple. Less populous states do not necessarily mean less demand on government. Even the most rural state, for example, still needs an educational system, roads, and law enforcement. These are all labor-intensive propositions. Indeed, they may be even more labor intensive in rural states. For example, to serve a widely dispersed population, an educational system either has to build lots of small schools or figure out a way to transport lots of students over considerable distances to a smaller number of large schools. More urban, densely populated states can take advantage of the economies of scale that come with centralized locations. Basically, less bureaucracy is needed when the citizens being served are close by.

The same tale is told by using expenditures—in this case, the amount of money states spent for services—to measure the size of bureaucracy. Three of the five states with the largest bureaucracies as measured by number of employees—Alaska, Delaware, and Hawaii—also have the largest bureaucracies in terms of per capita expenditure. (See Table 9-3.) Two of these are the only noncontiguous states—Alaska neighbors Canada rather than the United States, and Hawaii is an island chain in the Pacific. Geographic isolation requires these states to do more for themselves, which means more bureaucracy.

Expenditures and employees tell us something about the size of the bureaucracy, but they do not tell us much about its influence or power over the daily lives of citizens. An undermanned bureaucracy with a small budget still can have considerable impact on the interests of an individual. If you have ever spent time in a university financial aid office, you probably already understand the point here—when people complain about bureaucracy being too big, they often mean the red tape and rules that come with it, not its budget or payroll. For the number of forms you fill out at the financial aid office, you may feel that the bureaucracy owes you a free meal, but there is only so much money in the pot. It is very easy to recognize this sort of thing as a central part of bureaucracy. It is very hard to measure it objectively. Lacking good measures of "red tape" or "rules" makes it hard to make comparisons. If there are no comparative measures, it is harder to

TABLE 9-2

States with the Most and the Least Bureaucracy by Number of Employees

State	State Employees (per 1,000 citizens)
Top Five	
Alaska	361
Delaware	297
Hawaii	441
New Mexico	246
North Dakota	240
Bottom Five	
Wisconsin	124
Pennsylvania	124
Illinois	115
Florida	119
California	103

Source: U.S. Census Bureau. *Statistical Abstract of the United States: 2000.*

TABLE 9-3

States with the Most and the Least Bureaucracy by Expenditures

State	State and Local Expenditures (per capita)
Top Five	
Alaska	$8,501
Delaware	4,305
Hawaii	4,419
Massachusetts	4,094
Wyoming	4,000
Bottom Five	
Arizona	2,586
Colorado	2,546
Tennessee	2,554
Texas	2,354
Florida	2,459

Source: U.S. Census Bureau. *Statistical Abstract of the United States: 2000.*

use the comparative method to help show why some bureaucracies have more influence than others.

Despite this, there is little doubt that public bureaucracies in large, urban areas probably do have a more powerful role in the day-to-day lives of citizens than those in less populous rural areas. Why? It is not because bureaucracy is more power hungry in cities, but rather because more concentrated populations require more rules. Building codes are more critical in urban areas because of the associated fire safety and health risks—a problem with one building can pose risks for those working or living in surrounding buildings. Building regulations thus tend to be more detailed, and enforcement of these rules tends to be a higher priority, in urban than rural areas. In this sense, urban areas do have more bureaucracy than urban areas.

Measuring Bureaucratic Effectiveness: It Does a Better Job than You Think

So far, our application of the comparative method has given us a sense of how big bureaucracy is and why it is so big—because characteristics such as urbanization and geography result in different demands being placed on government. These different demands translate into different sized public agencies with varying levels of involvement in our day-to-day lives. What the comparative method has not told us is what sort of job public agencies do. The widespread belief is that public agencies are, at best, mediocre managers of public programs and services.[12] Although this negative stereotype is held by many, for the most part it turns out to be wrong. Public agencies, as it turns out, are very good at what they do.

How good? Well, in many cases at least as good, if not better, than their private sector counterparts. The assumption is that the private sector is more efficient and more effective than the public sector; however, numerous studies find this is based more on stereotypes than facts.[13] For example, in the early 1990s, officials in Fort Lauderdale, Florida, decided to shut down the city's pipe-laying operation and instead have the private sector bid on municipal pipe-laying jobs. The idea was to save the city money by getting competitive private sector bids and eliminating an entire public bureaucracy. A study undertaken by city engineers found that in-house costs for laying pipe were between $68 and $73 per linear foot. Much to everyone's surprise, the initial private sector bids were up to $130 per linear foot. The city undertook an extensive reorganization of its pipe-laying operations and managed to drop its costs to $43 per linear foot. The private sector responded by cutting its bids in half, into the $50 to $60 range. Even after these dramatic reductions, however, the private sector still could not do the job as cheaply as the "inefficient" public bureaucracy.

This not only shows that the public sector can be as cost-effective and efficient as the private sector, it also provides a cautionary tale about the downside of the profit motive. It turns out that the private sector is quite willing to feed at the public trough to fatten its bottom line.[14] There is not much glamour associated with laying utilities, filling potholes, and running public transportation systems, but these are highly valued public services that consume a lot of tax dollars. And contrary to popular perception, public bureaucracies provide these services efficiently and spend these dollars effectively.

It is not just about overall performance. Public agencies come out equal to or better than the private sector on a wide range of employee characteristics that are used to identify an effective organization. Public and private sector employees are roughly equal in terms of their job motivation, their work habits, and their overall competence. Compared to the private sector, however, public employees tend to have higher levels of education, express a greater commitment toward civic duty and public service, abide by more stringent codes of ethical behavior, and be more committed to helping other people.[15] Various studies show that over the past thirty years state and local agencies have become more productive and more professional, and they have done so during an era when they have shouldered an increasing share of the burden for delivering programs and services from the federal government.[16]

There *is* wide variation between and within the states on how well public bureaucracies are managed. Good management has an enormous impact on the capacities and effectiveness of programs and agencies. States that engage in prudent, long-range fiscal planning are better positioned to deal with economic downturns, and they can generally deliver programs more efficiently. States that do a better job of attracting qualified employees with a strong commitment to public service are almost certainly going to be rewarded with more effective public agencies. States that make training their employees a priority are likely to enjoy similar benefits. The bottom line is that well-managed public agencies lower costs and improve results, while the reverse is true for badly managed agencies.[17]

Bureacracies Put to the Test: Who Passes and Who Fails and Why

Which states and localities have the best run public agencies? The Government Performance Project (GPP) has devoted considerable resources to this question. A joint undertaking of the Pew Charitable Trusts, the Maxwell School of Citizenship and Public Affairs at Syracuse University, and *Governing* magazine, the GPP holds state and local governments publicly accountable for the quality of management at agencies within their jurisdictions.[18] It does this by researching management practices and performances in five areas: finance, capital projects (roads, bridges, and construction), human resources, managing for results (setting and achieving specific policy goals), and information technology. The GPP then issues grades for performance in each area. The result is an administrative report card for state and local governments, which is essentially an index of the relative performance of bureaucracy.

Table 9-4 shows the most recent grades issued to the states. The grades show that most state governments are doing at least an acceptable job, but that some are clearly doing better than others. These are differences that make a real difference. The quality of public schools and roads, and even the quality of the air we breathe is dependent in no small measure on the effectiveness of public bureaucracies.[19] States with the better run bureaucracies provide the best and most effective services and make the most efficient use of taxpayer dollars.

Why are some state and local bureaucracies run better than others? Why does California rate a C-plus, while Utah rates an A-minus? The answers to these questions are found not in the bureaucracy but in the broader political environment of the states. Ultimately, legislatures and governors are responsible for bureaucratic performance. This is not only because they set the laws that control personnel, management, and training practices. Their decisions on a wide range of policy issues have tremendous consequences even for a smoothly running agency. The most obvious example is budgets. States have gone through an extreme boom and bust cycle during the past ten years, with economic good times of the 1990s followed by a fiscal crisis shortly after the turn of the century. Some states practiced good fiscal management, with legislatures that resisted the temptation to spend excessively and enact large tax cuts. As the economy soured, these states also acted quickly to stabilize revenues.

Other states—like California—did the opposite. These states increased spending during the 1990s and then tried to put off the day of reckoning with creative accounting practices and by dipping into one-time revenue sources. The end result for California was a fiscal crisis that rocked the public sector, leaving it underfunded, understaffed, and a little shell-shocked—not exactly the ingredients for smoothly running public programs. The comparative method shows us that it is the states that avoided big tax cuts in the 1990s, states with divided governments in which the governor is from one party and the legislature is controlled by another, and states with powerful governors that are the states that spend less, have better financial management, and have public agencies with higher grades.[20]

Many of the faults attributed to public bureaucracies can actually be traced to legislatures, which give agencies conflicting and confusing missions, and often do not provide adequate resources to fulfill these missions. It is the legislatures that demand what is politically expedient, not what is effective

TABLE 9-4

Government Performance Project, Grades at a Glance, 2001

State	Financial Management	Capital Management	Human Resources	Managing for Results	Information Technology	Average Grade
Alabama	C+	D+	D+	D+	C–	C–
Alaska	C	C	C	C–	B	C
Arizona	C	C+	C	C+	B–	C+
Arkansas	B–	C	C	C–	C–	C
California	B–	C+	C	C–	B–	C+
Colorado	C+	B	B–	C+	C	C+
Connecticut	C	B–	C	C–	C+	C
Delaware	A–	B+	B	B	B	B+
Florida	B	B–	B–	B+	C+	R–
Georgia	B–	B–	B–	B–	C+	B–
Hawaii	C	B	C	C	C–	C
Idaho	C+	B–	B	C–	B	B–
Illinois	B+	B	B	B–	C+	B
Indiana	B–	B–	B	B–	B–	B–
Iowa	A–	B+	B+	A–	B	B+
Kansas	B–	B	B+	C+	A–	B
Kentucky	A–	B+	B+	B+	B+	B+
Louisiana	C	B	B	B+	B–	B–
Maine	B–	B–	B–	C+	B–	B–
Maryland	A–	A	B	B	B	B+
Massachusetts	B–	C+	B–	C	C	C+
Michigan	A–	A–	B+	B+	A–	A–
Minnesota	A–	B+	C+	B	B	B
Mississippi	B	C	B–	D+	C+	C+
Missouri	B+	B+	B+	A–	A–	B+
Montana	B	C+	C+	C	C	C+
Nebraska	A–	B	C	B–	C+	B–
Nevada	B–	B	D+	C	C–	C
New Hampshire	C+	C+	C+	D	C	C
New Jersey	B–	A–	C–	B–	B	B–

(Table continues on next page)

TABLE 9-4 *(continued)*

State	Financial Management	Capital Management	Human Resources	Managing for Results	Information Technology	Average Grade
New Mexico	C+	C−	B−	C	C+	C+
New York	C+	C+	C+	C−	B	C+
North Carolina	B	B	B+	B	B+	B
North Dakota	B−	B	B	C−	B−	B−
Ohio	B+	B	B	B	B−	B
Oklahoma	C+	C	C−	D+	B−	C
Oregon	B−	B−	C	B	C	C+
Pennsylvania	A−	B	B+	B	B+	B+
Rhode Island	B−	C+	C−	C	D	C
South Carolina	A−	C+	A	B	B	B+
South Dakota	B−	B−	B−	D	B	C+
Tennessee	C	C	B−	B−	B+	B−
Texas	B+	B	B	A−	B−	B
Utah	A	A−	B−	B+	A	A−
Vermont	B	B−	C	B	C+	B−
Virginia	B+	B+	B+	A−	A−	B+
Washington	B+	A−	A−	A−	A	A−
West Virginia	B−	C	C+	C	C−	C
Wisconsin	C+	B+	A−	C	B−	B−
Wyoming	B−	D	C+	C+	C−	C

Source: *Governing* magazine. http://governing.com/gpp/2001/gp1glanc.htm (accessed June 10, 2004).

or efficient, and then roundly and repeatedly criticize bureaucracy for not performing well. The real surprise is not that some bureaucracies are ineffective or poorly run, but that the vast majority of them, most of the time, manage to more or less serve the public interest. And they do so in spite of democratic institutions rather than because of them. At least one professional student of bureaucracy has suggested than any objective view of the joint performance of bureaucracy and representative democracy would lead to the conclusion that what we need is more bureaucracy and less democracy![21]

Is There a Better Way to Run Public Programs and Services?

Looking at bureaucracy comparatively, we learn how big it really is, why it is so big, and how well it performs. But is a traditional bureaucracy really the best way to run public programs and services? Do we really need less democracy and more bureaucracy? Do we really need eighteen million people on state and local government payrolls? The short answer is no. Public services and programs could be delivered through competitive bidding to the private sector. Public agencies could be staffed and run by political party loyalists or special interest supporters. Things could be done differently. Before abandoning the traditional public bureaucracy, however, it is worth considering why public agencies are so, well, bureaucratic.

> The real surprise is not that some bureaucracies are ineffective or poorly run, but that the vast majority of them, most of the time, manage to more or less serve the public interest. And they do so in spite of democratic institutions rather than because of them.

Remember the key characteristics of bureaucratic organizations listed earlier? These turn out to be important advantages when it comes to running public programs and services. For one thing, bureaucracies tend to be impartial because they operate using formal rules, not partisan preference, bribes, or arbitrary judgment. If you need some form of license or permit, if your shop is subject to some form of environmental or business regulation, or if you are trying to receive benefits from a public program, it does not matter to the bureaucracy if you are rich or poor, liberal or conservative, an influential high roller or an average citizen. What matters to the bureaucracy are the rules that define application, eligibility, and delivery of the necessary service or program. Following bureaucratic rules can be maddening, but those rules do help ensure that public agencies are more or less impartial.

The bureaucratic characteristics of hierarchy and record keeping help hold public agencies accountable. Public agencies are expected to be answerable for their actions. They have to justify why they did what they did to legislatures, executives, the courts, and citizens.[22] An action at a lower level of bureaucracy can almost always be appealed to a higher level. Students at most colleges and universities, for example, can appeal their grades. In such appeals the bureaucrat responsible for issuing the grade—your instructor— is expected to justify to the appeals board and the dean why it represents a fair and reasonable application of the rules of the class and the grading policies of the university. Setting rules, requiring records, and setting up a clear chain of authority helps ensure that bureaucrats and bureaucracies do not exceed their authority or act unfairly. If they do, these same factors provide a means for holding the bureaucrat or bureaucracy accountable.

Professionalization is another bureaucratic characteristic that is desirable in public agencies because it promotes competence and expertise. To get a job in most state and local bureaucracies, what you know is more important than who you know. Getting a job as a professor at a state university requires a specific set of professional qualifications. The same is true for an elementary school teacher, an accountant at the Department of Revenue, or a subway operator. Of course, setting and enforcing such qualifications as the basis for employment and promotion means another set of rules and regulations. These qualifications also help ensure that merit rather than partisan loyalty, family connections, or political influence are the basis for getting public sector employment.

The great irony of public bureaucracy is that the very characteristics that help ensure neutrality, fairness, and accountability also produce the things that people dislike about it: red tape and inefficiency. Formal rules help guarantee equity and fairness but—as anyone who has spent time filling out forms and waiting in line can attest—they can be a pain. Enforcing rules, or "going by the book," may mean bureaucracy is fair, but it is not particularly flexible. Treating everyone the same is an advantage from an equity standpoint, but the fact is, not everyone *is* the same. Surely there are ways to make bureaucracy more responsive to the individual? Well, yes, there are. But the history of bureaucratic reform in the United States suggests that the cures are often worse than the problem. Although going through this history is not a particularly comparative exercise, it is necessary in order to understand why bureaucracy is the way it is.

The Transformation of State Bureaucracy: From Patronage to Professionalism

Public agencies have undergone a remarkably radical transformation during the past century. They have become more professionalized, more organized, and more able to shoulder a large share of the political system's responsibilities.

For much of the early history of the United States there was little in the way of state and local bureaucracy. State and local government functions we now take for granted, such as public schools, libraries, and fire protection, were left largely to the private sector. In most cases, this meant they did not exist at all or were available only to those who could afford them. Public education is the single largest public program undertaken by state and local governments. Yet public education in the contemporary sense did not exist until the last half of the nineteenth century, roughly a hundred years after the nation's founding. As the nation grew, however, so did the demands on government. Roads needed to be built, commerce regulated, streets cleaned, and crime curtailed. Taxes had to be collected to make all this happen. There was no centralized plan to expand public bureaucracy—it evolved in fits and starts as governments took on the jobs citizens wanted done.

At the federal level, staffing bureaucracy was initially a job for which only the educated elite were considered qualified. This example was often followed at the state and local level. Public service was seen as an obligation of the aristocratic class of a community or state. This "gentlemen's" system of administration was swept away following the election of Andrew Jackson to the presidency in 1828.

Jackson believed in the **spoils system,** that is, the right of an electoral winner to control who worked for the government. The intent was to democratize government and make it more accountable by having regular citizens who supported the electoral winners run government agencies. This process of giving government jobs to partisan loyalists is called patronage.

Instead of producing a more democratic bureaucracy, the spoils system and patronage invited corruption. Following Jackson's example, the administrative arm of many state and local governments became a way for electoral winners to pay off political favors or reward partisan loyalty. Perhaps the most famous examples are the big city political "machines" that flourished well into the twentieth century and produced some of the most colorful characters ever to wield power in state and local politics. A political machine was an organization headed by a party committee or a by "boss." The committee or boss led a subset of ward or precinct leaders whose job it was to make sure voters in their district supported machine endorsed candidates. Supporters of the machine were in turn rewarded with government jobs and contracts. They also were often expected to contribute a set percentage of their salaries to the machine.[23] This created a well-regulated cycle, or machine—votes in one end, power and patronage out the other.

Machines dominated politics in many urban areas and even whole states in the nineteenth century and early twentieth century. They produced some of the most fascinating characters in U.S. political history: Boss Tweed of New York, Tom Pendergast of Kansas City, and Gene Talmadge of Georgia, to name just a few. These men wielded enormous power, aided in no small part by their ability to dole out government jobs and contracts. Some machines survived into the twentieth century. Mayor Richard Daley of Chicago ran what many would recognize as a political machine well into the 1960s.

While the machines made for lively politics and brought almost unlimited power to their leaders, they were often corrupt. Machine politics meant that getting a government job was based on who you knew rather than what you knew. Job security only lasted as long as you kept in your political patron's good graces or until the next election. Understandably then, there was tremendous incentive to make the most of a government position. Kickbacks and bribery inevitably made their way into many state and local agencies.

The founders of the modern conception of government bureaucracy were progressive reformers of the late nineteenth and early twentieth centuries. They wanted a lasting solution to the gross dishonesty and inefficiency they saw in public administration.

Political machines were powerful organizations that dominated many state and local governments for parts of the nineteenth and twentieth centuries. Their power was based on the ability to control government jobs, awarding these positions to supporters, or as the cartoon above suggests, to the highest bidder.

Toward this end, these reformers created a new philosophy. At its center was the idea that the administrative side of government needed to be more insulated from the political arena.[24] Reformers promoted the notion of **neutral competence**, the idea that public agencies should be impartial implementers of democratic decisions, not partisan extensions of whoever happened to win the election.

To achieve these ends, progressive reformers began to push for public agencies to adopt the formal characteristics of a bureaucratic organization. This was accomplished in no small part by lobbying for merit systems as an alternative to the spoils system. **Merit systems** are exactly that. They are systems in which jobs and promotions are earned on the basis of technical qualifications and demonstrated ability instead of given out as rewards for political loyalty. Merit systems also make it harder for public employees to be dismissed without due cause. This does not mean a guaranteed job. The idea is to create a system within which public employees can only be fired for failing to do their jobs and not because they missed a payment to a political boss. The overall goal was to make government bureaucracies less political and more professional.

The federal government shifted from the spoils system to the merit system in 1883, with the passage of the Pendleton Act. The main features of this merit system were: (1) competitive examination requirements for federal jobs; (2) security from political dismissals, meaning that you could not be fired simply because you belonged to the "wrong" party or supported the "wrong" candidate; and (3) protection from being coerced into political activities so that workers were no longer expected or required to contribute a portion of their salary to a political party or candidate. The basic principles of the merit system have since been expanded to include equal pay for equal work; recruitment, hiring, and promotion without regard to race, creed, national origin, religion, marital status, age, or disability; and protection from reprisal for lawful disclosure of lawbreaking, mismanagement, abuse of authority, or practices that endanger public health—so-called whistle blower laws.

States and localities once again followed the example of the federal government and began shifting from spoils systems to merit systems. New York State was the first to do so, adopting a merit system in the same year that the Pendleton Act became law. In 1935, the federal Social Security Act made merit systems a requirement for related state agencies if they wished to receive federal grants. This stimulated another wave of merit-based reforms of state and local bureaucracies. By 1949, nearly half of the states had created merit-based civil service systems. Fifty years later, virtually all states and many municipalities had adopted merit systems. All of this helped professionalize state and local bureaucracies and turned what had been sinkholes of patronage and corruption or marginally competent good-old-boy networks into effective instruments of democratic policymaking.

Politics and the Merit System

Although using merit as the basis for public bureaucracy has effectively created agencies that are competent and professional, it has its drawbacks. Remember the two key roles of the bureaucracy—policy implementation and policymaking? Merit systems have positive and negative implications for both.

In some ways, merit-based bureaucracy is a victim of its own success. The whole idea of shifting to a merit system was to insulate public agencies and their employees from undue political influence. We want bureaucrats to work for the public interest, not for that of a party boss. We want bureaucrats to apply rules neutrally, not to interpret them through the lens of partisan prejudices. To a remarkable extent, merit systems have done exactly that. Rules are rules, and bureaucracies more or less competently and impartially enforce them regardless of which party controls the legislature or who sits in the governor's mansion. The merit system has undoubtedly been an enormous positive for the policy implementation role of bureaucracy.

The impact of merit systems on the policymaking, or political, role of bureaucracy is more open for debate. Merit systems did not eliminate the political role of the bureaucracy. They merely changed it. Under the spoils system, bureaucracy was an agent of a particular boss, party, or political agenda, and it favored the supporters of electoral winners. The merit system cut the connection between the ballot box and the bureaucracy. Distancing bureaucracy from elections, however, arguably makes it less accountable to the democratic process—a big concern if bureaucracy is policymaker as well as a policy implementer.

Once distanced from the ballot box, public agencies and public employees discovered their own political interests and began to pursue them with vigor. Organized interests outside the bureaucracy also began to realize that being able to influence lawmaking and, especially, rulemaking offered enormous political opportunities. All you have to do is get your favored policy written into the rules and bureaucracy will enforce it well beyond the next election. These sorts of developments raise serious questions about the drawbacks of merit systems. As examples of how these concerns play out in state and local agencies, let us consider two issues: public labor unions and affirmative action.

Public Labor Unions

Public sector labor unions are a relatively new political force. Unions were almost exclusively a private sector phenomenon until the 1960s. This changed in 1962 when President John F. Kennedy issued an executive order that recognized the right of federal employees to join unions and requiring federal agencies to recognize them. The 1960s and 1970s saw a considerable expansion in the number of state and local employees joining unions. Today, roughly three to four times as many public sector as private sector workers belong to unions.[25]

The reasons for the expansion in public sector union membership are not hard to fathom. For much of their history, public employees received lower wages than their private sector counterparts. Public employees also had limited input in regard to personnel decisions. Despite the merit system, many still saw favoritism and good old boy networks having too much influence in pay and promotion decisions. Public sector labor unions pushed for **collective bargaining**, a process in which representatives of labor and management meet to negotiate pay and benefits, job responsibilities, and working conditions. The vast majority of states allow at least some public unions to bargain collectively.

What should not be missed here is that the outcomes of collective bargaining are important policy decisions. They are decisions that the voter—and sometimes the legislator—has little say in. Negotiations about pay and benefits for public employees are, in a very real sense, negotiations about taxes. A raise won by a public employee represents a claim on the taxpayer's pocketbook. A claim worked out not in an open democratic process, but often in closed-door negotiations. It is not just money. Collective bargaining agreements can result in fairly complex rules about what public employees are and are not expected to do. Such rules reduce the flexibility of agency managers—who are constrained from redirecting personnel from their assigned jobs—and reduce the responsiveness of bureaucracy to legislatures and elected executives.

Labor unions have given public employees more than just collective bargaining muscle, they also have started to do some heavy lifting in electoral politics. Unions that are able to deliver their members' votes can have a powerful say in who holds office. Understandably, people seeking public office pay attention to the policy preferences of public sector unions. By raising money, mobilizing voters, even running independent campaigns, unions exercise considerable political clout. Consider the Wisconsin Education Association Council (WEAC). Long recognized as an important political actor in the state, in the 2001–2002 state election cycle WEAC made $156,000 in political campaign contributions. That made the teachers' union Wisconsin's fifth largest campaign spender. Only the two major party organizations and the two major party gubernatorial campaigns spent more.[26] WEAC spends its money strategically. It has a well thought out set of legislative goals and supports candidates accordingly.[27]

Unions can have enough political clout to shape how the merit system actually works. A basic principle of the merit system is that competence is supposed to be rewarded. Expertise and job performance are supposed to be the basis of promotion and pay increases. In contrast, unions tend to advocate **seniority**—the length of time spent in a position. Public employees with more experience may—and often do—deserve such rewards. Yet it is

COLLECTIVE BARGAINING

A process in which representatives of labor and management meet to negotiate pay and benefits, job responsibilities, and working conditions.

SENIORITY

The length of time spent in a position

not always the most senior employee who is the most productive or contributes the most to the agency's success. Even in the absence of unions, seniority plays a considerable role in the pay and benefits of public employees. This is much to the chagrin of critics who view civil service protections as failing the public interest. For example, some critics view tenure at colleges and universities as a system that rewards laziness and allows "dead wood"—unproductive faculty members—to collect healthy paychecks.[28]

Unions are far from all bad—they have successfully fought for reasonable compensation packages and safer work environments for people who perform some of society's toughest, dirtiest, and most thankless jobs. In most instances, they support the merit system as long as it also protects seniority. And unions are far from incompatible with effectiveness and productivity. Comparative studies of student performance and the strength of teachers' unions have found that states with the strongest teachers' unions also tend to have the highest student achievement scores. (See Box 9-1).

The pros and cons of unions can be debated, but there is no doubt that unions have helped politicize the bureaucracy. It is a different sort of politics than the favoritism and outright corruption that marked the spoils system, but it is politics nonetheless.

Affirmative Action

Public unions show how a political role for bureaucracy can be generated internally—public employees get organized and pursue their interests in the political arena. Yet bureaucracies can be politicized from the outside as well. Consider **affirmative action**, the set of policies used to get government to make a special effort to recruit and retain certain categories of workers who have been historically underrepresented in order to achieve better and more fair representation. It is illegal for government agencies to have employment, evaluation, or promotion practices that discriminate on the basis of race, age, color, creed, gender, physical disability, or other characteristics that are not related to the job or job performance. Yet even though such discrimination has been banned outright, public bureaucracies are not particularly diverse on a number of these factors, especially race and gender.

About 55 percent of state and local government employees are males and about 70 percent are white. Males hold roughly 67 percent of the top management jobs in public agencies, and more than 80 percent of the individuals—male or female—in these positions are white. In contrast, racial and ethnic minorities tend to be much more concentrated in lower ranking positions. They constitute about 16 percent of the top management jobs in state and local government, but more than 40 percent of the service and maintenance positions.[29] Consider the New York Police Department (NYPD), which in 2001 had approximately 465 captains. Of these, only nine were black males. The proportion of the NYPD's frontline supervisors who are black males has actually been *decreasing*. Yet New York City's population is 25 percent black.

AFFIRMATIVE ACTION
Policies designed to help recruit and promote disadvantaged groups.

A Difference that Makes a Difference:
Teachers' Unions and Test Scores

Why do some states have better schools than other states? One possible answer is the level of unionization among teachers. A number of scholars have argued that strong teachers' unions may help determine educational outcomes and the overall quality of a state's public schools.

There is a disagreement, however, about whether the impact of stronger teachers' unions is positive or negative. Some argue that they are little more than self-interested political actors whose primary goal is to maximize pay, benefits, and working conditions for educators, regardless of how these educators shape student productivity and learning. Critics argue that unions flex their political muscle to prevent meaningful educational reform, leaving education to be run by large, rule-bound, unresponsive bureaucracies—public schools and school districts—that are good for teachers, but ultimately bad for students.

Union supporters do not deny that teachers' unions have negotiated for higher wages and better working conditions, but they argue that there is more than self-interest at stake here. The things unions fight for—higher wages, smaller classes, and time during the work-day to prepare lesson plans—attract better qualified people who are better able to do their jobs. The net result should be a more effective school and improved student performance.

Which of these perspectives is correct? Well, what is being posed here is a classic comparative question: Do the differences in the strength of state teachers' unions match up with differences in student performance? If union critics are correct, then states with higher performing schools should have lower levels of teacher unionization. If union supporters are correct, then the opposite should be found.

In a study published in the winter 2000 issue of *Harvard Educational Review,* a group of scholars put exactly this comparative question to the test by looking at the relative strength of teachers' unions in all fifty states and average SAT and ACT scores. The findings? Unfortunately for the critics, the greater the level of unionization, the higher the average SAT and ACT scores in that state. At least according to this study, teachers' unions are a difference between states that makes for an important difference in student performance.

Source: Lala Carr Steelman, Brian Powell, and Robert M. Carini, "Do Teacher Unions Hinder Educational Performance? Lessons Learned from State SAT and ACT Scores," *Harvard Educational Review* 70 (Winter 2000): 437–466.

The lack of diversity in the NYPD's management is probably not due to the outright racism of individuals. A bigger problem is that the nondiscriminatory hiring practices foundational to the merit system are passive—they ensure access to hiring opportunities, but make no guarantees of jobs or promotions. In choosing who should be hired or promoted, the merit system looks at things like experience and qualifications. It does not account for gender, race, or ethnicity. The problem here is that minorities historically have had fewer educational opportunities. Less education means fewer qualifications. This translates into a tougher time gaining access to jobs. The end result is that even if race is not an explicit factor in hiring and promoting, whites tend to have more education and better connections in bureaucratic hierarchies.[30] This strikes many as unfair.

One of the remedies offered to this is affirmative action. Policies that, in essence, are proactive attempts to increase diversity. Such policies are highly controversial—are they necessary to remove institutionalized racism from the merit system, or are they simply a way for certain groups to profit from a double standard that makes a mockery of the merit system? Defenders argue that such policies are necessary because of the political role of the bureaucracy. There is more than the desire for multiracial balance behind this argument. There is a fairly long-standing theory in the field of public administration that suggests that more diverse bureaucracies may actually be more effective bureaucracies. The theory of **representative bureaucracy** argues that public agencies that reflect the diversity of the communities they serve are more likely to account for the interests of all groups in managing programs and delivering services.[31] In order for bureaucracy to better serve a diverse and democratic society, affirmative action should be an important part of its hiring and promoting practices. Remember our street-level bureaucrat, the traffic cop deciding which speeders to stop? What if all the traffic cops were white and most of the speeders stopped were black—or vice versa? Regardless of who was going how fast, this sort of situation is likely to create friction. Some may view the agency as unfair, which can make the bureaucracy's job harder. If traffic cops are ethnically diverse, it is less likely that the bureaucracy is going to be seen as playing favorites and it is better able to focus on its job.

Opponents of affirmative action reject such arguments. Males and whites often resent establishing preferential recruitment and promotion policies for women and/or racial and ethnic minorities. Some see the policies as little more than reverse discrimination. From this perspective, affirmative action represents the success of special interests in getting their favored agendas written into the law and the rules that run bureaucracies. In a merit system, technical qualifications and job performance—not race or gender—are supposed to drive personnel decisions in the ideal bureaucracy. Opponents of affirmative action argue that it produces quotas and favoritism for certain groups. In effect, it has bureaucracy wage politics on behalf of the favored groups. Speeders should be stopped, and the race or gender of the driver and of whoever issues the ticket should be irrelevant.

Which of these viewpoints is correct is a matter of fierce debate. Whatever the underlying pros and cons, the fight comes down to what is the best way to recruit and promote public employees, and who—if anyone—should be given preferential treatment. This is ultimately a political fight about who gets government jobs.

If Not Merit . . . Then What?

Traditional bureaucracy and the merit system have some clear advantages: equity, competence, and something approaching neutrality. They also have

REPRESENTATIVE BUREAUCRACY
The idea that public agencies reflecting the diversity of the communities they serve will be more effective.

disadvantages: a measure of red tape and inefficiency, a lack of flexibility and accountability, and a political role that makes many uncomfortable. No clear answer exists on whether the pros outweigh the cons or vice versa, but this has not stopped the nearly constant search for a better way to do things. Bureaucratic reform is a perennial issue in American politics.

Many of the reform efforts are variations on a single theme that reflects a popular belief that government would be better if it were run more like a business. In practice this means introducing competition into the delivery of public programs and services, making the organizations that deliver these goods and services less hierarchical, and making greater use of the private sector to deliver public services.[32] The idea is to introduce the benefits of the market into the public sector, which in theory could lead to more efficiency through lower costs, while increasing responsiveness since competition means paying attention to your customers or going out of business. The great difficulty facing reformers is how do you get these benefits without leaving behind the advantages of the traditional, tried and true merit-based bureaucracy?

Over the past two decades reformers have made a sustained effort to try to change the entire philosophy of delivering public programs and services from the use of a traditional bureaucracy to the use of a more business-based model. Although these reforms come in many different packages, collectively they are often described as the New Public Management (NPM). NPM has six core characteristics that have been widely pursued and adopted by state and local governments:

1. A focus on productivity that emphasizes "doing more with less," that is, to provide public services with fewer resources.
2. A market orientation that increasingly looks to the private sector to deliver public services. This is typically done through a process of competitive bidding, during which private companies vie to gain a government contract to run a public program.
3. A drive to improve customer satisfaction with public services.
4. A decentralization of decision making power, an effort to push policy-making choices as close as possible to the people who are going to be affected by them.
5. A movement to improve the government's capacity to make, to implement, and to manage public policy and public programs.
6. An effort to maintain accountability, that is, to make the government deliver on its service promises.[33]

These characteristics all sound fairly positive when presented as a simple list. In practice, however, they have proven to be a mixed bag. It turns out that pursuing one of these goals often has negative implications for another. For example, in the effort to be more productive and to leverage the advantage of the market, many public policies and programs are now delivered through private sector contracts. So if a state government wants to implement a new mental-health care program, the NPM approach is to contract with private clinics and mental-health care professionals to deliver those services. This is considerably cheaper than building and staffing a mental-health care facility from scratch, since renting the expertise and facilities that already exist in the private sector costs a fraction of duplicating everything in the public sector.

Yet contracting public service delivery to the private sector can have considerable drawbacks. Consider the experience of Denver, Colorado. In the 1990s, the city shifted control of its public transportation services from a traditional bureaucracy to a system of competitive bidding from the private sector. Initially, eight companies submitted bids and three contracts were awarded, all to national transportation companies. The national companies submitted bids far below those submitted by local companies, and local operators were essentially cut out of the market. Two of the national companies that had been awarded bids soon merged, further reducing competition and leaving public transportation under the control of just two companies. Costs soon went up. In the late 1990s, another round of bidding yielded only three bids, all of which were awarded to a single company. Over a decade of contracting out, the costs of using private vendors turned out to be not that much different from using a public agency, the service quality was not noticeably different, and the public transportation services effectively ended up in the hands of a single for-profit company. The result, some critics argued, was a program that was more expensive, less effective, and less accountable than a traditional bureaucracy.[34]

The basic problem with trying to run government more like a business is that government is not a business. For the most part, we do not like rules and red tape—until there is a problem or a scandal. Then we want to know what went wrong and who is to blame. We want government agencies to act more like a business until a bureaucracy takes a calculated risk—as businesses do routinely—and loses taxpayer money. We want bureaucrats to be given the freedom to be flexible and make choices—until those choices result in favoritism or program failure. We like the idea of competition and the profit motive. We like it until a private company contracted to provide public services puts profit above the public interest.

Although most efforts to make government bureaucracy more market-like have produced very mixed results, they have done little to reduce the widespread belief that government is best run as a business. This belief has spawned a veritable alphabet soup of business-oriented reform movements. Reinventing government (REGO) stresses making public agencies entrepreneurial. Total Quality Management (TQM) emphasizes having public programs and services designed and shaped by the clients who actually consume those services and focuses on preventing problems rather than reacting to them. Management by Objectives (MBO) and Performance Based Management (PBM) are approaches that focus on setting goals and achieving them.

Policy in Practice: Florida Ends the Merit System

Frustrated with the drawbacks of traditional bureaucracy, the state of Florida has spent the past few years experimenting with an alternative to the merit system. On May 14, 2001, Florida governor Jeb Bush signed into law a civil service overhaul dubbed "Service First." Service First is technically a significant reform of public sector personnel policy. In practice, it eliminates the merit system.

Specifically, Service First does three things. First, it eliminates seniority for all state workers. Second, it classifies a large number of employees into a "serve at will" category, meaning that their superiors can hire or fire them at will. Third, it prepares the way for a massive reorganization of job titles and pay, all in an effort to give public sector managers the power to decide the salary and benefits of their individual employees.

The law has been controversial, to put it mildly. To its supporters, Service First is a long overdue change in the policies that regulate how public employees are hired, fired, promoted, and managed. It gives public sector managers the flexibility they need to hire workers who do the best job and fire those who do not and to compensate these employees according to their talents and contributions. The ability of agency personnel heads to freely and quickly hire, promote, transfer, or offer raises to employees arguably gives them the ability to better manage public employees and makes government agencies more businesslike.

To its detractors, however, Service First is little more than a re-institution of the spoils system. For example, bureaucrats who work for regulatory and licensing agencies may put their jobs on the line when they pursue

There are many others. All originated in private sector management trends that do not fully account for the unique problems of the public sector. Support and enthusiasm for making government more like a business tends to fade when these systems are put into practice and it becomes apparent that there are good reasons why government is not run like a business.

As the problems with these proffered replacements for traditional bureaucracy become apparent, public agencies gravitate back to their tried and true bureaucratic ways of doing things. At least until they get swept up in the next big reform movement. Some of these movements are counterproductive from the beginning because they spread more confusion than efficiency and leave public managers with a vague or complicated set of guidelines that is difficult to implement and is based on concepts that are hard to understand. "I'm just not sure what it has to offer, but maybe that's just because I don't understand what it is," was a typical public manager's response to Balanced Scorecard (BSC), a management reform movement that gained popularity in 2002.[35] This constant cycle of reform by acronym breeds cynicism among public sector administrators. Some refer to all reform movements as BOHICA, as in "bend over, here it comes again." BOHICA implies that the best response to reform is to just go through the motions. This fad too shall pass.

cases against politically well-connected businesses and individuals. The law also leaves higher-level bureaucrats exposed to the whims of budget cutters, who may be tempted to fire more experienced and higher salaried bureaucrats—not because of their job performance—but simply as an exercise in economizing.

There is evidence to suggest these concerns have merit. A watchdog Web site devoted to Florida government (www.whoseflorida.com) is packed with stories of political shenanigans in the state bureaucracy, including stories of those fired because they had the "wrong" political point of view. The shadow of a spoils system mentality is also evident in who is *not* covered by the Service First law. Several groups of employees, including police, fire fighters and dieticians, are exempt. What these groups have in common is that their unions sup-

ported Bush in his gubernatorial election campaign. To Service First critics this smacks of the sort of political payoff that is the cornerstone of the spoils system—support the electoral winner and get a secure job. Oppose the winner, and run the opposite risk. Even some groups that support Service First are opposed to these special exceptions.

Regardless of its pros and its cons, there is no doubt Service First has created a firestorm of controversy and no small amount of resentment among public employees. Thousands have lost their jobs and a number of lawsuits have been filed. Many believe the law's main goal is to downsize government and shift more public services into the private sector. Whether the result is a better or a worse public bureaucracy remains to be seen.

Source: Adapted from Jonathan Walters, "Civil Service Tsunami," *Governing* magazine, May 2003.

Another big drawback of trying to replace the traditional merit-based bureaucracy is that its advantages get overlooked until they are no longer there. Many of the attempts to radically reform the bureaucracy by either making agencies more like businesses or eliminating the merit system end up doing little more than returning public programs and services to the spoils system. (See Box 9-2.)

The ATM Bureaucracy

The history of reform shows us the difficulty in coming up with a viable alternative to traditional bureaucracy. This does not mean, however, that bureaucracy is not changing. Indeed, it is changing in fundamental ways. Perhaps the best example of this is how public agencies are increasing their use of information technology. The changes in technology are creating what is sometimes called the **ATM Bureaucracy**, or **e-government**. Both descriptions "refer to the delivery of information and services online via the Internet or other digital means."[36] All fifty states and most local governments now have at least some e-government operations that allow citizens to do everything from applying for hunting licenses to submitting small business applications to filing their taxes.[37] In Ventura, California, for example, build-

ATM BUREAUCRACY, OR E-GOVERNMENT

The delivery of public services and programs via the Internet or other digital means. Also known as "e-government."

ing contractors can apply online for 109 different sorts of permits that cover everything from rewiring a house to installing a new heating system. They can even schedule a visit from the building inspector to get final approval.

There are a number of key advantages to e-government. It is convenient for citizens—no more waiting in lines—and governments—shorter lines to deal with. It may even promote political participation by facilitating communication between the public and elected officials. A good example of this is the attempt by numerous states, especially in the Southwest, to make all of their Web sites available in Spanish as well as English to make it easier for non-native speakers to get the information they need. In Texas, all state government Web sites can be accessed in Spanish simply by clicking "en español."[38] Roughly two-thirds of state government Web sites have e-mail addresses. Governments post everything from laws and proclamations to bus schedules.[39] They also clearly hope that e-government will allow them to deliver information, public programs, and public services cheaper and faster, although it is still too early to make a general statement about how well this goal is being achieved.

States and localities, however, differ widely in their use of technology. A key indicator of the commitment to e-government is whether government Web sites are being used purely as communication tools or whether they actually allow transactions to take place online. In most states, 10 percent or fewer government sites actually allow transactions. In those states most committed to e-government, roughly half of government sites allow transactions. (See Table 9-5.) Why are some state and local governments more techno-savvy than others? The most important factors to explain the differences in e-government reform seem to be professionalism of state government and, to a lesser extent, party control. States that have more professionalized governments are considerably more committed to e-government reforms. States that are controlled by Republicans also tend to support the development of ATM bureaucracy.[40]

Unlike many other reform movements, the rise of e-government does seem to be bringing about important and permanent changes in the administrative arm of government. It is changing how people interact with government, changing expectations of government, and changing how public agencies are run. For example, in the virtual world there are no boundaries

TABLE 9-5

States that Offer Various Online Services

Service	Number of States
Taxes	
Download forms	43
Tax advice	38
Complete online filing, with refund	29
Complete online filing, no refund	23
Vehicle Registration	
Complete online registration	16
Download forms	11
Professional Licensing	
Download forms	50
Partial online registration	25

Source: Rob Gurwitt, "Behind the Portal," *Governing* magazine, August 2001. www.governing.com/archive/2001/aug/egweb.txt (accessed June 5, 2003).

between agencies—they are just a mouse click away. This is forcing those agencies to rethink how they work together. When you make it easier to do business with government online, one of the typical results is an increase in the workload of agency personnel. This can force a rethinking of who does what and why in a public agency. Management reform fads have had a very mixed impact on bureaucracy, but the shift toward e-government has brought broad changes that are here to stay.

Conclusion

Bureaucracy is in many ways the Rodney Dangerfield of government—it gets no respect. Although it is often despised and disparaged, it is also clear that government bureaucracy is underestimated and does not get the credit it actually deserves. A wide range of state and local agencies support and deliver the programs and services that make up our social and economic life as we know it. The comparative method shows us that bureaucracy is big, but only as big as we want it. If we want less bureaucracy, all we have to do is make fewer demands on government. The comparative method also shows that, for the most part, these bureaucracies do their jobs remarkably well. In contrast to the popular stereotype, most public agencies tackle difficult jobs that are unlikely to be done better by any other alternative. Perhaps the most astonishing thing about bureaucracy is how much we take it for granted. Public schools, safe drinking water, working utility grids, and roads are simply there. We rarely contemplate what an astounding administrative and logistical feat is required to make these aspects of everyday life appear so mundane.

Yet while bureaucracy almost certainly deserves more praise than criticism, there is cause for concern. Its growing role and responsibilities have raised worries about the power administrative agencies wield in a democratic society. Changes such as the rise of new information technology are forcing bureaucracy to change with the times. The high cost of public services and an on-going debate about what government should do is shifting more of what was traditionally considered public administration toward the private sector. Bureaucratic reform movements, at least in some ways, should be viewed with skepticism. Criticizing the bureaucracy is a traditional sport in American politics, and a lot of reforms turn out to be little more than fads that quickly fade when the pleasing rhetoric meets the real-life challenge of delivering the goods. Yet some reforms, like the rise of the merit system and of e-government, can radically reshape what bureaucracy is and what it does. One thing, however, will almost certainly remain constant. Whatever the government is, and whatever it does, it will rely on bureaucracy to get it done.

Key Concepts

affirmative action (p. 321)
ATM bureaucracy, or e-government (p. 327)
bureaucracy (p. 303)
bureaucrats (p. 303)
collective bargaining (p. 320)
merit systems (p. 318)
neutral competence (p. 318)
policy implementation (p. 304)
professionalization (p. 303)
representative bureaucracy (p. 323)
rulemaking (p. 306)
seniority (p. 320)
spoils system (p. 317)
street-level bureaucrats (p. 305)

Suggested Readings

Goodsell, Charles. *The Case for Bureaucracy: A Public Administration Polemic.* 4th ed. Washington, D.C.: CQ Press, 2004. A classic argument for why bureaucracy works and why it does not deserve its negative reputation.

Kerwin, Cornelius M. *Rulemaking: How Government Agencies Write Law and Make Policy* 3d ed. Washington, D.C.: CQ Press, 2003. A comprehensive look at rulemaking and bureaucracy.

Lipsky, Michael. *Street-Level Bureaucracy.* New York: Russell Sage Foundation, 1980. This is the classic work examining the policymaking role of the street-level bureaucrat.

Suggested Web Sites

www.aspanet.org. Official Web site of the American Society for Public Administration, the largest professional association for those who work for or study public agencies.

www.governing.com. Web version of *Governing* magazine, which is dedicated to covering state and local issues. Includes numerous stories and other resources on agency leaders and performance, e-government, and more.

CHAPTER 10

Local Government

Function Follows Form

Talking trash about recycling got city officials in Amsterdam, New York, into a heap of trouble. The New York state attorney general's office took the city to court after it dumped its popular but problematic curbside recycling program in January 2000. State law prohibits such an action. Community leaders were forced to toss out the suspension, negotiate a new contract for service that cost them double what the city previously had paid, and reinstate the program in August 2000. Such are the dilemmas of local governments. Caught among a mess of state and federal mandates, budgetary concerns, and citizen needs, elected officials often find it impossible to sweep even the smallest issue under the rug.

10

Why do local governments vary so much within and between states?

How and why have local governments changed over the years?

What are the positive and negative aspects of Dillon's Rule?

Alexis de Tocqueville, a nineteenth-century French aristocrat who wrote one of the most celebrated analyses of the American political system in history, once described local government as the "fertile germ" of democracy.[1]

He wasn't kidding about the fertile bit. In his day, the most common form of government in the United States was the New England township, typically a political jurisdiction with a relatively limited set of responsibilities that contains several thousand citizens.

Most northeastern states had dozens of townships. Some had considerably more.

What a difference two hundred years makes. Today, there are roughly eighty-seven thousand local governments in the United States, some of them with jurisdictions containing millions of citizens. The responsibilities of contemporary local governments include everything from running schools to repairing potholes to making sure sewage isn't, well, making germs too fertile.

The types of local government, as well as their institutional structure, responsibilities, and powers, vary enormously from state to state. For example, at the smaller end of the local government scale is the township. In twenty states, primarily in New England and the Midwest, this remains the most common form of government. In New York State, the smallest governing unit for centuries has been the village. There are 557 of these "one-horse" entities in the Empire State that range in population from 28 people in Deering Harbor to 50,000 in Hempstead. Contrast these relatively small enclaves with the Dallas-Fort Worth consolidated metropolitan area—locally known as the Metroplex—which had a population of 5,222,000 as of the 2000 census.

Broadly speaking, however, local government can be categorized into three basic forms: **counties, municipalities,** and **special districts.** Counties are administrative divisions of state government. States historically have divided themselves into smaller geographical units and given each of these separate jurisdictions a governance structure and set of policy responsibilities, such as road maintenance and law enforcement. This has made it easier to provide public services and attend to local concerns in what are often large and sparsely populated areas. Although modern county governments may be seated in very urban areas, they have their origins as the rural "branch offices" of state government.

COUNTIES

A geographic subdivision of state government.

MUNICIPALITIES

Political jurisdictions, such as cities, villages, or towns, incorporated under state law to provide governance to a defined geographic area. More compact and more densely populated than counties.

SPECIAL DISTRICTS

Local governmental units created for a single purpose, such as water distribution.

Municipalities are political units, including cities, towns, or villages, that are incorporated under state law to provide governance services to a clearly defined local area. The exact definition and role of these governments vary considerably from state to state. Generally speaking, municipalities are geographically more compact than counties, have denser and more urban populations, and have the legal status of independent corporations rather than simply being an administrative sub-unit of state government.

Special districts cover a huge range of local governments. Unlike counties and municipalities, special districts tend to be single—rather than general-purpose—governments. In other words, they are created to provide a specific public service rather than a range of services. School districts are a good example. These are geographically defined local units of government created to provide educational services. Other special districts include water management and sewage treatment districts.

Shoehorning the more than eighty-seven thousand local governments into just three categories, however, is a little misleading. What local government is, what it does, and how many local governments there are, varies wildly from state to state. The number of local governments in a state's boundaries, for example, depends on a state's history, culture, and administrative approach to service delivery. New England states have a highly educated citizenry. The region has a tradition of active civic participation and social spending that accommodates a large number of local governing units. By contrast, many residents of southern states traditionally have less education. Government was and still is regarded by many with suspicion. Individuals rely on a relatively small number of powerful county leaders for such services as school governance.

> Shoehorning the more than eighty-seven thousand local governments into just three categories, however, is a little misleading. What local government is, what it does, and how many local governments there are, varies wildly from state to state.

In terms of differences, local governments make state governments look like they were all stamped from the same cookie cutter. The populations of substate government areas range from single families of fewer than ten persons to millions. Geographically, they range from villages covering less than a square mile to counties that cover nearly 125,000 square miles. Within or adjacent to their borders may be mountains, deserts, beaches, urban centers, or vast stretches of nothingness. These differences help explain why some local governments are interested in maintaining subways and others worry about maintaining clean beaches.

Political and cultural traditions also vary at the local level. For instance, the degree of loyalty that citizens display toward a local governing entity often depends on whether they personally identify with the area or whether they ignore their membership and regard the area as an artificial construct. Put another way, a Manhattanite probably feels more community pride than, say, a user of the Susquehanna and Delaware River Basin.

Local governments must provide numerous public services, including police and fire protection. Here, firefighters in Gallup, New Mexico, struggle to beat back a blaze that threatened to consume an area historical landmark in April 2004.

All of these differences provide multiple opportunities to put the comparative method into practice, but they also can be confusing. Local authority, for example, overlaps—school districts sprawl across municipalities, which, in turn, are covered by counties. A couple may plan on getting married in the city of Chapel Hill, North Carolina, but their marriage certificate will carry the insignia of Orange County, North Carolina. That is because in most states the power to grant marriage licenses is vested in counties, not in cities. Adding to the confusion, the units of government at the substate level vary in their duties and obligations from state to state. Depending on where you live, you may rely on a different set of authorities to get a pothole filled on your street, arrange for a stop sign to be installed at a dangerous intersection, or register your opinion on a bond issue for a new high school.

Despite such challenges, it is worth putting in the effort to understand local government simply because it is at this level that government provides the services that most affect individual lives. Local governments spend much of their money on police and fire protection, sewage treatment, trash collection, roads, education, healthcare, and hospitals.[2] These are all things that the average household finds necessary, even if the tax bill to provide them is not welcome.

Local governments, however, go well beyond just providing efficient services. They must make political and philosophical decisions that affect their residents' quality of life and reinforce values. Many citizens believe local government has an obligation to provide a safety net for the poor, strike a balance between the need for sufficient revenues and public resistance to high taxation, and referee disputes over land-use planning that pit, say, developers against environmentalists or middle-income homeowners against low-income renters.

In short, local governments are worth getting to know. If states are the laboratories of democracy, then de Tocqueville was right to hint that local governments are democracy's petri dishes. This chapter examines the powers and responsibilities of specific forms of local government, how these forms evolved, how they differ by state and region, and how the democratic political process works at the substate level. The government of each community was set up according to some, but not all, of the available approaches discussed. The interesting thing is why.

Working within Limits: The Powers and Constraints of Local Government

Vital as the work of local governments is to the daily lives of Americans, anyone employed by one is constantly aware of its limits. Most of the services local governments provide are destined to be performed less visibly than those of the state and federal governments and always with an eye toward possible intervention from higher authority. State power nearly always trumps local power.

Therefore, the basic *modus operandi* of a local government is that it must do what it can do within some serious restrictions. Why is this the case? The Tenth Amendment to the U.S. Constitution says that the power to determine the scope of authority of local governments is among those "reserved to the States respectively, or to the people." In other words, to a very large extent, states get to say what localities can and cannot do. They set the limits and define the terms.

Dillon's Rule

One limit frequently imposed on localities by states is **Dillon's Rule**, named after Iowa Supreme Court justice John F. Dillon. In addition to having a fine legal mind, Dillon was a highly respected and well-read scholar of local government. An argument he formulated in 1868 has served ever since as the basis for understanding and justifying the power—or, more accurately, the lack of power—of local government. The rule is built around the legal principle of *ultra vires,* which means "outside one's powers." In a nutshell, it states that local governments are limited to the powers expressly granted to them by their state and to those powers indispensable to the stated objectives and purposes of each local government.

What Dillon essentially did was build a legal argument that the Tenth Amendment secured power for the states, but not for local governments. Local governments, in other words, are not sovereign; they only can exercise the powers granted to them by the state. Dillon's Rule has guided much legal thinking on the power of local governments, but it has always had its critics and opponents. It was challenged as early as the 1870s, when Missouri legislators rewrote the state constitution specifically to allow municipalities a degree of independence from the constraints of state government.[3]

For the most part, however, state legislators have been enthusiastic about employing Dillon's Rule. In Virginia, for example, antitax lawmakers continually prevent localities from restructuring their tax systems to raise revenue. It should come as no surprise that ambitious state legislators hoard power over their county and city counterparts.

That said, the independence and powers state governments grant to localities vary considerably. Some state governments are more willing than

> What Dillon essentially did was build a legal argument that the Tenth Amendment secured power for the states, but not for local governments. Local governments . . . only can exercise the powers granted to them by the state.

others to let local governments make their own decisions. Much of these differences can be explained by state culture and the degree of citizen participation. Idaho and West Virginia reserve the most local powers to the state. Oregon and Maine give localities the most freedom.[4]

The freedom, or lack thereof, that states allow local government can have significant consequences. For example, Virginia allows cities with populations greater than five thousand to operate independent of the counties of which they are a part. It also gives them the right to impose sales taxes on meals, lodging, or cigarettes. Counties are left with only funds from property taxes to pay their bills.[5] This can pose a serious dilemma for county leaders. When the housing market is booming, many homeowners watch their property assessments, and hence their annual taxes, rise inexorably. In many cases, the property taxes rise faster than their incomes. These homeowners, subsequently, take it out on county leaders come election time.

Similarly, the city of Buffalo, New York, is prevented from controlling the salaries and pensions of its uniformed workers because of New York State labor laws. The state limits the pool of candidates the city can consider when hiring managers. And state requirements for thorough hearings in cases of alleged disciplinary infractions by city employees make it tough for a city official to speedily fire an unsuitable staffer.

States also invoke Dillon's Rule to block localities from enacting what are called **living wage laws**. Living wage laws are part of a union-backed movement to require businesses that win contracts with a local government to pay prevailing area wages rather than just the federal minimum wage. This means that publicly financed workers can support a family without working multiple jobs. Such floors in wages can amount to twice the federal minimum wage. Proposals for such laws often clash with the desire of the business community to keep labor costs down.

Home Rule

There is one way for local governments to avoid the sometimes tight constraints imposed by Dillon's Rule. Cities and counties can petition the state legislature to grant **home rule,** or the freedom to make local decisions without interference from state government. Home rule typically is enshrined in a **charter,** which spells out the powers and purposes of the municipality.

The movement for such charters got started in the nineteenth century and peaked in the early 1970s. Charters can be adopted only after voters approve a council-approved or citizen-written petition. Thirty-six of the

LIVING WAGE LAWS

Laws that require businesses with government contracts to pay prevailing area wage rates rather than the national minimum wage.

HOME RULE

The right of localities to self-government, usually granted through a charter.

CHARTER

A document that outlines the powers, organization, and responsibilities of a local government.

forty-eight states that use a county form of government allow charters or some form of home rule, according to the National Association of Counties (NACo). This can free them from both state and county obligations.

In some instances, however, a measure of state control may be desirable. For instance, city or county employees may prefer state protections to giving local **mayor** or **city manager** too much authority. Antitax groups often fear that independent cities free of state regulation will raise new taxes.

Home rule can be granted in two basic forms. Legislatures may approve home rule in what are called **general act charters**, which apply to all cities, or **special act charters**, which affect only one community. Either type can be initiated by state legislators, local councils, or citizens groups. In cases of citizen initiatives, advocates gather the requisite number of signatures on petitions that are then converted to legislation or language for a ballot referendum that is put before voters.

For example, one fifth of all California cities are charter cities. In 2000, a ballot question for the city of Signal Hill asked voters whether the city should become a locally governed charter city, as opposed to a general law city that would be governed by all statewide laws. The question explained that the charter would serve as the city's constitution, giving it full control over its municipal affairs.

The ballot text specified that municipal affairs included "regulation of municipal utilities; procedures for bidding and contracting; regulation of parks, libraries, and other facilities; salaries of officers and employees; parking regulations; franchise and other fees; taxation; and zoning and election procedures." It also noted that the charter could exempt the city from some state sales taxes.

The city would remain subject to state law on "matters of statewide importance," however. This basically meant environmental regulations, General Plan requirements, open-meeting laws, public records, and redevelopment. Despite the complexity of the issue and the uncertainty about the fiscal impact of home rule, the charter city ballot question passed with 86 percent of the vote[6]. In principle, American voters warm to the notion of self-direction and autonomy, even though with such autonomy comes new responsibilities.

The downside of state and federal government oversight can be offset by the goodies that they can bestow. Much of what local leaders wish to accomplish requires infusions of funds from Washington and state capitals. So with oversight at least comes cold, hard cash. The superior capacities of state governments and the federal government to raise revenues is another limit on the powers of localities, and will be discussed in Chapter 11.

NACo's top priorities for 2004 clearly illustrate this love-hate relationship. Those county leaders surveyed said that they wanted the reauthorization of the federal Transportation Equity Act, which governs highway funding, road

MAYOR

The elected chief executive of a municipality.

CITY MANAGER

An official appointed to be the chief administrator of a municipality.

GENERAL ACT CHARTERS

Charters that grant powers, such as home rule, to all municipal governments within a state.

SPECIAL ACT CHARTERS

Charters that grant powers, such as home rule, to a single municipal government.

Local Focus: Sex and the City . . . Charter

Unless the discussion turns to sex, an ancient document written by city founders laying out the powers of a community's government seldom makes for popular reading. And that applies in spades to the sprawling and formless municipality of Los Angeles. There, a charter originally drafted in 1925 was for decades ignored by most neighborhood citizens but exploited by business lobbyists and downtown insiders who wanted their development projects approved with only minimal public debate.

When the Los Angeles city charter was revised and put to the voters in July 1999, a *Los Angeles Times* poll conducted three months before the vote showed that nine out of ten respondents said they did not know enough about the proposed charter to judge the reforms.[a]

The idea of charter reform was the work of Mayor Richard Riordan who, although he would not remain in office to enjoy it, had wanted to strengthen the city's famously weak mayoral powers and clip the wings of city council members who, many felt, had built their own personal fiefdoms across L.A.'s disconnected geography.

With city council members skeptical, two competing commissions were set up to research and draft the reforms. One was run by a law professor and another by a neighborhood negotiator. The two might never have seen eye-to-eye were it not for a stepped-up threat in 1998 from activists in the San Fernando Valley. Many of the 1.5 million suburbanites in this area, packed onto reclaimed farmland north of downtown, have long wanted to secede from Los Angeles and form their own city.

The prospect of such a loss prompted the two commissions to agree on a set of reforms that would simplify an intricate document that had been amended four hundred times. Their changes would strengthen the office of the mayor, allow voters to consider expanding the fifteen-member city council in the future, restrict civil service protection for high-level officials, and set up a new network of neighborhood councils.

There was resistance among council members who were wary of concentrating too much power with a mayor, such as the authority to fire department heads. Critics noted that the reforms would do nothing to exert more control over the vast Los Angeles Unified School System and that the new charter would leave intact the inconsistency between the Los Angeles planning commission boundaries and the political district boundaries used when electing the nonpartisan city council members. Finally, most neighborhood organizations were left as weakly organized as they had been before the reforms.

Still, the charter reforms passed with backing of 60 percent of L.A. voters. The new charter took effect in July 2002.[b]

Out of sight, out of mind. The next time many Los Angelinos would read about their new city charter was during a 2003 controversy over the regulation of strip clubs. Critics believe that the proliferation of "gentlemen's clubs" in certain L.A. neighborhoods increases public drunkenness and harms property values. Therefore, the city council unanimously passed an ordinance that banned the clubs from permitting male customers to go into private rooms and touch the female "lap dancers."

The adult entertainment industry stepped in, spending some $400,000 to make use of a provision in the city charter that allows any group of citizens to repeal a city ordinance if, within 30 days of its enactment, they gather signatures on a petition at a number equal to 10 percent of the people who voted for the mayor in the most recent election.

Under the threat of total repeal and leery of the costs of putting the measure to voters, the council retreated, working out a compromise with the clubs that included more narrow restrictions on sexual touching and stepped-up enforcement of rules in granting business permits.[c]

---

[a] Jim Newton, "Los Angeles: Voters Know Little of Candidates or Charter," *Los Angeles Times,* April 1, 1999. www.latimes.com (accessed January 14, 2004).

[b] William Fulton and Paul Shigley, "Putting Los Angeles Together," *Governing* magazine, June 2000.

[c] Robert Greene, "A Touch of Democracy: A Lap Dancer's Guide to Beating City Hall," *L.A. Weekly,* November 14–20, 2003. www.laweekly.com (accessed January 20, 2004).

safety, and related environmental protection and more funding for healthcare and homeland security.

They also requested the freedom to impose sales taxes for purchases made over the Internet, oversee mass transit planning, and manage social services and workforce programs. Surveyed officials voiced strong opposition to unfunded mandates such as the preemption of county authorities in telecommunications and cable television regulation.

The Organization and Responsibilities of Local Governments

There are a bewildering number of substate governments—from counties to townships to school districts, water districts, and airport authorities. It gets even more interesting. They all have different, although sometimes overlapping, governance structures.

Between the County Lines

The unglamorous, utilitarian governing unit known as the county grew out a thousand-year-old tradition brought over from Mother England, where it was known as the shire. (Americans also got the word sheriff from the merry old shire.) Counties "are nothing more than certain portions of the territory into which the state is divided for the more convenient exercise of the powers of government," wrote U.S. Supreme Court chief justice Roger B. Taney, in *Maryland ex. rel. Washington County v. Baltimore & Ohio Railroad Co.* (1845).[7]

Called parishes in Louisiana and boroughs in Alaska, more than three thousand counties are drawn on the maps of forty-eight states. There are no county governments in the fairly small states of Rhode Island and Connecticut. Hawaii and Delaware have only three apiece. Supporting the claim that everything is bigger in Texas, the state has 254 counties, the most in the nation.

Counties range in physical size from tiny Arlington, Virginia, which is just 42 square miles across, to North Slope Borough, Alaska, which arcs across a largely uninhabited 142,224 square miles. Measured by population, counties cross the spectrum from 9.5 million in Los Angeles County, California, to 67 persons in Loving County, Texas.[8] (See Tables 10-1 and 10-2.)

Because they generally cover the largest geographical territory, counties bear much of the burden of providing services widely, if not lavishly. The majority of the million citizens in California's Sacramento County, for example, live in **unincorporated territory**. This means that their property is not part of any city, town, or township that can provide municipal

UNINCORPORATED TERRITORY

A community or area in which there is no municipal corporation.

TABLE 10-1

Twenty-five Largest U.S. Counties by Population, 2000

County, State	Population	Rank	County, State	Population	Rank
Los Angeles, CA	9,519,338	1	Santa Clara, CA	1,682,585	14
Cook, IL	5,376,741	2	Broward, FL	1,623,018	15
Harris, TX	3,400,578	3	Riverside, CA	1,545,387	16
Maricopa, AZ	3,072,149	4	New York, NY	1,537,195	17
Orange, CA	2,846,289	5	Philadelphia, PA	1,517,550	18
San Diego, CA	2,813,833	6	Middlesex, MA	1,465,396	19
Kings, NY	2,465,326	7	Tarrant, TX	1,446,219	20
Dade, FL	2,253,362	8	Alameda, CA	1,443,741	21
Queens, NY	2,229,379	9	Suffolk, NY	1,419,369	22
Dallas, TX	2,218,899	10	Cuyahoga, OH	1,393,978	23
Wayne, MI	2,061,162	11	Bexar, TX	1,392,931	24
King, WA	1,737,034	12	Clark, NV	1,375,765	25
San Bernardino, CA	1,709,434	13			

Source: U.S. Census Bureau, *County and City Data Book 2000,* Table B-1.

services. Hence the burden falls on the county to provide these residents with such services as law enforcement, parks and recreation, and storm water management.

Counties have long differed from cities, although those differences began to blur as the nation's population and development exploded with the advent of the twentieth century. It helps, therefore, to think of the quintessential county government as a quiet, less visible keeper of public records such as property deeds, birth and death certificates, and mortgages. County governments are also the administrators of property taxes, local road maintenance, election results certification, criminal courts, and jails run by county sheriffs.

Contrast this, for simplicity's sake, with the image of a typical American city run by a government that performs such day-to-day functions as police and fire protection; sewage disposal; sanitation; and the maintenance of public parks and other infrastructure facilities, including stadiums, airports, and convention centers.

In the messy real world, however, many modern county governments—particularly urban ones—have their official fingers in these classic city functions as well. In many regions, there is substantial overlap between county and city functions. Indeed, in Phoenix, the city hall is directly across the street from the Maricopa County administration building.

Less visibly than cities, counties nonetheless are kept under tight control by states. In New Hampshire, for example, legislators still approve county

TABLE 10-2

Twenty-five Smallest U.S. Counties by Population, 2000

County, State	Population	Rank	County, State	Population	Rank
Loving, TX	67	1	Slope, ND	767	14
Kalawao, HI	147	2	Logan, NE	774	15
King, TX	356	3	Hooker, NE	783	16
Kenedy, TX	414	4	Hinsdale, CO	790	17
Arthur, NE	444	5	Harding, NM	810	18
Petroleum, MT	493	6	Banner, NE	819	19
McPherson, NE	533	7	Mineral, CO	831	20
San Juan, CO	558	8	McMullen, TX	851	21
Blaine, NE	583	9	Kent, TX	859	22
Loup, NE	712	10	Treasure, MT	861	23
Thomas, NE	729	11	Wheeler, NE	886	24
Borden, TX	729	11	Roberts, TX	887	25
Grant, NE	747	13			

Source: U.S. Census Bureau, *County and City Data Book 2000,* Table B-1.

Note: If two or more counties are tied, all counties are listed alphabetically by state.

budgets. In Texas, each county is required to appoint a county judge-at-large and four commissioners, regardless of whether the county's population numbers in the hundreds or the millions. Counties are still seen as the administrative units of the state government.

Yet for all of this, counties attract less money from federal and state appropriations than cities. For many counties, this is a problem, especially given their responsibilities as "backstop" in providing such services as welfare, healthcare, housing, and mass transit. Counties, according to a 1992 U.S. Census Bureau study, spend almost three times as much as cities on social services and twice as much on administration, but less on public safety and less on the environment than cities.

> [T]hink of the quintessential county government as a quiet, less visible keeper of public records such as property deeds, birth and death certificates, and mortgages.

Counties often get stuck with responsibilities involving costs they cannot cap. When the federal government appropriated funds to put more local cops on the beat in the 1990s, counties actually suffered. The resulting rise in arrests meant more prisoners to support in county jails.[9]

There are huge variations among counties in terms of priorities in spending. It all depends on geography, politics, and relations with neighboring jurisdictions. Merced County, California, for example, spent $618.07 per capita on public welfare and $747.35 on hospitals and healthcare for its residents in fiscal year 1991–1992, but recorded no spending for sewage treatment. Kent County, Delaware, by contrast, spent $78.78 per capita on sewer systems but nothing on welfare or hospitals or healthcare that same year.[10]

Most counties structure their local legislatures into **boards of commissioners**, also called county commissioners, supervisors, selectmen, county board members, or judges, depending on the state and county. In Louisiana, these locally elected legislators are called parish jurors. In New Jersey, they are boards of chosen freeholders. Whatever their official titles, these commissioners usually are elected to staggered two-year or four-year terms, along with a sheriff, an auditor, a district attorney, a coroner, a tax collector, a treasurer, and a county clerk. Elected commissions often appoint a top administrator to run programs, hire managers to staff the bureaucracy, and appoint citizens to serve on special boards. Power over day-to-day decisions usually is shared among elected and appointed officials.

County commissioners dominated city politics in the early twentieth century. Over time, reformers grew concerned that power under this arrangement was too diffused and that commissioners too often appointed friends to important positions. As a result, an increasing number of counties, as many as 15 percent, now are run by elected county executives who exert firm leadership on policy and hiring. This reduces the role of the commissioners to something closer to an advisory level. Another 12 percent of counties are led by appointed administrators. State policymakers have contributed to this trend—Arkansas, Kentucky, and Tennessee now mandate that their counties be headed by elected executives.

Although such reforms have reduced entrenched corruption, even today there are examples of county governments going very badly astray. When this happens, states are still known to step in and, in effect, put county government out of business. For example, in 1997, the Massachusetts House of Representatives voted to abolish the government of Middlesex County, which it believed had become a corrupt, debt-ridden, and expensive administrative burden. Although the county still survives as a legal venue and for other administrative purposes, legislators judged that the state could do better.

Municipal Governance

Governance arrangements at the city level vary even more than at the county level. In municipalities there is variation in the powers of the executive, or mayor, and the legislature, typically a **city council**. A strong role often is played by an appointed administrator, or city manager, who is given day-to-day responsibility for running municipal operations. There are three basic city-level governance systems: the **mayor-council system**, the **commission system**, and the **city manager system**. (See Table 10-3.)

Mayor-Council Systems

One of the most common forms of municipal governance is the mayor-council system. It is distinguished by a separation of executive and legislative powers. According to the International City/County Management Association (ICMA), approximately 43 percent of U.S. cities use this system. Executive power is vested in a separately elected mayor, although the powers a mayor actually is allowed to exercise vary considerably.

The mayor-council system can be broken down into **strong mayor** and **weak mayor** systems. In discussions of city governance, these terms have less to do with a politician's personality than with the powers that a given mayor enjoys when stacked up against the powers of the city council and the bureaucracy. Under the strong mayor system, the executive is roughly the municipal-level equivalent of a governor. Strong mayors exercise real power, and typically have the authority to make appointments to key city offices, to veto council decisions, to prepare budgets, and to run the day-to-day operations of municipal government in general.

The strong mayor system is most common in the Northeast and Midwest. One example of a strong mayor in action is Carleton S. Finkbeiner, who was elected mayor of Toledo, Ohio, in 1994. Early in his tenure, he overrode resistance from school authorities and placed uniformed police officers in every junior high school and high school as a way to reduce violence. The policy takes some cops off the street, but it also creates trust with

TABLE 10-3

Most Common Forms of City Government in the United States

Council-Manager	3,392 (48.2 percent)
Mayor-Council	3,013 (42.8 percent)
Commission	143 (2.0 percent)
Town Meeting	337 (4.8 percent)
Representative Town Meeting	63 (1.0 percent)

Source: International City/County Management Association, June 2003. Represents only those cities with populations of 2,500 or greater.

MAYOR-COUNCIL SYSTEM

A form of municipal governance in which there is an elected executive and an elected legislature.

COMMISSION SYSTEM

A form of municipal governance in which executive, legislative, and administrative powers are vested in elected city commissioners.

CITY MANAGER SYSTEM

A form of municipal governance in which the day-to-day administration of government is carried out by a professional administrator.

FIGURE 10-1 Strong Mayor–Council Form of Government

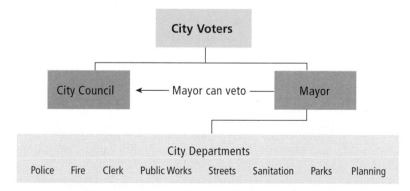

John P. Pelissero, "The Political Environment & Cities in the 21st Century." in *Cities, Politics & Public Policy: A Comparative Analysis,* ed. John P. Pelissero (Washington, DC: CQ Press, 2003), 15.

FIGURE 10-2 Weak Mayor–Council Form of Government

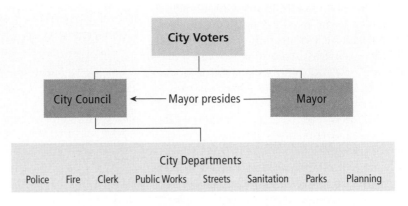

John P. Pelissero, "The Political Environment & Cities in the 21st Century," in *Cities, Politics & Public Policy: A Comparative Analysis,* ed. John P. Pelissero (Washington, DC: CQ Press, 2003), 15.

students and takes a preventive approach that reduces drug and gang problems by providing mentors and role models for students. The U.S. Conference of Mayors cited the program as an example of best practice in 2000.[11] What Finkbeiner demonstrated was the ability of a strong mayor to independently make important policy decisions.

A weak mayor system retains the elected executive, but this is more a ceremonial than a real policymaking office. In weak mayor systems real executive, as well as legislative, power is wielded by the council. Executives in weak mayor systems can still exercise considerable influence, but they have to do this using their powers of persuasion rather than the authority vested in their office. In many cities where mayors have limited powers, individuals with strong personalities have nevertheless been able to exert huge influence. They do this by fostering cooperative relationships with their powerful city managers. Examples are Pete Wilson, mayor of San Diego in the 1970s, and Henry Cisneros, mayor of San Antonio in the 1980s.

In both strong and weak mayor systems, the council serves as the municipal level legislature and can wield extensive policymaking power. No major policy or program can get far in a city without massaging from the city council. Councils average six members, but there are twelve members to fourteen members elected in many large jurisdictions. Los Angeles, for example, has fifteen. Chicago has a whopping fifty council members, and New York City has fifty-one.

City councils exert major influence over a city's livability. They steer policies on such vital issues as zoning and urban renewal, as have the councils in Los Angeles and Philadelphia, for example. In recent years, they have been pivotal in the pursuit of public-private partnerships. In Indianapolis, for instance, the city council has worked with the city's mayor and administrators to save taxpayers $100 million by opening up service contracts to competitive bidding. The money saved by contracting out such services as wastewater treatment, asbestos abatement, recycling, street sweeping, and server billing goes toward public safety and airport improvements.[12]

In cities where councils lack discipline, however, quirky personalities can impede progress. In St. Louis, the board of aldermen has twenty-nine members. Back in the 1950s, these aldermen enjoyed a major say in decisions that affected zoning, development, and highway location. But by the start of the twenty-first century, critics complained that the board micromanaged and encouraged parochialism—a limitation of views or interests—and balkanization—the division of an area into small, often hostile, units.

Elected with as few as eight hundred votes, some of these personally ambitious individuals have embarrassed their communities by spending more time squabbling among themselves than teaming up to make principled decisions. For many aldermen, however, the personal stakes are higher than is commensurate with their actual power. Neighborhood **wards** have little influence, for example, on developers and corporations whose view of the city includes many wards. Ward aldermen can't implement a broad vision because the real power is in the mayor's office. In addition, they do not always know about deals being cut in other wards. Yet, sometimes, just one or two individuals can hold up a hand and make the entire city come to a halt.[13]

A survey taken in 2001 by the National League of Cities showed an array of issues that cause frustration among city council members across the country. Local leaders resent state and federal controls over their decision making. They chafe at the degree to which their communities are polarized over such issues as taxation, traffic abatement, development, and race. And they are frustrated by conflict within their own ranks, interest group pressure, and the nature of media coverage.

The survey also found that council members—who work part-time—spend the bulk of their hours, in rank order, responding to constituent demands, reviewing and approving the budget, resolving complaints, addressing the city's "real problems," establishing objectives and priorities, establishing a vision for the community's future, establishing long-term goals, overseeing administrative performance, and overseeing program effectiveness.[14]

City councils have even been known to weigh in on national, and even international, issues with or without the approval of the mayor or city manager. In the 1980s, for example, when proposals for a joint U.S.-Soviet freeze on nuclear weapons was being discussed by U.S. arms control officials, "nuclear-free zones" were declared by city councils in Takoma Park, Maryland, and Santa Cruz, California. In February 2004, the New York City council joined with dozens of other city councils to pass a resolution that opposed the expanded FBI antiterrorism investigatory powers under the USA PATRIOT Act, passed in the wake of the September 11, 2001, terrorist attacks on New York City and the Pentagon.

WARDS
Political and administrative subdivisions of a municipality.

Commission Systems

Commission systems merge executive and legislative powers into city commissions. These bodies are elected and make key policy decisions in the same way a legislature does. Yet each commissioner is also the head of an executive department. Commissioners run for office not to be representatives in a legislative body, but to run a particular city department: commissioner for public safety, commissioner for public works, and so on. Most commission systems also have a mayor, but this is not an independent executive office. The position usually is held by a commissioner chosen to preside over commission meetings.

The commission system originated in Galveston, Texas, in the early 1900s. Galveston had suffered a devastating hurricane that killed thousands and left the city in ruins. The existing city government proved ineffective in dealing with the aftermath of this disaster. In response, the Texas legislature approved a completely new form of municipal government—the commission system—to try and deal with the huge task of rebuilding the city. It proved successful. Galveston was rebuilt and put back on the civic track.

This success led other municipalities to follow Galveston's lead and adopt the commission form of governance. The commission system's success, however, has been limited, and only a relative handful of cities currently operate under it. Its main drawbacks are twofold. First, the merging of elected and administrative positions leads to commissioners becoming entrenched advocates of their departments. Second, winning an election and administering a large bureaucracy turn out to be very different skills. Good politicians, in other words, do not always make good department heads.

The Council-Manager System

The council-manager system attempts to separate the political and administrative functions of government. This separation is achieved by having a council make policy decisions but placing their implementation into the hands of a professional administrator, usually called a city manager, hired by the council.

The origins of this system are in the Progressive reform movement that swept through government at all levels at the turn of the nineteenth century. As discussed elsewhere in the context of state-level party politics, a century ago, political machines ran the typical large city in the United States. Places like Boston, Chicago, and New York were governed by charismatic politicians who took advantage of ties to ethnic minorities, such as the Irish or the Italians. Patronage jobs were given out to personal friends whose chief qualification was that they were campaign supporters. Elections were fraught with partisanship, which produced high incumbent reelection rates. Many machine insiders got themselves elected as city commissioners, who were given authority to run individual departments, including police, fire, or sanitation services.

Governing States and Localities

During the first half of the twentieth century, reform groups began pressuring city governments to become more professionalized and less politicized. The National Municipal League (now the National League of Cities), which focuses on small to medium-sized cities, was one such group. The U.S. Conference of Mayors, whose members head larger cities, and the ICMA were two others. In the belief that the top vote-getters in a given city may not be the best managers, the National Municipal League drafted a model charter that laid out the powers of mayors, city councils, and administrators.

Dayton, Ohio, in 1913 became the first major U.S. city to create a position for a strong manager, largely in response to suburbanization—the establishment of residential communities on the outskirts of a city—and the rise of an educated middle class. The old machine became obsolete. The idea was that a government run by a professional city manager might be less prone to corruption and partisan favoritism than those led by the classic big-city mayor. Such managers are generally more interested in implementing organizational systems than they are in glad-handing voters and trolling for campaign cash.

This reform movement by no means eliminated urban political machines or the power wielded by strong executives. For example, Richard J. Daley, mayor of Chicago from 1955–1976, continued to run the city with unequaled influence. He swayed his city council members, the national Democratic Party, and the Chicago-area delegation to the U.S. Congress. New York City mayor Rudolph Giuliani, in leading the city's response to the terrorist attacks of September 11, 2001, was far more visible than any city council member or city administrator.

Still, what did take root was the idea of the professional manager. An individual who was appointed, not elected, and who could counter the powers of commissioners or city council members with nonpartisan technical administrative expertise. In some cities, this manager is paired with a mayor. The mayor acts as more of a ceremonial figurehead and seldom blocks anything wanted by the manager or the council members. Supported by a legislative body elected by popular vote meeting about every two weeks to deal with policy issues, the manager is empowered to hire and fire all city employees, set pay scales, prepare an annual budget that is approved by elected officials and implemented by staff, and make policy recommendations.

Today, the council-manager system of city government is seen in more than 3,000 cities, or 48 percent of communities with populations of more than 2,500. (See Table 10-3.) It is most popular in medium-sized cities primarily in the South and the West. Smaller cities can't afford a full-time manager's salary. Big cities want a more partisan mayor. However, there are exceptions to the rule. Large cities that use a manager-council system include Dallas, Texas, and San Diego and San Jose, California.[15]

And the trend toward professionalization continues. A survey conducted by the ICMA showed that the percentage of county managers with advanced degrees rose from 27 percent in 1971 to 73 percent in 1995. Managers are

FIGURE 10-3 Council-Manager Form of Government

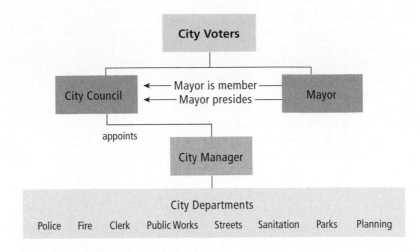

John P. Pelissero, "The Political Environment & Cities in the 21st Century," in *Cities, Politics & Public Policy: A Comparative Analysis,* ed. John P. Pelissero (Washington, DC: CQ Press, 2003), 16.

also less likely to use volunteer committees to farm out work and more likely to use a professional staff. They supervise the systems that provide detailed financial controls and reporting transparency. For example, in Phoenix, the city manager issues a monthly report that details the percentage of ambulance calls answered in less than ten minutes, the total number of nights individuals spent in homeless shelters, how many rounds of golf were played on public courses, and how many square miles of streets were swept.

Special Districts

One modern local government unit exists, for the most part, outside the consciousness of the average citizen. More than thirty thousand special districts have been created across the country—and often across borders of other units of government—to administer what usually is a single program or service. The most common are school districts, either dependent on or independent of the city or county. Next in line are sewer and water systems, which account for about one-third of special districts nationwide. These are followed by districts for such purposes as fire protection, housing, education, and sanitation.

Still other districts administer transportation, soil conservation, mosquito control, water, and even libraries. Commuters may not know it, but hundreds of thousands of them use some pretty well known special districts every day. The Port Authority of New York and New Jersey, Boston's Massachusetts Bay Transportation Authority, and the Washington Metropolitan Area Transportation Authority in the District of Columbia collectively cover hundreds of square miles and cross dozens of government borders.

Special districts sometimes are implemented as a way of heading off threats of political **annexation** of one local government by another. They also are used as a tool for community and business improvement. Freed of local tax authority, administrators of special districts often can get infrastructure items built and services provided without dipping into any one locality's funds. For example, farmers in special water districts, particularly in the West, are eligible for discounted federal loans to help them with irrigation. In addition, special districts can use private-sector business techniques in management, such as paying market rates instead of government rates to contractors.

The downside to special districts is the risk of balkanization, of reduced accountability to public trust. In 1996, the city of Alexandria, Virginia, declined a developer's proposal to convert an obsolete military installation into a shopping complex for fear of damaging its credit rating. The complex would have been run as a special district. A private townhouse community was eventually built, and the city acquired some of the former base as parkland. Indeed, some special districts have actually declared bankruptcy.[16]

Intragovernmental Politics

In the ongoing wars over suburban sprawl, traffic congestion, and uneven economic development, there are several weapons in a local government's arsenal. One of the more aggressive is the technique of annexation. A city's leaders may feel hemmed in by development along the community's borders that clashes with their own plans to expand the city's tax base. Cities like to create uniform requirements on area developers, but most developers favor unincorporated areas, where land is cheapest and there are fewer regulations.

Even so, many homebuilders count on selling to buyers who want to live within commuting distance of downtown and who want a city's services. A city government that wishes to annex a tract of land must organize

Sometimes crossing a bridge means more than just getting from one side to the other. Sometimes it means paying to leave one state to go work in another. These vehicles are steering through the Port Authority Trans-Hudson (PATH) toll plaza on the New Jersey side of the George Washington Bridge in January 2001. When fares and tolls are raised in the special district that is the Port Authority, the effects are felt far beyond the borders of New York City.

the citizens of an unincorporated area to sign a petition. Some communities seek to expand by annexing prospectively, working to incorporate a still-undeveloped parcel of land farther out from a suburban parcel already being transformed from woods or farmland to subdivisions. This, in turn, may alienate rural landowners, such as farmers, who value their traditional identity separate from that of the city.[17]

States make it tough for cities to annex new land, and the practice has long been controversial. Back in 1963, the California legislature created fifty-eight boundary watchdogs called local agency formation commissions to discourage annexations. Today, however, many Californians believe that these commissions are too weak to deal with rapid suburbanization and are unable to protect the tax base.

Plus, one community's gain from an annexation is often another's loss. In Ohio, for example, townships and counties are getting aggressive in demanding more say over annexations promoted by an alliance of developers and metropolitan areas such as Cleveland. Although thousands of annexations have taken place, all in all, the availability of annexation as a tool makes land-use planning tougher.[18]

Cities and counties often duplicate bureaucracies and paperwork, so one option available to willing parties is **city-county consolidation**. With as many as 75 percent of all major urban areas in the United States contained within single counties, it would seem logical that such mergers would be common and easy. On the contrary. According to NACo, of the nation's 3,069 county governments, only 31 have combined with cities. During the 1990s, only four of seventeen attempts were successful. Aborted efforts included Gainesville, Florida, with Alachua County; Des Moines, Iowa, with Polk County, and Spokane, Washington, with Spokane County.

The earliest consolidation dates back to 1805, when the city of New Orleans was consolidated with New Orleans Parish. The practice was especially popular in the 1960s and 1970s. State laws set the terms for a ballot initiative and determine how much of a majority is needed for approval. Turnout usually is not too high, which can make winning approval easier.

Proposals for consolidation often come in response to a state initiative or a regional challenge. For example, the citizens of Jacksonville, Florida, in Duval County, were experiencing industrial waste in their river, underachieving high schools, and clashes between city and county officials during the 1960s. Local business leaders lobbied the state legislature for help. The legislature created a study commission. The subsequent plan was approved in 1967 by the state legislature and then was passed as a referendum by voters.

Consolidation often is favored by business groups and editorial writers. These individuals seek a reorganization of government to reduce bureaucratic redundancy and to allow communities to speak "with one voice." Middle-class suburbanites are most likely to reject any plan that they believe

CITY-COUNTY CONSOLIDATION

The merging of city and county governments.

A Difference that Makes a Difference: Marrying a City with a County

January 2003 saw the birth of the Louisville-Jefferson Metro Government. The new government was the result of a long-disputed merging of Kentucky's most developed and populous entities—the city of Louisville and Jefferson County. Advocates of what would become the largest such consolidation in the United States since 1970 had finally driven home their case after three failed attempts to persuade voters going back to the 1950s.

The hope is that consolidation will allow struggling downtown Louisville to share the benefits of the job growth previously concentrated in the suburbs. Rivalry between competing bureaucracies should ease, paperwork for businesses in such areas as building codes should shrink, and regional planning to relieve traffic congestion should be streamlined.

No longer will the county, run by a judge-executive with authority over more than eighty municipalities, have veto power over tax and annexation proposals. Under the new rules, if both the county and the city have a law on the books for a certain issue, the county law prevails. If the city has a given law and the county doesn't, then the existing city law now covers both areas.

The idea seemed so promising that representatives from cities such as Fresno, California; Buffalo, New York; Milwaukee, Wisconsin; and Cedar Rapids, Iowa, came to study its implementation.[a]

For cities with expansion potential that is "inelastic," in the phrase of author and former Albuquerque mayor David Rusk, consolidation becomes a tempting alternative to annexation or boundary change. Rusk said this in his 1995 book *Cities without Suburbs* that consoli-

dation is a way to amplify economic power and project it over a greater area.

Resistance most commonly comes from suburbanites who do not feel attracted to forming a common identity with a city that in many cases is impoverished and suffering from crime and bad public schools. Perhaps suburban taxpayers are reluctant to pay for infrastructure improvements in other jurisdictions—urban sewer and water lines, for example—when many residents of rural areas and newly suburbanized neighborhoods paid for their own septic tanks and wells.

Politically, many urban minorities feel that their autonomy and influence would be diluted in a greater metropolitan entity. Those in surrounding unincorporated areas may feel left out of the political mix altogether.[b] Indeed, with the Louisville merger, the percentage of African Americans in the total population shrunk from 34 percent to 19 percent.

But there are grounds for optimism. With the area in square miles rising from 60 to 386, and the population tripling from 256,231 to 693,784, the average education levels, the median income, home price, homeownership rates, and employment rates all rose. The number of high school graduates rose from 76 percent to 82 percent, median household income rose from $28,843 to $39,457, homeownership rates rose from 52.5 percent to 64.9 percent.

[a] Alan Greenblatt, "Louisville: Anatomy of a Merger," *Governing* magazine, December 2002.

[b] *Handbook of Research on Urban Politics and Policy in the United States,* Ronald K. Vogel, ed. (Westport, Conn.: Greenwood Press, 1997), 139.

will raise their taxes to benefit downtown neighborhoods they seldom enter. Inner-city minorities fear the impact of their votes will be diluted.

Like a good marriage, the consolidation of a city and a county may depend on partners who make equal contributions. That is why a pairing is unlikely between the city of Phoenix, Arizona, which has won awards for its state-of-the-art management innovations, and surrounding Maricopa County, which has been hemorrhaging revenues and which has earned a reputation for management inefficiency.[19]

Even without the formal—sometimes drastic—steps of consolidation or annexation, governing units that span multiple jurisdictions have been created for nearly a century. The resulting movement toward regionalism has given birth in recent decades to a new form of metropolitics. Beginning in the 1930s, the federal government and various governors set up the Tennessee Valley Authority (TVA) to govern power generation and the routing of water in Appalachia. The Susquehanna and Delaware River Basin commissions were created during the 1960s for similar reasons. Other commissions in Appalachia and the Southwest were created in the 1960s to jointly administer federal antipoverty programs. Many such federal bodies were advisory in nature and had faded by the 1980s. But by then, fully 99 percent of U.S. counties had teamed up with their neighbors to form regional councils.[20]

Neither the distribution of natural resources nor exploding populations and the accompanying traffic congestion are respecters of local government borders. (See Table 10-4.) For this reason, metropolitics makes sense. People tend to congregate and to move to where the jobs are. That explains the

TABLE 10-4

Population Change for the Ten Fastest-Growing Metropolitan Areas, 1990–2000

Metropolitan area	Population		Change, 1990 to 2000	
	April 1, 1990	April 1, 2000	Number	Percent
Las Vegas, NV-AZ	852,737	1,563,282	710,545	83.3
Naples, FL	152,099	251,377	99,278	65.3
Yuma, AZ	106,895	160,026	53,131	49.1
McAllen-Edinburg-Mission, TX	383,545	569,469	185,918	48.5
Austin-San Marcos, TX	846,227	1,249,763	403,536	47.7
Fayetteville-Springdale-Rogers, AR	210,908	311,121	100,213	47.5
Boise City, ID	295,851	432,345	136,494	46.1
Phoenix-Mesa, AZ	2,238,480	3,251,876	1,013,396	45.3
Laredo, TX	133,239	193,117	59,878	44.9
Provo-Orem, UT	263,590	368,536	104,946	39.8

Source: U.S. Census Bureau, Census 2000; 1990 Census, *Population and Housing Unit Counts, United States* (1990 CPH-2-1).

boom of the **megalopolis** that grew up on the East Coast during the latter twentieth century and in the San Francisco Bay area.

Cities, their suburbs, and their neighboring cities and suburbs gradually blend together. According to the U.S. Conference of Mayors, nearly half of the fifty most populated cities in the United States were packed into just one hundred square miles of total territory at the start of the twenty-first century. These population centers account for an astonishing 85 percent of U.S. employment.[21]

Megalopolises often span across state borders. For example, one of the nation's largest starts at Philadelphia, Pennsylvania, and runs through the state of New Jersey. They even span national borders, such as Detroit, Michigan, and Windsor, Ontario, in Canada or El Paso, Texas, and Juarez, Mexico. Many jurisdictions have generated **edgeless cities**, sprawling, unplanned office and retail complexes that are not pedestrian friendly and that often become ghost towns at night when most of their residents commute home to greener residential areas.

These edgeless cities are fragmented and diverse, but interdependent nonetheless. They raise a whole host of planning challenges for city and county councils, including controversial efforts by some planners at density packing, or concentrating most development in designated corridors.[22] The rise of the edgeless city and the megalopolis is one reason for the emergence of **smart growth** movements. Advocates seek to temper development to preserve green space and use existing infrastructure more efficiently. (See Box 10-3.)

It should come as no surprise that some areas have moved to regularize their governing units to create a kind of regional land-use planning. Two well-known entities created for this purpose are the Metropolitan Services District in Portland, Oregon, and the Twin Cities Metropolitan Council in Minnesota. These have real authority and have done much to improve the urban environment and transportation systems and to spread economic development more evenly.

In the 1990s, a group of civic activists—former Albuquerque mayor David Rusk, Minnesota state representative Myron Orfield, and syndicated columnist Neal Peirce—began to champion a similar form of pan-regional metropolitan planning. The problem, Orfield writes, lies in the center cities. These "older areas, saddled with old infrastructure and housing, high taxes, social disorder, and industrial pollution, will have great difficulty competing with the heavily subsidized, socially exclusive periphery. These wasteful patterns also unnecessarily threaten groundwater, sensitive environmental habitats, and highly productive farmland."[23]

There are limits, however, to the advocates' ability to implement such a vision. Psychologically, locals still value their identity as residents of, say, Lake Oswego, Oregon, rather than greater Portland, or Edina, Minnesota, rather than the Twin Cities metropolitan area.

MEGALOPOLIS

A region made up of several municipalities that form a distinct urban area.

EDGELESS CITIES

A cluster of office and retail complexes with no clear boundaries.

SMART GROWTH

Development practices emphasizing more efficient infrastructure and less dependence on automobiles.

Local Focus: Loudoun County, Virginia: Caught between Sprawl and Smart Growth

In a county with a long geographical reach, local leaders can find themselves refereeing a citizenry whose interests diverge among those who live in towns, expanding suburbs, or preserved rural landscapes. Such is the case of Loudoun County in northern Virginia. The county is a 517-square-mile area bordered by the Blue Ridge Mountains on the west and exploding high-tech development surrounding Dulles International Airport to the east. In fact, it was *the* fastest growing county in the entire country in terms of population by.the early twenty-first century.

With quaint towns and "gentleman farmer" horse farms that date back to the eighteenth century, Loudoun has been torn by an ongoing cycle of zoning and land-use disputes since the early 1980s. Nearly every election for its board of supervisors hinges on the desirability of "smart growth" efforts to control encroaching suburban tracts and strip malls steadily pushed by developers eager to exploit Loudoun's commuting proximity to the nation's capital.

It was the arrival of world-class employers such as America Online and MCI that brought new demands to the county for housing, roads, and schools. So, in 1989, county officials drew up a 250-page 20-year growth vision with development guidelines that won the American Planning Association's "outstanding planning" award. It projected the likely impact of population growth, particularly school-age population, on demand for services, tax rates, and debt burden, as well as probable changes to infrastructure, water and air quality, and transportation needs. By the late 1990s, Loudoun was among the fastest-growing counties in the nation. Its population doubled in ten years and its economy expanded at a meaty 32 percent a year.

In 1999, however, angry voters turned out a board of supervisors perceived as being too much in the pocket of developers who many felt were making a killing at the expense of Loudoun's historically serene ambience. The incoming board vowed to make Loudoun a "land-use planning showcase." It would do this by using its powers to zone areas between towns that are beyond the control of small towns within Loudoun such as Purcellville, Middleburg, and Leesburg. This, the board stated, would help preserve the countywide vision voters wanted.

The smart-growth advocates had the backing of environmentalists and the "old money" landowners who wished to protect their idyllic heritage from the onslaught of traffic and cul-de-sacs lined with mini-mansions. Development would be restricted to compact, high-density areas. This encourages use of existing roads and sewer lines rather than digging expensive new ones. Sprawl can bankrupt a county government, they argued. For every $1 in tax revenues a new home brings in, the county shells out $1.55 in roads, sewers, and other services. This included the twenty-three new schools (at cost of $600 million) that Loudoun had had to plan for in recent years.[a]

But smart-growth restrictions on new subdivisions threaten to gore the oxes of developers, realtors, middle-class prospective homeowners, and longtime working farmers now ready to cash in on their land and retire. Their representatives warn against density packing, which they see as shifting all of the growth to eastern middle-class suburbs so that the gentry in the west can enjoy their horse country undisturbed.

"We're entitled to green space in the east as well," said one supervisor, adding that property owners have the right to sell their land for development.

In November 2003, the pro-growth Republican candidates from the eastern side of the county swept onto the board of supervisors. In January 2004, in a series of nineteen votes, six Republicans overrode the minority of two Democrats and one independent and voted to bring water and sewer services for planned home construction to a large chunk of central Loudoun. They set the stage for a new highway. They streamlined the business permit approval process and terminated public funding for a land preservation program that pays landowners who agree not to develop their property.

Finally, they promised to reduce government paperwork. The problem is "not the developers," said supervisor Stephen J. Snow. "It's the insidious growth of government."[b]

[a] Christopher Swope, "Sprawl: Rendezvous with Destiny," *Governing* magazine, March 2001, 32.

[b] Michael Laris and Maria Glod, "Loudoun GOP Eases Growth Restraints," *Washington Post,* January 6, 2004.

Participation in Local Government

What distinguishes local elections from state and national ones is that more than two-thirds are nonpartisan. Since the decline of the big-city political machines of the early twentieth century, candidates for county boards and city councils run on their personal competence for the most part rather than ideology or past affiliation. Only 17 percent of city councils hold partisan elections, according to the ICMA. Yet in some cities, partisan labels that have been officially abolished continue to play a role unofficially. This occurred in Chicago. Officially abolished since the 1930s, partisan labels have remained in play as Democrats continue to dominate the heavily African American city.

Council members usually run in **ward elections,** or **district elections.** The populations of such districts can reach as high as 246,000, as in Los Angeles, or 165,000, as in Phoenix. The advantage of such elections is that they assure each neighborhood of having a local on the city council who knows their streets and residents by name. This is especially important for minorities who may be grouped together by housing patterns.

Other jurisdictions permit candidates to run in **at-large elections.** This means that they can hail from any part of the jurisdiction. The advantage of having candidates run at-large, and the reason most cities opt for it, is that it makes room for a greater pool of highly qualified and talented people who, presumably, look at the interests of the city as a whole. Some city charters require a combination of ward representatives and at-large members. But it can get controversial. In 1991 in Dallas, court-ordered redistricting required a switch from an at-large system to fourteen members chosen by districts. The result was that more Hispanics and blacks won seats.

The townships of New England are famous for their town meetings. Usually held twice a year when the elected council or clerk issues a warrant, or agenda, these gatherings epitomize direct democracy in action. Citizens can do everything from pass a budget to resolve to oppose a developer's plan for a new golf course. Some townships have elected officials or town managers to tackle the everyday tasks. In a variation called the representative town meeting, citizens elect meeting members who then assemble to address community issues.

Turnout in local elections is often half of the national average of 55 percent voter turnout in a presidential election. This reflects a general indifference among many citizens toward the prosaic affairs of local government. Neighborhood volunteer and community development organizations, although often run by articulate and dedicated activists, often involve as little as 3 percent to 12 percent of the local population, according to one study done in Cincinnati in the 1980s.[24]

Yet the absence of popular fervor in local issues does not mean that local offices cannot serve as proving grounds for up-and-coming politicians. New immigrants, particularly Asians and Latinos, increasingly are working their

WARD, OR DISTRICT, ELECTIONS
Elections in which voters in a municipal ward vote for a candidate to represent them on a council or commission.

AT-LARGE ELECTIONS
Elections in which city or county voters vote for council or commission members.

When Kwame M. Kilpatrick was elected mayor of Detroit in 2002 at the age of thirty-one, he was the city's youngest mayor ever and the youngest big-city mayor in United States. Surrounded here by (from left to right) WJLB radio's MC Serch, Phat Farm's Russell Simmons, Dr. Benjamin Chavis, president and CEO of the Hip-Hop Summit Action Network, and RUN DMC's Rev. Run at the April 2003 Hip-Hop Summit, Kilpatrick is a strong mayor who has worked hard to embrace his city's youth culture.

way into public office. By the end of the twentieth century, a third of all cities with over two hundred thousand residents had elected either a Hispanic or black mayor.[25] The number of Hispanic or Latino officials, according to the 2003 *Directory of Latino Elected Officials,* is 438 among county officials, 1,522 among municipal officials, 1,694 among school board members, and 168 among special district officials.

The increase in black local officials over the final third of the twentieth century was dramatic. According to the Washington-based Joint Center for Political and Economic Studies, from 1970 to 2001, the number of black mayors rose from 48 to 454, the number of black city council members rose from 552 to 3,538, and the number of black county commissioners rose from 64 to 820.

Women also have made great gains, although far from their proportion as half the total population. According to the Center for American Women and Politics in Washington, D.C., as of June 2003, there were fourteen female mayors among the largest one hundred U.S. cities. One is African American, Shirley Franklin of Atlanta, Georgia; and one is Latino, Heather Fargo of Sacramento, California.

Historically, minority groups have tended to cast their ballots with Democratic candidates, who also drew Catholics and the liberal intelligentsia. Republicans tended to draw votes from WASPs, or white Anglo-Saxon Protestants; big business; and law-and-order enthusiasts. This is changing, however. In New York City in 2001, billionaire Michael Bloomberg, who had switched from the Democratic Party to the Republican Party, spent millions of dollars of his own money in an upset victory over Democratic public advocate Mark Green. Part of his success was that he was able to attract Hispanic voters.[26]

The payoff for winning local office is more likely to come in the form of visibility and personal satisfaction than in cold hard cash. Mayors, many of whom are part-time, earn an average $8,400. By contrast, the full-time mayor of Chicago earns $175,000. City and county managers make a median of $67,598, according to 1998 figures from the ICMA. The average salary of a council member in large council-manager jurisdictions is $23,335, but in large mayor-council cities, the average rises to $39,061, according to the National League of Cities.

The weekly average workload for council members in small, medium, and large cities is twenty, twenty-five, and forty-two hours, respectively. The typical number of hours they spend doing services for constituents rose to 35 percent of their time in 2001. In larger cities with mayor-council systems, more than 90 percent of elected officials have staffs at their disposal, compared with only half in smaller cities, says the National League of Cities.

Not surprisingly, 66 percent of city council members in the National League of Cities survey said they wanted a raise. Many citizens oppose large salaries for their local officials, particularly at the school board level, because they feel the nominal fees they receive are not an hourly wage, but a stipend that honors public spiritedness.

The Road Ahead

The forms and functions of local governments have evolved through myriad permutations, nearly all of them designed to produce leaders and practices that maximize both efficiency and responsiveness to voters. Yet few local governments can go it alone. When the National League of Cities did its 2002–2003 survey of city finance officers, cities both large and small were suffering the effects of a nationwide recession. It was their worst cash crunch in a decade. As a result, the responses were packed with pleas for help from the state and federal governments.

State aid was estimated to have declined by 2.1 percent. The George W. Bush administration had announced that increases in federal aid would not be forthcoming. Forty percent of city officials cited a negative impact from the recession on the quality of life in their areas. Given that when times get tough, demands for social spending intensify, this was particularly relevant.

Weighing in during the aftermath of the terrorist attacks of September 11, 2001, most officials agreed that their revenue gaps were created primarily by demands for new spending for public safety. With the added responsibilities of homeland security—Los Angeles alone was spending an extra $2 million a week by 2004—many cities have been forced to lay off employees, raise user fees, cut capital spending, and cut services. However, the budget items cited as most responsible for depleting revenues were city workers' health benefits (cited by 63 percent), costs of workers' pensions

Policy in Practice: The Feds Giveth, the Feds Taketh Away

In this era of color-coded terrorism warnings, local officials look to Washington for guidance as well as resources for protecting the homeland against terrorist threats. Many of the nation's mayors, therefore, found it odd when they learned that the George W. Bush administration's fiscal 2005 budget proposal requested cuts in the federal funds that had been flowing toward states and localities in the aftermath of the September 11, 2001, attacks.

In 2004, Washington's earmarked funds for helping local first responders, such as police and firefighters, with preventative approaches to combating terrorism totaled $4.1 billion. In an era of rising federal budget deficits, however, the proposal for fiscal 2005 was less than $3.5 billion

The funding that communities are getting currently is neither adequate nor direct, and many of the dollars get "stuck" at the state level, complained Baltimore mayor Martin O'Malley to the annual meeting of the U.S. Conference of Mayors in June 2004. "They're sending our first-responder money to second-responders," while too much of the money is backlogged.[a]

Officials in the federal Department of Homeland Security acknowledged delays in the delivery of federal dollars. But Josh Filler, senior director of the department's Office of State and Local Government Coordination, said that as much as $8 billion unspent from previous years' appropriations could bring the 2005 total to approximately $11.5 billion for local antiterrorism measures. The problem, he added, is that localities have legislative and procurement processes that sacrifice speed for caution in an effort to avoid waste and fraud.

Solutions being bandied about include streamlining state and local procurement procedures and introducing multistate cooperative purchasing. But no bureaucratic reforms are likely to alter the expectations of many mayors and county officials that their own communities deserve federal help with the all-important task of protecting the citizenry.

"There's not enough money for everyone, and, more importantly, it's not the wisest way to spend money," said Homeland Security's Filler. "Not everyone needs a SWAT team."[b]

---

[a] Ellen Perlman, "Mayors Slam Feds' Security Funding Plans," *Governing* magazine. www.governing.com/articles/6mayors.htm (accessed June 29, 2004).

[b] Ibid.

(30 percent), reduction of state aid (29 percent), the local economy (25 percent), and infrastructure (25 percent).

Some city officials have been drawing down their reserves, or rainy day funds. Understandably, such an approach causes them to worry about the impact on their bond ratings, which are a sign of a city's fiscal health. Anticipating bad times in the future, these officials have been pleading with their state governments to allow them to collect revenue from users of city services, in the form of a commuter or retail sales tax, for example, or to collect payments from nonprofit and government organizations currently exempt from property taxes.

So much for the superiority of government closest to the people. Still, the current vibrancy and long-term durability of governments at the town, city, county, and special-district levels continue to be seen in the variety of ways each responds to circumstances of geography, economics, and political culture. And there is no shortage of candidates willing to pay the price in time, sweat, and sacrificed income that it takes to make a go of it in the modern world of local elected office. These small-scale leaders continue to debate and organize to provide valued services using a process consistent with a loftier vision of democracy. It is a practice that still meshes with de Tocqueville's notion of "inhabitants with the same interests" from whose collective can be drawn "all the elements of a good administration."

Conclusion

De Tocqueville viewed local governments in the United States as sort of mini republics. He saw them as civic entities in which citizens were closest to government and government reflected accurately what citizens desired. In many ways, that perspective is still valid. Local governments wield real power, and they are responsible for important programs and services. They come in a bewildering variety of types, many of which reflect state or regional history, culture, and preferences. As a whole, all of these differences can seem confusing. Yet in any single place—your hometown, the local county—the government and what it does or does not do probably seems perfectly reasonable and natural. That's a testament to de Tocqueville's perceptiveness.

Local government certainly remains the most common form of government in the United States, and it is still the form of government the average citizen is most likely to come into contact with on a day-to-day basis. Counties, municipalities, and special districts build and maintain roads, police those roads, run schools, manage libraries, and provide other programs and services too numerous to list. And they do all of this while employing very different approaches to government. Some are run by powerful executives, others by more egalitarian councils or commissions. Still others are mostly run by professional managers.

Yet local government is far from ideal. These mini republics are constrained by Dillon's Rule. They tend to have relatively low voter turnout for elections. The idiosyncrasies of local government structure can mean electing someone with no real administrative experience to run a complicated bureaucracy with a multimillion-dollar budget. Local governments face significant challenges that range from the urban dysfunction brought on by sprawl to finding the money to hold up their end of the war on terror. Just because the politics are local does not mean they are less difficult.

Key Concepts

annexation (p. 351)

at-large elections (p. 357)

boards of commissioners
  (p. 344)

charter (p. 338)

city council (p. 344)

city manager (p. 339)

city-county consolidation
  (p. 352)

city manager system (p. 345)

commission system (p. 345)

counties (p. 334)

Dillon's Rule (p. 337)

edgeless cities (p. 355)

general act charters (p. 339)

home rule (p. 338)

living wage laws (p. 338)

mayor (p. 339)

mayor-council system (p. 345)

megalopolis (p. 355)

municipalities (p. 334)

smart growth (p. 355)

special act charters (p. 339)

special districts (p. 334)

strong mayor (p. 346)

unincorporated territory
  (p. 341)

wards (p. 347)

ward, or district, elections
  (p. 357)

weak mayor (p. 346)

Suggested Readings

Garvin, Alexander. *The American City: What Works, What Doesn't,* 2nd ed. New York: McGraw-Hill, 2002. A comprehensive reference to urban planning and design in the United States that analyzes key projects initiated in 250 urban areas.

Kemp, Roger L., ed. *Model Government Charters: A City, County, Regional, State, and Federal Handbook.* Jefferson, N.C.: McFarland, 2003. Each chapter covers a different level of government and the sample charters provided describe the laws that form the basis of government.

Orfield, Myron. *Metropolitics: A Regional Agenda for Community and Stability.* Washington, D.C.: Brookings Institution, 1997. Using the example of the Twin Cities, the author presents a system of regional government meant to improve schools, create affordable housing, and protect the environment and quality of life.

Pelissero, John P., ed. *Cities, Politics, and Policy: A Comparative Analysis.* Washington, D.C.: CQ Press, 2003. Through case studies and cross-sectional analyses of a variety of urban areas, this text shows how scholars find patterns and draw conclusions that offer insights beneficial to all communities.

Vogel, Ronald K., ed. *Handbook of Research on Urban Politics and Policy in the United States.* Westport, Conn.: Greenwood Press, 1997. This reference work provides access to research on urban politics and policy in the United States.

Suggested Web Sites

www.brookings.edu. Web site of the Brookings Institution, one of Washington, D.C.'s oldest think thanks, which pursues independent, nonpartisan research in such areas as metropolitan policy and governance.

www2.icma.org/main/sc.asp. Web site of the International City/County Management Association, whose mission is to create excellence in local government by developing and fostering professional local government management worldwide.

www.naco.org. Created in 1935, the National Association of Counties is the only national organization that represents county governments in the United States.

www.natat.org. The National Association of Towns and Townships seeks to strengthen the effectiveness of town and township governments by exploring flexible and alternative approaches to federal policies to ensure that smaller communities can meet federal requirements.

www.nlc.org. Web site of the National League of Cities, the oldest and largest national organization representing municipal governments in the United States.

www.usmayors.org. The web site of the U.S. Conference of Mayors, which is the official nonpartisan organization of the nation's 1183 U.S. cities with populations of 30,000 or more.

www.census.gov. Web site of the U.S. Census Bureau, which is responsible for collecting and tabulating data on the population and demographics of the United States.

CHAPTER 11

Finance

Filling the Till and Paying the Bills

Will that be cash or charge? Either way, these shoppers at the Mall of America in Bloomington, Minnesota, got a break from sales tax on their clothing purchases. Minnesota is one of numerous states that consider clothing an essential item and, therefore, waive any sales taxes. Other states, such as New Hampshire, have no sales tax at all, which makes their malls and shopping outlets very popular with shoppers from neighboring states.

What are the differences between progressive and regressive tax systems?

Why are many state and local politicians against Internet sales?

Why are property taxes so important to communities?

Tennessee is a state that prides itself on its low taxes. According to the Washington, D.C.-based Tax Foundation, residents of the Volunteer State pay 8.4 percent of their incomes in state and local taxes—the second lowest tax rate in the country.[1]

REVENUES

The money governments bring in, mainly from taxes.

TAX BURDEN

A measurement of taxes paid.

INCOME TAX

A tax on income.

SALES TAX

A tax levied by state and local governments on purchases.

BUDGET SHORTFALL

When the money coming into the government falls below the money being spent.

Only Alaska, which derives nearly 40 percent of its general **revenues** from taxes on the huge Prudhoe Bay oil field, has a lower **tax burden**. Tennessee is also one of only nine states with no **income tax**. Instead, Tennessee has long relied on a **sales tax** to generate most of the state's revenues. Back when the state sales tax rate hovered at 6 percent, that seemed like a good bargain to most Tennesseans. That was before Tennessee decided in 2002 to increase its sales tax from 6 percent to 9.75 percent in many parts of the state.

During the long economic boom of the 1990s, a decade in which Americans shopped like never before, Tennessee's sales tax more or less sufficed. But when the economy slid into recession in the spring of 2001, sales tax revenues dried up. By the summer of 2001, Tennessee found itself with an $880 million **budget shortfall**.

For the federal government, a budget shortfall is an embarrassment, not a crisis. Congress and the president usually agree to cover the shortfall by borrowing money, that is, by selling U.S. Treasury bonds. The situation at the state level is very different. Like virtually every state, Tennessee is required by law to balance its operating budget every year. As a result, its shortfall presented Tennessee legislators and Governor Don Sundquist with some very difficult choices. Policymakers could either slash programs or raise taxes or do some combination of both.

Governor Sundquist, a Republican, had been elected governor in 1994 and then again in 1998 due in large part to his opposition to a state income tax. After winning reelection, however, Sundquist changed his position and proposed replacing the state's 6 percent sales tax with a 3.75 percent sales tax and a 3.75 percent income tax.

Sundquist's proposal would have made Tennessee's tax system more **progressive**. Low-income Tennesseans would have gained more from the sales tax reduction than they would have lost from the new income tax. High-income residents would have their taxes increased. Of course, the new income tax also would have raised considerably more money for the state overall, decreasing the state's tax burden.

At first, the legislature resisted this proposal. By the afternoon of July 12, 2001, however, a majority of the state legislature was on the verge of accepting the governor's position. That is when Marsha Blackburn, a Republican state senator from Nashville, got on the phone. Blackburn, a vehement opponent of a state income tax, called two of Nashville's most popular—and most conservative—radio talk show hosts to sound the tax alarm.

Within forty minutes, more than two hundred protesters had entered the capitol building. Chants of "No new taxes"—and other, more explicit, phrases—soon filled the building and disrupted the debate. Soon an estimated two thousand protesters had converged on the building. State police locked them out, which made the crowd even angrier. As protestors pounded on the doors, someone hurled a rock through the window of the governor's office. Not surprisingly, the legislature decided to hold off on Governor Sundquist's income tax proposal.[2]

Tennessee's **tax revolt** was unusual, but strong feelings about taxes are not. Few things arouse stronger feelings among voters than taxes. Personal income taxes and property taxes are among the most visible and the most controversial. Yet many people have only a vague understanding of how state and local governments raise money.

That is because the taxes that state and local governments impose are less visible than, say, the federal income tax, which claims a large portion of most people's paychecks every two weeks. The largest source of money for state and local governments comes from a much less visible tax—the sales tax.[3] State and local governments also raise substantial sums from user fees and charges for tuition, sewage and water treatment, utilities, highway tolls, and various **user fees**. While a $19 resident fishing license may not sound like much, fees of that sort do add up.

In 1998, residents of the United States paid approximately $3.4 trillion in taxes and user fees—about $13,800 per person.[4] Just under half of this amount—$1.46 trillion—was raised by state and local taxes and user fees. State and local governments use these funds and a substantial influx of funds from the federal government to finance local schools and state universities, provide health insurance to very low-income families and people with disabilities, and build highways and mass transit. The money also helps maintain correctional facilities that house approximately 1.7 million people a year and provides police and fire protection to the remaining 260-odd million of the population. In short, state and local taxes pay for the programs that Americans care most about and most directly affect their daily lives.[5]

There's a tendency to think of taxes and budgets as dry, technical, and, yes, boring. That is a pretty good description of much of the literature on this subject, but a very mistaken view of the subject itself. Actually, budgets are the subject of

PROGRESSIVE TAX SYSTEM
System in which the tax rate paid reflects the ability to pay.

TAX REVOLT
A reaction to high taxes that often results in ballot initiatives to cap tax growth.

USER FEES
Charges levied by governments in exchange for services; a type of hidden tax.

> Budgets are fundamentally about policy. In many ways, they are the central policy documents of government. They determine and reflect much of the policy orientations of elected leaders. If you want to know what your state or local government's priorities are, its budget will tell you.

some of the most intense political struggles in state and local politics. It is not simply that people care about money, although they certainly do. Budgets are fundamentally about policy. In many ways, they are the central policy documents of government. They determine and reflect much of the policy orientations of elected leaders. If you want to know what your state or local government's priorities are, its budget will tell you.

This chapter discusses how state and local governments raise money, how they decide to spend it via the **budget process**, and what they spend it on. It examines why state and local governments make such different taxing and spending choices and explores the consequences of these very different choices. The chapter concludes with a discussion of how the growth of the **service economy** and the rise of Internet shopping are forcing many state and local governments to rethink how they pay for public services.

Show Me the Money: Where State Revenues Come From

Roughly half of the money that state and local governments took in in 1998, that is, about $773 million, came from six primary taxes. These were sales taxes, including **excise** taxes, often referred to as **sin taxes**, on tobacco and alcohol; property taxes; income taxes, motor vehicle taxes, **estate taxes**, also called death taxes; and **gift taxes**.

Sales Taxes

In 1998, state and local governments took in $274 million from sales taxes—about 35 percent of total state and local government tax revenues. About 80 percent of the money raised by sales taxes goes to state governments. However, most states allow at least some counties and cities to levy additional sales taxes. Currently, about 7,500 localities do. Some states, such as California, return a small percentage of sales taxes to the areas in which the purchases were made. Overall, sales tax revenues account for nearly 16 percent of local government revenues nationwide.[6]

State governments, and, to a much lesser extent, local governments, also take in significant sums from gasoline taxes and sin taxes on tobacco and alcohol. Different states interpret this type of tax very differently. Often, other factors influence what gets taxed and for how much. North Carolina has a large tobacco-growing industry and a small tax of only five cents on each pack of cigarettes. New York State has no large-scale tobacco industry and levies a tax of $1.50 per pack of cigarettes sold.

Politicians like sales taxes because they tend to be less visible than an income tax. As such, they are less likely to cause voters to retaliate against them at the polls. Economists like sales taxes because they are **focused consumption taxes** that do not distort consumer behavior. That is, sales taxes, even relatively high ones, often do not cause consumers to buy less.

This does not mean that they do not receive their share of criticism. Many liberals and advocates for low-income people complain that sales taxes are **regressive**, or flat. Everyone pays the same tax rate, regardless of income. If Bill Gates buys a grande latte on his way to work, he pays about twenty-eight cents in sales taxes. Freshmen at the University of Washington pay exactly the same.

The tax is the same but the students are paying a much higher percentage of their incomes to the government than Mr. Gates is. Put another way, if Bill Gates's income were even a mere $5 million a year, and a typical student's income is $2,500 a year, guess how much Bill Gates would have to pay in sales taxes to face the same tax burden as a typical student? Give up? His grande latte would have to cost him a whopping—but tax-proportionate—$566.20. Of course, as already noted, it doesn't really work that way. If and when Bill Gates goes to Starbucks, he pays the same price—and the same sales tax—as anyone else.

Often, states do attempt to make their sales tax less of a burden on low-income residents by exempting necessities such as food, clothing, and electric and gas utilities from taxation. In general, however, states that rely heavily on a sales tax tend to have more regressive tax systems than other states.

Take Tennessee again. Rich and poor alike paid a 7 percent sales tax at the cash register in 1998. However, Memphis residents earning $25,000 a year or less paid an average of 6.3 percent of their incomes in state and local taxes. That is about $1,575. In contrast, those residents earning $150,000 or more a year paid only 5.2 percent, or $9,450, of their incomes in taxes.

So, whereas it *looks* like the $150,000 wage earners paid more, the low-income residents paid a higher percentage of their incomes in taxes than they might have if they lived in a state that relied more on income taxes. That made Tennessee's tax system highly regressive—and this was before the state decided in 2002 to raise its sales tax even further.[7]

Sales taxes have another problem—they simply aren't bringing in as much revenue as they used to. In the words of James Hine, a finance expert at Clemson University, relying on the sales tax "is like riding a horse that is rapidly dying."

What that basically means is that the sales tax base is slowly eroding. Two factors seem to account for this. First, services have become a much more important part of the economy. In 1960, 41 percent of U.S. consumer dollars were spent on services. By 2000, that percentage had risen to 58 percent. Yet most sales taxes are skewed toward the purchase of products rather than the purchase of services. Buy a robotic massage chair at the Mall of America in Bloomington, Minnesota, and you'll pay $97.49 in sales

FOCUSED CONSUMPTION TAXES
Taxes that do not alter spending habits or behavior patterns and therefore do not distort the distribution of resources.

REGRESSIVE TAXES
Taxes that are the same rate for all taxpayers, regardless of income or ability to pay.

> [G]uess how much Bill Gates would have to pay in sales taxes to face the same tax burden as a typical student. Give up? His grande latte would have to cost him a whopping—but tax-proportionate—$566.20.

tax on that $800 item. Hire an acupuncturist for an hour from a holistic medical center in Bloomington, and you'll pay no sales tax.

Hawaii, New Mexico, and South Dakota have changed their tax codes so that sales taxes now cover most professional and personal services. However, most states have been reluctant to follow suit. Taxing services could put them at a competitive disadvantage. For instance, if Illinois starts to tax accounting services, there probably would be a sudden boom in business for CPAs in nearby Indiana.[8]

The second factor behind faltering sales tax revenues is the rise of the Internet and on-line shopping. In 1992, the U.S. Supreme Court ruled that states could not force companies to collect sales taxes for them in places where the companies had no physical presence. As a result, most on-line purchases are tax-free. A study by William F. Fox and Donald Bruce of the University of Tennessee, Knoxville put the overall losses of sales tax revenue from Internet sales at $13.3 billion in 2001 and predicted losses of $35.2 billion a year by 2006.[9]

For states such as Texas and Tennessee that don't have income taxes and rely heavily on sales tax revenue, this trend is a big problem. To make up for the kind of revenue loss that Fox and Bruce predict, Texas would have to raise its current statewide sales tax rate from 6.25 percent to 7.86 percent.[10]

Not surprisingly, states have made changing the federal government's mind on this issue a major priority. They have argued that giving on-line retailers a pass on sales taxes gives them an unfair competitive advantage over **bricks-and-mortar retailers** who are forced to add sales tax charges to customer purchases. So far, however, Congress has rejected such arguments. The main reason cited is the difficulty on-line retailers would have trying to comply with very different state sales tax codes. In 2001, Congress extended the moratorium on on-line taxation until 2003. As of August 2004, Congress was debating legislation that would make the ban permanent, despite heated opposition from many of the nation's governors.

TABLE 11-1

The Five States Most Reliant on Sales Tax for Revenue

State	Percentage of Total Collection
Washington	63.6
Florida	59.0
Tennessee	57.3
Nevada	53.5
South Dakota	52.7
State Average	32.1

Source: "The Government Performance Project: The Way We Tax," *Governing* magazine, February 2003, 26.

BRICKS-AND-MORTAR RETAILERS

Traditional retail stores, such as Wal-Mart, as opposed to on-line stores, such as Amazon.com.

Property Taxes

The second largest source of tax revenue for state and local governments comes from property taxes. In 1998, property taxes raised approximately 30 percent, or $230 million, of total state and local government tax revenues. Most sales tax revenues go to state governments, but almost all property taxes go to local governments. As a result, property taxes are by far the most important source of revenue for local government. Approximately 71 percent of local government revenues and only a tiny fraction—1 percent—of state tax revenues come from property taxes.

Just about every local government relies on property tax revenues, but property tax rates vary widely from community to community. Most Americans who own homes or condominiums face an effective tax rate of about 1.55 percent. The word "effective" simply acknowledges that some places have exemptions and adjustments that make the effective tax rate lower than the nominal tax rate. You can figure out the nominal tax rate by dividing the amount of tax paid by the amount of taxable income. The effective tax rate is found by dividing the amount of tax paid by the amount of total economic income.

In other words, if you own a condo worth $100,000, you probably pay about $1,550 a year in property taxes. In Manchester, New Hampshire, however, you'd pay $3,340 in property taxes on that same condo. That's because New Hampshire has an effective tax rate of 3.34, which is one of the highest in the country. Why are New Hampshire's property tax rates so high? Largely because the state has no income tax and no sales tax. That limits the state government's ability to raise funds. It also means that the state does not offer its towns the levels of financial support that most state governments do. As a result, while most local governments receive 24 percent of their total revenues from property taxes, local governments in New Hampshire are forced to rely on property taxes for 68 percent of their total revenues.[11]

The Education Connection. Property taxes are important for another reason. They pretty much finance elementary and high school education. On average, school districts receive about 40 percent of their funding from local governments. In most states, where you live determines how many education dollars your children receive.

Wealthy communities with high housing values raise the most money from property taxes. School districts in these areas tend to have the most educational resources. Conversely, school districts in the poorest areas have the fewest resources. For instance, in Illinois during the 1999–2000 school year, the most prosperous school districts spent about $2,060 more per student than the least prosperous school districts. That equals out to $7,460 per student versus $5,400 a student.

In recent years, this funding gap has begun to narrow. State governments have taken larger roles in financing public education in response to a string of lawsuits that has challenged the constitutionality of financing arrangements that provide the poorest children with the fewest resources. (See Box 11-3.) Nationwide, school districts with the highest levels of poverty spent $966 less per student during the 1999–2000 school year than school districts in areas with the lowest levels of poverty.[12]

Hawaii's state government has taken over financing local schools completely. Many view such a system as more equitable than a traditional, property tax–supported system. However, efforts to equalize school finances also can have unintended consequences, as the state of California discovered. (See Box 11-1.)

Policy in Practice: California's Misguided Effort to Equalize School Funding

Policymakers often look at different types of taxes and see interchangeable ways to raise revenue. Sometimes, however, the way policymakers decide to fund a program can have a dramatic impact on how the program itself works—or whether it works at all.

One example of a well-intentioned reform gone awry is California's effort to provide equal educational funding for all students in grades kindergarten to twelfth grade. In 1970, the California Supreme Court ruled in *Serrano v. Priest* that the state's existing education financing scheme was unconstitutional.

The system relied on local property taxes to support local schools. There was only one problem. Relying on property taxes meant that children in "property rich" communities often attended lavishly financed schools while children in "property poor" communities had to make do with facilities and instruction that were often completely inadequate.

In 1977, after years of such litigation, the California legislature responded. It voted to funnel money from the state's large budget surplus to local schools. However, the legislation didn't stop there. The state also required communities that wanted to boost school spending by raising local property taxes to share the additional funds they brought in with other school districts.

In hindsight, this "district power equalization" was ill conceived. Californians no longer had any incentive to raise local property taxes to pay for education. In fact, any incentive was to do just the opposite. Under the new system, each district received a base level of support regardless of its local tax revenue and tax rate. As a result, every district had an incentive to set its local property tax rate as low as possible. In other words, instead of raising education spending to a new, higher level for most students, equalization may have actually lowered the average amount spent on education.

By breaking the link between local property taxes and local school spending, some economists believe that the 1970 *Serrano* decision laid the groundwork for Proposition 13, which capped property taxes and banned reassessment of a house's value so long as the owner stayed in it. The result was less money for everyone.

According to Harvard economist Caroline Hoxby, "It appears that some students from poor households would actually have better funded schools if their states had not attempted such complete equalization."

New Mexico, South Dakota, and Utah—other states that have tried to equalize school funding by confiscating "extra" revenues raised by local school districts—also have ended up driving school funding *down* rather than up.*

* See Caroline Hoxby's paper, "All School Finance Equalizations Are Not Created Equal," forthcoming in *Quarterly Journal of Economics,* at http://post.economics.harvard.edu/faculty/hoxby/papers.html, and William Fischel's "How Judges Are Making Public Schools Worse," *City Journal,* Summer 1998.

The Pros and Cons of Property Taxes. Property taxes generally are paid twice a year as a large lump fee. As such, they tend to be highly visible and extremely unpopular with the public. However, local officials like them because property tax receipts are less volatile and more predictable than other types of taxes. Local revenue departments assess the value of houses and businesses and then send their owners a bill, so they know exactly how much revenue a property tax will yield.

In most instances, taxes seem worse when the economy is bad. Property taxes are the exception. They tend to rise most sharply when a town or city is experiencing an economic boom and housing prices are soaring. In these circumstances, an upsurge in property values can lead to a backlash.

The most famous of such backlashes occurred in California in 1978. In response to years of rising property values and related taxes, Californians passed Proposition 13. This piece of legislation capped the property tax rate at 1 percent of a property's purchase price and froze property assessments at their 1978 levels until the property is resold. Newcomers have to pay property taxes based on the actual value of the house.

To this day, Proposition 13 is hotly debated. Conservatives have long praised the movement that gave rise to it. They say that it was the harbinger of the conservative politics that former California governor Ronald Reagan would bring to Washington three years later. Most experts, however, believe that its effects have been devastating. These individuals point to Proposition 13 as the sole reason California transformed from one of the most generous contributors to public education to one of the least generous.

Eunice McTyre, one of the original activist proponents of Proposition 13, poses in front of her Los Angeles–area home with her property tax bill in February 2003. For individuals on fixed incomes, many of them elderly, Proposition 13 has been a tremendous financial boon. For parents, the legislation has been a disaster. Most communities use property taxes to pay for their public schools. Property taxes capped at rates well below the value of the property means millions of dollars less for education.

Even the most liberal electorates can be goaded into atypical action by rising property tax rates. In 1980, Massachusetts voters passed Proposition 2½. Property tax increases were capped to, you guessed it, 2½ percent. As a result, towns that want to increase spending by more than that, for such needs as increased funding for education, have to hold special override sessions. Towns also have come to rely on user fees, a phenomenon examined later in this chapter.

Many state and local governments have attempted to ease the burden of property taxes on senior citizens and, in some cases, on other low-income individuals. In about fifty Massachusetts towns, senior citizens can reduce their property taxes by performing volunteer work. Cook County, Illinois, limits property tax rate increases by tying them to the national rate of inflation.[13]

> Most economists believe that landlords pass the cost of property tax increases to renters in the form of rent increases.

Despite these efforts, tensions between retirees living on a fixed income and parents eager to spend more on local schools are commonplace. These pressures can be particularly acute in areas with large numbers of retirees living on fixed incomes. Indeed, some "active-adult retirement communities" in Florida ban young children altogether.[14]

It's worth noting another hidden cost of property taxes. You might think that commercial and residential property owners are the only ones who pay, right? You're off the hook if you rent, right? Wrong! Most economists believe that landlords pass the cost of property tax increases to renters in the form of rent increases.

Income Taxes

Personal income taxes account for 23 percent of all state and local tax revenues.[15] That makes income tax revenue the third most significant source of state and local government income. In some ways, however, this figure conceals more than it reveals. Almost all income tax revenues go to state governments.[16] Indeed, thanks to the rapid income growth of the 1990s, income tax revenues actually have edged out sales tax receipts to become the largest single source of state revenues.[17]

Of course, this is not true for every state. As previously stated, nine states make do without income taxes. Alaska, Florida, Nevada, South Dakota, Texas, Washington, and Wyoming impose no income taxes at all. New Hampshire and Tennessee impose taxes only on certain types of income.

As mentioned earlier, states that do not have an income tax usually rely heavily on the sales tax. But Alaska, Delaware, Montana, New Hampshire, and Oregon have no sales tax. Oregon has managed this by—you guessed it—relying heavily on a state income tax. In fact, Oregon's income tax provides more than two-thirds of its total tax revenues—the most of any state.[18]

So, Alaska and New Hampshire have neither income taxes nor sales taxes. How can that be? For Alaska, the answer is the Prudhoe Bay oilfields.[19] New Hampshire makes do. According to Donald Boyd of the Rockefeller Institute, New Hampshire's state government simply does less than most state governments. The state relies almost exclusively on local governments to finance elementary and secondary education rather than raising state revenue for this purpose. Unlike many other states, it also has managed to avoid court orders to spend dramatically more on secondary school education. It is able to do all of this, in part, because the income of the average New Hampshire resident is one of the highest in the country. People are able to pay for a lot of goods and services for themselves.

These states are the exceptions. On average, Americans pay about 2.6 percent of their personal incomes, or $694 a year, in state income taxes. However, residents of states with high taxes, such as Maryland, Massachusetts, New York, and Oregon, face much higher state income tax burdens. (See Table 11-2.)

Other Tax Revenue Sources: Cars, Oil, and Death

Car registrations, death, and oil and other natural resources also are major sources of state revenues. In 1998, car registration fees brought in more than $16 billion to state and local governments. Estate taxes, sometimes called death taxes, and gift taxes brought in another $7 billion.

TABLE 11-2

State Individual Income Tax Rates, 2004

State	Tax Rate (Percentage)		Number of Brackets	Income Brackets		Personal Exemption			Federal Tax Deductions
	Low	High		Low	High	Single	Married	Children	
Alabama	2.0 –	5.0	3	500 [b] –	3,000 [b]	1,500	3,000	300	*
Alaska	No State Income Tax								
Arizona	2.87 –	5.04	5	10,000 [b] –	150,000 [b]	2,100	4,200	2,300	
Arkansas [a]	1.0 –	7.0 [c]	6	3,999 –	27,500	20 [c]	40 [c]	20 [c]	
California [a]	1.0 –	9.3	6	5,962 [b] –	39,133 [b]	80 [c]	160 [c]	251 [c]	
Colorado	4.63		1	—Flat Rate—		—None—			
Connecticut	3.0 –	5.0	2	10,000 [b] –	10,000 [b]	12,500 [f]	24,000 [f]	0	
Delaware	2.2 –	5.95	6	5,000 –	60,000	110 [c]	220 [c]	110 [c]	
Florida	No State Income Tax								
Georgia	1.0 –	6.0	6	750 [g] –	7,000 [g]	2,700	5,400	2,700	
Hawaii	1.4 –	8.25	9	2,000 [b] –	40,000 [b]	1,040	2,080	1,040	
Idaho [a]	1.6 –	7.8	8	1,104 [h] –	22,074 [h]	3,100 [d]	6,200 [d]	3,100 [d]	
Illinois	3.0		1	—Flat Rate—		2,000	4,000	2,000	
Indiana	3.4		1	—Flat Rate—		1,000	2,000	1,000	
Iowa [a]	0.36 –	8.98	9	1,211 –	54,495	40 [c]	80 [r]	40 [c]	*
Kansas	3.5 –	6.45	3	15,000 [b] –	30,000 [b]	2,250	4,500	2,250	
Kentucky	2.0 –	6.0	5	3,000 –	8,000	20 [c]	40 [c]	20 [c]	
Louisiana	2.0 –	6.0	3	12,500 [b] –	25,000 [b]	4,500 [i]	9,000 [i]	1,000 [i]	*
Maine [a]	2.0 –	8.5	4	4,250 [b] –	16,950 [b]	4,700	7,850	1,000	
Maryland	2.0 –	4.75	4	1,000 –	3,000	2,400	4,800	2,400	
Massachusetts	5.3		1	—Flat Rate—		3,300	6,600	1,000	
Michigan [a]	4.0 [y]		1	—Flat Rate—		3,100	6,200	3,100	
Minnesota [a]	5.35 –	7.85	3	19,440 [j] –	63,860 [j]	3,100 [d]	6,200 [d]	3,100 [d]	
Mississippi	3.0 –	5.0	3	5,000 –	10,000	6,000	12,000	1,500	
Missouri	1.5 –	6.0	10	1,000 –	9,000	2,100	4,200	2,100	* [s]
Montana [a]	2.0 –	11.0	10	2,199 –	76,199	1,740	3,480	1,740	*
Nebraska [a]	2.56 –	6.84	4	2,400 [k] –	26,500 [k]	94 [c]	188 [c]	94 [c]	
Nevada	No State Income Tax								
New Hampshire	State Income Tax is Limited to Dividends and Interest Income Only.								
New Jersey	1.4 –	6.37	6	20,000 [l] –	75,000 [l]	1,000	2,000	1,500	
New Mexico	1.7 –	6.8	5	5,500 [m] –	26,000 [m]	3,100 [d]	6,200 [d]	3,100 [d]	
New York	4.0 –	7.70	7	8,000 [n] –	500,000 [n]	0	0	1,000	
North Carolina [o]	6.0 –	8.25	4	12,750 [o] –	120,000 [o]	3,100 [d]	6,200 [d]	3,100 [d]	
North Dakota	2.1 –	5.54 [p]	5	28,400 [p] –	311,950 [p]	3,100 [d]	6,200 [d]	3,100 [d]	
Ohio [a]	0.743 –	7.5	9	5,000 –	200,000	1,200 [q]	2,400 [q]	1,200 [q]	
Oklahoma	0.5 –	6.75 [r]	8	1,000 [b] –	10,000 [b]	1,000	2,000	1,000	* [r]

(Table continues on next page)

TABLE 11-2   *(continued)*

State	Tax Rate (Percentage)		Number of Brackets	Income Brackets		Personal Exemption			Federal Tax Deductions
	Low	High		Low	High	Single	Married	Children	
Oregon [a]	5.0 –	9.0	3	2,600 [b] –	6,500 [b]	151 [c]	302 [c]	151 [c]	* [s]
Pennsylvania	3.07		1	—Flat Rate—		—None—			
Rhode Island	25.0% Federal Tax Liability [t]			—		—	—	—	—
South Carolina [a]	2.5 –	7.0	6	2,400 –	12,300	3,100 [d]	6,200 [d]	3,100 [d]	
South Dakota	No State Income Tax								
Tennessee	State Income Tax is Limited to Dividends and Interest Income Only.								
Texas	No State Income Tax								
Utah	2.30 –	7.0	6	863 [b] –	4,313 [b]	2,325 [d]	4,650 [d]	2,325 [d]	* [u]
Vermont [a]	3.6 –	9.5	5	29,050 [v] –	319,100 [v]	3,100 [d]	6,200 [d]	3,100 [d]	
Virginia	2.0 –	5.75	4	3,000 –	17,000	800	1,600	800	
Washington	No State Income Tax								
West Virginia	3.0 –	6.5	5	10,000 –	60,000	2,000	4,000	2,000	
Wisconsin	4.6 –	6.75	4	8,610 [w] –	129,150 [w]	700	1,400	400	
Wyoming	No State Income Tax								
Dist. of Columbia	5.0 –	9.5 [x]	3	10,000 –	30,000	1,370	2,740	1,370	

Source: The Federation of Tax Administrators, from various sources. www.taxadmin.org/fta/rate/ind_inc.html (accessed August 12, 2004).

[a] Fourteen states have statutory provision for automatic adjustment of tax brackets, personal exemption or standard deductions to the rate of inflation. Michigan, Nebraska and Ohio index the personal exemption amounts only.

[b] For joint returns, the taxes are twice the tax imposed on half the income.

[c] Tax credits.

[d] These states allow personal exemption or standard deductions as provided in the IRC. Utah allows a personal exemption equal to three-fourths the federal exemptions.

[e] Plus a 3 percent surtax. A special tax table is available for low-income taxpayers reducing their tax payments.

[f] Combined personal exemptions and standard deduction. An additional tax credit is allowed ranging from 75 percent to 0 percent based on state adjusted gross income. Exemption amounts are phased out for higher income taxpayers until they are eliminated for households earning over $54,500.

[g] The tax brackets reported are for single individuals. For married households filing separately, the same rates apply to income brackets ranging from $500 to $5,000; and the income brackets range from $1,000 to $10,000 for joint filers.

[h] For joint returns, the tax is twice the tax imposed on half the income. A $10 filing tax is charge for each return and a $15 credit is allowed for each exemption.

[i] Combined personal exemption and standard deduction.

[j] The tax brackets reported are for single individuals. For married couples filing jointly, the same rates apply for income under $28,420 to over $112,910.

[k] The tax brackets reported are for single individuals. For married couples filing jointly, the same rates apply for income under $4,000 to over $46,750.

[l] The tax brackets reported are for single individuals. For married couples filing jointly, the same rates apply for income under $20,000 to over $150,000.

[m] The tax brackets reported are for single individuals. For married couples filing jointly, the same rates apply for income under $8,000 to over $40,000. Married households filing separately pay the tax imposed on half the income. Tax rate is scheduled to decrease in tax year 2005.

[n] The tax brackets reported are for single individuals. For married taxpayers, the same rates apply to income brackets ranging from $16,000 to $500,000.

[o] The tax brackets reported are for single individuals. For married taxpayers, the same rates apply to income brackets ranging from $21,250 to $200,000. Lower exemption amounts allowed for high-ncome taxpayers. Tax rate scheduled to decrease after tax year 2005.

[p] The tax brackets reported are for single individuals. For married taxpayers, the same rates apply to income brackets ranging from $47,450 to $311,950. An additional $300 personal exemption is allowed for joint returns or unmarried head of households.

[q] Plus an additional $20 per exemption tax credit.

[r] The rate range reported is for single persons not deducting federal income tax. For married persons filing jointly, the same rates apply to income brackets ranging from $2,000 to $21,000. Separate schedules, with rates ranging from 0.5 percent to 10 percent, apply to taxpayers deducting federal income taxes.

[s] Deduction is limited to $10,000 for joint returns and $5,000 for individuals in Missouri and to $5,000 in Oregon.

[t] Federal tax liability prior to the enactment of Economic Growth and Tax Relief Act of 2001.

[u] One half of the federal income taxes are deductible.

[v] The tax brackets reported are for single individuals. For married couples filing jointly, the same rates apply for income under $46,700 to over $307,050.

[w] The tax brackets reported are for single individuals. For married taxpayers, the same rates apply to income brackets ranging from $11,480 to $172,200. An additional $250 exemption is provided for each taxpayer or spouse age 65 or over.

[x] Tax rate decreases are scheduled for tax year 2005.

[y] Tax rate is scheduled to decrease to 3.9 percent after June 2004.

Governing States and Localities

Policy in Practice: Milking the Cash Cows

Many states have been raising just about every user fee, charge, and special tax in sight. In fact, a jumble of other taxes, such as those on alcohol and tobacco, and various other selective excise taxes and license fees, has grown by $17 billion in the past three years. This is more than the general sales tax has grown. A major line of attack has been increasing sin taxes. Sin taxes are levied on activities presumed to be unhealthy, frivolous, or otherwise contrary to public interest.

Sin taxes are alluring, but they have a major drawback: They cannot produce enough revenue to close the revenue shortfalls states have to contend with during economic downturns. All told, sin taxes on alcohol and tobacco produce only about 2 percent of state government revenues. Even doubling of rates would not increase revenues by more than 4 percent of any state budget.

As for gas taxes, states are in a pickle. In the good old days, federal highway aid was generous and gas prices were low. The tables are turned now. The federal transportation bill that would reauthorize the federal aid programs for highways and mass transit spending is stalled in Congress. War in the Middle East and production cutbacks by oil-producing countries have brought both current shortages and future uncertainties. Many states see their transportation funds lagging and their pennies-per-gallon revenue systems falling out of date. With oil prices spiking, the thought of raising gasoline taxes is politically unpalatable.

Some states, such as Florida, North Carolina, West Virginia, Wisconsin, and the Commonwealth of Puerto Rico, have taken an innovative approach to handling the ups and downs in fuel prices. A part of the gasoline tax is designed to increase as the price of oil decreases and to decrease when the price goes up. This leveling out helps maintain steadier gasoline prices at the pump overall while boosting revenues fairly painlessly when world prices drop. Averaging $150 million to $200 million a year in revenues, the inverse oil tax helps build a lot of highways in Puerto Rico.

Source: John E. Petersen, "Find Me the Money," *Governing* magazine, June 2004. www.governing.com/archive/2004/jun/muni.txt (accessed July 1, 2004).

Thirty-nine states levy **severance taxes** on natural resources that are removed, or severed, from the state. Some states are quite creative about devising severance taxes. Washington, for example, taxes oysters and salmon and other game fish caught in state. But despite some creative taxing, the only states that raise real money from severance taxes are states with significant coal, oil, and natural gas reserves, such as Wyoming and Alaska.

SEVERANCE TAXES

Taxes on natural resources.

Other Sources of Income: Fees, Charges, and Uncle Sam

The total tax revenues discussed so far add up to about $773 billion. That is a lot of money, but it accounts for only half of the $1.5 trillion that state and local governments spent in 1998. The rest of the money came from user fees and other charges, **insurance trust money,** and **intergovernmental transfers** account for most of the difference.

In 1998, state and local governments raised $336 million from "charges and miscellaneous fees." That is $62 million more than they raised from sales taxes. Little charges like university tuitions, public hospital charges,

INSURANCE TRUST MONEY

Money collected from contributions, assessments, insurance premiums, or payroll taxes.

airport use fees, school lunch sales, and park permits make a big difference. State and local governments earned another $81 million from utility fees and, yes, liquor sales and licenses.

Insurance Trust Funds

Looking at a pay stub before any deductions are taken out can be pretty impressive. Looking at the actual amount of the paycheck can be a bit disappointing. What people may not realize is that they are not the only ones paying these taxes and fees. Their employers often have to match these payroll taxes and deductions. These funds go to their state governments and to the federal government. Ultimately, the contributions are invested to support social security and retirement programs, workers' compensation and disability programs, and other related insurance programs that benefit the employees.

Intergovernmental Transfers

The final portion of state and local government revenues comes from intergovernmental transfers of money. In the case of state governments, that means transfers from the federal government. In the case of local governments, that means transfers from state governments. Localities do receive some funds directly from the federal government, but not much. In 2000, the federal government provided some $316 million to state and local governments. All told, federal funding made up approximately 31 percent of total state and local expenditures.[20]

Approximately 90 percent of federal funds go to specific state programs. Medicaid, the joint state-federal health insurance program for low-income people and people with disabilities, is by far the largest recipient. It receives about 44 percent of all federal funds that go to state governments. Education (both K–12 and post-secondary), transportation projects, and public welfare also receive significant federal funding. Most of these funds cannot be used on just anything. States must spend them on certain programs and often in a certain fashion.

During the 1960s, local governments and some neighborhood organizations also received substantial federal funding. Many of these programs have since ended or have been scaled back drastically. Today, local governments get only around 3 percent of their total revenues from the federal government. However, as the federal government has reduced support, state governments have stepped up their levels of assistance. In 1998, intergovernmental revenue transfers from state governments accounted for 30 percent of total local government revenues.

Localities generally have welcomed the money, but the relationship between state governments and county and city governments has not always been an easy one. Over the course of the past decade, many city and county governments have found themselves stuck with unfunded mandates. These requirements have been imposed upon them by federal or state legislation that forces them to perform certain tasks but fails to provide them with the money to carry out those tasks.

Even worse—from the perspective of local governments—some state governments have dealt with their own revenue shortfalls by cutting assistance to local budgets, shifting responsibilities from the state to the local level, or raiding local budgets outright. When Wisconsin's economy slid into recession early in his term, Governor Scott McCallum proposed to close the state's budget shortfall by eliminating the state's ninety-year-old system of revenue sharing. This move would have cost localities $1.1 billion. The legislature ultimately turned back McCallum's proposal. Less sweeping transfers of money and responsibilities, however, continue to be commonplace during economic downturns.[21]

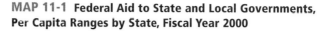

MAP 11-1 Federal Aid to State and Local Governments, Per Capita Ranges by State, Fiscal Year 2000

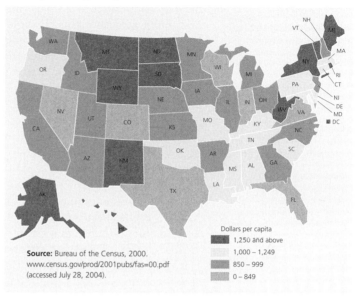

Dollars per capita
1,250 and above
1,000 – 1,249
850 – 999
0 – 849

Source: Bureau of the Census, 2000. www.census.gov/prod/2001pubs/fas=00.pdf (accessed July 28, 2004).

Taxing Variations among State and Local Governments

Generalizations about state and local finances should not obscure the fact that different states and localities tax themselves in very different ways and at very different rates. The first striking difference concerns the very different tax burdens that states choose to impose on themselves. Traditionally, New Yorkers pay the most per capita in taxes of any state in the country—$4,515 a year. However, in 2002, Maine residents faced the largest tax burden. They returned 12.9 percent of their incomes to state and local governments. This was the highest percentage of any state in the country. In contrast, residents of Alaska, New Hampshire, Tennessee, and Texas face some of the lowest state and local tax burdens in the country. On average, residents pay 9 percent or less of their incomes a year in state and local taxes.

State and local governments do not just choose to tax themselves at different rates. They also choose to tax themselves in different ways. Residents of many Tennessee counties pay sales taxes of almost 10 percent. New Hampshire relies on property taxes for two-thirds of its total state and local tax revenues. In contrast, property taxes contribute only about 3 percent of Alabama's revenues.

In thinking about a state's tax burden, it is helpful to distinguish between **tax capacities** and **tax efforts**. In Beverly Hills, California, for example, the median house price is a staggering $1.9 million. The typical family spends $62,000 a year shopping. Even low sales and property taxes are going to bring in serious money.[22] Conversely, Rio Grande City, Texas, a small border town of eighteen thousand, with a median household income of slightly more than $18,000 a year, is not going to have a lot of money to spend no matter how high its taxes are. Beverly Hills's tax capacity is high. Rio Grande City's tax capacity is low.

Many political scientists prefer to look at a different measurement—tax effort, or tax burden. Basically, measurements of tax effort seek to determine the proportion of its income that a given community chooses to pay out in taxes. A community's tax effort is also a good proxy for its appetite for public services. Some communities are willing to pay for street cleaning, and some communities are not. Some communities, such as Cambridge, Massachusetts, even are willing to pay a government employee to drive around and announce that street cleaning is about to commence.

Tax capacities and tax efforts often diverge markedly. Consider New Hampshire and Massachusetts. Both are comparatively affluent states. Personal income per capita in 2000 is $37,710 in Massachusetts and $33,042 in New Hampshire. The median household income nationwide is $29,451. In other words, the two states have very similar tax capacities.

However, they make very different tax efforts. New Hampshire has the second lightest tax burden in the country. Its residents pay about $2,590 a year in state and local taxes. In contrast, residents of neighboring Massachusetts pay about $3,606.[23]

Explaining Tax Variations

What accounts for such differences? Primarily, the two states have very different political cultures. New Hampshire prides itself on its rugged individualism. Its motto is "Live Free or Die." Residents tend to want the government to stay out of their way.

In contrast, Massachusetts was founded as a commonwealth. The founding document of the Massachusetts Bay Colony described a single "Body Politic" dedicated to the "general good" of the colony.[24] In this tradition, state and local governments are seen as effective ways of advancing "the general good." Higher taxes and larger governments are more acceptable.

Political culture is not the only important variable that explains the very different tax efforts among states. Factors such as geography, geology, demographics, and history also influence the choices that state and local governments make.

Geography. One obvious, but easy to overlook, factor that influences state tax policies is geography. It is no coincidence that Alaska and Wyoming, two huge states in which people drive a lot, have the lowest gas taxes in the country.

Geology. Geology plays an important role in some state economies too. This is most notably true in oil-rich and natural-gas-rich states like Alaska and Wyoming. Thanks in large part to Prudhoe Bay, state and local governments in Alaska were able to spend $13,041 per person in 1999 while maintaining the thirty-ninth lightest tax burden in the country. Indeed, Alaska's Permanent Fund sends each eligible citizen a yearly **dividend** check—typically, for around $1,500—as a way of distributing the oil wealth.

Demographics. Demographics play an important role in determining the attitudes of state and local governments toward taxes. This is particularly true at the local level. Consider a city with a strong local economy and rising house prices. Such a city attracts large numbers of young workers with children. These are people who might very well want to spend more money on local schools and are willing to deal with rising property tax revenues. However, as mentioned previously, for seniors living on fixed incomes, rising house prices and rising property taxes might spell disaster. During economic booms, conflicts between parents and retirees are a common feature of local politics.

The Economic Cycle. Even when states make similar tax efforts and have similar cultures, state and local finances are distributed very differently from state to state. That's because different states and cities have very different economies.

Different states are situated at different points on the economic cycle. Industrial states, such as Michigan and Indiana, experience economic downturns first. The good news is that they also emerge from such downturns earlier than other states. The reason is that manufacturers begin to rebuild inventories when they expect a recovery. Texas historically has had a counter-cyclical economy. When rising oil prices threaten to push industrial states into recession, Texas tends to do well. The same is true of Wyoming and Alaska.

Yet as important as demographics, geography, history, and political culture are, these variables do not always explain the actual financial choices that state and local governments make.

Take Mississippi. One of the most religious and politically conservative states in the country, Mississippi is the buckle of the Bible Belt. In 1990, however, Mississippi passed riverboat gambling legislation. This legislation allowed casino operators to build full-sized casinos on barges moored permanently to the shoreline. The goal was to turn the northwestern town of Tunica, which had gained a measure of renown after the television show *60 Minutes* profiled it as the poorest city in America, into Las Vegas East.

Nevada and Mississippi have completely different political cultures. Political scientist Daniel Elazar described Mississippi as a traditionalistic

Policy in Practice: Are Casinos and Lotteries a Good Bet?

Video poker casinos begin at the South Carolina state line and spread out in all directions from there. With hundreds of poker operators holding thousands of licenses in thousands of locations, it's difficult to drive very far without reaching the conclusion that the Palmetto State is hooked on electronic five-card draw.

It all happened startlingly fast. Ten years ago, there were seven thousand video poker machines in South Carolina. Now there are about thirty-four thousand. And they are not just in casinos. They have popped up in gas stations, convenience stores, bars, and restaurants.

As recently as 1996, the amount bet at the machines was $1.75 billion. Today, it is about $2.5 billion. In short, gambling has entrenched itself in South Carolina—and in some of the states around it—in a powerful way. That dependence, however, is accompanied by some persistent self-doubts—and by some determined opposition.

As gambling becomes more and more pervasive, the horror stories about its effects circulate more and more widely. In one well-publicized instance, a woman spent hours in a casino pouring change into a video game while her infant daughter suffocated to death inside her car. In another instance, an elderly couple not only spent their life savings on video poker but also went more than $50,000 into debt to finance their habit.

So, for all of its $2.5 billion success, video poker nonetheless occupies a precarious perch in the state. Although the state supreme court has legitimized the industry, it still could be banned by the legislature or voted out of existence in a referendum. That's why, on the day after the 2003 election, video poker interests paid for billboards that literally begged the state for more regulation. For them, it's been a constant theme. Although it might seem incongruous for a powerful industry to seek tighter regulation and higher taxes, there is a certain political genius to it.

If the industry is regulated and taxed, the state budget is certain to become permanently hooked on the revenue stream. "By legitimizing and then regulating them, you've further entrenched them," says former House Speaker Robert J. Sheheen. "If we get used to that, I think you'll see other forms of gambling come into the state."

One form of gambling that will almost certainly arrive soon is the lottery. When newly elected governor Jim Hodges took to the floor of the South Carolina

state and Nevada as an individualistic state. In short, Nevada has the kind of political culture that one might expect to produce, well, Las Vegas. Mississippi does not. Today, however, the hamlet of Tunica has more casino square footage than the East Coast gambling hotspot, Atlantic City, in the individualistic state of New Jersey. Clearly, political culture isn't everything.

BONDS

Certificates that are evidence of a debt on which the issuer promises to pay the holder a specified amount of interest for a specified length of time and to repay the loans on their maturity.

Bonds

The final source of money for state and local governments comes from **bonds.** These are financial instruments with which state and local governments promise to pay back borrowed money at a fixed rate of interest on a specified date.

State and local governments, as well as quasi-governmental entities like utility and water authorities, use bonds to finance **capital investments,** typically infrastructure upgrades such as a new road, a new school, or a new airport. There are two types of bonds—general obligation bonds, which are

General Assembly in January 1999 to offer his maiden state-of-the-state address, it almost seemed as if an aide had slipped him the wrong speech. He wanted to talk about Georgia. "Since 1993," he said, "lottery revenues have provided almost 400,000 Georgia students with more than $600 million in scholarship money. This year alone, 61,000 Georgia children will attend pre-kindergarten programs funded by lottery dollars."

Hodges was making a pitch for his campaign platform the best way he knew how—by pointing to the well-publicized successes of the lottery in a neighboring jurisdiction. "Whether you are pro or con, the lottery is here. From a practical standpoint, people know it's here, right on the Georgia border," says South Carolina state senator Glenn McConnell. "We're just not getting any money for it."

Lottery advocates argue that southeastern states without lotteries cannot afford to wait any longer. Georgia continues to drain its own dollars and those of South Carolina, and North Carolina and Alabama soon will have their own lotteries up and running.

It is the same argument that has powered gambling expansion all across the country. The horse racing industries in Pennsylvania and Maryland insist that they need slot machines at racetracks. They need them to compete against neighboring West Virginia and Delaware, where slots already are permitted. In Kansas, horse racing interests argue that slots are the only way they can survive against Missouri's riverboat casinos. In Nebraska, Iowa gaming is used for leverage. In Massachusetts, it is Connecticut and New Hampshire that play that role.

The rise of the Indiana gambling industry is instructive. A decade ago, legalized gambling was nearly non-existent in the state. It kicked off with a state lottery in 1989, progressed to riverboat legalization in 1993, and ended with a horse track in 1994. By 1996, just seven years after it began, legalized gambling had become a $1.6 billion industry.

"The adoption of a state lottery significantly increases the likelihood that a state will legalize casino gambling," says Patrick Pierce, a St. Mary's College political scientist who has studied the link between the two. "It tells policymakers that the forces that oppose gambling can be beaten. And if they can be beaten on a lottery, they can be beaten on a casino."

Source: Adapted from Charles Mahtesian, "The Lure of the Cards," *Governing* magazine, June 1999.

secured by the taxing power of the jurisdiction that issues them, and revenue bonds, which are secured by the revenue from a given project, such as a new toll road. For state governments, that means projects like highways, power plant construction and pollution control, or even land conservation. Local governments use bonds to finance programs like school construction, sewage and water lines, airports, and affordable housing. Investors like them too. The earnings from most state bonds are exempt from state income taxes.

In 2001, state and local governments issued $340 billion in bonds.[25] **Municipal bonds,** or "munis" to bond traders, are generally safe and attractive investments, particularly for the rich. Municipal bondholders usually are exempted from paying federal or state taxes on income they receive from bonds. Sometimes, however, municipal finances go disastrously awry. A recent example occurred in 1994 when Orange County, California, one of the nation's largest and richest counties, announced huge investment losses and defaulted on its bond payments after risky pension fund investments went bad.

CAPITAL INVESTMENTS
Investments in infrastructure, such as roads.

Boston's Central Artery/Tunnel Project, dubbed the "Big Dig" by locals, will have cost almost $15 billion by the time it is completed in 2005. City, state, and federal officials worked together to find ways to finance the massive undertaking. The most extensive—and expensive—project of its kind in the United States to date, construction had to take place around an existing city since work began in 1991. The ten-lane, one-of-a-kind Leonard P. Zakim Bunker Hill Bridge, opened in 2003, has already helped reduce traffic congestion and added beauty to the city skyline.

The Budget Process

Once state and local governments have raised money from taxes, user fees, and bonds and have received money from intergovernmental transfers, they must decide how to spend it. These decisions are made during the budget process.

Most state and local governments budget for one **fiscal year**. Unfortunately for fans of simplicity in government, the fiscal year is not the same as the calendar year. The federal government's fiscal year runs from October 1 to September 30. Most state and local governments generally begin the fiscal year on July 1. Alabama, Michigan, New York, and Texas are the exceptions. As a result, when legislatures debate the budget, they are almost always debating the budget for the coming fiscal year.[26] Twenty-three states pass two-year budgets.[27]

Budget timelines do vary from state to state, but the budget process itself is quite similar. It begins with instructions from the governor's budget office or the mayor's budget office. The executive branch agencies are told to draw up funding requests for the upcoming year. During the fall, the budget office reviews the spending requests and helps the chief executive develop a unified budget for the executive branch.

MUNICIPAL BONDS

Bonds issued by states, counties, cities, and towns to fund large projects as well as operating budgets. They are exempt from federal taxes and from state and local taxes for the investors who live in the state where they are issued.

FISCAL YEAR

The accounting period used by a government.

Most chief executives unveil their budgets in state-of-the-state addresses in January. In forty-five states, governors and mayors are legally required to submit a **balanced budget** to the legislature or city council. The legislative body reviews the budget, authorizes spending on certain programs, appropriates the necessary money, and presents its budget to the chief executive to sign into law.

As a guard against fiscal excess and abuse, forty-nine states have statutory or constitutional requirements that state legislatures must enact a balanced budget. Only Vermont is free to run up debts as it pleases.[28] All but five states also have laws that require lawmakers to save a certain portion of state revenues in so-called rainy day, or budget stabilization, funds. States can draw on these funds during times of recession, when revenues fall. Although rainy day funds rarely offset the revenue drops that occur during a recession, they do provide some cushion for the lawmakers who have to balance state budgets. Many local governments face similar requirements due to state requirements or their own municipal codes.

There are, of course, exceptions. In states such as Arkansas, Mississippi, and South Carolina, legislatures take the lead role in formulating the initial budget plan. Legislative bodies also take the lead in county and city governments with weak chief executives, such as Los Angeles, California. In many western states, citizens and special interests have become players in the budgeting process via ballot initiatives.

Expenditures, or Where the Money Goes

In fiscal year 1998, state and local governments spent approximately $1.5 trillion. That is $5,659 for every man, woman, and child in the country. So, where did the money go?

Wages. The single largest sources of **expenditures** for state and local governments are salaries—roughly $495 billion in 1998. State and local governments are the biggest employers in the United States. In 2001, state governments employed 4.9 million people nationwide. Local governments employed another 13.1 million people.[29]

What do all of these employees do? There's a good chance that someone from one large category of state government employees—a professor or lecturer—is teaching you this course.

Education. Education has long been the single largest functional spending category for state and local governments. In 1998, state and local governments spent $450 billion on education. Approximately 70 percent of that went to elementary and secondary schools. The remaining 30 percent went to community colleges and state universities.

Primary and secondary education traditionally has been the preserve of local governments. In most states, elected local school boards hire

BALANCED BUDGET

A budget in which current expenditures are equal to or less than income.

EXPENDITURES

Money spent by government.

TABLE 11-3

State Revenues, Expenditures, and Debt, 2000 (in millions of dollars)

State	Total Revenues	Total Expenditures	Total Debt Outstanding at End of Fiscal Year	State	Total Revenues	Total Expenditures	Total Debt Outstanding at End of Fiscal Year
Alabama	16,875	15,873	5,292	Montana	4,204	3,718	2,548
Alaska	8,584	6,611	4,150	Nebraska	6,136	5,772	1,680
Arizona	16,721	16,574	3,101	Nevada	7,235	6,047	2,990
Arkansas	10,789	9,589	2,746	New Hampshire	4,993	4,366	5,499
California	172,481	149,770	57,170	New Jersey	42,341	34,779	28,924
Colorado	17,060	13,930	4,431	New Mexico	10,570	8,700	3,627
Connecticut	17,857	16,723	18,456	New York	11,1492	97,654	78,616
Delaware	5,162	4,211	3,261	North Carolina	34,361	29,615	9,336
Florida	51,630	45,208	18,181	North Dakota	3,295	2,856	1,520
Georgia	29,567	24,739	7,086	Ohio	55,273	44,631	18,143
Hawaii	6,941	6,605	5,592	Oklahoma	13,116	10,271	5,663
Idaho	5,547	4,493	2,279	Oregon	21,228	15,776	6,235
Illinois	48,524	41,182	28,828	Pennsylvania	54,518	47,682	18,595
Indiana	20,456	20,289	7,894	Rhode Island	5,530	4,648	5,681
Iowa	11,340	11,453	2,362	South Carolina	15,870	16,237	7,057
Kansas	10,326	9,165	1,912	South Dakota	2,873	2,403	2,305
Kentucky	19,451	15,682	7,753	Tennessee	18,970	16,853	3,292
Louisiana	18,404	16,537	7,770	Texas	72,323	59,805	19,228
Maine	6,294	5,448	4,058	Utah	10,191	8,592	3,885
Maryland	21,367	19,432	11,365	Vermont	3,280	3,219	2,165
Massachusetts	32,011	29,748	38,961	Virginia	28,902	24,314	12,011
Michigan	49,512	42,748	19,445	Washington	30,616	25,902	11,734
Minnesota	26,889	22,026	5,602	West Virginia	8,256	7,552	3,730
Mississippi	12,181	10,972	3,222	Wisconsin	32,119	23,026	11,454
Missouri	20,327	17,293	9,820	Wyoming	5,740	2,553	1,250

Source: Adapted from *Book of the States 2003* (Lexington, Ky.: Council of State Governments, 2003), 334.

superintendents and principals, select curriculums that align with state standards, and develop school budgets. Local governments typically spend about 38 percent of their funds on schools.[30]

State governments now provide half of all funding for K–12 education. State dollars increasingly are used to train teachers, reduce the number of students in classrooms, promote the use of computers and high-speed Internet access, and fund "accountability" and testing regimes. In 2001, 22 percent of state general fund expenditures went to K–12 education.

State governments also devote a portion of their expenditures to higher education—about 11 percent of total expenditures in 2001. Spending on higher education is the third largest item on state budgets. Tuition covers about 20 percent of the costs of higher education.

As with other types of funding, different states evince different levels of enthusiasm for spending money on higher education. Delaware, Iowa, North Dakota, New Mexico, and Utah spend the most per capita on higher education. In Utah, that amount is $717 per state resident. In New Mexico, it is $658. Connecticut, Florida, Massachusetts, New Hampshire, and New York spend the least, with New Yorkers contributing a measly $315 per person to higher education.[31]

Unlike highways, which have their own dedicated stream of funding from gasoline taxes, legislatures typically appropriate funding for higher education from general revenue funds. This is known as **discretionary spending**. When economic times are good, institutions of higher learning and the voters and future voters who enroll in them often benefit from considerable largesse. Between 1996 and 2001, states such as California and Virginia increased higher education budgets by more than 10 percent a year.

When the economy slides into recession, however, the fact that institutions of higher education do not have a dedicated source of funding makes them particularly vulnerable to cutbacks. The economy stopped growing in the spring of 2001. State revenues plunged, and legislators responded in a familiar way. They cut higher education spending. The result in many states was higher tuitions at a time when family incomes and job prospects were often uncertain.

DISCRETIONARY SPENDING

Spending controlled in annual appropriations acts.

Healthcare. Since the late 1990s, healthcare spending has surged dramatically. In 1998, state and local governments spent $319 billion. For state governments, spending on healthcare is now larger than any other single item.

Medicaid is the largest and most expensive state-run health program. When established in 1965, it was viewed as a limited safety net for the very poor and disabled. However, the number of low-income, uninsured Americans has grown, and medical care has become more expensive. The program has grown at an enormous rate as a result. In 1970, state governments spent $2 billion on the program, and the federal government kicked in another $3 billion. By 2001, state governments spent $98 billion on the program, and the federal government came through with another $130 billion.[32] State Medicaid programs now provide health insurance to approximately forty-four million people and account for 15 percent of total state spending. And healthcare costs are growing much faster than any other category of government expenditures.

The Medicaid program is an excellent example of **fiscal federalism**. The federal government picks up most of the program's costs, while states take responsibility for administering the program itself.

Medicaid is also an **entitlement** program. Most programs receive a specific appropriation during the budget process and can spend no more. Entitlements like Medicaid are different. States and the federal government are legally obligated to provide health insurance to low-income individuals who qualify for the program, regardless of the cost. If states have an unexpected surge of applicants and they have not set aside enough money for Medicaid, tough.

States do have some leeway in determining how generous they want their state Medicaid programs to be. They enjoy similar discretion with another joint state-federal program, the State Children's Health Insurance Program (SCHIP). In most states, this program provides health insurance for children living in families whose primary wage earner makes up to twice the federal poverty level. In 2003, this amount was $18,400 for a family of four.[33]

During the boom of the late 1990s, some states made a major effort to extend health insurance via Medicaid and SCHIP. Mississippi raised the Medicaid eligibility to 135 percent of the federal poverty level—the highest in the country.

New Jersey extended health insurance to parents earning up to 350 percent of the federal poverty level, which equaled out to about $61,000 for a family of four.[34] Moreover, the state also offered health insurance to single adults earning up to $8,590, or 100 percent of the federal poverty level.[35]

Many healthcare advocates saw Medicaid and SCHIP expansions as the most promising approach to extending health insurance to some of the roughly forty-four million Americans who currently do without it. When the economy slid into recession in early 2001, however, states scaled back these efforts, sometimes dramatically. The state that made the most dramatic cuts in eligibility was New Jersey. In September 2001, it reduced the availability of health insurance for adults without children to people earning less than 30 percent of the federal poverty level—about $2,600 in 2002.

Medicaid increasingly serves another function as well. It is the only governmental program that pays for long-term care, such as nursing homes and assisted living facilities. Private nursing homes and assisted living facilities can cost anywhere from $1,000 a month to $3,500 a month. Few seniors or disabled individuals can afford these costs for very long. As the number of Americans age 85 and older increases from about 4.3 million in 2000 to a projected 6.5 million in 2020, a growing number of elderly citizens will find themselves in need of such services.

Local governments spend much less on healthcare than state governments, or only about 7 percent of total expenditures. This is not to say that local governments do not make an important contribution. In 1998, state and local governments spent $40 billion supporting local public hospitals, which is about the same amount they spent on police protection.[36] All of these funds came directly from the local governments. Many of these hospitals serve as healthcare providers of last resort to people without health insurance. In the event of a terrorist attack involving biological weapons, many of these hospitals would serve as society's defense of first resort.

Welfare. The topic of welfare has been one of the most contentious issues in U.S. politics for a long time. Welfare is an entitlement program. While states have some leeway to determine eligibility, they cannot deny or restrict benefits to qualified individuals. From 1965 to 1996, women with young children were eligible to receive monetary assistance through a welfare program known as Aid to Families with Dependent Children (AFDC).

Then in 1996, Republicans in Congress and President Bill Clinton joined forces to pass the Personal Responsibility and Work Reconciliation Act. The act abolished AFDC and replaced it with the Temporary Assistance for Needy Families (TANF) program. TANF ended welfare entitlement. Instead, it disbursed federal money to states in block grants and gave them considerable freedom in determining how they wanted to spend those funds. The new legislation also allowed states to require welfare recipients to work for their benefits and capped the duration of benefits at five years.

Many liberals predicted that such welfare "reform" would result in disaster. Instead, the number of people on welfare rolls declined dramatically. Between 1994 and 1999, the welfare caseload declined by nearly 50 percent, from approximately four million people to two million people.[37]

Welfare continues to be a politically contentious issue. Yet from a financial viewpoint, it is actually a pretty minor program. In 2001, state governments spent a total of $22.7 billion on TANF, that is, about 2.2 percent of total state expenditures.[38]

Fire, Police, and Prisons. In 1998, state and local governments spent $70 billion on fire and police protection. They spent an additional $40 billion on prisons and correctional facilities. State and local government spending on police protection and prisons varies widely. New York City, a city of eight million people, employs a police force of thirty-eight thousand. That works out to one police officer for every 211 people. In contrast, Los Angeles, a city of 3.8 million, employees only 9,200 police officers. That equals only one police officer for every 413 people.

TABLE 11-4

Department of Health and Human Services Poverty Guidelines, 2004

Size of Family Unit	48 Contiguous States and Washington, D.C.	Alaska	Hawaii
1	$ 9,310	$11,630	$10,700
2	$12,490	$15,610	$14,360
3	$15,670	$19,590	$18,020
4	$18,850	$23,570	$21,680
5	$22,030	$27,550	$25,340
6	$25,210	$31,530	$29,000
7	$28,390	$35,510	$32,660
8	$31,570	$39,490	$36,320
For each additional person, add	$ 3,180	$ 3,980	$ 3,660

Source: *Federal Register,* vol. 69, no. 30, February 13, 2004, 7333–7338.
Note: Amounts listed are maximum yearly income.

States also have very different levels of enthusiasm for building prisons. In fiscal year 2002, the Texas state government devoted 6.9 percent of state spending to prison construction. That is a level of spending nearly double that of the national average. In contrast, West Virginia's state government spent only 1.5 percent of its state budget on corrections.[39]

Highways. In 2001, state and local governments spent $91 billion on highways and roads. Most of this money came from dedicated revenue sources, such as the gasoline tax. In addition, the federal government kicked in another $25 billion from the federal highway trust fund and other sources.

Not surprisingly, states with wide open spaces spend more money on highway construction and transportation. In 2002, Wyoming devoted 26.4 percent of total state expenditures to transportation. This was the highest percentage of any state in the country, followed by North Dakota at 20 percent and South Dakota at 17 percent. Nationwide, state governments spent 8.9 percent of total revenues on transportation in 2002.[40]

Restraints on State and Local Budgeteers

Politicians and journalists usually talk about "the budget" in the singular tense, as if elected officials meet every year or two to divvy up a single pot of money. That's misleading. State and local officials cannot actually lay their hands on all the revenues flowing into state and local coffers. Most federal funds are devoted to specific programs, such as Medicaid. Revenue streams from many state sources, such as the car registration tax, are likewise dedicated to specific purposes, such as highway construction. State and local officials develop their budgets under several additional restraints as well.

Unfunded Mandates

For years, state officials complained bitterly about the federal government's habit of mandating that states achieve a goal, such as an environmental clean up, but then failing to provide any money to pay for it. State officials viewed such unfunded mandates as an affront to the notion of federalism itself. In 1995, Congress did something surprising. It passed legislation that dramatically curtailed the practice of imposing unfunded mandates on state governments. This measure alleviated some of the pressures on states, but it did not end the problem. Ironically, in the late 1990s, state governments increasingly imposed unfunded mandates on county and city governments. Evidently, many state governments were no more able to resist the temptation to set goals and make someone else pay for them than the federal government had long been.

The United States is a federation. Under this federal system, state governments and the federal government are coequal, at least in theory. If the federal government encroaches too much on state prerogatives, the U.S. Supreme Court can step in and strike federal actions down.

But states are not federations. Local governments are not equal partners with state governments. In most cases, state governments are free to intervene in local arrangements as they please. Beginning in the late nineteenth century, many states extended the sovereign powers of government to local governments by passing legislation that provided for home rule. Communities could enact charters and ordinances, change their names, and annex their neighbors without the permission of the legislature. They also controlled their own budgets and property taxes.

At the time, California was one of the strongest home-rule states. In recent years, however, that has changed. California cities now control less than half of their discretionary spending. The state tells them what they must do with the rest. The situation is even worse for California's counties. They now have the final say over less than one-third of the money they spend.[41]

Ballot Initiatives and the Budget Process

California's experience illustrates one of the most significant trends in state finances—the growing use of ballot initiatives to shape and restrain state tax systems. According to Bill Piper of the Initiative and Referendum Institute, voters put 130 tax initiatives on ballots nationwide between 1978 and 1999. Roughly two-thirds of them were antitax initiatives that cut, limited, or eliminated taxes in some way. Of these, forty-one passed. A whopping 67 percent of all antitax initiatives that came up for a vote between 1996 and 1999 passed.

When citizens put their hands directly on the tax levers, it often gets much harder for state and local governments to pay the bills. California is just one name on a list of states that are choking on tax policies put in place by voters. Colorado, Oregon, and Washington are only a few of the states dealing with financial problems caused by ballot initiatives.

By 2004, Washington State faced a budget shortfall of about $700 million, due in large part to antitax initiatives.

These maneuvers have influenced individual tax changes. They also have been known to paralyze state legislatures and local governments. Fifteen states have passed initiatives or referendums that require more than 50 percent of the vote, or supermajorities, on tax decisions made by the state legislatures. In Montana, for example, a supermajority is three-quarters of the legislature. Roy Brown, House majority leader for the state, sees changing tax policy as pretty much impossible. "We can't even get a three-fourths majority vote to go to the bathroom," he told the *Billings Gazette* in November 2002.[42]

Conclusion

State and local governments rely on six major types of taxes to fund the operations of government—property taxes; income taxes; sales taxes; sin, or excise, taxes; user fees; and gift taxes. Each of these taxes has distinct pros and cons. Local governments like property taxes because they set the rates and thus control exactly how much revenue is raised. However, when property taxes rise, seniors and people on fixed incomes often suffer. Income taxes tend to be more progressive; sales taxes are more regressive. The exact configuration of taxes in any given state reflects that state's history and political culture. Tax revenues, in turn, support the budget process by which state and local governments set their spending priorities.

State and local government finances can be difficult to unravel. However, it is an area that citizens are well advised to watch. Not only do the budget decisions of state and local governments determine the services individuals enjoy and how much they pay in taxes, it is also often the arena in which the priorities of public life are sorted out. Is it fair or unfair to ask wealthy citizens to pay a higher percentage of their income in taxes? States such as Texas and Florida that have no income taxes have in a sense decided that it is unfair. States like California, which does have an income tax, have reached a different conclusion. Should everyone pay more in taxes to extend healthcare to low-income citizens? Massachusetts's tax policies suggest that its answer is yes. Many states in the Deep South have reached different conclusions. In short, the consequences of budget decisions are very real.

There is another reason to pay close attention to state and local finances. Barring a repeat of the economic boom of the 1990s, they will almost certainly need to change. States like Tennessee that rely heavily on sales tax revenues face particularly serious challenges. As Internet sales continue to grow, sales tax revenues in particular will most likely continue to falter. This will create a need for new revenue-raising measures. Yet states with ballot initiatives may well find new approaches blocked by antitax sentiments at the voting booth.

Many states have turned to the federal government for help. In particular, states have asked Congress to relieve them of some of the fiscal burdens of Medicaid. Yet for now, large-scale federal assistance seems unlikely. As a result, in the coming years states will have to focus as never before on the programs and priorities that drive their taxing and spending decisions. The following three chapters examine some of the most important state and local government programs in more detail. In many states, they almost certainly will need to change soon.

Key Concepts

balanced budget (p. 385)

bonds (p. 382)

bricks-and-mortar retailers (p. 370)

budget process (p. 368)

budget shortfall (p. 366)

capital investments (p. 382)

discretionary spending (p. 387)

dividend (p. 381)

entitlement (p. 388)

estate taxes (p. 368)

excise, or sin, taxes (p. 368)

expenditures (p. 385)

fiscal federalism (p. 388)

fiscal year (p. 384)

focused consumption taxes (p. 368)

gift taxes (p. 368)

income tax (p. 366)

insurance trust money (p. 377)

intergovernmental transfers (p. 377)

municipal bonds (p. 383)

progressive tax system (p. 366)

regressive taxes (p. 369)

revenues (p. 366)

sales tax (p. 366)

service economy (p. 368)

severance taxes (p. 377)

tax burden (p. 366)

tax capacities (p. 380)

tax efforts (p. 380)

tax revolt (p. 367)

user fees (p. 367)

Suggested Readings

2004 State and Local Government Sourcebook. Washington, D.C.: *Governing* magazine. Annual publication that provides easy access to a wide range of information on state and local government finances.

Suggested Web Sites

www.census.gov/prod/www/statistical-abstract-03.html. The U.S .Census Bureau provides an on-line version of the *Statistical Abstract of the United States.* Section 8, "State and Local Government Finances and Employment," provides a wealth of information on state and local government revenue and spending.

www.cbpp.org/state/index.html. Web site of the Center on Budget and Policy Priorities. Founded in 1981, the center studies fiscal policy and public programs at the federal and state levels that affect low-income and moderate-income families and individuals. An excellent source of information on state budget controversies and debates.

www.nasbo.org/Publications/PDFs/budpro2002.pdf. The National Association of State Budget Officers rundown of budget processes in the states for 2002.

CHAPTER 12

Education

Reading, Writing, and Regulation

Making learning fun can be hard work. Here, Angela Lively plays word bingo with her kindergarten class in Indianapolis in December 2003. The job isn't made any easier when children come from low-income households. Lively keeps a box of shoes so that children can get a new pair when their old ones no longer fit. When she sends assignments home, she includes packets of crayons, glue sticks and scissors to make sure students have supplies to finish projects. Students at her school can get hats, coats, gloves, belts, socks, backpacks, and even underwear if their parents can't afford them.

Why do some localities still have much better schools than others when there is such a strong national push for standards in education?

Why is there such variation in what schools teach from state to state?

Why are there so many different brands of school reform?

As father of the American **common school**, nineteenth-century Massachusetts education chief Horace Mann would have much to say about the federal **No Child Left Behind Act**, signed into law by President George W. Bush at the dawn of the twenty-first century.

Mann spent the 1840s riding from village to village pushing for local taxes to be raised to pay for the education that he argued should be the right of every child.

COMMON SCHOOL

In a democratic society, a school in which children of all income levels attend at taxpayer expense.

NO CHILD LEFT BEHIND ACT

Federal law enacted in January 2002 that introduced new accountability measures for elementary and secondary schools in all states that wish to receive federal aid.

STATE BOARD OF EDUCATION

Top policymaking body in each of the fifty states, usually consisting of appointees selected by governors.

At a time when schooling was reserved mostly to families able to afford tutors or boarding schools, Mann's endeavor was school reform for radicals. The one-room schoolhouses he inspected as First Secretary of Massachusetts's **State Board of Education** were crude and ill equipped. Many of the teachers were poorly paid and trained, and regular attendance by students was not even required by law. Through personal advocacy and his widely circulated writings, Mann did much to build up the state as the primary actor in the fledgling experiment of public education in the United States.

So, one would guess that Mann would be pleased to learn of the No Child Left Behind Act's demands that all schools make "adequate yearly progress" in bringing students of all races and ethnic backgrounds to an achievement level deemed proficient by state education leaders. That he would approve of the law's demand for a qualified teacher in every classroom by the 2005–2006 school year. He might look kindly on the new emphasis on reading instruction based on what some advocates tout as "scientific research."

But Mann would be less likely to warm to the law's penalties for schools that do not raise student test scores. Penalties such as the loss of federal funds, the dismissal of staff, or the humiliation of being slapped with the label of "failing." Mann was a Unitarian who championed the public school in which the children of doctors and lawyers would learn alongside the children of manual laborers.

He might be wary of the law's potential to bankroll families who seek to leave bad neighborhood schools. This nod to free-market competition eventually might send taxpayer funds to selective religious and private schools. Most dramatically, he might be stunned by the degree of federal intrusion into responsibilities that he had worked so hard to give the states.

A century and a half of impassioned debate has passed since Mann's time. The years have yielded few certainties in American education. What is undisputed, however, is the way the quest for good schools is intertwined with democratic civic ideals. The everyday rough-and-tumble over curriculum and budgets pays constant heed to this country's founding ideals of individual dignity, the promise of social mobility, and government by consent of the governed.

It was not just for public relations that President Lyndon B. Johnson viewed education as "the answer to all our national problems." [1] A former teacher himself, Johnson launched what he called the Great Society initiative. This was a series of new federal programs design to curb poverty and expand opportunities to the nation's disadvantaged. It rested, as he said in one speech, on "abundance and liberty for all" and led the federal government to make its first major forays into education policy.

Given the variety of policy approaches permitted under the U.S. system of federalism, education has always been governed, to the extent possible, by the units closest to the citizenry, the states and localities. Education accounts for the largest share of state government spending—35.4 percent of general funds—according to the National Association of State Budget Officers. One-fourth of all U.S. citizens either attend a public school or are employed by one. Members of all parties and followers of various philosophical leanings agree that education has the most impact on economic growth and civic engagement.

The nation's universal compulsory education laws mean that all taxpayers, not just families with school-age children, are required to support society's bid for an educated citizenry. Education is a field that brings out the panic in some parents who feel their child's whole future is at stake with every report card. It is a field that allows ambitious politicians to make names for themselves by vowing to make schools more accountable. Candidates vow to get better results in the classroom from taxpayer dollars. They do this despite occasional resistance by professional educators who value autonomy and resent burdensome regulation.

The stakes have always been high. But it was in the final decades of the twentieth century that political leaders and many in the general public shifted to a mindset that public education was in dire and ongoing need of fixing. The 1983 report *A Nation at Risk* was commissioned by the Reagan administration. It declared that the United States was just that because a rising tide of mediocrity in schools invited defeat by a foreign power.

That report set in motion a continual movement with themes such as **back to basics**, new curriculum **standards**, and **high-stakes standardized testing**. The movement involved not just teachers and parents, but also federal and state legislators, local **school boards**, courts, advocacy groups, even the national political parties. It is a wave of reform that continues well into the twenty-first century.

BACK TO BASICS

A movement against modern education "fads" and a return to an emphasis on traditional core subjects such as reading, writing, and arithmetic.

STANDARDS

Fixed criteria for learning that students are expected to reach in specific subjects by specific grade years.

HIGH-STAKES STANDARDIZED TESTING

Testing of elementary and secondary students in which poor results can mean either that the student fails to get promoted or that the school loses its accreditation.

SCHOOL BOARDS

Elected or appointed bodies that determine major policies and budgets for each of the nation's school districts.

Organization and Leadership: Schools Have Many Bosses

DEPARTMENTS OF EDUCATION

State-level agencies responsible for overseeing public education.

TEACHER LICENSURE PROCEDURES

The academic degrees, work experience, and performance on adult standardized tests a state requires before a teacher candidate can be certified to work in a school district.

ACCREDITATION

Certification process in which outside experts visit and evaluate a school or college to vouch for minimum quality standards.

The United States is one of the few industrialized countries with no national ministry of education. The U.S. Department of Education was created in 1978, but the primary authority for running schools rests with the fifty states. This is in accordance with the Tenth Amendment edict that the powers not delegated by the Constitution to the federal government are reserved to the states. An exception is the District of Columbia. Its board of education derives its funds from the city's appropriation from Congress.

As far back as the 1780s, state legislatures were tasked with schooling the citizenry. For example, in 1857, Minnesota's constitution proclaimed that the "stability of a Republican form of government depending upon the intelligence of the people, it is the duty of the legislature to establish a general and uniform system of public schools."[2] In other words, the consensus was that creating a well-educated population not only helped individual citizens prosper, it also helped entrench the democratic process.

Fifty varying traditions make for a lot of bosses in a democratic approach to education. A system that permits local innovations and variations is a far cry from systems in Europe. Legend has it that a national education chief there can look at a clock on any given weekday and know precisely what lesson is being taught in classrooms across the country.

Modern state legislatures, working with state **departments of education**, are the players who deal with major state policy questions and large-scale resource issues. A state legislature can raise teacher salaries statewide, equalize funding between districts, and set up health benefits and retirement plans for the state's pool of teachers. It can borrow money by "floating" state bonds to provide schools with construction funds, which commits taxpayers to long-term debts.

The states are also the main players in determining **teacher licensure procedures**. For example, they determine whether or not teacher candidates take a standardized test and how education schools are awarded **accreditation**.

The more complex state decisions are proposed and implemented by an experienced educator who is the chief state school officer. The governor can appoint these officials, as in Iowa, Maine, and New Jersey. They can be appointed by a state board of education, as in Utah, Louisiana, and Vermont. Sometimes, they are elected on a partisan ballot, as in North Carolina and Oklahoma or on a nonpartisan ballot, as in North Dakota and Oregon. They work closely with state boards of education. These boards also can be appointed or elected, depending on the state, and their members usually represent each region of a state.

> A system that permits local innovations and variations is a far cry from systems in Europe. Legend has it that a national education chief there can look at a clock on any given weekday and know precisely what lesson is being taught in classrooms across the country.

Further down the chain are the **local education agencies** (LEAs), which have been formed in nearly fifteen thousand **school districts** scattered over cities, counties, and townships. School districts are staffed with full-time professionals, but they carry out policies set by school boards or other locally elected officials.

The extent of policymaking authority enjoyed by each LEA or district is determined by a state's legislature. In Horace Mann's region of New England, local control is strong. The population of states in the Deep South traditionally has been poor and rural. Many citizens are suspicious and untutored in the workings of government. As a result, these states have retained a more centralized role.

Even within states, there are huge differences in economies, traditions, and demographics. Think of rural, mountainous northern California versus densely populated, arid southern California, which some want to turn into separate states. Northern Virginia, an affluent suburban area of Washington, D.C., that favors active government, is very different from Virginia's rural areas, in which folks favor limited government.

The degree of flexibility states can give to localities in education depends greatly on scale. It also depends on the degree to which local citizens feel passionate about participating in school governance. The nation's school districts are a patchwork quilt that evolved as individually as the states themselves. Texas, for example, contains more than one thousand school districts. These vary widely, from the liberal college town of Austin to the conservative business center of Dallas. By contrast, rural, and still largely undeveloped, Hawaii is administered as one district.

In large cities, such as Los Angeles, schools are administered under a centralized authority. This is why the district is called Los Angeles Unified. New York City, the nation's largest school district with more than one million students, has tried both centralized and decentralized approaches. In 2002, Mayor Michael Bloomberg won approval from the state legislature to eliminate the city's thirty-two separate school boards and centralize control. The intent is to reduce what some view as administrative bloat, so that the new chancellor, Joel Klein, can experiment with such reforms as charter schools and be held accountable for results. Is it working? More time is needed to tell.

School boards are quintessentially U.S. democratic institutions that got their start in the Progressive Era at the end of the nineteenth century. These citizen boards were envisioned as a way to end the spoils system. Individuals would no longer be able to show partisan and political favor by awarding jobs to their followers. This would make way for the shared pursuit of effective public education.

Looking back now, that promise seems quaint, given that political interest groups continue to target school board elections. In Virginia, for example, school board elections were abolished in the early 1950s because southern white traditionalists feared that too many candidates were sympathetic to the then-growing school desegregation movement. It was not until 1992

LOCAL EDUCATION AGENCIES

School districts, some of which may be cities, or counties, or subsets thereof.

SCHOOL DISTRICTS

Local administrative jurisdictions that hire staff and report to school boards on management of area public schools.

Policy in Practice: Do School Board Races Improve Education or Simply Create More Bumper Stickers?

At the bottom of the ballot, far below the household names seeking the presidency or a seat in Congress, appear the names of candidates for your local school board. Most, rest assured, are fine people. But with voter turnout often as low as 20 percent in off-year elections, school board races are sometimes derided as wasteful exercises dominated, in the worst cases, by personally ambitious, underqualified, single-issue ideologues.

According the National School Boards Association (NSBA), 95 percent of the members of the nation's 14,890 school boards are elected, 2.8 percent are appointed. The remainder serve on boards with both elected and appointed members.

Today, only 10 percent of the country's ninety-five thousand school board members declare a party affiliation. Most run and pay for their bumper stickers using their own funding, without the typical baggage of campaign donations from business groups or trade unions (other than the teachers' associations). In large cities, such as San Diego, Milwaukee, and Los Angeles, candidates can spend tens of thousands of dollars. In the poorer communities of the Deep South, fundamentalist candidates may rely instead on tactical support from the Costa Mesa, California-based National Association of Christian Educators.

Although some complain that school board incumbents are firmly entrenched, school board races actually

TABLE 12-1

Voter Turnout and the Timing of School Board Elections

	Percent Turnout When School Board Elections Are		Percent Increase When Board Elections Are Held on the Same Day as
	Always Held on the Same Day as	Never Held on the Same Day as	
National or State Elections	43.8	25.8	+18.0
Mayoral or City Council Elections	41.8	29.1	+12.7

Source: Frederick M. Hess, "School Boards at the Dawn of the 21st Century: Conditions and Challenges of District Governance," National School Boards Association, 2002.

Note: Turnout percentage is respondents' estimate of the percentage of registered voters who voted in the most recent local school board election.

seem competitive. Compared with congressional races, that is. An NSBA survey shows that from 1998 to 2001, 47.4 percent of the races produced no defeats for incumbents. In the U.S. Congress, the incumbency re-

that elected members would once again replace appointed members. In addition, during the 1990s, conservative Christian political activists zeroed in on school board elections as battlegrounds for the agenda of promoting school prayer and eliminating sex education.

Some critics say school boards actually produce fewer school improvements than they do campaign bumper stickers. (See Box 12-1.) That is one reason they were curbed by city governments during the 1990s in Boston, Chicago, Cleveland, Detroit, and, to a lesser extent, the District of Columbia.[3] Faced with stagnating test scores and an exodus of families to private or parochial schools, urban leaders argued that emergency action to arrest

tention rate is well over 90 percent. Turnout for school board elections is highly influenced by the presence of state and national races, with turnout improving substantially when school board races take place at the same time as those other more visible races. (See Table 12-1.) The average school board term of office is 4 years; the average member serves six or seven years. Many win a second term, serve, and then go on to run for higher office. Those whose children have graduated, however, can find themselves losing energy and credibility.

Among the most vocal critics of elected school boards are the superintendents, whose function as chief executive officers of school districts can sometimes be thwarted by boards, which have power to hire and fire them. They argue that school board members, who are paid little or nothing, often take office with little understanding of nuts-and-bolts management issues and that many need training. "With some exceptions for members who serve purely as a civic duty, many board members' interests are either ideological, political, or both," writes William J. Price, a former superintendent in Michigan. "The more highly politicized and single issue-oriented the school board election is, the more difficult it is to create a governance culture in which the school board operates within a carefully defined and crafted set of role expectations, while maximizing the role of the CEO."[a]

Princeton University molecular biology professor Lee Silver, after a frustrating term as an elected school board member in his college town, proposed that boards be abolished and replaced by a committee of professional educators. "There isn't a single thing school boards do well," he wrote. "On the contrary, what they do more often than not is to get in the way of school district administrators who are perfectly able to run the schools by themselves."[b]

But abolition of elected school boards is unlikely in today's political climate. So-called education "experts" don't carry much weight among average citizens—and many of today's pushy baby-boomer parents will simply call in another expert with opposing views. Parents want a role in picking the superintendent and assigning budget priorities, which is why they value board members who seek their votes. And the low turnout for school board elections could easily be a sign that constituents are satisfied with the way boards run things.

[a] William J. Price, "Policy Governance Revisited," *School Administrator* Web edition, February 2001.

[b] Lee M. Silver, "Why I'm Giving Up on School Boards," *School Administrator,* Web edition, February 1998.

the decline of the schools was more important than the democracy of a thousand voices.

The idea is that a centralized authority figure, such as a mayor or school chief, is accountable in the mystifying field of school reform. Appointees from an elected mayor are more likely to take decisive action and worry less about glad-handing, returning campaign favors, and seeking reelection. The jury is still out on such propositions, and proposals to abolish elected school boards tend to appear only in districts that are in dire straits.

The challenges facing school boards are formidable. Keep in mind that by law a public school must accept all students who live within its jurisdiction. This makes planning tricky. School boards do not have taxing authority, but most prepare budgets for approval by the county board or city council, which must balance education spending against spending on police and fire protection and transportation. It is the board that hires the superintendent . . . who hires the principals . . . who hire the teachers who taught you to read.

Money Matters

The lion's share of school funding comes from the states. On average, states paid for 49.9 percent of a school's costs in 2003, according to the U.S. Census Bureau's Annual Survey of Local Government Finances. This is in comparison to 43 percent from local jurisdictions and just 7 percent from the federal government.

Washington's contributions are invaluable as a way to target and upgrade schools mired in poverty through the **Title I** program. Their relatively small size, however, leads some critics of the No Child Left Behind law to question its effectiveness. They wonder how much leverage distant federal officials in D.C. can have on boosting academic achievement in local schools nationwide. Especially when there is so much variation in curriculums, tests, and student performance standards.

Many states and localities raise school funds from income tax and sales taxes. Forty-one states support education through the morally controversial practice of running a state lottery. The bulk of school funds, however, come from the local property tax. This tax is based on the assessed value of a taxpayer's home, usually a percentage of each $100 in assessed value.

There is a logic to this. All taxpayers in a given community are believed to benefit from a quality school system—it helps maintain attractive real estate values and helps create an educated workforce. That tax system is progressive. Homeowners whose property is worth more pay more in nominal amounts, although all pay the same percentage. Most mortgage companies inconspicuously collect most of these tax funds for homeowners. The money is then kept in the homeowner's personal escrow account until the tax is due.

The downside of property taxes is that as property values gain in value, the assessment and corresponding property taxes also rise—irrespective of whether a homeowner's income is rising along with it. As mentioned in Chapter 11, this vicious circle is what fueled passage of California's famous Proposition 13 in 1978. This statewide ballot measure capped property taxes and ignited a tax revolt. This revolt is credited with launching former California governor Ronald Reagan, a champion of curbing the size of government, toward the White House.

An even deeper problem with funding schools via the property tax is the fact that wealthier districts are able to keep theirs attractively low as a percentage rate and still produce enough revenue dollars to support good schools. For example, in affluent Beverly Hills, California, property was—and still is—very expensive. Yet the tax rate cited in *Serrano v. Priest* (1971) was only $2.38 per $100 in assessed value.

Place this up against the $5.48 per $100 in the low-income Baldwin Park area. Schools were demonstrably inferior, and the community was able to spend only half of what was spent in Beverly Hills. In this famous school funding equity case, the California Supreme Court agreed that families in Baldwin Park were being denied a "fundamental right" to quality schools.[4] The court ordered the legislature to find a way to make school funding more equitable.

A slightly different principle was spelled out by the U.S. Supreme Court in the 1973 ruling in *San Antonio Independent School District v. Rodriguez*. In this case, attorneys for a largely Mexican American population found that their clients were paying a tax rate 25 percent higher than nearby affluent school districts. These less affluent districts, however, were only able or willing to fund schools at only 60 percent of that enjoyed by wealthy San Antonio neighborhoods.

The Supreme Court acknowledged the disparities but ruled that equal school funding is not a federal constitutional right: "The Equal Protection Clause does not require absolute equality or precisely equal advantages" the justices wrote. Still, the precedent was set. State courts began to see themselves as protectors of poor and rural students, and the school funding equity movement at the state level gathered more steam.

These two cases launched a decades-long movement of constitutional litigation on school funding that has spread to forty-five states. It pits the principle of local control against pressures to close the gap between wealthy and poor districts. Jurists, educators, parents, and tax activists continue to fight over the key to school equity. Must the funneling more resources into disadvantaged communities require penalizing affluent communities?

Understandably, citizens in affluent districts like to see their tax dollars spent in their own communities, and they will lobby and push to keep their schools the best. Many middle-class and upper-class taxpayers say they paid extra for their homes so that their children could attend schools that lack for no essentials. Citizens in poor districts, by contrast, argue that dilapidated school buildings, meager resources, and teachers at the low end of the profession's already low pay scale are the chief reasons for the achievement gap between their children and those in wealthier districts. (See Map 12-1.)

In the 1970s, most courts, like California's, ruled in favor of greater equalization among districts. After some judicial setbacks, the momentum slowed in the 1980s before gaining ground again in the courts of the 1990s. Nowhere was this drama played out more visibly than in Vermont, where a 1997 state supreme court ruling prompted the legislature to enact the controversial Act 60. The act forces wealthier districts that want to upgrade their schools to share their added funds with schools in poor districts.

Responses among state legislatures to court orders on school funding have varied. The issue has not always broken down easily along conservative-liberal lines. Indeed, the percentage of per-pupil expenditures has risen most steeply during periods of conservative ascendancy, such as the 1920s and 1950s.[5] This all demonstrates the degree to which creating quality schools is a near-universal value.

Researchers examining the role that money plays in learning—referred to as the "production function"—have created models that attempt to factor in such variables as the school's percentage of student dropouts, graduation rates, teacher salaries, and enrollment. (See Map 12-2.) These models also look at the percentage of children living in poverty and those in female-headed households, how many students have disabilities and how many of these have severe disabilities, and how many students possess limited English proficiency.[6]

Few believe that pouring in money automatically produces school improvements. As a result, they also attempt to consider such human factors as the degree of cooperation among teachers, rates of absenteeism, and the extent of disruptive behavior in classrooms.

Most importantly, researchers try to isolate precisely how monies are best spent inside schools to derive the most benefit. Areas in which increased funding translates into student learning gains, according to one study, included spending on instruction, central office administration, and teacher-student ratios. Areas that demonstrated less of a payoff included funds for school-level administration, overall **capital outlays** and salaries for teachers with advanced degrees.[7]

Since the movement for new standards and accountability gained ground in the 1990s, school funding battles have shifted from an emphasis on equalization toward an effort to achieve adequacy, or what is required to get students to meet high standards.[8] To determine how much per-pupil spending is adequate for a school district, some states convene a panel of experts who use their professional judgment to pick the resources needed by schools, determine the costs of acquiring these resources, and then adjust their recommendations in favor of the needier districts. Examples of such states are Maine, Oregon, and Wyoming. Other states use the **successful**

MAP 12-1 Spending Per Student by State, 1999–2000

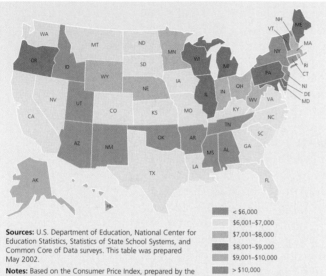

Legend:
- < $6,000
- $6,001–$7,000
- $7,001–$8,000
- $8,001–$9,000
- $9,001–$10,000
- > $10,000

Sources: U.S. Department of Education, National Center for Education Statistics, Statistics of State School Systems, and Common Core of Data surveys. This table was prepared May 2002.

Notes: Based on the Consumer Price Index, prepared by the Bureau of Labor Statistics, U.S. Department of Labor, adjusted to a school-year basis. These data do not reflect differences in inflation rates from state to state. Beginning in 1980–1981, state administration expenditures are excluded. Beginning in 1989–1990, extensive changes were made in the data collection procedures. There are discrepancies in average daily attendance reporting practices from state to state. Some data have been revised from previously published figures.

CAPITAL OUTLAYS

A category of school funding that focuses on long-term improvements to physical assets.

schools model, wherein groups of schools whose students have achieved well according to state standards are examined for their average per-pupil costs, which are then applied across the state. Examples of these states are Ohio, Illinois, and Mississippi.[9]

The funding appropriated by state legislatures depends on the input expected of localities. New York State, for example, reports the nation's largest disparity in per-pupil spending between affluent and less affluent districts.[10] The amounts also vary by regional costs of living and a state's philosophy on the proper reach of government.

Furthermore, affluent suburban communities often differ from their urban counterparts in funding priorities. Parents in downtown Detroit or Cleveland, for example, may want extra monies for crime prevention and building upgrades, whereas suburbanites in places such as Bloomfield Hills, Michigan, and Shaker Heights, Ohio, want more money spent on computer technology and extracurricular programs.

Rural districts in states such as South Dakota or Wyoming have their own problems. They may have trouble raising teacher salaries, for example, if it means pushing those salaries out of line with comparable local salaries in other professions.

In rankings compiled annually by *Education Week,* the states determined most generous in terms of multiple-factor "resource adequacy" in 2002 in rank order were West Virginia, New York, Wyoming, Vermont, Delaware, and Wisconsin. States ranked at the bottom were Utah, Arizona, California, Tennessee, Florida, and Mississippi. States that did the most to equalize disparities among districts were, in order, Hawaii, Utah, Delaware and New Mexico.[11]

Looking strictly at per-pupil spending, the state offering the least was Utah at $4,769. The jurisdiction spending the most was the District of Columbia at $11,009. Unfortunately for the nation's capital, its high per-pupil spending for years has been accompanied by some of urban America's lowest student test scores. This has made it a favorite whipping boy for conservatives who argue the futility of "throwing money at problems." (See Box 12-2.)

Understandably, school funding is affected by economic downturns. Nearly all states are required to balance their budgets. As a result, they must

MAP 12-2 Student Enrollment in Public Schools by State, Fall 2000

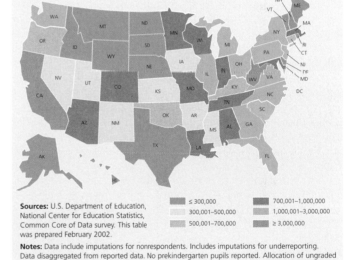

Sources: U.S. Department of Education, National Center for Education Statistics, Common Core of Data survey. This table was prepared February 2002.

≤ 300,000
300,001–500,000
500,001–700,000
700,001–1,000,000
1,000,001–3,000,000
≥ 3,000,000

Notes: Data include imputations for nonrespondents. Includes imputations for underreporting. Data disaggregated from reported data. No prekindergarten pupils reported. Allocation of ungraded students to elementary and secondary levels based on proportions derived from prior years.

Local Focus: Got an Alternative to Throwing Money at Schools? Tell It to Kansas City

In August 2003, a judge in Kansas City, Missouri, issued a ruling that ended a labyrinthine, high profile lawsuit over school desegregation and unequal funding between the city's urban and suburban schools. The postmortems offered by attorneys and educators were eye-popping: In twenty-six years, $2 billion had been spent; multiple court rulings had gone back and forth that had required tax increases and redrawing of boundaries; and fifty-five dilapidated schools were renovated while seventeen new ones were built, including a new $32 million magnet high school designed to attract suburban students by featuring, among other assets, an Olympic-sized pool and indoor track. Magnet schools place a strong emphasis in a particular subject area, for example, music, science, drama, or math. Students are selected through an application process instead of being assigned based on residence as in traditional public schools.

The main goals of the litigation, however—the recruitment of more white students to the mostly black inner-city schools and improved academic achievement by minorities—went largely unfulfilled. One of the series of judges who handled the epic case was reported to have confessed, "Maybe I created too expensive a school system." [a]

The degree to which money should factor as an ingredient in any recipe for school improvement is among the least settled disputes in education research.

Conservatives have long argued against the futility of "throwing money at problem schools." Indeed, school districts plagued by "bureaucratic bloat," embezzlement scandals, and rigid regulation and paperwork do not inspire school reformers to push additional funds as a panacea. If a funding shortage is the cause of underperformance, critics ask, how do you explain the fact that students often perform better at private and Catholic schools, some with tuitions under $3,000? How to explain the fact that students in the other countries of the Organization for Economic Cooperation and Development outperform American children on reading and math tests, even though the per-

pupil spending rates in these mostly European countries are nearly half the U.S. average? [b]

Such critics argue that competently run schools provide "added value." This, they say, has as much to do with academic rigor as with simple dollars. They offer case studies in which infusions of cash failed to prompt a noticeable rise in test scores. [c]

Backers of increased school spending argue that in most cases, higher test scores are linked to affluent districts. They dramatize the "savage inequalities" in resources between districts, using a phrase coined from Jonathan Kozol's 1991 book of the same name. Who wants to teach or learn inside a run-down and filthy building? Liberals emphasize that greater spending is needed in districts with a preponderance of children from low-income homes and uneducated parents. They note that some children also are more expensive to educate—the National Center on Education Statistics calculates that special education students need 2.3 times the student average, poor students 1.2 times the average.

The lack of consensus on this question is one reason the fifty states and the District of Columbia vary so widely in what they spend. (See Map 12-1.) The jury is still out on measuring the role of funding. As the Kansas City drama confirmed, money may not be a guaranteed solution to troubled schools. But most communities feel obliged to spend goodly amounts in the course of finding one.

[a] Donna McGuire," Judge Ends Desegregation Case after 26 Years and $2 Billion," *Kansas City Star,* August 14, 2003.

[b] Center for Education Reform, "Spending More but Educating Less" www.edreform.com (accessed October 24, 2003). See also Thomas B. Fordham Foundation, "Spending More while Learning Less: U.S. School Productivity in International Perspective," report by Herbert J. Walberg, 1998. www.edexcellence.net (accessed October 24, 2003).

[c] Eric A. Hanushek, "Assessing the Effects of School Resources on Student Performance: An Update. *Educational Evaluation and Policy Analysis.* 19 (1997):141–164.

choose among raising taxes, drawing from budget stabilization (rainy day) funds, or cutting spending in areas such as corrections and welfare. In the fall of 2002, states suffered their weakest two-year growth rates since the recession of the early 1980s.

In 2003, California ceased paying its $10,000 merit awards to mid-career teachers who earned national certification.[12] Washington State suspended teacher cost-of-living salary hikes for two years. Oregon, faced with a protracted funding crisis and a legislature determined not to raise income taxes, watched as its largest communities around Portland approved a temporary new sales tax, narrowly avoiding having to end the school year early.

To school reformers, these state funding cuts were embarrassing. Occurring at a time when the federal No Child Left Behind law was just getting moving, critics were blasting the Bush administration for underfunding the program by some six billion dollars less than what had been agreed upon in the bipartisan authorization bill. Bush education secretary Roderick Paige took after them in an opinion piece, lamenting, "No matter how much we spend, it will never been enough for them."[13]

New Pressure to Perform

Except in the minds of some nostalgists, it is doubtful there ever was a halcyon era of consensus among education's disparate stakeholders. There are far too many disparate views about the nation's public schools to have all parties agree that they had achieved a satisfactory level of quality. Today's charge that schools are going to the proverbial hell in a hand basket also was heard throughout the 1940s and 1950s.

This charge intensified in 1957 after the Soviet Union launched its *Sputnik* satellite. Americans feared that U.S. students had fallen behind the country's cold war rivals in science and math. Traditionalists who hearken back to the classic education taught in the early twentieth century sometimes forget that in 1900, only 6 percent of children in the United States finished high school. Back then, the best that most could count on was a solid job in, say, manufacturing. College wasn't even an option for many.[14]

> Traditionalists who hearken back to the classic education taught in the early twentieth century sometimes forget that in 1900, only 6 percent of children in the United States finished high school.

The current crisis over performance was set in motion during the early 1980s by the Reagan administration. Education secretary Dr. Terrell Bell lit a fire under sometimes resentful educators in 1983 by publishing *A Nation at Risk*. This annual report ranked states by school achievement data. Today, there are continuing laments that test scores are plummeting, kids don't know U.S. history, and that graduates arrive in college or in the workplace unable to write a declarative sentence.

Grade inflation and boasts of widespread rising test scores have caused some critics to bemoan the **Lake Woebegon Effect,** taken from humorist Garrison Keillor's immortal town where "all the children are above average." The phrase personifies critics' fears and has become routine in the ears of educators, many of whom respond simply by waiting for the next reform "fad" to come and go.

It is true that school test scores in many years have been stagnate. It is hard to argue that a yawning achievement gap has not persisted between the preponderance of black and Hispanic students at the lower end of the achievement scale and the frequently more affluent whites and Asians near the top. Eighty-one percent of respondents to a 2001 Gallup Poll said that most American students achieve only a small part of their potential.[15]

Those who chose to see the glass as half full, however, point to the nation's ever-replenishing supply of successful entrepreneurs. Look at the country's proliferation of Nobel Prize winners, they say. Step back and admire how its corporations continue to dominate the world economy. Yes, a disturbing 67 percent of respondents to the annual Gallup Poll for *Phi Delta Kappan* magazine gave the nation's overall school system a grade of less than A or B. But defenders point out that far more assigned good grades to the performance of their own local schools. In addition, they note, parents in urban areas tend to be more critical of local schools than do suburban parents.[16]

Is it fair to blame a school for its students' performance, defenders ask, without considering each child's opportunity to learn? What about the income disparities that subject poorer kids to inferior schools? Schools that, however well-intentioned their staff, present a less rigorous curriculum, underqualified teachers, low expectations, resource disparities, and a disruptive climate? These students also tend to suffer from performance anxiety, negative peer influences, racial discrimination, sketchy preschool attendance, and homes in which the value of learning is not emphasized. So the debate roars on.

Meanwhile, in the front lines of education, the main performance indicator for schools remains not grades, not satisfaction surveys, not oral exams, but rather the standardized test. A thriving commercial testing industry has grown up to supply schools with inexpensive, mass-produced tests for quick, computerized scoring of large numbers of students from kindergarten to twelfth grade. Familiar giants in the multibillion-dollar industry include the Comprehensive Test of Basic Skills; the Iowa Test of Basic Skills; and the Stanford Achievement Test, or SAT.

Each publisher has developed procedures to continually rotate questions, keep the tests statistically valid and as free as possible from cultural bias, and minimize scorekeeping errors. And all for good reason. When things go awry, the result can be lawsuits. Some of these tests are **criterion referenced** and are intended to measure mastery of a given subject as defined by state standards. Most, however, are **norm referenced,** meaning that students are graded on how well they approach the mean student score on that same test administered around the country.[17]

Forty-two states have their own tests. Resistance among advocates of local control to proposals made in the 1990s for a national student test caused such tests to continue to be permitted under the No Child Left Behind Act. Florida has its Florida Comprehensive Assessment Test (FCAT), Virginia has its Standards of Learning, and New York has its Regents Exam. Critics still question whether these tests are properly aligned with a given district's or state's curriculum and if such tests are comparable to those used in other states.

After eight decades of standardized testing, sometimes it seems that the more experts learn, the more they learn there is to learn. In New York State, for example, a special panel of math and testing experts concluded in October 2003 that the state's new high school end-of-course tests were of unacceptably bad quality. They came to this conclusion after a poor showing on state tests by high school seniors. The tests were the first under No Child Left Behind. Unfortunately, the experienced professionals who had prepared them ignored their own guidelines for the number of students needed for a valid sample in testing the questions.

In an effort to provide some uniformity and continuity in testing, the federal government has administered its own test since 1969—the **National Assessment of Educational Progress** (NAEP). Nicknamed "the nation's report card," it is administered in volunteer sample districts to students in grades four, eight, and twelve. Over the years, NAEP scores have remained essentially flat, with subgroups' scores rising and falling. At a release of new scores in November 2003—the first time all fifty states contributed students to the national sampling—U.S. education secretary Roderick Paige hailed improvements in math scores among fourth graders and eighth graders, particularly minorities, although gains in reading scores were slight.[18]

Another key performance indicator coordinated by the U.S. Department of Education is the **Trends in International Mathematics and Sciences Study** (TIMSS). Designed to compare the academic achievement of students in thirty-two countries, the TIMMS study for 1999 found, for example, that the score for U.S. eighth graders is just above average for that of industrialized countries. Students in the United States beat out those in Mexico and Israel, but were far behind Finland and superstars like Japan and Singapore.[19]

Testing, testing, and still more testing. That's the way of things for students at Sun Path Elementary School in Shakopee, Minnesota. After poor test scores in the spring of 2003, the school was placed on the state's list of underachieving schools. Not a place a school wants to be, especially in Minnesota, one of the nation's best education states. Sun Path's way off the list? Testing earlier and more often.

NATIONAL ASSESSMENT OF EDUCATIONAL PROGRESS

Known as the "nation's report card," this is the only regularly conducted independent survey of what a nationally representative sample of students in grades 4, 8, and 12 know and can do in various subjects.

TRENDS IN INTERNATIONAL MATHEMATICS AND SCIENCES STUDY

Launched by the United States in 1995, it is a regularly updated study that compares performance in science and mathematics of students from thirty-two countries.

Policy in Practice: How College Tuition Gets Raised

College students who get irked when tuition goes up should nail down one key detail before rounding up their dorm mates to stage a protest. Who has the power to make education more expensive?

The answer depends on the state and its policies on the question of who pays for whom to gain access to public higher education.

In the decade ending in 2003–2004, average tuition and fees at public and private four-year colleges and universities, after adjusting for inflation, climbed a steep 47 percent and 42 percent, respectively, according to the College Board.

Tuition hikes grew thicker and faster with the economic downturn and state budget crunches during the first few years of the twenty-first century. State higher education appropriations were cut at a time when the children of the baby boomers were creating record-size freshman classes. In 2003, the average increase was 14 percent, but several public institutions imposed larger hikes. UCLA led the pack with a 43.1 percent increase, while the University of Arizona system raised tuition at all three major campuses by 39 percent.

Some students don't take it lying down. In Arizona, four students in 2003 filed suit against the Arizona Board of Regents to challenge the legality of the $1,010 tuition hike.[a] The Arizona students said the hike violated the state constitution's provision that tuition

be "as nearly free as possible." After the University of Maryland announced tuition hikes in the middle of academic year, seven students challenged the move—unsuccessfully—in circuit court. The Maryland students said the hike violated a contract.[b]

A whopping 80 percent of college students in the United States attend taxpayer-funded public institutions. This means that most family pocketbooks are squeezed by tuition decisions made by legislators, governors, and public higher education boards.

Tuition at private colleges is set by the board of trustees in consultation with administrators. In the public system, tuition is set using governance structures worked out over the decades by state statute. Nine states vest their legislatures with full authority on tuition. Twenty-eight states give that authority to a statewide higher education system coordinating body, and thirteen allow tuition to be set by institutional governing boards, which are composed of distinguished volunteers either appointed by the governor or elected.[c]

In some cases the decision-making authority on tuition is total, in others it is shared. In South Carolina and Washington State, for example, the legislature has complete decision-making authority for state colleges and universities. In North Carolina, the legislature considers recommendations from the governor and university board of governors and sets tuition rates as part of

U.S. school reform advocates frequently point out the superior academic performance of students in many other countries. They cite the relatively poor showing of U.S. students as a sign of an urgent need to introduce more resources and more accountability measures to get students up to speed. Others note, however, that many countries run schools that are rigidly tracked between a college-bound elite of students and the remainder who normally attend vocational schools. In the United States, all students have an equal opportunity to advance, at least in theory. (See Box 12-3.)

Then there are the stomach-churning tests known to every college applicant, the SAT and the less widely used ACT, which is used primarily in the Midwest. Designed by the private nonprofit Educational Testing Service and run by the private nonprofit College Board, the SAT is designed to be a preits annual appropriations bill. In Connecticut and Wisconsin, the authority resides with system boards, but the legislature can appropriate funding to freeze tuition rates and, in times of economic hardship, require increases. In Pennsylvania, the institutions and the state system share authority, but four legislative representatives serve on its board of governors.

Victims of tuition hikes point to an increasing chunk of the American family's income that is required to finance college—more than $11,000 on average for public institutions and $27,000 for private institutions. That is just tuition, fees, and room and board. That's like buying a new car every year. They complain that colleges have become profligate spenders. The burden on students and parents clearly has grown. Tuition in 1990 covered 20 percent of public institutions' costs; by 2002 that share had risen to 30 percent.[d]

It is true that colleges feel pressure to remain competitive in attracting students by outfitting campuses with health facilities, entertainment centers, and state-of-the-art electronic and computer equipment. There also is constant pressure to raise professors' salaries. Tuition, however, doesn't begin to cover the actual cost per student. This means that all students are to some extent subsidized. For example, public medical schools derive a mere 3 percent of their revenues from student tuition payments, according to the American Medical Student Association (AAMC). Because their state appropriations have been dropping for two decades, public colleges and universities have been striving for efficiencies and creating alternative sources of revenue such as university-affiliated foundations.

Those who raise tuition are aware of the pain they inflict. In Arizona, the 39 percent hike was combined with a 140 percent increase in need-based student aid, and the tuition increase was done after the regents conducted a comprehensive study of the missions, strengths, and finances of the state schools, along with the needs of the state economy.

In Maryland, a lone regent in 2003 proposed doubling tuition in order to improve campus finances while attracting a higher caliber of student. In most of higher education, however, that is a minority view. Nationwide surveys show there is consensus that all of society benefits from widespread access to college.

[a] *Arizona Republic,* August 27, 2003.

[b] *Baltimore Sun,* April 16, 2003.

[c] *Survey of State Tuition, Fees, and Financial Assistance Policies, 2003,* State Higher Education Executive Officers. www.sheeo.org (accessed October 22, 2003).

[d] "Why Does College Cost So Much?: A Forthright Discussion about Tuition in Public Colleges and Universities," Association of Governing Boards of Universities and Colleges, 2003.

dictor of college achievement. The test has been renamed and recalibrated on several occasions. What began as the Scholastic Aptitude Test became the Scholastic Assessment Test. Thirty years of annual scores from this test have prompted much anguish.

In the early 1980s, a study found that average scores had fallen by 81 points from 1963–1977—from 478 down to 429 on the verbal test and from 502 to 470 on the math test. More recently, however, the College Board has been upbeat. During the 1990s, reading and math scores for the college-bound rose to over 500. In an August 2003 report, the board reported the highest level of math scores in thirty-five years. Verbal scores also were back up to the level reached in 1987. And all of this with a record number of students taking the exam.

Beyond standardized testing—and both before and after passage of the No Child Left Behind Act—one performance indicator that is gaining ground is the measurement of high school graduation rates. The states are a patchwork of methods for figuring these rates, which has led to a policy conundrum. Experts point out that it is tempting for districts to arrive at a school's rate simply by subtracting the number of dropouts from the number collecting a diploma. The problem with that is that some dropouts transfer to other schools in a **General Equivalency Degree (GED) program**, get their GEDs on their own, or are incarcerated.

These missing students are hard to track down. Only ten states spent the money required to perform a longitudinal study of the fate of such students. Some schools are embarrassed by such "failures" and choose to sweep them under the rug. Indeed, in 2003, the school district for Houston, Texas, previously run by Education Secretary Paige, suffered under the glare of the national spotlight when it was revealed that the city's high schools had been underreporting dropout rates in order to perform better under the state's accountability plan. (See Table 12-2.)

The underreporting—a city-wide dropout rate of 1.5 percent, when the actual figures were between 25 percent and 50 percent—was uncovered by a principal. His school reportedly had had no dropouts. Unfortunately, he personally knew of some. Fallout from the scandal caused several high officials to be fired.[20]

For these reasons and others, graduation rates are not fully reliable. Methods for creating uniform measures are still works in progress. For instance, if raising standards merely creates pressure that produces more dropouts, it should not count as true education reform.[21]

Many Brands on the School Reform Shelf

It is one thing to theorize on how to improve schools and quite another to implement real-world programs that get results. Decades of promising techniques—and sometimes utopian promises—have rotated through solutions that span everything from **site-based management** to early-reading programs to smaller class sizes, to name just a few. No consensus has materialized, only more debate. Still, the main schools of thought on school reform can be boiled down to the following:

Standards and Accountability

The **standards movement** first drew attention at a 1989 education summit in Charlottesville, Virginia. Attended by state governors, including future president Bill Clinton, and the elder George Bush, the summit created a national panel to set and monitor education targets that would become **Goals 2000**. That same year, the Kentucky Supreme Court struck down the

GENERAL EQUIVALENCY DEGREE (GED) PROGRAM

A series of tests that can be taken to qualify for a high school equivalency certificate or diploma.

SITE-BASED MANAGEMENT

Movement to increase freedom for building administrators such as school principals to determine how district funds are spent at a given school.

TABLE 12-2

Dropout Numbers and Rates in Grades 9–12 by State, 2000–2001

State	Total 9th–12th Graders[1]	Dropouts		Grade			
		Number	Total 9th–12th rate	9th	10th	11th	12th
Alabama[2]	200,923	8,238	4.1	3.4	4.4	4.7	4.1
Alaska[2]	38,914	3,177	8.2	6.6	8.4	8.5	9.8
Arizona[2]	234,367	25,632	10.9	11.3	10.2	11.0	11.3
Arkansas	131,898	6,987	5.3	3.4	4.9	6.7	6.6
California	†	—	—	—	—	—	—
Colorado	†	—	—	—	—	—	—
Connecticut	155,731	4,649	3.0	2.9	3.0	3.2	2.8
Delaware	33,875	1,420	4.2	4.9	4.6	3.7	3.1
District of Columbia	†	—	—	—	—	—	—
Florida[2]	674,817	29,965	4.4	4.8	4.1	4.0	4.7
Georgia	384,954	27,543	7.2	6.5	7.3	7.2	8.1
Hawaii[2]	52,053	2,968	5.7	3.9	5.8	6.2	7.8
Idaho	74,357	4,143	5.6	4.1	5.7	6.6	6.0
Illinois[2]	564,633	34,008	6.0	6.0	6.0	6.2	5.9
Indiana	†	—	—	—	—	—	—
Iowa	158,050	4,193	2.7	1.5	2.4	3.2	3.7
Kansas	143,763	4,565	3.2	1.7	3.1	3.9	4.2
Kentucky	185,003	8,557	4.6	3.9	5.1	5.0	4.6
Louisiana	196,040	16,361	8.3	9.1	8.2	7.7	8.2
Maine	61,426	1,926	3.1	1.8	3.1	4.3	3.6
Maryland[2]	242,502	9,930	4.1	4.1	4.2	4.1	4.0
Massachusetts	272,497	9,380	3.4	3.3	3.4	4.0	3.0
Michigan	†	—	—	—	—	—	—
Minnesota	275,502	11,014	4.0	1.4	3.1	4.6	7.1
Mississippi	131,787	6,108	4.6	4.3	4.9	4.8	4.7
Missouri	271,455	11,447	4.2	3.1	4.4	5.2	4.4
Montana	49,668	2,095	4.2	3.2	4.3	4.7	4.9
Nebraska	90,344	3,614	4.0	3.0	4.1	4.5	4.6
Nevada	90,125	4,730	5.2	3.4	1.7	5.2	12.2
New Hampshire[3]	51,592	2,763	5.4	2.3	4.6	7.6	8.0
New Jersey[2]	351,496	9,882	2.8	2.9	2.8	2.9	2.6
New Mexico	95,427	5,092	5.3	5.4	5.8	5.7	4.1
New York[2]	809,036	30,898	3.8	2.7	4.0	5.5	3.6

(Table continues on next page)

TABLE 12-2 *(continued)*

State	Total 9th–12th Graders[1]	Dropouts Number	Total 9th–12th rate	Grade 9th	10th	11th	12th
North Carolina	346,424	21,773	6.3	6.3	6.9	6.4	5.2
North Dakota	36,230	784	2.2	1.1	2.4	2.5	2.7
Ohio	590,120	22,822	3.9	3.6	3.4	3.7	4.8
Oklahoma[2]	177,577	9,202	5.2	5.1	5.1	5.7	4.7
Oregon	163,106	8,696	5.3	3.1	4.5	5.8	8.6
Pennsylvania	548,125	19,568	3.6	2.1	3.3	4.5	4.7
Rhode Island	44,499	2,212	5.0	5.0	5.0	4.9	5.0
South Carolina	183,896	6,089	3.3	3.5	3.7	3.1	2.6
South Dakota	40,784	1,571	3.9	2.9	3.8	4.2	4.6
Tennessee[2]	244,897	10,499	4.3	2.8	3.6	5.1	6.6
Texas	1,116,518	46,973	4.2	3.4	4.4	4.0	5.5
Utah	147,086	5,449	3.7	1.2	2.5	4.1	7.1
Vermont[2]	31,138	1,476	4.7	2.9	4.6	5.8	5.9
Virginia	329,575	11,415	3.5	3.3	3.3	3.4	3.9
Washington	†	—	—	—	—	—	—
West Virginia	85,100	3,570	4.2	3.5	4.8	4.6	4.0
Wisconsin	259,047	6,002	2.3	1.8	1.6	1.9	4.2
Wyoming	29,758	1,900	6.4	3.0	6.5	8.0	8.4

Department of Defense (DoD) dependents schools, Bureau of Indian Affairs, and outlying areas							
DoD schools (overseas)	†	—	—	—	—	—	—
DoD schools (domestic)	†	—	—	—	—	—	—
Bureau of Indian Affairs	†	—	—	—	—	—	—
American Samoa	3,773	73	1.9	1.2	1.5	2.3	3.2
Guam	8,775	1,001	11.4	7.6	17.6	13.5	8.6
Northern Marianas	2,206	134	6.1	8.6	7.4	2.4	2.9
Puerto Rico[2]	166,476	1,737	1.0	0.7	1.4	1.3	0.8
Virgin Islands	5,454	215	3.9	6.8	2.4	2.8	2.2

Source: Data are reported by states to the U.S. Department of Education, National Center for Education Statistics, Common Core of Data (CCD), "Local Education Agency Universe Dropout and Completion Data File: School Year 2000–01," version 1a.

—Not available. These states do not report dropouts that are consistent with the NCES definition.

†Not applicable. Total 9th–12th graders not reported for states without conforming dropout data.

[1] Ungraded students are prorated into the 9th–12th grade total for dropout rate calculation purposes. For those states that did not report dropouts, no prorated 9–12th grade enrollment was calculated.

[2] These states reported on an alternative July through June cycle rather than the specified October through September cycle.

[3] New Hampshire is missing reported dropouts for fourteen of their seventy-six school districts that operate high schools (16.3 percent of enrollment in the 76 school districts).

entire state education system, which prompted the enactment of the **Kentucky Education Reform Act** the following year. This paved the way for the standards movement nationwide.

The premise was simple. Standards mean laying out in advance what students should be able to do at each grade in each subject, aligning tests to the content, and then evaluating who reaches the standard. Determining what students should know was a task for the professional association. The National Council of Teachers of Mathematics produced the earliest standards. As momentum built in the early 1990s, the Clinton administration worked to give the movement a national framework in its reauthorization of the **Elementary and Secondary Education Act**, originally passed in 1994 as Goals 2000, the Educate America Act.

Prodding from governors and the business community produced much progress on the integration of a standards-based approach. Fully forty-nine states laid out standards. Iowa—the lone holdout—proudly leaves standards to local school districts. By summer 2002, forty-seven states were issuing "report cards" on student achievement. Not quite half were breaking the data down by racial subgroups, poverty, or limited English proficiency. Among teachers, according to an *Education Week* survey, eight in ten reported that their curricula were now more demanding. Six out of ten said their students were writing more.

The problem with standards, teachers say, is that there are too many to cover in one school year. The problem with accountability is that teachers are forced to tailor their instruction to state tests.[22] There is no consensus that standardized tests truly measure learning, given that some children who perform well in written and oral and problem-solving situations do not test well, perhaps due to pressure. Plus, many who test well forget what they memorized soon after.[23]

There is also the issue of textbooks and curriculum development. Twenty-nine states are open territory states that allow individual districts to purchase their own textbooks and develop their own curriculums. This means that children are using different learning materials in different grades at different schools, even if the state has subject standards. Actual learning levels may not be represented accurately on standardized tests, state-authored or otherwise. (See Map 12-3.)

The other twenty-one states are adoption states. This means that not only are there state standards, there is also a standard statewide curriculum. Often, the state legislature or a specially appointed panel determines what books will be used at every grade in every public school in the state. Even among adoption states, however, curriculums and standards vary widely. This also can cause students' education levels to be misrepresented. For example, a student moving from Texas to California will not have learned the same material in the same grade. Forced to take a standardized test, especially a state-sponsored one, the child may fail.

STANDARDS MOVEMENT

Effort to create benchmarks of adequate learning in each subject for each grade level so that students and teachers can be evaluated on mastery of this predetermined material.

GOALS 2000

The Educate America Act, signed into law in March 1994 that provided resources to states and communities to ensure that all students reached their full potential.

KENTUCKY EDUCATION REFORM ACT

1990 law, passed in response to court findings of unacceptable disparities among schools, considered the most comprehensive state school reform act ever.

ELEMENTARY AND SECONDARY EDUCATION ACT

Federal law passed in 1965 as part of President Johnson's Great Society initiative; steered federal funds to improve local schools, particularly those attended primarily by low-income and minority students.

MAP 12-3 Textbook Adoption and Open Territory States

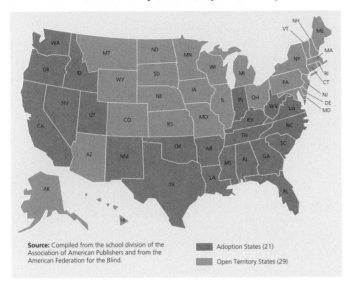

Source: Compiled from the school division of the Association of American Publishers and from the American Federation for the Blind.

Adoption States (21)

Open Territory States (29)

Open territory state or adoption state, at the high school level, standardized tests are truly high stakes. By 2003, nineteen states had policies in place to deny diplomas to students who fail end-of-course exams. That means students can fail to graduate even if they had passing grades. This not only breaks the hearts of families, it can cost a student a college acceptance. It also opens schools up to embarrassment from lowered graduation rates. Such fears are the reason that Alaska, Arizona, Maryland, and other states have delayed implementation of high-stakes tests.[24]

The achievement aims expressed in the standards movement were undeniably noble. Goals 2000 included such aspirations as all children beginning school ready to learn and then graduating with demonstrated competencies. It vowed that there should be more professional development for teachers and greater parental involvement. Graduate rates were to be increased to 90 percent. All schools would be drug-free and violence-free, and U.S. students would rocket to first place in the world in math and science.

The question the standards movement never fully answered, however, dealt with accountability. What happens if students fail? Should students, teachers, principals, schools, or all of the above be penalized? As the turn of the millennium came and went, no one could argue that whoever was accountable had done their jobs. Nor could anyone claim that the lofty goals had been achieved. The George W. Bush administration abolished the Goals 2000 infrastructure to make way for the No Child Left Behind program.

Recruiting Good Teachers

Recent research has demonstrated that the single most important factor in student learning, more important than curriculum, family income, student health, or parental involvement, is good teaching.[25] Economists have even quantified the effect, estimating that the best teachers give their students an extra year's worth of learning and perhaps fifty points on standardized tests.[26] This is particularly true for minorities, so many of whom enter school socially or economically disadvantaged.

Problem is, demographic projections point to a shortage of teachers that could exceed two million during the first decade of the twenty-first century. The absence of qualified teachers also is worse in high-poverty schools.

Governing States and Localities

These schools suffer from heavy turnover, and the number of teachers with less than three years experience is 13 percent versus only 9 percent for other school districts.

The shortage is acute in certain subject areas: special education, mathematics, science, bilingual education, and technology. This is in part due to the fact that teacher salaries often are too low to attract candidates who can earn more at high-tech firms and corporations. The use of teachers, however reluctantly, to instruct in areas outside their academic specialty affects 11 percent to 22 percent of middle school students and 5 percent to 11 percent of high school students in the liberal arts, says the Department of Education.[27]

Solutions are slowly gaining traction. Kentucky is the only state to bar teachers who lack a degree in their subject matter, while only California and Massachusetts give bonuses to teachers willing to go into high-poverty schools. The reason for so little change? There's no one answer. Basically, states are tremendously varied, and it's tough to account for why some legislators or advocates in a given state pushed for a certain solution and it passed, whereas in another state, the whole chain of events turned out differently.

Colleges and universities that have schools of education are working to improve the quality of their graduates and to provide aspiring educators with more substantive knowledge—less jargon and abstract pedagogy. Many current researchers believe that teachers with the most content knowledge in their field are most effective in raising student achievement. This suggests that the techniques of working with young people and diagnosing student impediments are best acquired on the job.[28]

Alternative licensure programs that provide appropriate training, mentoring, and testing to interested individuals are now permitted in twenty-four states and the District of Columbia. Examples of such programs include Troops to Teachers, which opens up classroom jobs to former military personnel, and Teach for America, which involves recent college graduates who want to fight poverty.

The problem of shrinking teacher numbers has many in education feeling like they are banging their heads against the wall. Or, in this case, the table. DeSoto, Texas, Independent School District Athletic Director Fred Hedgecoke pretty much sums up the frustration and helplessness felt by recruiters at this poorly attended teacher career day at the University of Texas in April 1998. The years that have passed since then haven't changed the seriousness of the teacher shortage situation.

Charter Schools

Entrepreneurs who want to launch their own schools with public money have been applying to run **charter schools**, since the early 1990s. They are less an educational philosophy than a variation on school governance. Charter schools range in theme from Montessori to the fact-based niche curriculum called Core Knowledge to ranching to online (distance) learn-

CHARTER SCHOOLS
Public schools, often with unique themes, managed by teachers, principals, social workers, or nonprofit groups. The movement was launched in the early 1990s.

ing. Sponsors have included former public and private school principals, parent groups, universities, social service agencies, and nonprofits such as the YMCA. By 2004, approximately 3,000 charter schools had sprung up in the 39 states that have enacted charter laws, although the number of students involved was less than 700,000.

In principle, students who attend charter schools are given the same per-pupil expenditure as students in mainstream schools, although the founders often must scrounge to find facilities. The willingness of a state to encourage the establishment of charter schools depends on the condition of its public schools and the energies of would-be charter school founders. Some states set up special chartering boards. Others allow local school boards to approve applications.

Overall, state charter laws vary. Arizona's loose regulations provide startup funds, a fifteen-year authorization, and the freedom for existing private schools to convert to charter status. States with strict charter laws, such as Kansas, provide no start-up funds, allow perhaps only a three-year term before a charter must seek a renewal, and cap the number of schools permitted.

Backers see charter schools as laboratories of innovation that bypass staid bureaucracies and satisfy the parental desire for choice. Evidence of the academic achievement of charter schools is modestly favorable, but not spectacular. Some have been forced to close due to corruption, such as embezzlement by administrators, or a failure to attract enough families or maintain a physical facility. California's largest charter school operator announced in August 2004 that it would be closing at least sixty campuses. This left ten thousand children stranded just weeks before the start of the school year.

In addition, critics worry that charter schools will balkanize public education and that they may be exploited as a way to avoid dealing with unionized teachers. They also fear that these schools may present an administrative headache to those school superintendents charged with monitoring against abuses of funds.

To determine whether charter schools should be scaled up and duplicated around the country, researchers do not just want to know whether a charter's own students test scores improve. They also want to know if the schools these children's families chose to leave are using the departures as an incentive to do better.[29]

Advocates of charter schools, including the George W. Bush administration, suffered a blow in August 2004. An article in the *New York Times* showed that fourth graders in charter schools scored significantly below their peers in traditional public schools. (See Table 12-3.) Critics were quick to cite a lack of accountability by school officials as the leading cause for the poor showing by the students.

An earlier study mentioned in the same article, however, suggested that tracking students over time might present more favorable findings. Tom

TABLE 12-3

Charter School Scores

| | Percent of Fourth Graders at or above Basic Level in | | | |
| | Math | | Reading | |
	Charter Schools	Other Public Schools	Charter Schools	Other Public Schools
Race				
White	84	87	71	74
Black	50	54	37	40
Hispanic	58	62	45	43
Income				
Eligible for Public Lunch	53	62	38	45
Not Eligible	80	88	70	76
Location				
City	58	68	50	52
Suburb/large town	78	80	64	66
Small town/rural area	84	80	64	67

Source: Adapted from data compiled by the American Federation of Teachers from the National Center for Education Statistics, 2004.

Loveless, director of the Brown Center on Education Policy at the Brookings Institution, conducted a two-year study of 569 charter schools in 10 states. He found that although charter school students do score lower on state tests, over time they progress faster than students in traditional public schools. Other proponents believe that students in charter schools also score lower in part because they were farther behind to begin with in their last schools.[30]

There are plenty of individual charter school success stories. They have been embraced by the chancellor of the nation's largest school system, that of New York City. For all of this, the jury is still out on whether the concept of charter schools will emerge as a strong force behind future school reform.

Vouchers

Considered a more radical reform than charter schools, **school vouchers** have been proposed in some form since the 1950s. The idea is to mimic government grants used in higher education by giving interested families a set amount of public money that can be used at any accredited school—public, private, or religious. Voucher enthusiasts want to provide parents with more choice, break up the "monopoly" of the public education bureaucracy

SCHOOL VOUCHERS

Movement dating to the 1950s to allow taxpayer dollars to be given to families to use at whatever public, private, or parochial schools they choose.

Education

419

to boost competition, and, more recently, advance as a civil right the rescue of low-income black families from failing schools in low-income neighborhoods.

Opponents worry that vouchers spell the beginning of the end of society-wide efforts to maintain and improve universal public education. They note that private schools can be selective about which students they accept. In addition, the proposed amounts for vouchers are often less than half of actual tuition. In some communities, the number of available slots at area private schools sometimes is insufficient for the number of interested applicants. This is true in the District of Columbia, where a congressionally authorized experimental voucher plan has been launched.

Critics also object to the potential for religious indoctrination at parochial schools. However, in June 2002, the U.S. Supreme Court ruled that vouchers can go to a religious school as long as the school's chief purpose is education. In other words, a school that offers a comprehensive secular curriculum, albeit with religious rituals and instructors, as opposed to a Sunday school or bible study. For each of the above reasons, vouchers generally have failed when put to voters on state ballot initiatives.

Since the early 1990s, voucher experiments have been underway at long-troubled and racially isolated schools in Cleveland, Ohio, and Milwaukee, Wisconsin. More recently, the state of Florida has explored them on a smaller scale. As described in an important study on voucher effectiveness by the newly renamed Government Accountability Office (GAO), 90 percent of the schools accepting voucher students in Cleveland and Milwaukee are religious.

Wisconsin funds the Milwaukee program, which involved 7,621 students at 91 schools in 1999, with general state education funds. This means that all citizens across the state help pay for the $38.9 million program. Ultimately, however, the state accounts only for half. The Milwaukee school district puts up the cash for the rest.

Ohio funds the $6.2 million Cleveland program through a "Disadvantaged Pupil Impact Aid fund. The fund is limited by the state legislature's annual appropriation. At the time of the study, the Cleveland program involved 3,400 voucher students at 52 private schools.

Many studies have been released that document achievement gains among students using vouchers.[31] Certainly any program that is selected by parents eager for change has an improved chance for students to gain ground. But the congressionally requested GAO study of the Milwaukee and Cleveland experiments "found little or no difference in voucher and public school students' performance" in the schools of those two cities.[32]

Privatization

Beginning in the 1990s, critics who believe public school management is riddled with waste and fraud have teamed up with groups of business investors to bid on contracts to run public schools. In essence, they have moved towards **privatization**. Groups such as National Heritage Academies and Edison Schools have promised to use their portable expertise and high-volume resource strategies to reorganize troubled schools, install new management, and upgrade the physical school facility, including providing new computers.

In Florida, companies such as Chancellor-Beacon Academies actually team up with developers of new subdivisions to construct buildings to be used for charter schools. Best known of the school-management companies is Edison Schools, founded in 1991 by entrepreneur Christopher Whittle. Acting on a desire to do good by doing well, Whittle was also founder of Channel One, which offered schools television news shows for the classroom. These programs, however, were supported by product advertising. This was a compromise that some educators feel is inappropriate to a captive audience of students.

By 1999, Edison was selling public stock. By 2003, it had won contracts in 2,000 schools in 20 states and was serving some 132,000 students. Following highly visible controversies in San Francisco and Philadelphia, however, Edison was dismissed from many schools. Complaints surfaced about failures to deliver promised equipment and supplies, heavy teacher turnover, discipline problems, and dwindling attendance. Its stock price sunk to under a dollar, and it was again taken private. Reports released in spring 2003 by Edison and the American Federation of Teachers reached opposite conclusions about whether students at Edison schools had outperformed those at comparable schools managed by local authorities.

PRIVATIZATION
Movement to contract out responsibilities traditionally done by the government to for-profit businesses in hopes of achieving greater efficiencies.

Home Schooling

The most surprising of the major school reform movements is **home schooling**. According to a 1999 survey by the U.S. Department of Education, an estimated 850,000 students were taught at home. By 2004, that number had jumped by 29 percent to 1.1 million. This is according to the National Center for Education Statistics (NCES), a part of the U.S. Department of Education.

Home schooling champions have organized a legal defense network and a lobbying effort. They put out national publications, including *Homeschooling Today* and *Homeschooling Helper*. As the movement has grown, it has organized sports leagues, field trips, proms, and graduation ceremonies. And there are plenty of home-school success stories, including Harvard acceptances and solid scores on standardized tests.

Home schooling advocates are a diverse group, but the two main strands are fundamentalist Christians and "free-school" advocates who favor more student choice of subject matter. Parents who can make the time to home-school like the security and personal imprint they can leave on their youngsters. The NCES study found that 30 percent of those surveyed wanted the

HOME SCHOOLING
The education of children in the home; a movement to grant waivers from state truancy laws to permit parents to teach their own children.

For those who choose to home school their children, the rewards can be great. Christine and Paul Pressau (second from left and second from right, respectively) have home schooled each of their four daughters since pre-kindergarten. Oldest daughter Tatiana (not shown) went on to graduate in May 2004 from Geneva College with highest honors. Eighteen-year-old Jacquelyn (center) graduated in June 2004 from high school and began college in fall 2004. Fifteen-year-old Arielle (far left) and thirteen-year-old Desirée (far right) continue to be educated at home and also through the Cedar Brook Academy in Clarksburg, Maryland, from which Jacquelyn's diploma was issued. The academy was started in 1983 as resource for families who home school. More than 550 students from 250 families take part in classes, sports, and other activities offered by the academy.

flexibility to teach moral or religious lessons. Another 31 percent cited concerns about the environment of traditional schools.

Of course, throughout the history of this country, there have always been those who have chosen to teach their children at home. The modern movement, however, really started taking off in the 1980s. State governments have accommodated home schoolers to varying degrees. Some require parents to have a bachelor's degree to home-school. Others require a curriculum to be submitted for approval, and still others give parents a choice whether to give their children a standardized test selected by the school district or to hire their own qualified evaluator.

Michael Farris, leader of the Purcellville, Virginia-based Home School Legal Defense Association, has been at the forefront of the national movement. His organization ranks states based on how tightly or loosely they regulate home schooling. States with no requirements for notifying state authorities include Idaho, Michigan, and Texas. States with low regulation include Alabama, Kentucky, and Mississippi. Most states in the Southwest moderately regulate home schooling, while most states in New England regulate a great deal.

Critics fear that home-schooled students miss important opportunities for social development and that many parents are not qualified to teach. They also worry that some parents isolate their children and instill them with religious prejudice. Some state and local officials consider home schooling an inconvenience. It forces them to come up with policies on home visits, gauge assessments that may be out of sync with conventional report-card grades, and wrestle with dilemmas such as whether a home-schooled student can play in the public high school band. Finally, there have been cases of severe child abuse among the more hermit-like home schoolers. These are cases that short-staffed state education departments can't always track.

Can't Tell the Players without a Program

When the Texas Supreme Court struck down school funding disparities in *Edgewood Independent School District v. Kirby* (1989), it declined to specify a precise solution to the problem. Instead, it opted to launch a dialogue with legislators and education officials. In Kentucky, the state supreme court was even more activist. That same year, it declared the state's school system unconstitutional and not adequate to meeting "an efficient system of public schools." The court went on to lay out a set of goals and ability standards to be pursued.[33]

In both cases, judges knew that no legal ruling on the subject of education would hold sway without public support and buy-in from key stakeholders. That meant going far beyond a small elite of education officials. In Texas, the Mexican-American Legal Defense and Education Fund (MALDEF) played an influential role in developing and supporting the state's new education reforms.

In Kentucky, the legislation and landmark school reform program that resulted from the state court's ruling gained ground largely because of support from such players as newspaper editorialists and a group of education and business leaders called the Prichard Committee for Academic Excellence. The following is a roster of the familiar players in the education dramas that unfold around the country.

Teachers' Unions

For decades, the major **teachers' unions** have been the National Education Association (NEA), which today boasts 2.7 million members, and the American Federation of Teachers (AFT), reporting 1.3 million members, as of 2004. These groups organize employees from the pre-school level to the K–12 level to the university levels to form state and local affiliates. They engage in collective bargaining, lobby for resources, and seek to upgrade teacher professionalism through training and publications.

For years, the two Washington, D.C.-headquartered unions have flirted with a merger, but style differences always intervene. The AFT was quicker than the NEA to join the school reform parade, by participating in creation of standards and charter schools, for example. By the late 1990s, however, both had turned sour on the school choice movement, which they consider a threat to public education and their members' livelihoods. Both unions align themselves with the Democratic Party, one reason most Republicans blame them for obstructing school reform.

Parents' Groups

The **National PTA**, with 6.5 million members, bills itself as the "largest volunteer child advocacy organization in the United States." For decades, this umbrella group for local parent-teacher associations and organizations was stereotyped as a klatch of moms putting on bake sales. Today, however, the PTA has school-based state and national organizations that combine to form a sophisticated lobbying and policy force. For the most part, the organization works to boost parent involvement and to encourage parent-teacher cooperation.

TEACHERS' UNIONS
Primarily the National Education Association and the American Federation of Teachers, both headquartered in Washington, D.C.

NATIONAL PTA
Founded in 1897, this umbrella organization of state-based and school-based parent-teacher associations consists of volunteers who work to improve and support schools.

The PTA is under strict rules to remain nonpartisan. Despite this, occasional endorsement of state legislative candidates based on school funding commitments has gotten some locals in hot water. Other parent groups have emerged over the years to focus on narrower issues, such as the school desegregation efforts of the Mississippi-based Parents for Public Schools.

National Political Parties

For much of the latter part of the twentieth century, education was Democratic Party turf, mostly because of the Great Society legislation pushed through in the mid-1960s. The Democrats traditionally wanted to expand government spending to close the gap between affluent and low-income schools. Republicans, on the other hand, emphasized local control and social issues, such as efforts to overturn the ban on school prayer. During the Reagan administration, Republicans vowed to abolish the federal Department of Education set up by President Jimmy Carter. Many of them opposed proposals made during the mid-1990s to introduce a national standardized test. They based their protests on the need to preserve local control of schools.

By 2000, however, Texas governor George W. Bush moved the Republicans dramatically to the center of the education debate while campaigning for the Oval Office. His eventual victory in enacting the No Child Left Behind Act, which is modeled in part on the system used since the early 1990s in Texas and borrows its name from the liberal Children's Defense Fund, was attributable to support from key Democratic lawmakers.

Sen. Edward M. Kennedy, D-Mass., and Rep. George Miller, D-Calif., carry a lot of weight in their respective congressional houses, and they were able to sway others in their party to cross partisan lines. Polls soon after showed that Republicans had caught up with Democrats on the question of which party was the "education party." Republican efforts to woo Democrats on the more controversial proposals for school vouchers have been less successful. This is due in great part to the strong support Democrats depend on from anti-voucher teachers' unions and their general skepticism about market-based alternatives to government programs.

Business Groups

Corporations and small businesses have been among the most vocal in pushing for school reform. They cite what they perceive as a decline in the writing and math skills of young job applicants as industry has become more complex technologically. Business leaders, such as IBM chief executive Louis V. Gerstner Jr., joined with business groups, such as the Business Roundtable and the National Alliance of Business, to meet with governors, educators, and school reform activists to press for higher standards for students and teachers.

Professional and Advocacy Groups

Within the education "establishment," each of the managerial groups—administrators, principals at the elementary and secondary levels, and school boards—have their own associations. These official decision makers usually win their jobs through a prerequisite set of academic credentials, years of experience in the classroom, and dues paid in the front lines of management.

In addition, there are research groups, such as the Washington, D.C.-based Education Trust. This organization performs research to encourage higher education to help with elementary and secondary school reforms. There are also teacher professional development providers and school design consultants, such as Arlington, Virginia-based New American Schools. Then there are the advocacy groups, such as the Center for Education Reform, which promotes school choice, and the Public Education Network, which organizes local funds to improve public engagement in school reform.

Finally, there are the single-issue activists, most prominent of which are Texas textbook critics Mel and Norma Gabler. For forty years, this fundamentalist Christian couple has been the bane of the multimillion-dollar school textbook industry, taking advantage of the fact that Texas is a "bellwether" state in the intricate nationwide school textbook adoption process. Focused and persistent, the Gablers challenge books for factual errors, forcing the publishers, in some cases, to tone down discussions of such tricky topics as evolution or unhappy chapters of American history such as the Vietnam War.[34]

Ever-Unsettled Issues

The No Child Left Behind Act signed in January 2002 was less radical than advertised. For instance, it built on a standards and accountability movement that was already a decade old. It was *more* radical than advertised in that it dramatically boosted the federal role in education, intensified accountability pressures, and did much to place all state and local school entities on a similar path toward change. All of this is quite contrary to Republican orthodoxy. Under the previous federal law, there was great variation in how strictly the standards were enforced.

Some of the buzz was due to clever marketing, as well. The Clinton administration had been active, for example, in efforts to get all students to read by third grade. What the Bush approach did, however, was side with pro-phonics advocates in the reading debate. This stand then was installed in the federal machinery and touted as a fresh idea.

By June 2003, all fifty states had submitted and won the Department of Education's approval of their compliance plans for No Child Left Behind.

States in the early years were making the most progress in areas where they already had experience, such as developing state standardized tests in reading and math tests for grades three through eight. But because the states all began compliance with the new law from different points, their beginning definitions of "adequate yearly progress" vary by as much as fifty percentage points.

In 2001, only twenty-two states had "unitary accountability systems" that treat all schools the same, while twenty-eight had dual systems that treat low-income (Title I) schools differently.[35] Progress has come more slowly on new procedures, such as an approval process that allows public school students to be tutored by outside nonprofits and for-profit companies. Why? Again, states come to the education table with very different appetites and very different views.

Resistance to the act, however, began as soon as schools and districts began facing the prospect of penalties. (See Table 12-4.) The idea of lost federal aid, fired staff, and new expenses for private tutoring and transport of kids switching away from "failing schools" left a bad taste in the mouths of state and local officials. In Vermont in summer 2003, two schools announced that they would do without the federal funds and ignore No Child Left Behind. Complaints that the law is burdensome and impractical were heard from Chicago mayor Richard Daley and former Oklahoma governor Frank Keating.

Although each state has its own internal timeline for success, No Child Left Behind requires that all schools bring every single student to proficiency by the 2013–2014 school year. Until that day comes, it is a safe bet that the debates over performance, accountability, funding, and teacher quality will continue to passionately invoke lofty themes of democracy and civic ideals. Efforts at strengthening the federal role in public education will continue to run up against a centuries-old tradition of local control. Advocates of increased funding targeted at the poor will still lock horns with those who stress reforms in pedagogy and new incentives.

In February 2004, the entire state of Utah considered opting out of the No Child Left Behind program because of its cost.

Conclusion

If Horace Mann is watching from school-reformers' heaven, he probably isn't surprised that ancient debates over school reforms remain unsettled. The governance system of the U.S. public education system is rooted in local control and wide variations in state and community traditions. This guarantees that it will always be characterized by diverse approaches and active political maneuvering. The quest for the ideal school continues to be more art than science. The results? They are as glorious—and as messy—as democracy itself.

TABLE 12-4

Types of Sanctions and Assistance for States with Policies Regarding School Sanctions, 2000

	Sanctions							Assistance			
	Written warning	Place on probation	Remove accreditation	Withhold funding	Reconstitute school	Close school	Take over school	Technical assistance	More funding	Improvement plan by school	Improvement plan by other entity
Alabama	No	No	No	No	No	No	Yes	Yes	No	Yes	Yes
Alaska	No	No	No	No	No	No	No	No	No	Yes	No
Arkansas	Yes	No	No	No	Yes	Yes	Yes	Yes	No	Yes	Yes
California	No	No	No	No	Yes	Yes	Yes	Yes	Yes	Yes	No
Colorado	No	Yes	Yes	No	Yes	No	Yes	Yes	No	Yes	Yes
Connecticut	No	No	No	No	Yes	Yes	No	Yes	No	Yes	No
Delaware	No	No	Yes	No	No	No	No	Yes	No	Yes	Yes
Florida	No	No	No	Yes	Yes	No	No	Yes	No	Yes	Yes
Georgia	No	No	No	No	Yes	No	Yes	Yes	No	Yes	Yes
Illinois[1]	No	No	No	No	Yes	No	Yes	No	Yes	No	Yes
Indiana	No	Yes	No	No	No	No	No	Yes	Yes	Yes	Yes
Kansas	Yes	No	Yes	Yes	Yes	No	No	No	No	Yes	No
Kentucky	No	No	No	No	No	No	No	Yes	Yes	Yes	No
Louisiana	No	No	Yes	Yes	Yes	No	No	Yes	No	Yes	Yes
Maryland	No	Yes	No	No	Yes	Yes	Yes	Yes	Yes	Yes	Yes
Massachusetts	No	Yes	No	No	Yes	No	No	No	No	Yes	Yes
Michigan	No	No	Yes	No	No	Yes	No	Yes	No	No	No
Missouri	No	Yes	No	No	Yes	No	No	No	Yes	No	Yes
Nevada	Yes	Yes	No	No	No	No	Yes	No	No	Yes	Yes
New Mexico	Yes	Yes	Yes	No	No	No	Yes	Yes	No	Yes	No
New York[2]	Yes	Yes	Yes	No	Yes	Yes	No	Yes	No	Yes	Yes
North Carolina	No	No	No	No	Yes	No	Yes	Yes	No	No	Yes
Oklahoma	No	No	Yes	No	Yes	Yes	Yes	Yes	No	No	No
Oregon	No	No	No	No	No	No	No	Yes	No	Yes	No
Rhode Island	No	Yes	Yes	Yes	Yes	Yes	Yes	Yes	Yes	Yes	Yes
South Carolina	No	No	No	No	Yes	No	Yes	Yes	Yes	Yes	Yes
Tennessee	No	Yes	No	No	No	No	No	No	No	No	Yes
Texas	No	No	No	No	Yes	Yes	Yes	No	No	Yes	No
Vermont	No	Yes	Yes	No	Yes	Yes	Yes	Yes	No	Yes	No
Virginia	No	No	Yes	No	No	No	No	Yes	No	Yes	No
West Virginia	No	No	Yes	No	No	No	No	Yes	No	Yes	Yes
Wyoming	No	No	Yes	No	No	No	No	Yes	No	Yes	No

Source: Education Commission of the States, *Clearinghouse Notes: Rewards and Sanctions for Districts and Schools: August 2000,* 2000.

Notes: The District of Columbia was not reported in the original source. States not listed did not sanction schools on the basis of performance in 2000 according to original sources.

[1] Illinois has enacted legislation that allows the Chicago Public Schools to sanction its low-performing schools. The school district provides technical assistance to its low-performing schools, requires low-performing schools to create and implement an improvement plan, and requires another entity, such as the school district, to create an improvement plan for low-performing schools. In addition, the school district has the authority to place a low-performing school on probation, reconstitute a low-performing school, and close a low-performing school.

[2] New York has enacted legislation that allows the chancellor of the New York City Public Schools to sanction schools in the school district on the basis of performance. The chancellor may require that a low-performing school create and implement an improvement plan, may create an improvement plan for a low-performing school, and has the authority to take over a low-performing school.

Key Concepts

accreditation (p. 398)

back to basics (p. 397)

capital outlays (p. 404)

charter schools (p. 417)

common school (p. 396)

criterion referenced tests (p. 408)

departments of education (p. 398)

Elementary and Secondary Education Act (p. 415)

general equivalency degree (GED) program (p. 412)

Goals 2000 (p. 412)

high-stakes standardized testing (p. 397)

home schooling (p. 421)

Kentucky Education Reform Act (p. 415)

the Lake Woebegon Effect (p. 408)

local education agencies (p. 399)

National Assessment of Educational Progress (p. 409)

National PTA (p. 423)

No Child Left Behind Act (p. 396)

norm referenced tests (p. 408)

privatization (p. 421)

school boards (p. 397)

school districts (p. 399)

school vouchers (p. 419)

site-based management (p. 412)

standards (p. 397)

standards movement (p. 412)

state board of education (p.396)

successful schools model (p. 404)

teacher licensure procedures (p. 398)

teachers' unions (p. 423)

Title I (p. 402)

Trends in International Mathematics and Sciences Study (p. 409)

Suggested Readings

Boswell, Matthew H. *Courts as Catalysts: State Supreme Courts and Public School Finance Equity.* Albany, N.Y.: State University of New York Press, 2001. Examines the effectiveness of state supreme courts in Kentucky, North Dakota, and Texas in achieving funding equity between rich and poor public school districts.

Rothman, Robert. *Measuring Up: Standards, Assessment, and School Reform.* San Francisco: Jossey-Bass, 1995. Examines the shift in thinking about testing, including a look at assessment programs in California, Colorado, Kentucky, and Vermont. Also explores the problems reformers are encountering.

Rothstein, Richard. *The Way We Were?: The Myths and Realities of America's Student Achievement.* New York: Century Foundation, 1998. Provides a counter-argument to the claim that education in the United States is bad and getting worse.

Smith, Kevin. *The Ideology of Education: The Commonwealth, the Market, and America's Schools.* Albany, N.Y.: State University of New York Press, 2003. The author examines the ideological underpinnings of school choice and other market-based reforms in education.

Tyack, David, and Larry Cuban. *Tinkering toward Utopia: A Century of Public School Reform.* Cambridge: Harvard University Press, 1995. Explores some of the basic questions of education reform.

Suggested Web Sites

www.aasa.org. Web site of the American Association of School Administrators. Founded in 1865, AASA has over thirteen thousand members worldwide. Its mission is to support and develop individuals dedicated to the highest quality public education for all children.

www.aft.org. Web site of the American Federation of Teachers, which represents the economic, social, and professional interests of classroom teachers. The AFT has more than 3,000 local affiliates nationwide, 43 state affiliates, and more than 1.3 million members.

www.charterfriends.org. The Charter Friends National Network has helped start charter support organizations in states that are passing and strengthening charter school laws.

www.ed.gov. Web site of the U.S. Department of Education, which oversees the federal government's contributions to public education.

www.edexcellence.net. The mission of the Thomas B. Fordham Foundation is to advance understanding and acceptance of effective reform strategies in primary and secondary education.

www.edreform.com. Web site of the Center for Education Reform, a national organization dedicated to the promotion of more choices in education and more rigorous education programs.

www.nea.org. The National Education Association is dedicated to advancing public education. The organization has 2.7 million members at every level of education, from preschool to university graduate programs, and affiliates in every state, as well as in more than 13,000 local communities across the United States.

www.nsba.org. Web site of the National School Boards Association, a not-for-profit federation of state associations of school boards across the United States.

CHAPTER 13

Crime and Punishment

Just because these women got their cake and were allowed to eat it too doesn't mean that crime pays. In fact, these female chain gang members were headed back to their work details in downtown Phoenix, Arizona, in August 1998. All are residents of Maricopa County, Arizona, sheriff Joe Arpaio's "Tent City." Arpaio opened the outdoor tent compound in 1994 as an inexpensive way to battle prison overcrowding. About 185,000 individuals have been incarcerated in the facility since then. In 2004, the facility housed nearly two thousand men and women and there are plans to expand. Supporters laud Arpaio as a criminal justice hero for his creative strategy. Critics say his tactics are too harsh.

Why did different types of policing develop in the United States?

Why has creative problem solving become so important to law enforcement?

How does political culture affect law enforcement in the different states and localities?

Think back for a moment and consider this question: Over the past decade, have state or local governments done anything really notable?

Something that has improved the lives of everyone in the country in an unquestionably good way?

Anything come to mind? No? If not, then criminologist George Kelling thinks you're missing something pretty big. "The most impressive achievement of city governance during the urban renewal of the 1990s," writes Kelling, "was the enormous decline in crime."[1] The numbers speak for themselves. In 1990 alone, 23,440 people were murdered in the United States. By 2000, that number had fallen to 15,517—and this at a time when the population of the country as a whole grew by 40 million people.

Overall, violent crime rates have declined to less than half that of 1973. Property crimes, robbery, burglary, and auto theft, which make up 75 percent of total crimes committed, fell by a similar amount. The lives, trauma, and money saved by this crime reduction are immense. New York City alone experienced approximately sixty thousand fewer crimes than it would have if crime rates had not declined.[2]

This crime drop of the mid-1990s to late 1990s was one of the most welcome developments of the past decade, and state and local officials and law enforcement were quick to take the credit. But is it really their accomplishment to boast about? To many, including Kelling, the answer is clearly yes. They credit the crime reduction to a revolution in policing. Further reductions are possible, advocates believe, as more police departments adopt the new methods. Given that the vast majority of law enforcement officers in the United States work for local police departments, county sheriffs' offices, and state law enforcement agencies, it might seem reasonable to credit local and state governments with this improvement.

However, not all criminologists are applauding. Many doubt that improved law enforcement had much at all to do with the crime decline. University of Cincinnati criminologist John Eck recently summed up the resurgent conventional wisdom, "The bottom line is that one can't really give a lot of credence to the strong statement about the police having a huge *independent* role in reducing crime, particularly homicide."[3] In the view of Eck and most other criminologists, crime rates are primarily the function of larger societal trends like the changing nature of the drug market, changing demographics, improved economic conditions, and increased incarceration rates.

Still other researchers attribute the crime drop to such factors as improved trauma procedures in hospital emergency rooms and even legalized abortion.[4] Many of these criminologists believe that the crime drop is over and that rising crime rates will be the norm for the future. For anyone new to the field, the wide divergence in opinions about what happened, what works, and what is likely to occur in law enforcement may be startling. Welcome to the fractious world of the criminal justice system.

This chapter is about the U.S. criminal justice system. It explores not just how the system works but also whether it works. Can police reduce crime? Do tougher penalties and longer jail terms deter criminals? Do Americans as a society have or want to have a penal system that emphasizes punishment? Or one that stresses correction instead?

Are antidrug laws too tough? Should we be concerned that 18 percent of African American males currently cannot vote because of state laws that penalize criminal activity? Is capital punishment fair or racially biased? Why is crime so much higher in some cities and some states than in others? In examining these questions, we not only take a tour of the criminal justice system, we also explore the causes of crime in a world where the connections between crime and punishment are often uncertain and unclear.

These days the local news is filled with stories of unexpected crimes happening in unexpected places and involving unexpected individuals. Pure sensationalism? Not quite. While alarming, those reports actually do reflect the fact that while crime rates have declined in cities, they are on the rise in suburban areas. Alda Larios lives in the quiet neighborhood of South Miami, Florida. In January 2004, one of her children's eleven-year-old playmates and her mother were arrested for the dealing and possession of heroin.

Gangs, guns, murder, drugs, and hard time are just some of what this chapter examines. Exploration of the criminal justice system also offers an opportunity to investigate our society's most basic values. After all, crime is about the transgression of a society's ethical norms and punishment about the enforced adherence to them. Understanding how a society disciplines itself and punishes people also provides insights into the nature and limits of state power, into the society's conception of justice, and ultimately, into the nature of democracy itself.

Private Wrongs, Public Justice

Americans are fascinated with crime. Books about private eyes, detectives, and the courts regularly top the best-seller lists. Television shows about cops top the Nielsen charts. In fact, anyone who watches TV has a pretty good idea of how the criminal justice system in the United States works. The police enforce the law and make arrests.

However, they do not have the power to punish. That authority rests with the state. District attorneys initiate prosecutions. Elected at the county level—except in Alaska, Connecticut, and New Jersey, where they are appointed by the governor—these individuals represent the state's interests in a case. Most of the time, the defendant is represented by either a defense attorney or a public defender and agrees to a plea bargain without ever going to trial.

If a case does go to trial, a jury decides the guilt or innocence of the accused. If the accused is found guilty—and most are—then a circuit judge metes out a penalty, in accordance with relevant law. Judges may be appointed or elected, depending on the state, but their responsibilities are the same in this situation. Defendants who believe they received an unfair trial may file an appeal request with an appeals court or even with the state supreme court.

That is the U.S. criminal justice system—as seen on *CSI* or *Law and Order*. It's a pretty accurate picture, as far as it goes. The problem is, it doesn't go very far. In fact, Americans' very familiarity with the system obscures some very basic facts about it. Take, for instance, the fact that punishment is a public function at all.

One of the most (pardon the pun) arresting features of the U.S. criminal justice system is that the state initiates and dispenses punishment for such crimes as homicide, assault, robbery, or burglary. To Americans, this seems entirely natural. People in the United States instinctively note the differences between civil and criminal affairs. Civil disputes are private. Your neighbors knock down your fence and then refuse to put it back up or pay to repair it. You've never much liked them, so you decide to sue. The state offers a forum for the dispute—the court—and carries out the penalty, but the dispute is between two private individuals and their lawyers, and the penalty is a fine. No one expects the county district attorney to initiate criminal proceedings against your neighbors. No matter how precious your fence or how guilty your neighbors, you cannot lock them away. In short, a civil offense is a crime against an individual.

Criminal offenses are thought of in an entirely different way. These are offenses not just against an individual, but also against society itself. As a result, the state initiates the punishment—and the punishment can be severe. It can take the form of imprisonment or **parole**. Cruel and unusual punishment, such as torture, may not be allowed, but for the most serious offenses, death is still an option.

When you stop to think about it, however, the distinction between civil and criminal cases is not really an obvious one at all. It's all well and good to say that the guy who pulls a gun on you, takes your wallet, and whacks you upside the head has committed a crime against "the public order." Yet you might be forgiven for thinking that what he really has done is commit

PAROLE

Supervised early release from prison.

a crime against *you*. If you happen to actually know the guy who mugged you, it might seem natural, just, and appropriate for you to try to punish him. If he hurt you, you might want to hurt him. As it says in the Book of Deuteronomy, "An eye for an eye, a tooth for a tooth, a hand for a hand, a foot for a foot."

A look at the historical record reveals something interesting—the beliefs that Americans see as natural are, in fact, not natural at all. For most of human history, from ancient Greece to monarchical Europe, private prosecution was the norm.[5] In medieval Britain, the attorney general initiated cases only for the king. Justices of the peace began prosecutions only when there was no private individual to initiate punishment.

Until comparatively recently, all that the governments of most nations really did was set the rules for how offended parties should pursue justice. Their role was essentially that of umpire. Governments had to fight long and hard to establish that they had the *exclusive* right to punish wrongdoers.[6] A key figure in this transference of the right of retaliation from the wronged party to the state was the public prosecutor. For reasons that historians still do not fully understand, public prosecutors first appeared in North America—in Great Britain's Atlantic colonies.

On the whole, the state's successful monopoly on punishment has brought enormous benefits to the United States. Conflicts like those between the Hatfields and McCoys notwithstanding, the nation is essentially free of ongoing feuds or vendettas. However, there are also drawbacks to such efforts to monopolize authority. Today, for instance, state and local governments in forty-eight states actively conceal what may be the greatest power U.S. citizens enjoy.

Common Law, Sovereign Power

The criminal justice system in the United States is rooted in the tradition of English common law. Forty-nine states operate within this common law tradition. (The exception is Louisiana. As a former French colony, the state instead operates under the Napoleonic code. Emperor Napoleon I put forth this body of law in the early nineteenth century.) The common law tradition makes the U.S. system quite unlike the legal systems of most other countries. In most of the world, law is enacted by a single sovereign power, be that a legislature, a monarch, or some other combination.

This is partially true in the United States as well, of course. The nation is a federation, in which the federal government and the state governments are both sovereign. Congress and state legislatures both make laws—as do county and city governments, at the discretion of the state. Citizens must obey these laws or risk punishment. However, lawmakers are not the only source of laws. Americans are governed by a mixture of formal—or statute—law and case—or common—law. The common law is made up of

A Difference that Makes a Difference:
Jury Power: What the Courts Don't Want You to Know

The origins of the modern jury go back to the early 1200s, when the English crown enlisted the most notable men in local communities across England into administrative divisions called "hundreds." Clearly, the right to mete out punishment was not something the state intended to hand over to just anyone.

Nor was the early English justice system troubled by any presumptions of innocence. Twice a year, the king's circuit court judges rode out. In each village, they would meet with these hundreds of notable individuals and ask them to identify all of the miscreants in the area who had violated the king's peace. Fines and other forms of punishment were then allotted accordingly.

By the fourteenth century, it had become clear that this approach was subject to abuse. As a result, it was decided that jury verdicts had to be unanimous. The presiding judge could punish juries that couldn't come to an agreement. Restricting their access to food and providing unpleasant accommodations were two favorite techniques. Despite the strong arming, the right to issue a verdict remained firmly in the hands of the local juries.[a]

In the mid-sixteenth century, the criminal justice system took a big step towards law and order as it is known today, when Queen Mary decreed that henceforth justices of the peace had the power to investigate accusations, take statements from the accused and the accuser, and indict potential criminals. Justices of the peace were then to present their findings to the jury.

They even could instruct the jury on how to proceed. In short, the state was asserting ever more control over the way the criminal justice system worked.

All well and good for the state, save for a problem that has continued to this day. Sometimes, juries refused to play along. This was particularly true when it came to enforcing laws about religion. In 1670 William Penn, a Quaker, was brought to trial for illegally preaching to the public. Under English law, only state-sanctioned Anglican priests could preach in public. Penn freely admitted that he had broken the law, but he argued that the law itself was illegal. He asked the jury to acquit him. It did, despite instructions from the presiding judge to enforce the law.

The Crown was profoundly displeased, for in a sense the jury's challenge raised a very fundamental issue: Who really held sovereign power? When a jury could set aside laws made by the queen in Parliament, the clear implication was that the jury, not the government, was the ultimate power in society. To demonstrate where power really lay, all twelve jury members were fined.

Juryman Bushel, however, refused to pay. His appeal went to the court of Chief Justice Robert Vaughan who ruled, believe it or not, in favor of the stubborn juror. He rejected the practice of penalizing jurors for ruling in defiance of the law, and his opinion established something remarkable. Juries truly became the final authority in English society. This was the case that made the power of the jury clear. It had all been rather vague until

legal opinions written by judges that recognize commonly accepted community practices and evolves gradually over time as a community's ideas change.

One of American society's most important inheritances from the common law tradition is the institution of the jury. Serving on a jury is *the* defining act of citizenship. It is just about the only thing every citizen must do. (Men between the ages of eighteen and twenty-five must also register with the Selective Service in the event that the government needs to reinstitute the draft.) In most states, ignoring a jury summons is a crime. Failing to appear for jury duty without being properly exempted constitutes contempt of court

that moment, which marked a turning point in judicial history. Today, the practice whereby juries set aside laws or penalties they disagree with is known as jury nullification. The right to a trial by jury is one of the basic constitutional rights, enshrined in the Sixth Amendment.

William Penn went on to establish the colony of Pennsylvania in North America. Like Penn, jury nullification also quickly jumped across the Atlantic. In the tumultuous years leading up to the Revolutionary War, American juries repeatedly refused to convict John Hancock and other agitators who were brought to trial on charges of smuggling. Their activities were viewed as principled acts of defiance rather than as crimes. During the 1850s, juries in the North regularly refused to enforce the Fugitive Slave Act, which had been passed at the insistence of the South in 1850 and made it illegal for anyone to assist a runaway slave.[b] Southern anger at Northern "lawlessness" and Northern anger at Southern "overreach" became major issues of contention in the years leading up to the Civil War.

The practice of jury nullification and the spirit of civil disobedience that inspired it also inspired other, less savory actions. For instance, in the 1950s and 1960s, many white juries in the South would not convict citizens who assaulted and sometimes killed civil rights workers. The federal government responded by enacting new guidelines for jury selection that made juries more representative of the community as a whole and not just the whole white elite. Women, minorities, and poor whites began to sit on juries after centuries of nonrepresentation.

Despite the important role that jury nullification has played, no government in the United States is very keen on letting folks know about it. In fact, the 1992 federal criminal law instructions read: "You will . . . apply the law which I will give you. You must follow that law whether you agree with it or not." Forty-eight states bar defense lawyers and judges from even mentioning that jurors may set aside a law. Indiana and Maryland are the exceptions. As in the days of Juryman Bushel, the state remains uneasy about the discretion that juries enjoy.

Does the fact that jurors can find whatever they want mean that they should? Not necessarily. Chief Justice Vaughan upheld the right of an English jury to reject laws promulgated by a thoroughly undemocratic monarchical government. In contrast, the United States today is a democracy in which nearly every adult citizen has the right to vote. Today, jury nullification can be seen as a profoundly undemocratic act. After all, laws are passed by democratically elected bodies. However, it is also a right that jurors can continue to enjoy it. It may be a secret, but under the U.S. system of law, the jury is still sovereign.

[a] Danielle S. Allen, *The World of Prometheus: The Politics of Punishing in Democratic Athens,* (Princeton: Princeton University Press, 1999), 7.

[b] Ibid., 5–6.

and may present a somewhat less appealing opportunity to experience the criminal justice system, such as fines or even imprisonment. Unless you commit a crime or have the misfortune of being one of the roughly five million people who fall victim to a crime every year, serving on a jury probably will be your primary mode of interaction with the criminal justice system.[7]

As discussed in Chapter 8, there are two types of juries. In most states east of the Mississippi River, a grand jury determines whether there is sufficient evidence for the state to prosecute someone for a crime. In states west of the Mississippi, district attorneys usually have the authority to take someone to trial on their own. Presented with a less clear instance of wrongdoing, a prosecutor also may impanel an investigative grand jury to study the evidence and determine exactly who should be targeted for prosecution. Once a grand jury or the district attorney has indicted an individual, another trial begins and another jury is formed to hear the case.

So what is the role of a juror? Most are given clear instructions by the presiding judge. The word **verdict** comes from the Latin phrase *vera dicere,* "to speak the truth." Jurors usually are told that their role is to determine exactly what the truth of a case is. They are to apply the law, regardless of whether they personally agree with it or not. As a result, the role of the juror often is that of a cog—albeit a very important one—in the criminal justice machine.

This official story conceals the fact that the role of jurors historically has not been limited to deciding whether the prosecutor's charges are true or not and delivering a verdict. Since the seventeenth century, jurors, like judges, also have enjoyed the legal right to set aside laws. (See Box 13-1.) The effort to limit juries to mere fact-finding bodies is part of an ongoing and largely hidden struggle between the state and the citizenry over who should wield the power to punish.

The jury system is not the only inheritance left to the United States by the British legal system. Many of the other institutions that characterize the U.S. criminal justice system have their roots in the English justice system as well. County sheriffs are the most notable example. More than one thousand years old, the office of sheriff is the oldest law enforcement office within the common law system. The King of England appointed a representative called a "reeve" to act on behalf of the King in each shire or county. The "shire reeve," or King's representative, became the "sheriff" as the English language changed. These days, sheriffs remain the primary law enforcement official in most communities.

Together with state law enforcement agencies like the highway patrol, county sheriffs make up the vast bulk of law enforcement capacity in the United States. In most states, each law enforcement agency focuses on maintaining order in a specific geographic area, although agencies frequently do cooperate.

The Purpose of Punishment

The criminal justice system of nearly every state comes out of the same English common law tradition. As a result, most states share an idea of what is permitted and what is a crime. The ancient Greeks may have tolerated slavery while harshly cracking down on the crime of hubris—not knowing your place in society—but even Minnesota and Mississippi more or less agree on what constitutes a crime these days.

This is much less true of punishment, however. Here the differences among the states become more evident. The Deep South, for instance, imprisons people at a much higher rate than other parts of the country. (See Map 13-1.) In one sense, this is not surprising. Different states and localities do have very different political cultures. It should come as no shock that they define some crimes differently and punish them differently.

Still, efforts to better understand this dynamic have produced some interesting findings. Studies have shown that the percentage of African American residents in a state's population correlates closely with the severity of penalties. The more black residents a state has, the tougher its laws tend to be.[8] Social scientists question the degree to which what is supposed to be an objective, color-blind criminal justice system—one that is administered largely by whites—systematically disadvantages blacks.[9]

The severity of punishment also is tied closely to the political parties. States with more Democratic legislators tend to have less severe penalties than states with more Republican legislators. Not surprisingly, election years tend to produce calls for tough new penalties as well.[10] The fairness and effectiveness of these penalties is a hotly debated issue that is taken up later in this chapter.

Cultural differences cannot be dismissed when studying criminal justice at the state and local levels. They play an important role in explaining why states approach crime differently. New England, with its Puritan heritage, has always been a region that took a strong interest in saving people's souls, whether they wanted saving or not. During the nineteenth century, it was the center of the national abolitionist movement. The region exported missionaries, built universities, and fostered the temperance movement. It also sent hundreds of thousands of emigrants west, where they settled much of the Upper Midwest and Pacific Northwest. As a result, these regions share many cultural similarities. To use the typology of the political scientist Daniel Elazar, they all have a strong moralistic streak.[11]

MAP 13-1 Incarceration Rates (Rank) Per 100,000 Population, 2000

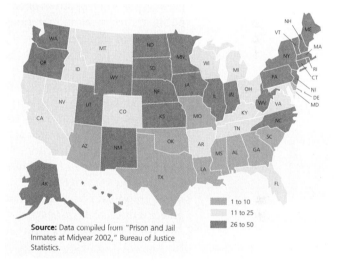

Source: Data compiled from "Prison and Jail Inmates at Midyear 2002," Bureau of Justice Statistics.

Given this cultural background, it should be evident why New Englanders and their descendants and other moralistic groups, such as Quakers, view punishment in a certain light. By the early nineteenth century, a growing number of people in the Northeast were turning against the viewpoint that painful punishments deterred crime and were fitting "just desserts" for criminal activity. Instead, they embraced a new idea—protecting society while rehabilitating criminals.

A new kind of institution soon spread across the landscape—the penitentiary. Unlike prisons, penitentiaries were designed for correction, not for punishment. The most famous penitentiary in early America was located in Philadelphia. Eastern State Penitentiary was designed to force criminals to face their consciences. It operated under a system of maximum solitary confinement. The facility went to extremes to achieve its goal. For example, until 1903, inmates were required to wear face masks when they left their cells. An unfortunate side effect of this "reform" was that many inmates, faced with such extreme isolation, suffered mental breakdowns.[12] It would not be the last unsuccessful criminological reform.

Of course, correction and penance are not the only purposes a criminal justice system serves. There is also deterrence, incapacitation, and even vengeance. The debate over the proper purpose of punishment is very old. Different societies have addressed it in different ways at different times. Three centuries before the birth of Christ, in ancient Athens, public punishment was administered to salve the wounds and ease the anger of the injured party. The philosopher Socrates was the first Athenian to argue that public punishment should aim at correcting the deficiencies of the criminal and not just at revenge. For his efforts, Socrates eventually was tried and sentenced to die by drinking poison hemlock for "corrupting youths" and for heresy.

Here in the United States, punishments also have changed to reflect evolving political cultures. To Pennsylvania Quakers, accustomed to silent contemplation, forcing inmates to confront their misdeeds in silent isolation was a natural idea. In the traditionalistic Deep South, governments chose another model of correction. Facilities like Parchman Farms in Mississippi and Angola Prison in Louisiana were organized as working plantations until well into the twentieth century. For their overwhelmingly African American inmate populations, the similarities to antebellum slavery were unmistakable.[13] Different histories and cultures produced very different institutions. Nonetheless, reformers believed that correction, not punishment, was the future. Then came the 1960s.

New Freedoms, New Fears

The 1960s was a decade of extremes. Its early years saw the birth of arguably the two most significant social movement of recent times—the civil rights movement and the modern feminist movement. Congress started to dismantle the Jim Crow laws that states had erected during the 1890s. Federal monitors were placed at polling stations throughout the South. Housing and real estate discrimination were outlawed. Women, who identified themselves as feminists, persuaded both Congress and most state legislatures to outlaw the practice of paying women less than men who performed the same job.[14]

Yet despite these accomplishments, the decade ended in a social inferno. A wave of riots nearly snuffed the life out of several inner city neighborhoods, jump-started the move to the suburbs, and ushered in a new era focused largely on public safety issues. The first such urban disturbance occurred in the summer of 1964 in the historically African American neighborhood of Harlem in New York City. The event that triggered it all was the police shooting of a fifteen-year-old African American boy.

The shooting tapped into a widespread belief that law enforcement in minority neighborhoods was arbitrary, ineffective, and sometimes brutal. One year later, a police stop in the Los Angeles neighborhood of Watts set off riots that lasted six days, cost thirty-nine people their lives, and caused hundreds of millions of dollars in damages. In the summer of 1967, large swaths of Newark, New Jersey, and Detroit, Michigan, went up in flames.

Then, on April 4, 1968, Martin Luther King Jr., was assassinated in Memphis, Tennessee. Within days of King's death, Washington, D.C., Chicago, Illinois, and many other cities were torn apart by riots. By one estimate, 329 "important" racial disturbances took place in 257 cities between 1965 and 1968. The result was nearly three hundred deaths, eight thousand injuries, sixty thousand arrests, and hundreds of millions of dollars in property losses.[15] The decade-long increase in crime showed no sign of stopping.

Confronted by the specter of race riots, most social scientists concluded that racism and inequality were the real fuel behind violence in urban America. These experts argued that, far from solving the problem, the police actually inflamed it on occasion with discriminatory and sometimes violent misconduct. The idea that better policing might be an appropriate response to the riots and rising crime rates was largely dismissed.

To support the belief that the police had little to do with the crime rate, researchers pointed to a decade of studies that documented what police actually did on the job. These seemed to show that the answer was, well, not much. Police officers spent most of their time walking around, talking to people, and occasionally mediating disputes. They did little actual crime fighting. Social scientists suggested that cities should look for other solutions that did not involve law enforcement. Programs to address inner-city poverty and a society-wide effort to reduce income inequality were the solutions.

Federal money began to flow to neighborhood community groups, with few apparent results. One possible reason for this is that all of this funding was going to sometimes erratic community groups that were primarily interested in advocacy. This "me first" attitude did not accomplish much. Another reason for the lack of success was that many mayors resented the

The riots that swept the Watts neighborhood of Los Angeles in August 1965 confirmed the beliefs of many nationwide that the law enforcement system needed an overhaul. In a spiral of violence, a police action started a retaliatory backlash from blacks that caused further violence on the part of law enforcement. Nearly four thousand people, like the young man in this picture, were arrested for looting and destruction of property.

FIGURE 13-1 The Rise and Fall of Crime Rates: Aggravated Assault, Robbery, and Homicide Rates, 1960–2000

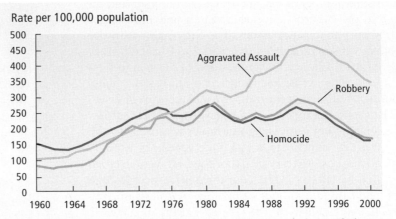

Source: Jeremy Travis and Michelle Waul, "Reflections on the Crime Decline: Lessons for the Future?" Urban Institute, 2002. www.urban.org/uploadedpdf/410546_crimedecline.pdf.

fact that federal money was flowing to someone other than them. The result was dissension and not much else.

No massive redistribution of income from wealthy Americans to poor Americans was ever tried. It is impossible to know if such a large-scale move would have worked. Empowering neighborhood groups did not. Crime continued to rise throughout the 1970s. (See Figure 13-1.) In many U.S. cities, there was a belief that authority was collapsing and anarchy was at hand. Nowhere was this sense of imminent disaster more apparent than in New York.

On the evening of July 13, 1977, lightening strikes, coupled with a Con Edison repair mistake, plunged the city into darkness. In many neighborhoods, riots and looting broke out. Thousands of fires were set. Although the police ultimately arrested more than three thousand people, much of the city experienced what *Time* magazine described as "a night of terror."[16] The country was entering a world of fear that would last for several decades.

The War on Drugs

As policymakers cast about for a way to make sense of the growing crime problem in the United States, one problem in particular stood out—illegal drugs. By 1978, one-third of all kids age twelve to seventeen admitted to having tried an illegal drug.[17] In the country's inner cities, heroin usage was a particular problem. Many government officials first viewed the upsurge in drug use as a public health issue. However, as a strong link between illegal drug use and crime became clear, most turned to the criminal justice system for solutions.

Faced with a seemingly unstoppable rise in violence, more and more cities responded by increasing the penalties for dealing and possessing drugs. Nelson Rockefeller, the liberal Republican governor of New York State, led the way. In 1973, Rockefeller and the New York state legislature agreed to impose new drug laws that were among the toughest in the nation. Suddenly, anyone found in possession of four or more ounces of a narcotic like heroin or cocaine faced the likelihood of a *mandatory* fifteen-year prison sentence. Selling as little as two ounces of the same narcotic could result in similar penalties. The hope was that such harsh penalties would drive up prices and deter potential users.

Other states and many cities quickly followed suit. State legislatures upped the penalties for the possession of illegal narcotics. Local and county law enforcement officers focused their resources on catching dealers.[18]

However, sometimes efforts did seem to be at cross-purposes. The same year Governor Rockefeller and the New York state legislature created tough new penalties for heroin and cocaine, they essentially decriminalized the use and possession of small portions of marijuana. In New York today, possession of less than eight ounces of marijuana typically leads to a small fine for a first-time offender.[19]

By contrast, in the state of Arkansas, possession of more than one ounce of marijuana can open you up to prosecution on felony charges. Penalties can range from four years to ten years in prison. In Montana, first-time offenders can face a life sentence for selling a pound of marijuana. The maximum penalty for selling ten thousand pounds of marijuana is three years in New Mexico.[20] Why such wide variations in penalties? At least part of the answer can be traced back to the differing political cultures of these states.

Unfortunately, toughening laws did not work as well as policymakers hoped. Efforts to deter drug use and dealing by setting draconian penalties probably did drive up prices somewhat. Higher prices probably stopped at least some casual users from experimenting with illegal drugs. However, for the hard-core user, the "high" of heroin or the rush of cocaine was worth the fairly long-shot chance of a stint in prison.[21]

All in all, the tough new penalties directed against drug users had a minor effect at best on drug use. What they did succeed in doing is putting a lot more people in jail. In 1973, New York State incarcerated approximately ten thousand people. By 1980, that number had reached twenty thousand. To many, it seemed that things could hardly get worse. By the mid-1980s, they were.

Crack Cocaine

In the early 1980s, intrepid drug dealers discovered that they could add baking soda and water to high-quality powder cocaine and bake up small rocks. These rocks could be smoked in homemade pipes. Nicknamed

Policy in Practice: Is It Time to Admit Defeat in the War on Drugs?

Listen to the nightly news or read the daily paper and it's easy to conclude that the "war on drugs" has been something of a disaster. Billions of dollars spent and tens of thousands of Americans in prison, and yet drug usage remains constant. The price of drugs actually has gone down. So is it time to raise the white flag and do something different?

Most criminologists would say, yes, it is time to do something different. However, few see the most commonly proposed solution—legalization—as a good answer. The problem with legalizing drugs is who uses them. Basically, disproportionate numbers of young people do. According to University of California, Los Angeles, criminologist Mark Kleiman, the number of middle-school students who report using marijuana has more than doubled since 1991.

Use among high school students has risen 50 percent. Even if drugs are legalized, these are not the people society wants using drugs, just as it currently does not want teenagers to smoke cigarettes. So most likely, even if most narcotics were legalized, say, for people

twenty-one years old and up, there would still be a serious illegal drug problem. Which leads Kleiman to this opinion about legalizing marijuana

My view is that the risks [related to cannabis use] are substantially greater than most of my well-educated boomer friends believe. Taking the entire population of people who have used cannabis at least five times, the risk in that group of becoming a heavy daily cannabis user for a period of at least months is something like one in nine. Being a pothead isn't nearly as bad for you as being a drunk, and it usually doesn't last as long, but it's still not a good place to be.

That seems a strong enough reason to oppose the legalization of marijuana on any commercial basis. Think about how aggressively tobacco and alcohol already are marketed. Imagine what big business could do with legalized marijuana.

Source: Mark Kleiman, "Revenge of the Killer Weed," www.markarkleiman.com, October 9, 2002.

"crack," for the crackling sound the rocks made when broken, it could be bagged and sold for as little at $5. Cocaine had been a "yuppie" drug available only to those with the right connections and the right amount of cash. Now it could be bought for a week's allowance.

Crack delivered a potent high at a bargain price. As a result, it quickly found users—with devastating results. Many heroin addicts managed to maintain functioning lives while also indulging their habit. That drug provides a comparatively gentle high. Crack was different. Highly concentrated, the craving it created in most users was so intense that they would do almost anything to get more. Children were abandoned. Prostitution was embraced. Condemned buildings were broken into and stripped of their contents, even their pipes.

A new urban type was born—the "crackhead" or "fiend." On their best days, crack addicts resembled urban zombies. In particularly hard hit neighborhoods, police recount seeing dozens of addicts wandering the streets in search of their next "fix." At their worst, they could be very violent. Hardcore crack users would rob the grandmother next door or do much worse.

To serve this new market, open-air drug markets sprang up on street corners across urban America. In drug-infested neighborhoods, teenagers often occupied the perfect dealing niche. Many were juveniles and thus were hard to arrest. But dealing drugs on a street corner could be a violent business. These open-air drug markets were profitable. Street-level dealers became popular robbery targets. So they started carrying handguns. Neighborhood fistfights and gang brawls turned into running gun battles. Homicides, which had been rising slowly for years, skyrocketed.

Harsher Punishments and Penalties: Prison Nation

State and local government officials responded to this frightening surge in violence and crime in much the same way that legislators had responded to drug use concerns a decade earlier. They imposed tough new penalties for the use and possession of crack. Many states also made fundamental changes to their sentencing practices. For most of the post–Second World War era, U.S. courts had enjoyed considerable leeway in determining the severity of punishment they delivered. In academic-speak, this was known as indeterminate sentencing.

By the 1980s, however, the public's rising fears led to more strident demands to get tough on crime. Most judges obliged, if only to placate voters. Federal judges are nominated by the president and approved by the Senate for life service. However, most states rely at least in part on elections to select judges—even state supreme court justices.[22]

Stories of judges releasing hardened criminals with little more than a slap on the wrist resulted in a growing number of states moving toward determinate sentencing. "Truth in sentencing" laws were passed. These restricted a judge's ability to set penalties and curtailed a parole board's freedom to release prisoners early. Some states went even further. Fourteen states abolished discretionary parole and parole boards altogether. In 1994, California voters approved a "three strikes" law. Individuals arrested and convicted of three felony crimes must be imprisoned for a minimum of twenty-five years, if not for the rest of their lives.

The increased reliance on incarceration had a big effect on state budgets. In 1978, state governments spent about $5 billion on maintaining prisons and jails. By 2000, prison spending had risen to $40 billion. Two million people were under lock and key. (See Figures 13-2 and 13-3.) States now spend an average of 7 percent of total general revenue funds—$1 out of every $14—on prisons.[23]

Not everyone felt the weight of determinate sentencing equally. By 1995, 7 percent of all black males in the United States were serving time either in a state prison or in a city or county jail on any given day. This was double the percentage of a decade earlier. It also was in sharp contrast to the 1 percent

FIGURE 13-2 U.S. Incarceration Rate, 1920–2000

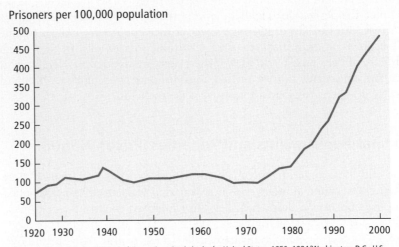

Prisoners per 100,000 population

Sources: M. W. Cahalan, *Historical Corrections Statistics in the United States, 1850–1984* (Washington, D.C.: U.S. Department of Justice, 1986) and Federal Bureau of Investigation, *Uniform Crime Reports.*

of white males jailed during the same period. By 1999, African American males made up only 13 percent of the total population, but 49 percent of prison inmates. Every day, nearly one-third of all black males age twenty to twenty-nine were either in prison or under some form of supervision, such as **probation** or parole. A black male born in 1991 currently has a 29 percent chance of going to prison at some point in his life. In contrast, Hispanic males born that same year have a 16 percent chance of being imprisoned and white males have a 4 percent chance.[24]

The high incarceration rate for black males has meant that many no longer can vote. Forty-eight states—Maine and Vermont being the exceptions—have laws that prohibit prisoners from voting. Felons on probation or out on parole are barred from voting in thirty-five states. The exceptions are Hawaii, Illinois, Indian, Massachusetts, Michigan, Missouri, New Hampshire, North Dakota, Ohio, Oregon, Pennsylvania, South Dakota, and of course, Maine and Vermont. Alabama, Florida, Iowa, Kentucky, Mississippi, and Virginia deny convicted felons the right to vote *ever* again. As a result, more than four million Americans can no longer vote. Of this total, 1.4 million are black males. An estimated 13 percent of all black men cannot vote. In comparison, two million white males are barred from voting.[25]

Longer prison terms undoubtedly kept some violent offenders off the streets, but they had little impact on rapidly escalating crime problem. Between 1985 and 1992, the number of people incarcerated rose by 79 percent. Far from dropping, crime rates instead rose by 17 percent.[26] Policymakers were at a loss. However, a handful of academics and police chiefs already had started to experiment anew with an old idea—better policing.

PROBATION

Supervised punishment in the community.

Governing States and Localities

FIGURE 13-3 **U.S. Incarceration Rate for Six Types of Crime**

Prisoners per 100,000 Adult Population

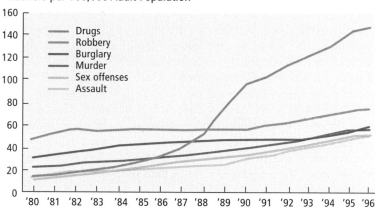

Source: A. Blumstein and A. Beck, "Population Growth in U.S. Prisons, 1980–1996," in *Prisons,* ed. M. Tonry and J. Petersilla, vol. 26 of *Crime and Justice* (Chicago: University of Chicago Press, 1999), 17–61.

The Return of Policing

In the 1820s, Sir Robert Peel founded London's Metropolitan Police, the first recognizably modern police department. "The basic mission for which the police exist," wrote Peel, "is to prevent crime and disorder."[27] Peel's vision defined policing until the 1960s. Race riots and rising drug abuse convinced criminologists and many police departments that there was little they could do to reduce crime in the face of shifting demographic trends.[28] By the 1970s, however, a handful of people began to rethink the role that law enforcement agencies should play. In time, these ideas would revolutionize the practice of policing.

The first big idea came in the late 1970s. Put forward by Herman Goldstein, a professor at the University of Wisconsin Law School in Madison, it argued that the proper role of the police was not to enforce the law. It was to solve problems. Goldstein's work encouraged police chiefs in cities such as Madison, Wisconsin, and Newport News, Virginia, to think in more creative ways about how to deal with such issues as street-level drug problems. He urged local officials to search for ways to solve underlying societal problems. This philosophy came to be known as problem-oriented policing. Although it would be more than a decade before Goldstein's theory began to take root in police departments, the idea that police ought to function as creative problem solvers eventually would transform the way in which many departments thought about policing.

The second breakthrough came in the early 1980s. A pair of criminologists, James Q. Wilson and George Kelling, hatched an idea that changed the future of policing in the United States. Arguably, it changed the future of urban America. Their basic premise was simple—minor disorders, such as shoplifting and vandalism, often give rise to much more serious types of disorder and crime, such as robbery and arson.

To support this claim, Wilson and Kelling pointed to a famous experiment conducted by Stanford psychologist Philip Zimbardo in the 1960s. Zimbardo took two identical cars, popped their hoods, and then abandoned them on two very different streets. One car was left on a high crime street in the Bronx neighborhood of New York City. The other car was parked in Stanford's hometown of Palo Alto, California. The two cars met with very different fates. Within ten minutes of its being abandoned, vandals—most of whom were respectably dressed, clean-cut whites—began to strip the car left in the Bronx. One day later, virtually everything of value had been removed. In contrast, the car in Palo Alto sat untouched, hood up, for an entire week.

Then Zimbardo changed the equation. He smashed out the windshield of the car in Palo Alto. Within hours, the car had been turned upside down and essentially destroyed. Once again, most of the perpetrators were whites. He concluded that untended property—particularly property that looks as if it actually has been neglected—sends the signal that disorder is tolerated. This quickly gives rise to more serious forms of disorder.

Wilson and Kelling extended this idea to neighborhoods as a whole. They theorized that seemingly minor signs of neglect, such as graffiti, trash, or broken windows, signal that authority is absent and give rise to much more serious problems such as violent crime. The two criminologists went on to make a larger point about policing. Those police officers whom researchers in the 1950s observed walking around and resolving disputes actually might have been doing something important. By their very presence, they had been maintaining order. It was time, Wilson and Kelling wrote, to go back to the future.[29]

Community Policing vs. the Professional Model

PROFESSIONAL MODEL

An approach to policing that emphasizes professional relations with citizens, police independence, police in cars, and rapid responses to calls for service.

Wilson and Kelling argued for a dramatic break from the **professional model** of policing. This approach to crime emphasizes squad cars and quick response times. Police departments across the country embraced it during the 1970s. The reason was an important new innovation—the 9-1-1 emergency number. Cops who had once walked the beat and played the role of friendly neighborhood supervisor now were put into squad cars. Response time—how quickly the police responded to a call for assistance—became the criterion by which departments were judged as successes or failures. It was an all-or-nothing situation, since there simply were not enough police officers available to both monitor neighborhoods and answer emergency calls.

The professional model originated on the fast-growing West Coast. Long before the advent of 911, many West Coast police departments emphasized technology. They prided themselves on their small, highly mobile forces. The influence of the Los Angeles Police Department (LAPD) in particular on police technique nationwide cannot be understated. For many years, it was seen as the prototype for effective police departments. Its cool professionalism ("Just the facts, ma'am.") was captured in the TV show *Dragnet*. The department was the first to buy helicopters. It pioneered the use of the now ubiquitous Special Weapons and Tactics, or S.W.A.T., teams.

When widespread use of 911 pushed things even further toward the professional model, East Coast departments changed the most because they had been most unlike the professional model in the first place. West Coast officials long had thought of East Coast police departments as dinosaurs with troubling opportunities for corruption. With many more police officers per capita than West Coast police departments, East Coast departments were portrayed as sources of patronage jobs, not as effective law enforcement agencies. A beat cop walking past the same gambling den or house of ill repute every day could be tempted all too easily to accept payoffs and look the other way.

West Coast police departments were convinced that they could do the same job better—or at least as well. Good tactics and high-tech equipment would prevail. And, for a while, departments such as the LAPD did maintain order, but at a cost. Their smaller forces used aggressive tactics—sometimes in a very arbitrary fashion. Senseless stops by the police became an all too familiar experience for residents of many predominantly minority areas. Consequently, a considerable number of African Americans and Hispanic Los Angelinos came to mistrust the police department.

This state of affairs was underscored by violence that broke out following the 1992 acquittal of police officers involved in the beating of Rodney King.[30] Earlier that year, a bystander had videotaped LAPD officers violently subduing King, a black motorist who had led them on a high-speed chase and then resisted arrest.[31] When an all-white jury found the officers not guilty, riots erupted throughout the city. For six days, the police force, caught unprepared in part because of political maneuvering in its top levels, struggled to regain control.

A Return to Community Policing

By the early 1990s, it was obvious that a different model was needed. That model was community policing. In a sense, it represented a return to one of Sir Robert Peel's earliest ideas—the belief that police officers should walk a beat and get to know their neighborhoods. Community policing emphasizes the importance of good relations with local neighborhoods and the need for residents and police officers to solve problems jointly. Isolated experiments with community policing began to appear in a handful of police departments, including that of San Francisco, California, as early as the late 1960s.

Momentum did not begin to build, however, until the late 1980s and early 1990s. Departments like those in Madison, Wisconsin, and Houston, Texas, embraced and developed the model during this period.[32] The Rodney King riots spotlighted the problems of the professional model. They also pushed other departments toward the community policing model. The most significant variation on community policing appeared in New York. During the early 1990s, Mayor David Dinkins introduced its precepts to the nation's largest police department, the New York Police Department (NYPD).

At the same time the NYPD was experimenting with community policing, the city's transit police were attempting to test James Q. Wilson and George Kelling's belief that disorder left unattended bred crime. **Broken windows policing**, which emphasizes the maintenance of public order, was instituted. The result was immediate and dramatic. The transit police discovered that many of the vandals and turnstile jumpers they arrested were ex-felons who also were carrying guns or skipping out on warrants. By getting to these people early, the police were, in effect, disarming them. After two years in which crime underground had increased by 48 percent, the transit police under the leadership of Chief Bill Bratton managed to bring it down by 40 percent.[33]

Bratton's successes caught the attention of an equally ambitious U.S. attorney, Rudolph Giuliani. Two years later, Giuliani won a close race to become mayor of New York. Reducing crime was one of his major priorities. The young chief who had done so much with the transit police immediately went to the top of Giuliani's list to head the NYPD. What secured the job offer for Bratton was his promise to Giuliani. If he offered Bratton the job, Bratton would deliver a 40 percent crime reduction for the whole of New York City within three years.

It was an unprecedented and—in the eyes of most criminologists—outlandish commitment. Most experts believed that other factors, such as demographics, were far more important than any type of policing. And the demographics were bad. The problem was young people. People between the ages of eighteen and twenty-five commit crimes at disproportionate rates—more than five times the rate of people age thirty-five and older. (See Figures 13-4a and 13-4b.) During the 1990s, the proportion of young people in the population as a whole was growing fast. Demographers described it as "the echo of the baby boom." Criminologists saw it in different terms—they predicted the coming of the juvenile **superpredator**.

Fortunately for New York City, Mayor Giuliani was not much interested in criminology's conventional wisdom. Bratton's bold offer and the promise that broken windows policing had shown underground appealed to the

BROKEN WINDOWS POLICING

Policing that emphasizes maintaining public order.

SUPERPREDATOR

Ultra-violent youths that experts predicted would drive up the nation's crime rate.

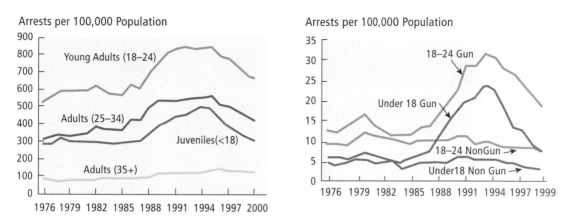

Source: Jeffrey A. Butts and Jeremy Travis, *The Rise and Fall of American Youth Violence: 1980 to 2000* (Washington, D.C.: Urban Institute, 2000).

new mayor. Bratton got the nod. When he resigned two years later, homicides in New York had fallen by 39 percent.

So what happened? Officials in the NYPD say the answer is simple—better policing. The key innovation was a new computerized crime-mapping system known as Compstat. This system allowed the police to map crime in virtual real time, identify patterns or problems, and then shift resources and devise solutions accordingly. Before the creation of Compstat, the NYPD compiled crime statistics every quarter. Compstat provided fresh numbers every week and allowed police commanders to look for crime patterns and "hot spots." It also encouraged officers to try new tactics and introduced an element of accountability to policing.[34] Today, nearly 70 percent of large police departments in the United States use some version of this system. More police officers and a focus on broken windows, or quality of life offenses, rounded off the prescription for success.

In the mid-1990s and late 1990s, these concepts were exported to other cities nationwide. Former NYPD officials were hired as consultants in such cities as New Orleans, Louisiana; Newark, New Jersey; Philadelphia, Pennsylvania; and Baltimore, Maryland. These consultants put NYPD-style techniques into place. Many of these transplants generated dramatic results, especially at first. However, another dynamic soon became evident that caught public officials off guard. Many cities that had done nothing to improve their police departments also were enjoying dramatically falling crime rates.

Los Angeles was a case in point. Once one of the most admired police forces in the country, by the early 1990s, the LAPD had fallen on hard times.

FIGURE 13-5 **Homicides in Large U.S. Cities, 1995, 2000, 2001.**

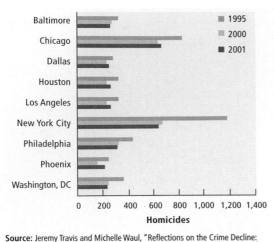

Source: Jeremy Travis and Michelle Waul, "Reflections on the Crime Decline: Lessons for the Future?" Urban Institute, 2002. www.urban.org/uploadedpdf/410546_crimedecline.pdf.

TABLE 13-1

Percent Change in Homicides

City	1995–2000	2000–2001
Baltimore	−20%	−2%
Chicago	−23%	6%
Dallas	−16%	4%
Houston	−27%	16%
Los Angeles	−35%	7%
New York City	−43%	−4%
Philadelphia	−26%	−3%
Phoenix	−37%	38%
Washington, DC	−34%	−3%

In the years that followed the Rodney King riots, the department went through two chiefs and struggled with sagging officer morale. Yet despite all of this, homicides in LA fell from 983 in 1990 to 425 in 1999. (See Figure 13-5 and Table 13-1.)

As crime fell almost everywhere, regardless of policing techniques, questions about Bratton's accomplishment in New York and his philosophy of crime reduction reappeared. Criminologists began to look for factors other than improvements in policing. They explored such areas as changes in the structure of urban drug markets, demographics, the economic boom of the 1990s, and the high rates of incarceration during the 1980s and 1990s.[35]

The dispute between those who give the police most of the credit for the crime reduction of the 1990s and those who do not continues. There is, however, a more subtle and widely accepted explanation for what happened in New York and across the country that both sides more or less agree with. It's called the "tipping point." This concept comes from epidemiology, the study of diseases. Early in the history of the discipline, epidemiologists noted that diseases do not tend to spread in a linear fashion. Rather, a handful of people come down with a disease, then a few more, and then BOOM!, doctors are dealing with a full-fledged epidemic.

Moreover, the scientists noted that epidemics often end suddenly too. Some diseases spread too fast and then "burn out" or, if checked by quarantine, die out as infected people are isolated from the rest of the population. As a result, epidemiologists developed the concept of the tipping point, literally, the number at which a disease either "tips" into a full-fledged epidemic or burns out.

Many observers now see the crack-fueled violent crime wave of the 1980s as a kind of epidemic. An epidemic that eventually burned out as a new generation saw how addictive the narcotic really was and stayed clear and as the police developed new techniques that reduced related violent crimes. Under this model, no single factor caused the crime reduction. Rather, a series of interventions were tried, each of which had some effect. First, the at-risk population came to appreciate the dangers of the "disease," and then—at some point—violent crime "tipped." The epidemic crashed, and crime rates plummeted.

Crime, Punishment, and the Essence of Modern America

At the beginning of this chapter, we stated that the way a society chooses to define crime and mete out punishment offers fundamental insights into the nature of that society. When the young French nobleman Alexis de Tocqueville decided in the early 1830s to visit and investigate the fledgling democracy of the United States, his first stop was the prisons. When British author Charles Dickens visited in 1842, he too sought out prisons and asylums.

Today, many Europeans view punishments like the death penalty as evidence of American cruelty and racism. They use the death penalty to argue against American "justice" in much the same way that critics of U.S. actions in the Middle East seized on the abuses at Abu Ghraib to criticize the U.S. occupation of Iraq. Most U.S. citizens these days are shielded from the reality of the nation's criminal justice system. It operates largely out of sight. Only a small percentage of Americans see what modern punishment looks like in this country. A tour of its state prisons and county and city jails may prove enlightening.

First, the system is rife with violence.

Prisons can be dangerous places. A surprise sweep of the Big Muddy Correctional Center in Ina, Illinois, in March 1998 resulted in more than thirty positive drug tests and the discovery of one weapon. Prisoners often find creative ways to manipulate the system to gain access to forbidden items.

A recent report by Human Rights Watch estimated that approximately 20 percent of all inmates are sexually assaulted in some way and at least 7 percent are raped. That equals approximately one million assaulted individuals over the past twenty years. For many of these prisoners, rape may be just the beginning. Prisoners who are passive or effeminate may end up as slaves, forced to do menial jobs and sometimes "rented out" to other inmates to satisfy their sexual needs.[36]

Second, the prison population is a sick population. In the 1960s, most states disbanded the psychiatric hospitals that held many of society's mentally ill. At the time, the goal was to replace the old, often cruel, networks of state mental hospitals with more humane, community-based clinics. Unfortunately, the states did away with the hospitals without building the clinics. An estimated two hundred thousand to three hundred thousand of those in prison suffer from mental disorders. This includes serious illnesses like schizophrenia, bipolar disorder, and depression. There are three times more mentally ill people in prisons than in mental hospitals.

Once in prison, do people with mental illnesses receive adequate treatment? For the most part, the answer is no. In the words of a recent report by Human Rights Watch, "across the nation, many prison mental health services are woefully deficient, crippled by understaffing, insufficient facilities, and limited programs. All too often, seriously ill prisoners receive little or no meaningful treatment. They are neglected, accused of malingering, treated as disciplinary problems."[37]

A century-and-a-half ago, many visitors to the United States praised the prisons and asylums. Today, they do not. A recent study by the international human rights group Amnesty International stated,

> The death penalty continued to be used extensively. There were reports of police brutality and unjustified police shootings and of ill treatment in prisons and jails. Human rights groups and others voiced concern at the lack of public information given about the circumstances under which more than 1,200 people, mainly foreign nationals, were detained during investigations into the . . . attacks [of September 11] on the Pentagon and World Trade Center. . . .[38]

The organization found that more than twenty thousand prisoners continued to be held in conditions of extreme isolation in **supermax security prisons**. Between 1976 and 2002, 749 people have been executed in the United States. Roughly 40 percent of those executed have been black.

What most shocks the rest of the developed world, however, is this country's treatment of children. According to Amnesty International, the United States has "continued to use life imprisonment without the possibility of parole against defendants who were under eighteen at the time of the crime, in violation of international law." The nation also leads the world in the execution of juveniles (people under the age of eighteen) and people with mental impairments. Amnesty International estimates that over the course of the past decade, the United States executed roughly two-thirds of the total children age seventeen and under who were put to death worldwide. It is the only developed country that has made child execution a regular part of its criminal justice system.[39]

Should the United States care about such criticisms? Do such statistics tell something important about the society, as Tocqueville and Dickens did

SUPERMAX SECURITY PRISONS

High security prisons designed for violent criminals.

150 years ago? While such questions are being asked, why is corporal punishment—inflicting pain on the body of someone else—now viewed as "cruel and unusual" in the words of the U.S. Constitution, but capital punishment is viewed as acceptable, as long as it's painless? Is locking someone away for five years really more humane than a public flogging?

> [W]hy is corporal punishment . . . now viewed as "cruel and unusual" . . . but capital punishment is viewed as acceptable, as long as it's painless? Is locking someone away for five years really more humane than a public flogging?

Trends to Watch in Criminal Justice

After the long crime decline of the 1990s, most experts are uncertain about what to expect in the future. Crime rates in the United States still are well above the post–Second World War rate. Granted, the world has changed a lot since the 1950s. It may seem unrealistic and idealist to think that such an old benchmark is relevant anymore. However, if the goal is the lowest crime rates possible, then maybe it is not so crazy.

Many police chiefs and most criminologists do seem to believe that the decline of the 1990s is over and that crime is likely to increase in the future. But if the 1990s showed anything, it was that making predictions about crime rates is an uncertain thing. Radical improvement is still the goal in cities such as Los Angeles. Today, the city has one of the country's highest homicide rates. The LAPD estimates that approximately one hundred thousand of LA County's residents are gang members, one of the largest populations in the nation.

Despite these daunting numbers, Los Angeles's elected leadership insists that it is committed to making the city the nation's safest. With enough law enforcement personnel and creative problem solving, it just might happen. Even with the inherent uncertainty of predicting the future, some important trends already are evident in LA and nationwide. Such trends are likely to remain.

Policing

Experts predict that the retreat from the professional model of policing will continue. The belief that the professional model was a misguided reform is now conventional wisdom. Even the West Coast, the one-time citadel of the professional model, now is trying to revamp its departments. Given its commitment to improved safety, it should be no surprise that the biggest change is taking place in Los Angeles. In the fall of 2002, Mayor James Hahn hired Bill Bratton of New York City fame to head LA's police force. Since taking over, Bratton has introduced his Compstat to the city and pushed hard to put an additional three thousand officers on the payroll.

Yet despite Bratton's efforts, the legacies of the professional model linger. Even now, residents of East Coast cities continue to enjoy a far higher level of protection than residents of West Coast cities. To police a city of 3.8 million people, the LAPD relies on approximately 9,200 officers. New York City has a population of eight million and thirty-nine thousand police officers. That is more than twice the number of police officers per capita for New York than for Los Angeles. Granted, Los Angeles and New York are extreme examples of (comparatively) small and large police forces, but such differences are visible between other cities as well. Cities in the Upper Midwest, including Chicago, Illinois; Milwaukee, Wisconsin; and Detroit, Michigan, tend to have larger police departments, in line with the size of East Coast forces. Cities in the Southwest and the Southeast, such as Dallas and El Paso, Texas; Phoenix, Arizona; Charlotte, North Carolina; and Memphis, Tennessee, often have smaller departments comparable to West Coast cities like Los Angeles and Las Vegas.[40]

Cooperation among Law Enforcement

Despite the incarceration boom, most people who are arrested do not go to prison. Probation—a punishment that permits people to remain in the community under the supervision of a probation offer—is far more common. At the close of 2002, approximately two million people were locked away in state or federal prisons and county jails, whereas four million others were on probation. Another 750,000 people had been released from prison after serving part of their sentence and were out on parole.[41]

In theory, people on probation or on parole are monitored. In practice, parole officers and probation officers are stretched very thin in most states. As a result, people on probation and parole frequently commit crimes. Within three years of their release from prison, two-thirds of former prisoners are rearrested for one or more serious crimes.[42]

Fortunately, in recent years, the police and the probation and parole officers have begun to work together, with heartening results. This is particularly true of Boston. During the mid-1990s, an interagency team of police, probation officers, corrections officers, social workers, and others agencies targeted a rapidly growing juvenile violence epidemic fed by gangs with guns. The interagency team developed a system. Probation officers inspected the homes of gang members with police officers at the ready. Corrections officials and cops kept track of who was being released when. Social workers talked with gang members and warned them that gun play would result in constant police attention. The result was a dramatic reduction in juvenile gun violence. In 1990, seventy-three people under the age of twenty-four were murdered in Boston. By 1997, that number had fallen to fifteen.[43]

Recidivism and the Limits of Improvement

The increased rate of imprisonment during the 1980s and 1990s most likely contributed to the impressive crime decline that began in the 1990s. But 95 percent of the people who are sent off to state prisons and county jails eventually are released. For too many, prison now functions as a kind of criminal finishing school. It is an educational facility whose graduates usually return to a life of crime. Roughly two-thirds of the people who leave prison after serving time for a felony return within three years. That percentage is growing. Unless state and local governments figure out an effective strategy to reverse this recidivism, millions of those locked away during the "tough on crime" 1980s and 1990s will almost certainly commit crimes again.

In 2002, Kentucky released 567 nonviolent offenders from prison an average of three months early because of budget constraints.

The End of Federal Support

This chapter has discussed crime and punishment as almost an entirely local matter. Basically, this is true. According to the Bureau of Justice Statistics, there are roughly 708,000 state and local law enforcement officers nationwide and only 88,000 federal law enforcement officers. This does not mean that the federal contribution to law enforcement is insignificant. Federal agencies take the lead in responding to crimes that cross state boundaries. They also are in charge of certain categories of crime, including counterfeiting, and, to a lesser extent, gun trafficking. Sometimes the division of responsibility between federal law enforcement, such as the Drug Enforcement Agency or the FBI, and state and local agencies can be quite unclear.

The most significant federal contribution to state and local law enforcement, however, has been financial. During the late 1960s, the federal government created the Law Enforcement Assistance Administration. This agency funneled hundreds of millions of dollars to local law enforcement agencies. In the mid-1990s, President Bill Clinton and Republicans in Congress passed legislation that provided nearly $20 billion to states and localities to build more prisons and helped localities add about seventy thousand police officers to their forces.

Today, the picture is very different. At a time when many departments are facing a manpower crisis as police officers hired in the 1970s begin to retire, direct federal funding of local departments has virtually ended. This is in part because of longstanding Republican antipathy toward such funding and plain old part belt-tightening.[44]

The New Criminal Frontier

There also is a sense that the locus of crime is shifting. During the 1960s, 1970s, and 1980s, the notion of the city as a dangerous place established a

Policy in Practice: Does Gun Control Work?

The late 1980s and early 1990s witnessed a huge surge in homicide rates. The rising numbers can be attributed to just one thing—the rise in the use of handguns by people under the age of twenty-five. Between 1985 and 1993, firearm homicides increased by 53 percent. Other homicides actually declined slightly.[a] Handgun homicides committed by juveniles under the age of eighteen *quadrupled*.[b]

The huge surge in juvenile gun violence in the mid-1980s raises an obvious question: Would tougher gun control laws have saved lives? For some people, the answer is obvious. In 1992, the United States suffered 13,200 gun-related homicides. Countries with strict gun control laws, such as Great Britain and Japan, suffered thirty-three and sixty gun-related deaths, respectively.

For others, the very suggestion of outlawing handguns is outrageous. Many gun owners view firearms ownership as a basic constitutional right. The Second Amendment proclaims "A well-regulated militia being necessary for the security of a free state, the right to keep and bear arms shall not be infringed." Some have even attempted to argue that allowing citizens to carry concealed weapons would improve overall public safety. They claim that the country would be safer if more Americans carried guns, although the research supporting these claims has largely been undermined.

In general, the courts have not agreed with this more expansive interpretation of the Constitution. States and individual cities enjoy considerable discretion to restrict gun laws as they see fit—or not at all. As a result, the right to bear arms depends very much on where you live. Twenty-nine states essentially require law enforcement agencies to provide a concealed weapon license to any law-abiding citizen who applies. Fourteen states—Alabama, California, Delaware, Georgia, Hawaii, Iowa, Maryland, Massachusetts, Michigan, Minnesota, New Jersey, New York, Rhode Island, and South Carolina—give law enforcement agencies the discretion to issue or deny weapons based on a variety of factors. In most of these states, relatively few permits are issued. Only Illinois, Kansas, Missouri, Nebraska, New Mexico, Ohio, and Wisconsin ban concealed weapons altogether.[c] In Vermont, no permit is needed to carry a concealed weapon. Many cities have also passed laws banning concealed firearms although in gun-friendly states, state preemption laws typically mean that people with concealed weapon licenses do not have to disarm before entering otherwise "firearm-free" cities.

Both sides believe that their position will increase public safety. Advocates of gun ownership point out that localities with strict gun control laws often have very high crime rates and that all bans on handgun

powerful hold on the American mind. *Law and Order* is not set in Oklahoma City, Oklahoma, or suburban Indianapolis, Indiana. It is set in New York City. These days, more and more these images of danger are just that—creations of the imaginations. Today, New York is one of the safest cities, not just in the country, but also in the world. Although gun crimes are still much, much more rare in European cities, London residents are more than twice as likely to be victims of crime than New Yorkers.

In fact, a new dynamic is now at play in cities that reduced their rates of violent crime dramatically during the 1990s—cities such as New York and Boston. These communities have exported much of their crime to their surrounding suburbs. The places that were once the first step away from troubled inner-city neighborhoods are now struggling. Guns, gangs, and drug problems are no longer limited to cities. Moreover, suburban communities

do is ensure that only criminals have guns. Gun control advocates acknowledge the problems but say the real problem is that borders are porous and other surrounding jurisdictions often have very weak gun control laws. Handguns may be illegal, period, in Washington, D.C., but cross the Potomac into Virginia and anyone can buy an assault rifle as long as no criminal record shows up in a background check. If someone does have a criminal record, a gun still can be picked up at a firearms show, since vendors there don't have to run background checks on buyers.

In fact, according to criminologist Garen Wintemute at the University of California–Davis, a dispassionate look at the evidence seems to support key claims of both sides. Studies have shown that certain types of gun restrictions—waiting periods, background checks, and some level of screening for gun buyers—work. In Wintemute's words, "they reduce rates of criminal activity involving guns and violence among people who are screened out and denied purchase of a gun—about 25 percent to 30 percent of those who are screened." Others, such as gun "buy-backs," do not. They often encourage people to turn in old, sometimes inoperable guns.

Some measures, such as requiring gun manufacturers to install trigger-locks on new handguns, are still too new to fully evaluate. However, the argument for treating gun violence as a public health problem is a strong one. Gun-related deaths, mainly accidental, are the second leading cause of death in the United States, second only to automobile accidents.[d] At the same time, there is no evidence to suggest that gun control laws reduce violent crime. Which raises an intriguing question: How can gun control laws work and yet not work at the same time?[e]

[a] Jeremy Travis and Michelle Waul, "Reflections on the Crime Decline: Lessons for the Future?" *Proceedings from the Urban Institute Crime Decline Forum,* August 2002, p. 2.

[b] Alfred Blumstein, "Why Is Crime Falling—Or Is It?" February 14, 2001 presentation.

[c] Figures come from www.bradycampaign.org/facts/gunlaws/ccw.asp and www.packing.org.

[d] See David Hemenway, *Private Guns, Public Health* (Ann Arbor: University of Michigan Press, 2004), for a discussion of the public health approach to gun violence.

[e] Wintemute's answer is this: "The resolution of the apparent paradox is that under current criteria so few people are denied the purchase of a firearm under Brady and its state level analogs relative to the number of people who purchase guns every year that an impact on that select group is too small at the population level to be noticed." Travis and Waul, "Reflections on the Crime Decline," 16.

Source: John Buntin, *Assertive Policing, Plummeting Crime: The NYPD Takes On Crime* (1530.0) case study written for use by the John F. Kennedy School of Government, Harvard University (0799). Copyright © 1999 by the Presidency and Fellowes of Harvard College.

are dealing with these problems without the resources or the experience of big city police departments. The next decade may need to witness an explosion of suburban public safety creativity to match the urban innovations of the 1990s.

The Uncertain Future of the Death Penalty

In 1972, the U.S. Supreme Court found that the application of the death penalty in many states had been cruel, arbitrary, and unconstitutional. A moratorium, or indefinite delay, was placed on all executions. Four years later, the Court lifted the moratorium. By then, the states had passed sentencing guidelines that addressed the Court's concern that the death penalty was being applied in an arbitrary fashion. Today, the statutes of thirty-eight states allow prosecutors to request the death penalty. Since 1976, 879 people have been executed in state prisons. As of July 1, 2003, another 3,517 people were on death row.[45] Roughly three-quarters of Americans consistently indicate that they support capital punishment.

The fact that most states sanction capital punishment does not mean that they use it in a similar way. Some counties and states are much more enthusiastic than others. A 1999 *USA Today* investigation found that suburban counties tend to apply the death penalty with more zeal than urban counties. For example, San Mateo County, a suburb of San Francisco, had seventeen people on California's death row at the time. San Francisco itself, a larger city with twice as many murders, had sentenced only four people to death. The newspaper found that "fifteen counties account for nearly a third of all prisoners sentenced to death but only one-ninth of the population of the states with capital punishment."[46] One reason for this may be the rising crime rates in suburban areas and a "fight back" reflex felt by residents who have seen their safe communities become danger zones.

During the 1990s, a scientific breakthrough—DNA testing—shook up the capital punishment systems of most states. In state after state, lawyers and public interest groups convinced courts and prosecutors to reexamine forensic evidence. What they found was that innocent people had been convicted for crimes they had not committed. By mid-2002, post-conviction DNA testing had cleared 108 Americans. Thirty-two of these people had been wrongfully convicted of murder, and thirteen had been sentenced to death.[47]

The impact of this new research has been felt. In January 2000, Illinois governor George Ryan, a Republican and an avowed supporter of capital punishment, became the first governor in the nation to halt executions. By the summer of 2004, nineteen states had introduced laws intended to reform their capital punishment systems.[48] It is doubtful, however, that capital punishment is going anywhere. More likely, the effect of the new DNA discoveries and system reform will be marginal improvements to the status quo. Only a slim majority of the public may believe that the death penalty is applied fairly, but approximately 57 percent of those polled remain opposed to a moratorium.[49]

A New Interest in Alternative Punishment

A serious curtailment of executions seems unlikely, but other changes to state criminal justice systems already are becoming evident. It is yet to be seen if these will do more harm than good. For instance, during the 2001–2002 economic recession, many states concluded that they could no longer afford to warehouse ever-growing numbers of prisoners. Some states, notably Oregon and Alabama, responded with a simple but perhaps shortsighted solution—they released inmates early. Given current recidivism rates, law enforcement officials may be placing many of these individuals back behind bars for other crimes. By letting criminals out of jail early, states may save some money in the short term, but at a potentially high cost in the long run.

Early release programs are not the only option states are exploring. During the late 1980s and early 1990s, states such as Arizona and Georgia pioneered the use of military-style boot camps for offenders. The camps reflected the belief that many young individuals lack direction, discipline, and self-control. Exposure to military-style discipline might correct that. However, while studies found some evidence of improved attitudes, boot camp seemed to have no impact on future criminal activities. Recidivism rates for juveniles who had gone through boot camps were no lower than recidivism among juveniles who did not. Since the mid-1990s, the number of juvenile boot camps has declined by a third.[50]

In recent years, state and local governments have experimented with a number of promising options. One initiative that got underway during the Clinton administration involves **drug courts**. Drug courts are special tribunals that offer non-violent drug offenders a chance to reduce or dismiss charges in exchange for undergoing treatment or other rehabilitation. As of May 2004, 1,160 drug courts were operating in all fifty states, and more than five hundred new drug courts were planned.[51]

Drug courts are closely connected with the **community, or restorative, justice movement**. The movement's basic goal is to give neighborhoods a voice in determining what kinds of criminals that prosecutors should choose to pursue. In practice, community justice initiatives range from the modest—placing prosecutors in local police stations where they can see neighborhood needs firsthand—to the ambitious—alternative courts that may require juvenile offenders to apologize to the people they harmed and perform community service in an attempt to rectify the harm done by the crime committed.

Another reform that states have recently embraced has been a restoration of voting rights for convicted criminals. Most of the impetus for this effort has come from civil rights organizations, which in recent years have argued that state laws that deny felons the right to vote penalize African American males, who are incarcerated at much higher rates than white and Hispanic men. Between 1996 and 2003, eight states—Connecticut, Delaware, Maryland, Nevada, New Mexico, Texas, Virginia, and Wyoming—responded to these concerns by removing or scaling back voting restrictions on ex-cons.[52]

DRUG COURTS
An alternative forum for sentencing drug offenders.

COMMUNITY, OR RESTORATIVE, JUSTICE MOVEMENT
A movement that emphasizes nontraditional punishment.

More Young People, More Crime?

For the past twenty years, the proportion of eighteen-year-olds to twenty-four-year-olds in the overall population has declined. However, that trend is now beginning to reverse. During the first decade of the twenty-first century, the proportion of eighteen-year-olds to twenty-four-year-olds will increase. The proportion of young African American males, a group who commits and suffers from crimes at a much higher rate than the population as a whole, will continue to increase through 2020.

From the standpoint of a criminologist, this is bad news. As mentioned earlier, young people, particularly young men, commit crimes at a much higher rate than older people.[53] Young people are also much more likely to be victims of crime than older people. According to the Centers for Disease Control, homicide is the second leading cause of death among young people age fifteen to nineteen.[54] As a result, more young people usually means more crime.

Of course, demography is not destiny. During the mid-1990s, society dodged the dreaded juvenile superpredator and managed to actually reduce crime during "the echo of the baby boom." To do so again may require another outburst of creative policing and community problem-solving. Other- wise, look for crime to return once more to the top of the public agenda.

Conclusion

Crime is one of the most complex—and contentious—issues in public policy. Its causes are not well understood, and the fairness of the criminal justice system and the best strategies for responding to crime are hotly debated. Nevertheless, the past decade has been a period of remarkable progress. Such innovations as community and broken windows policing and Compstat have given law enforcement agencies new tools and a new sense of purpose. Contrary to some alarmist predictions, crime rates have fallen sharply and youth violence also has declined. However, serious issues, notably the high incarceration and victimization rates of African American males, remain. Moreover, the future remains uncertain. Will new innovations push crime back down, or is the crime decline of the 1990s finally over? Only time will tell.

Key Concepts

broken windows policing (p. 450)

community, or restorative, justice movement (p. 461)

drug courts (p. 461)

parole (p. 434)

probation (p. 446)

professional model (p. 448)

supermax security prisons (p. 454)

superpredator (p. 450)

verdict (p. 438)

Suggested Readings

Blumstein, Alfred, and Joel Wallman. *The Crime Drop in America.* New York: Cambridge University Press, 2000. Presents a comprehensive overview of current thinking on a wide range of issues.

Goldstein, Herman. *Problem-Oriented Policing.* New York: McGraw-Hill, 1990. One of the classics of modern policing.

Wilson, James Q., and George Kelling. "Broken Windows," *Atlantic Monthly,* March 1982. The authors set forth what became an extremely influential vision of policing. Available online at www.theatlantic.com/politics/crime/windows.htm.

Sherman, Lawrence W., et al. "Preventing Crime: What Works, What Doesn't, What's Promising," National Institute of Justice, July 1998.

Simon, David and Edward Burn. *The Corner: A Year in the Life of an Inner-City Neighborhood.* New York: Broadway, 1998. Offers a gripping and sympathetic account of life in a troubled Baltimore neighborhood.

Suggested Web Sites

http://virlib.ncjrs.org/Statistics.asp. The Web site of the National Criminal Justice Reference Service provides statistics on a variety of topics involving crime.

www.amnesty.org. Amnesty International's Web site gives readers a sense of how the rest of the world views the criminal justice system of the United States through recent and archived material.

www.fbi.gov. Web site of the Federal Bureau of Investigation, which offers information on national and international criminal activities as well as crime prevention tips.

www.manhattan-institute.org. The Manhattan Institute's Web site includes archived articles from the institute's *City Journal,* which addresses such issues as the affects of racism.

www.ojp.usdoj.gov/nij/welcome.html. The National Institutes of Justice is the research, development, and evaluation agency of the U.S. Department of Justice. The agency researches crime control and justice issues, particularly at the state and local levels.

www.sentencingproject.org. The Sentencing Project's Web site offers data and information about racial disparities in the U.S. criminal justice system.

CHAPTER 14

Health and Welfare

State, Heal Thyself!

Open up and say, "Ahhh . . . ." Undeniably, the patients aren't the only ones who are sick in the U.S. healthcare system. The system itself will need more than an aspirin and an apple a day to heal itself. While the debate continues to rage over a national healthcare plan, states and localities are forced to pick up the slack. And the flu doesn't care if someone has insurance or not. Here, Beverly Cowart, a nurse at NAN Healthcare in Hattiesburg, Mississippi, checks for signs of influenza in 6-year-old Devon Kraeger in January 2003.

Why is long-term healthcare becoming more important?

Why has creating a universal healthcare program in the United States been so difficult?

When are Medicaid benefits generous? When are they realistic or stingy?

P erris, California, is located eighteen miles south of the city of Riverside. Headquarters of the Riverside County fire department and not much else, the town has a rural, easygoing feel to it.

On December 14, 1998, however, the slow tempo of Perris was disrupted dramatically.

At approximately 4:30 P.M., the director of special education at an elementary school in the small town of Perris, California, opened a letter. Inside, he found a moist paper towelette and a note that read, "You have been exposed to anthrax."

Anthrax is an infectious disease caused by the spore-forming bacterium *Bacillus anthracis*. In the wild, it primarily infects sheep. People who come in close contact with infected animals or infected animal products—such as wool—also may contract it. In its early stages, anthrax can be treated with antibiotics, but it can be fatal if left untreated. Consequently, many people employed in occupations that require them to work closely with animals receive anthrax vaccinations.

There's more. The spore form of the bacterium is extremely durable and can be delivered as an aerosol. It is largely invisible—at best, a fine dust—and hence difficult to detect. Symptoms typically do not appear for one to five days. The evidence is extremely limited, but mortality rates from anthrax inhalation may exceed 85 percent.[1] What all of this means is that anthrax is well suited for use as a biological weapon.

Even before September 11, 2001, government officials had become increasingly concerned about the dangers of chemical and biological weapons. So when the Riverside County fire department got a call about a possible anthrax attack, it treated the situation seriously. Firefighters arrived in Level B protective gear—essentially, full-protection suits with self-contained breathing gear. Then they quarantined everyone who might have been exposed to the purported anthrax.

In keeping with the standard protocol for dealing with people exposed to hazardous materials, the fire department proceeded to decontaminate everyone on the scene. With the temperature hovering below thirty degrees Fahrenheit, people were forced to take off of all their clothes. Their garments were sealed in plastic bags. Quarantined individuals then had to stand in small inflatable plastic containers like child-sized swimming pools while they were hosed down with a bleach solution. At the end of the process, they were issued temporary clothing.[2]

Once FBI agents arrived on the scene, however, they quickly ascertained that the letter was almost certainly a hoax. Even if it had been a real incident of terrorism involving anthrax, local officials were not really doing the right thing. Anthrax is not a dangerous chemical that needs to be washed off with a strong solution. Proper treatment involves antibiotics. Local first responders were responding to a novel and frightening public health threat in a traditional—and ineffectual—way.

Riverside County's reaction underscores one of the most important functions of government—protecting public health. Public health is the area of medicine that deals with the protection and improvement of citizen health and hygiene by government agencies. Since the earliest days of the United States, state and local governments have met this need. This is especially true in regard to the poorest and to the disabled members of society.

State and local governments also have taken the lead in responding to public health crises. In practice, this includes responses as simple as making sure an ambulance or fire truck responds to a 911 call and responses as complex as managing an epidemic. A century ago that might have involved yellow fever, cholera, or influenza. A flu outbreak in 1918 killed an estimated six hundred thousand Americans and one hundred million people worldwide.[3]

Today, such a crisis is more likely to be a new illness. Sudden Acute Respiratory Syndrome (SARS) altered travel worldwide in 2003, and sporadic outbreaks continued in 2004. A terrorist attack involving a chemical or biological weapon is another very real possibility. Only three years after Riverside County's anthrax scare, the residents of New York, New York; Washington, D.C.; and Boca Raton, Florida, were victims of real anthrax attacks.

SARS, anthrax, and the specter of bioterrorism are frightening new developments in the field of public health. But they are not the only threats to the public. Sometimes the public is its own worst enemy. The impact of recent "outside" health threats pales beside more long-standing public health concerns. According to the Surgeon General, smoking causes more than four hundred thousand deaths a year in the United States. And a growing percentage of Americans are overweight or suffer from **obesity**.

Just how active state and local governments should be on these issues is often a source of heated debate. Terrorism experts warn that the United States has far too few hospital beds in the event of a real emergency.[4] Many communities cannot even keep an adequate blood supply available to healthcare facilities when things are quiet and uneventful. Despite the dangers posed by illnesses like SARS, most counties maintain only skeletal public health departments.

Some governors, including Mike Huckabee of Arkansas—who has himself lost more than a hundred pounds—have made combating obesity a major

OBESITY

A medical term used to describe people who are excessively overweight.

Can yoga do as much good for the body as for the spirit? At P.S. 5 in New York, administrators hope so. A Head Start program started in late 2003 is aimed specifically at preventing childhood obesity. More and more Americans are tipping the scales, and educators and public health officials are scrambling to curb the trend.

priority. They have pushed for educational programs for parents and have restored physical education classes in schools while removing soft drink machines. Others pooh-pooh the problem. Some states are generous providers of health insurance, which covers the expenses associated with illness and hospitalization, to their low-income citizens. Other states are much more restrictive. Explanations for these differences will be explored in this chapter.

For all the variation among state and local governments, it is clear that over the course of the past decade they have become much more assertive. During the economic boom of the mid-1990s and late 1990s, the states worked with the federal government to find new ways to extend health insurance to low-income parents and children. When the economy slipped into recession, states led the effort to find ways to reduce the costs of medical care, particularly prescription drugs, and to improve the quality of care.

The newfound activism on the part of the states regarding prescription drug costs reflects what may prove to be a momentous realignment of the United States' system of federalism. Forty years ago, most states were minor players in the nation's healthcare system. Proponents of expanded health coverage and healthcare reform looked to the federal government for solutions. Today, the situation is very nearly reversed. A decade of inaction and partisan division in Washington has shifted the most important—and most difficult—healthcare issues to state and local governments. The lawmakers tackling tough issues like rising rates of obesity, health insurance for the uninsured, rising prescription drug costs, long-term care, AIDS and other sexually transmitted diseases, and drug use are more likely to be sitting in state capitols than under the Capitol dome in Washington, D.C.

In addition, states have taken the lead in rethinking such safety net programs as welfare. In 1996, Congress abolished the existing Aid for Families with Dependent Children (AFDC), or welfare, program and replaced it with a system of block grants to the states. These grants gave state governments the leeway to design their own personalized, work-oriented, time-limited welfare programs. The result has been a profusion of sometimes very different welfare-to-work programs.

For instance, Oklahoma, a traditionalistic state, used TANF funds to train government workers and religious volunteers to administer a program developed by the U.S. military and designed to strengthen marriages to people moving from welfare to work. Arizona, Michigan, Oklahoma, Tennessee, and Utah also have focused on encouraging welfare recipients to embrace more traditional family arrangements. Utah's state-run program focuses on providing long-term assistance. This is largely because the Church of Jesus Christ of Latter-day Saints already provides care to Mormons in need, and Mormons make up two-thirds of the state's population.

In contrast, states like New York have downplayed so-called "family formation" policies. Part of this difference in emphasis reflects states' different political cultures. However, the structure of state government also plays an important role. New York's welfare system is decentralized. It relies on county governments to administer programs. So does Colorado. Despite having a political culture that would seem to be supportive of "family formation," Colorado has made few efforts in that direction, largely because its decentralized structure makes the system unresponsive to directives of any sort.[5]

The Influence of Culture

How state governments define public health has a lot to do with a given region's distinctive political culture. All public health officials would agree that certain issues, such as terrorism and AIDS, are important public health issues. No one would argue that a flu epidemic or the contamination of a major watershed also qualify.

Other topics are not so easily categorized. Is gun violence a public health issue? Researchers at the Centers for Disease Control and Prevention (CDC) think so. They point out that gun-related deaths, most of which are accidental, are the country's second leading cause of death. The American Medical Association (AMA) now advises doctors to talk with patients about the proper handling and storage of any guns they may own. Many gun owners, however, vehemently reject the idea that guns are a public health issue.

On other health fronts, some cities have attempted to reduce the transmission of dangerous blood-born illnesses like HIV and Hepatitis C by providing addicts with clean needles. Others have rejected these needle exchange programs. They charge that such programs give rise to disorder and crime and send the message that intravenous drug use is okay.

Then there is the always controversial question of sexual education. Should parents, educators, and other adult role models emphasize **abstinence** or teach teenagers to use condoms? Or is instruction in a variety of options that includes both abstinence and birth control the answer?

As these examples demonstrate, state and local governments are responding to such public health challenges in very different ways. Often these different positions reflect very different political cultures. Oregon has granted terminally ill patients the right to physician-assisted suicide. Most other states continue to classify such an action as a felony, even if it is rarely prosecuted, for obvious reasons. Nebraska passed legislation to ban late-term abortions, and even though the U.S. Supreme Court later struck down the law, the voters had made their preferences known.

ABSTINENCE
Refraining from sexual activity, usually intercourse.

It doesn't stop there. California, Connecticut, Delaware, Georgia, Hawaii, Iowa, Maine, Missouri, Nevada, New Hampshire, New Mexico, North Carolina, Rhode Island, Texas, Vermont, and Washington have passed legislation that requires health insurers to pay for all contraceptive devices. Communities such as Berkeley, California; Boulder, Colorado; New Haven, Connecticut; and Tacoma, Washington, cautiously have embraced needle exchange. Many other cities have rejected the idea in the face of strong community opposition.

Different states have very different notions about the roles state governments should fill. Wisconsin's innovative early attempts at welfare reform in the late 1980s and early 1990s, which have been discussed in previous chapters, laid the groundwork for the federal decision to junk welfare altogether in 1996 and return most welfare responsibilities to the states. States such as Oregon and Tennessee have sought to transform state Medicaid programs into comprehensive, state-run health insurance plans. Other states have shown no great enthusiasm for providing healthcare to low-income citizens.

Yet even states that have shown little interest in taking on new responsibilities are finding that healthcare is fast becoming *the* unavoidable issue. This is due largely to Medicaid, the joint state-federal health insurance program for low-income mothers and children, the elderly, and people with disabilities. When Congress created the program in 1965, it was supposed to be a modest program that served only a small number of extremely poor people. It hasn't worked out that way.

As soon as it was created, Medicaid expenditures started growing quickly—and never stopped. Today, it provides health insurance and services to approximately 44 million Americans. This includes 22.6 million children, 12 million elderly and people with disabilities, and 9.2 million adults in low-income families. States now devote an average of about 15 percent of their total general revenue funds to Medicaid.[6]

> Yet even states that have shown little interest in taking on new responsibilities are finding that healthcare is fast becoming *the* unavoidable issue. This is due largely to Medicaid . . . . When Congress created the program in 1965, it was supposed to be a modest program that served only a small number of extremely poor people. It hasn't worked out that way.

The continuing growth of Medicaid has huge implications for the future of state governments. If the program continues to grow at its current rate—and there are good reasons to believe it will—healthcare eventually will become the major function of state governments. That means either higher taxes or less money for other state priorities like education, transportation, and criminal justice.

County and city governments spend significant amounts on healthcare as well. In many parts of the country, hospitals and clinics funded by counties and cities continue to function as a critical social safety net for people without health insurance. These are people who earn too much to qualify for Medicaid but too little to pay for private health insurance. If the United States ever experiences a large-scale biological attack, such as smallpox or anthrax, the capacities of these facilities will determine how well this society survives such an attack.

How Government Got into the Healthcare Biz

Any serious discussion of healthcare soon arrives at a basic question: "Who should pay for what?" Over the past decade, the answer has varied widely. During the early 1990s, the solution offered by many Democrats was, "The federal government should provide health insurance to everyone who does not have it."

By the early twenty-first century, a lot of those same Democrats were arguing that state governments, not the federal government, should lead the way. Universal—or nearly universal—coverage, they stated, should be created by gradually extending existing health insurance programs, notably Medicaid. Such programs should be expanded to encompass various populations not currently eligible for it. In contrast, some Republicans argued that health insurance should be extended via federal tax credits. How much health insurance should be provided has been another hotly contested topic.

It wasn't always so complicated. For most of the nation's history, elected officials believed that the government should serve as the health and welfare provider of last resort for society's poorest and sickest members. The level of government that officials had in mind, however, was not the federal government. Not even state governments. It was local government.

The role of local governments in health and welfare goes back to the very beginning of U.S. history. In colonial America, local communities maintained almshouses to feed and clothe people who could not care for themselves and who had no families to care for them. Back then few distinctions were made between the sick, the mentally ill, and people without a means of support. As sociologist Paul Starr has noted, almshouses "received dependent persons of all kinds, mixing together promiscuously the aged, the orphaned, the insane, the ill, the debilitated."[7] Those with infectious diseases, such as typhoid fever and cholera, were sent to pesthouses to survive as best they could.

Colonial almshouses made few distinctions between the poor and the sick for a reason. Put simply, the two conditions often were interrelated. Sickness quickly led to poverty and poverty to sickness. Each contributed to the other.

That began to change in the nineteenth century. By the middle of the century, elected officials, social reformers, and physicians—who were just beginning to establish themselves as a respectable profession—came to believe that mixing juveniles, beggars, the mentally ill, widows, and others in almshouses was no longer the best course of action. In effect, physicians and public officials began to distinguish between the sick and the destitute. A new institution was needed—the hospital.

From the early 1800s to mid-1800s, cities like Philadelphia and New York transformed some of their almshouses into hospitals.[8] Privately organized charitable hospitals, many run by religious groups, appeared in many cities too. Even state governments made a modest foray into health care. By 1860, most states had established mental hospitals and homes for the blind and the deaf.

Like almshouses, the first hospitals were institutions for unfortunates without money or family. For people with families or money, a house call from the doctor was the preferred form of medical care. According to Starr, "[a]lmost no one who had a choice sought hospital care."

Hospitals were regarded with dread, and rightly so. They were dangerous places, in part because of the medical and hygienic practices of the time. Sick people were safer at home. The few who became patients went into hospitals because of special circumstances. They might be seamen in a strange port, travelers, the homeless, or the solitary aged. Individuals who, whether traveling or destitute, were unlucky enough to fall sick without family, friends, or servants to care for them.[9]

Hospitals and physicians made a spirited effort to improve their image. Hospitals moved their sickest residents—as well as patients who were dissolute or morally objectionable—to other institutions. In 1847, for instance, Bellevue Hospital in New York decided to move the penitentiary and almshouse off its grounds and concentrate on medical care.[10] Previously, there had been a tendency to mingle them together. However, this practice did vary widely by facility. The hospital was beginning to emerge as a distinctive institution.

As hospitals sought more respectable clientele, almshouses took on a harder edge. During the seventeenth and eighteenth centuries, many almshouses were patterned on conventional homes and sought to serve as a kind of surrogate family for their residents. During the nineteenth century, however, local governments refashioned almshouse to serve a different purpose. Such facilities now were used to illustrate the consequences of idleness, sinfulness, and poverty and to shame their residents. Shabby facilities and neglect became commonplace.[11]

The Idea of a Social Safety Net

This arrangement continued in the United States until well into the twentieth century. The duty of providing healthcare and welfare remained firmly in the hands of local governments. States assisted with those with mental illnesses and people with disabilities. The federal government ran a compulsory health insurance system for the merchant marine, so that sick sailors could get care in any port, and provided pensions and healthcare to military veterans.

By the end of the nineteenth century, a new idea was percolating in progressive circles. Many social reformers came to believe that the federal government should take a much larger role in securing healthcare and pensions for the working class.

Such an idea first arose in Germany. In 1883, the conservative government of German chancellor Otto von Bismarck created the world's first compulsory sickness and unemployment insurance fund, which required employees and employers to set aside money to cover the costs of medical treatment for workers. Bismarck later created a compulsory retirement program, whose cost was divided among employees, employers, and the national government, in much the same way that it is done in the United States today.

These innovations were momentous in the development of the state. Before Bismarck, talk of healthcare, unemployment insurance, and pensions had been largely the arena of socialists and communists. He showed that conservative, capitalist countries could enact such programs too. Indeed, they could take the lead in developing a generous social safety net. Over the course of the next thirty years, other European countries followed Germany's lead.

The United States, however, did not. During the heyday of the Progressive movement in the early twentieth century, discussions about national health insurance were widespread. Eventually, opposition from physicians and from the country's largest labor union, the American Federation of Labor (forebearer of today's AFL-CIO) effectively derailed the idea. During the 1920s, many states took the small, first steps toward creating a social safety net by setting up workers' compensation funds for injured workers. However, amidst the affluence of the times, there was little support for a more ambitious social safety net.[12] That changed with the start of the Great Depression.

The Birth of the American Safety Net

On Thursday, October 24, 1929, the stock market in New York City collapsed in what the *New York Times* called "the most disastrous trading day in the stock market's history."[13] By the spring of 1933, it was clear that the United States had entered an unprecedented economic slump—the Great Depression.

In response to this economic disaster, the federal government for the first time took on some of the social safety net functions that European governments had pioneered decades earlier.[14] In 1935, President Franklin Delano Roosevelt and Congress teamed up to pass the Social Security Act. This act established two social safety net programs. The first was a joint federal-state program of unemployment compensation. The second was a federally run program of retirement benefits for senior citizens, which soon would be known simply as Social Security.

The federal government also created the Aid for Families with Dependent Children program. AFDC's purpose was to provide monetary assistance to widowed women with children, women who had been abandoned by their husbands, or women who were in some way incapacitated. Funded by the federal government, the program was administered by the states.

The Roosevelt administration briefly considered adding compulsory health insurance program to the Social Security Act as well. However, given the American Medical Association's vehement opposition to the idea, the proposal was eventually dropped as too controversial. Instead, the Social Security Act provided federal grants to help states pay for programs for the disabled and the aged and to provide child welfare services, public health services, and vocational rehabilitation.[15] As a result, responsibility for providing a healthcare safety net remained in the hands of state and local governments.

A Multibillion-Dollar Afterthought

State governments became major participants in the U.S. safety net system almost by accident. After the assassination of President John F. Kennedy in 1963, Lyndon B. Johnson ascended to the Oval Office. Johnson and congressional Democrats were determined to pass legislation that would cover hospital costs for senior citizens. Congressional Republicans, however, had a different proposal in mind. They supported a voluntary health insurance program that would cover the cost of physician visits for seniors. So in 1965, the two parties decided to compromise in classic Washington fashion—by doing both. The result was Medicare, the federal health insurance program for the elderly.

But Congress didn't stop there. While it was on a roll, it also created Medicaid. Despite their very similar names, Medicare and Medicaid are very different programs. Medicare is run and paid for entirely by the federal government. As with Social Security, every senior who worked for ten years and paid taxes—or whose spouse worked for ten years and paid taxes—is eligible to participate, as are people with certain types of disabilities. The program is financed in part by a small payroll tax. Most retirees, however, take far more out of Medicare than they contribute.[16] Understandably, Medicare almost immediately became a popular program.

Medicaid, on the other hand, is a joint state-federal program that is paid for in part by the general revenue funds of state and local governments. The federal government picks up most of the cost. On average, it covers 59 percent of Medicaid expenditures. For poorer areas, the percentage is higher. Alabama, Arkansas, the District of Columbia, Idaho, Louisiana, Montana,

New Mexico, Oklahoma, Utah, and West Virginia all receive more than 70 percent of their Medicaid expenditures from the federal government. Wealthier states split the cost 50–50. States do not have to participate. However, since 1982—when Arizona finally signed on—all states have.

Therefore, Medicaid is not an unfunded mandate. The federal government does not force states to participate in it. It is, however, an entitlement program. That is, it does create legally enforceable rights. In fact, it is a double entitlement program. For one, states have a right to a certain amount of federal money every year. And then, individuals who meet its eligibility thresholds are entitled to its services, regardless of the cost.

The states enjoy considerable leeway to setting those eligibility standards. (See Table 14-1.) They have created health care safety nets with very different levels of generosity. As of July 2000, the least generous state in the country was Alabama. It allowed only those earning less than 21 percent of the federal poverty level—the threshold set by the U.S. Bureau of the Census to measure poverty—to receive Medicaid. That means that a working parent with two children who earned more than $254 a month—slightly more than $3,000 a year—earned too much to qualify.

The most generous state was Minnesota. It allowed families earning up to 275 percent of the federal poverty level to receive Medicaid benefits. In other words, a working parent with two children could earn up to $3,372 a month—more than $40,000 a year—and still qualify for Medicaid. Even controlling for the fact that most parts of Alabama have considerably lower costs of living than Minnesota, that is a dramatic difference. The United States may have one safety net for seniors, but for everyone else, it is a country with fifty-one safety nets.

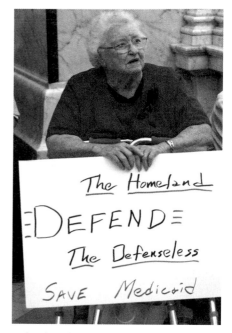

Medicaid may be guaranteed to those who qualify, but the qualifications are determined by state legislatures and affected by a variety of factors. And the qualifications can change. Maybelle Brewer, an eighty-two-year-old Medicaid recipient from Gulfport, Mississippi, was sent a letter informing her that she was being dropped from the Medicaid rolls. Rallying at the state capitol in Jackson in June 2004, Brewer was protesting not only her own change in circumstances, but that of sixty-five thousand other residents as well.

Oops!: The Unexpected Cost of Health Insurance

Medicare and Medicaid were structured very differently, but the two programs soon revealed a common trait. They both quickly proved to be fantastically expensive. From 1965 to 1970, the annual rate of increase in state and federal health expenditures was 20.8 percent. By fiscal year 2000, the federal government and state governments spent more than $200 billion on Medicaid alone.[17]

Even as state officials were watching with alarm as Medicaid spending soared, another disturbing trend was becoming evident. The number of women with children receiving financial assistance under the AFDC

TABLE 14-1

Amount a Working Parent with Two Children Applying for Publicly Funded Coverage May Earn and Still Be Eligible (as of July 1, 2000)

State	Monthly Income-Eligibility Threshold	Annual Income-Eligibility Threshold	Percent of 2001 Federal Poverty Line	State	Monthly Income-Eligibility Threshold	Annual Income-Eligibility Threshold	Percent of 2001 Federal Poverty Line
Alabama	$254	$3,048	21%	Montana	$836	$10,032	69%
Alaska	$1,208	$14,496	79%	Nebraska	$535	$6,420	44%
Arizona	$437	$5,244	36%	Nevada	$1,055	$12,660	87%
Arkansas	$365	$4,380	30%	New Hampshire	$815	$9,780	67%
California	$1,309	$15,708	107%	New Jersey	$533	$6,396	44%
Colorado	$511	$6,132	42%	New Mexico	$704	$8,448	58%
Connecticut	$866	$10,392	71%	New York	$974	$11,688	80%
Delaware	$1,309	$15,708	107%	North Carolina	$750	$9,000	62%
District of Columbia	$2,438	$29,256	200%	North Dakota	$988	$11,856	81%
Florida	$806	$9,672	66%	Ohio	$1,219	$14,628	100%
Georgia	$514	$6,168	42%	Oklahoma	$591	$7,092	48%
Hawaii	$1,403	$16,836	100%	Oregon	$1,219	$14,628	100%
Idaho	$407	$4,884	33%	Pennsylvania	$557	$6,684	46%
Illinois	$882	$10,584	72%	Rhode Island	$2,345	$28,140	192%
Indiana	$378	$4,536	31%	South Carolina	$668	$8,016	55%
Iowa	$1,065	$12,780	87%	South Dakota	$796	$9,552	65%
Kansas	$493	$5,916	40%	Tennessee	$930	$11,160	76%
Kentucky	$909	$10,908	75%	Texas	$396	$4,740	32%
Louisiana	$323	$3,876	26%	Utah	$673	$8,076	55%
Maine	$1,309	$15,708	107%	Vermont	$2,345	$28,140	192%
Maryland	$524	$6,288	43%	Virginia	$448	$5,376	37%
Massachusetts	$1,621	$19,452	133%	Washington	$2,438	$29,256	200%
Michigan	$622	$7,464	51%	West Virginia	$380	$4,560	31%
Minnesota	$3,352	$40,224	275%	Wisconsin	$2,255	$27,060	185%
Mississippi	$458	$5,496	38%	Wyoming	$790	$9,480	65%
Missouri	$1,309	$15,708	107%	**U.S. Median**	**$806**	**$9,672**	**66%**

Source: Matthew Broaddus et al., "Expanding Family Coverage: States' Medicaid Eligibility Policies for Working Families in the Year 2000," Center for Budget and Policy Priorities, rev. February 13, 2002, 23. www.cbpp.org/1-2-02health.pdf (accessed July 18, 2004).

program was soaring too. After two decades of slow growth, the number of AFDC beneficiaries took off in the late 1960s, rising from slightly more than two million recipients in 1960 to more than ten million recipients by 1972.

The composition of AFDC recipients also was changing. The widows of the 1940s were being replaced by divorced and separated women with children as well as single mothers who had never been married. By 1979, single mothers made up nearly 80 percent of all AFDC recipients.[18]

As those benefiting from welfare changed, the program became increasingly unpopular with the public. During the late 1970s and early 1980s, Ronald Reagan and other conservative politicians railed against what they saw as the excesses of the welfare state. They evoked images of "welfare queens" who drove Cadillacs and paid for steak dinners with fat rolls of food stamps.[19] Reagan's welfare queen proved to be more of a myth than reality, but it was arguably true that the United States had created a set of permanent dependents of the sort that Franklin Delano Roosevelt had warned against when he called government relief "a narcotic, a subtle destroyer of the human spirit."[20]

The 1970s were a difficult decade for proponents of expanding the nation's social safety net. As the boom of the 1960s gave way to the stagflation of the 1970s, cities such as New York ran into serious problems. These were urban centers that had long prided themselves on generous housing subsidies and social programs. However, as manufacturing jobs vanished and businesses and middle-class residents abandoned many urban downtowns, cities were forced to radically scale back their efforts. In 1976, after years of lavish overspending and declining federal subsidies, New York City was forced to declare bankruptcy. Even state and local governments that had not attempted to forge comprehensive social safety nets were forced to dramatically reduce their social welfare programs.

The Devolution Revolution

Supporters of Ronald Reagan weren't the only people fed up. State and local officials were too. Many were frustrated by the high-handed way that the federal government administered welfare and Medicaid. Medicaid was theoretically a joint state-federal program, but the federal government always held the whip over state governments. The Centers for Medicare and Medicaid Services (CMS) is the federal agency responsible for administering both Medicare and Medicaid. Formerly the Health Care Financing Administration, this agency monitors state governments in much the same way that a reform school principal might monitor juvenile offenders.

Of course, the federal government sometimes had reason to be suspicious. Many states, most notably Louisiana, have long sought to shift as many Medicaid expenses to the federal side of the ledger as possible. Indeed, in 2004, the federal government chided both Louisiana and Missouri for improper reimbursements totaling $116 million and $87 million, respectively.[21]

Despite sometimes questionable actions on the part of the states, such as Louisiana, even federal officials began to come around during the 1980s. Maybe the states should be given greater freedom to experiment with their welfare and Medicaid programs. In the late 1980s, the U.S. Department of

Health and Human Services, the parent organization of the CMS, began to grant states "demonstration waivers." This allowed states to experiment with how they provided welfare and healthcare. By 2001, eighteen states had received waivers. States were able to extend or augment health insurance to more than seven million who otherwise would not have been able to receive it.[22]

Welfare Reform

One of the first states to take advantage of this new federal flexibility was Wisconsin. In 1987, Tommy Thompson entered the governor's office. One of Thompson's first acts was to bring together about a dozen people for lunch at the executive mansion to discuss one of the most contentious topics in American politics—welfare reform. For years, conservatives had charged that welfare encouraged births outside of marriage and created multiple generations of dependence. Liberals had decried the "demonization" of welfare recipients and called for more generous programs. Amidst the furor, reform had lost out to partisan rancor.

Thompson's first lunch underscored that he was eager to think outside the box and achieve real reform. Unlike most governors, Thompson didn't invite policy wonks or advocates, either pro or con. Instead, he invited welfare mothers so that he could hear first-hand about obstacles that made it difficult for them to get and keep jobs.[23]

Thompson took the answers he got that day and during his subsequent yearly lunches and set out to radically reorient welfare in Wisconsin. In doing so, he managed to avoid the dead ends that previous reformers had encountered. In the past, most states had attempted to move welfare recipients into the job market by providing training and education opportunities. All of these programs were expensive. Only some were successful. Thompson decided to focus on getting welfare recipients a job. Any job. Virtually all recipients were required to work. If they were unable to find a job, then a subsidized one or one in community service was made available.

If welfare recipients needed childcare or transportation to get to work, the state provided it. Essentially, Thompson subverted one of the major arguments for ending welfare—namely, that welfare recipients were free riding on the taxpaying public. Instead, he actually increased funding for childcare, healthcare, and transportation. Once recipients were working, they were provided with one-on-one job counseling, education, training, and other support services.[24]

Not all of Thompson's actions to reform welfare were as touchy-feely as his yearly lunches or as supportive as providing childcare and transportation. Some of them were downright coercive. Funds were cut off to parents of truant children. Marriage incentives were created for teenage parents.

By *forcing* welfare recipients to get jobs *and* offering them the support they realistically needed to enter the job market, Thompson disarmed both conservative and liberal critics and pointed the way to workable reforms to the system. Other states soon followed suit. Work requirements were strengthened and time limits on benefits were imposed. New assistance with childcare and transportation was offered. By the summer of 1996, more than forty states had received statewide waivers that allowed them to vary work requirements for AFDC recipients.[25]

Thompson's reforms, coercive or otherwise, were remarkably effective. Providing services such as childcare and transportation increased per capita welfare costs in the short run, but in the long run it paid off. State welfare costs fell by about 65 percent over the course of the decade. The state saved more than $1 billion. Such successes later earned Thompson the position of secretary of health and human services under President George W. Bush.

It was in 1996 that Congress and President Bill Clinton formally embraced the reforms that states had initiated. The AFDC program was replaced with TANF. As part of this new program, the Personal Responsibility and Work Opportunity Reconciliation Act put a five-year cap on federal payments to welfare recipients. It also required states to put a large portion of welfare recipients to work.

What the new legislation was most notable for, however, was for what it did not require. Gone were most of the requirements that the federal government sign off on state plans. TANF gave states the freedom to set benefit levels, eligibility requirements, and financial incentives and penalties as they saw fit.

TANF also converted welfare from an entitlement program to a block grant program. In the past, people who met eligibility guidelines had been legally entitled to welfare, no matter the cost. Now, the federal government would provide only a finite amount of money to the states. At first, the federal payout was quite generous. The intent was to give states plenty of funds to devise and implement the support programs of their choice. Over time, however, the federal contribution grew smaller and smaller.

Opponents of the reforms were deeply upset by the loss of the entitlement aspect of welfare. This seemed to announce a retreat from the progressive goal of expanding the social safety net. Democratic senator Daniel Patrick Moynihan warned of children in the streets and "something approaching the Apocalypse."[26]

So far, such predictions have proven to be off base. The number of welfare recipients has declined sharply, from approximately six million in 1996 to less than half that number by 2000. Poverty rates for single-parent households also fell during this period. By and large, the alarming predictions have failed to materialize.

The fact that this happened during the longest economic expansion since the Second World War undoubtedly played an important part in the success

MAP 14-1 TANF Income Eligibility Thresholds

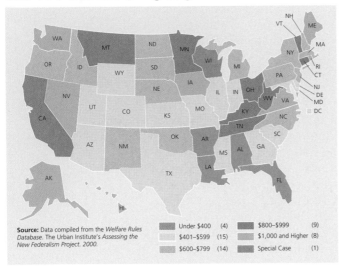

Source: Data compiled from the *Welfare Rules Database*. The Urban Institute's *Assessing the New Federalism Project*. 2000.

Under $400	(4)	$800–$999	(9)	
$401–$599	(15)	$1,000 and Higher	(8)	
$600–$799	(14)	Special Case	(1)	

of welfare reform. However, even when the economy slid into recession in the spring of 2001, the number of people on welfare rolls stayed low. So too did the expansion of the Earned Income Tax Credit and the expansion of Medicaid in many states, a development examined in the next section.

However, as with the AFDC program, states have created TANF programs with very different levels of benefits. (See Map 14-1.) A dollar in Mississippi goes a lot farther than a dollar in California. Even a cursory look at the map reveals that states' TANF spending tends to track their political orientation. Simply put, Democratic states continue to spend more on welfare than Republican states.

The Feds Falter

When Bill Clinton took office in 1993, he and his administration were prepared to let states take the lead on welfare reform. After all, the president's previous job had been governor of Arkansas. However, the president and his wife, Hillary, did see the problem of the uninsured as primarily a federal one. In early 1994, Clinton introduced the Health Security Act. This was legislation that would have provided universal health insurance to all Americans.

Senate Republicans initially countered with a proposal that would have extended health insurance coverage dramatically but would still have fallen short of universal health insurance. Clinton rejected this counterproposal, vowing to veto any measure that failed to provide 100 percent coverage.[27] Politics being politics, the two major parties were unable to find common ground. Nine months later, the Clinton health insurance proposal went down in defeat.[28]

Fast forward six years. In 2000, there were an estimated 38.5 million Americans without health insurance.[29] (See Map 14-2.) That means that during the longest economic expansion since the Second World War, the number of people without insurance actually grew. In the decade since the defeat of the Health Security Act, the federal government has largely given up the effort to find a federal solution to the problem of the uninsured or such new problems as the soaring cost of prescription drugs. In the absence of federal initiative, the states stepped up to the plate.

The Rise of the Healthcare State

The collapse of healthcare reform efforts at the federal level left states in a tricky position. They were being squeezed between the pincers of the rising costs of state Medicaid programs and the rising demands for assistance from citizens struggling with drug costs and a lack of health insurance. Finally, in the mid-1990s, states found what looked like a good way to both contain costs and expand coverage—**managed care.**

Under managed care, instead of paying doctors a fee for each service provided, states typically paid a health maintenance organization (HMO) a flat fee for each Medicaid patient enrolled in a plan. The fee that states offered HMOs was designed to be lower than the expenses the states would have incurred if patients had remained in a traditional "fee for service" Medicaid program. HMOs agreed to these lower rates because they believed that even with lower reimbursement rates, they would still be able to squeeze inefficiencies out of the system and turn a profit.

Medicaid beneficiaries benefited too. They were able to join health plans that gave them access to physicians and services that often had been unavailable under the old program. Traditional Medicaid reimbursement rates are so low that many physicians simply refuse to see Medicaid beneficiaries. Ultimately, the states saved money, at least theoretically.[30] (See Box 14-1.)

Some states pocketed the savings. Others viewed the windfall as an opportunity to achieve more ambitious goals. In 1994, Tennessee governor Ned McWherter, a Democrat, converted Tennessee's entire Medicaid program into a managed care program—TennCare. The new program was opened up to an estimated four hundred thousand people who lacked health insurance but earned too much to qualify for Medicaid. That same year Oregon governor John Kitzhaber received permission from the HHS to try an even more radical approach: Oregon was allowed to explicitly ration its healthcare dollars to cover as many people as possible in the most cost-effective fashion.

A Promising Beginning

For a while, this approach seemed to work. By 1998, approximately half of all Medicaid recipients nationwide were in managed care programs.[31] As

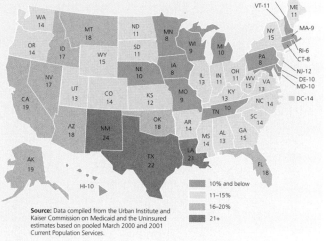

MAP 14-2 Highest Rates of Uninsurance

Source: Data compiled from the Urban Institute and Kaiser Commission on Medicaid and the Uninsured estimates based on pooled March 2000 and 2001 Current Population Services.

MANAGED CARE

An arrangement for the provision of healthcare whereby an agency acts as an intermediary between consumers and healthcare providers.

A Difference that Makes a Difference:
When States Go It Alone

In recent years, advocates of universal health insurance have lost patience. Legislation that would provide universal health insurance continually has been stalled in Washington. Instead, proponents have expanded their lobbying efforts to the states.

Can states really extend healthcare to uninsured citizens on their own? During the 1990s, three states—Tennessee, Oregon, and Washington—made a major effort to find out. Each devised a bold plan to rationalize and revise its Medicaid program in a way intended to control costs while expanding coverage. The experiences of these states show that such efforts can indeed work—up to a point.

In 1994, Tennessee governor Ned McWherter, a Democrat, struck a deal with the federal government to completely transform Tennessee's Medicaid program. Essentially bypassing the legislature, McWherter junked Medicaid and replaced it with TennCare, a managed care plan. This plan was designed to provide access to healthcare not just to the state's eight hundred thousand former Medicaid beneficiaries but also to an additional four hundred thousand people who were either too sick or too poor to purchase private insurance.

TennCare has not run as smoothly or inexpensively as many had hoped. Most observers, however, believe the program is, in fact, doing its job. They point out that the number of uninsured has shrunk significantly. "We're making corrections," says Tony Garr, head of the Ten-nessee Health Care Campaign, a patient-advocacy group, "but the damn thing works."

Oregon, a state with a long history of bold governmental programs, took the most radical approach of all. At the behest of John Kitzhaber, then president of the state senate and himself a physician, in the early 1990s a panel of experts created a list of 709 important medical procedures. They then ranked these procedures according to the importance of the treatment. The common cold, for instance, is low in the pecking order. Each item also comes with a price tag—how much it costs the state to provide treatment to its roster of Medicaid patients.

When costs escalate and money becomes scarce, the state drops coverage for less important procedures instead of reducing the number of participants in the program—the traditional government response to tough financial times. The idea is to treat the most severe illnesses for the largest number of people possible.

Oregon's program began smoothly. In the first three years, the state added 120,000 people to its Medicaid coverage—much of it in managed care. This increased the number of people with health insurance by more than a third. But then health reformers ran into an unexpected obstacle—education reforms.

As a result of several ballot initiatives, Oregon has moved toward state funding of education. Fifty percent of the state budget now goes toward providing for pri-

enrollment increased, health costs slowed. Between 1995 and 1999, Medicaid expenditures grew at the relatively modest rate of 4.3 percent annually. This was dramatically lower than the unprecedented 27 percent growth of the early 1990s.[32] In addition, as the economic expansion that began in the early 1990s gained momentum and swelled state coffers, a growing number of state officials and healthcare advocates began to think about addressing other problems of the uninsured.

Who should do what? In 1993, Democrats and other advocates of universal health insurance had said that nothing less than universal coverage would do. After the defeat of the Health Security Act, however, many advocates set their sights on a different model. Instead of a new federal

mary and secondary schools. "The growth of the fiscal commitment to education has placed enormous pressure on other state programs, including human service programs," says Mark Gibson, point man on healthcare for Kitzhaber, who is now governor.

Washington State took a somewhat different approach. In 1993, state lawmakers passed legislation that required everyone to have health insurance. Insurers were required to accept all comers, regardless of health problems. They also had to cover treatment for pre-existing conditions after three months, foregoing the usual nine-month to twelve-month waiting period. The theory was that by creating the largest possible pool and spreading the costs around to all, insurers could afford to cover everyone. Lawmakers in Olympia also created a barebones health insurance program for workers who were not eligible for insurance through their jobs but who earned too much to qualify for the state's low-income health insurance program.

Of the three reform attempts, Washington State's was perhaps the least effective. The package was somewhat troubled from the start because federal law precluded the state from forcing employers to provide insurance for their workers—one of the plan's critical ingredients. Then in 1995, the Republican-controlled legislature stripped away some of the reforms.

What it left in place were two of the original requirements that were very popular with Washington consumers. Pre-existing health problems still are covered within three months, and people still can buy insurance whenever they want—even if it is only when they feel sick. Sue Crystal, health policy adviser for Governor Gary Locke, has likened this to buying fire insurance when your house is burning down. "The whole principle of insurance is you buy it before you need it," she said.

The result was what insurers call "a death spiral." Three of the state's top insurers said they would stop selling individual health insurance entirely unless changes were made to improve business conditions for them. The legislature ultimately okayed a compromise that lengthened the waiting period on pre-existing conditions and let insurance companies raise rates without permission from the state insurance commissioner.

The lesson for other states is that what Tennessee, Oregon, and Washington set out to do—control costs and expand coverage—is very hard. "It's not that the leading states have done things wrong," says John Holahan, director of health policy research at the Urban Institute. "They have more problems because they have tried to address more of the issues."

Source: Penelope Lemov, "Critical Condition: Several States' Widely Heralded Managed-Care Plans Are in Serious Trouble," *Governing* magazine, October 1999.

program, they sought a new state-federal partnership. The first goal—to extend health insurance to uninsured children in families that earned too much to qualify for Medicaid but too little to pay for health care on their own.

In August 1997, Congress created the State Children's Health Insurance Program at the behest of President Clinton. SCHIP (as it came to be known) was designed to provide health insurance to roughly six-and-a-half million children in low-income families without health insurance.[33] As with Medicaid, SCHIP would be designed and administered by the states and paid for primarily by the federal government. The federal government would spring for about 80 percent of total costs.

MAP 14-3 States as Innovators in Low-Income Health Coverage

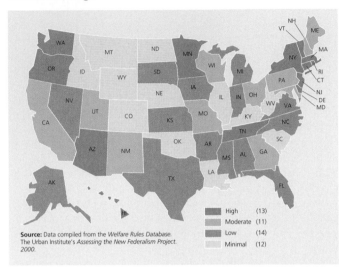

High (13)
Moderate (11)
Low (14)
Minimal (12)

Source: Data compiled from the *Welfare Rules Database*. The Urban Institute's *Assessing the New Federalism Project*. 2000.

The states were given considerable flexibility in designing their child health programs. They were free to fold SCHIP into their Medicaid programs or create stand-alone SCHIP programs. As with Medicaid, they determined eligibility levels. They also could cap SCHIP enrollments and force recipients to pay some of the costs for the health insurance they received.[34]

Not surprisingly, states have taken full advantage of this flexibility. Twenty-seven states currently allow children living in families earning up to 200 percent of the federal poverty level to qualify for health insurance. Thirteen states cover children in families with even higher incomes—sometimes significantly higher. New Jersey, Connecticut, Missouri, New Hampshire, and Vermont all set their eligibility levels from 300 percent to 350 percent of the federal level. Other states set much lower eligibility thresholds. Eleven—Colorado, Idaho, Illinois, Kentucky, Louisiana, Montana, Nebraska, North Dakota, South Carolina, West Virginia, and Wyoming—set their eligibility levels well below 200 percent of the federal poverty level or failed to amend regulations that reduced benefits for welfare recipients who worked too long.[35]

What effect do these different policies have on the residents of these states? It's hard to say. Not having health insurance does not necessarily translate into no healthcare. Government-supported community health clinics provide healthcare to more than six million Americans in thousands of communities across the country every year. These clinics treat people regardless of their ability or inability to pay. According to the National Association of Community Health Centers, these facilities are the primary source of healthcare for one-fifth of all uninsured low-income Americans.[36] In addition, hospitals are required to provide treatment to people who come into their emergency rooms, whether these people can pay or not.

Nevertheless, researchers have found a strong link between health insurance and access to and use of healthcare.[37] Giving more people access to public healthcare probably is the most direct way to increase their healthcare use. Vermont and Connecticut are two states that have made major efforts to expand eligibility for public health insurance. Subsequently, they have lower numbers of uninsured children than states like Idaho or Montana. (See Map 14-3.) However, that is not universally the case. During the

2001–2002 fiscal year, "generous" New Jersey and "stingy" Illinois both had an 11 percent uninsured rate among children.[38]

Does It Work?

By the end of 2003, SCHIP programs had enrolled more than five million children in the program. That's clearly a significant accomplishment. Unfortunately, it also has become clear that the SCHIP approach hasn't reached everyone it was supposed to reach. The Urban Institute estimates that over a quarter of all poor children—those in families with incomes below 100 percent of the federal poverty level—continue to go without insurance. Indeed, data from 1999 showed that 12 percent of children in the United States are not covered by insurance. Among poor children—who make up about one-fifth of all children—that figure is significantly higher. And this despite the fact that almost all of this population qualifies for SCHIP.[39]

Why? The problem seems to be that families in certain states simply have not signed up. Knowledge of Medicaid and SCHIP varies substantially across states. In Texas, only 41 percent of low-income families had heard of these programs. In Massachusetts, 71 percent had. As a result, in Massachusetts, the vast majority of people eligible for Medicaid and SCHIP participate. Subsequently, only 6 percent of children in Massachusetts lack health insurance. In contrast, roughly 22 percent of children in Texas lacked health insurance in 2002.

Despite these problems, by the late 1990s, many health policy experts and advocates had come to see the gradual expansion of Medicaid and SCHIP and of the state-federal partnership as the best way to address the widespread lack of health insurance in the United States. The next step was to extend Medicaid and SCHIP funds to cover the parents of SCHIP-eligible children. In January 2001, New Jersey, Rhode Island, and Wisconsin received special waivers to do just that.[40]

The Return of Rising Costs

However, these aspirations and good intentions soon got a nasty jolt. In late 1999, health inflation began to revive. In fiscal year 2000, Medicaid expenditure grew by 9 percent. By 2002, it was running at 12.8 percent.

What was behind this surge in healthcare spending? Three factors stand out: prescription drugs, the decline of managed care, and the growing numbers of people in need of "long-term care," such as nursing homes, assisted living, or at-home care.

Prescription Drugs

One of the primary forces behind rocketing drug spending is the appearance of a new generation of prescription drugs. Consumers naturally want the newest and best products, particularly when they don't directly bear the costs. Subsequently, seniors with arthritis ask for Celebrex at $2.20 a pop rather than Advil, which costs five cents a pill. Drug manufacturers have brought more and more innovative but expensive prescription drugs to market, and state Medicaid programs and private health insurance plans alike have devoted ever more of their limited resources to buying these products.

It is somewhat difficult to gauge the true costs of rising prescription drug usage. While new drugs are often very expensive, drug companies and some health economists have argued that many seemingly "expensive" drugs actually pay for themselves by mitigating the effects of a condition, preempting surgical care, and reducing hospital admissions and lengths of hospital stays.[41]

Few states have much time for this claim. Many officials, particularly in border states, are enraged by the fact that prescription drugs in the United States cost so much more here than in Canada or Mexico. "The price difference is so dramatic, it just strikes people as something that's unfair," says Chellie Pingree, a primary sponsor of Maine's prescription drug price-control legislation.[42]

State Medicaid programs are legally entitled to receive the "best available price." In practice, many don't. Drug pricing is a notoriously murky matter, but health policy experts say that some large private sector customers actually get bigger discounts than state Medicaid programs. A recent study by the Lewin Group estimated that the biggest HMOs buy drugs for 30 to 39 percent below retail. That is at least twice as much as the discounts state Medicaid programs receive.[43]

Not surprisingly, a growing number of states are attempting to do something about this. As mentioned previously, Maine has sought to pass legislation that would force drug companies to offer drugs at lower prices or provide additional rebates. Florida, Michigan, and several other states have done the same. Delaware, Missouri, New Hampshire, New Mexico, Vermont, and West Virginia have teamed up to create regional purchasing pools. These pools negotiate more favorable deals with the big drug companies. However, it's too early to tell if either of these approaches will prove effective.

The Decline of Managed Care

Proponents of managed care originally saw HMOs as a way to improve the quality of care that patients received. Most medical care patients receive in the United States is poorly coordinated. Different doctors often cannot easily share a patient's medical records. Physicians have little incentive to offer preventive services because they get paid for dealing with sickness. Paul Ellwood, the physician who coined the phrase "health maintenance organization" in the early 1970s, believed that HMOs would rationalize and coordinate the care patients received. This would improve the quality of the healthcare the members of an HMO received. Moreover, HMOs would reduce costs by emphasizing preventive health care. (See Maps 14-4 and 14-5.)

As discussed earlier, corporate America and state and federal governments alike signed on to the managed care movement during the 1990s.[44] But after an initial surge of success, many HMOs failed to meet the high hopes of their boosters. Consumers were dismayed by the ways in which HMOs limited their choices of doctors to a small group of physicians who had agreed to lower reimbursement rates. In some cases, the programs demanded that doctors receive pre-approval before performing certain procedures. By the late 1990s, many consumers turned against HMOs. In 2002, Hollywood sent actor Denzel Washington into battle against an evil HMO in the movie *John Q.* Washington played the aggrieved and angry father of a son in need of an organ transplant. HMOs had gone from healthcare salvation to healthcare savages.

Eager to separate themselves from the HMOs they had initially supported, state legislators acted on their residents' desires. More than forty states passed laws that prohibited "drive-by deliveries" in which mothers with newborns were discharged within less than twenty-four hours of admission. These laws were passed more for public relations purposes than anything else because medical evidence showed that such practices were not harmful.[45]

Many states also passed "patients' bill of rights" legislation. These laws made it easier for patients to sue HMOs and generally made it more difficult

MAP 14-4 **Medicaid Managed Care**

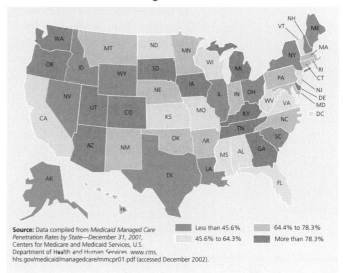

Source: Data compiled from *Medicaid Managed Care Penetration Rates by State—December 31, 2001,* Centers for Medicare and Medicaid Services, U.S. Department of Health and Human Services. www.cms.hhs.gov/medicaid/managedcare/mmcpr01.pdf (accessed December 2002).

Less than 45.6%   64.4% to 78.3%
45.6% to 64.3%   More than 78.3%

MAP 14-5 **HMO Penetration Rate**

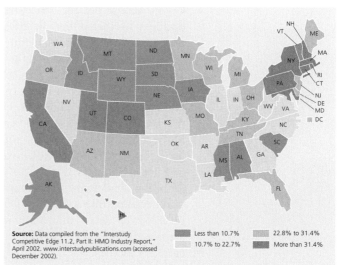

Source: Data compiled from the "Interstudy Competitive Edge 11.2, Part II: HMO Industry Report," April 2002. www.interstudypublications.com (accessed December 2002).

Less than 10.7%   22.8% to 31.4%
10.7% to 22.7%   More than 31.4%

for managed care plans to restrict healthcare. Such acts may have curbed some of the HMOs' more egregious practices, but they also came with a cost of their own. By making it harder for HMOs to limit care and access to physicians, lawmakers also deprived HMOs of negotiating leverage and reduced their ability to hold down costs. Costs were again on the rise by the late 1990s.

Long-Term Care

Unlike private sector health insurance plans, state Medicaid programs have an additional responsibility. Medicaid provides long-term care to the elderly and other services to people with disabilities. These services can range from providing nursing home care for low-income Medicaid recipients to developing rehabilitation plans for people with disabilities. All of these services are extremely expensive. Although the elderly and disabled make up only about 27 percent of the 47.2 million people enrolled in Medicaid programs, they account for more two-thirds of total Medicaid spending. In 2002, Medicaid spent $150 billion providing services to thirteen million elderly and disabled patients. The remaining thirty-four million adults and children in Medicaid cost the program $62 billion.[46]

Moreover, the cost of long-term care is growing fast. According to the Congressional Budget Office, the increased cost of the caring for elderly and disabled Medicaid beneficiaries was the single largest factor behind the $12.4 billion increase in federal Medicaid spending between 2000 and 2001.

Some states, such as Oregon, have kept costs down by shifting the elderly away from expensive care in nursing homes and toward less expensive at-home care and assisted-living centers. Seniors overwhelmingly support such alternatives to nursing homes. However, the strong nursing home lobby and the legislation creating Medicaid have hobbled the efforts. The nursing home lobby obviously does not want to lose its bread and butter, and the legislation provides explicit coverage only for nursing homes.

Even if these problems can be resolved, states will continue to face a daunting challenge—demographics. According to the Census Bureau, the number of people eighty-five years of age and older will grow by 16 percent by 2009. By 2054, that population is expected to grow by nearly 350 percent. As it does, the number of people with serious disabilities will almost certainly increase also. Many of these people will be unable—or unwilling—to pay for long-term care on their own. (See Box 14-2.)

To make matters worse, Medicaid spending was rising sharply just as the economy began to falter. State revenues soon followed. By early 2003, states were experiencing the most dramatic revenue decreases in history. Some states saw income tax revenues fall by as much as 25 percent in a matter of months. As Medicaid spending accelerated and state revenues shriveled, states retreated from plans to expand their SCHIP programs and shifted their emphasis to containing costs as best they could.

Policy in Practice: Felonious Seniors

In 2002, about seven million older Americans needed long-term care in the form of home health aides, nursing homes, or assisted-living facilities. By 2020, experts estimate that number will jump to nearly twelve million.

How much will it cost? According to a recent survey by the AARP (formerly the American Association of Retired Persons), most Americans don't have a clue. Only about twenty percent of responders came close to guessing the actual monthly cost of a nursing home (more than $4500 a month) or of an assisted living facility (about $2200). Needless to say, most Americans underestimate these costs.

Moreover, a considerable portion of Americans believe that their private health insurance covers long-term care services. It doesn't. Long-term care requires a separate policy, and according to the Health Insurance Association of America, only about 6 percent of Americans had purchased such a policy as of 1998.

The general lack of knowledge about long-term care means that families are often unprepared for when a family member requires such care. Many people are shocked to discover that Medicare provides for only very limited long-term care services. Medicaid pays for long-term care, but only for individuals who qualify.

Many senior citizens are forced to spend all of their money on medical care and then, when sufficiently impoverished—typically, seniors must have less than $2,000 in assets—receive care through Medicaid. However, a small but not insignificant group of seniors choose another course of action. They break the law by transferring their assets to their children on the sly in order to qualify for Medicaid faster.

Source: Linda L. Barrett, "The Costs of Long-Term Care: Public Perceptions Versus Reality," AARP Research Center, December 2001.

The full significance of this strategic retreat is as yet unclear. State cost-saving measures may merely represent a temporary fallback in the face of the sharpest economic contraction in recent history. However, there are reasons to believe that at least some states are rethinking the idea that they should play the leading role in expanding the health insurance safety net. In other words, the answer to the question "Who should do what?" may be about to change yet again.

Groups such as the National Governors Association have petitioned lawmakers in Congress to relieve states of the burden of providing long-term care in particular. As Kentucky governor Paul Patton told the Senate Special Committee on Aging in March 2002,

> At a time when state Medicaid budgets are rising annually at double digit inflation rates and most states face budget deficits, we must find long range solutions or we will be ill-prepared to meet the long-term care needs of seventy-seven million **baby boomers** when they retire. . . . This is not an issue that can be put on the back burner until Social Security and Medicare are reformed. It is an issue that will not wait.[47]

However, with deficits at the federal level rising too, a grand bargain of this sort seems unlikely.

BABY BOOMERS

The generation of people born following World War II, between the late 1940s and the early 1960s.

The Return of Public Health

As Medicaid costs have risen and SCHIP has emerged as the major means for expanding health insurance coverage, states have become major players in the field of healthcare. However, local governments at both the county and city levels continue to play important roles as well. In many parts of the country local governments, unlike state governments, are direct healthcare providers.

Along with community health clinics, public hospitals have long assumed a particularly important role in providing services to the uninsured. For many low-income individuals, the emergency room of a public hospital is their first and only way to access medical care. Many public hospitals border high-crime neighborhoods and provide essential advanced emergency and trauma services, as well as outpatient clinics for these same communities.

These are critically important functions. They are not, however, very profitable ones. The 1990s were a tough decade for public hospitals. HMOs squeezed hospitals' fees and private competitors scooped up desirable patients with private health insurance. Between 1979 and 1998, the number of public hospitals fell from 211 to 139. The share of total hospital beds provided by public institutions fell from 31 percent to 24 percent.[48]

Whether this is a good or a bad development is a hotly debated question. Proponents of public hospitals insist that public hospitals play a vital role in serving groups that often do not have traditional health insurance. They warn that private hospitals will close emergency rooms and find ways to make people without insurance feel unwelcome. Detractors say private hospitals are more efficient and that local governments have no real reason to be direct health care providers.

During the 1990s, Hillsborough County, Florida, and communities such as Boston and Milwaukee converted public hospitals into private facilities. (See Box 14-3.) A survey of users conducted by the Urban Institute after these conversions found that most were equally or more satisfied with the new arrangements. However, respondents also expressed fear about diminished access in the future.[49]

In the wake of September 11, 2001, many government officials have come to view public hospitals and the public health system in general in a new light. They now are seen as responders to possible biological terrorism. Some experts now believe that instead of downsizing public hospitals, governments should look for ways to keep them available in case a terrorist attack generates high numbers of casualties.[50]

Local communities also tend to be on the frontlines for sorting out many of the most controversial public health issues. One such issue is needle exchange. In recent years, the sharing of contaminated needles among intravenous drug users has become a major conduit for the spread of AIDS/HIV and Hepatitis C, which is an inflammation of the liver that is often fatal. In response, some communities have begun to support needle cleaning and needle exchange programs. Studies of needle exchange programs in San Fran-

Local Focus: Rising from a Hospital's Ruins: Milwaukee

It was the "hospital of last resort." For 135 years, County General—later Doyne Hospital—served the poor of Milwaukee. Located eight miles in the suburbs, the county hospital was as solid in its commitment to providing care as its massive brick-and-stone architecture. It mattered not if the patient was from the inner city or from across the street.

By the 1980s, however, that commitment got expensive. Hospital managers had to make regular visits to the county board of supervisors to report yet another budget shortfall. The county bailed the hospital out, but the board was growing increasingly tired of the ritual. All of this in addition to the drain on county resources and the threat to the county's bond rating.

By 1995, the supervisors had had enough. They closed Doyne down, an act that cut a psychological hole in the fabric of the community. Generations of families had been born or treated at Doyne. The fear was that the poor would have nowhere to go when they got sick or just needed to get a prescription filled.

However, five years after Doyne's closing, Milwaukee is looking pretty good. The city has been fortunate. The county was able to convince the area's private hospitals and clinics that all health providers, not just the county, were responsible for the healthcare safety net. All ten of the area's private hospitals and fifteen neighborhood clinics have signed contracts with the county to treat the medically indigent.

The county's medically indigent have, by most accounts, roughly the same access to medical care that they had before. For some residents, particularly in the inner city, access actually has improved. What's more, the nature of that care is changing for the better. Fewer people use emergency rooms and more people visit clinics for preventive care.

And all of this is being accomplished for less money and with a more stable budgeting process. "We can provide for indigent care without running a county hospital," says county executive Tom Ament. "We can provide it in a better way. And we can provide it in a more cost-effective way."

This does *not* mean that the burden comes cheap. The hospitals especially have had to suck up big financial losses to make it work. "When Doyne was there, it was easy for other hospitals to say that the uninsured and underinsured were Doyne's problem," says county health director Paula Lucey, who also worked as a nurse at Doyne for twenty years. "Now, taking care of the poor is everybody's problem."

Fears of closures similar to that of Doyne have been running through neighborhoods in Austin, Texas; Boston, Massachusetts; Detroit, Michigan; Tampa, Florida; and dozens of other places in which public hospitals have closed recently or been turned over to private management. With the dramatic upheaval and rising costs in the healthcare industry, more and more local governments are getting out of the hospital business. In 1980, 1,800 hospitals were considered "public." Today, after a wave of closures, consolidations, and privatizations, fewer than 1,200 remain.

For local officials, closing a public hospital is politically risky. The hospital—its history, its difficulties, and its successes—is often a symbol of the community itself. Just ask Anthony Williams, the mayor of Washington, D.C. Facing budget woes, Williams sought to close D.C. General, the city's lone public hospital for nearly two hundred years. Many African American residents relied on the hospital for care, and they were proud of the generations of black physicians who had been trained there. Williams eventually won the battle and the hospital closed in June 2004, but the backlash is likely to be a factor in the mayoral election.

Source: Adapted from Christopher Swope, "Rising from a Hospital's Ruins," *Governing* magazine, September 2001.

cisco, California; Portland, Oregon; Tacoma, Washington; and Baltimore, Maryland, have shown that they decreased needle sharing by anywhere from 16 percent to 72 percent and reduced the risks of contamination.[51] However, critics worry that needle exchange programs attract drug users and send a message that drug use is okay.

Often, the ideal is not the reality. It would be ideal if drugs were not part of the landscape of the United States, but the reality is that thousands of individuals abuse illegal substances every day. This makes them vulnerable to diseases and health issues, such as Hepatitis C and AIDS. Some individuals feel that public health officials must work in the reality and worry about achieving the ideal later. Which is why Ngozi Ibeh of Prevention Point, a Philadelphia-based needle exchange program, spoke at an Atlantic City, New Jersey, city council meeting in June 2004. Advocates hope that such a program in New Jersey will help lower rising AIDS numbers.

Another controversial issue in many communities involves sex education. One in nine girls between the ages of sixteen and nineteen currently becomes pregnant outside of marriage, yet a considerable number of parents remain opposed to their children learning about sexuality in the classroom. These parents have resurrected abstinence-only sex education programs. In 1998, only 2 percent of schools offered such programs. By 2002, the number of schools teaching abstinence as the only way to avoid sexually transmitted diseases and pregnancy had risen to 23 percent, despite the dearth of evidence that abstinence-only sex education works.[52]

Some advocates of abstinence say this effort is working. A report by the Centers for Disease Control and Prevention found that 54 percent of high school students graduating in 2001 claimed to be virgins. Forty-six percent did not. A decade earlier, those percentages were reversed. Of course, lower pregnancy rates could reflect the fact that sex education has taught teenagers something about contraception as well.

It also may reflect the fact that teenagers' definitions of "virgin" are quite different from those of most adults. A 1994–1995 survey of 1,101 college freshmen and sophomores in the South, the most traditionalistic part of the country, found that 61 percent of students considered mutual masturbation to the point of orgasm to be abstinent behavior. Thirty-seven percent said the same of oral sex. Twenty-four percent believed it true for anal sex. Conversely, nearly 25 percent said that kissing or showering together was not abstinent. And students aren't the only people who have difficulty defining abstinence. A 1999 e-mail survey of health educators found that nearly one-third agreed that oral sex and masturbation qualified as abstinence.[53]

What Is Good Health Anyway?

As if these issues were not enough, local health officials are increasingly wrestling with another question. What exactly constitutes a health issue anyway?

Consider obesity. Media attention has turned to this issue more and more as an ever-growing list of health studies appears proclaiming just how out

MAP 14-6 **Obesity Trends among U.S. Adults**

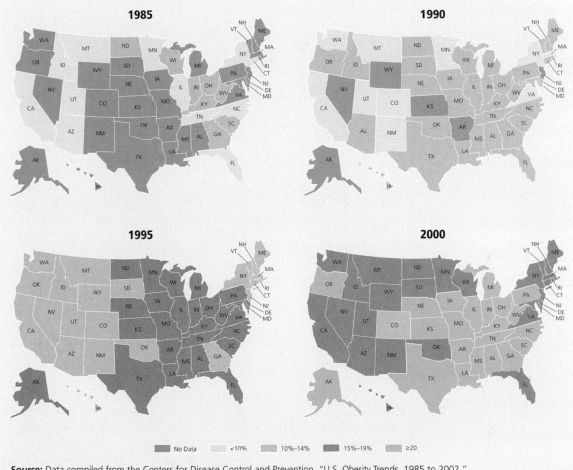

Source: Data compiled from the Centers for Disease Control and Prevention, "U.S. Obesity Trends, 1985 to 2002."

Note: BMI ≥30, or ~30 lbs. overweight for 5' 4" woman

of shape Americans are. The documentary film *Super Size Me!* addresses people's obsession with fast food. The latest figures show that two-thirds of all adults in the United States are overweight or obese. Kids are getting heavier too. In the past two decades, the number of overweight and obese children has nearly tripled. Today, roughly 13 percent of children between the ages of six years and eleven years are overweight. That number rises to 14 percent for adolescents between the ages of twelve and nineteen.

Obesity contributes to a variety of ailments, among them heart disease, certain types of cancer, diabetes, stroke, arthritis, breathing problems, and psychological disorders such as depression. Overweight individuals suffer from these and other related conditions at a much higher rate than people who are not overweight. Indeed, researchers attribute about three hundred thousand deaths to obesity each year in the United States alone. The estimated cost of obesity in the United States was about $117 billion in 2000.[54]

The Future of Devolution

Who should do what? The answer to that question is as unclear now as it has ever been. Democrats in Washington want to expand health insurance coverage by helping states do more with their Medicaid and SCHIP programs without loosening the rules. Republicans want to loosen the rules for Medicaid but move towards universal coverage via tax credits. States want more flexibility, more money, and less responsibility. And these positions will probably shift again.

However, two things seem certain. One is that healthcare costs will continue to rise at a faster rate than any other item of government spending. The other is that there will be a lot more discussion of this issue as more and more of the seventy-seven million baby boomers enter retirement.

Conclusion

State and local governments have played an important role in providing healthcare and assistance to the poorest members of society for a long time. They also have the responsibility of protecting and promoting public health. Things changed in the 1960s, however. Congress passed legislation that created the Medicare program for the elderly and the Medicaid program for low-income Americans. This set into motion a process that continues to this day. In recent decades, Medicaid has emerged as one of the most expensive and most important functions of state government.

Rising costs and the failure of the federal government to address the problem of the uninsured has put state governments in a difficult position. They have been forced to look for ways to save money on the one hand and extend health insurance coverage on the other. Despite the difficulty in reconciling these tasks, state governments have achieved some notable successes. The SCHIP program has made health insurance available to most American children—and, in some cases, to their parents as well. In addition, states have begun to make headway in reducing the costs of prescription drugs.

At the same time, state and local governments are grappling with new public health challenges. Illnesses like SARS show that local governments still have a role to play in guarding public health. The threat of biological and chemical terrorism also presents local public health officials with a grave new threat. All of this means that healthcare will almost certainly continue to be a major concern of state and local governments for the foreseeable future.

Key Concepts

abstinence (p. 459)
baby boomers (p. 489)
managed care (p. 481)
obesity (p. 467)

Suggested Readings

Starr, Paul. *The Social Transformation of American Medicine.* New York: Basic Books, 1992. Provides a wonderful account of the evolution of American healthcare.

Weil, Alan. "Ten Things Everyone Should Know about Welfare Reform," Urban Institute, May 9, 2002. Provides a concise yet thorough overview of welfare reform. Available online at www.urban.org/url.cfm?ID=31048.

Gingrich, Newt. *Saving Lives, Saving Money.* Washington, D.C.: Alexis de Tocqueville Institution, 2003. Former House Speaker Gingrich provides a spirited, conservative review of healthcare and possible future innovations.

Cutler, David. *Your Money or Your Life.* New York: Oxford University Press, 2003. For a sophisticated and sometimes eye-opening introduction to healthcare policy.

Suggested Web Sites

www.familiesusa.org. Web site of FamiliesUSA, a liberal advocacy group that promotes a more activist government policy.

www.kaiseredu.org. Developed by the Kaiser Family Foundation, the Kaiser.edu.org Web site offers instructors modules focused on specific issues of health policy.

www.kff.org. Web site of the Henry J. Kaiser Family Foundation that offers a wealth of detail on state health care initiatives in general and Medicaid in particular.

www.statehealthfacts.kff.org. This Kaiser Family Foundation site provides detailed information on state healthcare policies.

Notes

Chapter 1

1. Andrew Ritz, "More than Votes Drive Democracy," *USA Today,* March 6, 2003, 13A.

2. Statistical profile taken from National Center for Education Statistics, *Digest of Education Statistics* (Washington, D.C.: Department of Education, 2001); Institute of Politics, "Attitudes toward Politics and Public Service: A National Survey of College Undergraduates," Harvard University, 2000; Higher Education Research Institute, "CIRP Freshman Survey," 2001. www.gseis.uscla.edu/heri/01_press_release.htm (accessed March 21, 2002); and Bureau of the Census, *Statistical Abstract of the United States, 2001* (Washington, D.C.: U.S. Government Printing Office, 2001).

3. Higher Education Research Institute. "CIRP Freshman Survey." See also the Panetta Institute, "Volunteerism, Education, and the Shadow of September Eleventh: A Survey of American College Students," 2002. www.panettainstitute.org/lib/hart_05.html (accessed September 16, 2003).

4. Bureau of the Census, *Statistical Abstract of the United States, 2001.*

5. National Center for Education Statistics, "Finance FY 95," January 1998.

6. National Center for Education Statistics, "Average Amounts of Federal, Institutional, or State Aid Received by Undergraduates: 1999–2000," 2000. www.nces.ed.gov/surveys/npsas/table_library/tables/npsas.04.asp (accessed March 25, 2002).

7. National Center for Education Statistics, "Enrollment in Educational Institutions, by Level and by Control of Institution: 1869–70 to Fall 2010," 2002. http://nces.ed.gov/pubs2001/digest/dt003.html (accessed March 27, 2002).

8. Kenneth J. Meier, *Politics and the Bureaucracy* (Pacific Grove, Calif.: Brooks/Cole, 1993), 2.

9. Christopher Z. Mooney, "Why Do They Tax Dogs in West Virginia? Teaching Political Science through Comparative State Politics," *PS: Political Science & Politics* 31 (June 1998): 199–203.

10. Federation of Tax Administrators, "State Tax Guide." www.taxadmin.org/fta/rate/sl_sales.html (accessed March 13, 2002).

11. Based on a standard OLS regression analysis in which average tuition bills are the dependent variable and state appropriations as a percentage of higher education revenue are the independent variable.

12. Bureau of the Census, *Statistical Abstract of the United States, 2002.* www.census.gov/prod/2002 pubs/01statab/stat-ab01.html (accessed March 13, 2002).

13. Daniel Elazar, *American Federalism: A View from the States* (New York: Crowell, 1966).

14. Russell Hanson, "Political Culture Variations in State Economic Development Policy," *Publius* 21, no. 2 (Spring 1991): 63–81, and Kevin B. Smith, *The Ideology of Education* (Albany: SUNY Press, 2003).

15. *Governing* magazine, "State Economies," *State and Local Sourcebook,* supplement to *Governing* magazine, April 2002, 3.

16. Phillip W. Roeder, *Public Opinion and Policy Leadership in the American States* (Tuscaloosa: University of Alabama Press, 1994).

17. Bruce Wallin, "State and Local Governments Are American Too," *Political Science Teacher* 1 (1988): 1–3.

18. Bureau of Labor Statistics. www.bls.gov/oco/cg/cgs041.htm (accessed April 8, 2002).

19. *Governing* magazine, *Sourcebook.*

20. Ronald E. Weber and Paul Brace, "States and Localities Transformed," in *State and Local Politics,* ed. Ronald E. Weber and Paul Brace (New York: Chatham House, 1999).

21. Bureau of the Census, *Statistical Abstract of the United States, 2001.*

22. Evan J. Ringquist and James C. Garand, "Policy Change in the American States," in *State and Local Politics,* ed. Ronald E. Weber and Paul Brace (New York: Chatham House, 1999).

23. David Osborne and Ted Gaebler, *Reinventing Government: How the Entrepreneurial Spirit Is Transforming the Public Sector* (New York: Plume, 1993).

Chapter 2

1. Martin Merzer, *The Miami Herald Report: Democracy Held Hostage* (New York: St. Martin's Press, 2001), 32–36.

2. Ibid., 33.

3. Cass Sunstein, "The Return of States' Rights," *American Prospect.* www.prospect.org/print/V11/24/sunstein-c.html (accessed November 27, 2002).

4. The Constitution was adopted by a convention of the states in 1787 and met the requirements for ratification in 1788. The First Congress under the Constitution assembled in 1789.

5. James Collier and Christopher Collier, *Decision in Philadelphia* (New York: Random House, 1986), 3.

6. Ibid.

7. Ellen Perlman, "The Preemption Beast: The Gorilla that Swallows State Laws," *Governing* magazine, August 1994, 46–51.

8. Harry Scheiber, "The Condition of American Federalism: An Historian's View," in *American Intergovernmental Relations,* ed. Laurence J. O'Toole Jr. (Washington, D.C.: CQ Press, 2000), 71.

9. Ibid.

10. Ibid.

11. Paul L. Posner, *The Politics of Unfunded Mandates: Whither Federalism?* (Washington, D.C.: Georgetown University Press, 1998), 13.

12. David S. Broder, "President's Unfunded Mandates Criticized," *Washington Post,* March 11, 2004, A25.

13. Timony Conlon, "Federalism and Competing Values in the Reagan Administration," *Publius: The Journal of Federalism* 16, no. 4 (1986): 29–47.

14. Thomas J. Anton, "New Federalism and Intergovernmental Fiscal Relationships: The Implications for Health Policy," *Journal of Health Politics, Policy and Law* 22, no. 3 (1997).

15. Richard L. Cole and John Kincaid, "Public Opinion and American Federalism: Perspectives on Taxes, Spending and Trust," *Spectrum: The Journal of State Government* 74, no. 3 (2000): 14–18.

16. "Same-Sex Marriage: Federal and State Authority," *Congressional Digest* 75 (November 1996): 263.

17. Rueben Morales, "Federalism in the Bush Administration," *Spectrum: The Journal of State Government* 75, no. 2 (2001): 5–6.

18. Bardon Aronson, "The Rising Tide of Federalism." CNN.com. www.cnn. com/2001/LAW/02/columns/fl.aronson.federalism.02.01/ (accessed November 25, 2002).

19. Michael S. Greve, *Real Federalism: Why It Matters, How It Could Happen* (Washington, D.C.: AEI Press, 1999), 17.

20. Jeffrey G. Homrig "*Alden v. Maine:* A New Genre of Federalism Shifts the Balance of Power," *California Law Review* 89, no. 1 (2001): 183–205.

21. Brady Baybeck and William Lowry, "Federalism Outcomes and Ideological Preferences: The U.S. Supreme Court and Preemption Cases," *Publius: The Journal of Federalism* 30, no. 1 (2000): 73–96.

22. Greg Shaw and Stephanie Reinhart, "Devolution and Confidence in Government," *Public Opinion Quarterly* 65, no. 2 (2001): 369–388.

Chapter 3

1. "Old Alabama Won't Leave Politely," *Economist,* March 16, 2002.

2. Edwin I. Gardner Jr., Robert S. Montjoy, and Douglas J. Watson, "Moving into Global Competition: A Case Study of Recruitment of Daimler-Benz," *Policy Studies Review,* 18, no. 3 (September 2001).

3. Anna M. Tinsley, "State to Consider Updating Constitution: Voters Divided on Whether There Is a Need to Delete Outdated Provisions," *Corpus Christi Caller-Times,* October 11, 1999.

4. See Chapter 1 for a discussion of Elazar's typology.

5. Donald Kettl, "Governor Rehnquist," *Governing* magazine, July 1999.

6. Christopher Hammons, "Was James Madison Wrong? Rethinking the American Preference for Short, Framework-Oriented Constitutions," *American Political Science Review* 93, no. 4 (December 1999): 837.

7. Ibid., 840.

8. Ibid. See also John G. Kester, "Amendment Time," *Washingtonian,* March 1995.

9. Janice C. May, "Trends in State Constitutional Amendment and Revision," in *The Book of the States 2003* (Lexington, Ky.: Council of State Governments, 2003), 8.

10. Robert J. Taylor, ed., *Massachusetts, Colony to Commonwealth* (New York: Norton, 1961).

11. Willi Paul Adams, *The First American Constitutions: Republican Ideology and the Making of the State Constitutions in the Revolutionary Era* (Chapel Hill: University of North Carolina Press, 1980).

12. Ibid.

13. Ibid., 207

14. Alan Tarr, *Understanding State Constitutions* (Princeton, N.J.: Princeton University Press, 1998), 121.

15. W. B. Stouffer, Cynthia Opheim, and Susan Bland Day, eds., *State and Local Politics: The Individual and the Governments* (New York: Harper-Collins College Publishers, 1996).

16. Bruce Sundlun, "R.I.'s Martyr for Democracy," *Providence Journal-Bulletin,* August 11, 2002.

17. Delaware is the only state that does not refer constitutional amendments to the electorate as a whole. The legislature may enact constitutional amendments on its own if a measure receives support in two consecutive legislative sessions.

18. *The Book of the States 2001* (Lexington, Ky.: Council of State Governments, 2001), 5. In South Carolina, a majority of both houses of the legislature must vote to approve a constitutional amendment a second time, after it has passed a popular referendum, before it can go into effect.

19. *The Book of the States 2003,* (Lexington, Ky.: Council of State Governments, 2003), 7. The precise criterion is 3 percent of the number of votes cast in the last gubernatorial campaign.

20. Juan B. Elizondo Jr., "Ratliff: Time to Rewrite Constitution; Lawmaker Joined by Watchdog," *Austin American-Statesman,* October 28, 1999.

21. *The Book of the States 2003,* 3–4.

22. Warren Richey, "Unique Law Lets Florida Voters Make Changes to Constitution," *Christian Science Monitor,* May 8, 1998.

23. Alan Ehrenhalt, "Vermont's Judicial Distillery," *Governing* magazine, February 2000.

24. Hammons, "American Preference," 839.

25. Joni James, "Voters Hold Key to Big Shake-Up in State Cabinet: The Revision Would Eliminate Three Posts, Give the Governor More Power, and Shift Control of Education Policy," *Orlando Sentinel*, October 20, 1998, D1.

26. Stuart MacCorkle and Dick Smith, *Texas Government* (New York: McGraw-Hill, 1960).

27. Daniel Elazar, *American Federalism: A View from the States*, 3rd ed. (New York: Harper & Row, 1984).

28. Hammons, 846.

29. See Hammons for a more complete argument along these lines.

30. Melinda Gann Hall, "State Judicial Politics: Rules, Structures, and the Political Game," in *American State and Local Politics*, ed. Ronald Weber and Paul Brace (New York: Chatham House, 1999).

31. Ibid., 136.

32. Andrew Taylor, "Line Item Budget Barely Trims Spending at State Level," *Denver Rocky Mountain News*, January 15, 1995.

33. Scott Milfred, "Some Want to Clip Gubernatorial Wings: A Resolution in the Legislature Would Curtail Wisconsin Governor's Exceptionally Broad Veto Power," *Wisconsin State Journal*, September 23, 2001, A1.

34. Virginia Gray, Herbert Jacob, and Kenneth N. Vines, eds. *Politics in the American States: A Comparative Analysis* (Boston: Little, Brown, 1983).

35. In 2003 the U.S. Supreme Court invalidated laws prohibiting sodomy. Until that time, Alabama, Florida, Idaho, Louisiana, Massachusetts, Mississippi, North Carolina, South Carolina, Utah, and Virginia had laws that explicitly prohibited sodomy. Kansas, Oklahoma, and Texas prohibited only same-sex sodomy. Lambda Legal Defense and Education Fund Web site: www.lambda.org.

36. Alexander Hamilton, James Madison, and John Jay, *The Federalist Papers,* ed. Charles Kesler and Clinton Rossiter (New York: Penguin Putnam, 1961).

37. Hamilton, Madison, and Jay, envisioned other safeguards as well. One is the well-known principle of the separation of powers among the three branches of government. The other was the large size of the republic itself. Previous theorists of democracy had worried about republics that became too large to govern. In *The Federalist*, No. 10, Madison makes the novel claim that a more extensive republic would be less likely to succumb to factionalism than the smaller republics of old.

38. David Broder, *Democracy Derailed: Initiative Campaigns and the Power of Money* (New York: Harcourt, 2000), 27.

39. Ibid.

40. Richard Ellis, *Democratic Delusions: The Initiative Process in America* (Lawrence: University Press of Kansas, 2002).

41. Broder, *Democracy Derailed.*

42. Ibid.

43. Lawrence F. Keller, "Municipal Charters," *National Civic Review* 91, no. 1: 55–61.

Chapter 4

1. Franklin E. Zimring, *The Contradictions of American Capital Punishment* (New York: Oxford University Press, 2003).

2. Quoted in Roy Blount Jr., *Robert E. Lee* (New York: Viking, 2003), 76.

3. Quoted in Associated Press, "Judge Blocks Effort to Bar Plutonium," *New York Times*, June 19, 2002, A21.

4. "Census 2000 beyond the Numbers: Census Survey Shows Pennsylvanians Stay Put," *Pittsburgh Post-Gazette,* August 6, 2001. www.post-gazette.com/census/20010806censusnat2p2.asp (accessed May 2004).

5. Bureau of the Census, "County to County Migration Flow Files," August 11, 2003. www.census.gov/population/www/cen2000/ctytoctyflow.html.

6. Daniel J. Elazar, *American Federalism: A View from the States* (New York: Crowell, 1966). See

especially Chapter 4. This book has gone through three editions, most recently in 1984.

7. Ibid., 90.

8. Ibid., 88.

9. See William G. Jacoby and Saundra K. Schneider, "Variability in State Policy Priorities: An Empirical Analysis," *Journal of Politics* 63, no. 2 (May 2001): 544.

10. Maureen Moakley, "New Jersey," in *The Political Life of the American States,* ed. Alan Rosenthal and Maureen Moakley (New York: Praeger, 1984), 222.

11. Associated Press "Many in N.J. Don't Know Enough about Politics to Complain," *Daily Journal* (Vineland, N.J.), June 3, 2003, 4A.

12. Moakley, 221.

13. Elazar, *American Federalism,* 93.

14. Quoted in Robert D. Putnam, *Bowling Alone* (New York: Simon & Schuster, 2000), 293.

15. Personal email, September 9, 2003.

16. Phone interview, September 3, 2003.

17. See, for instance, David R. Morgan and Sheilah S. Watson, "Political Culture, Political System Characteristics, and Public Policies among the American States," *Publius: The Journal of Federalism* 21, no. 2 (Spring 1991): 31–48.

18. Steven Hill, *Fixing Elections* (New York: Routledge, 2002), 119

19. "Q&A with Bob Levey," *Washington Post,* September 16, 2003. http:// discuss.washingtonpost. com/wp-srv/zforum/03/r_metro_levey091603. htm.

20. Election Data Services, *The Election Data Book: A Statistical Portrait of Voting in America* (Lanham, Md.: Bernan Press, 1992), Appendix.

21. Kevin J. Coleman, Thomas H. Neale, and Joseph E. Cantor, "The Election Process in the United States," Congressional Research Service, Washington, D.C., July 6, 1995, 69.

22. Kay Lawson, "How State Laws Undermine Parties," in *Elections American Style,* ed. A. James Reichley (Washington, D.C.: Brookings Institution, 1987), 241.

23. Cited in William C. Binning, Larry E. Esterly, and Paul A. Sracic, *Encyclopedia of American Parties,* *Campaigns, and Elections* (Westport, Conn.: Greenwood Press, 1999), 95.

24. Phone interview, September 11, 2003.

25. "Jimmy Carter Supports Ballot Access Reform," *Ballot Access News,* August 1, 2003, 3. www. ballot-access.org/2003/0801.html.

26. Lawson, "State Laws," 246.

27. Binning, Esterly, and Sracic, *American Parties,* 95.

28. Phone interview, September 4, 2003.

29. Phone interview, September 11, 2003.

30. Barbara G. Salmore and Stephen A. Salmore, *New Jersey Politics and Government,* 2nd ed. (Lincoln: University of Nebraska Press, 1998), 128.

31. See Liberal Arts Instructional Technology Services, University of Texas at Austin, "Texas Politics." http://texaspolitics.lamc.utexas.edu/html/ exec/index.html.

32. Associated Press, "The Decatur Daily on Windom Candidacy," October 4, 2001.

33. Rob Gurwitt, "The Lone Comptroller," *Governing* magazine, October 2003, 68.

34. Quoted in Alan Greenblatt, "Where Campaign Money Flows," *Governing,* magazine, November 2002, 44.

35. Alan Greenblatt, "The Avengers General," *Governing* magazine, May 2003, 54.

36. Roy A. Schotland, "2002 Judicial Elections and State Court Reforms," in *The Book of the States, 2001.* (Lexington, Ky.: Council of State Governments, 2003), 233.

37. Initiative & Referendum Institute. www. iandrinstitute.org.

38. John F. Camobreco, "Preferences, Fiscal Policy, and the Initiative Process," *Journal of Politics* 60, no. 3: (August 1998): 822.

39. Alan Greenblatt, "Total Recall." *Governing* magazine, September 2003, 27.

40. Ibid.

41. Phone interview, August 7, 2003.

42. V. O. Key, *Public Opinion and American Democracy* (New York: Knopf, 1964), 7.

43. See especially Robert S. Erikson, Gerald C. Wright, and John D. McIver, *Statehouse Democracy: Public Opinion and Policy in the American States* (New York: Cambridge University Press, 1993).

44. Paul Brace, Kellie Sims-Butler, Kevin Arceneaux, and Martin Johnson, "Public Opinion in the American States: New Perspectives Using National Survey Data," *American Journal of Political Science* 46, no. 1 (January 2002): 173–189.

45. Susan Herbst, "How State-Level Policy Managers 'Read' Public Opinion," in *Navigating Public Opinion: Polls, Policy, and the Future of American Democracy*, ed. Jeff Manza, Fay Lomax Cook, and Benjamin I. Page (New York: Oxford University Press, 2002), 176.

46. Phone interview, September 3, 2003.

47. Phone interview, September 10, 2003.

Chapter 5

1. Gabriel Garcia Marquez, *One Hundred Years of Solitude*, trans. Gregory Rabassa (New York: Everyman's Library, 1995), 171.

2. Alan Greenblatt, "The Disengaging Voter," *CQ Weekly*, October 24, 1998, 2880.

3. Quoted in Alan Greenblatt, "Politics and Marketing Merge in Parties' Bid for Relevance," *Congressional Quarterly Weekly Report*, August 16, 1997, 1967.

4. Jeff Greenfield, "Hayes's Ride," *Washington Monthly*, March 2003.

5. Alvin Kess, *Politics in New York State* (Syracuse, N.Y.: Syracuse University Press, 1965), 29.

6. David R. Mayhew, *Placing Parties in American Politics: Organization, Electoral Settings and Government Activity in the 20th Century* (Princeton, N.J.: Princeton University Press, 1986), 24ff.

7. Quoted in Bertil L. Hanson, "County Commissioners of Oklahoma," *Midwest Journal of Political Science* 9 (1965): 396.

8. Joel H. Sibley, "The Rise and Fall of American Political Parties, 1790–1990," in *The Parties Respond: Changes in the American Party System*, ed. L. Sandy Maisel (Boulder, Colo.: Westview Press, 1990), 9.

9. Mayhew, *Placing Parties*, 105.

10. Ibid., 185.

11. John F. Bibby and Thomas M. Holbrook, "Parties and Elections," in *Politics in the American States: A Comparative Analysis*, ed. Virginia Gray, Russell L. Hanson, and Herbert Jacobs (Washington, D.C.: CQ Press, 1999), 71.

12. John F. Bibby, "State and Local Parties in a Candidate-Centered Age," in *American State and Local Politics: Directions for the 21st Century*, ed. Ronald E. Weber and Paul Brace (New York: Chatham House, 1999), 198.

13. Rhodes Cook, "Republican Brawls through the Century Helped Define Party for Years to Come," *Congresional Quarterly Weekly Report*, April 6, 1996, 942.

14. Alan Greenblatt, "History: Winds of War Blew through Chicago." *Congresional Quarterly Weekly Report*, August 17, 1996, 23.

15. Bibby "State and Local Parties," 1999, 199.

16. Peter W. Wielhower and Brad Lockerbie, "Party Contacting and Political Participation, 1952–90," *American Journal of Political Science* 38 (February 1994): 213.

17. See John H. Kessel, "Ray Bliss and the Development of the Ohio Republican Party during the 1950s," in *Politics, Professionalism and Power: Modern Party Organization and the Legacy of Ray C. Bliss*, ed. John C. Green (Lanham, Md.: University Press of America, 1994), 49–50.

18. Interview with Lee Herrington, September 2002.

19. Leon D. Epstein, *Political Parties in the American Mold* (Madison: University of Wisconsin Press, 1986), 155.

20. Malcolm E. Jewell and Sarah M. Morehouse, *Political Parties and Elections in American States*, 4th ed. (Washington, D.C.: CQ Press, 2001), 76.

21. Bibby, "State and Local Parties," 1999, 198.

22. Bibby and Holbrook, "Parties and Elections," 1999, 70.

23. Ibid., 71.

24. Quoted in Ruth Marcus, "Party Spending Unleashed; Justices Say Independence from Candidate Is Key," *Washington Post*, June 27, 1996, A1.

25. Alan Greenblatt, "Soft Money: The Root of All Evil or a Party-Building Necessity?" *Congressional Quarterly Weekly Report,* September 26, 1997, 2064.

26. Don Van Natta Jr. and Richard A. Oppel Jr., "Parties Set Up Groups to Elude Soft Money Ban," *New York Times,* November 2, 2002, A1.

27. Richard A. Oppel Jr., "Political Donations Thriving at State Level," *New York Times,* June 26, 2002, A19.

28. Interview with Larry J. Sabato, May 2002.

29. Tim Storey and Gene Rose, "GOP #1 First Time in 50 Years," *State Legislatures* 12 (December 2002).

30. Jewell and Morehouse, *Political Parties and Elections,* 22–23.

31. "Changing Hands," *Governing* magazine, January 2003, 24.

32. Daniel J. Elazar, *American Federalism: A View from the States* (New York: Crowell, 1966).

33. G. David Garson, "Researching and Teaching Political Culture through Web-Based Content Profile Analysis" (paper presented at the Annual Meeting of the American Political Science Association, Boston, 2002).

34. Alan Greenblatt, "Enemies of the State," *Governing* magazine, June 2002, 28.

35. Alan Rosenthal, *The Third House: Lobbyists and Lobbying in the States,* 2nd ed. (Washington, D.C.: CQ Press, 2001), 75.

36. "Texas," *Governing* magazine, February 2003, 88.

37. Mayhew, *Placing Parties,* 291.

38. Ibid., 292–293.

39. David S. Broder, "Edwards Criticizes Bush's Policies on Family," *Washington Post,* March 13, 2003, A8.

40. Alan Greenblatt, "California House Race Shapes Up as a Duel of Interest Groups," *Congressional Quarterly Weekly Report,* January 17, 1998, 1172.

41. Alan Ehrenhalt, "Political Pawns," *Governing* magazine, July 2000, 20.

42. Alan Greenblatt, " 'Big Tent' Advocates Look Likely to Defeat Abortion Measure," *Congressional Quarterly Weekly Report,* January 10, 1998, 89.

43. Martin P. Wattenberg, *The Decline of American Political Parties, 1952–1992* (Cambridge, Mass.: Harvard University Press, 1994), x.

44. Quoted in Joel Siegel, "Party's over for Liberals," *Daily News,* February 24, 2003, 20.

45. Greenblatt, "Politics and Marketing," 1967.

46. Larry M. Bartels, "Partisanship and Voting Behavior, 1952–1996," *American Journal of Political Science* 44 (January 2000): 35.

47. Ibid., 36–37.

48. Quoted in Greenblatt, "Politics and Marketing."

49. Frank J. Sorauf, *Political Parties in the American System* (Boston: Little, Brown, 1964), 13.

50. Rosenthal, *The Third House.*

51. Virginia Gray and David Lowery, "Interest Representation in the States," in *American State and Local Politics: Directions for the 21st Century,* ed. Ronald E. Weber and Paul Brace (New York: Chatham House, 1999), 267.

52. Quoted in Rosenthal *Third House,* 17

53. Christopher Swope, "Winning Without Steaks and Cigars," *Governing* magazine, November 2000.

54. Rosenthal *Third House,* 78.

55. Ibid., 45.

56. Quoted in Alan Greenblatt, "Secondhand Spokesmen," *Governing* magazine, April 2002.

57. Quoted in Rosenthal *Third House,* 61.

Chapter 6

1. Alan Greenblatt, "Segway Rolls," *Governing* magazine, September 2002, 18.

2. National Conference of State Legislatures, "Overview: Public Health Preparedness," July 22, 2002.

3. Rob Gurwitt, "The Riskiest Business," *Governing* magazine, March 2001, 21.

4. Interview with bill status clerk, New York legislature, October 7, 2002.

5. Interview with Montana Legislative Services Division, October 7, 2002.

6. Associated Press, "Wisconsin Governor Signs Bill to Increase Efforts to Kill Deer to Fight Fatal Disease," May 20, 2002.

7. Greenblatt, "Fit to Be Tied," *Governing* magazine, August 2001, 20.

8. Judith C. Meredith, *Lobbying on a Shoestring*, 2nd ed. (Dover, Mass.: Auburn House Publishing Company, 1989), 4.

9. Alan Greenblatt, "Health Crusader," *Governing* magazine, November 2001, 33.

10. Greenblatt, "Fit to Be Tied," 20.

11. Richard Perez-Pena, "Legislating the New York Way in a Chronic Case of Gridlock," *New York Times*, October 19, 2002, 1.

12. Virginia Gray and David Lowery, "Where Do Policy Ideas Come From? A Study of Minnesota Legislators and Staffers," *Journal of Public Administration Research and Theory* 10 (January, 2000): 573–597.

13. See Gary F. Moncrief, Joel A. Thompson, and Karl T. Kurtz, "Old Statehouse Ain't What It Used to Be," *Legislative Studies Quarterly* 21, no. 1 (February 1996): 57–72.

14. Interview with Rosalind Kurita, October 7, 2002.

15. Alan Rosenthal, *Governors and Legislatures: Contending Powers* (Washington, D.C.: CQ Press, 1990), 187.

16. Diane D. Blair, *Arkansas Politics and Government* (Lincoln: University of Nebraska Press, 1988), 182, cited in Rosenthal, *Governors and Legislatures*.

17. Alan Rosenthal, Burdett A. Loomis, John R. Hibbing, and Karl T. Kurtz, *Republic on Trial: The Case for Representative Democracy,* (Washington, D.C.: CQ Press, 2003), 26.

18. Wes Clarke, "The Divided Government and Budget Conflict in the U.S. States," *Legislative Studies Quarterly* 23, no. 1 (February 1998): 5.

19. Greenblatt, "Fit to Be Tied."

20. Meredith, *Lobbying on a Shoestring*, 34.

21. Edmund Burke, "The English Constitutional System," in *Representation*, ed. Hannah Pitkin, (New York: Atherton Press, 1969).

22. Christopher Swope, "Winning without Steak and Cigars," *Governing* magazine, November 2000, 40.

23. Quoted in Alan Ehrenhalt, "Putting Practice into Theory," *Governing* magazine, November 2000, 6.

24. Alan Ehrenhalt, *The United States of Ambition: Politicians, Power and the Pursuit of Office* (New York: Times Books/Random House, 1991), 158.

25. Foster Church, "Just Like a Woman," *Governing* magazine, September 1990, 26.

26. Richard A. Clucas, "Principal-Agent Theory and the Power of State House Speakers," *Legislative Studies Quarterly* 26, no. 2 (May 2001): 319–338.

27. Alan Greenblatt, "The Mapmaking Mess," *Governing* magazine, January 2001, 23.

28. Ibid., 22.

29. David Rosenbaum, "Campaign Season," *New York Times,* October 3, 2002, 24.

30. Rosenthal et al., *Republic on Trial*, 69.

31. Howard Troxler, "Choice for Attorney General Not So Easy," *St. Petersburg Times*, October 18, 2002.

32. Alan Greenblatt, "The Regency Shuffle," *Governing* magazine, March 2001, 31.

33. Otis White, "Making Laws Is No Job for Lawyers These Days," *Governing* magazine, June 1994, 27.

34. Kathleen Dolan and Lynne E. Ford, "Change and Continuity among Women Legislators: Evidence from Three Decades," *Political Research Quarterly* 50 (March 1997): 137–152.

35. Donald E. Whistler and Mark C. Ellickson, "The Incorporation of Women in State Legislatures: A Description," *Women and Politics* 20, no. 2 (1999): 82.

36. National Conference of State Legislatures, "Women in State Legislatures," 2001. www.ncsl. org/programs/legman/about/women.htm (accessed October 14, 2002).

37. Interview with Barbara Lee, October 8, 2002.

38. Thomas H. Little, Dana Dunn, and Rebecca E. Dean, "A View from the Top: Gender Differences in Legislative Priorities among State Legislative Leaders," *Women and Politics* 22, no. 4 (2001): 29–50.

39. Whistler and Ellickson, "Women," 84.

40. Ibid.

41. Michael B. Berkman and Robert E. O'Connor, "Do Women Legislators Matter: Female Legislators and State Abortion Policy," *American Politics Quarterly* 21, no. 1 (January 1993): 105.

42. Kerry L. Haynie, *African American Legislators in the American States* (New York: Columbia University Press, 2001), 19.

43. Ibid., 2.

44. Ibid., 25.

45. Bernard Grofman and Lisa Handley, "Impact of the Voting Rights Act on Black Representation in Southern State Legislatures," *Legislative Studies Quarterly* 16 (1991): 111–128.

46. Malcolm E. Jewell and Samuel C. Patterson, *The Legislative Process in the States* (New York: Random House, 1966), 138.

47. William Pound, "State Legislative Careers: Twenty-Five Years of Reform," in *Changing Patterns in State Legislative Careers,* ed. Gary F. Moncrief and Joel A. Thompson (Ann Arbor: University of Michigan Press, 1992).

48. James D. King, "Changes in Professionalism in U.S. State Legislatures," *Legislative Studies Quarterly* 25, no. 3 (May 2000): 327–343.

49. Wade Rawlins, "Lawmakers Adjourn," *News and Observer* (Raleigh), October 4, 2002.

50. Ellen Perlman, "The 'Gold-Plated' Legislature," *Governing* magazine, February 1998, 37.

51. Bob Mahlburg, "Special Session to Cost Taxpayers $25,000 a Day," *Orlando Sentinel,* April 30, 2002, A1.

52. Alan Ehrenhalt, "An Embattled Institution," *Governing* magazine, January 1992, 30.

53. Interview with John Hibbing, October 15, 2002.

54. William Powers, "The Saturation Fallacy," *National Journal,* September 7, 2002, 2565.

55. Jonathan Walters, "How to Tame the Press," *Governing* magazine, January 1994, 30.

56. Charles Layton and Jennifer Dorroh, "The State of the American Newspaper," *American Journalism Review,* June 2002, 18.

57. Peverill Squire, "Professionalization and Public Opinion of State Legislatures," *Journal of Politics* 55, no. 2 (1993): 479–491.

58. Interview with Gary Moncrief, October 2, 2002.

59. Anita Chadha and Robert A. Bernstein, "Why Incumbents Are Treated So Harshly: Term Limits for State Legislators," *American Politics Quarterly* 24 (1996): 363–376.

60. Interview with Stacie Rumenap, October 4, 2002.

61. Rosenthal et al., *Republic on Trial,* 52.

62. Patricia Lopez, "Coleman's Journey Crosses Typical Divide," *Minneapolis Star Tribune,* October 16, 2002. www.startribune.com/stories/462/3367928.html.

63. Rob Gurwitt, "Southern Discomfort," *Governing* magazine, October 2002, 32.

Chapter 7

1. Quoted in Alan Greenblatt, "Governing in the Fast Lane: A Frantic First Year in New Mexico," *Governing* magazine, January 2004, 28.

2. Quoted in Larry J. Sabato, *Goodbye to Good-Time Charlie,* 2nd ed. (Washington, D.C.: CQ Press, 1983), 4.

3. Lynn R. Muchmore, "The Governor as Manager," in *Being Governor: The View from the Office,* ed. Thad Beyle and Lynn R. Muchmore (Durham, N.C.: Duke University Press, 1983), 83.

4. Terry Sanford, *Storm over the States* (New York: McGraw-Hill, 1967), 185–188, as quoted in Eric B. Herzik and Brent W. Brown, "Symposium on Governors and Public Policy," *Policy Studies Journal* 17 (1989): 761.

5. David Nitkin, "Maryland's Governor Ranks Second to None in Chief Budget Power," *Baltimore Sun,* January 21, 2004, 4B.

6. E. Lee Bernick, "Gubernatorial Tools: Formal vs. Informal," *Journal of Politics* 42 (1979): 661.

7. Quoted in Alan Rosenthal, *Governors & Legislatures: Contending Powers* (Washington, D.C.: CQ Press, 1990), 14.

8. Muchmore, *Governor as Manager,* 13.

9. Quoted in H. Edward Flentje, "The Political Nature of the Governor as Manager," in *Being Governor: The View from the Office,* ed. Thad Beyle and Lynn R. Muchmore (Durham, N.C.: Duke University Press, 1983), 89.

10. Alan Ehrenhalt, "Myths and Realities of Statehouse Power," *Governing* magazine, December 2002, 6.

11. Sabato, *Goodbye,* 4.

12. See Muchmore, "Governor as Manager."

13. Rob Gurwitt, "The Governor's People," *Governing* magazine, March 1991, 28.

14. Alan Greenblatt, "Why Are We Meeting Like This?" *Governing* magazine, August 2002, 40.

15. Rosenthal, *Governors & Legislatures,* 28.

16. Garry Young and Vicky M. Wilkins, "The Influence of Governors on Veto Override Attempts: A Test of Pivotal Politics," *Legislative Studies Quarterly* 27, no. 4 (November 2002), 557.

17. Laura A. Van Assendelft, *Governors, Agenda Setting and Divided Government* (Lanham, Md.: University Press of America, 1997), 1.

18. Wes Clarke, "Divided Government and Budget Conflict in the U.S. States," *Legislative Studies Quarterly* 23, no. 1 (February 1998), 5.

19. Quoted in Van Assendelft, *Governors,* 71.

20. Raphael J. Sonenshein, "Can Black Candidates Win Statewide Elections?" *Political Science Quarterly* 105 (1990): 219.

21. We are indebted for these figures to Professor Thad Beyle of the University of North Carolina, who compiled them for a forthcoming edition of *The Book of the States.*

22. Quoted in Thomas Clouse, "Kempthorne at the Helm," *Idaho Statesman,* January 5, 1999, 1A.

23. Interview with author, January 5, 2004.

24. Quoted in Alan Greenblatt, "Where Campaign Money Flows," *Governing* magazine, November 2002, 44.

Chapter 8

1. Robert A. Carp, Ronald Stidham, and Kenneth Manning, *Judicial Process in America,* 6th ed. (Washington, D.C.: CQ Press, 2004), 53, 70.

2. Molly McDonough, "Gay Marriage Decision Harks Back 55 Years," *ABA Journal* 46, E-Report 1 (November 21, 2003).

3. National Center for State Courts Online *Examining the Work of State Courts, 2003.* www.ncsconline.org/D_Research/CSP/2003_Files/2003_Overview.pdf (accessed May 20, 2004).

4. David Rottman et al., *State Court Organization, 1998* (Washington, D.C.: Bureau of Justice Statistics, 2000), KF8736.582. www.ojp.usdoj.gov/bjs/pub/pdf/sco9801.pdf (accessed June 3, 2004).

5. Ibid., Table 2: Courts and Judges.

6. Victor Flango and Carol Flango, "A Taxonomy of Appellate Court Organization," *Caseload Highlights: Examining the Work of the State Courts,* vol. 3, no. 1 (July 1997), citing R. Leflar, *Internal Operating Procedures of Appellate Courts* (Chicago: American Bar Foundation, 1976).

7. Sari S. Escovitz, *Judicial Selection and Tenure* 4 (Chicago: American Judicature Society, 1975).

8. Caleb Nelson, "A Re-Evaluation of Scholarly Explanations for the Rise of the Elected Judiciary in Antebellum America," *American Journal of Legal History*, 37 (April 1993).

9. Larry C. Berkson, "Judicial Selection in the United States: A Special Report," *Judicature*, vol. 64, no. 4, (October 1980, updated in 1999 by Seth Andersen): 176–193. www.ajs.org/ selection/berkson.pdf (accessed June 2, 2004).

10. G. Alan Tarr, "Rethinking the Selection of State Supreme Court Justices," *Willamette Law Review*, 39, no. 4 (Fall 2003): 1445.

11. Ibid.

12. Mark S. Hurwitz and Drew Noble Lanier, "Women and Minorities on State and Federal Appellate Benches: A Cross-Time Comparison 1985 to 1999," *Judicature*, 85 (September– October 2001): 84.

13. National Center for State Courts, "African American Justices Serving the State Supreme Courts," and "Women Justices Serving on State Courts of Last Resort and Intermediate Appellate Courts," 2002 (last comprehensive revision May 2003).

14. American Judicature Society, "Judicial Selection in the States: Appellate and General Jurisdiction Courts" (1986, revised October 2002). www.ajs. org/js/judicialselectioncharts.pdf (accessed June 2, 2004)

15. Ibid.

16. David B. Rottman, Anthony Champagne, and Roy A. Schotland, *Call to Action: Statement of the National Summit on Improving Judicial Selection* (Williamsburg, Va.: National Center for State Courts, 2002).

17. Frontline, "Justice for Sale: Interview with Justices Stephen Breyer and Anthony Kennedy." www.pbs.org/wgbh/pages/frontline/shows/justice/ interviews/supremo.html (accessed, June 10, 2004).

18. Ibid.

19. Paul Brace and Melinda Gann Hall, "Studying Courts Comparatively: The View from the American States," *Political Research Quarterly* 48 (1995): 5–29.

20. Ibid.

21. Gerald F. Uelmen, "Crocodiles in the Bathtub: Maintaining the Independence of State Supreme Courts in an Era of Judicial Politicization," *Notre Dame Law Review* 72 (1997): 1133, 1135–1142.

22. Ibid., 1133, 1137.

23. Stephen J. Ware, "Money, Politics and Judicial Decisions: A Case Study of Arbitration Law in Alabama," *Journal of Law and Politics* 15 (1999): 645.

24. Rottman, Champagne, and Schotland, *Call to Action*.

25. Mark A. Behrens and Cary Silverman, "The Case for Adopting Appointive Judicial Selection Systems for State Court Judges," *Cornell Journal of Law and Public Policy* 11 (2002): 273, 275, citing William Glaberson, "States Taking Steps to Rein in Excesses of Judicial Politicking," *New York Times*, June 15, 2001, A1.

26. Rottman, Champagne, and Schotland, *Call to Action*.

27. Kaplan, "Justice for Sale," *Common Cause Magazine*, May–June 1987, 29–30.

28. Rottman, Champagne, and Schotland, *Call to Action*.

29. Uelman, "Crocodiles in the Bathtub."

30. Deborah Goldberg, Craig Holman, and Samantha Sanchez, *The New Politics of Judicial Elections* (Washington, D.C.: Justice at Stake Campaign, 2002), 17.

31. Behrens and Silverman, "Case for Adopting."

32. Charles H. Sheldon and Linda S. Maule, *Choosing Justice: The Recruitment of State and Federal Judges* (Pullman: Washington State University Press, 1997).

33. Rottman, Champagne, and Schotland, *Call to Action*.

34. Behrens and Silverman, "Case for Adopting."

35. "Judicial Selection in the States: Appellate and General Jurisdiction Courts," *American Judicature Society*, 1986 (updated January 2004). www.ajs.org/js/ judicialselectioncharts.pdf (accessed June 10, 2004).

36. Behrens and Silverman, "Case for Adopting."

37. Berkson, "Judicial Selection.

38. Ibid.

39. Behrens and Silverman, "Case for Adopting."

40. Ibid., 303.

41. Ibid.

42. Rottman, Champagne, and Schotland, *Call to Action.*

43. Behrens and Silverman, "Case for Adopting."

44. Luke Bierman, "Beyond Merit Selection," *Fordham Urban Law Journal* 29 (2002): 851, 864–865.

45. Ibid., citing, American Bar Association, "An Independent Judiciary, Report of the Commission on Separation of Powers and Judicial Independence," (1997), 48–49, and Henry J. Abraham, *The Judicial Process: An Introductory Analysis of the Courts of the United States, England, and France,* 6th ed. (New York: Oxford University Press, 1993), 42.

46. Brace and Hall, "Studying Courts Comparatively."

47. Drew Noble Lanier and Roger Handberg, "In the Eye of the Hurricane: Florida Courts, Judicial Independence, and Politics," *Fordham Urban Law Journal* 29 (2002): 1033.

48. Robert L. Misner, "Recasting Prosecutorial Discretion," *Journal of Criminal Law and Criminology* 86 (1996): 717, 741.

49. Carol J. DeFrances, "Prosecutors in State Courts 1996," *Bureau of Justice Statistics Bulletin,* NCJ-170092, July 1998.

50. Ibid.

51. Misner, "Recasting."

52. Carol J. DeFrances, "State Court Prosecutors in Large Districts 2001," *Bureau of Justice Statistics Special Report,* NCJ-191206, December 2001.

53. Ibid. "About two-thirds of Part I Uniform Crime Report (UCR) offenses reported to the police in 1998 occurred in the prosecutorial district served by these offices."

54. Misner, "Recasting."

55. Shelby A. Dickerson Moore, "Questioning the Autonomy of Prosecutorial Charging Decisions: Recognizing the Need to Exercise Discretion— Knowing There Will Be Consequences for Cross-ing the Line," *Louisiana Law Review* 60 (Winter 2000): 371, 374.

56. Wayne R. LaFave, "The Prosecutor's Discretion in the United States," *American Journal of Comparative Law* 18 (1970): 532, 533.

57. Misner, "Recasting."

58. William T. Pizzi, "Understanding Prosecutorial Discretion in the United States: The Limits of Comparative Criminal Procedure as an Instrument of Reform," *Ohio State Law Journal* 54 (1993): 1325, n.88 citing a telephone interview with Kenneth Noto, the deputy chief of the narcotics section at the U.S. Attorney's Office for the Southern District of Florida.

59. John M. Dawson, "Prosecutors in State Courts," 1990, *Bureau of Justice Statistics Bulletin,* NCJ-134500, March 1992.

60. Moore, "Questioning."

61. Floyd D. Weatherspoon, "The Devastating Impact of the Justice System on the Status of African-American Males: An Overview Perspective," *Capital University Law Review* 23 (1994): 23, 43.

62. Steven K. Smith and Carol J. DeFrances, "Indigent Defense," *Bureau of Justice Statistics Selected Findings,* NCJ-158909, February 1996.

63. Carol J. DeFrances and Marika F. X. Litras, "Indigent Defense Services in Large Counties 1999," *Bureau of Justice Statistics Bulletin,* NCJ-184932, November 2000.

64. Ibid.

65. Carol S. DeFrances, "State Funded Indigent Defense Services 1999," *Bureau of Justice Statistics Special Report,* NCJ-188464, September 2001.

66. DeFrances and Litras, "Indigent Defense Services in Large Counties."

67. Ibid. Public defenders offices in the largest 100 counties employed more than 12,700 individuals during 1999, including more than 6,300 assistant public defenders; 1,200 investigators; 300 social workers; 21,700 support staff; and nearly 400 paralegals.

68. Criminal Justice Standards Committee, *Standards for Criminal Justice: Providing Defense Services,*

3d ed. (Chicago: American Bar Association, 1992).

69. Smith and DeFrances, "Indigent Defense."

70. Ibid.

71. Adele Bernhard, "Take Courage: What the Courts Can Do to Improve the Delivery of Criminal Defense Services," *University of Pittsburgh Law Review* 63 (2002): 293, 305.

72. DeFrances and Litras, "Indigent Defense Services in Large Counties."

73. Brian Ostrom, Robert LaFountain, and Neal Kauder, "Profiling Felony Cases in the NACM Network," *Caseload Highlights: Examining the Work of State Courts,* 7, no. 1 (August 2001). In seventeen courts surveyed, nearly three-quarters of all felony cases resulted in pleas of guilty by the defendant.

74. *Improving Criminal Justice Systems through Expanded Strategies and Innovative Collaborations: Report of the National Symposium on Indigent Defense,* NCJ-181344, (Washington, D.C.: U.S. Department of Justice, Office of Justice Programs, 2000); Richard Klein and Robert Spangenberg, *The Indigent Defense Crisis* (Washington, D.C.: ABA Section of Crime Justice 1993), 25.

75. David Cole, *No Equal Justice: Race and Class in the American Justice System* (New York: New Press, 1999), 92.

76. ACLU press release, "ACLU Files Class-Action Lawsuit against Montana's Indigent Defense Program," February 14, 2002.

77. Kevin Clermont and Theodore Eisenberg, "Trial by Jury or Judge: Transcending Empiricism," *Cornell Law Review* 77 (1992): 1124.

78. See *Williams v. Florida,* 399 U.S. 78 (1970), approving six-member juries; *Apodaca v. Oregon,* 406 U.S. 404 (1972), allowing non-unanimous verdicts.

79. David Rottman et al., *State Court Organization, 1998.*

80. *New Directions from the Field: Victims' Rights and Services for the 21st Century,* Executive Summary (Washington, D.C.: U.S. Department of Justice, Office of Justice Programs, Office for Victims of Crime, 1998).

81. Wayne A. Logan, "Through the Past Darkly: A Survey of the Uses and Abuses of Victim Impact Evidence in Capital Trials," *Arizona Law Review* 41 (1999): 143, 177–178.

82. See *Payne v. Tennessee,* 501 U.S. 808 (1991), which reversed *Booth v. Maryland,* 482 U.S. 496 (1987).

83. Robert Mosteller, "New Dimensions in Sentencing Reform in the Twenty-First Century," *Oregon Law Review* 92 (2003): 1, 13.

84. Ibid., 14–15.

85. In *Ring v. Arizona,* 536 U.S. 584 (2002), the Supreme Court invalidated Arizona's capital sentencing procedures, holding that the jury, not the judge, must find the aggravating factors necessary to impose the death penalty. Similar procedures in Colorado, Idaho, Montana, and Nebraska also were ruled unconstitutional.

86. Rottman et al., *State Court Organization 1998.*

87. Michael M. O'Hear, "National Uniformity/ Local Uniformity: Reconsidering the Use of Departures to Reduce Federal-State Sentencing Disparities," *Iowa Law Review* 87 (2002): 721, 756.

88. Ibid., 749.

89. Robert Mosteller, "New Dimensions in Sentencing Reform in the Twenty-First Century," *Oregon Law Review* 92 (2003): 1, 16–17.

90. Arizona, California, Delaware, Florida, Illinois, Maine, Minnesota, Mississippi, New Mexico, North Carolina, Ohio, Virginia, and Washington have adopted determinate sentencing laws. *1996 National Survey of State Sentencing Structures* NCJ-169270 (Washington, D.C.: Bureau of Justice Assistance, 1998), 4–5.

91. Marguerite A. Driessen and W. Cole Durham, Jr., "Sentencing Dissonances in the United States: The Shrinking Distance between Punishment Proposed and Sanction Served," *American Journal of Comparative Law* 50 (2002): 623, 635.

92. Bureau of Justice Statistics, National Corrections Reporting Program 1999. www.ojp.usdoj.gov/bjs/abstract/ncrp92.htm.

93. *1996 National Survey of State Sentencing Structures,* exhibit 1-1.

94. Rottman et al., *State Court Organization, 1998.*

95. Driessen and Durham, "Sentencing Dissonances."

96. Rottman et al., *State Court Organization, 1998.*

97. *1996 National Survey of State Sentencing Structures.*

98. Rottman et al., *State Court Organization, 1998.*

99. Ibid., Table 47.

100. B. Ostrom, N. Kauder, and R. LaFountain, *Examining the Work of the State Courts, 1999–2000: A National Perspective from the Court Statistics Project* (Williamsburg, Va.: National Center for State Courts, 2000).

101. Judith S. Kaye, "The State of the Judiciary, 2003: Confronting Today's Challenge" (annual address, Albany, N.Y., January 13, 2003), 4.

102. Alan Greenblatt, "Docket Science," *Governing* magazine, June 2001, 40

103. Ibid.

104. Ibid.

105. Ibid.

106. Rottman, Champagne, and Schotland, *Call to Action.*

107. Ibid., 61.

108. Michael M. O'Hear, "National Uniformity/ Local Uniformity."

109. Ibid., n.70, citing Ralph Ranalli, "Crack Sentence Debate Reopened: Proof Whites, Blacks Treated Equally Asked," *Boston Globe,* September 26, 1999, B1.

Chapter 9

1. Larry Hannan, "Police Shut Down Girl's Lemonade Stand: City Later Offers Free Permit," *Naples Daily News.* www.bonitanews.com/03/06/naples/d945350a.htm (accessed June 20, 2003).

2. H. H. Gerth and C. Wright Mills, *Max Weber: Essays in Sociology* (New York: Oxford University Press, 1943).

3. Ronald C. Moe and Robert S. Gilmour, "Rediscovering Principles of Public Administration: The Neglected Foundation of Public Law," *Public Administration Review* 55, no. 2 (March/April 1995): 135–146.

4. John J. Gargan, "Introduction and Overview of State Government Administration," in *Handbook of State Government Administration,* ed. John J. Gargan (New York: Marcel-Dekker, 2000).

5. Jerrell D. Coggburn and Saundra K. Schneider "The Quality of Management and Government Performance: An Empirical Analysis of the American States," *Public Administration Review* 63, no. 2 (March/April 2003): 206–213.

6. National Center for Education Statistics, "Quick Tables and Figures: 2001." http://nces.ed.gov/quicktables/Detail.asp?Key=495 (accessed April 29, 2003).

7. Charles Barrilleaux, "Statehouse Bureaucracy: Institutional Consistency in a Changing Environment," in *American State and Local Politics,* ed. Ronald E. Weber and Paul Brace (New York: Chatham House, 1999).

8. Michael Lipsky, *Street-Level Bureaucracy* (New York: Russell Sage Foundation, 1980).

9. Cornelius Kerwin, *Rulemaking: How Government Agencies Write Law and Make Policy,* 3d ed. (Washington, D.C.: CQ Press, 2003).

10. Deil S. Wright, Chung-Lae Cho, and Yoo-Sun Choi, "Top-Level State Administrators: Changing Characteristics and Qualities," *The Book of the States 2002* (Lexington, Ky.: Council of State Governments, 2002).

11. Charles T. Goodsell, *The Case for Bureaucracy: A Public Administration Polemic* (Chatham, N.J.: Chatham House, 1994).

12. Ibid.

13. George W. Downs and Patrick D. Larkey, *The Search for Government Efficiency* (Philadelphia: Temple University Press, 1986).

14. Elliott Sclar, *You Don't Always Get What You Pay For* (Ithaca, N.Y.: Cornell University Press, 2000).

15. J. Norman Baldwin, "Public Versus Private Employees: Debunking Stereotypes," *Review of Public Personnel Administration* 12 (Winter 1991): 1–27.

16. Barrilleaux, "Statehouse Bureaucracy," 106–107.

17. John J. DiIulio Jr., Gerald Garvey, and Donald F. Kettl, *Improving Government: An Owner's Manual* (Washington, D.C.: Brookings Institution, 1993).

18. The Government Performance Project. www.maxwell.syr.edu/gpp/about/goals.asp (accessed May 20, 2003).

19. Coggburn and Schneider, "Quality of Management," 206–213.

20. Dennis Cauchon, "Bad Moves, Not Economy behind Busted State Budgets," *USA Today,* June 23, 2003, P1A.

21. Kenneth J. Meier, "Bureaucracy and Democracy: The Case for More Bureaucracy and Less Democracy," *Public Administration Review* 57, no. 3 (May/June 1997): 193–199.

22. Barbara Romzek and Melvin Dubnick, "Accountability in the Public Sector: Lessons from the Challenger Tragedy," *Public Administration Review* 47, no. 3 (May/June 1987): 227–238.

23. Alfred Steinberg, *The Bosses* (New York: MacMillan, 1972).

24. Dwight Waldo, *The Administrative State* (New York: Holmes & Meier, 1948).

25. "Union Membership Edges Up, but Share Continues to Fall," *Monthly Labor Review,* January 1999, 1–2.

26. Wisconsin Democracy Campaign, "2001–2002 Committee Contributions to Candidates and LCCs," 2003. www.wisdc.org/WEB_PAC_Amt 2002.html (accessed Dec. 9, 2003).

27. WEAC's legislative goals are available on its Web site: www.weac.org/capitol/ ltlo.htm.

28. Charles J. Sykes, *Profscam: Professors and the Demise of Higher Education* (New York: St. Martin's Press, 1989).

29. Bureau of the Census, *Statistical Abstract of the United States,* 2000 (Washington, D.C.: U.S. Government Printing Office, 2000), Table 527.

30. C. J. Chivers, "For Black Officers, Diversity Has Its Limits," *New York Times,* April 2, 2001.

31. Sally Selden, *The Promise of Representative Bureaucracy: Diversity and Responsiveness in a Government Agency* (Armonk, N.Y.: M. E. Sharpe, 1997).

32. Donald F. Kettl, *The Global Public Management Revolution: A Report on the Transformation of Governance* (Washington, D.C.: Brookings Institution, 2000).

33. H. George Frederickson and Kevin B. Smith, *The Public Administration Theory Primer* (Boulder, Colo.: Westview Press, 2003), 215.

34. Sclar, *You Don't Always Get,* 84–88.

35. Jonathan Walters, "The Buzz over Balance," in *Governing: Issues and Applications from the Front Lines of Government,* ed. Alan Ehrenhalt (Washington, D.C.: CQ Press, 2002).

36. D. M. West, "Assessing E-Government: The Internet, Democracy and Service Delivery by State and Federal Governments," World Bank, 2000. www1.worldbank.org/publicsector/egov/Egov ReportUs00.htm (accessed May 15, 2003).

37. Ramona McNeal, Caroline J. Tolbert, Karen Mossberger, and Lisa J. Dotterweich, "Innovating in Digital Government in the American States," *Social Science Quarterly* 84, no. 1 (March 2003): 52–70.

38. Ellen Perlman, "eGovernment Special Report," *Governing* magazine, 2002. www.governing.com/archive/2002/sep/eg2c.txt (accessed June 3, 2003).

39. McNeal et al., "Innovating."

40. Ibid.

Chapter 10

1. Alexis De Tocqueville, *Democracy in America: A New Translation* by George Lawrence, ed. by J. P. Mayer (New York: Doubleday/Anchor, 1969).

2. *Cities, Politics, and Policy: A Comparative Analysis,* ed. John D. Pelissero (Washington, D.C.: CQ Press, 2003), 222.

3. Ibid., p. 40.

4. *Handbook of Research on Urban Politics and Policy in the United States,* ed. Ronald K. Vogel (Westport, Conn.: Greenwood Press, 1997), 133.

5. *Model Government Charters: A City, County, Regional, State, and Federal Handbook,* ed. Roger L. Kemp (Jefferson, N.C.: McFarland Publishers, 2003), 59.

6. League of Women Voters of California. http://smartvoter.org (accessed January 20, 2004).

7. Jonathan Walters, "Cry, the Beleaguered County," *Governing* magazine, August 1996.

8. See the National Association of Counties Web site, www.naco.org/Template. cfm?Section= About_Counties (accessed Feb. 5, 2004). See also Kemp, *Model Government,* 55.

9. Walters, "Cry."

10. "A Brief Overview of County Government," National Association of Counties, August 2003. www.naco.org/Content/NavigationMenu/About_ Counties/ County_Government/Default271.htm (accessed August 4, 2004).

11. U.S. Conference of Mayors Web site. www. usmayors.org (accessed January 12, 2004).

12. Penelope Lemov, "Infrastructure Conference Report: Building It Smarter, Managing It Better," *Governing* magazine, October 1996.

13. Rob Gurwitt, "Are City Councils a Relic of the Past?" *Governing* magazine, April 2003.

14. National League of Cities, *Research on America's Cities,* Issue 2003–5, September 2003.

15. Kemp, *Model Government,* 10.

16. Lemov, "Infrastructure."

17. Vogel, *Handbook,* 139.

18. Rob Gurwitt, "Annexation: Not So Smart Growth," *Governing* magazine, October 2000.

19. Alan Ehrenhalt, "Maricopa County: Good Government, Bad Government," *Governing* magazine, April 1995.

20. Kemp, *Model Government,* 101.

21. Vogel, *Handbook,* 138, 141.

22. Robert E. Lang, *Edgeless Cities: Exploring the Elusive Metropolis* (Washington, D.C.: Brookings Institution, 2003).

23. Myron Orfield, *Metropolitics: A Regional Agenda for Community and Stability* (Washington, D.C.: Brookings Institution, 1997), 95.

24. Pelissero, *Cities,* 81.

25. Ibid., 162.

26. Ibid., 71.

Chapter 11

1. Tax Foundation, "Comparing the 50 States' Combined State/Local Tax Burdens in 2002." www.taxfoundation.org/statelocal02.html (accessed May 10, 2004).

2. Jason Zengerle, "Radio City Dispatch," *New Republic,* August 9, 2001.

3. Alaska, Delaware, Florida, Nevada, South Dakota, Texas, Washington, and Wyoming have no personal income taxes. New Hampshire imposes a 5 percent tax on interest and dividend income only. Tennessee also only imposes an income tax on certain types of interest, dividend, and partnership income.

   See Tracy C. Von Ins's, "Some Cities Turning to Local Income Taxes for Revenue," July 9, 2001, published by the National League of Cities, for information on local income taxes.

4. These figures and the figures that follow come from the Bureau of the Census, *Statistical Abstract of the United States, 2001* and refer to the fiscal year that concluded in 1998, one of the last years for which such data are available.

5. "Facts about Prisons and Prisoners," The Sentencing Project, briefing sheet, August 2002. www.sentencingproject.org/pubs_02.cfm (accessed July 23, 2004).

6. *Statistical Abstract, 2001,* 284.

7. Ibid., 288.

8. Katherine Barrett, Richard Greene, Michele Mariani, and Anya Sostek, "The Way We Tax: A 50-State Report," *Governing* magazine, February 2003.

9. Cited in Penelope Lemov, "The Untaxables," *Governing* magazine, July 2002.

10. Ibid.

11. *Statistical Abstract, 2001,* 284.

12. Greg F. Orlofsky, *The Funding Gap: Low-Income and Minority Students Receive Fewer Dollars* (Washington, D.C.: The Education Trust, 2002). Based on 1999–2000 U.S. Department of Education and U.S. Census Bureau data.

13. Alan Greenblatt, "The Loathsome Local Levy," *Governing* magazine, October 2001.

14. Jeff Kunerth, "Retiree Dreams Come True at the Villages: Residents Find Clean Streets, Cheerful Neighbors, and Plenty of Golf Courses and Beer," *Orlando Sentinel,* November 24, 2002, A1.

15. Corporate income taxes account for an additional 4 percent of state and local tax revenues.

16. Fifteen states allow certain localities to impose income taxes as well, but for the most part, income tax receipts are a minor source of funds for cities and counties.

17. Donald J. Boyd, "State Fiscal Issues and Risks at the Start of a New Century," Fiscal Studies Program, Nelson A. Rockefeller Institute of Government, presented June 2000.

18. Ibid.

19. Recently, however, Alaska's oil-dependent tax structure has been shaken. Alaska entered 2003 with the most serious revenue shortfall of any state.

20. *Statistical Abstract, 2001,* 262.

21. Alan Greenblatt, "Enemies of the State," *Governing* magazine, June 2002.

22. Reality Times, "Market Conditions." http://realtytimes.com/rtmcrloc/California~Beverly_Hills (accessed November 12, 2003).

23. *Governing* magazine, *State and Local Sourcebook, 2002,* supplement to *Governing* magazine, 33.

24. See the Mayflower Compact for further insights into the mindset of the founders of the Massachusetts Bay Colony.

25. *Governing Sourcebook,* 2002, 40.

26. See *Budget Processes in the States,* National Association of State Budget Officers, Washington, D.C., January 2002, for a detailed discussion of the state budget process.

27. These states are Arizona, Arkansas, Connecticut, Hawaii, Indiana, Kansas, Kentucky, Maine, Michigan, Minnesota, Montana, Nebraska, Nevada, New Hampshire, North Carolina, North Dakota, Ohio, Oregon, Texas, Virginia, Washington, Wisconsin, and Wyoming. *Budget Processes in the States,* (Washington, D.C.: National Association of State Budget Officers, January 2002).

28. See "Legislative Budget Procedures: A Guide to Appropriations and Budget Processes in the States, Commonwealths and Territories," National Conference of State Legislatures, for a detailed discussion of state balanced budget requirements. www.ncsl.org/programs/fiscal/ balbud2.htm (accessed December 15, 2003).

29. *Governing Sourcebook, 2002,* 47.

30. *Statistical Abstract, 2001.*

31. *Governing Sourcebook, 2002,* 12.

32. *2001 State Expenditure Report* (Washington, D.C.: National Association of State Budget Officers), 47.

33. "The 2003 HHS Poverty Guidelines," Office of the Assistant Secretary for Planning and Evaluation, Department of Health and Human Services. http://aspe.hhs.gov/poverty/03poverty.htm (accessed July 22, 2004).

34. John Buntin, "Medicaid: the Incredibly Expansive Medicaid Machine," *Governing* magazine, October 2001.

35. The Urban Institute's John Holahan et al., "The State Fiscal Crisis and Medicaid: Will Health Programs Be Major Budget Targets?" a report for the Kaiser Commission on Medicaid and the Uninsured, January 2003. www.kff.org/medicaid/loader.cfm?url=/commonspot/security/getfile.cfm&PageID=14313 (accessed November 15, 2003).

36. *Statistical Abstract, 2001,* Section 8.

37. Cynthia Miller, "Leavers, Stayers, and Cyclers: An Analysis of the Welfare Caseload," Manpower Demonstration Research Corporation, November 2002. Submitted to the Office of the Assistant Secretary for Planning and Evaluation, U.S. Department of Health and Human Services. See also Alan Weil's "Ten Things Everyone Should Know about Welfare Reform," Urban Institute, May 9, 2002, for a full discussion of the effects of welfare reform.

38. *2001 State Expenditure Report,* 30.

39. *2001 State Expenditure Report,* 58.

40. *2001 State Expenditure Report,* 67.

41. Alan Greenblatt, "Enemies of the State," *Governing* magazine, June 2002.

42. This section is adapted from the February 2003 *Governing* special issue on state tax systems. See Katherine Barrett et al., "The Way We Tax."

Chapter 12

1. David Tyack and Larry Cuban, *Tinkering toward Utopia: A Century of Public School Reform* (Cambridge: Harvard University Press, 1995), 2.

2. Michael A. Rebell, "Fiscal Equity Litigation and the Democratic Imperative," *Journal of Education Finance* 24, no. 1 (Summer 1998): 23–50.

3. Charles Mahtesian, "Too Much Democracy," Governing.com, January 24, 2000. www.governing.com/view/vu012400.htm (accessed November 14, 2003).

4. Rebell, "Fiscal Equity."

5. Tyack and Cuban, *Tinkering toward Utopia,* 47.

6. William Duncombe, John Ruggiero, and John Yinger, "Alternative Approaches to Measuring the Cost of Education," in *Holding Schools Accountable: Performance-Based Reform in Education,* ed. Helen F. Ladd (Washington, D.C.: Brookings Institution, 1996), 338. See also Christopher B. Swanson, "Ten Questions (and Answers) about Graduates, Dropouts, and NCLB Accountability," Urban Institute, 2003.

7. Harold Wenglinsky, "School District Expenditures, School Resources and Student Achievement: Modeling the Production Function," in *Developments in School Finance, 1997—Does Money Matter?* ed. William J. Fowler Jr. (Washington, D.C.: National Center for Education Statistics, 1998).

8. Allan Odden, "Equity and Adequacy in School Finance Today," *Phi Delta Kappan* (October 2003): 120–125.

9. "Money Matters: A Reporter's Guide to School Finance," Education Writers Association, 2003, 5.

10. "Government Performance Project," *Governing* magazine, February 2003.

11. "Quality Counts 2003," *Education Week,* 98–100.

12. "Quality Counts 2003," 22.

13. Rod Paige, "It's Not about the Money," *Wall Street Journal,* October 30, 2003.

14. Richard Rothstein, *The Way We Were: The Myths and Realities of America's Student Achievement* (New York: Century Foundation, 1998), 19.

15. Jean Johnson and Ann Duffett, "Where We Are Now: 12 Things You Need to Know about Public Opinion and Public Schools," Public Agenda, 2003, 8.

16. Anthony Carnevale and Donna M. Desrochers, "School Satisfaction: A Statistical Profile of Cities and Suburbs," Educational Testing Service, 1999. See also Keith Gayler et al., "State High School Exit Exams: Put to the Test," Center on Education Policy, 2003, 8.

17. Robert Rothman, *Measuring Up: Standards, Assessment, and School Reform* (San Francisco: Jossey-Bass, 1995), 53.

18. "National Assessment of Educational Progress," National Center for Education Statistics, November 2003. www.ed.gov/news/speeches/2001/11/011120. html (accessed July 16, 2004).

19. National Center for Education Statistics. www.NCES.ed.gov/timss (accessed November 3, 2003).

20. "The Texas Miracle," CBSNEWS.com. www.cbsnews.com/stories/2004/01/06/ 60II/main591676.shtml (accessed August 13, 2004).

21. Swanson, "Ten Questions (and Answers)."

22. "Quality Counts 2001," *Education Week.*

23. Kevin Smith, *The Ideology of Education: The Commonwealth, the Market, and America's Schools* (Albany: SUNY Press, 2003), 59.

24. Gayler et al., "State High School Exit Exams," 8.

25. Kati Haycock, "Good Teaching Matters: How Well-Qualified Teachers Can Close the Gap," *Thinking K–16,* 3, no. 2 (Summer 1998).

26. Economists Steven G. Givkin and Eric A. Hanushek cited, along with researcher William Sanders, in "Quality Counts 2003," *Education Week,* 10.

27. John Wirt et al., "The Condition of Education 2003: Out-of-field Teacher in Middle and High School Grades," U.S. Department of Education, 2003.

28. Michael Allen, "Eight Questions on Teacher Preparation: What Does the Research Say?" Education Commission of the States, July 2003.

29. Brian P. Gill et al., *Rhetoric versus Reality: What We Know and What We Need to Know about Vouchers and Charter Schools* (Santa Monica, Calif.: RAND Corporation, 2001), xviii; Charles S. Clark, "Charter Schools," *CQ Researcher,* December 20, 2002.

30. Diana Jean Schemo, "Nation's Charter Schools Lagging Behind, U.S. Test Scores Reveal," *New York Times,* August 17, 2003. www.nytimes.com/ 2004/ 08/17/education/17charter.html?hp (accessed August 17, 2004).

31. See the work of Paul Peterson at Harvard University School of Education. Paul E. Peterson and David E. Campbell, eds., *Charters, Vouchers, and Public Education* (Washington, D.C.: Brookings Institution Press, 2001).

32. "School Vouchers: Publicly Funded Programs in Cleveland and Milwaukee," GAO-01-914, Government Accountability Office, 2001, 4.

33. Matthew H. Boswell, *Courts as Catalysts: State Supreme Courts and Public School Finance Equity* (Albany: SUNY Press, 2001), 125.

34. Charles S. Clark, "School Censorship," *CQ Researcher,* February 19, 1993, 159; Gabler Web site, www.textbookreviews.org (accessed November 6, 2003).

35. "The Future of the Federal Role in Elementary and Secondary Education," Center on Education Policy, 2001, 53.

Chapter 13

1. George Kelling and Ronald Corbett, "This Works: Preventing and Reducing Crime," *Civic Bulletin* 32 (March 2003): 1.

2. Ibid., 3.

3. Jeremy Travis and Michelle Waul, "Reflections on the Crime Decline: Lessons for the Future?" *Proceedings from the Urban Institute Crime Decline Forum,* August 2002.

4. See John Donohue and Steven Levitt's National Bureau of Economic Research working paper, "The Impact of Legalized Abortion on Crime," November, 2000. www.nber.org/papers (accessed July 13, 2004).

5. Danielle S. Allen, *The World of Prometheus: The Politics of Punishing in Democratic Athens* (Princeton: Princeton University Press, 1999), 3.

6. See Sir Frederick Pollock and F. W. Maitland's *History of English Law before the Time of Edward I* (Cambridge: Cambridge University Press, 1969) for a brilliant discussion of how this transformation came to pass.

7. Marc Mauer, "The Crisis of the Young African American Male and the Criminal Justice System." Presentation to the U.S. Commission on Civil Rights in Washington, D.C., April 15–16, 1999, 6.

8. Kevin Smith, "The Politics of Punishment: Evaluating Political Explanations of Incarceration Rates," *Journal of Politics* 66, no. 3 (August 2004): 925.

9. Katherine Beckett, *Making Crime Pay: Law and Order in Contemporary Politics* (New York: Oxford University Press, 1997).

10. Smith, "Politics."

11. Daniel J. Elazar, *American Federalism: A View from the States* (New York: Crowell, 1972), 106–107.

12. See Norman Johnston's *The Crucible of Good Intentions* (Philadelphia: Philadelphia Museum of Art, 1994), for more details on nineteenth-century views of incarceration and on the Quakers' longstanding opposition to corporal punishment.

13. See David Oshinksy's *Worse than Slavery: Parchman Farm and the Ordeal of Jim Crow Justice* (New York: Free Press, 1996). As Oshinsky's title makes clear, the author is no fan of Parchman Farm. It is therefore interesting that he concludes in the book's final chapter that the modern penal institution that replaced the farm in the 1970s is in many ways worse.

14. Discrimination, however, persists. Women continue to earn only three quarters of what men with similar backgrounds and experience earn. Francine Blau and Lawrence Kah, "The Gender Pay Gap," in the *National Bureau of Economic Research Report* (Summer 2001).

15. Stephan Thernstrom, remarks, Heritage Foundation symposium on the Kerner Commission, March 13, 1998. www.heritage.org/Research/ PoliticalPhilosophy/ hl619.cfm (accessed July 13, 2004).

16. "Night of Terror," *Time Magazine,* July 25, 1977.

17. This figure—from the Office of National Drug Control Policy—does not include alcohol, which is considered the most popular drug of all.

18. See Robert MacCoun and Peter Reuter's *Drug War Heresies: Learning from Other Vices, Times, and Places* (New York: Cambridge University Press, 2001), 26, 29.

19. See the National Organization for the Reform of Marijuana Laws for state-by-state drug laws. www.norml.org (accessed July 12, 2004).

20. Eric Schlosser, *Reefer Madness: Sex, Drugs, and Cheap Labor in the American Black Market* (Boston: Houghton Mifflin, 2003), 26.

21. See David Simon and Edward Burns's *The Corner: A Year in the Life of an Inner-City Neighborhood* (New York: Broadway Books, 1998), for an exploration the drug culture in one inner city Baltimore neighborhood. Later made into an HBO mini-series.

22. Kathleen Hunger, "Money Mattering More in Judicial Elections," Stateline.org, Wednesday, May 12, 2004.

23. "Cutting Correctly: New Prison Policies for Times of Fiscal Crisis," Center on Juvenile and Criminal Justice, December 15, 2002. www.cjcj.org/pdf/cut_cor.pdf (accessed July 13, 2004).

24. Mauer, "The Crisis."

25. Information comes from "Felony Disenfrachisment Laws in the United States of America," The Sentencing Project. www.sentencingproject.org (accessed July 12, 2004). The Sentencing Project also notes that every state has some process for restoring voting rights to ex-offenders, although some of these are quite cumbersome: "In Alabama, for example, ex-offenders are required to provide a DNA sample to the Alabama Department of Forensic Sciences as part of the process of regaining the right to vote."

26. Mauer, "The Crisis."

27. Kelling and Corbett, "This Works."

28. See Fred Siegel's *The Future Once Happened Here: New York, D.C., LA, and the Future of America's Big Cities* (New York: Free Press, 1997), for an account of how well-intentioned policies went horribly wrong.

29. James Q. Wilson and George L. Kelling, "Broken Windows: The Police and Neighborhood Safety," *Atlantic Monthly*, March 1982.

30. For an account of the Rodney King beating and the LAPD, see Lou Cannon's, *Official Negligence: How Rodney King and the Riots Changed Los Angeles and the LAPD* (New York: Westview Press, 1999).

31. Ibid.

32. See George L. Kelling and Mary A. Wycoff's "Evolving Strategy of Policing: Case Studies of Strategic Change," National Criminal Justice Reference Center Document No. 198029, for a detailed account of early experiments with community policing and problem-oriented policing.

33. William Bratton, *Turnaround: How America's Top Cop Reversed the Crime Epidemic* (New York: Random House, 1998), 143, 180.

34. See John Buntin's "Assertive Policing, Plummeting Crime: The NYPD Takes on Crime in New York City," Kennedy School of Government Case Study, Harvard University, August 1999 for an account of how Compstat was created and how it is used.

35. This section draws from an August 2002 seminar at the Urban Institute. "Reflections on the Crime Decline: Lessons for the Future," 12–19.

36. Robert Weisberg and David Mills, "Violence Silence: Why No One Really Cares about Prison Rape." *Slate*, October 1, 2003. See also "No Escape: Male Rape in U.S. Prisons," Human Rights Watch, 2001. www.hrw.org/reports/2001/prison/report.html (accessed July 13, 2004).

37. "Ill-Equipped: U.S. Prisons and Offenders with Mental Illnesses," Human Rights Watch, 2003. www.hrw.org/reports/2003/usa1003 (accessed July 12, 2004).

38. "Amnesty International's Concerns Regarding post-September 11 Detentions in the U.S.," Amnesty International, March 14, 2002.

39. "Rights of Children Must be Respected," Amnesty International, April 25, 2003. Currently, eighty child offenders await execution in the United States for crimes committed when they were sixteen or seventeen years old. Nineteen children were executed in the United States between 1995 and 2003.

40. Brian A. Reaves and Matthew J. Hickman, "Police Departments in Large Cities, 1990–2000,"

Bureau of Justice Statistics Special Report, NCJ-175703, May 2002.

41. Lauren E. Glaze, "Probation and Parole in the United States, 2002," *Bureau of Justice Statistics Bulletin,* NCJ-301135, August 2003.

42. Patrick A. Langan and David J. Levin, "Recidivism of Prisoners Released in 1994," *Bureau of Justice Statistics Special Report,* NCJ-193427, June 2002.

43. John Buntin, "A Community Responds: Boston Confronts an Upsurge of Youth Violence," Kennedy School of Government Case Study, Harvard University, June 1998.

44. Benjamin Wallace-Wells, "Bush's War on Cops" *Washington Monthly,* September 1, 2003, 30.

45. Figures are current up to November 5, 2003. They are compiled from "Death Row USA," a quarterly report by the Criminal Justice Project, the NAACP Legal Defense and Educational Fund, Summer 2003, and the Death Penalty Information Project. www.deathpenaltyinfo.org (accessed May 2004).

46. Richard Willing and Gary Fields, "Geography of the Death Penalty," *USA Today,* December 20, 1999, A1.

47. Barry Scheck, co-founder, the Innocence Project, testimony before the U.S. Senate Judiciary Committee, June 18, 2002.

48. Alan Ehrenhalt, "Tragic Official of the Year," *Governing* magazine, October 2002.

49. NBC News/*Wall Street Journal* poll conducted by the polling organizations of Peter Hart (Democrat) and Robert Teeter (Republican). January 19–21, 2003. N=500 adults nationwide. www.pollingreport.com/crime#Death (accessed on July 13, 2004)

50. "Correctional Boot Camps: Lessons from a Decade of Research," National Institute of Justice, U.S. Department of Justice, June 2003.

51. "In the Spotlight: Drug Courts," National Criminal Justice Research Center. www.ncjrs.org/drug_courts/summary.html (accessed July 13, 2004).

52. "National Movement to Restore Ex-Felon Voting Rights Grows with Legislative Changes in Eight States between 1996–2003," The Sentencing Project, September 24, 2003.

53. In 2000, 44 percent of the 625,243 people arrested nationwide were age 24 or under. Jeremy Travis and Jeffrey Butts, "The Rise and Fall of Youth Violence," Urban Institute, March 2002, 9.

54. Fact sheet, National Center for Injury Prevention and Control, Center for Disease Control. www.cdc.gov/ncipc/dvp/bestpractices/FactsYV-BP.htm. (accessed July 12, 2004).

Chapter 14

1. Internal memorandum from G. Marshall Lyon, M.D., National Center for Infectious Diseases, Centers for Disease Control and Prevention, January 21, 1999. The medical evidence strongly suggests that people who have inhaled anthrax can be successfully treated with antibiotics within twenty-four hours of the incident and perhaps later.

2. John Buntin, "Anthrax Threats in Southern California," Case No. 1577, a part of the Case Program: Case Studies in Public Policy and Management, Harvard University, John F. Kennedy School of Government, May 2000.

3. John Barry, *The Great Influenza: The Epic Story of the Deadliest Plague in History* (New York: Viking Penguin, 2004).

4. "Third Annual Report to the President and Congress of the Advisory Panel to Assess Domestic Response Capabilities for Terrorism Involving Weapons of Mass Destruction," RAND Corporation, December 15, 2001, 44.

5. Gary Bryner, "Welfare Reform in Utah," Nelson A. Rockefeller Institute of Government, Report No. 14, August 2002. See also Deborah A. Orth and Malcolm L. Goggin, "How States and Counties Have Responded to the Family Policy Goals of Welfare Reform," Report to the U.S. Department of Health and Human Services, Administration for Children and Families (Grant No. 90XP0028/01), Nelson A. Rockefeller Institute of Government, State University of New York, 2003.

6. "The Role of Medicaid in State Budgets," Kaiser Family Foundation, October 2001.

7. Paul Starr, *The Social Transformation of American Medicine* (New York: Basic Books, 1992), 149.

8. Ibid., 72.

9. Ibid.

10. NYU Medical Center. www.med.nyu.edu/Bellevue (accessed July 20, 1994).

11. Starr, *Social Transformation*, 150.

12. Samuel Gompers, the head of the AF of L, viewed compulsory health insurance as "paternalistic" and worried that it might weaken the labor movement by causing workers to look to employers instead of to unions for benefits. Starr, *Social Transformation*, 254–255.

13. "Stocks Collapse in 16,410,30-Share Day, but Rally at Close Cheers Brokers," *New York Times*, October 30, 1929.

14. Scholars such as Theda Skocpol have argued that the federal government's first major foray into safety net programs actually came much earlier in the form of lavish pensions for Union veterans of the Civil War. Theda Skocpol, "America's First Social Security System: The Expansion of Benefits for Civil War Veterans," *Political Science Quarterly* 108 (Spring 1993): 85–86.

15. *Columbia Encyclopedia*, 6th ed., (New York: Columbia University Press, 2001). Entry for "social security."

16. Jay Bhattacharya and Darius Lakdawalla, "Does Medicare Benefit the Poor? New Answers to an Old Question," working paper w9280, National Bureau of Economic Research, October 2002.

17. John Klemm, "Medicaid Spending: A Brief History," *Health Care Financing Review*, 22, no. 1 (Fall 2000).

18. By 1983, the number of single mothers had fallen back to about 50 percent of AFDC recipients. By 1992, that number had crept back up to 55 percent of AFDC recipients. *Evaluating Welfare Reform in an Era of Transition*, (Washington, D.C.: National Academy of Sciences, 2001), 17.

19. Steven Roberts, "Food Stamps Program: How It Grew and How Reagan Wants to Cut It Back, *New York Times*, April 4, 1981.

20. Lou Cannon *Governor Reagan: His Rise to Power* (New York: Public Affairs, 2003), 349. Of course, FDR made this statement to argue for government-funded work programs—a measure that Reagan never supported as president.

21. General Accountability Office, "Medicaid: Improved Federal Oversight of State Financing Schemes Is Needed," GAO-04-228, February 2004.

22. Andy Schneider, *Medicaid Resource Book* (Washington, D.C.: Kaiser Commission on Medicaid and the Uninsured, July 2002), 97–98.

23. "Public Officials of the Year: Leading in Good Times and in Bad," *Governing* magazine, December 1997.

24. Charles Mahtesian, "Captains of Conservatism," *Governing* magazine, February 1995.

25. *Evaluating Welfare Reform*, 19.

26. Mickey Kaus, "Has Welfare Reform Worked? Yes, Smashingly." *Blueprint Magazine*, January/February 2002.

27. See Haynes Johnson and David Broder's *The System: The Way of American Politics at the Breaking Point* (New York: Little, Brown 1996), for a comprehensive account of the health care debate.

28. Ibid.

29. "Rising Unemployment and the Uninsured," Kaiser Family Foundation, January 2002.

30. In practice, states might not save money if HMOs managed to enroll the healthiest Medicaid recipients who would not have used many medical services anyway—a practice known as "risk selection."

31. Christopher Swope, "The Medicaid Windfall: Enjoy It While It Lasts," *Governing* magazine, September 1998.

32. Medicaid expenditures grew at an annual rate of 27.1 percent between 1990 and 1992. "Medicaid 101 Briefing Charts," Kaiser Commission on Medicaid and the Uninsured/Alliance for Health Care Reform, February 28, 2003.

33. "Enrolling Uninsured Low Income Children In Medicaid and SCHIP," Kaiser Commission on Medicaid and the Uninsured, May 2002.

34. In practice, states might not save money if HMOs managed to enroll the healthiest Medicaid recipients who would not have used many medical services anyway—practice known as "risk selection."

35. Lisa Dubay, Ian Hill and Genevieve M. Kenney, "Five Things Everyone Should Know about SCHIP," Urban Institute, October 1, 2002. No. A-55 in Series *New Federalism: Issues and Options for States.*

36. Dan Hawkins and Michelle Proser, Special Topics Issue Brief #5 "A Nation's Health at Risk: A National and State Report on America's 26 Million People without a Regular Health Provider," National Association of Community Health Centers, March 2004.

37. John Holahan and Brend Spillman, "A Strong Safety Net Is Not the Same as Insurance," Urban Institute, January 15, 2002. www.urban.org/url.cfm?ID=31041.

38. Kaiser Family Foundation. www.statehealthfacts.kff.org (accessed July 20, 2004).

39. Dubay, Hill and Kenney, "Five Things Everyone Should Know about SCHIP."

40. Statistics come from the Kaiser Family Foundation's State Health Facts On-Line. www.statehealthfacts.org. (accessed July 20, 2004). Participation figures come from Dubay, Hill, and Kenney, "Five Things Everyone Should Know about SCHIP." See also the Urban Institute "Parents' Reasons for Not Obtaining Public Health Insurance for Children More Complex Than Once Thought," July 02, 2001. www.urban.org/url.cfm? ID=900396.

41. J. R. Kleinke, "The Price Of Progress: Prescription Drugs in the Health Care Market," *Health Affairs,* September/October 2001.

42. John Buntin "Why Do Drugs Cost Less in Canada?", *Slate,* May 25, 2000, provides a partial explanation of this cost difference.

43. John Buntin, "Rx RELIEF: With Prescription Drug Costs Soaring, States Are Taking Bold Steps to Bring Them Down," *Governing* magazine, September 2000, provides more details.

44. However, they emphasized different things. Corporate America and its employees were most attracted by the low costs at which HMOs offered medical insurance. For young employees of companies offering more than one health plan, the low-cost HMO is often an attractive option. In contrast, both Medicaid and Medicare programs put a greater emphasis on using cost savings to add extra benefits (such as prescription drug coverage).

45. Jeanne M. Madden et al. "Effects of a Law against Early Postpartum Discharge on Newborn Follow-up, Adverse Events, and HMO Expenditures," *New England Journal of Medicine* 347, no. 25 (December 19, 2002): 2031–2038.

46. "Medicaid 101 Briefing Charts."

47. March 21, 2002 testimony by Kentucky governor Paul E. Patton before the Senate Special Committee on Aging. National Governors Association. www.nga.org/nga/legislativeUpdate/1,1169,C_TESTIMONY%5ED_3671,00.html (accessed on June 7, 2004).

48. Randall R. Bovbjerg, Jill A. Marsteller, and Frank C. Ullman, "Health Care for the Poor and Uninsured after a Public Hospital's Closure or Conversion," Occasional Paper 39, Urban Institute, September 2000.

49. Ibid.

50. Statement by Janet Heinrich, GAO, "Public Health and Medical Preparedness." Testimony before the Subcommittee on Public Health, Committee on Health, Education, Labor, and Pensions, U.S. Senate, Tuesday, October 9, 2001.

51. Eric Nagourney, "A Closer Look at Needle Exchanges," *New York Times,* August 7, 2001.

52. Nicholas Kristof, "Shaming Young Mothers," *New York Times,* August 23, 2002 and Jane Brody, "Abstinence-Only: Does It Work?" *New York Times,* June 1, 2004.

53. See P. F. Horan, J. Phillips, N. E. Hagan's, "The Meaning of Abstinence for College Students," *Journal of HIV/AIDS Prevention & Education for Adolescents & Children,* 2, no. 2 (1998): 51–66 and J. G. Mercer's "Defining and Teaching Abstinence: An E-mail Survey of Health Educators," unpublished thesis, North Carolina State University, Raleigh, N.C., 1999.

54. See Alan Greenblatt's "Obesity Epidemic: Can Americans Change Their Self-Destructive Habits?" *CQ Researcher*, January 31, 2003, for a comprehensive overview of the problem.

APPENDIX A

State Capitals and Date of Admission to the Union

State	Capital	Date	State	Capital	Date
Alabama	Montgomery	December 14, 1819	Montana	Helena	November 8, 1889
Alaska	Juneau	January 3, 1959	Nebraska	Lincoln	March 1, 1867
Arizona	Phoenix	February 14, 1912	Nevada	Carson City	October 31, 1864
Arkansas	Little Rock	June 15, 1836	New Hampshire	Concord	June 21, 1788
California	Sacramento	September 9, 1850	New Jersey	Trenton	December 18, 1787
Colorado	Denver	August 1, 1876	New Mexico	Santa Fe	January 6, 1912
Connecticut	Hartford	January 9, 1788	New York	Albany	July 26, 1788
Delaware	Dover	December 7, 1787	North Carolina	Raleigh	November 21, 1789
Florida	Tallahassee	March 3, 1845	North Dakota	Bismarck	November 2, 1889
Georgia	Atlanta	January 2, 1788	Ohio	Columbus	March 1, 1803
Hawaii	Honolulu	August 21, 1959	Oklahoma	Oklahoma City	November 16, 1907
Idaho	Boise	July 3, 1890	Oregon	Salem	February 14, 1859
Illinois	Springfield	December 3, 1818	Pennsylvania	Harrisburg	December 12, 1787
Indiana	Indianapolis	December 11, 1816	Rhode Island	Providence	May 29, 1790
Iowa	Des Moines	December 28, 1846	South Carolina	Columbia	May 23, 1788
Kansas	Topeka	January 29, 1861	South Dakota	Pierre	November 2, 1889
Kentucky	Frankfort	June 1, 1792	Tennessee	Nashville	June 1, 1796
Louisiana	Baton Rouge	April 30, 1812	Texas	Austin	December 29, 1845
Maine	Augusta	March 15, 1820	Utah	Salt Lake City	January 4, 1896
Maryland	Annapolis	April 28, 1788	Vermont	Montpelier	March 4, 1791
Massachusetts	Boston	February 6, 1788	Virginia	Richmond	June 25, 1788
Michigan	Lansing	January 26, 1837	Washington	Olympia	November 11, 1889
Minnesota	St. Paul	May 11, 1858	West Virginia	Charleston	June 20, 1863
Mississippi	Jackson	December 10, 1817	Wisconsin	Madison	May 29, 1848
Missouri	Jefferson City	August 10, 1821	Wyoming	Cheyenne	July 10, 1890

Glossary

abstinence. Refraining from sexual activity, usually intercourse. (Chapter 14)

accreditation. Certification process in which outside experts visit and evaluate a school or college to vouch for minimum quality standards. (Chapter 12)

activist governor. A governor who takes a leading role in setting the political agenda of the state, as opposed to a governor who views himself or herself more as a manager, or caretaker. (Chapter 7)

activist judges. Judges who act as independent policymakers by creatively interpreting constitutions and statutes. (Chapter 8)

ad hoc federalism. The process of choosing a state-centered or nation-centered view of federalism on the basis of political or partisan convenience. (Chapter 2)

affirmative action. Policies designed to help recruit and promote disadvantaged groups. (Chapter 9)

alternative dispute resolution. A way to end a disagreement by means other than litigation. It usually involves the appointment of a mediator to preside over a meeting between the parties. (Chapter 8)

annexation. The incorporation of additional land into a municipality. (Chapter 10)

appeal. A request to have a lower court's decision in a case reviewed by a higher court. (Chapter 8)

appointment powers. A governor's ability to pick individuals to run state government, such as appointing cabinet secretaries. (Chapter 7)

apportionment. The allotting of districts according to population shifts. The number of congressional districts a state has may be reapportioned every ten years. (Chapter 6)

appropriations bills. Laws passed by legislatures authorizing the transfer of money to the executive branch. (Chapter 3)

assigned counsel. Private lawyers selected by the courts to handle particular cases and paid from public funds. (Chapter 8)

at-large elections. Elections in which city or county voters vote for council or commission members. (Chapter 10)

ATM bureaucracy. The delivery of public services and programs via the Internet or other digital means. Also known as "e-government." (Chapter 9)

baby boomers. The generation of people born following World War II, between the late 1940s and the early 1960s. (Chapter 14)

back to basics. A movement against modern education "fads" and a return to an emphasis on traditional core subjects such as reading, writing, and arithmetic. (Chapter 12)

balanced budget. A budget in which current expenditures are equal to or less than income. (Chapter 11)

ballot initiatives. The process through which voters directly convey instructions to the legislature, approve a law, or amend the constitution. (Chapter 3)

bench trials. Trials in which no jury is present and a judge decides the facts. (Chapter 8)

bicameral legislatures. Legislatures that possess two chambers, typically a house of representatives, or assembly, and a senate. (Chapter 3)

Bill of Rights. The first ten amendments to the Constitution. These amendments set limits on the power of the federal government and set out the rights of individuals and, to a lesser extent, the states. (Chapter 2)

blanket primaries. Elections in which all voters may cast ballots for any candidate for any office regardless of party. (Chapter 5)

block grants. Federal grants-in-aid given for general policy areas that leave states and localities with wide discretion on how to spend the money within the designated policy area. (Chapter 2)

boards of commissioners. The legislatures of county government. (Chapter 10)

bonds. A certificate that is evidence of a debt on which the issuer promises to pay the holder a specified amount of interest for a specified length of time and to repay the loan on its maturity. (Chapter 11)

bricks-and-mortar retailers. Traditional retail stores, such as Wal-Mart, as opposed to on-line stores, such as Amazon. (Chapter 11)

broken windows policing. Policing that emphasizes maintaining public order. (Chapter 13)

budget process. The procedure by which state and local governments assess revenues and set budgets. (Chapter 11)

budget shortfall. When the money coming into the government falls below the money being spent. (Chapter 11)

bureaucracy. Public agencies and the programs and services they implement and manage. (Chapter 9)

bureaucrats. Employees of public agencies. (Chapter 9)

candidate-centered politics. Politics in which candidates promote themselves and their own campaigns rather than relying on party organizations. (Chapter 5)

capital investments. Investments in infrastructure, such as roads. (Chapter 11)

capital outlays. A category of school funding that focuses on long-term improvements to physical assets. (Chapter 12)

casework. The work undertaken by legislators and their staffs in response to requests for help from constituents. (Chapter 6)

categorical grants. Federal grants-in-aid given for specific programs that leave states and localities with little discretion on how to spend the money. (Chapter 2)

caucus. A closed meeting of members of a political party. (Chapter 6)

cause lobbyist. A person who works for an organization that tracks and promotes an issue, for example, environmental issues for the Sierra Club or gun regulation for the National Rifle Association. (Chapter 5)

charter. A document that outlines the powers, organization, and responsibilities of a local government. (Chapter 10)

charter schools. Public schools, often with unique themes, managed by teachers, principals, social workers, or nonprofit groups. The movement launched in the early 1990s. (Chapter 12)

city council. A municipality's legislature. (Chapter 10)

city-county consolidation. The merging of city and county governments. (Chapter 10)

city manager. An official appointed to be the chief administrator of a municipality. (Chapter 10)

city manager system. A form of municipal governance in which the day-to-day administration of government is carried out by a professional administrator. (Chapter 10)

civil cases. Cases that involve disputes between parties. (Chapter 8)

closed primaries. Nominating elections in which only voters belonging to that party may participate. Only Democrats can vote in a closed Democratic primary, for example. (Chapter 5)

coalition building. The assembling of an alliance of groups to pursue a common goal or interest. (Chapter 6)

collective bargaining. A process in which representatives of labor and management meet to negotiate pay and bene-fits, job responsibilities, and working conditions. (Chapter 9)

colonial charters. Legal documents drawn up by the British crown that spelled out how the colonies were to be governed. (Chapter 3)

commission system. A form of municipal governance in which executive, legislative, and administrative powers are vested in elected city commissioners. (Chapter 10)

committee. A group of legislators formally tasked with considering and writing bills in a particular issue area. (Chapter 6)

common school. In a democratic society, a school in which children of all income levels attend at taxpayer expense. (Chapter 12)

community, or restorative, justice movement. A movement that emphasizes nontraditional punishment. (Chapter 13)

compact theory. The idea that the Constitution represents an agreement among sovereign states to form a common government. (Chapter 2)

comparative method. A learning approach based on studying the differences and similarities among similar units of analysis (such as states). (Chapter 1)

compromise. The result when there is no consensus on a policy change or spending amount but legislators find a central point on which a majority can agree. (Chapter 6)

concurrent powers. Powers that both federal and state government can exercise. These include the right to tax, borrow, and spend. (Chapter 2)

confederacy. A political system in which power is concentrated in regional governments. (Chapter 2)

constituents. Residents of a district. (Chapter 6)

constituent service. The work done by legislators to help those in their voting districts. (Chapter 6)

constitutional amendments. Proposals to change the constitution, typically enacted by a super-majority of the legislature or through a statewide referendum. (Chapter 3)

constitutional convention or assembly. An assembly convened for the express purpose of amending or replacing a constitution. (Chapter 3)

constitutional revision commissions. Expert committees formed to assess a constitution and suggest changes. (Chapter 3)

contract attorneys. Private attorneys who enter into agreements with a state, a county, or a judicial district to work on a fixed-fee basis per case or for a specific length of time. (Chapter 8)

contract lobbyist. A person who works for different causes for different clients in the same way that a lawyer will represent more than one client. (Chapter 5)

cooperative federalism. The notion that it is impossible for state and national governments to have separate and distinct jurisdictions and that both levels of government must work together. (Chapter 2)

counties. A geographic subdivision of state government. (Chapter 10)

court of first instance. The court in which a case is first introduced and nothing has been determined yet. (Chapter 8)

criminal cases. Cases that involve violations of the law. (Chapter 8)

criterion referenced. Standardized tests designed to gauge a student's level of mastery of a given set of materials. (Chapter 12)

crosscutting requirements. Constraints that apply to all federal grants. (Chapter 2)

crossover sanctions. Federal requirements mandating that grant recipients pass and enforce certain laws or regulations as a condition of receiving funds. (Chapter 2)

crossover voting. When members of one party vote in another party's primary. This practice is not allowed in all states. (Chapter 5)

dealignment. When no one party can be said to dominate politics in this country. (Chapter 5)

delegates. Legislators who primarily see their role as voting according to their constituents' beliefs as they understand them. (Chapter 6)

departments of education. State-level agencies responsible for overseeing public education. (Chapter 12)

determinate sentencing. The judge sentences an offender to serve a specific amount of time in prison depending on the crime. (Chapter 8)

devolution. The process of taking power and responsibility away from the federal government and giving it to state and local governments. (Chapter 1)

Dillon's Rule. The legal principle that says local governments only can exercise the powers granted them by state government. (Chapter 10)

direct democracy. The means for citizens to make laws themselves, rather than relying on elected representatives. (Chapters 3 and 4)

discretionary jurisdiction. Occurs when a court decides whether or not to grant review of a case. (Chapter 8)

discretionary spending. Spending controlled in annual appropriations acts. (Chapter 11)

districts. Geographical areas represented by members of a legislature. (Chapter 6)

dividend. Income paid out by stocks. (Chapter 11)

drug courts. An alternative forum for sentencing drug offenders. (Chapter 13)

dual constitutionalism. A system of government in which people live under two sovereign powers. In the United States this is government of their state of residence and the federal government. (Chapter 3)

dual federalism. The idea that state and federal governments have separate and distinct jurisdictions and responsibilities. (Chapter 2)

edgeless cities. A cluster of office and retail complexes with no clear boundaries. (Chapter 10)

electorate. Individuals who can vote. (Chapter 3)

Elementary and Secondary Education Act. Federal law passed in 1965 as part of President Johnson's Great Society initiative; steered federal funds to improve local schools, particularly those attended primarily by low-income and minority students. (Chapter 12)

en banc. Refers to appeals court sessions in which all of the judges hear a case together. (Chapter 8)

entitlement. A service that government must provide, regardless of cost. (Chapter 11)

enumerated powers. Grants of authority explicitly given by the Constitution. (Chapter 2)

estate taxes. Taxes levied on a person's estate or total holdings after that person's death. (Chapter 11)

excise, or sin, taxes. Taxes on alcohol, tobacco, and other similar products that are designed to raise revenue and reduce usage. (Chapter 11)

exclusive powers. Powers given by the Constitution solely to the federal government. (Chapter 2)

executive orders. Rules or regulations with the force of law that governors can create directly under the statutory authority given them. (Chapter 7)

expenditures. Money spent by government. (Chapter 11)

factional splits, or factions. Groups that struggle to control the message within a party; for example, a party may be split into competing regional factions. (Chapter 5)

federalism. Political system in which national and regional governments share powers and are considered independent equals. (Chapter 2)

felony. A serious crime, such as murder or arson. (Chapter 8)

filibusters. Debates that under Senate rules drag on, blocking final action on the bill under consideration and preventing other bills from being debated. (Chapter 6)

fiscal federalism. The system by which federal grants are used to fund programs and services provided by state and local government. (Chapter 11)

fiscal year. The accounting period used by a government. (Chapter 11)

focused consumption taxes. Taxes that do not alter spending habits or behavior patterns and therefore do not distort the distribution of resources. (Chapter 11)

for cause challenge. Occurs when a lawyer asks the judge to excuse a potential juror because the individual appears to be biased or unable to be fair. (Chapter 8)

formal powers. The powers explicitly granted to a governor according to state law, such as vetoing legislation or appointing heads of state agencies. (Chapter 7)

Fourteenth Amendment. Prohibits any state from depriving individuals of the rights and privileges of citizenship and requires states to provide due process and equal protection guarantees to all citizens. (Chapter 2)

the franchise. The right to vote. (Chapter 3)

full faith and credit clause. The constitutional clause requiring states to recognize each other's public records and acts as valid. (Chapter 2)

general act charters. Charters that grant powers, such as home rule, to all municipal governments within a state. (Chapter 10)

general elections. The decisive elections in which all registered voters cast ballots for their preferred nominees for a political office. (Chapter 5)

General Equivalency Degree (GED) program. A series of tests that can be taken to qualify for a high school equivalency certificate or diploma. (Chapter 12)

general jurisdiction trial courts. Hears any civil or criminal cases that have not been assigned to a special court. (Chapter 8)

general revenue sharing grants. Federal grants-in-aid given with few constraints, leaving states and localities almost complete discretion over how to spend the money. (Chapter 2)

general welfare clause. An implied power giving Congress the authority to provide for the "general welfare." (Chapter 2)

gerrymanders. Districts clearly drawn with the intent of pressing partisan advantage at the expense of other considerations. (Chapter 6)

gift taxes. Taxes imposed on money transfers made during an individual's lifetime. (Chapter 11)

Goals 2000. The Educate America Act, signed into law in March 1994, that provided resources to states and communities to ensure that all students reached their full potential. (Chapter 12)

grand jury. A group of between sixteen and twenty-three citizens that decides if a case should go to trial; if yes, an indictment is issued. (Chapter 8)

grants-in-aid. Cash appropriations given by the federal government to the states. (Chapter 2)

habitual offender laws. These statutes impose harsher sentences for offenders who previously have been sentenced for crimes. (Chapter 8)

high-stakes standardized testing. Testing of elementary and secondary students in which poor results can mean either that the student fails to get promoted or that the school loses its accreditation. (Chapter 12)

home rule. A form of self-governance granted to towns and cities by the state. (Chapter 3); The right of localities to self-government, usually granted through a charter. (Chapter 10)

home schooling. The education of children in the home; a movement to grant waivers from state truancy laws to permit parents to teach their own children. (Chapter 12)

impeachment. A process by which the legislature can remove the executive branch officials, such as the governor, or judges, from offices for corruption or other reasons. (Chapter 7)

implied powers. Broad, but undefined, powers given to the federal government by the Constitution. (Chapter 2)

income tax. A tax on income. (Chapter 11)

incumbent. A person holding office. (Chapter 6)

independent expenditures. Ad campaigns or other political activities that are run by a party or an outside group without the direct knowledge or approval of a particular candidate for office. (Chapter 5)

indeterminate sentencing. The judge sentences an offender to a minimum and a maximum time in prison. A parole board decides how long the offender actually will remain in prison. (Chapter 8)

indictment. A formal criminal charge. (Chapter 8)

individualistic. A political culture where politics and government are seen as just another way to achieve individual goals. (Chapter 1)

informal powers. The things a governor is able to do, such as command media attention or persuade party members, based on position, not on formal authority. (Chapter 7)

initiative. When citizens collect signatures to place on the ballot measures that will be approved or rejected by voters, such as new laws or constitutional amendments. (Chapter 4)

insurance trust money. Money collected from contributions, assessments, insurance premiums, or payroll taxes. (Chapter 11)

interest groups. Individuals who organize to support policy issues that concern them. (Chapter 1)

intergovernmental transfers. Funds provided by the federal government to state governments and by state governments to local governments. (Chapter 11)

intermediate appellate court. A court that reviews court cases to find possible errors in their proceedings. (Chapter 8)

interstate commerce clause. The constitutional clause that gives Congress the right to regulate interstate commerce. This clause has been broadly interpreted to give Congress a number of implied powers. (Chapter 2)

Jim Crow laws. Measures passed in the last decade of the nineteenth century that sought to legally and systematically separate blacks and whites. (Chapter 3)

judicial federalism. The idea that the courts determine the boundaries of state-federal relations. (Chapter 3)

judicial review. The power of courts to assess whether a law is in compliance with the constitution. (Chapter 3)

jury nullification. Occurs when a jury returns a verdict of "Not Guilty" even though jurists believe the defendant is guilty. The jury cancels out a law that it believes is immoral or was wrongly applied to the defendant. (Chapter 8)

Kentucky Education Reform Act. 1990 law, passed in response to court findings of unacceptable disparities among schools, considered the most comprehensive state school reform act ever. (Chapter 12)

laboratories of democracy. Term for the states that emphasizes their ability to engage in different policy experiments without interference from the federal government. (Chapter 1)

the Lake Woebegon Effect. The tendency to treat all members of a group as above average, particularly with respect to such numerical values as test scores. (Chapter 12)

legislative overcriminalization. The tendency of government to make a crime out of anything the public does not like. (Chapter 8)

liability. A legal obligation or responsibility. (Chapter 8)

limited, or special jurisdiction, trial courts. Hear cases that are statutorily limited by either the degree of seriousness or the types of parties involved. (Chapter 8)

line-item veto. The power to reject a portion of a bill while the rest remains intact. (Chapter 3)

living wage laws. Laws that require businesses with government contracts to pay prevailing area wage rates rather than the national minimum wage. (Chapter 10)

lobbying. Trying to persuade legislators or other policy makers to take a position favorable to one's own. (Chapter 6)

local education agencies. School districts, some of which may be cities, or counties, or subsets thereof. (Chapter 12)

logrolling. The practice in which a legislator will give a colleague a vote on a particular bill in return for that colleague's vote on another bill to be considered later. (Chapter 6)

magistrates. Local officials or attorneys granted limited judicial powers. (Chapter 8)

majority-minority districts. Districts in which a minority group, such as African Americans or Latinos, makes up a majority of the population or electorate. (Chapter 6)

majority rule. The process in which the decision of a numerical majority is made binding on a group. (Chapter 6)

malapportionment. A situation in which the principle of equal representation is violated. (Chapter 6)

managed care. An arrangement for the provision of healthcare whereby an agency acts as an intermediary between consumers and healthcare providers. (Chapter 14)

mandatory jurisdiction. Occurs when a court is required to hear every case presented before it. (Chapter 8)

mandatory minimum sentences. The shortest sentences that offenders may receive upon conviction for certain offenses. The court has no authority to impose a shorter sentence. (Chapter 8)

mayor. The elected chief executive of a municipality. (Chapter 10)

mayor-council system. A form of municipal governance in which there is an elected executive and an elected legislature. (Chapter 10)

megalopolis. A region made up of several municipalities that form a distinct urban area. (Chapter 10)

merit systems. Systems in which employment and promotion in public agencies are based on qualifi-

cations and demonstrated ability. Blends very well with the organizational characteristics of bureaucracy. (Chapter 9)

migration patterns. The ways in which people move about the country, with different groups of settlers choosing different places to live. (Chapter 4)

misdemeanor. A less serious crime, such as shoplifting. (Chapter 8)

model constitution. An expert-approved generic or "ideal" constitution that is sometimes used by states as a yardstick against which they can measure their existing constitutions. (Chapter 3)

moralistic. A political culture where politics and government are seen as the means to achieve the collective good. (Chapter 1)

municipal bonds. Bonds issued by states, counties, cities, and towns to fund large projects as well as operating budgets. They are exempt from federal taxes and from state and local taxes for the investors who live in the state where they are issued. (Chapter 11)

municipal charter. A document that establishes operating procedures for local governments. (Chapter 3)

municipalities. Political jurisdictions, such as cities, villages, or towns, incorporated under state law to provide governance to a defined geographic area. More compact and more densely populated than counties. (Chapter 10)

National Assessment of Educational Progress. Known as the "nation's report card," this is the only regularly conducted independent survey of what a nationally representative sample students in grades 4, 8, and 12 know and can do in various subjects. (Chapter 12)

National PTA. Founded in 1897, this umbrella organization of state-based and school-based parent-teacher associations consists of volunteers who work to improve and support schools. (Chapter 12)

national supremacy clause. The constitutional clause stating that federal law takes precedence over all other laws. (Chapter 2)

nation-centered federalism. The belief that the nation is the basis of the federal system and that the federal government should take precedence over the states. (Chapter 2)

natural, or higher, law. A set of moral and political rules based on divine law and binding on all people. (Chapter 3)

necessary and proper clause. An implied power giving Congress the right to pass all laws considered "necessary and proper" to carry out the federal government's responsibilities as defined by the Constitution. (Chapter 2)

neutral competence. The idea that public agencies should be impartial implementers of democratic decisions. (Chapter 9)

New Federalism. The belief that states should receive more power and authority and less money from the federal government. (Chapter 2)

No Child Left Behind Act. Federal law enacted in January 2002 that introduced new accountability measures for elementary and secondary schools in all states that wish to receive federal aid. (Chapter 12)

nonpartisan ballots. Ballots that do not list candidates by political party; still often used in local elections. (Chapter 5)

nonpartisan elections. Elections in which candidates do not have to declare party affiliation or receive a party's nomination; local offices and elections are often nonpartisan. (Chapter 4)

norm referenced. Standardized tests designed to determine how a student's mastery of a set of materials compares with that of a specially designed sampling of students determined to be the national "norm" for their age group. (Chapter 12)

nullification. The process of a state rejecting a federal law and making it invalid within state borders. (Chapter 2)

obesity. A medical term used to describe people who are excessively overweight. (Chapter 14)

office group (Massachusetts) ballot. Ballots in which candidates are listed by name under the title of the office they are seeking. (Chapter 4)

open primaries. Election races that are open to all registered voters regardless of their party affiliation. (Chapter 5)

oversight. The role the legislature takes in making sure that the implementation of its laws by the executive branch is being done properly. (Chapter 6)

panels. U.S. courts of appeal usually sit in groups of three judges to hear a case. (Chapter 8)

parole. Supervised early release from prison. (Chapter 13)

party column (Indiana) ballot. Ballots in which the names of candidates are divided into columns arranged according to political party. (Chapter 4)

party conventions. A meeting of party delegates called to nominate candidates for office and establish party agendas. (Chapter 5)

patronage. The ability of elected officials or party leaders to hand out jobs to their friends and supporters, rather than hiring based on merit. (Chapter 5)

peremptory challenges. Used by lawyers to dismiss potential jurors for any reason except race or gender. (Chapter 8)

plea bargain. An agreement in which the accused admits guilt, usually in exchange for a promise that a particular sentence will be imposed. (Chapter 8)

plural executive system. A state government in which the governor is not the dominant figure in the executive branch, but instead is more of a first among equals, serving alongside numerous other officials who were elected to their offices rather than appointed by the governor. (Chapter 4)

plurality. The highest number of votes garnered by a candidate for a particular office but short of an outright majority. (Chapter 4)

policy implementation. The process of taking the expressed wishes of government and translating them into action. (Chapter 9)

political action committees. Groups formed for the purpose of raising money to elect or defeat political candidates. They usually represent business, union, or ideological interests. (Chapter 5)

political culture. The attitudes and beliefs broadly shared in a polity about the role and responsibility of government. (Chapter 1); A set of beliefs that prevails within a state over an extended period of time. (Chapter 4)

political machines. Political organizations controlled by a small number of people and run for selfish or partisan ends; controlled party nominations for public office and rewarded supporters with government jobs and contracts. (Chapter 5)

political parties. Organizations that choose, support, and nominate candidates for elected offices. (Chapter 5)

precedent. In law, the use of the past to determine current interpretation and decision making. (Chapter 8)

preemption. The process of the federal government overriding areas regulated by state law. (Chapter 2)

prejudicial error. An error that affects the outcome of a case. (Chapter 8)

primary elections. Elections that determine a party's nominees for offices in general elections against other parties' nominees. Participation in primary elections is sometimes limited to voters registered as members of that particular party. (Chapter 5)

privatization. Movement to contract out responsibilities traditionally done by the government to for-profit businesses in hopes of achieving greater efficiencies. (Chapter 12)

privileges and immunities clause. The constitutional clause prohibiting states from discriminating against citizens of other states. (Chapter 2)

probation. Supervised punishment in the community. (Chapter 13)

professional model. An approach to policing that emphasizes professional relations with citizens, police independence, police in cars, and rapid responses to calls for service. (Chapter 13)

professionalization. The process of making legislators' positions full-time jobs. (Chapter 6); Bureaucratic employees earn their jobs based on qualifications and merit. (Chapter 9)

progressive tax system. System in which the tax rate paid reflects the ability to pay. (Chapter 11)

prosecutor. A government official who conducts criminal cases on behalf of the people. (Chapter 8)

public defender. A government lawyer who provides free legal services to those accused of a crime who cannot afford to hire a lawyer. (Chapter 8)

pure appointive systems. Judicial selection systems in which the governor appoints judges alone without a nominating commission. (Chapter 8)

rank and file members. Legislators who do not hold leadership positions or senior committee posts. (Chapter 6)

ratification. A vote of the entire electorate to approve a constitutional change, referendum, or ballot initiative. (Chapter 3)

realignment. When popular support switches from one party to another. (Chapter 5)

recall. An occasion for citizens to collect signatures and then vote on the ouster of an incumbent politician prior to the next regularly scheduled election. (Chapter 4)

recidivism. A return to, or relapse into, criminal behavior. (Chapter 8)

Reconstruction. The period following the Civil War when the southern states were governed under the direction of the Union Army. (Chapter 3)

redistricting. The drawing of new boundaries for congressional and state legislative districts, usually following a decennial census. (Chapters 4 and 6)

referendums. A procedure that allows the electorate as a whole to either accept or reject a law passed by the legislature. (Chapter 3)

regressive taxes. Taxes that are the same rate for all taxpayers, regardless of income or ability to pay. (Chapter 11)

representation. When individual legislators act as the voices of their constituencies within the House or Senate. (Chapter 6)

representative bureaucracy. The idea that public agencies reflecting the diversity of the communities they serve will be more effective. (Chapter 9)

representative government. A form of government in which citizens exercise power indirectly by choosing representatives to legislate on their behalf. (Chapter 2)

retention elections. Judges run uncontested and voters are asked to vote "yes" if they wish to retain a judge in office for another term or "no" if they do not. (Chapter 8)

responsible party model. The theory that political parties offer clear policy choices to voters, try to deliver on those policies when they take office, and are held accountable by voters for the success or failure of those policies. (Chapter 5)

revenues. The money governments bring in, mainly from taxes. (Chapter 11)

riders. Amendments to a bill that are not central to its intent. (Chapter 6)

rocket docket. Fast-track cases that often have limited, specific deadlines for specific court procedures. (Chapter 8)

rulemaking. The process of translating laws into written instructions on what public agencies will or will not do. (Chapter 9)

runoff primary. An election held if no candidate receives a majority of the vote during the regular primary. The two top finishers face off again in a runoff to determine the nominee for the general election. Such elections are held in some states, primarily in the South. (Chapter 5)

sales tax. A tax levied by state and local governments on purchases. (Chapter 11)

school boards. Elected or appointed bodies that determine major policies and budgets for each of the nation's school districts. (Chapter 12)

school districts. Local administrative jurisdictions that hire staff and report to school boards on management of area public schools. (Chapter 12)

school vouchers. Movement dating to the 1950s to allow taxpayer dollars to be given to families to use at whatever public, private, or parochial schools they choose. (Chapter 12)

secession. The process of a government or political jurisdiction withdrawing from a political system or alliance. (Chapter 2)

secret (Australian) ballot. Ballots printed by the states that allow voters to pick and choose among different candidates and party preferences in private, replacing older systems in which voters openly picked an all-Democratic or all-Republican ballot. (Chapter 4)

sectionalism. Another word for regionalism, referring to major sections of the country, usually the North, the South and the West. (Chapter 4)

seniority. The length of time spent in a position. (Chapter 9)

separation of powers. The principle that government should be divided into separate legislative, executive, and judicial branches, each with its own powers and responsibilities. (Chapter 3)

service economy. An economy that relies primarily on services rather than manufacturing. (Chapter 11)

settlement. A mutual agreement between parties to end a case before going to trial. (Chapter 8)

severance taxes. Taxes on natural resources. (Chapter 11)

site-based management. Movement to increase freedom for building administrators such as school principals to determine how district funds are spent at a given school. (Chapter 12)

smart growth. Development practices emphasizing more efficient infrastructure and less dependence on automobiles. (Chapter 10)

sociodemographics. The characteristics of a population, including size, age, and ethnicity. (Chapter 1)

soft money. Money that is not subject to federal regulation that can be raised and spent by state parties. A 2002 law banned the use of soft money in federal elections. (Chapter 5)

sovereign immunity. The right of a government to not be sued without its consent. (Chapter 2)

special act charters. Charters that grant powers, such as home rule, to a single municipal government. (Chapter 10)

special districts. Entities created by state legislatures that enjoy some attributes of government. (Chapter 3); Local governmental units created for a single purpose, such as water distribution. (Chapter 10)

spoils system. The right of an electoral winner to decide who works for public agencies. (Chapter 9)

standards. Fixed criteria for learning that students are expected to reach in specific subjects by specific grade years. (Chapter 12)

standards movement. Effort to create benchmarks of adequate learning in each subject for each grade level so that students and teachers can be evaluated on mastery of this predetermined material. (Chapter 12)

state board of education. Top policymaking body in each of the fifty states, usually consisting of appointees selected by governors. (Chapter 12)

state-centered federalism. The belief that states are the basis of the federal system and that state governments should take precedence over the federal government. (Chapter 2)

states' rights. The belief that states should be free to make their own decisions with little interference from the federal government. (Chapter 2)

state supreme court. The highest level of appeals court in a state. (Chapter 8)

straight ticket. Originally, ballots that allowed voters to pick all of a party's candidates at once; today, straight ticket voting is the practice of voting for all of one party's candidates for various offices—for instance, voting for all Democrats or all Republicans. (Chapter 4)

street-level bureaucrats. Lower-level public agency employees who actually take the actions that represent law or policy. (Chapter 9)

strong mayor. A mayor with the power to perform the executive functions of government. (Chapter 10)

successful schools model. Education model that uses observed spending levels in the highest-performing schools as models from which to calculate necessary spending in other, lower-performing schools. (Chapter 12)

supermajority vote. A legislative vote of much more than a simple majority, for instance, two-thirds of a legislative chamber voting to override a governor's veto. (Chapter 7)

supermax security prisons. High security prisons designed for violent criminals. (Chapter 13)

superpredator. Ultra-violent youths that experts predicted would drive up the nation's crime rate. (Chapter 13)

swing voters. Individuals who are not consistently loyal to candidates of any one party. They are true independents whose allegiance is fought for with every election. (Chapter 5)

tax burden. A measurement of taxes paid. (Chapter 11)

tax capacities. Measurement of the ability to pay taxes. (Chapter 11)

tax efforts. A measure of taxes paid relative to the ability to pay taxes. (Chapter 11)

tax revolt. A reaction to high taxes that often results in ballot initiatives to cap tax growth. (Chapter 11)

teacher licensure procedures. The academic degrees, work experience, and performance on adult standardized tests a state requires before a teacher candidate can be certified to work in a school district. (Chapter 12)

teachers' unions. Primarily the National Education Association and the American Federation of Teachers, both headquartered in Washington, D.C. (Chapter 12)

Tenth Amendment. Guarantees a broad, but undefined, set of powers be reserved for the states and the people, as opposed to the federal government. (Chapter 2)

tenure. The time a governor spends in office. (Chapter 7)

ticket splitting. When voters or districts vote for different parties' nominees for different offices—for instance, supporting a Republican for president, while supporting a Democrat for Congress. (Chapter 5)

Title 1. The largest federal program in elementary and secondary education, it sends money to school districts based primarily on the number of children from low-income families that attend each. (Chapter 12)

traditionalistic. A political culture where politics and government is dominated by elites (Chapter 1)

Trends in International Mathematics and Sciences Study. Launched by the United States in 1995, it is a regularly updated study that compares performance in science and mathematics of students from thirty-two countries. (Chapter 12)

trial court. The first level of the court system. (Chapter 8)

trustees. Legislators who believe they were elected to exercise their own judgment and to approach issues accordingly. (Chapter 6)

truth-in-sentencing laws. These laws give parole boards less authority to shorten sentences for good behavior by specifying the proportion of a sentence an offender must serve before becoming eligible for parole. (Chapter 8)

unfunded mandates. Federal laws that direct state action but provide no financial support for that action. (Chapter 2)

unicameral legislatures. Legislatures that possess only one chamber. Nebraska is currently the only state with a unicameral legislature. (Chapter 3)

unincorporated territory. A community or area in which there is no municipal corporation. (Chapter 10)

unitary systems. Political systems in which power is concentrated in a central government. (Chapter 2)

user fees. Charges levied by governments in exchange for services; a type of hidden tax. (Chapter 11)

variance. The difference between units of analysis on a particular measure. (Chapter 1)

verdict. A jury's finding in a trial. (Chapter 13)

veto. The power to reject a proposed law. (Chapter 7)

voir dire. The interviewing and examination of potential jurors. (Chapter 8)

voter identification. When a voter consistently identifies strongly with one of the parties and can be considered, for example, a Democrat or Republican. (Chapter 5)

voter turnout. The percentage of eligible citizens who register to vote and do vote. (Chapter 4)

ward, or district, elections. Elections in which voters in a municipal ward vote for a candidate to represent them on a council or commission. (Chapter 10)

wards. Political and administrative subdivisions of a municipality. (Chapter 10)

weak mayor. A mayor who lacks true executive powers, such as the ability to veto council decisions or appoint department heads. (Chapter 10)

Index

NOTE: Page numbers with *f* indicate figures; with *m*, maps or cartograms; with *t*, tables.

A

AARP (formerly American Association of Retired Persons), 126, 489
Abortion(s), 270, 433, 469
Abstinence, sexual education and, 469, 492
Abu Ghraib prison, 453
Accountability, jurisdictional federalism and, 34
    judges and, 265
Accreditation, 398
Activist governors, 214
Activist judges, 256. *See also* New Judicial Federalism
Activists, political party, 153, 154–155
Adams, John, 71
Ad hoc federalism, 52, 56–57
Admission of new states, 39t
Adoption states, for textbooks and curriculum development, 415–416
Advertisements, political, 143
Advocacy groups, 425. *See also* Interest groups
Affirmative action, 88, 321–323
African Americans
    Democratic Party and, 134
    as elected city officials, 358
    franchise for, 72
    as governors, 236, 239m, 240t
    incarceration rates for, 445–446
    as legislators, 199, 200–201t, 201, 203

majority-minority districts and, 194
    state populations and incarceration rates of, 439
    as state supreme court justices, 267
    traditionalistic cultures and, 102
    voter turnout by, 111
    and voting rights for felons, 461
Age factors, voting and, 114
Agricultural Adjustment Act, 53
Agriculture secretaries, 252
AIDS, 468
Aid to Families with Dependent Children (AFDC)
    abolishment of, 50, 389, 468, 479
    growth and changes in, 475–477
    purpose, 474
Akers, Dominic, 214
Alabama
    ballot access regulations in, 109
    constitutional conventions in, 78
    constitution of, 62–64, 66
    death penalty in, 94
    early prison releases in, 460
    executive branch elections in, 118
    federal funding of Medicaid programs in, 474–475
    fiscal year of, 384
    gun control laws in, 458
    home schooling regulations in, 422

    intermediate appellate court in, 263
    judicial elections in, 120, 267
    jury qualifications in, 287
    legislative culture in, 206
    Medicaid qualifications in, 475
    political machine in, 139–140
    Reconstruction and, 81
    Supreme Court, 260, 269
    unions in, 181–182
    voter registration in, 112–113
Alabama v. Garrett (2001), 56t
Alaska
    ballot initiatives in, 87, 88, 89
    boroughs in, 341
    bureaucracy in, 309
    chief justice appointment in, 273
    constitutional conventions in, 78–79
    constitutional revision commission in, 79
    culture and history of, 12
    education achievement tests in, 416
    intermediate appellate court in, 263
    merit selection for justices in, 266
    Permanent Fund dividend in, 381
    severance taxes in, 377
    tax burden in, 366, 379
    tax system in, 374
    third-party governor in, 159

Alcohol treatment, as alternative sentencing, 292

Alden v. Maine (1999), 55, 56*t*

Alexander, Lamar, 229–230

Alexandria, Va., special districts and, 351

Allen, Cheryl, 295

Allen, Paul, 89

Almshouses, 471–472

Alternative dispute resolution, 294

Amendments, constitutional, 65, 83. *See also specific amendments*
  formal procedures for, 74–75, 76–77*t*, 78–80
  initiatives, by state, 123*t*
  initiatives and state judicial independence, 270
  number adopted per state, 72*m*
  ratification of, 79–80

Ament, Tom, 491

American Bar Association, 272, 284, 285, 286

American Federalism (Elazar), 98

American Federation of Labor, 473

American Federation of Teachers, 421, 423

American Journalism Review, 208

American Medical Association (AMA), 161, 469, 474

American Medical Student Association, 411

American Planning Association, 356

Amnesty International, 454

Anaconda Copper Company, Mont., 141

Angola Prison, La., 440

Anheuser-Busch, 164

Annapolis Convention (1786), 31

Annexation, 351–352

Anthrax exposure, 466–467

Anti-Federalists, 36–37, 38

Appeals, legal, 260

Appeals (appellate) courts, 261, 263–264, 274–275*t*

Appointments
  governors powers' of, 216, 217, 219–220, 224, 227–228
  judicial, 265, 271–273

Apportionment, 193–195

Appropriations bills, 68

Approval ratings, legislative, 206

Arizona
  ballot initiatives in, 88, 89
  boot camps for offenders in, 461
  charter schools in, 418
  chief justice appointment in, 273
  college tuition-setting in, 410, 411
  constitution of, 68
  education achievement tests in, 416
  judicial selection in, 265
  legislative leadership change in, 182
  lieutenant governor in, 249
  nonpartisan judicial elections in, 267
  political party competition in, 150
  TANF-funded programs in, 468

Arkansas
  ballot access regulations in, 109
  budget formulation in, 385
  constitutional revision commission in, 79
  county administrators in, 344
  drug possession penalties in, 443
  federal funding of Medicaid programs in, 474–475
  legislative sessions in, 204
  legislators in, 195–196
  nonpartisan judicial elections in, 267
  parole board discretion in, 292
  Reconstruction and, 81
  sentencing in, 289
  on state constitutional conventions, 78
  term limits in, 209

Arkansas Livestock and Poultry Commission, 184

Arpaio, Joe, 430

Articles of Confederation, 30, 31, 32, 216

Asians
  as elected city officials, 357–358
  as governors, 236, 239*m*, 240*t*

Assigned counsel, 283–284

Association of Trial Lawyers of America, 162

At-large elections, 357

ATM bureaucracies, 327–329, 328*t*

Attorneys, private, 279. *See also* Defense attorneys

Attorneys general, 116, 118–119, 249–250, 251*t*

Australian ballots, 108

B

Baby boomers, 489

Back to basics movement, 397

Baer, Max, 295

Balanced budgets, 385

Balanced Scorecard (BSC), 326

Ballot access, 108, 160

Ballot initiatives, 63. *See also* Referendums
  budget formulation and, 385, 391
  constitutional amendments by, 75
  direct democracy and, 87–89, 120–121
  elections for, 116
  by state, 123*t*

Ballots, styles of, 106, 108, 140

Barbers, state licensing and regulation of, 305

Barnburners, 133

Barnes, Roy, 235–236

Bartels, Larry M., 161

Base, political party, 154

Bell, Terrell, 407

Bench trials, 261

Benson, Craig, 236

Beyle, Thad, 244

Bicameral legislatures, 71, 185, 187

Biden, Joe, 247

Bill of Rights, 38, 288. *See also* Amendments, constitutional

Bills
  annual introductions of, 178
  appropriations, 68
  process for becoming state law, 174*f*

Bioterrorism, 467, 490. *See also* Terrorism

Bismarck, Otto von, 473

Blackburn, Marsha, 367

Blagojevich, Rod, 235

Blank, Robert H., 112

Blanket primaries, 141
Blanton, Roy, 229–230
Bliss, Ray, 144
Block grants, 46, 49, 389, 468–469, 479. *See also* Federal grants; Grants-in-aid
Bloomberg, Michael, 358, 399
Boards of commissioners, 344
BOHICA, 326
Bonds, 382–383
Boot camps, prison overcrowding and, 292, 461
Bowling Alone (Putnam), 116
Boyd, Donald, 374
Brace, Paul, 126–127, 268, 275
Brandeis, Louis, 20, 33
Bratton, Bill, 450–451, 452, 455–456
Brennan, William J., 64, 258
Brewer, Maybelle, 475
Breyer, Stephen G., 146–147, 268
Bricks-and-mortar retailers, 370
Broder, David, 89
Broken windows policing, 450–451
Brooklyn, N.Y., judicial selection in, 270
Brown, Jerry, 87, 249
Brown, Roy, 391
Brown, Willie, 158, 209
Bruce, Donald, 370
Bryant, Kobe, 290–291
Budget process, 368, 384–391
Budgets, local. *See also* Finance
    fire protection, 389
    healthcare, 388–389
    police protection, 389
    prisons, 389–390
    wages, 385
Budgets, state. *See also* Appropriations bills; Finance
    education, 385–387
    fire protection, 389
    governors and, 218–219
    healthcare, 387–389
    highways, 390
    police protection, 389
    prisons, 389–390
    restraints on, 390
    revenues, expenditures, and debt, 2000, 386*t*
    unfunded mandates, 390–391

wages, 385
welfare, 389
Budget shortfalls, 366
Budget stabilization funds, 385
Bullock, Bob, 85
Bureaucracies
    affirmative action and, 321–323
    ATM, 327–329, 328*t*
    definition of, 303–304
    effectiveness measures for, 310–312, 314–316
    employee selection for, 316–318
    employment by function of, 308*t*
    function of, 304
    GPP performance measures, 311–312, 313–314*t*, 314
    merit system alternatives, 323–327
    paradoxical nature of, 302–303
    as policy implementer, 304–305
    as policymaker, 305–307
    politics and merit system of, 319–323
    private sector versus, 310–311
    public labor unions and, 319–321
    size and role of, 307–310
    states with most and least, by employee numbers, 309*t*
    states with most and least, by expenditures, 310*t*
Bureaucrats, 303
    affirmative action and, 321–323
    diversity of, 323
    public labor unions and, 319–321
    selection systems, 316–318
    street-level, 305–306
Burke, Edmund, 191
Burke, Kevin, 294
Burnham, Walter Dean, 137
Bush, George H. W., 49, 54, 412
Bush, George W. *See also* No Child Left Behind Act
    on constitutional amendment banning gay marriage, 50, 256, 258
    election of 2000 and, 26–27, 86, 134, 159
    electoral college vote allotments and, 105

gubernatorial elections and, 243
gubernatorial endorsements for, 222
gubernatorial experience of, 49
New Federalism and, 51–52
presidential appointments of, 247
as second term presidential candidate, 246
as Texas governor, 85
Thompson and, 225, 479
Bush, Jeb, 26–27, 221, 326
Bush (George W.) administration, 359, 360, 418, 425–426
Bush v. Gore (2000), 27, 55, 56*t*, 57
Business groups, 154, 424. *See also* Corporations
Business permits, 302
Business Roundtable, 424
Butterfly ballot design, 27
Byrd, Harry F., 102, 153

C

Cain, Bruce, 122
Calhoun, John, 42
California
    ballot access regulations in, 108
    ballot initiatives in, 75, 89
    bureaucracy in, 309
    candidate-centered politics in, 136
    charter cities in, 339
    charter schools in, 418
    constitutional revision commission in, 79
    constitution of, 63, 65–66, 83
    counties in, 341, 344
    direct democracy in, 87–88
    education funding in, 407
    education policymaking in, 399
    governor recall in, 122
    GPP performance grade, 312
    gun control laws in, 458
    habitual offenders law in, 291
    Hispanics and redistricting in, 195
    as individualistic culture, 101
    intermediate appellate court in, 263
    Johnson & Johnson's corporate presence in, 164

judicial appointments in, 271, 272
judicial elections in, 267
judicial retention elections in, 273
legislative professionalism in, 205
legislative sessions in, 204
legislators in, 195
lieutenant governor in, 249
local agency formation commissions, 352
political parties in, 134, 140
political party competition in, 150–151
Proposition 13, 87–88, 121, 372, 373
school financing in, 371, 372
Senate president pro tem in, 188
sentencing in, 290
Supreme Court, 257
term limits in, 209
"three strikes" law in, 445
unfunded mandates in, 391
California Democratic Party v. Jones (2000), 141
Camden, N.J., individualistic culture of, 101
Campaign finance, 146–147, 149
for gubernatorial elections, 244
for judicial elections, 269–270, 271, 296
laws on, 137
public, 148
public labor unions and, 320
Campbell, Carroll, 236
Canavan, Marilyn, 148
Candidate-centered politics, 136, 153, 155–156
Cantor, Dan, 160
Capital investments, bonds and, 382–383
Capital outlays, 404
Capital punishment. *See* Death penalty
Car registrations, 374
Carter, Jimmy, 49, 246, 424
Cartograms, 10
Casework, 183. *See also* Constituents, legislators' service to
Casinos, 381–382
Categorical grants, 46. *See also* Grants-in-aid

Catholic Alliance, 155
Caucuses, 188
Cause lobbyists, 163
Censor, councils of, 71
Center for American Women and Politics, 358
Center for Education Reform, 425
Centers for Disease Control and Prevention (CDC), 176, 462, 469, 492
Centers for Medicare and Medicaid Services (CMS), 477
Chancellor-Beacon Academies, 421
Channel One, 421
Chard, Nancy, 67
Charles II, king of England, 69, 70
Charter of Privileges, Pennsylvania's, 71
Charters, home rule and, 338–339
Charter schools, 417–419, 419*t*
Chavis, Benjamin, 358*f*
Checks and balances, 68
oversight and, 183–185
Chicago, Ill.
individualistic culture of, 101
nonpartisan elections in, 357
political machine in, 138–139
race riots in (1960s), 441
Chicago Tribune, 138
Children. *See also* State Children's Health Insurance Program
truant, welfare reform and, 478
U.S. death penalty for, 454
Children's Defense Fund, 424
Christian Coalition, 155
Circuit judges, 434
Cisneros, Henry, 346
Cities. *See also* Local governments; Municipalities
counties versus, 342
drugs, war on, 442–443
healthcare expenditures by, 470–471
inner city, crime prevention and, 441–442
Cities without Suburbs (Rusk), 353
City councils, 344, 346–347
City-county consolidation, 352–353
City manager systems, 339, 344, 345. *See also* Council-manager governments

Civil cases, 259–260
criminal cases versus, 434–435
growth in, 293–294
Civil liberties, judicial federalism impact on, 258
Civil rights movement, 440
Civil War Amendments, 38, 110
Clements, Bill, 118
Cleveland, Ohio, school vouchers in, 420
Clinton, Bill, 246, 247
federal support for prisons under, 457
gubernatorial elections and, 243
gubernatorial experience of, 49
impeachment of, 245–246
San Francisco mayoral race and, 158
SCHIP and, 483
school standards movement and, 412
welfare reform and, 479, 480
Clinton, Hillary, 480
Clinton administration, standards movement and, 425
Closed primaries, 141
Coalition building, 172
Cocaine, crack, 443–445
Cole, David, 285
Coleman, Garnet, 180–181
Coll, Max, 214
Collective bargaining, 320
College Board, 410, 411
College students
demographic profiles of, 4–5
political engagement by, 4, 5
state government subsidies for, 5–6
tuition rates and, 410–411
Colonial charters, 69
Colorado
ballot initiatives in, 391
chief justice appointment in, 273
constitution of, 68
legislative sessions in, 205
magistrate system in, 294–295
political party competition in, 151
sex offense statutes in, 291
TANF-funded programs in, 469
Columbine High School shootings, 178

Commentaries on the Law of Municipal Corporations (Dillon), 51

Commerce Clause, 39*t*

Commission systems, 344, 345, 348

Committees, legislative, 173, 188, 190

Common law, 435–438

Common schools, 396

Communication, governor's ability for, 234–235

Community justice movement, 461

Compact theory of federalism, 42

Comparative method for study
  of economy, 13–15
  of geography and topography, 15–16
  of history and culture, 12–13
  on politics and women's status, 9
  of sociodemographics, 10–12
  as systemic approach, 7–10

Comprehensive Test of Basic Skills, 408

Compromises, 175

Compstat, 451, 455

Concurrent powers, 36, 40*f*

Confederacy, as system of power, 29, 30

Congressional Budget Office, 488

Connecticut
  college tuition-setting in, 411
  counties in, 341
  education funding in, 387
  gross state product of, 13
  homeland security legislation in, 176–177
  judicial nominating process in, 273
  judicial retention in, 273
  political party regulation in, 146
  population of, 11–12
  public health insurance in, 484–485
  rank-and-file legislators in, 191
  third-party governor in, 159
  voting rights for felons in, 461

Conservatism, traditionalistic cultures and, 102

Constituents, 175
  legislators' representation for, 180–182

legislators' service to, 177, 183, 184

Massachusetts legislation and, 178–179

Constitution, U.S., 8. *See also* Amendments, constitutional
  on compensation for federal judges, 277
  federalism provisions in, 39*t*
  judicial selection under, 265
  ratification of, 30
  representative government under, 86–87
  state constitutions versus, 65–69
  on state management of elections, 106
  state powers and interpretation of, 38, 40

Constitutional Convention of 1787, 30, 32

Constitutional conventions, state, 62, 78–79

Constitutional revision commissions, 79

Constitutions, state. *See also* Amendments, constitutional
  Alabama corporate recruitment and, 62–63
  democratic structures in, 68
  differences among, 83–89
  evolution of, 69–71
  financial mandates of, 68
  first generation of, 71–72, 74
  formal changes to, 74–75, 76–77*t*, 78–80
  geography and, 83
  history and, 81–82
  impact on state governments, 63–64
  informal changes to, 80–81
  judicial activism and educational equity under, 66–67
  length of, 66, 83
  model, 82–83
  number per state, 72*m*
  operating rules and selection for office under, 83–84
  permanence of, 65–66
  political cultures and, 83
  power distribution under, 84–85

representative government versus direct democracy under, 86–89

rights granted under, 64–65, 85–86

specificity of, 66–67, 83

Tenth Amendment and, 68–69

Continental Congress, 69–70

Contract attorneys, 283–285

Contract lobbyists, 162

Cooney, Mike, 159

Cooperative federalism, 43, 45–47

Core Knowledge program, 417

Corporations. *See also* Business groups
  Alabama recruitment of, 62–63
  lobbying by, 162, 163
  state political parties funding by, 140–141

Corruption
  individualistic cultures and, 100, 101
  political machines and, 139–140

Council-manager governments, 348–350, 350*f*

Council-mayor governments, 116. *See also* Mayor-council systems

Counties, 334, 341–344. *See also* Local governments
  healthcare expenditures by, 470–471
  twenty-five largest by population, 2000, 342*t*
  twenty-five smallest by population, 2000, 343*t*

County commissioners, 116, 344

County sheriffs, 438

Courts of first instance, 260, 261

Courts of last resort, 263, 278*t*. *See also* Supreme courts, state

Cowart, Beverly, 464–465

Crack cocaine, 443–445, 453

Crime
  arrest rates by age, 1976–2000, for murder, 451*f*
  arrest rates by age, 1976–2000, for violence, 451*f*
  changes in locus of, 457–459
  Compstat mapping system of, 451, 455
  decline in, 432–433

homicides in large cities, 1995, 2000, 2001, 452*f*
longer prison terms and, 446
percent change in homicides, 452*f*
rise and fall, 1960–2002, 442*f*
Criminal cases, 259–260, 278–279
civil cases versus, 434–435
federalization of, 296
growth in, 293
Criminal justice system. *See also* Death penalty
alternative punishment and, 460–461
common law and sovereign power, 435–438
community policing, 449–453
as county burden, 343
crack cocaine and, 443–445
as essence of modern America, 453–455
federal support and, 457
gun control laws and, 457–459
harsher punishments and penalties, 445–446
incarceration rates, 2000, 439*m*
law enforcement cooperation, 456
1960s changes in, 440–442
penitentiaries versus prisons, 440
policing return, 447–448
professional policing model, 448–449
prosecution procedures, 433–435
punishment purpose, 438–440
recidivism and, 457
trends in, 455–462
war on drugs, 442–443, 444
young people and, 461–462
Criterion-referenced tests, 408
Crosscutting requirements, for grants-in-aid, 46–47
Crossover sanctions, for grants-in-aid, 47
Crossover voting, 141
Cruel and unusual punishment, death penalty versus, 455
Crump, Edward Hull "Boss," 103
Crystal, Sue, 483
Culture, 12–13

Curb, Mike, 249
Curriculums, development of public school, 415

D

Daley, Richard J., 317, 349
Daley, Richard M., 426
Dallas, Tex.
council-manager system in, 349
elections in, 357
Davis, Gray, 122, 244
Davis, Sylvester, 257
Dayton, Ohio, council-manager system in, 349
Dealignment, 144
Dean, Howard, 246
Death penalty, 434
elected judges and, 84
European view of, 453
federal sentencing guidelines and, 297
future of, 459–460
judicial independence and, 269–270
judicial selection and, 268–269
judicial terms of office and, 275
pardons after DNA tests, 229
Phoenix's flat fees for contract attorneys and, 285
states holding executions, 95*m*
statutes on, 94
U.S. executions 1976–2002, 454
U.S. Supreme Court on sentence of, 289
Death taxes, 368, 374
Defendants' rights, 287–288
Defense attorneys, 281–286, 434. *See also* Attorneys, private; Public defenders
Defense of Marriage Act (1996), 50
Delaware
appellate courts in, 263
bureaucracy in, 309
constitutional amendments in, 75, 79–80
counties in, 341, 344
education funding in, 387
gubernatorial elections in, 240
gun control laws in, 458
judicial retention in, 273

Penn and, 70
prescription drugs plan in, 486
slot machines in, 383
state political party funding in, 141
tax system in, 374
voting rights for felons in, 461
Delaware River Basin Commission, 354
Delegates, 191
DeLeon, James, 295
Democratic Farmer-Labor Party, 160
Democratic Party
dealignment and, 145
factional splits in, 133–134
federal spending for congressional districts of, 48
gubernatorial elections and, 243
on health insurance, 471
professional staff for, 144
Republican Party versus, 132
in the South, 105
states' regulation of, 108
supporters of, 135
trial lawyers and, 181–182
Democratic Republicans, 133
Demographic factors
taxes and, 381
voter turnout and, 113, 114
Demonstration waivers, for welfare, 478, 479
Denver, Colo., transportation privatization in, 325
Departments of education, 398
Determinate sentencing, 290, 291
De Tocqueville, Alexis, 334, 361, 453, 454–455
Detroit Free Press, 271
Devolution, 18–20, 50, 477–478
Dewhurst, David, 118
Dickens, Charles, 453, 454–455
Dillon, John F., 51, 337
Dillon's Rule, 51, 337–338
Dingell, John, 173
Dinkins, David, 450
Direct democracy, 63, 86–89, 120–122, 123*t*
Directory of Latino Elected Officials, 358
Discretionary jurisdiction, 263
Discretionary spending, 387

Distance (online) learning, 417–418
District attorneys, 434, 437
District of Columbia
    appeals process in, 264
    appellate courts in, 263
    board of education in, 398
    as federal city, 19
    federal sentencing guidelines in, 297
    judicial compensation in, 278
    judicial selection in, 272
    Medicaid programs in, 474–475
    per-pupil spending in, 405
    public hospital closing in, 491
    race riots in (1960s), 441
    school vouchers in, 420
Districts, 175. *See also* Redistricting
    elections in, 357
    special, 90
Diversity, judicial selection method
    and, 267
Divided power, 234
Dividends, 381
Division of labor, bureaucracies and, 303
DNA testing, 460
Dogs, taxation of, 7
Dorr, Thomas Wilson, 74
Dorr War (Dorr's Rebellion), 74
Drug courts, 293, 461
Drug Free School Zone Act of 1990, 55
Drugs
    blood-borne diseases, needle-
        exchange programs and, 469
    treatment for, as alternate
        sentencing, 292
    war on, 442–443, 444
Dual constitutionalism, 65
Dual federalism, 41–43
Duplication, jurisdictional, 34
DuPont Corporation, Del., 141
Dyer, Buddy, 196

E

Earned Income Tax Credit, 480
East Jersey, 70
Eck, John, 432
Economy, 13–15
    devolution and, 20–21

education funding and, 405, 407
    post–Revolutionary War
        recession, 31
    by state, 14m
    tax variations and, 381–382
Edgeless cities, 355
*Edgewood Independent School
    District v. Kirby* (1989), 422
Edison Schools, 421
Educate America Act, 415
Education, public
    advocacy groups and, 425
    business groups and, 424
    charter schools, 417–419, 419t
    dropouts, grades 9–12, by state,
        2000–2001, 413–414t
    equalization funding plans for, 372
    funding, 402–407
    home schooling, 421–422
    national political parties and, 424
    New Hampshire's funding for, 374
    organization and leadership,
        398–402
    parents' groups, 423–424
    performance pressure, 407–412
    privatization, 420–421
    "production function" of, 404
    professional groups and, 425
    property taxes and, 371
    reform programs, 412, 415–422
    "resource adequacy" rankings, 405
    sanctions and assistance types
        by state, 2000, 427t
    school vouchers, 419–420
    spending-per-student by state,
        1999–2000, 404m
    state constitutions and equity
        versus adequacy in, 66–67
    state funding for, 5–6, 8, 10–11,
        385–387
    state supreme courts and,
        422–423
    student enrollment by state, fall
        2000, 405m
    teacher recruitment, 416–417
    textbook adoption and open
        territory states, 415–416,
        416m

Educational Testing Service,
    410–411
Education Trust, 425
Education Week, 415
E-government, 327–329, 328t
Ehrlich, Robert, 127
Eisenhower, Dwight, 49
Elastic Clause, 39t
Elazar, Daniel J.
    on criminal punishment and
        political culture, 439
    political culture classifications
        of, 82, 97–103, 100t, 151–152
    on political culture of Nevada
        versus Mississippi, 381–382
Elderly
    Democratic Party and, 134
    heathcare for, 10
    political parties and, 154
Elected positions, 83–84. *See also*
    Term limits
Election of 2000, 26–27, 86, 134.
    See also Bush v. Gore
    Florida ballot styles and, 107
    percentage of population voting
        in, 114–115t
    third party competition in, 159
Elections, 104–116
    direct democracy and, 120–122
    executive branch, 117–118
    gubernatorial, 236, 239–240
    judicial, 265, 266–271, 295, 296
    judicial retention, 272, 273
    legal offices, 118–120
    local government, 357
    party regulations, 108–109
    political culture and, 95
    public opinion and, 123–127
    purposes for, 116–117
    school board, 400–401
    state supervision of, 106, 108
    voter restrictions, 110
    voter turnout, 110–111, 114, 116
Electoral college, 26–27, 86, 105
Electorate, 63, 209–210
Electric utility deregulation, New
    Federalism and, 51
Elementary and Secondary
    Education Act, 415
Eleventh Amendment, on sovereign
    immunity of states, 55

Ellwood, Paul, 487
Eminent domain, 28
En banc appellate court hearings, 263–264
Engler, Jim, 224
Entitlements, 388, 475, 479
Enumerated powers, 35–36, 54
Environmentalists, political culture and, 151
Equal Protection Clause, education funding and, 403
Estate taxes, 368, 374
Ethics
    laws on lobbying and, 163, 191
    scandals, legislative process and, 177–178
Ethnicity, indeterminate sentencing and, 290
Excise taxes, 368
Exclusive powers, 36
Executive branch, 32. *See also* Governors
    attorneys general, 249–250
    election of, 117–118
    legislative oversight and, 183–185
    lieutenant governors, 248–249
    other offices of, 251–252
    powers of, 251t
Executive orders, 249
Expenditures, budgetary, 385
Experiencing Politics (McDonough), 191

F

Factional splits, 133
Family courts, integrated, 293
Fargo, Heather, 358
Farmer-Labor Party, 160
Farris, Michael, 422
Federal Cigarette Labeling and Advertising Act, 55–56
Federal Communications Commission, 37
Federal employees' labor unions, 319–320
Federal government. *See also* Constitution, U.S.; Senate, U.S.; Supreme Court, U.S.; White House
    devolution of power and policy from, 18–20

education funding by, 402
fiscal year of, 384
origins of, 30–32
powers of state governments versus, 40f
state-administrated programs of, 304
state and local government versus, 16–18
Washington, D.C., government and, 19
Federal grants. *See also* Block grants
    under (George W.) Bush administration, 359, 360
    cooperative federalism and, 45–47
Federalism
    ad hoc, 52
    advantages and disadvantages of, 33–35, 35t
    compact theory of, 42
    constitutional basis for, 35–38, 39–40f
    cooperative, 43, 45–47
    development of, 40–52
    dual, 41–43
    election of 2000 and, 26–27
    judicial, 64
    key dates in history of, 44f
    New, 47–52
    shared powers under, 28
    Supreme Court rulings 1992–2001 on, 56t
    as system of power, 29
    U.S. development of, 30–32
Federalist, The
    No. 10, 86, 89
    No. 73, 173
Federalists, 133
Federal sentencing guidelines, 290, 296–297
Felonies, 281–282
Feminist movement, modern, 440
Fifteenth Amendment, 110
Files and records maintenance, bureaucracies and, 303, 315
Filibusters, 173
Filler, Josh, 360
Finance, 364–393
    ballot initiatives and, 391
    bonds, 382–383

budget process, 384–391
budget restraints, 390
education, 385–387
factors in tax variations, 380–382
fees and charges, 377
fire protection, 389
healthcare, 387–389
highways, 390
income taxes, 374, 375–376t
insurance trust money, 378
intergovernmental transfers, 378–379
other sources, 374, 377
police protection, 389
prisons, 389–390
property taxes, 370–374
revenues, expenditures, and debt, 2000, 386t
sales taxes, 368–370
severance taxes, 377
taxing variations, 379–380
Tennessee's tax revolt, 366–367
unfunded mandates, 390–391
wages, 385
welfare, 389
Finkbeiner, Carleton S., 345–346
Fire protection, funding for, 389
First Amendment, interest groups, judicial elections and, 296
First World War, federal government centralization and, 43
Fiscal federalism, 388
Fiscal year, 384
Fishing industry regulations, 13–14
Fixed fee contracts, 284–285
Florida, 26–27. *See also* Bush v. Gore
    ballot initiatives in, 87
    constitutional revision commissions in, 79
    constitution on judicial compensation, 277–278
    death penalty in, 94, 268–269
    education funding in, 387
    judicial selection in, 266, 267, 268–269
    political machine in, 139–140
    political parties in, 134, 151
    prescription drugs plan in, 486

prosecution of drug cases in, 280
public hospitals' privatization in, 490
Reconstruction and, 80–81
retirees on fixed incomes in, 373
school privatization in, 421
Service First program, 326–327
special legislative session costs in, 205–206
statehouse reporters in, 208
tax system in, 374
Florida Comprehensive Assessment Test (FCAT), 409
Focused consumption taxes, 368–369
Folsom, Jim, 62–63
For cause challenges, in jury selection, 287
Ford, Gerald, 49
Ford, Tim, 188, 230
Ford-Coates, Barbara, 26–27
Ford Foundation, 206
Formal powers, of governors, 223, 224, 226–227t, 227–230
Formal rules, bureaucracies and, 303
Fort Lauderdale, Fla., private bids for pipe-laying in, 310–311
Fourteenth Amendment, 38, 39, 39t, 72
Fox, Vincente, 221
Fox, William F., 370
Frame of Government, Pennsylvania's, 71
Franchise, 72, 74. *See also* Voters
    ballot styles and, 107
    for felons, 446, 461
    importance of, 105
Franklin, Benjamin, 71
Franklin, Shirley, 358
Frazier, Lynn, 122, 245
Free Soilers, 133
Fugitive Slave Act (1850), 437
Full faith and credit clause, 36, 38

G

Gabler, Mel and Norma, 425
Gallup Organization, 161
Galveston, Tex., commission systems and, 348

Gambling addictions, 382
Gann, Paul, 87
Gans, Curtis, 111
Garfield, James, 246
Garr, Tony, 482
Garson, Gerald, 270
Gay marriage, 50–51, 94, 158, 256, 258
General act charters, 339
General Assemblies, 180, 187, 205
General elections, 141
General Equivalency Degree (GED) program, 412
General jurisdiction trial courts, 261
General Motors (GM), 303
General obligation bonds, 382–383
General revenue sharing grants, 46. *See also* Federal grants; Grants-in-aid
General welfare clause, 36
Geography, 15–16
    state constitution variations and, 82
    taxes and, 380–381
    voter turnout and, 111
Geology, taxes and, 381
Georgia
    ballot access regulations in, 109, 160
    boot camps for offenders in, 461
    constitutional conventions in, 78
    death penalty in, 94
    executive branch elections in, 118, 243
    gun control laws in, 458
    HMO regulation in, 207
    judicial elections in, 267
    legislative leadership in, 188
    lieutenant governor power in, 248
    lottery in, 383
    Republican legislators from, 7
    state superintendent of education in, 252
    unicameral legislature in, 71
Germany, social safety net in, 473
Gerry, Elbridge, 194
Gerrymanders, 194, 195
Gerstener, Louis V., Jr., 424
Gibson, Mark, 483
Gideon v. Wainwright (1963), 281

Gift bans, lobbyists and, 163, 191
Gift taxes, 368, 374
Giuliani, Rudolph, 18, 349, 450–451
Glendening, Parris, 225
Gnant, Randall, 123–124
Goals 2000, 412, 415, 416
Goldstein, Herman, 447
Gonzalez, Matt, 158
Gore, Al, 26–27, 134, 159, 209
Governing (magazine), 311
Government Performance Project (GPP), 311–312, 313–314t
Governors, 214–216. *See also* Appointments; Executive branch; Veto power
    activist, 214
    backgrounds of, 241–242t
    ballot initiatives on recall of, 88
    budgetary power of, 228
    as chief legislator, 218–219
    as chief spokesperson for state, 220–221
    colonial, 216
    communication ability of, 234–235
    election of, 116, 236, 239–240, 243–244
    formal and informal powers of, 235–236
    formal powers of, 223, 224, 227–230
    as head of state agencies, 219–220
    informal powers of, 223, 230, 233–235
    institutional powers of, by state, 2004, 231–232t
    job of, 216–223
    keeping and leaving office, 244–247
    as National Guard commander-in-chief, 222–223
    pardons by, 229–230
    as party chief, 221–222
    party support in legislature for, 233–234
    personal powers of, by state, 2004, 237–238t
    popular support for, 233
    powers of, 223–235

as presidents, 246–247
selection rules for, 83
special sessions and, 230
third-party, 159
Grand juries, 281, 437, 438
Grand Old Party, 134. *See also*
Republican Party
Grannis, Alexander, 177
Grants-in-aid. *See also* Block grants;
Federal grants
(George W.) Bush on red tape
and, 52
cooperative federalism and,
46–47
New Federalism and, 48–49
to Republican districts, 48
Great Britain, post–Revolutionary
War actions by, 31
Great Depression, 45, 473–474
Great Society initiative, 397, 424
Greeks, ancient, on criminal
punishment, 440
Green, Mark, 358
Green, Paul, 193
Green Party, 158, 159
Griswold v. the State of Connecticut
(1965), 85–86
Groscost, Jeff, 144
Gross state product, 13–15
Gun control laws, 21, 178, 458–459
Gun lobby, 119, 163. *See also*
National Rifle Association
Gunthor, George, 176
Gun violence, public health and, 469

H

Habitual offender laws, 291–292
Hahn, James, 455
Halfway houses, prison
overcrowding and, 292
Hall, Melinda Gann, 268, 275
Hamilton, Alexander, 32, 40–41,
133, 173. *See also* Federalist, The
Hammonds, Christopher, 67, 91
Hancock, John, 437
Harvard Education Review, 322
Haskell, Dean, 67
Hawaii
ballot initiatives in, 89
bureaucracy in, 309

counties in, 341
culture and history of, 12
gubernatorial elections in, 243
gun control laws in, 458
hurricane and tsunami response
legislation in, 176
intermediate appellate court in,
263
judicial retention in, 273
local school financing in, 371
political party competition in,
150
professional and personal
services taxes in, 370
school districts in, 399
Haynie, Kerry L., 199, 201
Health Care Financing
Administration, 477
Healthcare funding, 387–389
Health Care Industry Manufacturers
Association, 166
Health insurance. *See also* Health
maintenance organizations;
Medicaid programs
for contraceptive devices, 470
healthcare and, 484–485
Health Security Act, 480
for low-income citizens, 468, 470
SCHIP program, 483–484
states as innovators in low-
income coverage, 484*m*
universal coverage under, 471
Health Insurance Association of
America, 489
Health maintenance organizations
(HMOs), 164, 206–207, 481, 486,
487*m. See also* Managed care
Health Security Act, 480, 482
*Heart of Atlanta Motel v. United
States* (1964), 54
Hedgecoke, Fred, 417
Heineman, Dave, 248
Help America Vote Act, 107
Hepatitis C transmission, needle-
exchange programs and, 469
Herbst, Susan, 125–126
Herron, John, 295
Hibbing, John, 207
Hickel, Walter, 159
Hierarchies, bureaucracies and, 303,
315

Higher law, 65
High school graduation rates, 412
High-stakes standardized testing,
397
Highway patrol, 438
Highways, funding for, 390
Hiler, Bob, 156
Hill, Steven, 105, 111
Hine, James, 369
Hispanics. *See* Latinos
History, 12–13
political culture and, 96
state constitution variations and,
81–82
HIV transmission, needle-exchange
programs and, 469
Hodges, Jim, 382
Holahan, John, 483
Home rule, 101. *See also* Municipal
home rule
local powers and, 338–339, 341
Home schooling, 421–422
Homeschooling Helper, 421
Homeschooling Today, 421
Hospitals
development of, 472
emergency treatment by, 484
public beds in, 490
House arrest, 292
House of Representatives (states), 187
Houston, Tex., school dropout rates
in, 412
Hoxby, Caroline, 372
Huckabee, Mike, 467–468
Human Rights Watch, 453, 454
Humphrey, Hubert H., 142, 143
Hunkers, 133
Hunt, Guy, 246
Hunter, Tye, 285
Hurst, Julia, 249
Hynes, Charles, 270

I

Ibeh, Ngozi, 492
IBM, 303
Idaho
federal funding of Medicaid
programs in, 474–475
home schooling regulations in,
422

intermediate appellate court in, 263

local powers in, 338

nonpartisan judicial elections in, 267

political parties in, 134–135

public health insurance in, 484–485

Republican Party domination in, 127

term limits in, 208–209

Illinois

ballot initiatives in, 75, 87

constitution on environmental goals of, 258

Cook Co. property taxes, 373

education funding in, 405

gun control laws in, 458

as individualistic culture, 101

Johnson & Johnson's corporate presence in, 164

local school financing in, 371

partisan judicial elections in, 267

party affiliation and government jobs in, 146

political party competition in, 150

public health insurance in, 485

statehouse coverage in, 208

state supreme court elections in, 120

trial courts in, 261

truth-in-sentencing in, 292

Immigrants, illegal, ballot initiatives on services for, 88

Impeachment, 244, 273

Implied powers, 36, 38

Incarceration rates, 439*m*, 443. *See also* Prisons

Income taxes, 374

education funding and, 402

state systems, 2004, 375–376*t*

state versus federal, 367

Incumbents, 163, 183, 193, 259

Independence Party, Minnesota's, 159

Independent candidates, 157–159

ballot access regulations and, 108–109

difficulties of building support for, 159–160

elected governor, 239

major party support for, 160–161

Independent expenditures, 146

Indeterminate sentencing, 290–291

Indiana

constitutional amendments in, 75

constitution of, 74

economic cycle and, 381

gambling industry in, 383

gubernatorial elections in, 240

judicial selection in, 265, 267

legislators in, 195–196

lieutenant governor power in, 249

on state constitutional conventions, 78

Indiana ballots, 106

Indianapolis, Ind., city council, 346–347

Indictments, 281

Individualistic cultures, 12, 13

characteristics of, 99–100, 100*t*

party competition and, 151–152

states with, 98*m*

Influenza, 464–465, 467

Informal powers, of governors, 223, 230, 233–235

Initiatives. *See* Ballot initiatives

Insurance commissioners, election of, 118, 252

Insurance companies, 177, 181. *See also* Health maintenance organizations

Insurance trust money, 377, 378

Interagency Working Group on Federalism, 52

Interest groups, 161–164, 166–167. *See also* Business groups; Lobbies

campaign financing for judicial elections by, 269–270, 271

devolution and, 20–21

government expansion and, 153

judicial elections and, 296

moralistic cultures and, 127

political party competition and, 151, 154–155

school board elections and, 399–400

Intergovernmental transfers, 377–379

Intermediate appellate courts, 260, 263, 264, 266*m*, 278*t*

International City/County Management Association, 345, 349

Internet

public opinion polling using, 125

sales taxes and, 341, 370

Interracial marriage, state courts and, 257

Interstate commerce clause, 54

Iowa

chief state school officer in, 398

constitutional amendments in, 75

constitutional conventions in, 78

education funding in, 387

gun control laws in, 458

redistricting in, 194

school standards administration in, 415

Iowa Test of Basic Skills, 408

Iraq war, New Federalism and, 52

Issue ads, 155

J

Jackson, Andrew, 133, 134, 266, 316–317

James I, king of England, 69

Jamestown (Va. colony), 69

Jarvis, Howard, 87

Javits, Jacob, 160

Jefferson, Thomas, 41, 133

Jenness v. Fortson (1971), 109

Jersey City, N.J., political machine in, 139

Jim Crow laws, 72

Johanns, Mike, 248

John Q (movie), 487

Johnson, Gary, 228–229

Johnson, Lyndon B., 49, 142–143, 397, 474

Johnson & Johnson, 164

Johnston, Henry, 245

Joint Center for Political and Economic Studies, 358

Judges. *See also* Justices; State court systems

activist, 256

appellate court, 263–264, 274–275t
circuit, 434
compensation, 277–278, 278t
as county legislators, 344
independence, impartiality of, 268
managerial, 294
merit selection for, 266, 271, 272–273
popular elections for, 266–271
pure appointment systems for, 271–272
retention elections for, 272, 273
selection of, 116, 264–273, 266m, 275, 295–296
sentencing and, 289
terms of office, 273, 275
trial court terms and reappointment methods by state in 2004, 276–277t
Judicial branch, 32, 83–84, 119–120. See also State court systems
Judicial compensation commissions, 278
Judicial federalism, 64
Judicial review, 80
Juries, 286–287, 289, 434, 436–438
Jury nullification, 281, 436–437
Justices, state supreme court, 267. See also Judges; State court systems
Justices of the peace, 436

K

Kansas
charter schools in, 418
gubernatorial elections in, 243
gun control laws in, 458
judicial selection in, 266, 267
political party competition in, 150
Kansas City, Mo., school desegregation and education funding in, 406
Katz, Vera, 192
Katzenback v. McClung (1964), 54
Keating, Frank, 426
Keillor, Garrison, 408

Kelling, George, 432, 447–448, 450
Kempthorne, Dirk, 247–248
Kennedy, Anthony, 268
Kennedy, Edward M., 424
Kennedy, John F., 49, 319, 474
Kennedy, Robert F., 143
Kentucky
county administrators in, 344
Education Reform Act, 415
gubernatorial elections in, 240
home schooling regulations in, 422
judicial independence in, 270
judicial selection in, 267
legislators in, 196
lieutenant governor power in, 249
lobbying ethics laws of, 163
lobbying in, 191
Louisville-Jefferson Metro Government, 353
sex acts legislation in, 86
state legislators on activist judges in, 259
state supreme court on public schools in, 422–423
Kerry, John, 246
Key, V. O., 108
Kilpatrick, Kwame M., 358f
King, Angus, 148, 239
King, Martin Luther, 441
King (Rodney) riots, 449, 450, 452
Kitzhaber, John, 481, 482, 483
Kleiman, Mark, 444
Klein, Joel, 399
Know-Nothings, 133
Knox, John, 62
Kozol, Jonathan, 406
Kraeger, Devon, 464–465
Ku Klux Klan, 102
Kurita, Rosalind, 183

L

Laboratories of democracy, 20–22
Labor unions, 134, 151, 154, 196, 319–320
LaBrant, Bob, 119, 250
La Follette, Robert M., 87
Lake Wobegon Effect, 408
Land-grant colleges, 43

LaPore, Theresa, 26–27
Larios, Alda, 433
Latinos
as elected city officials, 357–358
as governors, 236
incarceration rates for, 446
as legislators, percentage by state of, 2004, 202–203t
redistricting and, 195
voter turnout by, 111
Law Enforcement Alliance of America, 119
Law Enforcement Assistance Administration, 457
Lawmaking, 178–180
Laws, odd-sounding, 179t
Lawson, Kay, 108
Leadership, legislative, 188, 190, 192–193
Lee, Barbara, 197
Lee, Richard Henry, 69–70
Lee, Robert E., 96, 102
Legal offices, elections for, 118–120
Legislative branch, 32. See also Legislatures, state
bicameral houses, 71
constitutional amendments and, 74–75, 76–77t
judicial selection by, 272
unicameral houses, 70, 71
Legislative over-criminalization, 280
Legislative referendums, 120
Legislative Services Agency, 194
Legislators, state, 195–196
African Americans, percentage by state of, 2004, 200–201t
demographic diversity of, 196–197, 199
election of, 116
governor as chief, 218–219
Latinos, percentage by state of, 2004, 202–203t
lobbyists and, 162–163
professional backgrounds of, 196
professional versus citizen, 203–206
public opinion and, 125–127, 206–210
state ranking by total number of, 2004, 186–187t

third-party, 159–160
women, percentage by state of, 2004, 198–199*t*
Legislatures, state, 172–175. *See also* General Assemblies; Legislative branch
  apportionment and, 193–195
  bicameralism of, 185, 187
  committees, 190
  constituent service by, 183
  education policymaking by, 399
  full-time, hybrid, and part-time, 205*m*
  governor's party support in, 233–234
  job of, 175–177
  lawmaking by, 178–180
  leadership in, 188, 190
  organization and operation of, 185, 187–188, 190–195
  oversight by, 183–185
  partisan control of, 1954 versus 2000, 189*m*
  process for bill becoming state law, 174*f*
  purposes of, 177–178
  rank-and-file members, 191–193
  representation by, 180–182
Lewin Group, 486
Lewis, Peter, 88
Liability cases, 287
Liberal Party, 160
Licensing requirements, state and local, 34
Lieutenant governors, 118, 188, 248–249, 251*t*
Limited jurisdiction trial courts, 261
Lincoln, Abraham, 134
Lindsay, John, 160
Line-item veto, 84–85, 229
Liquor sales and licenses, 378
Literacy tests, voting and, 110, 112
Living wage laws, 338
Lobbies, 161–164, 165–166*t*, 166–167. *See also* Interest groups
Lobbying, 162, 173, 175–176, 221
Local education agencies, 399
Local governments, 332–362. *See also* Budgets, local; Finance
  constitutions and, 90
  counties, 341–344

devolution of power and policy to, 18–20
  education funding by, 402
  elections in, 116–117
  employees by state, 17*m*
  federal aid to, 379*m*
  federal government versus, 8, 16–18
  federalism and, 33
  franchise limitations and, 72, 74
  intragovernmental politics, 351–355
  as laboratories of democracy, 20–22
  lobbying by, 162
  municipalities, 344–351
  New Federalism and, 49
  participation in, 357–359
  powers and constraints of, 337–339, 341
  Social Security Act and, 474
  special districts, 350–351
  state and federal aid to, 359–361
  state powers and, 51
Local political parties, 134, 140
Local politics
  comparative method of studying, 7–10
  daily impact of, 5–7
  policymaking constraints on, 21–22
Locke, Gary, 180, 483
Loeb, William, 153
Logrolling, 172
Long, Huey, 139, 140
Long Island, N.Y., political machine in, 138–139
Long-term care, 388, 468, 485, 488–489
Lorillard Tobacco Co. v. Reilly (2001), 55–56, 56*t*
Los Angeles (city). *See also* Los Angeles Police Department
  budget formulation in, 385
  city charter, 340
  city council, 346
  elections in, 357
  homeland security and, 359–360
  homicide rates in, 455
  public schools' administration in, 399

race riots in (1960s), 441
  school board races in, 400
Los Angeles County, district attorney's office staff, 279–280
Los Angeles Police Department, 449, 451–452, 456
Lotteries, 382–383
Louisiana
  Angola Prison, 440
  chief state school officer in, 398
  constitutional conventions in, 78
  constitution of, 65, 66
  death penalty in, 94
  drinking age law of, 177
  federal funding of Medicaid in, 474–475
  gubernatorial elections in, 240
  judicial selection in, 267
  jury verdicts in, 287
  Medicaid reimbursement claims by, 477
  parishes in, 341
  parish jurors in, 344
  parole board discretion in, 292
  political machine in, 139
Louisville-Jefferson Metro Government, Ky., 353
Loveless, Tom, 418–419
Low Level Waste Policy Amendments Act of 1985, 54–55
Lucey, Paula, 491
Lynching, 94, 103
Lynn, James, 295

M

Madison, James, 31, 32, 37–38, 86, 89. *See also* Federalist, The
Madrid, Mike, 51
Magistrates, 294
Magna Carta, 69
Maine
  ballot initiatives in, 89
  chief state school officer in, 398
  constitutional conventions in, 78
  education funding in, 404
  independents and ballot access regulations in, 109
  judicial appointments in, 271–272
  legislators in, 196

lieutenant governor in, 249
local powers in, 338
political party competition in,
150
prescription drug plan in, 206,
486
public campaign financing in,
148
tax burden in, 379
term limits in, 209
third-party governor in, 159
Majority leaders, 188
Majority-minority districts, 194
Majority rule, 172
Malapportionment, 194
Malvo, Lee Boyd, 289
Managed care, 481, 485, 486–488.
See also Health maintenance
organizations
Management by Objectives (MBO),
325–326
Mandatory jurisdiction, 263
Mandatory minimum sentences, 291
Mann, Horace, 396, 426
Marbury v. Madison (1803), 259
Maricopa County (Ariz.) Public
Defender's Office, 285
Marijuana, medical, referendums on,
88, 89, 120–121
"Marissa's Law," 214
Markham, William, 70–71
Marquez, Gabriel Garcia, 132
Marriage. *See also* Gay marriage;
Interracial marriage
incentives for teenage parents,
478
Marshall, John, 53
Mary, queen of England, 436
Maryland
budgetary control in, 219
college tuition-setting in, 410,
411
constitution of, 67
Democratic Party domination
in, 127
education achievement tests in,
416
gubernatorial elections in, 243
gun control laws in, 458
as individualistic culture, 101
judicial selection in, 272–273

legislative leadership in, 188
political party competition in,
150
on slot machines, 383
Smart Growth Act in, 225
tax burden in, 374
voting rights for felons in, 461
*Maryland v. Baltimore & Ohio
Railroad* (1845), 341
Massachusetts
ballot initiatives in, 75
constitutional amendments in,
75
constitution of, 63
county government corruption
in, 344
Democratic legislators from, 7
education funding in, 387
gun control laws in, 458
introduction of legislative bills
in, 178–179
Johnson & Johnson's corporate
presence in, 164
judicial review in, 80
judicial terms of office in,
257–258, 273
legislative sessions in, 204
lobbying ethics laws of, 163
politics and women's status in, 9
privatization of public hospitals
in, 490
property tax ballot initiative in,
121
Proposition 2½, 373
SCHIP enrollment in, 485
Senate president in, 188
on state constitutional
conventions, 78
supercabinet in, 220
Supreme Court, 50, 55–56, 257
tax capacity versus tax effort in,
380
Massachusetts ballots, 106
Massachusetts Bay Colony, 69, 70, 71
Massachusetts Bay Transportation
Authority, 350
Masset, Royal, 132
Mathy-Zvailer, Marissa, 214
Maxwell School of Citizenship and
Public Affairs, Syracuse University,
311

Mayhew, David R., 234
Mayor-council systems, 344,
345–347. *See also* Council-mayor
governments
Mayors, 116, 339, 357–358, 359
McCain-Feingold campaign finance
law, 147
McCallum, Scott, 152, 379
McCarthy, Eugene, 142–143
McConnell, Glenn, 383
McCulloch v. Maryland (1819), 41,
53
McDonough, John, 191–192
McGovern, George, 143
McGreevey, James, 101
McLaughlin, Ed, 148
MC Serch, 358f
McWhorter, Ned, 233–234, 481,
482
Mecham, Evan, 245
Media. *See also* Newspapers;
Television advertising
adversarial view of government
by, 207–208
gubernatorial elections coverage
by, 243–244
public opinion shaping and, 126
on special legislative session
costs, 205–206
Medicaid programs, 180–181, 207
costs for, 475–477, 481–482,
485–489
creation of, 474–475
demonstration waivers for, 478
devolution of, 477–478
funding, 387–389
future of, 494
long-term care and, 488–489
managed care for, 481, 487m
state and local governments and,
470–471
Medical malpractice cases, 287
Medicare programs, 474, 475–477,
478
Medinger, John, 184
Megalopolises, 355
Membership groups, 161
Memphis, Tenn., traditionalistic
culture in, 103
Mental health treatment, as
alternative sentencing, 292

Mercedes-Benz, 62–63, 64

Merit selection, for judgeships, 266, 271, 272–273, 295–296

Merit systems, bureaucratic, 318
Florida's alternative to, 326–327
politics and, 319–323

Metropolitan areas. *See also* Local governments
ten fastest growing, 1990 to 2000, 354*t*

Mexican-American Legal Defense and Education Fund, 423

Michigan
economic cycle and, 381
fiscal year of, 384
gun control laws in, 458
habitual offender law in, 292
history and constitution of, 82
home schooling regulations in, 422
judicial selection in, 267, 269, 271
political machine in, 139–140
political party competition in, 150
prescription drugs plan in, 486
property tax ballot initiative in, 121
statehouse reporters in, 208
state supreme court elections in, 120
TANF-funded programs in, 468

Microsoft, attorneys general consumer protection case against, 249

Mid-America Regional Council (MARC), 33–34

Mid-term vacancies, judicial appointments and, 265

Midwest (region)
police departments in, 456
unions in, 182

Migration patterns, political culture and, 98

Miller, George, 424

Miller, Mike, 188

Milwaukee, Wis.
public health by private hospitals in, 490, 491
school board races in, 400
school vouchers in, 420

Minnesota
competitive elections in, 116
constitution on public schools in, 398
Democratic Farmer-Labor Party in, 160
governor recall in, 122
gun control laws in, 458
history and constitution of, 82
Independence Party of, 159
independents and ballot access regulations in, 109
judicial selection in, 267
legislative ideas in, 182
legislative professionalism in, 204–205
lieutenant governor power in, 248
lobbying ethics laws of, 163
moralistic culture in, 127
political party regulation in, 146
public campaign financing in, 148
third-party governor in, 159
voter registration in, 113

Minority leaders, 188

Minor (minority) parties, 143, 157–159
ballot access regulations and, 108–109
difficulties of building support for, 159–160
major party support for, 160–161

Misdemeanors, 281–282

Mississippi
ballot initiatives in, 87
budget formulation in, 385
casinos in, 381–382
constitution of, 74
death penalty in, 94
education funding in, 405
gubernatorial elections in, 240
home schooling regulations in, 422
judicial selection in, 267
jury qualifications in, 287
legislative leadership in, 188
lieutenant governor power in, 249
Medicaid eligibility in, 388

Parchman Farms in, 440
politics and women's status in, 9
Reconstruction and, 80–81
on state constitutional conventions, 78
state supreme court elections in, 120
tort laws changes in, 181
unions in, 181–182

Missouri
ballot initiatives in, 75
Dillon's Rule challenge in, 337
gubernatorial elections in, 240
gun control laws in, 458
as individualistic culture, 101
judicial selection in, 266, 267
jury qualifications in, 287
legislators in, 187
Medicaid reimbursement claims by, 477
prescription drugs plan in, 486
riverboat casinos, 383
sentencing in, 289

Missouri Compromise (1820), 42–43

Missouri Plan, for justice selection, 84, 266

Moakley, Maureen, 101

Moberly, Harold, 196

Model constitutions, 82–83

Molnau, Carol, 248

Moncrief, Gary, 208

Montana
appellate courts in, 263
ballot initiatives in, 391
bills before 2002 legislature of, 178
constitutional conventions in, 79
constitutional right to privacy in, 86
drug possession penalties in, 443
federal funding of Medicaid programs in, 474–475
gubernatorial elections in, 240
judicial selection in, 267
political parties in, 134–135
public health insurance in, 484–485
state superintendent of education in, 252
tax system in, 374

Montessori schools, 417
Moore, Roy S., 260
Morales, Reuben, 52
Moralistic cultures, 12, 13
    characteristics of, 99, 100*t*
    party competition and, 151–152
    states with, 98*m*
    voter registration and, 112
    voter turnout and, 111, 116
Mormons, social services provided
    by, 469
Motor-voter registration, 110,
    112–113
Mountain West, political party
    competition in, 150
Moynihan, Daniel Patrick, 479
Muchmore, Lynn, 217
Municipal bonds, 383, 384. *See also*
    Local governments
Municipal charters, 90
Municipal home rule, 90. *See also*
    Home rule
Municipalities, 334–335
    commission systems, 348
    governance of, 344–351, 345*t*
    mayor-council systems, 345–347

N

Nader, Ralph, 159
Naples, Fla., business permits in, 302
Napoleonic code, 435
NASCAR dads, 136
Nassau County, N.Y.
    individualistic culture of, 101
    political machine in, 139
National Alliance of Business, 424
National Assessment of Educational
    Progress (NAEP), 409
National Association of Christian
    Educators, 400
National Association of Community
    Health Centers, 484
National Association of Counties
    (NACo), 339, 341, 352
National Association of State Budget
    Officers, 397
National bank, 40–41
National Center for Education
    Statistics, 421–422
National Center for State Courts, 278

National Center on Education
    Statistics, 406
National Conference on State
    Legislation, 47, 49
National Council of Teachers of
    Mathematics, 415
National Education Association, 423
National government. *See* Federal
    government
National Governors Association, 49,
    225, 489
National Guard, governors as
    commander-in-chief of, 222–223
National Heritage Academies, 421
National League of Cities, 347, 359
National Municipal League, 82, 349
National PTA, 423
National Restaurant Association,
    162
National Rifle Association, 79, 126
National School Boards Association,
    400
National supremacy clause, 35–36,
    37, 39*t*, 96
Nation at Risk, A (Bell), 397, 407
Nation-centered federalism, 42
Natural law, 65
Natural resources, state revenues
    and, 374, 377
Nebraska
    Games and Park Commission,
        306
    gun control laws in, 458
    Iowa gaming and, 383
    jury qualifications in, 287
    late-term abortions in, 469
    lawmaking in, 187
    legislative process in, 174*f*
    lieutenant governor power in,
        248
    nonpartisan culture in, 136,
        145, 188
    state superintendent of
        education in, 252
    unicameral legislature in, 116,
        185
Necessary and proper clause, 36, 38,
    41
Needle-exchange programs, 469,
    470, 490–492
Neutral competence, 318

Nevada
    ballot initiatives in, 88
    casinos in, 381–382
    constitutional amendments in,
        75
    constitution of, 68
    governor recall in, 122
    as individualistic culture, 101
    judicial selection in, 267
    mandatory minimum sentencing
        in, 291
    statehouse reporters in, 208
    tax system in, 374
    term limits in, 209
    voting rights for felons in, 461
New American Schools, 425
New Deal, 45, 53, 134, 145
New England
    citizen participation in local
        government of, 335
    criminal punishment and culture
        of, 439
    education policymaking in, 399
    home schooling regulations in,
        422
    sentencing in, 290
    town meetings in, 357
New Federalism, 47–52, 306–307
New Hampshire
    appeals process in, 264
    constitutional conventions in,
        78–79
    counties in, 342–343
    education funding in, 387
    franchise in, 72
    governor's term of office in, 217
    gubernatorial elections in, 240
    judicial selection in, 271,
        272–273
    judicial terms of office in, 273
    legislative professionalism in,
        205
    lieutenant governor in, 249
    population characteristics of, 10
    prescription drugs plan in, 486
    state constitution and
        educational adequacy in,
        66–67
    tax burden in, 379
    tax capacity versus tax effort in,
        380

tax system in, 374
term limits in, 246
New Jersey
    boards of chosen freeholders in, 344
    chief state school officer in, 398
    constitution on education goals of, 258
    executive branch elections in, 117, 248
    freeholders, 344
    funding insurance for parents of SCHIP-eligible children in, 485
    gubernatorial elections in, 240
    gun control laws in, 458
    healthcare funding in, 388
    as individualistic culture, 101
    intermediate appellate court in, 263
    Johnson & Johnson's corporate presence in, 164
    judicial appointments in, 271, 272
    legislative sessions in, 204
    legislators in, 195
    lieutenant governor in, 249
    political parties in, 146
    public health insurance in, 485
    redistricting in, 194
    Senate president in, 188
    on state constitutional conventions, 78
    state constitution and educational adequacy in, 67
    Supreme Court, 256
    taxation in, 7
New Judicial Federalism, 257, 258
New Mexico
    activist governor in, 214, 220–221
    constitution on bilingual education goals of, 258
    drug possession penalties in, 443
    education funding in, 387
    federal funding of Medicaid programs in, 475
    gun control laws in, 458
    judicial selection in, 273
    mandatory minimum sentencing in, 291

population of, 11–12
prescription drugs plan in, 486
professional and personal services taxes in, 370
school funding in, 372
voting rights for felons in, 461
New Orleans, La.
    New Orleans Parish consolidation with, 352
    political machine in, 139
New Public Management (NPM), 324–325
Newsom, Gavin, 158
Newspapers, partisan, 138
New York (city)
    bankruptcy of, 477
    Bellevue Hospital, 472
    blackout and crime wave in (1977), 442
    Liberal Party in, 160
    public schools' administration in, 399
    race riots in (1960s), 441
New York (city) Police Department, 321–322, 450, 456
New York (state)
    ballot access regulations in, 109
    bills before 2002 legislature of, 178
    budgetary control in, 219
    constitutional amendments in, 75
    constitutional revision commission in, 79
    constitution of, 63, 66
    drug possession penalties in, 443
    education funding in, 387, 405
    fiscal year of, 384
    gun control laws in, 458
    Integrated Domestic Violence Court, 293
    judicial retention in, 273
    judicial terms of office in, 273
    legislative sessions in, 204
    legislators in, 196
    local powers in, 338
    long-term party control of legislature in, 182
    partisan judicial elections in, 267
    per capita taxes in, 379
    post–Sept. 11 terrorist attacks concerns of, 18

redistricting in, 193
Regents Exams in, 409
statehouse reporters in, 208
TANF-funded programs in, 469
tax burden in, 374
trial courts in, 261
New York Times, 418–419
New York v. United States (1992), 54–55, 56t
9-1-1 emergency number, 448–449, 467
Nineteenth Amendment, 72, 110
Nixon, Richard M., 49, 207
No Child Left Behind Act, 52, 396
    achievement testing in states and, 409
    education funding and, 407
    national political parties and, 424
    standards movement and, 416, 425–426
Nominating committees, judicial selection by, 272–273
Nomination, political party, 135
Nonbinding referendums, 120
Nonpartisan ballots, 140
Nonpartisan elections, 116–117, 265, 266
Norman, Clarence, 270
Norm-referenced tests, 408–409
Norris, George, 136–137
North Carolina
    ballot access regulations in, 109
    chief state school officer in, 398
    college tuition-setting in, 410–411
    gubernatorial elections in, 240
    judicial selection in, 267, 296
    lawmaking in, 218
    legislative sessions in, 205
    Reconstruction and, 81
    veto power and, 228
North Dakota
    appellate courts in, 263
    bureaucracy in, 309
    chief state school officer in, 398
    education funding in, 387
    governor recall in, 122
    gubernatorial elections in, 240
    judicial compensation in, 278
    nonpartisan judicial elections in, 267

on state constitutional
conventions, 78
voting in, 110, 113
Northeast (region)
legislative professionalism in,
205
political party competition in,
150
unions in, 182
Nuclear-free zones, city councils and,
347
Nullification, 42

O

Obesity, 467–468, 492–494, 493*m*
Office group ballots, 106
Off-year elections, 240, 243
Ohio
annexations in, 352
ballot access regulations in, 108
education funding in, 405
gun control laws in, 458
judicial independence in, 270
judicial selection in, 120, 267
mandatory minimum sentencing
in, 291
state constitution and
educational adequacy in, 67
voter registration and turnout
in, 143
Ohio State Bar, 269
Oil, state revenues and, 374
Oklahoma
ballot access regulations in, 109
chief state school officer in, 398
civil and criminal appeals in,
264
constitutional revision
commission in, 79
constitution of, 67, 68, 83
federal funding of Medicaid
programs in, 475
gubernatorial elections in, 243
judicial selection in, 267
political machine in, 139
political party competition in,
150
sentencing in, 290
TANF-funded programs in, 468
term limits in, 209

Old Regulars, 139
O'Malley, Martin, 125, 360
One Hundred Years of Solitude
(Garcia Marquez), 132, 157
Online (distance) learning, 417–418
Open primaries, 141
Open territory states, for textbooks
and curriculum development,
415–416
Orange County, Calif., bond
payments default by, 383
Oregon
ballot initiatives in, 75, 88, 89,
391
chief state school officer in, 398
early prison releases in, 460
education funding in, 404, 407
judicial selection in, 267
jury verdicts in, 287
lieutenant governor in, 249
local powers in, 338
long-term care in, 488
Medicaid programs in, 470, 481
physician-assisted suicide in,
469
social safety net in, 482–483
state superintendent of
education in, 252
tax system in, 374
voting in, 113
Orfield, Myron, 355
Organization for Economic
Cooperation and Development,
406
Orlando Sentinel, 205–206
O'Rourke, P. J., 184
Oversight, legislative, 183–185

P

Pacific Coast, political party
competition along, 150
Paige, Roderick, 407, 409, 412
Panels, for appellate court hearings,
264
Parchman Farms, Miss., 440
Pardons, by governors, 229–230
Parents for public Schools, 424
Parents' group, school reform and,
423–424
Parole, 434, 445, 456

Partial veto, 229
Partisan judicial elections, 267, 270
Party column ballots, 106
Party conventions, 141, 142, 143
Party machines, 139, 153, 317
Pataki, George, 18, 229, 244
Patients' bill of rights legislation,
487–488
Patronage, 139–140, 317
Patton, Paul, 489
Peel, Robert, 447, 449
Peirce, Neal, 355
Pence, Stephen, 249
Pendergast, Tom, 317
Pendleton Act, 318
Penitentiaries, prisons versus, 440
Penn, William, 70–71, 436–437
Pennsylvania
constitutional amendments in, 75
evolution of constitution of,
70–71
as individualistic culture, 101
partisan judicial elections in,
267, 295
political machine in, 139
on slot machines, 383
on state constitutional
conventions, 78
supreme court elections and
education equity in, 181
unicameral legislature in, 71
Peremptory challenges, in jury
selection, 287
Perez, Andrea, 257
Performance Based Management
(PBM), 325–326
Performance measures, legislative,
206
Permanence, of state versus U.S.
Constitutions, 65–66
Perot, Ross, 157–158, 159
Perry, Rick, 94
Personal Responsibility and Work
Reconciliation Act (1996), 389,
479
Pew Charitable Trusts, 311
Pew Research Center for the People
and the Press, 161
Pharmaceutical Research and
Manufacturers of America, 164,
166

Phi Beta Kappan magazine, school
performance poll, 408
Philadelphia, Penna.
city council, 346
Eastern State Penitentiary in,
440
founding of, 70–71
population characteristics of, 10
Philip Morris, 166
Phillips, Thomas, 271, 294
Phoenix, Ariz.
elections in, 357
Maricopa Co. consolidation
with, 353
population characteristics of, 10
Physician-assisted suicide, 469
Pierce, Patrick, 383
Pigs, pregnant, ballot initiatives on,
121
Pinchbeck, P. B. S., 236
Pingree, Chellie, 486
Pioneer Press (St. Paul, Minn.), 182
Piper, Bill, 391
Plea bargains, 259, 260, 281
Plethismograph tests, 291
Plural executive systems, 117–118
Plurality, 104
Police protection, funding for, 389
Policing
community, 449–453
problem-oriented, 447
professional model versus
community, 448–449
trends in, 455–456
Policy implementation, 304–305
Political action committees (PACs),
147
Political agendas, bureaucratic,
306–307
Political cultures, 12, 94–96
dominant, by state, 98*m*
Elazar's classifications of,
98–103, 100*t*
Elazar's methodology on,
103–104
elections and, 104–116
incarceration rates and, 439
party competition and, 151–153
political party effects on, 153
prosecution of local crimes and,
281

public health and, 467–469
state constitution variations and,
82
state variations in, 96–98
tax variations and, 380,
381–382
voter turnout and, 111,
112–113
Political machines, 139–140
Political parties, 132–133. *See also*
Local political parties; State
political parties
campaign reform and, 143–145
competition among, 149–157
criminal punishment severity
and, 439
governor's support in legislature
by, 233–234
historical characteristics of,
138–140
judicial selection and, 267
local governments and, 358
party activists and, 153,
154–155
political culture and, 151–153
pragmatism versus idealism of,
156–157
primer on, 133–138
public school reform and, 424
redistricting and, 194
third parties and independents,
157–161
transfers to state parties,
1999–2000, 147*t*
twentieth century, 140–143
Pollsters, 143
Poll taxes, 110
Poor people, Democratic Party and,
134
Popular initiatives, 120
Popular referendums, 120, 123*t*
Popular support, of governors, 233
Population
party competition and mobility
of, 150
by state, 10–11, 11*m*
Port Authority of New York and
New Jersey, 350
Trans-Hudson toll plaza, 351*f*
Portland, Ore., Metropolitan
Services District in, 355

Poverty rates. *See also* Poor people
decline in, 479
health insurance and, 485
HHS guidelines, 2004, 389*t*
SCHIP eligibility and, 484
state welfare programs and,
475, 476*t*
Power, systems of, 28–30. *See also*
Formal powers; Informal powers;
Separation of powers
divided, 234
Precedents, legal, 260
intermediate appellate courts
and, 263
Preemption, 36
credit regulations in Vermont
and, 37
New Federalism and, 49–51
Prejudicial errors, 261
Prescription drug plans, 206, 468,
485, 486
Presidential elections
electoral college and, 26–27
former governors in, 246–247
President of the Senate, 188
President pro tem, 188
Press. *See* Media
Price, William J., 401
Primary elections, 108, 141, 142*m*,
156
Printz v. United States (1997), 56*t*
Prisons. *See also* Incarceration rates
Abu Ghraib abuses, 453
determinate sentencing and,
445–446
early release programs, 460–461
federal support cutbacks for,
457
funding for, 389–390
mental illness in, 454
overcrowding in, 292
supermax security, 454
violence in, 453
Pritchard Committee for Academic
Excellence, 423
Privacy, right to, 85–86
Private colleges and universities, 5–6,
410
Private sector
bureaucratic effectiveness versus,
310–311, 315

New Public Management and, 324–325

Privatization, of public schools, 420–421

Privileges and immunities clause, 36, 38

Probation
    intensive, 292
    supervision of, 456

Problem-oriented policing, 447

Problem-solving courts, 293

Products liability cases, 287

Professional groups, public schools reform and, 425

Professionalization, 193
    bureaucracies and, 303, 315–316
    legislatures and, 203–206

Professional policing model, 448–449

Progressive Corporation, 88

Progressive Era
    council-manager governments and, 348–349
    direct democracy and, 87
    national health insurance discussions during, 473
    popular referendums, popular initiatives and, 120
    state constitutional changes during, 68

Progressive Party, 160

Progressive taxes, 366

Property rights, New Federalism and, 51

Property taxes, 367, 370–374
    education funding and, 402–403
    state and local variations in, 379

Proposition 2½, Mass., 373

Proposition 13, Calif., 87–88, 121, 372, 373, 402

Prosecutors, 278–281
    public, 435
    salary range in large districts, 2001, 280t
    staff and operations in large districts, 280t

Providence, R.I.
    individualistic culture of, 101
    political machine in, 138

Public colleges and universities, 5–6, 410–411

Public defenders, 279, 281–286, 434
    annual salary ranges in state-funded systems, 1999, 282t
    staff and operations statistics, 1999, 283t

Public Education Network, 425

Public health. *See also* Health maintenance organizations; Medicaid programs; Medicare programs; Welfare funding
    anthrax exposure and, 466–467
    costs for, 475–477
    devolution of control, 477–478
    historical review of government programs, 471–472
    long-term care, 488–489
    obesity and, 492–494, 493m
    political cultures and, 469–471
    prescription drug plans and, 486
    private hospitals and, 490, 491
    SCHIP, 483–485
    social safety net concept, 472–473
    states' involvement in, 467–469

Public opinion
    elections and, 123–127
    political culture and, 95
    on state and local governments, 49–50
    state legislators and, 206–210

Public schools, 305. *See also* Education

Punishment
    alternative, 460–461
    criminal, purpose of, 438–440

Pure appointive judicial selection systems, 271–273

Putnam, Robert, 116

Q

Quakers, 70–71, 439

Quality of healthcare, 468

R

Race riots
    1960s, 441
    policing and, 447

Racial discrimination
    Congressional regulations against, 54
    indeterminate sentencing and, 290
    prosecution of local crimes and, 281

Rainy day funds, 385

Rank-and-file members, 191–193

Ranney, Austin, 150

Rants, Christopher, 230

Ratification, 75, 79–80

Ratliff, Bill, 152

Raytheon, Massachusetts legislation affecting, 191–192

Reagan, Ronald, 246
    New Federalism and, 47–49
    Proposition 13 and, 373, 402
    Supreme Court appointments by, 54
    taxpayer revolt and, 88
    on welfare state, 477

Realignment, 145

Recall elections, 88, 122, 123t, 245t

Recht, Don, 291

Recidivism, 293, 457

Reconstruction, 80–81, 82

Record-keeping, bureaucratic, 303, 315

Redistricting, 103, 193–195. *See also* Districts
    party competition and, 151, 156

Referendums, 63, 75, 116, 120–121. *See also* Ballot initiatives

Reform Party, 157–159

Regional land-use planning, 355, 356

Regressive taxes, 369

Rehnquist, William, 54, 64

Reinventing government (REGO), 325–326

Religious freedom, 70–71, 258

Reno v. Condon (2000), 56t

Renters, property taxes and, 374

Representation, 180–182

Representative bureaucracies, 323

Representative governments, 32, 86–89

Republican Attorneys General Association (RAGA), 119, 250

Republican government, enforcement of, 39t

Republican National Committee, 135, 156
Republican Party
  dealignment and, 145
  Democratic Party versus, 132
  elections of 2002 and, 149
  federal spending for congressional districts of, 48
  formation of, 134
  gubernatorial elections and, 243
  on health insurance, 471
  in Ohio, 144
  professional staff for, 144
  in the South, 104–105
  states' regulation of, 108
  supporters of, 135
Republican Party of Minnesota v. White (2002), 295
Reserved powers, 38
  Supreme Court interpretation of, 54
Responsible party model, 137–138
Restorative justice movement, 461
Retention elections, 272, 273
Retired legislators, 196
Retirees on fixed incomes, property taxes and, 373
Retirement benefits for senior citizens, 473–474
Rev. Run (of RUN DMC), 358f
Revenue bonds, 383
Revenues, 366
Revision, councils of, 71
Revolutionary War, economic recession after, 31
Rhode Island
  appellate courts in, 263
  counties in, 341
  funding insurance for parents of SCHIP-eligible children in, 485
  governor's appointment power in, 228
  gun control laws in, 458
  illegal constitutional convention in, 74
  judicial terms of office in, 273
  legislative power in, 80, 84
  legislative sessions in, 204
  political machine in, 138
Richards, Ann, 224
Richardson, Bill, 214, 220–221, 220f, 251

Richmond, Va., council-mayor government in, 116
Riders, 173
Riordan, Richard, 340
Rivas, Richard, 285
Robertson, James, 269
Rockefeller, Nelson, 443
Rocket dockets, 294
Romney, Mitt, 220
Roosevelt, Franklin D.
  court "packing" plan of, 53
  federal government centralism and, 45
  political realignment and, 145
  Socialist candidate influences on, 159
  Social Security and, 473–474
  on welfare dependents, 477
Roosevelt, Theodore, 142, 159
Rosenstone, Steven J., 112
Rowland, John, 244
Rulemaking, 306
Rumenap, Stacie, 209
Runoff primaries, 141
Rural areas
  bureaucracies in, 309
  healthcare in, 466–467
Rusk, David, 353, 355
Ryan, George, 229–230, 460

S

Sabato, Larry J., 102, 149
Sales taxes, 8, 366, 368–370, 379, 402
San Antonio Independent School District v. Rodriguez (1973), 403
Sanchez, Tony, 244
San Diego, Calif.
  council-manager system in, 349
  school board races in, 400
Sanford, Terry, 217–218
San Francisco
  mayoral race competition in, 158
  same sex marriages in, 50
San Jose, Calif., council-manager system in, 349
SARS (Sudden Acute Respiratory Syndrome), 467
SAT (Scholastic Assessment Test), 410–411

SAT (Stanford Achievement Test), 408
Schair, Fern, 270
Scholastic Assessment Test (SAT), 410–411
School boards, 397, 400–402
School districts, 399
  rural versus urban, 405
School vouchers, 419–420
Schwarzenegger, Arnold, 122, 136, 236, 244
Scott, Dred, 42–43
Scott v. Sandford (1857), 42–43
Search and seizure laws, state courts on, 258
Seattle, Wash., ballot initiative for football stadium in, 89
Secession, 42
Second Amendment, 458–459
Second World War, federal government centralization and, 43, 45
Secretaries of state, 116, 118, 251t, 252
Secret ballots, 108
Sectionalism, political culture and, 98, 103–104
Securities Market Enhancement Act (1999), 37
Securities regulation, 164
Segway LLC, 175–176, 180
Selectmen, county, 344
Seminole Tribe of Florida v. Florida (1996), 55, 56t
Senate, state, 187
Senate, U.S., 86, 105
Seniority, 320–321
Sentencing, criminal, 289–292, 296–297
Separation of powers, 70
Sept. 11 terrorist attacks (2001)
  faith in government after, 207
  FBI antiterrorism investigatory powers after, 347
  Giuliani's leadership after, 349
  local government revenue gaps after, 359–360
  New Federalism and, 52
  New York State concerns after, 18
  public hospitals and public health plans after, 490

state and local terrorism
response funding after, 33–34
Serrano v. Priest (Calif. 1970), 372,
403
Service economy, 368
Service First, Florida, 326–327
Settlements, legal, 259, 260
Severance taxes, 377
Sex discrimination, indeterminate
sentencing and, 290
Sex education, abstinence-only, 469,
492
Sex offenders, penalties for, 214
Sexually transmitted diseases, 468
Sharp, Milton, 222–223, 227
Shaw, Greg, 103, 126
Shays, Daniel, 31–32
Shays's Rebellion, 31–32
Sheheen, Robert J., 382
Sheriffs, county, 438
Sherman, Bobby, 191
Shiprack, Bob, 192
Sibley, Joel, 139
Sieben, Bill, 294
Siegelman, Don, 78
Sierra Club, 126, 161
Silver, Lee, 401
Simmons, Russell, 358*f*
Sin taxes, 368
Site-based school management, 412
Sixth Amendment, 281–282, 286,
437
Smart growth, 355, 356
Smart Growth Act, 225
Smith, David, 285
Smoking, warnings about, 467
Snow, Stephen J., 356
Social safety net. *See also* Public
health; Welfare funding
American development of,
473–474
costs for, 475–477
development of, 472–473
state eligibility levels for, 476*t*
Social Security Act (1935), 53, 318,
473–474
Social status, indeterminate
sentencing and, 290
Social trust, voting and, 116
Sociodemographics, 10–12
Socrates, 440

Soft money, 147
Softshells, 133
Sorauf, Frank J., 161
Soros, George, 88
South (region)
citizen participation in local
government of, 335
criminal punishment of,
438–439
Democratic Party and, 134
jury nullification in, 437
labor unions in, 151
majority-minority districts in,
194
police departments in, 456
political party competition in,
149–150
Republicans in, 104–105, 134
traditionalistic culture in, 102
trial lawyers in, 181–182
voter turnout in, 111, 113
South Carolina
budget formulation in, 385
casinos in, 382
college tuition-setting in, 410
constitutional amendments in,
75, 79
constitutional conventions in, 78
constitution of, 74
federal supremacy and, 96
gun control laws in, 458
judicial selection in, 273
jury qualifications in, 287
legislative sessions in, 204
lotteries and, 382–383
South Dakota
appellate courts in, 263
ballot initiatives in, 75
constitutional conventions in, 78
constitution of, 67, 68
judicial selection in, 267
professional and personal
services taxes in, 370
school funding in, 372
statehouse reporters in, 208
tax system in, 374
Southwest (region)
home schooling regulations in,
422
police departments in, 456
Sovereign immunity, 55

Sovereignty, 435
Soviet Union, educational
performance and, 407
Spain, Mississippi shipping and, 31
Speaker of the House, 188
Special act charters, 339
Special districts, 90, 334, 335,
350–351
Special jurisdiction trial courts, 261
Special sessions, governors' power to
call, 230
Sperling, Jon, 88
Spitzer, Eliot, 250
Spoils system, 317
Sputnik, 407
Standardized testing, high-stakes, 397
Standards, curriculum, 397, 404
Standards movement, 412, 415–416,
425–426
Stanford Achievement Test (SAT),
408
Starr, Paul, 471, 472
Star Tribune (Minneapolis, Minn.),
182
State agencies, governors as head of,
219–220
State board of education, 396
State-centered federalism, 42, 43
State Children's Health Insurance
Program (SCHIP), 388, 483–485,
494
State court systems. *See also* Judges;
Judicial branch; Justices
activist judges and, 256–259
defendants' rights versus
victims' rights, 287–289
increasing case loads of,
293–295
judicial appointments, 271–273
judicial compensation, 277–278,
278*t*
judicial elections, 266–271
judicial selection, 264–273,
266*m*, 274–275*t*, 276–277*t*
judicial selection reforms,
295–296
judicial terms of office, 273,
274–275*t*, 275, 276–277*t*
juries, 286–287
prosecutors, 279–281

reforms, 292–297
role and structure of, 259–261, 263–264
sentencing, 289–292
sentencing uniformity reform, 296–297
trial process, 278–292
State governments. *See also* Budgets, state; Finance; *specific branches of*
devolution of power and policy to, 18–20, 50, 477–478
education funding by, 402
employees by state, 17*m*
federal aid to, 379*m*
federal government versus, 8, 16–18
federalism and, 33
franchise limitations and, 72, 74
as laboratories of democracy, 20–22
lobbying in, 163–165, 164*t*
local government powers and, 51
New Federalism and, 49
powers of national government versus, 40*f*
Social Security Act and, 474
State political parties, 134, 145
campaign finance and, 146–147, 149
corporate funding of, 140–141
governor as chief of, 221–222
professional staff for, 144
public campaign financing and, 148
regulation of, 145–146
transfers from national party committees to, 1999–2000, 147*t*
State politics
comparative method of studying, 7–10
daily impact of, 5–7
States' rights
dual federalism and, 42
New Federalism and, 50
Reagan and, 48–49
State supreme courts. *See* Supreme courts, state
Stolberg, Irving, 192

Straight tickets, 108, 160
Strayhorn, Caroline Keeton, 118
Street-level bureaucrats, 305–306, 323
Strong mayor–council systems, 345–346, 345*f*
Subnational government, 17–18
Suburban areas
crime in urban areas versus, 457–459
death penalty and, 460
Successful schools model, 404–405
Sudden Acute Respiratory Syndrome (SARS), 467
Suffrage Movement, 72
Suicide, physician-assisted, 88, 120–121
Sundquist, Don, 366, 367
Supermajority votes, 218
Supermax security prisons, 454
Superpredators, juvenile, 450
Super Size Me! (movie), 493
Supervisors, county, 344
Supremacy clause. *See* National supremacy clause
Supreme Court, U.S.
activism by, 256
on California's anti-political party law, 140
on education funding, 403
federalism and, 52–53
on jury verdicts, 287
nation-centered federalism and, 53–54
on party affiliation and government hires, 154
on political expenditures as free speech, 149
on political party regulation, 146
on school vouchers, 420
on state laws and regulations, 64
states' rights or ad hoc federalism under, 54–57
on term limits, 121
Supreme courts, state, 260. *See also* Courts of last resort
activist judges in, 256–257
assertiveness of, 64–65

demographics of justices serving, 267
judicial review by, 80
judicial selection for, 84, 119–120, 265, 266*m*
jurisdiction of, 257
New Judicial Federalism, 257, 258
teachers' unions and, 423
Susquehanna River Basin Commission, 354
S.W.A.T. (Special Weapons and Tactics) teams, 449
Swing voters, 135
Symington, Fife, 246
Syracuse University, Maxwell School of Citizenship and Public Affairs, 311

T

Taft, William Howard, 142
Talmadge, Gene, 317
Taney, Roger B., 53, 341
Tax burden, 366, 379–380
Tax capacities, 380
Tax codes, state and local, 34
Tax efforts, 380
Taxes. *See also* Finance
ballot initiatives on, 121
demographics and, 381
economic cycle and, 381–382
effective versus nominal rates of, 371
geography and, 380–381
geology and, 381
on Internet sales, 341
political culture and, 380
Tax Foundation, 366
Taxpayer revolts, 88, 367. *See also* Proposition 13, Calif.
Teachers
licensure procedures for, 398
recruitment of, 416–417
Teachers' unions, 196, 320–321, 322, 423
Teach for America, 417
Telecommunications Act (1996), 37
Television advertising, party conventions and, 143

Temporary Assistance for Needy
Families (TANF), 389, 468–469,
479, 480, 480*m*
Ten Commandments display in
Alabama Supreme Court, 260
Tennessee
constitutional amendments in,
75
county administrators in, 344
judicial retention elections in,
273
judicial selection in, 267, 272
jury qualifications in, 287
lieutenant governor in, 249
Medicaid programs in, 470,
481, 482
Reconstruction and, 81
regressive taxes in, 369
sales taxes in, 370
sex acts legislation in, 86
TANF-funded programs in, 468
tax burden in, 366–367, 379
tax revolt in, 367
Tennessee Valley Authority (TVA),
354
Tenth Amendment, 39, 39*t*, 187
reserved (state) powers under, 38
state constitutions and, 69
state governmental authority
and, 337
Supreme Court on, 53–54
U.S. Department of Education
and, 398
Tenure
of governors, 223
in public higher education, 321
Term limits, 88, 121, 208–209, 246
Terms of office, judicial, 273,
274–275*t*, 275
Terribile, Mike, 285
Terrorism. *See also* Bioterrorism;
Sept. 11 terrorist attacks
anthrax used for, 466–467
New Federalism and war on, 52
Texas
ballot access regulations in, 109
civil and criminal appeals in,
264
college level state politics
courses in, 6

constitution of, 63
counties in, 341, 343
death penalty in, 94, 268–269
economic cycle and, 381
executions in, 7
executive branch elections in,
117, 118
executive branch legislation in,
218
fiscal year of, 384
governmental power in, 85
government services and
political culture of, 152–153
Hispanics and redistricting in,
195
history and constitution of,
81–82
HMO regulation in, 207
home schooling regulations in,
422
judicial selection in, 267,
268–269, 271
legislative professionalism in,
204
lieutenant governor in, 188
lieutenant governor power in,
249
Medicaid programs in, 180–181
political culture in, 94
prisons funding in, 390
Reconstruction and, 80–81
Republican control of, 151
sales taxes in, 370
SCHIP enrollment in, 485
school districts in, 399
sentencing in, 289
Spanish-language e-government
in, 328
state constitutional conventions
in, 78
state supreme court on public
schools in, 422
statewide officials elected in,
219–220, 248
tax burden in, 379
tax system in, 374
voting rights for felons in, 461
Textbooks, development of, 415
Think tanks, state-level, 127
Third-party candidates, 157–159

difficulties of building support
for, 159–160
elected governor, 239
major party support for,
160–161
presidential election of 2000
and, 27
Thomas, Norman, 159
Thompson, Tommy, 85, 221, 225,
229, 478–479
Ticket splitting, 160
"Tipping point" concept, 452–453
Title 1, 407
Tobacco companies, 119, 166–167,
249–250
Tocqueville, Alexis de, 334, 361,
453, 454–455
Topography, 15–16
Tort laws, changes in, 181
Total Quality Management (TQM),
325–326
Towns. *See* Municipalities
Townsend, Kathleen Kennedy, 127
Townships, 334
Trade associations, 161–162
Traditionalistic cultures, 12–13
ballot access regulations in,
109
characteristics of, 100*t*,
101–103
party competition and, 151–152
states with, 98*m*
voter registration and, 112
Transportation Equity Act, 341
Treasurers, state, 118, 252
Trends in International Mathematics
and Sciences Study (TIMSS), 409
Trial courts, 259–260
description of, 260–261
judicial compensation range for,
278*t*
judicial selection for, 265, 266*m*
terms of office and
reappointment methods by
state in 2004, 276–277*t*
Trial lawyers, 162, 181–182, 250
Troops to teachers, 417
Truman, Harry, 49
Trustees, 191
Truth-in-sentencing laws, 291, 292

Tucker, Jim Guy, 246
Twain, Mark, 247
Tweed, Boss, 317
Twenty-Fourth Amendment, 110
Twin Cities Metropolitan Council, 355

U

Uelmen, Gerald, 269–270
Ultra vires principle, 337
Unemployment compensation, Social Security Act (1935) and, 473–474
Unfunded mandates, 47, 49, 390–391, 475
Unicameral legislatures, 70, 71. *See also* Nebraska
Unincorporated territories, 341–342
Uninsured persons, 468, 480, 481*m*, 485
Union Leader (Manchester, N.H.), 153
Unions. *See* Labor unions
Unitary systems, 29, 30, 32
United Kingdom, unitary power system in, 30
U.S. Census Bureau, 402, 488
U.S. Chamber of Commerce, 119, 250
U.S. Conference of Mayors, 349, 355
U.S. Council of Mayors, 346
U.S. Department of Education, 398
  on home schooling, 421
  national political parties and, 424
  No Child Left Behind Act and, 425
  on teachers' responsibilities, 417
  Trends in International Mathematics and Sciences Study and, 409
U.S. Department of Health and Human Services, 389*t*, 477–478
U.S. Department of Homeland Security, 360
U.S. Term Limits, 209
United States v. Darby Lumber Co. (1941), 53
United States v. Lopez (1995), 55, 56*t*

United States v. Morrison (2000), 55, 56*t*
Universal health insurance coverage, 471, 482
Urban areas
  bureaucracies in, 310
  crime in suburban areas versus, 457–459
  death penalty and, 460
Urban Institute, 484, 490
USA PATRIOT Act, 347
User fees, 367
Utah
  chief state school officer in, 398
  constitutional revision commissions in, 79
  education funding in, 372, 387
  GPP performance grade, 312
  gubernatorial elections in, 240
  judicial appointments in, 272–273
  Medicaid programs in, 475
  per-pupil spending in, 405
  political party competition in, 151
  TANF-funded programs in, 468–469
  term limits in, 209, 246
Utility fees, 378

V

Vanna White veto, 85
Variances, definition of, 7–8
Vaughan, Robert, 436–437
Ventura, Calif., e-government in, 327–328
Ventura, Jesse, 159, 236, 239
Verdicts, 438
Vermont
  appellate courts in, 263
  chief state school officer in, 398
  education funding and Act 60 in, 403
  governor's term of office in, 217
  gubernatorial elections in, 240
  gun control laws in, 458
  HMO regulation in, 207
  judicial retention in, 273
  judicial review in, 80
  Medicaid programs in, 181

No Child Left Behind and, 426
parole board discretion in, 292
political culture in, 94
preemption and credit regulations in, 37
prescription drugs plan in, 486
public health insurance in, 484–485
state constitution and educational equity in, 66–67
Supreme Court, 294
term limits in, 246
unicameral legislature in, 71
voting rights in, 71–72
Veto power, 84–85, 218, 228–229
Victim impact evidence, 289
Victims' rights, 288–289
Vigilantes, death penalty statutes and, 94
Villages, 334, 335. *See also* Municipalities
Vilsack, Tom, 230
Violence Against Women Act (VAWA, 1994), 55
Virginia
  ballot access regulations in, 108–109
  candidate nomination in, 141
  constitutional amendments in, 75
  constitutional conventions in, 78
  counties in, 341
  education policymaking in, 399
  franchise in, 72
  governor's term of office in, 217
  gubernatorial elections in, 240
  Lee's loyalty to, 96
  legislative appointment of judges in, 272
  lieutenant governor power in, 248
  local powers in, 337, 338
  Loudoun Co. land use plan, 356
  public defender funding in, 285–286
  rocket dockets in, 294
  school board elections in, 399–400
  sentencing in, 289
  Standards for Learning, 409

traditionalistic culture in, 102–103
voting rights for felons in, 461
Virginia Company of London, 69
Voir dire examinations, 287
Voter identification, 137, 157, 161
Voter participation, in judicial elections, 271
Voter registration, 110, 112–113, 144. *See also* Franchise
Voters
    perception of legislatures by, 174
    swing, 135
Voter turnout, 110–111, 114, 116
    analysis of, 105–106
    local and state parties and, 144
    for local elections, 357
    moralistic culture and, 99
    school board elections and, 400*t*, 401
Voting Rights Act of 1965, 110
Voting Rights Act of 1982, 194
Voting technology, costs of, 107

W

Wardein, Avigayil, 302
Wards, 347, 357
Ware, Steven, 269
Warner, John, 103
Warner, Mark, 236
Washington (state)
    ballot initiatives in, 89, 391
    college tuition-setting in, 410
    education funding in, 407
    health policy reform in, 483
    judicial selection in, 267
    Puget Sound transportation funding in, 179–180
    severance taxes in, 377
    tax system in, 374
Washington, D.C. *See* District of Columbia
Washington, Denzel, 487
Washington, George, 31, 32, 132
Washington Metropolitan Area Transportation Authority, 350–351
Watergate scandal, 207
Wattenberg, Martin, 157

Weak mayor–council systems, 345, 346, 346*f*
Weekend sentencing, prison overcrowding and, 292
Weicker, Lowell, 159
Welfare funding, 389. *See also* Block grants; Public health; Social safety net
    Clinton's Health Security Act, 480
    state eligibility levels for, 476*t*
    uninsured persons, 480, 481*m*
Welfare reform, 478–480
West Virginia
    appeals process in, 264
    ballot access regulations in, 109
    federal funding of Medicaid programs in, 475
    gross state product of, 13
    judicial selection in, 267
    local powers in, 338
    political machine in, 139
    prescription drugs plan in, 486
    prisons funding in, 390
    slot machines in, 383
    state constitution and educational adequacy in, 67
    taxation in, 7
    tort laws changes in, 181
Whigs, 133, 134
Whistle blower laws, 318
White, Mark, 118
White House, 162, 246–247
Whiteley, Leslie, 181*f*
Whitman, Christine Todd, 156
Whittle, Christopher, 421
Wickard v. Fillburn (1942), 54
Wilder, L. Douglas, 103, 236
Williams, Anthony, 491
William v. Rhodes (1968), 108
Wilson, James Q., 447–448, 450
Wilson, Pete, 346
Wilson, Woodrow, 142
Windom, Steve, 118
Winger, Richard, 108
Winner-takes-all system, 157
Wintemute, Garen, 459
Winthrop, John, 69, 70
Wisconsin. *See also* Milwaukee, Wis.
    ballot access regulations in, 160
    college tuition-setting in, 411

constitutional amendments in, 75
direct democracy in, 87
funding insurance for parents of SCHIP-eligible children in, 485
governor recall in, 122
governor's veto power in, 85
gun control laws in, 458
history and constitution of, 82
judicial selection in, 267, 296
legislative professionalism in, 204–205
as moralistic culture, 99
political party competition in, 150
Progressive Party in, 160
public campaign financing in, 148
shared-revenue system in, 152
wasting disease in deer legislation of, 179
welfare reform in, 470, 478–480
Wisconsin Education Association Board, 155
Wisconsin Education Association Council (WEAC), 320
Wisconsin Manufacturers and Commerce, 155
Wisconsin Territory, Missouri Compromise (1820) and, 42–43
Wisconsin Works, 225
Wolfinger, Raymond, 112
Women
    as elected city officials, 358
    franchise for, 72, 110
    governors, 236, 239*m*, 240*t*
    legislators, 196–197, 198–199*t*, 199
    as state supreme court justices, 267
    status of, 9
Women's Policy Research (WPR), 9
Working Families Party, 160
Work Opportunity Reconciliation Act (1996), 50
Work release programs, prison overcrowding and, 292
World wars. *See* First World War; Second World War
World Wildlife Fund, 126

Wyoming
appellate courts in, 263
ballot initiatives in, 87
economic cycle and, 381
education funding in, 404
franchise for women in, 72
gubernatorial elections in, 243
individualistic culture in, 127
lieutenant governor in, 249
parole board discretion in, 292
political party competition in, 150
severance taxes in, 377
state constitution and
educational adequacy in, 67
tax system in, 374
voting rights for felons in, 461

Y

Yoga, 468

Young people
criminal justice system and,
461–462
political parties and, 154
as superpredators, 450

Z

Zimbardo, Philip, 448
Zimring, Franklin, 94